THE ESSENTIALS
OF REAL ESTATE LAW
FOR PARALEGALS

DELMAR
™
THOMSON LEARNING

Africa • Australia • Canada • Denmark • Japan • Mexico • New Zealand • Philippines
Puerto Rico • Singapore • Spain • United Kingdom • United States

Cover Design: Susan Mathews, Stillwater Studio

Cover Photo: PhotoDisc, Inc.

Delmar Staff

Publisher: Susan Simpfenderfer
Acquisitions Editor: Joan Gill
Developmental Editor: Rhonda Dearborn

Production Manager: Wendy Troeger
Production Editor: Laurie A. Boyce
Marketing Manager: Katherine Hans

COPYRIGHT © 1999 Delmar, a division of Thomson Learning, Inc. The Thomson Learning™ is a trademark used herein under license.

Printed in the United States of America
10 11 12 XXX 08 07 06

For more information, contact Delmar, 5 Maxwell Dr., PO Box 8007, Clifton Park, NY 12065-8007; or find us on the World Wide Web at http://www.delmar.com

International Division List

Asia
Thomson Learning
60 Albert Street, #15-01
Albert Complex
Singapore 189969
Tel: 65 336 6411
Fax: 65 336 7411

Australia/New Zealand:
Nelson/Thomson Learning
102 Dodds Street
South Melbourne, Victoria 3205
Australia
Tel: 61 39 685 4111
Fax: 61 39 685 4199

Latin America:
Thomson Learning
Seneca, 53
Colonia Polanco
11560 Mexico D.F. Mexico
Tel: 525-281-2906
Fax: 525-281-2656

Spain:
Thomson Learning
Calle Magallanes, 25
28015-MADRID
ESPANA
Tel: 34 91 446 33 50
Fax: 34 91 445 62 18

Japan:
Thomson Learning
Palaceside Building 5F
1-1-1 Hitotsubashi, Chiyoda-ku
Tokyo 100 0003 Japan
Tel: 813 5218 6544
Fax: 813 5218 6551

UK/Europe/Middle East
Thomson Learning
Berkshire House
168-173 High Holborn
London
WC1V 7AA United Kingdom
Tel: 44 171 497 1422
Fax: 44 171 497 1426

Canada:
Nelson/Thomson Learning
1120 Birchmount Road
Scarborough, Ontario
Canada M1K 5G4
Tel: 416-752-9100
Fax: 416-752-8102

Library of Congress Cataloging-in-Publication Data
Slossberg, Lynn T.
    The essentials of real estate law for paralegals / Lynn T.
Slossberg.
        p. cm.
    Includes bibliographical references and index.
    ISBN 0-7668-0395-3
    1. Real property—United States. 2. Vendors and purchasers—
United States. 3. Conveyancing—United States. 4. Legal
assistants—United States—Handbooks, manuals, etc. I. Title.
KF665.Z9S58   1998   98-8347
3463.7304'3—dc21   CIP

To my family, with love

SUMMARY OF CONTENTS

CONTENTS

PREFACE

The Essentials of Real Estate Law for Paralegals embraces a systems approach. This text shall first provide a basic foundation of legal concepts necessary for an understanding of real estate transactions. The text shall then guide the student, by providing not only procedural checklists the paralegal may utilize daily in the law office, but also hypothetical client scenarios worked through each step of the way, resulting in a final product that shows the paralegal how to handle various client matters. Finally, this text shall involve the paralegal through exercises in the text and in the accompanying student workbook, building proficiencies in real estate file management, from handling closings start to finish to handling common real estate litigation.

I believe students learn most effectively by doing. The process of involving students in the course materials by mimicking their functions in the legal environment serves three purposes. The first is the creation of excitement in the material presented. This is a constant challenge for both student and instructor. Faced with a lengthy narrative of new legal concepts followed simply by questions geared toward memorization rather than assimilation, the student tends to lose interest. Active participation with practical applications speeds and reinforces the assimilation process.

The second purpose is increase in self-esteem. Traditional examinations are limited in the way they test learning. Because of this, the student is not certain that examination results truly reflect performance capability on the job. By performing typical paralegal tasks first in the receptive environment of the classroom, the paralegal receives helpful feedback and reassurance that he or she is leaving the course with the requisite knowledge to do the job demanded of him or her.

The third purpose is competitive edge. Utilizing these materials, the student will have a portfolio of work at the completion of the course that may be used to great effect in the employment interview. Most students taking a basic real estate law course will lack prior law office experience and will need a marketing tool in "selling" their skills to attorneys. Indeed, most attorneys I know are "show me" people, more interested in the efficient output of quality product than examination results. An interviewee armed with a portfolio of "experience" is more likely to become a desired employee.

Although this text addresses itself to the entry-level paralegal, more experienced paralegals may benefit from its contents. Each chapter sets forth clear objectives that are reinforced at the end of the chapter in a chapter summary. After the presentation of major concepts, most chapters include hypothetical client scenarios illustrating the application of these concepts by showing a real estate paralegal performing the responsibilities discussed in the chapter. Additionally, each chapter includes review questions, an ethical question related to real estate practice, and numerous practical assignments, allowing the student to implement his or her knowledge of the presented material.

The text is divided into four major sections: Part I, Fundamental Concepts of Real Estate Law; Part II, The Closing: Residential, Commercial, and Construction Loan Closings; Part III, Landlord/Tenant Law; and Part IV, Real Estate Litigation.

Part I provides the foundation for the rest of the text. In this section, the basic principles of real estate law are set forth. The section begins with a chapter on ethics and real property practice that first outlines basic ethical principles and then discusses potential ethical problems that may arise in real estate practice. The next chapter introduces the student to the concept of real property, basic ownership rights, estates and tenancies, and methods of title holding. This is followed by a chapter on various categories of real property, both residential and commercial. Subsequent chapters include governmental and private ownership restrictions, legal descriptions, real estate brokers, the basic real estate contract, deeds, liens on property, real estate financing, recording real estate documents, and title examination and insurance. The chapters on real estate contracts, deeds, financing, and title examination include hypothetical client scenarios highlighting paralegal responsibilities in these areas.

Part II of the text concentrates on the closing. The first chapter in this section is an introduction to the closing process, concentrating on the opening of a client file and its management, preclosing arrangements, document preparation for closing, the presently available real estate closing software, the closing itself, postclosing matters, tax matters, and escrow closings. The next three chapters are devoted to different closing situations: a residential real estate closing, a commercial real estate closing, and a construction loan closing. Included in each of these chapters is a discussion of special considerations pertaining to that type of closing, checklists, and a hypothetical client closing showing a paralegal in each step of the process.

Part III centers on landlord/tenant law. It covers the basic areas of residential and commercial leases and includes a chapter on eviction procedures. Each of the chapters in this section includes a hypothetical client matter, including a hypothetical eviction proceeding.

The focus of Part IV is on real estate litigation, a topic too often overlooked in real estate texts. This section explores many common litigation situations, including breach of sale contract, actions by real estate brokers, partition of property, and mortgage foreclosures. Each chapter in this section includes checklists, an explanation of pleadings to be filed, and a hypothetical client lawsuit.

Students have an opportunity to apply their knowledge further in the accompanying student workbook that creates a fictional law office environment in which the student will adapt checklists to meet state law requirements and handle client matters delegated by their supervising attorney including, but not limited to, such matters as the drafting of real estate contracts and leases; preparing title commitments and policies; handling residential, commercial, and construction loan closings including the preparation of all pertinent documents; and handling mortgage foreclosure proceedings. The student workbook provides instructions for setting up a resource portfolio of checklists, worksheets, and completed work product to be used as a constant resource tool.

Lynn T. Slossberg

ACKNOWLEDGMENTS

This text would not be possible without the assistance of several people. First, I would like to thank all those at West Publishing Company and Delmar Publishers who believed in this project for their guidance and patience. Special thanks to Elizabeth Hannan, Patricia Bryant, Rhonda Dearborn, and Linda Ireland.

I would like to thank Stuart M. Rapée of Attorneys' Title Insurance Fund, Inc. for his invaluable assistance with materials for the chapters on legal descriptions and title examinations and Elayne Prince for her input on commercial leases.

Thanks also to Henry Watson of Real Estate Expert Systems Associates, Inc. (REESA) for permission to use forms generated by REESA software in the chapters on real estate closings. I would like to thank John M. McCabe of The National Conference of Commissioners on Uniform State Laws for his assistance in obtaining permission for the reproduction of sections of various uniform acts, and Diane M. Noetzel for her assistance in obtaining permission for the reproduction of the Code of Ethics and Standards of Practice of the National Association of Realtors®. Additional thanks goes to Weldon Spencer of Spencer Systems, Inc. for permission to reprint materials and to Scott Murphy of Bankers Systems, Inc. for providing the loan application form found in the financing chapter.

Lastly, special thanks to the reviewers of this book for their invaluable input, including:

Carl Cone
South College

Lisa Dean
Georgetown University
Legal Assistant Program

John DeLeo
Central Pennsylvania
Business School

Ronald Goldfarb
Middlesex County College

Paul Guymon
William Rainey Harper
College

Flora F. Hessling
Briarcliffe College

Jane Johnson
May Technical College

Melissa Jones
Sanford University

Dianna Juettner
Mercy College

John Kaplan
New York City Technical
College

Ann Kastle
Edmonds Community
College

Cheryl Kirschner
Bentley College

Edward Kissling
Ocean County College

Nance Kriscenski
Manchester Community
Technical College

Victoria Combs Owen
Midway College

Mary Pavlovich
Duff's Business Institute

Paul Rausch
Interstate Business College

Chris Sadler
Denver Paralegal Institute

Paula Sinopoli
Mississippi Gulf Coast
Community College

Christine Taylor
Volunteer State Community
College

TABLE OF ILLUSTRATIONS

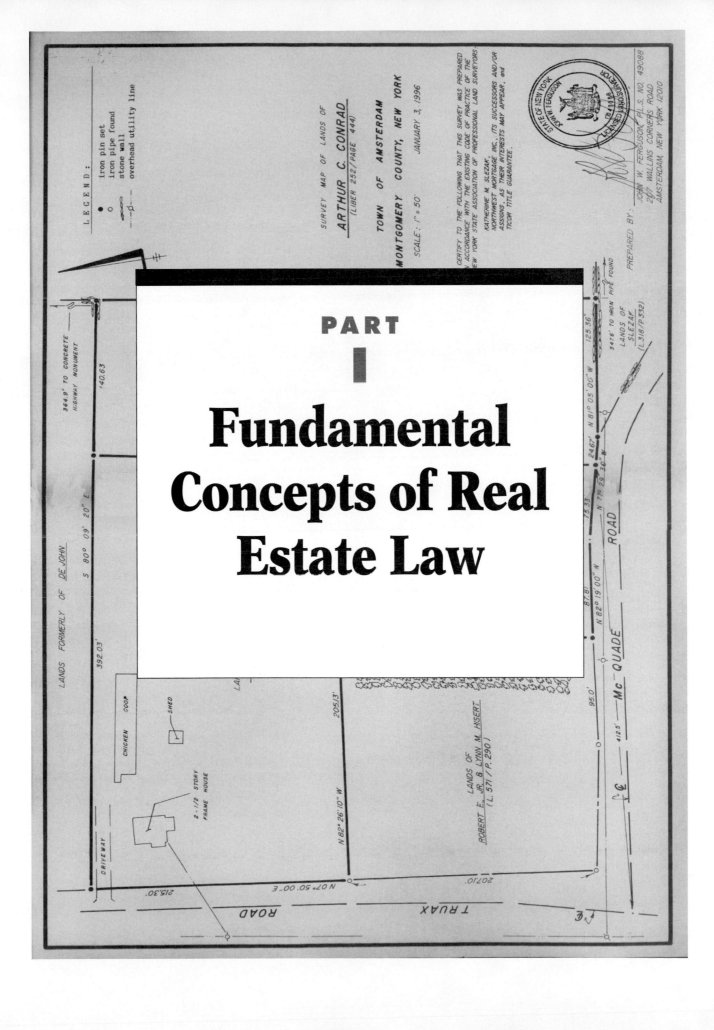

PART

I

Fundamental Concepts of Real Estate Law

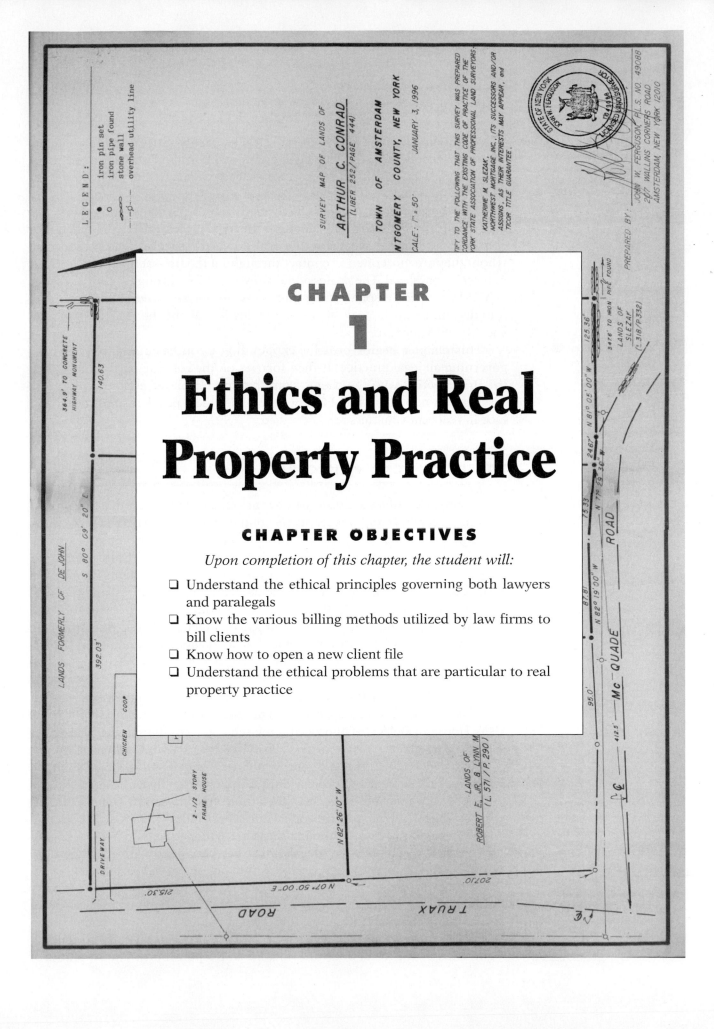

CHAPTER

1

Ethics and Real Property Practice

CHAPTER OBJECTIVES

Upon completion of this chapter, the student will:

❑ Understand the ethical principles governing both lawyers and paralegals
❑ Know the various billing methods utilized by law firms to bill clients
❑ Know how to open a new client file
❑ Understand the ethical problems that are particular to real property practice

INTRODUCTION

Real estate law offers you, the paralegal, a richly satisfying and challenging experience. It requires knowledge of a wide array of subjects: contracts, mortgages, surveys, and title insurance, just to name a few. It puts you in contact with an equally wide array of people: buyers and sellers, real estate brokers, mortgage brokers, bankers, lawyers from various firms, and others. The first exposure many individuals have to the legal profession occurs when they contact a law firm to aid them in a real estate transaction. The person with whom they are most often in contact throughout the transaction process is the real estate paralegal. The professionalism you exhibit through your knowledge of the law, your personal skills, and, most important, your ethics can profoundly influence the way these individuals feel about the legal system and, specifically, your firm.

This chapter begins broadly, expounding upon basic ethical principles governing all legal practice. It then focuses on the role the paralegal plays in the first meeting with the client, from the first telephone contact to the processing of a new client file. Finally, potential ethical problems that often surface in real estate matters are addressed.

BASIC ETHICAL PRINCIPLES

Professional ethics are governed by various regulations establishing guidelines for acceptable and unacceptable conduct within a particular profession. The legal profession abounds with such regulations to ensure that the profession responsibly serves the society in which it practices. These regulations take into consideration the interests of the general public, clients, the lawyer, nonlawyers working in legal environments, including paralegals, and the legal system as a whole. Further, these regulations come from state statutory and case law, rules of court, and codes of ethical conduct adopted by the American Bar Association (ABA) as well as state bar associations. In addition, professional paralegal associations provide guidelines for the ethical conduct of their members.

The ABA's Code of Professional Responsibility has been adopted by most states' bar associations as the official standard for legal conduct. In 1983, the ABA's House of Delegates approved a revised code, combining the prior rules with a set of ethical considerations clarifying and, in some instances, imposing more stringent restraints on legal conduct. This revised code was named the ABA's Model Rules of Professional Conduct. Together, these two codes commonly are referred to as the **ABA standards.** Presently, some state bar associations follow the original code while others follow the Model Rules, and still others embrace both. Although these regulations speak to a lawyer's conduct and responsibilities, paralegals must be acquainted with them because the supervising attorney is responsible for all actions of the paralegal.

The National Association of Legal Assistants (NALA), a voluntary national association of paralegals, has issued ethical canons in its Code of Ethics and Professional Responsibility, encompassing the ABA standards and applying them to paralegals. The last canon states a paralegal's ethical conduct is governed by the ABA's Code of Professional Responsibility. The emphasis of

ABA standards: Standards of ethical conduct for persons in the legal profession set forth in the American Bar Association's Model Code of Professional Responsibility and Model Code of Professional Conduct.

National Association of Legal Assistants (NALA): A voluntary national paralegal association.

the NALA code is to clarify the role the paralegal plays in a legal environment, noting the tasks that may and may not be undertaken by the paralegal, and stressing lawyer supervision and ultimate responsibility for the work product.

Ethical guidelines in statutes, court decisions, and association rules all state that paralegals must not engage in the *unauthorized practice of law.* This includes such practices as advising a client of his or her legal rights and remedies, representing a client in court, making strategy decisions in client matters, negotiating settlements, accepting cases, and setting fees. Each state has a statute that defines the practice of law, and many states have an "unauthorized practice of law" statute, the violation of which results in the imposition of sanctions. Although it is generally the law firm, not the transgressing paralegal, that incurs civil liability for any damage to a client resulting from the violation, the end result for the paralegal is often termination of employment. In some states, the unauthorized practice of law is considered a criminal offense and the offender may suffer fines or possible imprisonment.

Paralegals may engage in many aspects of legal work as long as the work is performed under the direction and supervision of an attorney. This means that the attorney maintains direct contact with the client and that all paralegal tasks are delegated by the attorney who personally examines, ultimately approves, and assumes full responsibility for the work product.

In supervising a paralegal, an attorney should give consideration to the paralegal's knowledge, training, and experience and delegate responsibilities accordingly. Within these parameters, paralegals may perform a multitude of functions such as conducting client interviews, locating and interviewing witnesses, conducting factual and legal research, drafting legal documents and correspondence, and assisting at depositions, hearings, trials, and real estate closings.

When first introduced to a client, a paralegal's nonlawyer status must be made clear. Similarly, when communicating with persons outside of the law firm, including other attorneys, a paralegal must disclose his or her status. Many states allow paralegals to carry business cards as long as their status appears next to or under their name. Many states also allow a paralegal's name to appear on law firm letterhead, again as long as he or she is listed as a paralegal or support staff. Letters signed by paralegals must indicate their status and must not contain legal advice.

Both attorneys and paralegals should assist in maintaining integrity and **competence** in the legal profession. An attorney must act competently in the representation of a client, which means that he or she not only must have the necessary legal skill required but also must devote adequate time and thorough preparation to the client matter. In like manner, a paralegal must be competent in fulfilling tasks delegated by the attorney. Competency is of particular concern in real estate practice because so many areas of the law may have an influence on any given real estate transaction. If asked to handle a responsibility totally outside his or her capabilities or experience, a paralegal must admit that the responsibility is beyond his or her present skills. The attorney will then determine whether the matter is one in which there is adequate time for the paralegal to become competent in the skill area, or whether the matter is best handled by another staff member.

Incompetent representation includes not only taking on a legal matter one is not competent to handle but also neglecting a client matter. Failure to

competence: Having the necessary legal skill to perform a given task and devoting the requisite time to that task to do a thorough job for the client.

handle a client matter in a timely fashion is one of the most frequent complaints heard before a state bar's grievance committee. Promptness and **diligence** (attentiveness and care) are as important in real estate practice as they are in any other area of law. Although real estate lawyers usually do not deal with court dates or **statutes of limitations** (statutes indicating the time periods within which suit must be brought or be forever barred) as often as civil trial lawyers, real estate contracts and closing documents do contain numerous deadlines that must be met.

Paralegals often are responsible for keeping track of all deadlines in each assigned client file and are involved directly in managing the workload. A good **tickler system** is crucial to prevent missed deadlines. A tickler system is a method of keeping track of priorities and deadlines. Tickler systems may be as simple as listing daily tasks on a calendar or as sophisticated as utilizing one of the many docketing softwares on the market. Many insurance companies require that law firms use at least two different systems as a condition for providing legal malpractice insurance.

Clients deserve attention. Communication is central to client satisfaction. Clients must be kept informed of the status of their legal matter on a regular basis. This task usually falls into the lap of the paralegal. Telephone calls should be returned promptly, preferably on the same day on which the original call was made. Many times the client simply wants a progress report. If this is the case, the paralegal may be in a better position to provide such a report than the attorney because the managing of client files is his or her domain. There are times, however, when the client will raise a question a paralegal may not ethically answer, even if the paralegal believes he or she knows the proper answer, because the answer necessarily contains legal advice or legal judgment (for example, rendering an opinion of title or the tax consequences of a particular real estate transaction). These matters must be addressed by the attorney, and if the attorney is not presently available, the client should be informed that the matter will be forwarded to the attorney who will return the client's call promptly.

Sacrosanct in the practice of law is the concept of **confidentiality.** All persons working in a law firm must preserve the confidences of clients. This rule pertains to potential clients who decide not to engage the firm, current clients, and former clients. Note that confidentiality is a different concept than **attorney-client privilege.** Attorney-client privilege is a rule of evidence law that prevents a court from compelling the revelation of communications between attorney and client. The privilege belongs to the client, not the attorney, and only the client may waive it. Confidentiality is an ethical concept and is considerably broader in scope than attorney-client privilege. It prohibits an attorney, and others in the legal environment, from voluntarily disclosing information about a client matter. It covers not only direct confidential communications between client and attorney but also any other information the attorney obtains during representation of the client from whatever source. Further, it pertains to both the disclosure of this information and to the use of it, which prevents an attorney and his or her support staff from using confidential information without the client's consent.

The most complex ethical issues are found in the context of **conflicts of interest,** particularly in the field of real estate law, as discussed in a later section of this chapter. In general terms, situations giving rise to conflicts of

diligence: Attentiveness and care.

statute of limitations: A statute indicating the time periods within which a suit must be brought or be forever barred.

tickler system: A method of keeping track of priorities and deadlines.

confidentiality: An ethical concept prohibiting a lawyer and others in a law firm from voluntarily disclosing information about a client matter.

attorney-client privilege: A rule of evidence law that prevents a court from compelling the revelation of communications between lawyer and client.

conflict of interest: A situation in which a lawyer's professional judgment might be affected because of business or personal interests.

interest are set forth in the ABA standards as well as each state's adopted code of professional responsibility. A basic definition of a conflict of interest is any situation in which an attorney's professional judgment might be affected because of business or personal interests. Taking on a new client who wishes to sue a current client is an obvious example of a conflict of interest inasmuch as an attorney in this situation is prevented from properly representing one party without adversely affecting the other. If the conflict is apparent before the attorney takes on a matter, the attorney must not represent the conflicting client. If the conflict becomes apparent only after the attorney has taken on the matter, the attorney must withdraw from the representation of one or both clients.

The ABA standards state that an attorney cannot represent a client if to do so would adversely affect the interests of another *unless* the attorney informs the parties of the conflict and each party consents after consultation. The problem here is that consultation necessarily includes the disclosure of all relevant facts. If the attorney were to disclose these facts, he or she could very well be breaching the duty of confidentiality.

A subtler but equally discomfiting situation pertains to third parties. Sometimes the attorney's compensation will come from a third party. The attorney's ethical responsibilities are to the client. The client is the individual or entity requiring the legal representation, not the individual or entity paying the legal fees. If the attorney believes that the third party's interest will prevent proper representation of the client (for example, it might conflict with the interest of the client or the third party might request that the lawyer violate the duty of confidentiality), the attorney must address these issues before assuming representation.

In real estate practice, third-party issues often surface in other ways, usually through the form of a real estate broker, title agent, or lender who refers business to the attorney in anticipation that the grateful attorney will act as a "deal maker." In order to properly represent the client, the attorney may be forced to disappoint the third party who referred the matter. The loyalty must always be to the client.

INITIAL MEETING WITH THE CLIENT

As a paralegal, you may become involved with your firm's clients as early as the initial client meeting. Law firms today realize that under the direction and supervision of an attorney, a knowledgeable paralegal can competently and cost-effectively provide many services for the client and, as noted earlier, is often the client's major contact in the firm. Clients who understand the role a paralegal plays in a law firm welcome the assistance of a paralegal with their legal matters, especially when apprised of the fact that paralegal services are billed at a lower rate than attorney services.

When a potential client telephones the law firm to make an appointment, the receptionist will turn the call over to you. Be sure to check your attorney's calendar for availability and to obtain certain basic information, such as the date and time of the call, the client's name and telephone number, and a brief description of the client matter. Before ending the telephone conversation, give the client precise directions to the office and inform him or her of appropriate documents to bring to an initial meeting. For example, the attorney may need the client to bring a real estate contract, existing title policy, surveys, or other pertinent documents. Once you have concluded your telephone conversation with the client, note the date, time, client's name, and telephone number directly on the attorney's calendar. This provides both you and the attorney immediate access for reviewing the client schedule for the day first thing in the morning, as well as for quick rescheduling of appointments.

The new client's name should be checked against the firm's current client case listings for a conflict of interest before the initial meeting with the client. If your law firm has more than one attorney, you must check not only your own attorney's client list but also the case listings for all attorneys in the firm. Under the **doctrine of imputed disqualification,** the entire body of attorneys in a firm is treated as one for conflict of interest purposes. Conducting such a check may reveal, for instance, that another attorney in the firm is representing an established client in a matter directly in conflict with the matter of the person for whom you set up an initial appointment, in which case the conflict of interest must be brought to your supervising attorney's attention.

A conflict of interest can also arise when an attorney or paralegal leaves a law firm, government agency, title company, bank, or mortgage company for other employment. If the new firm, agency, or company represents a client whose interests are adverse to those of a party represented by the old firm, agency, or company, a conflict of interest exists. If the new firm has yet to agree to represent the client, the firm may decline representation. Alternatively, the new firm may agree to representation and isolate the attorney or paralegal from the old firm from all contacts with the client's case. This tactic of isolation is sometimes referred to as a **Chinese Wall.**

When checking for conflicts of interest, even though a business client will be the business entity and not the individual who represents the entity, both names must be checked. For example, if the new client is Douglas Harrington of Country Estates Development Corporation, a thorough check would include both names. A corporate client may conduct business under a **fictitious name,** a name other than the corporation's legal name on the articles of incorporation. If this is the case, the fictitious name would need to be checked as well.

Once you are assured that no conflict appears, your next step is to open a file for the new client. Many firms have a new client data sheet to initiate this procedure, such as the one provided in Figure 1–1. Basic background information on the client is included on this form, such as the nature of the client matter, the name of the individuals to be handling the matter, and the pertinent billing information. After the form is completed, it will be forwarded to the legal secretary for data entry, assigned a client number and matter number, forwarded to the billing department, and placed in the client file.

Every new client is assigned his or her own client number, which may be numeric (for example, 4839) or alphanumeric (for example, T4839). If an alphanumeric system is used, the letter may refer to the client's name or the responsible attorney's name. The assignment of a client number helps not only to organize office files but also to preserve the confidentiality of a client. The names of clients are as confidential as any other client information and must not be revealed to others coming into the law office. Attorneys and paralegals often have several client files stacked on their desks or elsewhere in their

doctrine of imputed disqualification: A doctrine which provides that the entire body of lawyers in a firm are treated as one for conflict of interest purposes.

Chinese Wall: A situation in which an attorney or paralegal is isolated from a client case for conflict of interest reasons.

fictitious name: A name other than one's legal name under which one operates a business.

FIGURE 1–1
New client data sheet

NEW CLIENT DATA SHEET

DATE: _____

REFERRED BY: _____

INITIATING ATTORNEY: _____

ASSIGNED ATTORNEY(S): _____

ASSIGNED PARALEGAL(S): _____

CLIENT NUMBER: _____

MATTER NUMBER: _____

TYPE OF CASE: _____

(Supply one of the following):

01	Real estate closing	08	Personal injury
02	Real estate litigation	09	Contracts
03	Commercial litigation	10	Corporate
04	Probate	11	Bankruptcy
05	Divorce	12	Trusts and estates
06	Medical malpractice	13	Workers' compensation
07	Other professional malpractice	14	Other

BILLING METHOD: _____

(Supply one of the following):

01	Hourly fee: standard rate	04	Contingency fee: special rate
02	Hourly fee: special rate	05	Flat fee: (supply fee in special
03	Contingency fee: standard rate		rate line below)

SPECIAL RATE (Please describe in detail):

_____

_____

RETAINER FOR COSTS: _____

BILLING FREQUENCY : COSTS: _____ FEES: _____

(Supply one of the following):

01	Annually	04	Monthly
02	Semiannually	05	End of case
03	Quarterly	06	Other

CLIENT NAME: _____

CLIENT BILLING ADDRESS: _____

_____

CLIENT PHONE: HOME: _____ OFFICE: _____ FAX: _____

CASE NAME: _____

OPPOSING PARTY (PARTIES): _____

ADDRESS OF OPPOSING PARTY (PARTIES): _____

_____

_____

OPPOSING COUNSEL: _____

ADDRESS OF OPPOSING COUNSEL: _____

_____

OPPOSING COUNSEL'S PHONE: _____ FAX: _____

CASE NUMBER: _____ COURT: _____

JUDGE: _____ JUDICIAL ASSISTANT: _____

offices. If a client's name appeared on the outside of the file, this could present an ethical problem should another client enter the office. The use of client numbers prevents a breach of confidentiality.

It is common for an attorney to handle several different matters for a client, and so a client matter number must be assigned to each matter. This number is added to the end of the client number, for example, in 4839.0001, the 0001 refers to the first client matter the firm is handling for this client.

In addition to the new client data sheet, a **retainer agreement** should be placed in the file. A retainer agreement is a contract spelling out the fee agreement reached between the attorney and the client should the client decide to hire the attorney after the initial consultation. The retainer agreement will reflect one of the three common billing methods used in law firms: flat fees, hourly fees, and contingency fees.

One type of fee arrangement common in real estate practice is the charging of **flat fees,** which are sometimes referred to as *fixed fees*. These fees make the most sense when dealing with routine legal matters in which the amount of work involved is fairly easy to determine. In real estate, flat fees may be used in simple closings, the preparation of a title opinion letter, or the preparation of a residential lease.

In handling other matters, such as a mortgage foreclosure or other types of real estate litigation in which the amount of time required on the matter is difficult to determine, the **hourly fee** agreement may be more appropriate. Here the client pays for the attorney's services based upon the amount of time spent on the client matter. A hierarchical fee structure typically prevails in law firms, with a client paying more per hour for the services of a senior partner than for those of an associate, and still less for those of a paralegal.

Contingency fees are not used in standard real estate practices. They are most commonly used in personal injury cases and certain other tort matters. The fee for the attorney's services, set forth as a percentage of the judgment or settlement, is contingent upon the client settling the case or winning in court. Caps are set by statute on the percentage that may be charged in contingency fee cases in many states. Additionally, clients often are given the right to cancel the contingency fee agreement within three business days from the date they signed it. It is important to note that the contingency fee refers only to payment to an attorney for the time spent on the case and does not include any costs incurred on behalf of the client (for example, filing fees, expert witness fees, and the like). The client is responsible for these costs whether or not the client settles, wins, or loses.

Understandably, it is imperative to keep meticulous track of time when working on a client matter. Many law firms bill in tenths of an hour (six-minute intervals). Each attorney and paralegal is required to record the time he or she spends on each client matter on time slips. Time slips specify the time each task was started and completed and contain a description of the work done. These time slips may be manual forms, or they may be entered on a computer time slip program.

An attorney may require a retainer to be paid upon the signing of a retainer agreement. This sum must be deposited in the firm's **client trust fund account,** which is an account separate from the firm's regular business account. This retainer amount may be put toward fees, costs, or both,

retainer agreement: A contract between an attorney and client that sets forth the manner in which the client will be billed for the attorney's work.

flat fee: An attorney's fee set forth as a sum certain for the performance of a specified task.

hourly fee: An attorney's fee based upon the amount of time the attorney spends on a client matter.

contingency fee: An attorney's fee that is contingent upon the client reaching settlement or winning in court. The payment the attorney receives is set forth as a percentage of the settlement or court award.

client trust fund account: An account separate from the law firm's regular business account in which fee advances, deposit money, closing proceeds, and/or escrowed funds are placed.

according to the terms of the retainer agreement, with withdrawals made in installments as the costs are incurred or the fees are earned. Any unearned portion of the retainer must be refunded to the client. In addition to retainer fees, any deposit money, closing proceeds, or escrowed funds must be deposited in the client trust fund account. State professional codes of ethics impose very strict rules for the handling of client trust accounts, and therefore, it is crucial to understand the manner in which your firm's accounts are administered.

Finally, the new client file should contain an interview information worksheet to be used during the initial client conference. The client will have provided you with a basic summary of his or her legal matter when speaking with you to set up the appointment. This information will enable you to select the appropriate specialized worksheet to aid in preparing the initial client documents (for example, a specialized worksheet for a residential real estate closing, a commercial real estate closing, and so on). Numerous specialized worksheets are provided throughout this text. Such worksheets aid significantly in ensuring that all details are addressed. A well-organized paralegal will have the new client file containing these basic contents sitting on the attorney's desk prior to the initial client meeting.

An initial conference with a client will start with a discussion between the client and the attorney. The attorney should introduce the client to all staff members who will be working on the client matter and may ask you to attend. Your status as a paralegal, as well as the status of all other staff members, should be clearly indicated to the client. The consultation fee, if any, may have been discussed by the attorney and client over the telephone. The attorney should explain to the client that all fee arrangements will be discussed thoroughly before the client must pay any additional amounts.

The attorney also should indicate to the client that both the attorney and the client are free to withhold judgment on representation until the end of the consultation. The attorney may spend enough time in this initial conference to assess the client's legal matter and then turn the client over to you, asking you to take the client into a conference room to obtain further detailed information.

Should the client decide to hire your firm to represent him or her in a particular transaction, the attorney and client will sign the retainer agreement before the client leaves the office, and the client will receive a copy of the agreement for his or her files. If a retainer fee is required, it will be collected at this time.

Before the client leaves the office, you or your supervising attorney should review with the client any additional information the client must provide before the client matter can proceed further. Additionally, a follow-up letter should be sent to the client as a reminder. If the client was unable to provide all of the information required on the worksheet, make a photocopy of the partially completed worksheet and give it to the client to complete at home, together with an addressed, stamped envelope for return to your office. Again, a reminder letter should be sent.

The importance of a reminder letter cannot be stressed too strongly. The letter serves not only as a common courtesy but also as protection against miscommunication between attorney and client and possible malpractice. Without a reminder letter, a client may assume that his or her legal matter is progressing when, in fact, the client file has remained inactive awaiting further information from the client. It is advisable to follow up the reminder letter with a telephone call to motivate the client to return papers or provide necessary information promptly.

In some instances, the client may not be certain that he or she wants to proceed after the initial meeting with the attorney, and the results of the consultation may be unclear because the client has neither accepted nor declined legal representation. If this happens, rather than closing the file, it should be retained as an inactive file for a prescribed period of time (for example, 90 days, 120 days). Prior to the expiration of this time period, a letter should be sent to the prospective client, informing him or her that the firm will be closing the client file if it does not hear from the client by a set date.

Should the client decide not to hire the firm, or the attorney decline representation for any reason, the file should be closed, but not without first sending the client a letter confirming that the client met with the attorney and declined representation, such as the sample letter found in Figure 1–2. Although paralegals are allowed to draft these letters, the ethical code prohibits paralegals from signing them; such a letter must be signed by the attorney.

FIGURE 1–2
Follow-up letter

August 1, 1997

CERTIFIED MAIL #P112264551
RETURN RECEIPT REQUESTED

Madeline Stevenson
22 Granville Terrace
Any City, Any State

Re: Stevenson v. Dutton Construction Company

Dear Ms. Stevenson:

Thank you for consulting our office concerning your legal matter. It is my understanding that as a result of our meeting on July 28, 1997, you have decided to decline our services with respect to your proposed lawsuit against Dutton Construction Company for breach of a construction contract.

Should you choose to pursue this matter further, I advise you to consult another attorney immediately. There are certain statutory time periods during which lawsuits must be filed and claims must be made. Any delay could prevent you from exercising your rights.

Sincerely,

Ava Ross, Esquire

POTENTIAL ETHICAL PROBLEMS

The majority of ethical problems confronting the real estate attorney fall within the realm of conflict of interest. Problems occur because real estate attorneys commonly are requested to take dual representation in several scenarios. One such scenario involves a seller who hires an attorney to represent him or her in a closing and a buyer who requests that the attorney represent both the buyer and seller. Sometimes the attorney is hired by one party and agrees to prepare closing documents for the other party for a small fee. Another scenario is one in which one party retains the attorney, and then that party enters into an agreement with the other party to split the fee. Still another dual representation scenario occurs when a buyer or seller retains the attorney, who is then requested to represent the lender financing the transaction.

Although the ABA standards allow dual representation in a transaction if the parties are informed of the potential conflict and agree to the dual representation after full disclosure, the better practice is to decline such representation, suggesting that either the buyer or the seller seek independent counsel. If the attorney believes, in his or her own professional judgment, that multiple-party representation will adversely affect his or her legal judgment, then the attorney must decline such representation, even if the parties consent to it.

Special problems are presented in the area of title examination. An attorney must be able to exercise fully his or her independent professional judgment when rendering an opinion of title. This judgment is easily challenged when the attorney takes on any form of dual representation. If an attorney representing a seller provides a title insurance policy to the buyer at the seller's expense, no problem presents itself. If the buyer pays for the policy, however, the ethical question arises. Many real estate attorneys become title insurance agents with commercial title companies. If the attorney providing the title examination of a property is an agent and is charging a party for the title work separately from the charges for other real estate services, the attorney must disclose his or her interest in the title insurance company.

Often one party to a real estate transaction will choose to forego legal representation and the other party's lawyer will draft all necessary closing documents. Dealing with unrepresented parties poses its own problems. The unrepresented party may seek legal advice from the attorney or may assume that because the attorney is drafting all of the documents the attorney is a disinterested party. The attorney should guard his or her conduct carefully in these situations, declining to provide legal advice and clarifying his or her role in the transaction. Some courts have held that when a party is unrepresented at a real estate closing, the attending attorney must not only disclose to the unrepresented party that he or she is representing an adverse interest but must also explain the material terms of all closing documents to the unrepresented party so the party understands the effect of signing the documents. The better practice is to provide a form to the nonrepresented party advising him or her that the attending attorney represents the seller (or buyer, as the case may be) and advising the nonrepresented party to consult his or her own counsel.

The situation of unrepresented parties may arise not only in cases in which the attorney represents the buyer or the seller but also when the attorney represents the lender in the real estate transaction. In such a situation, the buyer (borrower) may be unrepresented, yet may be contributing to the payment of the lender's attorney fees as part of the loan costs. If the attorney representing the lender has any direct dealings with the buyer, the attorney may have certain disclosure duties, such as disclosing any title defects to the buyer.

Many real estate transactions are considered "routine," while others may be quite complex. An attorney must educate himself or herself on the law pertaining to aspects of the transaction with which he or she is unfamiliar. The complexities of the transaction may require the hiring of additional counsel specialized in other areas such as federal and state tax laws, securities regulations, or environmental law. The client must be informed of and agree to the hiring of additional counsel. Further, nonlegal experts may be required to ensure a successful transaction. No experts should be retained without the informed consent of the client. The client should be informed not only of the costs of employing experts but also of the potential detriment to the client if the expert is not employed.

CHAPTER SUMMARY

1. State bar associations have adopted the American Bar Association's (ABA's) Code of Professional Responsibility, the ABA's Model Rules of Professional Responsibility, or a combination of both. Although these codes address the ethical conduct of attorneys, they pertain to paralegals as well. Additionally, the National Association of Legal Assistants (NALA) has encompassed the major tenets of the ABA standards in its Code of Ethics and Professional Responsibility.

2. Paralegals may avoid the unauthorized practice of law by following certain guidelines: (1) only accepting tasks delegated by a supervising lawyer, (2) alerting clients and third parties to one's paralegal status, (3) avoiding any request for legal advice, and (4) making certain that the lawyer personally examines and approves of the work product produced.

3. A paralegal's ethical duties include preserving clients' confidences, alerting attorneys of potential conflicts of interest by conducting a conflict of interest check prior to opening a new client file, and ensuring that clients are routinely updated on the status of their cases.

4. An initial client folder should be prepared prior to the client's first conference at the law office. This folder should include a new client data sheet, a retainer agreement, and a client interview worksheet. Each new client is assigned a client number, and each client project is assigned its own matter number. These numbers are assigned to promote efficiency in handling client files as well as client confidentiality.

5. The three types of retainer agreements are contingency fee, flat fee, and hourly fee agreements. Many routine real estate transactions are handled on a flat fee basis, while most real estate litigation is billed at hourly rates.

6. Upon the completion of the initial consultation, the client file may be given an active, inactive, or closed file status. If the client hires the attorney, the client will receive a copy of the retainer agreement. Before leaving the office, additional information to be provided by the client should be

reviewed, followed by a reminder letter. If the client remains undecided about representation, the file is labeled inactive and remains so for the firm's prescribed inactive period. At the close of this period, a letter is sent to the client indicating the firm's intentions to close the file. The file will be closed if the client declines representation, and a letter is sent to the client confirming the client's decision.

7. The most common ethical problems facing real estate attorneys occur in one of two contexts: (1) dual representation and (2) the unrepresented party. Dual representation may arise when: (1) a buyer or seller hires a lawyer and the lawyer is later asked to represent both, (2) buyers and sellers decide amongst themselves to split a lawyer's legal fees, (3) a lawyer represents one party and also prepares documents for an unrepresented party for a small fee, and (4) a buyer or seller hires a lawyer and the lawyer is later asked to also represent a lender. The best practice is to decline dual representation, suggesting that all parties obtain independent counsel.

REVIEW QUESTIONS

1. Which of the three billing options (contingency fee, flat fee, hourly fee) would be most appropriate in the following situations?
   a. Preparing a residential lease
   b. Representing a client in a construction litigation lawsuit
   c. Handling a complex commercial closing
2. Distinguish between the concept of attorney-client privilege and the concept of confidentiality.
3. How may a paralegal avoid the unauthorized practice of law?
4. What are the two most common ethical problems facing real estate attorneys? What should be done when confronted with these situations?
5. What items should be included in an initial client folder?

ETHICAL QUESTIONS

Your supervising attorney is representing client CBH Properties, Inc. CBH Properties is in the business of buying and selling real property for investment purposes and has found a commercial property it would like to attain. Rather than purchase the property, CBH Properties wants to do a like-kind property exchange, exchanging one of the commercial properties it presently owns for the one it wants. Your supervising attorney hands you some notes pertaining to the two properties in question and asks you to research the relevant tax laws to determine whether the proposed transaction will satisfy the statutory criteria to defer the paying of capital gains taxes on the transaction. Your supervising attorney wants you to provide her with a memorandum and copies of all relevant statutes. She needs an answer by this afternoon. You have no experience with tax law and once you begin your research you realize you are in over your head, yet you do not want to disappoint her. What should you do?

PRACTICAL ASSIGNMENTS

Assignment 1:1. Set up a resource portfolio according to the instructions in your student workbook. As you progress through this text, the portfolio will contain checklists, worksheets, and documents you have drafted for your supervising attorney.

Assignment 1:2. Obtain a copy of your state's code of legal conduct. After reading through the regulations, for each rule write a sentence indicating how that rule impacts your ethical responsibility as a paralegal.

Assignment 1:3. Research your state statutes to determine how your state defines the practice of law and, conversely, the unauthorized practice of law. What sanctions are imposed for violation of these statutes?

Assignment 1:4. Your supervising attorney, Deborah Sanders, has just met with a new client, Justin Foster, president of Monteagle Condominium Association, Inc. The condominium association has placed a lien on the condominium unit owned by Susan Wright for delinquent condominium assessments and now wants to foreclose on the lien. After meeting with Deborah, Justin has decided to hire her to handle the case. Deborah has asked you to write a follow-up letter for her signature, thanking Justin Foster, as representative of the condominium association, for retaining your firm, Hernandez, Sanders, and Norris, P.A., and reminding him to provide Deborah with the following: (1) a copy of the declaration of condominium of Monteagle Condominium, (2) a copy of the letter sent by the condominium association to Susan Wright indicating the association's intention to foreclose on the lien, and (3) a copy of the recorded lien. The client condominium association's office address is 300 Montbank Drive, #100 (your city and state).

Assignment 1:5. Brenda Hoskins has called your supervising attorney for legal advice. She is very upset, having just attended the closing on her home. She sold her home to Paul and Priscilla Watson, who have used the services of Middleton Mortgage Company in obtaining a loan to purchase the property. Middleton Mortgage Company is represented by attorney Nathaniel Cowling, who regularly represents Middleton Mortgage Company and is representing the Watsons as well. Nathaniel Cowling is known to run his real estate practice like a "closing mill," handling several closings a day. When Brenda asked Nathaniel whether she needed to hire an attorney to represent her at the closing, he told her that most sellers do not bother because the lending institution prepares the necessary documents. Brenda arrived at Nathaniel's office this morning to close on her house, only to find that she has been charged on the closing statement an attorney's fee of $200 for the preparation of legal documents. This morning was the first time she was made aware of this fee. When she questioned Nathaniel about the fee, he told her that as a courtesy he prepares and furnishes a package of forms that are to be executed by the seller, and that the fee charged is considerably less than what an attorney would charge to represent her at the closing. She did not want to pay the fee, but she also did not want to hold up the closing, so she signed the closing statement. She now wants to know if Nathaniel's actions were proper and if there are any grounds for complaint. Deborah has asked you to research the matter. Are there any cases in your jurisdiction that address this matter? If not, does your state's ethical code provide any commentary that would be relevant?

Assignment 1:6. Deborah has also received a telephone call from a potential client, Jack Barlow, a real estate broker she met with last week. He consulted Deborah regarding a lawsuit he wanted to bring on behalf of his brokerage firm, Barlow Realty, Inc., against a seller, Oliver Edmonds, for failure to pay a real estate commission. He has telephoned today to tell Deborah that he has decided not to have your firm represent him in the matter. Deborah has asked you to send him a letter confirming that he has declined representation. Barlow Realty, Inc.'s address is 240 Turnbull Drive (your city and state).

Assignment 1:7. Define the following key terms.

ABA standards	doctrine of imputed disqualification
attorney-client privilege	fictitious name
Chinese Wall	flat fee
client trust fund account	hourly fee
competence	National Association of Legal Assistants
confidentiality	(NALA)
conflict of interest	retainer agreement
contingency fee	statute of limitations
diligence	tickler system

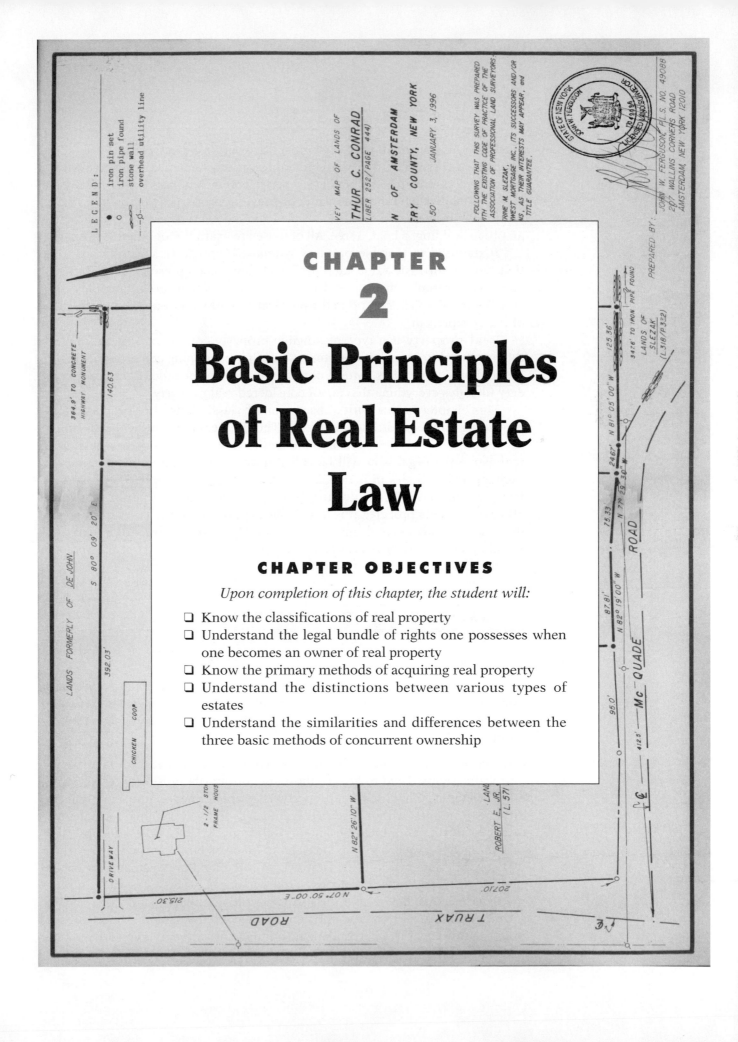

CHAPTER
2

Basic Principles of Real Estate Law

CHAPTER OBJECTIVES

Upon completion of this chapter, the student will:

❑ Know the classifications of real property
❑ Understand the legal bundle of rights one possesses when one becomes an owner of real property
❑ Know the primary methods of acquiring real property
❑ Understand the distinctions between various types of estates
❑ Understand the similarities and differences between the three basic methods of concurrent ownership

INTRODUCTION

Property is a broad term, encompassing everything subject to ownership. There are various ways of classifying property, some of which necessarily overlap. One classification is tangible property. *Tangible property* is property that can be touched. The intrinsic value of tangible property is embodied in the physical subject matter itself. Examples abound everywhere: a desk, a plate, an office building, a boat, a tree. All of these are examples of tangible property.

Juxtaposed to tangible property is *intangible property*, which is property that has no intrinsic value in and of itself but that represents something of value. For example, checks, stock certificates, and patents are intangible property. Their value is not found in the physical slips of paper but in what the slips of paper represent.

Real property is a type of tangible property comprised of land and all things affixed to it, such as apartment buildings, shopping centers, and single-family homes as well as natural objects growing on the land. **Personal property** includes everything that is not considered real property.

This chapter begins with a discussion of classifications of property, concentrating on the physical components. The chapter continues with a explanation of basic ownership rights and the methods of acquiring these rights. As a real estate paralegal, you will be called upon to draft numerous documents exchanged by parties in a real estate transaction, such as deeds, financing instruments, and bills of sale, just to name a few. In order to draft these and other documents properly, it is important to understand the types of interests that can be conveyed and the various methods of holding title to property, so the chapter details these issues. The chapter concludes with special spousal rights that may impact the title to and transfer of real property.

CLASSIFICATIONS OF PROPERTY

Real Property

Real property, also referred to as *real estate* or *realty,* is a general term pertaining to land and all things permanently attached to the land. It also refers to a composite of physical components including surface, subsurface, and air space, and the rights attendant to each.

Surface Rights. Surface rights in property may be divided into land rights and water rights. *Land rights* are those one ordinarily presumes to have and enjoy when one purchases real property. They are defined as property rights in all land contained within specified boundaries, plus everything permanently attached to the land, including natural elements such as trees, shrubs, and other foliage, as well as manmade elements such as buildings and other artificial constructions. Certain items growing on the land are deemed part of the real property, and others are considered personal property. The determining factor is whether the item is the result of cultivated labor, as in the case of farming crops. In such a case, the item is considered personal property. If the item is naturally growing, requiring no annual cultivation, it is considered real property.

real property: Property comprised of land and all things affixed to it, as well as natural objects on or growing on the land.

personal property: All property that is not considered real property.

Water rights are those rights pertaining to property covered by water on or adjacent to a landowner's boundaries as well as rights in the use of the water itself. Water has always been considered a scarce and prized resource in this country—valuable for consumption, recreation, and industry. Because of this fact, a landowner's rights in a body of water adjacent to his or her property are an important factor in assessing the value of that property. Factors determining the extent of the landowner's rights in water are (1) the source and (2) the characteristics of the water.

One source of water is groundwater, found below the surface of the land. It may be created by underground streams or by the accumulation of rainwater that has penetrated the soil. Groundwater is considered part of the property on which it is found and therefore belongs to the property owner to use as he or she deems fit, as long as that use does not divert water away from or harm an adjoining property owner. The same is true of surface water formed by rainwater accumulating on the surface of the land. In neither case may the property owner divert the natural flow of the water.

Natural bodies of water, such as rivers, lakes, and streams, are governed by one of two doctrines: the riparian doctrine or the appropriation doctrine. The word *riparian* derives from the Latin *ripa*, meaning "river." The *riparian doctrine*, dating back to ancient times, is premised on the theory that citizens should share water rights equally for their daily needs. This doctrine divides water rights into riparian rights and littoral rights.

Littoral rights are those pertaining to a landowner whose land abuts a lake, ocean, or sea. Littoral rights give the landowner access to and use of the water, but the landowner owns only up to the high-water line.

Riparian rights are those pertaining to a landowner whose land abuts a river, stream, or similar watercourse. To determine the extent of a landowner's riparian rights, one must look to the body of water and first determine whether it is navigable or nonnavigable. If the water adjacent to a landowner's property is deemed navigable, it is considered a public waterway, and the submerged land underneath this waterway is owned by the state. Therefore, the landowner may use the water just as a member of the public may, with the landowner's property rights extending only to the water's edge. Nonnavigable waters generally are shallow lakes, small ponds, and rivulets. A landowner whose property is adjacent to nonnavigable water owns the submerged land up to the center of the water.

Under the riparian doctrine, a landowner whose property abuts a natural body of water may make use of the water as long as he or she does not preclude a neighboring landowner's use of it. Additionally, this doctrine affords the landowner ingress and egress between the property and the water, as well as the right of view from the property to and over the water.

The *appropriation doctrine* developed out of necessity as American settlers moved west to claim homesteads at the same time that a new mining industry expanded. Increasing conflict over the scarce water supply resulted in a doctrine of first in use, first in right. In order to substantiate a claim under this doctrine, a landowner must be able to show diversion of the water with the intention to use it in a beneficial manner. Those states that still follow this doctrine (primarily western states) issue water permits to landowners who can show valid appropriation.

littoral rights: Water rights pertaining to a landowner whose property abuts a lake, ocean, or sea.

riparian rights: Water rights pertaining to a landowner whose property abuts a river, stream, or similar watercourse.

The understanding of a few other terms is necessary to round out this discussion of surface rights. They are *accretion, erosion, avulsion,* and *reliction.* Accretion and reliction pertain to the addition to land, whereas erosion and avulsion pertain to the loss of land.

Accretion is the addition to land by the gradual and seemingly imperceptible deposit of water-borne material, called *alluvian,* on the shore. The landowner who has riparian rights continues to own the land up to the edge of the water, thus owning this addition to his or her property.

The process of *reliction* works differently. Instead of materials washing up on shore and adding to the property, water gradually recedes and dries up, uncovering land. The same rule applies, however, when applying riparian rights. The landowner, owning to the water's edge, has gained the additional land uncovered by reliction.

Erosion, sometimes referred to as *submergence,* is the opposite of accretion. In this instance, material is gradually washed away from the shore by tides or currents. Erosion causes the owner of riparian rights to lose portions of property that are submerged by this process.

Avulsion is the result of a sudden or violent natural disturbance, such as a tropical storm or hurricane, that causes a loss of property bordering on the water. When avulsion occurs, unlike erosion, the landowner retains ownership of the now-submerged property lost during the upheaval.

Air Rights. In addition to owning the surface of his or her parcel of property, the landowner owns the air space above the parcel extending up to heights established by law. Up to these legal limits, the property owner has *private air rights.* Above the legal limit, the air space necessarily is subject to *public air rights* to allow use for communications technology and aerial transportation. Local government regulates air rights near airports.

Depending on the location of the parcel, the value of private air rights may be insignificant or quite valuable. In congested cities, such as Manhattan and Chicago, for instance, buildings have been constructed on the air space of another's property. The Pan Am Building in Manhattan and the Merchandise Mart in Chicago are two examples of landmark structures built on private air "lots," both located in strategic city centers.

Air space also is important to a property's value if the property is in a scenically desirable location. In this situation, one wants to prevent another from building a structure that would obstruct the view. A possible solution to ensure a continued view would be to buy the air space of adjoining properties.

Subsurface Rights. *Subsurface rights,* sometimes referred to as *mineral rights,* are rights in land extending from the surface boundaries of a parcel of land downward, toward the center of the earth, and include oil, gas, ore, and other minerals, but not water. When a purchaser purchases a parcel of land, subsurface rights generally are included with the surface rights to the property unless they have been previously severed or the real estate contract for sale and purchase provides otherwise.

In some instances, the subsurface rights may be more valuable than the surface rights, such as in the case of property located in areas rich in mineral, gas, or oil resources. Under such circumstances, the property owner may choose to sell or lease subsurface rights to another, allowing the purchaser or lessee of such rights to enter the property to extract the natural resource, while keeping the surface rights for himself or herself.

Personal Property

Personal property, also referred to as *chattel* or *personalty,* is a catch-all term referring to all property that is not real property and the basic characteristic of which is movability. Whereas real property is transferred legally by deed (discussed in detail in Chapter 8), personal property is transferred by a document called a **bill of sale,** or *receipt.* Although a real estate contract for sale and purchase may contain a personalty provision that itemizes any personal property (for example, a dining room set, patio furniture, area rugs) sold to the buyer of a residential property, most attorneys also prepare a bill of sale.

In assisting your supervising attorney in preparation for a real estate closing, you may be asked to draft this document. The bill of sale may include items that are being sold outside of the real estate contract for sale and purchase. Additionally, the bill of sale may state the condition the personal property must be in at time of sale. A sample bill of sale is found in Figure 2–1.

If a real estate transaction involves both real and personal property and financing is involved, a lending institution may require the pledging of personal property as part of the collateral for the loan. In this situation, it is important for the lending institution to *perfect* its security interest in the personal property. Perfecting a security interest is a way of indicating priority status among creditors. This is done by filing a UCC-1 financing statement, sometimes referred to as a filing statement or financing statement, in the same office in which mortgages on real property are recorded.

The abbreviation UCC refers to the Uniform Commercial Code, which is a uniform set of laws drafted by the National Conference of Commissioners on Uniform State Laws. The UCC has been adopted by every state except Louisiana. The code governs commercial transactions, including sales of goods and secured transactions. By filing a UCC-1 financing statement, the lender is giving notice to third parties of its security interest in the personal property described in the statement.

If your law firm represents a lending institution, you may be asked to prepare a UCC-1 financing statement. If you assist legal counsel of a title company, you may be asked to search the Uniform Commercial Code financing statement index to determine whether any UCC-1 filing statements have been filed in connection with particular property. An example of a UCC-1 financing statement can be found in Figure 2–2.

Fixtures

A **fixture** is an object that at one time was personal property but that has, through the process of attachment to real property, become part of the real property. Examples of fixtures are gasoline pumps installed on the real property on which a gasoline station is located, bathtubs installed in a bathroom, and customized built-in wall units installed in a den. Each of these items started out as personal property but, after being affixed to the real property, may be seen as part of it.

Are fixtures legally treated as real property or personal property that may be removed by the owner when the owner sells the real property? What about

bill of sale: A document that transfers title to personal property.

fixture: An object that at one time was personal property but has, through the process of attachment to real property, become part of the real property.

FIGURE 2–1
Bill of sale

BILL OF SALE

KNOW ALL MEN BY THESE PRESENTS that ROBERT PRENTISS and REBECCA PRENTISS, Husband and Wife, Parties of the First Part, for and in consideration of the sum of Ten and No/100 Dollars ($10.00) lawful money of the United States, paid by JOHN HALL and JUDITH HALL, Husband and Wife, Parties of the Second Part, the receipt whereof is hereby acknowledged, have granted, bargained, sold, transferred and delivered, and by these presents do grant, bargain, sell, transfer and deliver unto the said Parties of the Second Part, their heirs, executors, administrators and assigns, all those certain goods located at 22 King's Court, Any City, Any State and described as follows:

> Imported crystal chandelier in dining room, black-out draperies in master bedroom, mahogany Empire-style bedroom set in master bedroom, tan leather sofa and loveseat in family room, cream brocade sofa and loveseat in living room, glass and marble coffee table in living room, and etched glass mirror in foyer

TO HAVE AND TO HOLD the said personal property unto the said Parties of the Second Part, their heirs, executors, administrators and assigns forever.

AND we do, for ourselves and our heirs, successors and assigns, covenant to and with the said Parties of the Second Part, their heirs, executors, administrators and assigns, that we are the lawful owners of the said goods and chattels; that they are free from all encumbrances; that we have good right to sell the same aforesaid, and that we will warrant and defend the sale of said personal property hereby made, unto the said Parties of the Second Part, their heirs, executors, administrators and assigns against the lawful claims and demands of all persons whomsoever.

IN WITNESS WHEREOF, the Parties of the First Part have hereunto set their hand this 5th day of August, 1997.

Signed, sealed and delivered in the presence of:

_____   _____
                                                              Robert Prentiss

_____   _____
                                                              Rebecca Prentiss

STATE OF ANY STATE
COUNTY OF ANY COUNTY

The foregoing instrument was acknowledged before me this 5th day of August, 1997 b/ ROBERT PRENTISS and REBECCA PRENTISS, Husband and Wife.

Witness my hand and official seal at Any City, County of Any County, State of Any State, this 5th day of August, 1997.

_____
Notary Public, State of Any State
My commission expires:_____

the situation in which a tenant of an apartment or office installs items that are affixed to the real property? May the tenant remove the items at the end of the lease?

The answer to these questions depends first and foremost upon the intentions of the parties involved. Unless a contract indicates otherwise, an item that is determined to be a fixture is considered part of the real property and therefore stays with the real property. However, real estate contracts and

STATE OF FLORIDA
UNIFORM COMMERCIAL CODE—FINANCING STATEMENT—FORM UCC-1 REV. 1981
THIS FINANCING STATEMENT is presented to a filing officer for filing pursuant to the Uniform Commercial Code:

DEBTOR (Last Name First if a Person)	THIS SPACE FOR USE OF FILING OFFICER

NAME
1A MRT Properties, Inc.
MAILING ADDRESS
260 Norbrook Drive
CITY New City   STATE Florida

MULTIPLE DEBTOR (IF ANY) (Last Name First if a Person)
NAME
1B
MAILING ADDRESS
CITY   STATE

MULTIPLE DEBTOR (IF ANY) (Last Name First if a Person)
NAME
1C
MAILING ADDRESS
CITY   STATE

SECURED PARTY (Last Name First if a Person)
NAME Millennium Bank
2A
MAILING ADDRESS
500 Main Street
CITY New City   STATE Florida

MULTIPLE SECURED PARTY (IF ANY) (Last Name First if a Person)
NAME
2B
MAILING ADDRESS
CITY   STATE

AUDIT	UPDATE

ASSIGNEE OF SECURED PARTY (IF ANY) (Last Name First if a Person)
NAME
3
MAILING ADDRESS
CITY   STATE

VALIDATION INFORMATION

4. This FINANCING STATEMENT covers the following types or items of property (include description of real property on which located and owner of record when required) If more space is required, attach additional sheets 8½" x 11" All furniture, equipment, and other tangible personal property of any kind attached to or located at TRIDENT INDUSTRIAL PARK No. 2, according to the plat thereof recorded at Plat Book 70, Page 15, Middle County, Florida.

5. Proceeds of collateral are covered as provided in Sections 679.203 and 679.306, F.S.

6. Filed with as per statute

7. No. of additional Sheets presented none

8. (Check ☐) ☒ All documentary stamp taxes due and payable or to become due and payable pursuant to Section 201.22, F.S., have been paid
☐ Florida Documentary Stamp Tax is not required

9. This statement is filed without the debtor's signature to perfect a security interest in collateral (Check ☐ if so)
☐ already subject to a security interest in another jurisdiction when it was brought into this state or debtor's location changed to this state
☐ which is proceeds of the original collateral described above in which a security interest was perfected
☐ as to which the filing has lapsed
☐ acquired after a change of name, identity, or corporate structure of the ☐ debtor or ☐ secured party

10. (Check ☐ if so)
☐ Debtor is a transmitting utility
☐ Products of collateral are covered

11. SIGNATURE(S) OF DEBTOR(S)
MRT Properties, Inc.
By Miranda Thomas, President

12. SIGNATURE(S) OF SECURED PARTY(IES) OR ASSIGNEE
Millennium Bank
By Kay Holmes, V. Pres.

13. Return copy to
NAME Brian Munden, Esquire
ADDRESS 600 Bushnell Street, Suite 201
CITY New City
STATE Florida   ZIP CODE 00000

NAME AND ADDRESS OF PREPARER: Brian Munden, Esquire, 600 Bushnell St., #201, New City, FL 00000

FILING OFFICER COPY   STANDARD FORM—FORM UCC-1   Approved by Secretary of State, State of Florida

FIGURE 2–2 UCC-1 financing statement

leases are governed by contract law, and the terms of the contract, as long as they are not illegal, govern the transaction between the parties. Contracts are negotiable, and therefore, a buyer and seller may decide between themselves whether the gas pumps or the bathtub or the wall units "go with" the property or may be removed by the seller. If the intentions of the parties are clear from a reading of the contract, the resolution of these matters is equally clear.

Fixture Provisions. From the previous discussion, one can gather how important it is to carefully draft the fixtures provision of a real estate contract or a lease. Nothing should be assumed. The buyer may assume that the wall-to-wall carpeting in the living room will remain in the living room after closing on the property while the seller may intend to use that carpeting in his or her next home. Fixtures are deemed part of the real property, but if there is a question, these matters should be determined at the time of negotiating the contract. Misunderstanding may lead to forestalling the closing or to the closing not taking place at all. If the parties fail to include a fixtures provision when negotiating the contract, they should include one in a later addendum that can be attached to it.

As a real estate paralegal, you may be asked to draft or review real estate contracts for sale and purchase or leases. The fixtures provision should be as specific as possible. Anything that is not structurally part of the house, apartment, or office (for example, anything other than the walls, ceiling, floors, stairways, and so on) should be addressed in this provision. Thus, floor coverings, window treatments, air-conditioning units, appliances, lighting fixtures, and the like should be addressed. The provision should indicate whether the items are considered personal property that will be removed by the seller, or whether they will be treated as fixtures to be included with the real property. Additionally, these items should not only be named but, if possible, described. For example, the dishwasher should not be described simply as a dishwasher but rather as the "white General Electric Potscrubber 600 dishwasher," or at least as the "existing dishwasher."

This may seem excessive, but numerous lawsuits abound where a seller has switched appliances from superior to inferior ones before a closing, taking the superior appliances with him or her. This drafting method may appear time-consuming and premised on lack of trust between the parties, but one must remember that the primary aim of both buyer and seller is a problem-free closing, and a well-drafted fixtures provision helps the parties meet their goal. A real estate contract for sale and purchase also may include a provision pertaining to personal property in which the parties describe furniture, paintings, or other items of personal property that may be sold together with the real property.

In drafting a lease, a fixtures provision should indicate what items may be attached to the real property and whether or not the tenant has the right to remove them upon termination of the lease. If removal is allowed, the lease should stipulate that the tenant agrees to return the real property to the condition it was in before the item was attached.

Judicial Tests for Fixtures. In the event that the parties to a real estate contract for sale and purchase or a lease fail to include such provisions, how do the courts settle disputes that arise? Over the years courts have devised various tests to aid them in determining whether an article is a fixture that must remain with the real property. The courts generally look at four things: (1) the intention of the parties, (2) the method of annexation of the item to the real property, (3) the adaptation of the item, and (4) the relationship of the parties involved.

The intention of the parties is of primary importance in determining whether an item is a fixture if there is some way in which this intention can be shown. It is possible a court will allow and consider evidence of an oral agreement if no provision is contained in the written contract stating whether or not the attached items are to be sold to the buyer along with the house. If no oral agreement can be proven, the courts consider the intention of the party who attached the item to the real property. Did this party intend the item become a fixture? How did he or she intend to use the item? Did he or she say anything to a third party such as a real estate agent to indicate his or her intent? Although the "intention test" is an important criterion because the courts wish to enforce the intentions of the parties when they enter into a voluntary agreement rather than rewrite the contractual terms of the parties, the courts do utilize other tests when the intentions of the parties cannot be ascertained.

One such test is the "annexation test" in which the courts look to see how the item was annexed, or attached, to the real property. The more permanent the method of annexation, as in the case of central air conditioning for instance, the more likely the courts will determine that the item can no longer be considered personal property and must be considered a fixture. Using this test, the courts also consider the amount of damages resulting if the item were to be removed. The more potential damage to the real property, as in the case of ripping out kitchen cabinets, the more likely the courts will consider the item a fixture that must remain with the real property.

Some courts have stretched the concept of annexation to include not only actual annexation but also "constructive annexation," where the courts will construe annexation has occurred because of the relationship between the item and the real property, even if the item has not been attached in any manner that may be considered permanent or damaging if the item were to be removed. In some instances, courts have determined that items customized to fit into or onto real property, such as window screens or storm shutters, are fixtures even though they could easily be removed.

A third test that courts utilize in determining whether an item is a fixture is the "adaptation test," looking at the manner in which the item has been adapted for use with the real property. For example, the gasoline pumps mentioned earlier may be considered fixtures if a court determines that they have been adapted for use with the rest of the gasoline station and that the pumps are necessary for the continued use of the real property as a gasoline station and, therefore, are considered intrinsically part of the purpose or use to which the previous and new owners have made of the land.

The fourth test is the relationship between the parties involved in the transaction. Is the relationship that of a buyer and seller of real property or that of a landlord and tenant? And if it is that of a landlord and tenant, is it one concerning a residential lease or a commercial lease? Over the years special statutory and common law principles have evolved in the area of tenant's fixtures.

Domestic Fixtures. It is quite common for a residential tenant to want to improve the leased premises by installing built-in bookshelves or ceiling fans, for instance. Items installed by residential tenants to make the premises more attractive or more functional are called *domestic fixtures*. While many states treat domestic fixtures as the personal property of the tenant, some states do not and, instead, maintain that anything a residential tenant annexes to the leased premises must remain with the premises. Therefore, state statutes should be checked carefully.

Trade Fixtures. Commercial tenants often need to install certain items before they can open their doors for business. A tenant in the retail clothing business needs to install display counters, garment racks, and mirrors. A dentist renting space in a professional building needs to install his dental chairs and cabinets for dental equipment. Those items used in carrying out a trade or business are called *trade fixtures*. Absent a fixtures provision in the lease, most courts routinely allow removal of trade fixtures as long as (1) they are installed by the tenant, not the landlord; (2) they are removed prior to or at the expiration of the lease (any fixtures remaining after the expiration of the lease become the property of the landlord except in the circumstance of eviction, which is discussed in later chapters); and (3) the premises are restored to their original condition.

BASIC OWNERSHIP RIGHTS

Now that the classifications of property have been established, it is important to understand the legal rights that go along with real property ownership. When one acquires real property, one acquires both the real estate and certain legal rights in that real estate. These legal rights are sometimes referred to as a "bundle of rights."

The first of these rights is the *right of disposition*, which is the right to "dispose" of one's property by transferring rights to the property or any portion of it during one's lifetime or at time of death. One may do this through sale, lease, gift, or will. It is possible to lose this right by operation of law in certain circumstances, such as the nonpayment of property taxes, the failure to pay a mortgage loan, or criminal forfeiture.

The second of these rights is the *right of use*, which is sometimes referred to as the *right of enjoyment* because it allows one to use one's property in any manner one sees fit as long as that use is lawful, or to give a general or limited right of use of the property to another. Until the mid-nineteenth century, this right was virtually absolute. As the population grew and density increased, however, so did the restrictions placed on the use of one's property. (These restrictions are addressed in Chapter 4.) Nonetheless, the legal concept of right of use remains intact.

The third of these rights is the *right of possession*, which allows a property owner to occupy his or her property in privacy. Unauthorized entry onto the property by others constitutes trespass that can be stopped by requesting injunctive relief from the court as well as money damages for violation of this right.

The last of these rights is the *right of exclusion*, which is a means of exercising control over one's property. This right has been limited through the introduction of fair housing laws (discussed in Chapter 4) that disallow most forms of discrimination in the sale or lease of one's property.

Rights to real property are transferred by sale, gift, inheritance, or operation of law. Real property rights may be transferred voluntarily and deliberately, as in the basic real estate transaction in which property is bought and sold, a person makes a gift of real property to another, or a person dies and leaves a will specifying to whom real property is to pass. In other circumstances, property rights may pass by operation of law. This may occur when a property owner dies without a will indicating the intended beneficiary, which requires the real property to pass according to state inheritance statutes. Property rights also may arise by operation of law when a property owner "sleeps" on his or her rights and neglects to enforce them, as in the case of adverse possession, which is discussed in the following text. Further, state statutes may give special rights to certain categories of people, such as surviving spouses and dependent children.

METHODS OF ACQUIRING REAL PROPERTY

Purchase

The sale and purchase of property is the most common way in which property changes hands. The agreement between the buyer and seller is reduced to writing by the drafting of a real estate contract for sale and purchase, which is signed by the parties. If a real estate broker was instrumental in bringing the parties together, another contract, generally known as a *listing agreement*, is involved as well. The listing agreement specifies the terms under which the seller "lists" his or her property with the broker as well as the circumstances under which the commission will be paid and the amount of commission to be paid to the broker. If financing is required by the buyer, a separate contract, such as a *mortgage agreement* or a *deed of trust*, must be signed by the buyer and the lender. This contract will specify the conditions under which the financing will be arranged, the amount of financing, and the terms for repayment. Each of these contracts is discussed in detail in later chapters. As a real estate paralegal, you may be involved actively in the drafting of these contracts.

Devise and Descent

Another common way to acquire property is by inheritance. Upon the death of a real property owner, the manner in which his or her real property will pass depends upon whether he or she died *testate* (with a valid will) or *intestate* (without a will). The person executing a valid will is called a *testator*. When a valid will exists, real property passes according to the terms of the will. A gift of real property made to a beneficiary in a will is called a *devise* and the recipient is known as the *devisee*.

Generally, the devisee will take the real property subject to all encumbrances and liens. If the testator intends for the real property to pass clear of any liens, then he or she must make provision elsewhere in the will for any mortgages to be paid off and must indicate the source of funds from which the mortgages are to be paid. A general provision in a will that all debts be paid from the *residue* (remainder of an estate after specific gifts have been distributed) is not sufficient to pass title of the property without encumbrances. The primary family residence must pass according to state statutory law pertaining to homestead property, which is discussed further in the following text. When a person dies intestate, his or her property passes according to the *intestacy laws,* sometimes referred to as the *laws of inheritance* or *laws of descent,* of the state in which the property is located. For example, if Fred Franklin dies intestate leaving real property in New York and in California, the intestacy laws of New York will govern how the New York property passes and the intestacy laws of California will govern how the California property passes.

Gift

A person may also obtain title to real property by *gift.* The person making the gift of real property is called the *donor* and the recipient is called the *donee.* A gift of real property generally is revocable prior to the execution and delivery of a deed indicating transfer of title from the donor to the donee. Should the donor change his or her mind prior to delivering a deed, the donee rarely has legal grounds to bring suit to enforce the gift.

In most states, the oral gift of real property is not legally enforceable. However, some states have provided that the oral gift may be enforced if the donee can prove the donor's intent to give the land and can show that the donee took possession of the land in reliance upon the gift and that the donee made permanent and valuable improvements upon the land. Other states will allow the donee to recover the costs of any detrimental reliance (for example, purchasing insurance, payment of taxes, repair costs) but will not enforce the gift of real property.

Adverse Possession

Acquiring title through **adverse possession** means acquiring title through taking possession of land that belongs to another without the owner's consent and retaining possession for a statutory period of time. This statutory period varies from state to state from a period of several years to a period of a few decades. Many states have statutes prohibiting individuals from acquiring federal, state, or local land through adverse possession.

The principle behind adverse possession is an English common law principle that land is of value and should be put to use. Thus, if the legal owner of the property does nothing to enforce his or her rights to the property within the statutory time period, the owner may lose title. The property in question may be a few feet, as in the case where a neighbor installs a fence a few feet beyond his or her property boundaries, or several acres, as in the case where a cattle farmer grazes his or her stock over a large acreage and extends the grazing into acreage belonging to another.

Adverse possession must be *hostile,* meaning it must be without the owner's consent. It must be *actual,* meaning there must be physical dominion and control exerted over the property. Although there is no requirement that

adverse possession: The acquisition of title to real property through taking possession of land that belongs to another without the owner's consent and retaining possession for a statutorily prescribed period of time.

the adverse possessor live on the property, in some states, the adverse possessor must pay the real property taxes on the land for the statutory time period to be said to have actual possession.

Adverse possession must be *open and notorious,* meaning anyone would be able to determine that possession was taking place through inspection of the property. This does not mean that the owner actually is aware that possession has taken place, only that he or she could find out if he or she made proper inspection.

Many states require the adverse possessor to take possession *under claim of right,* meaning the adverse possessor has the intent to claim the land as his or her right. In most states, however, the physical possession meets the intent requirement and there is no additional requirement that the adverse possessor subjectively intend to lay claim to the land of another.

Taking possession under claim of right is not synonymous with taking possession *under color of title.* In the latter instance, the adverse possessor possesses documentation that is in some way defective (for example, the deed may be lacking witnesses or notarization or fails to meet some other statutory requirement for validity) but that allegedly gives title to the property to the adverse possessor. In this situation, the adverse possessor truly believes he or she is the title owner of the property. Many states shorten the requisite time period for the person who takes possession under color of title and give him or her title to the entirety of the property described in the defective document rather than giving title only to the actual property possessed.

The adverse possessor must be in *continuous* possession for the entire statutory period. However, most states apply the concept of *tacking* to adverse possession. Tacking allows one adverse possessor to "tack on" the time periods of previous adverse possessors if there is privity of contract or a blood relationship between them. For example, suppose the state of Any State has an adverse possession statute permitting tacking and setting the statutory time period of possession for seven years. If adverse possessor *A* continuously used the property in question for five years and then the property was taken over by his son, the son would be allowed to "tack on" his father's five years to the amount of time the son had been in possession of the property to meet the statutory requirements.

Finally, the adverse possession must be *exclusive.* This means the adverse possessor cannot share use of the land in question with its title owner. Generally, possession by only one co-owner on property in which title is held jointly (joint ownership is discussed in detail later) does not constitute adverse possession unless the other co-owners are excluded from possession through *ouster.* In that event, the ousted co-owners must bring suit to regain possession within the statute of limitations for adverse possession or else lose all rights to the property to the ousting co-owner.

ESTATES AND TENANCIES

When one acquires real property by one of the methods discussed previously, one is acquiring an interest in the land and the improvements thereon. This interest may include full or limited property rights. The interest a person receives in real property is based on the type of *estate* or *tenancy* conveyed.

These terms are used to denote the nature, extent, and duration of a person's interest in the property.

The concept of estates and tenancies derives from feudal English law. Feudal law was pervasive throughout Europe in the twelfth to the fourteenth centuries. It was introduced in England in the early twelfth century during the Norman Conquest and has formed the basis of all real property law in England until very recently. Certain feudal concepts still survive and were incorporated into American real property law, particularly the concept of freehold and leasehold estates. Figure 2–3 diagrams the most common freehold and leasehold estates.

Freehold Estates

A **freehold estate** is an estate of indeterminate duration. If ownership rights are granted for a period of time capable of being accurately fixed and determined at the time of granting, the estate is not a freehold estate. Thus, freehold estates last indefinitely, either for the lifetime of an individual (and who is to say what the duration of that lifetime may be) or continuously as the property is passed from one generation to the next. A freehold estate is created through the combination of *words of purchase* (indicating the party to be granted the estate, for example, "To Hilary Hodgson") and *words of limitation* (indicating the extent of the estate created, for example, "to have and to hold for her lifetime"). Although several types of freehold estates exist, as a real estate paralegal, you will primarily encounter the two most common types: the fee simple absolute and the life estate.

freehold estate: An estate of indeterminable duration.

FIGURE 2–3
Types of estates

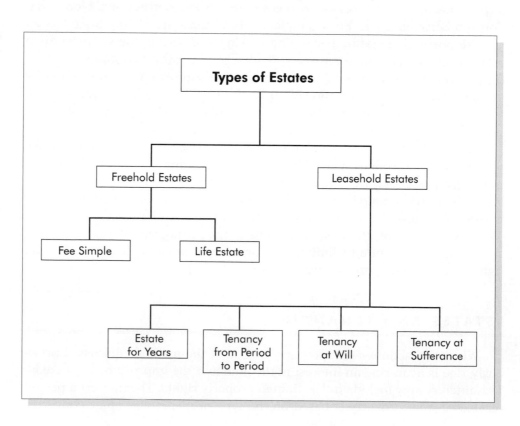

Fee Simple Absolute. The greatest estate one may hold is a **fee simple absolute,** also known as a *fee simple* or a *fee.* A fee simple absolute grants to the owner each of the four basic ownership rights. The estate is generally conveyed through the words "To . . . and his/her heirs forever." Thus, the owner may dispose of the property in any manner he or she chooses during his or her lifetime and may leave the property to whomever he or she chooses upon death. The majority of real property transactions convey a fee simple absolute to the grantee unless words to the contrary appear in the deed.

Life Estates. Another type of freehold estate is a **life estate.** As the name implies, the owner (the grantor) gives title to the property to another (the grantee, also referred to as the life estate holder) for a period of time measured by someone's life, which can be the life of the grantee, the life of the grantor, or the life of a third party. Words creating a life estate are "To . . . for [some person's] lifetime, then to. . . ."

If the owner does not specify who takes title to the property once the lifetime ends, the grantor retains a *reversionary interest* in the property. This means that upon termination of the lifetime specified, the property reverts back by operation of law to the grantor, if still alive, or to his or her estate if the grantor is deceased at that time.

If the grantor does specify to whom title to the real property passes upon termination of the life estate, the person so indicated is referred to as a *vested remainderman.* This person has a present interest in the property but will not get the right to exercise his or her interest until the life estate ends, at which time he or she receives a fee simple absolute.

For example, suppose Paul Peterson had a daughter, Pamela, from his first marriage. Paul is presently married to Priscilla. Paul and Priscilla live a lavish lifestyle, spending time in various properties Paul owns in Manhattan, Boulder, and Scottsdale. The primary domicile of the Petersons is located in Scottsdale, and they hold title to the property jointly. Paul would like Priscilla to retain her present lifestyle after he dies but would also like his daughter to eventually inherit the properties he holds in his own name. In his will, Paul might devise the Manhattan and Boulder properties "to my wife, Priscilla Peterson, for her lifetime, then to my daughter, Pamela." Thus, Priscilla would get a life estate and Pamela would be a vested remainderman. This means that a present interest in the properties would pass to Pamela but she would not get the right to exercise it until Priscilla's death, at which time Pamela would get title to the properties in fee simple absolute, as illustrated in Figure 2–4. If instead of giving the remainder to Pamela, Paul wanted his yet-to-be-born grandchild to have it, the grandchild would be a *contingent remainderman,* whose interest in the properties would be contingent upon being born.

When a life estate is granted for the lifetime of someone other than the grantee, it is called a **life estate pur autre vie.** For example, parents of an adult retarded child might want to leave a life estate to the child's caretaker for the life of the child and then have the property revert back to the parents' estate. The life estate is given to the caretaker, but another person's life, in this instance, the life of the adult retarded child, is the measuring life.

The owner of a life estate enjoys the same rights of use, possession, and exclusion as the owner of a fee simple absolute, but not the right of disposition. While in theory a life estate may be sold, the purchaser will only take title

fee simple absolute: An estate that grants the property owner each of the four basic property rights.

life estate: An estate in which the grantor conveys title to real property to another for a period of time measured by somebody's life.

life estate pur autre vie: A life estate granted for the lifetime of someone other than the grantee.

FIGURE 2–4
Interest of a
life estate

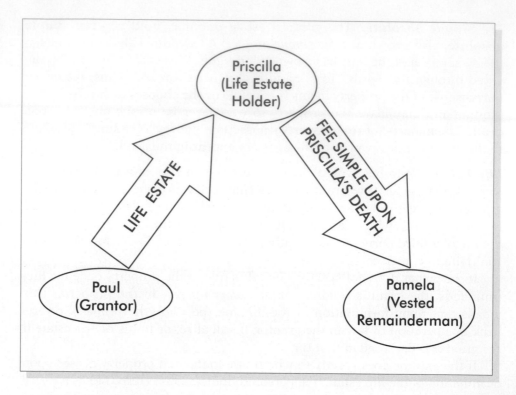

to the same interest the seller possesses, and thus, in actuality, the right of disposition virtually evaporates. However, the life estate holder may rent out the property and keep all income from the rental. The life estate holder may use the property in any manner not contrary to law as long as the life estate holder does nothing to diminish the value of the property (that is, the life estate holder cannot commit *waste*). The law recognizes three types of waste: (1) permissive, (2) voluntary, and (3) ameliorative (also known as ameliorating). *Permissive waste* occurs when the life estate holder fails in the upkeep of the property (for example, fails to make necessary repairs or to keep the grounds in good condition). *Voluntary waste* occurs when the property is actively used in a manner that reduces its market value. *Ameliorative waste* is, in many respects, a misnomer because it increases the property value. It occurs when the original condition of the property is altered by improvements (for example, tearing up the back lawn to install a swimming pool). A life estate holder may commit ameliorative waste because it actually improves, rather than reduces, the value of the property.

Life estate holders have various obligations as well as rights. State law may require them to pay all real property taxes. Additionally, they may be required to obtain adequate insurance on the property and keep any mortgage payments current.

Leasehold Estates

leasehold estate: An estate of
determinable duration.

A **leasehold estate** is an estate of determinable duration. This estate conveys the rights of use, possession, and exclusion, but not disposition, and is initially created by a lease agreement between a landlord and a tenant. There are four basic leasehold estates: (1) an estate for years (sometimes referred to as a *tenancy for years),* (2) a tenancy from period to period, (3) a tenancy at will, and (4) a tenancy at sufferance.

Estate for Years. An **estate for years** is an estate that continues for a designated period, be it three months, or longer than the average lifetime (for example, ninety-nine years), the estate automatically extinguishing upon a fixed date. If an estate for years is created for a period of more than one year, the lease conveying the interest must be in writing in order to be enforceable. An estate for years does not convey actual title that allows the estate holder to sell the real property (although the estate holder may be able to rent out the property) but simply conveys for a temporary period the rights of possession and use.

Tenancy from Period to Period. A **tenancy from period to period** is a leasehold that continues for successive intervals until one party to the agreement provides the other party with notice of termination of the tenancy. The agreement between the parties may be *express* (reduced to words, either oral or written) or *implied* (created by the actions of the parties—for example, a landlord accepting monthly payments of rent may imply a tenancy from month to month).

Tenancy at Will. A **tenancy at will** is similar to a tenancy from period to period. The primary distinction is that a tenancy at will typically begins as an estate for years and then converts to a tenancy at will once the estate for years expires and the tenant remains on the property by agreement with the landlord. Originally a tenancy at will meant exactly what its name implies, that the tenancy could be terminated at the will of either party by the sale of the property, or by the death of one of the parties. However, most state statutes now require appropriate notice by the terminating party. Appropriate notice generally is determined not by the notice requirements of the original written or oral lease, but by the intervals between rent payments. For example, if the tenant had a two-year lease that expired and under that lease he or she made monthly rental payments, then the applicable notice requirements are those pertaining to a month-to-month lease (for example, fifteen days). Some state statutes distinguish between the notice requirements for residential leaseholds and those for commercial leaseholds.

Tenancy at Sufferance. At common law, a **tenancy at sufferance** did not create any rights in the tenant. This situation occurred when a tenant remained on the leased premises after the lease expired without the agreement of the landlord. Under these circumstances, the landlord could choose to "suffer" the party's presence and treat the party as a tenant at will, or choose to evict the party. No notice was required to remove the party from the property. Today, most state statutes disallow this common law principle, requiring statutory notice prior to termination of a tenancy.

METHODS OF TITLE HOLDING

Title to real property may be held in the name of a single owner, or it may be held jointly by two or more persons in one of several types of *joint* or *concurrent ownership.* Each method of concurrent ownership confers different

estate for years: An estate that continues for a designated period.

tenancy from period to period: A leasehold that continues for successive intervals until one party to the agreement provides the other party with notice of termination of the tenancy.

tenancy at will: A tenancy that begins as an estate for years, with the tenant remaining on the property by agreement with the landlord after the estate for years expires.

tenancy at sufferance: A tenancy occurring after the expiration of a lease, in which a tenant remains in possession of the property without the landlord's consent.

rights on the titleholders. Title to real property also may be held in the name of a business entity such as a partnership, corporation, or limited liability company. As noted at the beginning of the chapter, title to real property typically is obtained through a *conveyance* (for example, through the conveyance of a deed granting title). Additionally, title to real property may come about through operation of law, such as in the case of community property shared equally by husband and wife in community property states, or by statutory rights afforded surviving spouses in a percentage of a deceased spouse's real property.

Individual Ownership

An individual may hold title to real property in his or her own name as a single owner. This method of ownership is termed *ownership in severalty*. The individual taking title in fee simple absolute has the right to use and ultimately dispose of the property in any manner he or she chooses, subject to law. Additionally, the individual is personally liable for all real property taxes, income taxes arising from any income produced by the property (for example, rents or sale of the property), and any claims made against the property.

Although it usually is a single person who takes title in this fashion, a married or widowed person also may take title as a sole owner. It is necessary to indicate the sole owner's marital status after his or her name on the deed (for example, "Greg Grayson, a single man"; "Nancy Nelson, a married woman") because of special rights afforded widows and widowers in some states. These are the rights of *dower*, which allow a widow a certain percentage of her deceased husband's property, and *curtesy*, which allow a widower a certain percentage of his deceased wife's property. A few states afford married persons *community property rights*, which are rights to share equally in property acquired during marriage. Many states also afford spouses special rights in *homestead property*, which is the primary domicile of the family. Dower, curtesy, community property, and homestead rights are discussed in detail later in the chapter.

In states that afford special spousal rights, Nancy Nelson's husband would have to join her as a grantor on a deed granting title to a buyer should Nancy decide to sell her property, even though title to the property is held in her name, to indicate his relinquishment of any curtesy, community property, or homestead rights he may have in the property.

Types of Concurrent Ownership

Joint or concurrent ownership of real property occurs when more than one individual (or entity) holds title to the same property at the same time. The joint owners are termed *co-owners* or *cotenants* in the real property. Co-owners share certain rights, such as the right to enjoy possession of the entire property and the right to their proportionate share of any rents or profits derived from the property. Further, they share certain responsibilities with regard to the real property. Co-owners cannot commit waste that reduces the market value of the property, and each is responsible to the other(s) for any contribution toward the maintenance of the real property. The most common forms of concurrent ownership are a tenancy in common, a joint tenancy, and a tenancy by the entirety.

Tenancy in Common. **Tenancy in common** is the most commonly used method of concurrent ownership, because if two or more persons are co-owners of real property and there is no indication to the contrary, the law in most states presumes they are tenants in common. This may vary in some states where the co-owners are a husband and wife.

Any number of persons may own property together as tenants in common and need not acquire title at the same time. Each co-owner may have obtained separate title from the same or from different grantors. Further, they may own equal or unequal shares in the real property. For example, Eve Enderby, Joyce Johnson, and Henry Hickson may be tenants in common, with Eve owning a one-half interest in the real property and Joyce and Henry each owning a one-quarter interest in the real property. Nonetheless, tenants in common share *unity of possession*, which is the right each has to possession of the entire property. Additionally, each co-owner is said to own an *undivided interest* in the real property, which means that the interests of the cotenants, although fractional interests, are not physically separate. If the fractional shares of each co-owner are not documented, the law presumes that each co-owner owns an equal share in the real property.

This method of concurrent ownership does not confer *right of survivorship*, the right of the co-owners to inherit a deceased co-owner's share in the real property. Thus, each co-owner's share passes to his or her heirs or to beneficiaries designated in a will. In addition, each co-owner has the right, during his or her lifetime, to mortgage or convey his or her undivided interest in the real property without obtaining the consent of the other co-owners, unless there is an agreement to the contrary. Should a co-owner transfer his or her interest, it may be necessary for that co-owner to have his or her spouse join in the execution of the deed for the same reasons indicated in the previous discussion of transfer of property in severalty.

Should a dispute arise among tenants in common over the use of the property or any other rights associated with it, any of the co-owners may file a legal action requesting *partition* of the property, which is the division of real property into distinct portions so that co-owners may hold them in severalty. In granting partition, a court will divide the real property into parcels according to the percentage owned by each co-owner. If this is not possible for some reason, then the court may order the property sold and the proceeds of the sale allocated proportionately. Partition of property is discussed in detail in Chapter 19.

Joint Tenancy. A **joint tenancy** is sometimes referred to as a *joint tenancy with right of survivorship*. The most striking characteristic of a joint tenancy is the right of survival each co-owner has in the undivided interests of the other co-owner(s). For example, assume Burt Bryant, Patrick Pickering, and Lisa Lawson are co-owners in a joint tenancy. Should Burt die, his heirs will not inherit his undivided share in the real property; rather, it will pass to Patrick and Lisa. Should Patrick then die, Lisa will own the real property in severalty. Because of this feature, many states presume that co-owners are tenants in common unless the words "as joint tenants with right of survivorship" appears on the deed to indicate the contrary.

Another characteristic of a joint tenancy is the presence of the *four unities:* (1) unity of possession, (2) unity of interest, (3) unity of time, and (4) unity of

tenancy in common: A form of concurrent ownership in which two or more persons have undivided interests in property but which does not confer the right of survivorship.

joint tenancy: A form of concurrent ownership in which two or more persons have undivided interests in property, with right of survivorship.

title. As in a tenancy in common, each co-owner in a joint tenancy has the right to enjoy the use of the entire property. Unlike a tenancy in common, however, in a joint tenancy, each co-owner's interest is identical. Further, for a joint tenancy to exist, each co-owner must take title under the same deed at the same time. If one or more of these unities is not present, the co-owners are deemed tenants in common.

Even if the four unities are initially present, the sale or mortgage of a co-owner's interest will sever the joint tenancy. Using the above example, should Burt sell his interest to Richard Runnells, Patrick and Lisa remain joint tenants with respect to each other and become tenants in common with Richard. Therefore, Richard's heirs may inherit his interest; however, Patrick's heirs will not receive Patrick's interest, which will pass to Lisa.

Tenancy by the Entirety. A **tenancy by the entirety,** sometimes referred to as a *tenancy by the entireties,* is a distinct form of joint ownership that can occur only when property is owned by a husband and wife. This form of ownership has its origins in the early English common law principle that a husband and wife are one person and that their joint ownership could be divided only by the death of one or the other spouse. If state law provides, neither spouse has an individual interest in the property to convey, and therefore, neither can mortgage or convey the property without the consent and signature of both parties. Each spouse owns a one hundred percent interest in the property, preventing the creditors of one spouse from obtaining a judgment against property held in this fashion. If a debt is owed jointly by the spouses, however, a creditor may obtain judgment against tenancy by the entirety property. Because right of survivorship exists in this form of joint ownership, neither spouse may dispose of the property by will, the property instead passing automatically to the surviving spouse upon the death of the other.

Although this form of joint ownership is not recognized in all states, in some states that do recognize it, a tenancy by the entirety will be presumed, unless there is evidence to the contrary, any time a conveyance is made to a husband and wife, even if the words "as tenants by the entirety" do not appear on the deed. In a minority of states, the words "as tenants by the entirety" must appear on the deed. Should the spouses divorce, a divorce decree terminates the tenancy by the entirety and the ex-spouses become co-owners in a tenancy in common.

Figure 2–5 provides a chart indicating the characteristics of each type of concurrent ownership, while Figure 2–6 indicates the types of concurrent ownership recognized by each state.

OWNERSHIP BY A BUSINESS ENTITY

tenancy by the entirety: A form of concurrent ownership by husband and wife, in which each spouse has an undivided interest and right of survivorship.

The manner in which title to real property is held by a business is determined by the laws governing the particular business structure. There are five basic business structures: (1) sole proprietorships, (2) general partnerships, (3) limited partnerships, (4) corporations, and (5) limited liability companies.

FIGURE 2–5
Characteristics of
concurrent ownership

Characteristics of Concurrent Ownership

Characteristics	Tenancy in common	Joint tenancy	Tenancy by the entirety
Owners	Two or more persons	Two or more persons	Husband and wife only
Nature of interest	Undivided	Undivided	Undivided
Right of survivorship	No	Yes	Yes
Right of partition	Yes	In some states	Only in event of divorce
Quantity of interest	Equal or unequal shares	Equal shares	Each spouse has 100% interest
Co-owner's right to sell interest	Yes	Yes	No

States Recognizing Forms of Concurrent Ownership

State	Tenancy in common	Joint tenancy	Tenancy by the entirety	State	Tenancy in common	Joint tenancy	Tenancy by the entirety
Alabama	X	X		Missouri	X	X	X
Alaska	X		X	Montana	X	X	
Arizona	X	X		Nebraska	X	X	
Arkansas	X	X	X	Nevada	X	X	
California	X	X		New Hampshire	X	X	
Colorado	X	X		New Jersey	X	X	X
Connecticut	X	X		New Mexico	X	X	
Delaware	X	X	X	New York	X	X	X
District of Columbia	X	X	X	North Carolina	X	X	X
Florida	X	X	X	North Dakota	X	X	
Georgia	X	X		Ohio**	X		X
Hawaii	X	X	X	Oklahoma	X	X	X
Idaho	X	X	X	Oregon	X		X
Illinois	X	X		Pennsylvania	X	X	X
Indiana	X	X	X	Rhode Island	X	X	X
Iowa	X	X		South Carolina	X	X	
Kansas	X	X		South Dakota	X	X	
Kentucky	X	X	X	Tennessee	X	X	X
Louisiana*				Texas	X	X	
Maine	X	X		Utah	X	X	X
Maryland	X	X	X	Vermont	X	X	X
Massachusetts	X	X	X	Virginia	X	X	X
Michigan	X	X	X	Washington	X	X	
Minnesota	X	X		West Virginia	X	X	X
Mississippi	X	X	X	Wisconsin	X	X	
				Wyoming	X	X	X

*Louisiana does not recognize these forms of concurrent ownership; joint ownership interests are created by its state statutes.
**Instead of a joint tenancy, Ohio recognizes a type of joint ownership conveyed by an instrument called a joint and survivorship deed.

FIGURE 2–6 States Recognizing Forms of Concurrent Ownership

Sole Proprietorships

The most common business structure in the United States continues to be the sole proprietorship, although it is the least likely to acquire substantial real estate holdings. A *sole proprietorship* is exactly what the term implies, an unincorporated business owned and operated by a single individual. The inclusion of the term *unincorporated* is important because many states allow incorporation of a business with a single shareholder. The central concept is one-person ownership. A sole proprietor may hire employees but may never share ownership of the business with someone else. If this happens, the business ceases to be a sole proprietorship.

A sole proprietorship cannot be separated from the identity of its owner. Therefore, any real property acquired by the sole proprietor is acquired in his or her name, and the sole proprietor is personally responsible for the mortgage note.

Partnerships

There are two types of partnerships: general partnerships and limited partnerships. A *general partnership* is the voluntary association of two or more individuals or entities, acting as co-owners of a business for profit. Profits and losses, as well as management responsibilities, are shared among the partners according to the terms of a partnership agreement. Each partner in a general partnership is personally responsible for the financial obligations of the general partnership.

Each partner has a *partnership interest* in the general partnership, usually proportionate to his or her capital contribution, which is considered a personal property right. This partnership interest does not entitle any partner to particular partnership property; instead, it typically reflects that partner's equity interest in the business. Therefore, although real property may be acquired or conveyed either in the partnership name or in the names of the partners, it is the partnership that holds title to real property, not the individual partners. Additionally, because the real property owned by a partnership is owned by the business, not the partners themselves, spouses of partners do not have dower, curtesy, or community property rights in the real property.

A *limited partnership* is similar to a general partnership, requiring the joining of two or more individuals or entities to run a business based on the terms set forth in a partnership agreement. In a limited partnership, however, there must be at least one general partner and at least one limited partner. The limited partner is limited in terms of both personal liability (he or she is liable personally for business losses only up to the amount of his or her capital contribution) and managerial responsibility (he or she may not actively participate in the running of the business).

Limited partnerships require more formalities in formation than do general partnerships. They do not officially exist until a *certificate of limited partnership* is filed with the appropriate state authority, usually the secretary of state. If a limited partnership wishes to expand operations outside of the state of its creation, it must apply to do so as a foreign limited partnership. With regard to the sale and acquisition of real property, conveyance to or from a limited partnership is similar to that of general partnerships.

A *joint venture* is similar to a partnership but is established to create a relationship between the parties only for a single transaction or business venture. Joint ventures are often chosen as the preferred business structure for the acquisition and development of real property. A joint venture is not considered a separate legal entity in many states, and therefore, real property acquired by a joint venture is considered the real property of the joint venturers, who hold title as tenants in common. Because the property is considered the property of the individual joint venturers, conveyance of the property may require the signatures of any spouses.

Corporations

A *corporation* is a business structure that is a legal entity separate from the owners of the business and is created according to the dictates of statutes. It does not exist until a document called *articles of incorporation* is filed with the secretary of state or other designated authority. The owners of a corporation are called shareholders, and their shares of the profits are apportioned by the number and types of shares of stock they hold in the corporation. An important feature of a corporation is the shielding from personal liability of the owners for the debts of the corporation.

All corporations are managed by a board of directors, elected by the shareholders. The board of directors, in turn, appoints corporate officers who oversee the daily affairs of the business. A document called the *bylaws* serves as a procedural guide for the running of a corporation. It specifies voting procedures, meetings to be held, the powers of the board of directors and of the officers, as well as the procedures for removal of directors and officers.

The bylaws typically indicate that the officers of the corporation, acting on behalf of the board of directors, may enter into contracts for the purchase or sale of real property. Such a contract would have to be ratified by the board of directors. This is done by the board of directors meeting to pass a resolution adopting the actions of the officer. An example of a resolution is found in Figure 2–7. Because a corporation is a separate legal entity, title to real property of a corporation is held in the name of the corporation, not in the name of its shareholders.

Limited Liability Companies

A recently recognized business entity is the *limited liability company*, which encompasses characteristics of a partnership as well as characteristics of a corporation. The formation of a limited liability company requires at least two owners, called members. A creature of state statute, a limited liability company comes into creation when *articles of organization* are filed with the appropriate state authority. The document governing the daily operations of a limited liability company is the *operating agreement*, a hybrid between a partnership agreement and corporate bylaws. The company may be manager-managed or member-managed. A limited liability company, as its name implies, provides its members with limited liability for business debts and, in so providing, is similar to a corporation. However, it presently is taxed as a partnership, at least at the federal tax level. A limited liability company acquires title and conveys title to real property in the name of the company.

FIGURE 2–7
Board of directors
resolution to purchase
real property

BOARD OF DIRECTORS RESOLUTION TO PURCHASE REAL PROPERTY

RESOLUTION OF BOARD OF DIRECTORS
OF AMERICAN LAND ACQUISITIONS, INC.

WHEREAS, CONTINENTAL DEVELOPMENT CORP., owner of the land located in Any City, Any County, Any State, has offered to sell certain real property to this Corporation for the sum of ONE MILLION FIVE HUNDRED THOUSAND DOLLARS ($1,500,000.00), upon the terms hereinafter set forth, and

WHEREAS, the Board of Directors deems it advisable that the Corporation acquire said land from CONTINENTAL DEVELOPMENT CORP. for the price aforementioned, be it

RESOLVED, That this Corporation purchase from CONTINENTAL DEVELOPMENT CORP. the land more specifically described as follows:

Tract 16 of KENSINGTON MANOR ESTATES, 2nd Edition, according to the plat thereof recorded at Plat Book 56, page 23 of the public records of Any County, Any State.

RESOLVED, FURTHER, That the President and Secretary of this Corporation are hereby authorized to enter into an agreement on behalf of this Corporation with said Seller to purchase the above described property pursuant to agreement annexed.

RESOLVED, FURTHER, That the President and Secretary of this Corporation are hereby authorized to execute all instruments and make all payments necessary to carry the foregoing resolution into effect, and to accept all documents, duly executed, which may be necessary for the transfer and conveyance of the land to this Corporation.

I do hereby certify that I am the duly elected and qualified Secretary, and that the above is a true and correct copy of a resolution duly adopted at a meeting of the Board of Directors thereof, convened and held in accordance with law and the Bylaws of said Corporation on August 5, 1997, and that such resolution is now in full force and effect.

IN WITNESS WHEREOF, I have affixed my name as Secretary and have caused the corporate seal of said Corporation to be hereunto affixed, this 5th day of August, 1997.

A True Record
Attest

AMERICAN LAND ACQUISITIONS, INC.

_____
Secretary

DOWER AND CURTESY

dower: The provision the law makes for a widow to lay legal claim to an interest in her deceased husband's real property.

Dower is an old legal right that used to exist in the majority of states. It still survives intact in a few states but has been considerably altered in others. **Dower** is the provision the law makes for a widow to lay legal claim to an interest in her deceased husband's real property (that is, in property he held in severalty). Traditionally, the claim could be made only by a widow with children by the deceased husband. The widow was entitled to a life estate in one-third of the deceased husband's real property, the children being the vested remaindermen, with the remainder of the property passing to the children outright. This entitlement was given to the widow so she had property upon which to bring up the children and from which she could support herself. Because of this rationale, the widow's rights to the property took precedent over those of the husband's creditors.

Some states have retained the concept of dower but have allowed widows with no children the same right. In some other states, the widow, with or without children, is entitled to a one-third interest, or some other fractional interest, in fee simple rather than simply a life estate in the property.

Until the death of a husband, a wife's dower rights are *inchoate*, meaning that they are contingent upon her outliving her husband and will vest only upon his death. Nonetheless, because this inchoate right exists in states that continue to recognize dower rights, a husband cannot sell real property without his wife's signature accompanying his own on a deed. Her signature acts as a release or satisfaction of her inchoate interest in that particular real property.

In a number of states, if the buyer accepts the deed without the signature of the grantor's wife, the buyer risks the chance that the wife may make a claim against the property after her husband's death. In the event that she does so, her claim may be found to be superior to that of the buyer. This would not be the result in other states in which the widow has dower rights only in real property that the husband owned at the time of his death.

Should a husband and wife divorce, her dower rights terminate. In the event the wife predeceases her husband, his property passes to his heirs; her heirs have no legal claim to a one-third share of the real property because the deceased wife's inchoate rights never vested.

In some states, a similar right is given to a widower in his deceased wife's real property. This right is known as **curtesy.** Traditionally, the widower's curtesy rights were not limited to a fractional share; instead, he was given a life estate in all real property his wife owned during their marriage, provided that there were children born from the marital union. Most states have forfeited the requirement that there be children from the marriage, and a number of states have reduced the widower's curtesy rights to an interest in a fractional share of the deceased wife's property, similar to dower rights. As with dower, some states recognize rights in all lands owned during the marriage while other recognize rights only in lands owned at the time of the wife's death. Thus, it is safe practice to require the husband's signature on all conveyances of real property by the wife.

Many states have abolished both the concept of dower and of curtesy in favor of gender-neutral statutes that allow the surviving spouse to choose between taking the property passed to him or her by the deceased spouse's will or taking an **elective share,** sometimes referred to as a *marital share,* which is a fractional share of the property (usually both real and personal) in fee simple owned by the deceased spouse at the date of death. This guarantees the surviving spouse a certain interest in the deceased spouse's property should a will leave the surviving spouse less than he or she would be entitled to under state intestacy statutes. In states providing for an elective share, the surviving spouse is entitled to take that share even if he or she contests the will and the deceased spouse's will provides that the surviving spouse is to receive nothing if the will is contested.

curtesy: The provision the law makes for a widower to make a legal claim to an interest in his deceased wife's real property.

elective share: A spouse's statutory right to a fractional share of real and personal property owned by the deceased spouse at the date of death.

COMMUNITY PROPERTY

Community property law developed in certain, but not all, states that were founded under Spanish or French rule. The states with community property systems are Louisiana, California, Nevada, Arizona, Idaho, New Mexico, Washington, and Texas. In 1986, Wisconsin adopted a concept called *marital property* that is very similar to community property. All other states follow a common law system of real property in which each spouse owns whatever he or she earns or has rights to by conveyance. Under the community property law system, all property falls within one of two categories: separate property and community property.

Separate property is (1) all property acquired by a spouse prior to marriage; (2) all income from property acquired by a spouse prior to marriage, unless commingled in such a manner that it is difficult to separate it from community property; (3) property acquired solely through separate funds; and (4) all property acquired by gift, will, or descent, unless the gift or will clearly indicates that the property is given to both husband and wife.

Community property is all property, both personal and real, acquired during marriage by either spouse. It pertains only to marital relationships. Community property is owned equally by the spouses, regardless of each spouse's contribution to the acquisition of the property (indeed, it applies even if one spouse makes no financial contribution) or the manner in which title to the property is held.

Thus, if Monica Montrose purchases a vacation home in her own name during her marriage to Martin Montrose, there is a legal presumption in community property states that the vacation home is community property by operation of law regardless of the fact that only Monica is listed on the deed as grantee unless she can show that the vacation home was purchased entirely from funds legally considered her separate property. If Martin contributed anything to the purchase of the vacation home or if community property were used in part to purchase the vacation home, apportionment would take place and a proportionate percentage of the vacation home would be considered Monica's separate property while the remaining percentage would be considered community property owned equally by Monica and Martin. Because community property cannot be sold by one spouse without the other spouse's consent, if the vacation home were deemed community property, even though Monica's sole name appeared on the present deed, both Monica and Martin would have to sign a new deed as grantors when the home was sold.

Most community property states honor *prenuptial agreements*. Therefore, spouses in community property states may desire to determine among themselves what property is to be considered separate property and what property is to be considered community property. Prenuptial agreements must be in writing in order to be enforceable. As with any other type of contract, consideration must be given on both sides for a prenuptial agreement to be valid, but in this circumstance, the exchange of mutual promises to marry may be determined to be sufficient consideration. Further, each party must make full financial disclosure to the other prior to signing the agreement. It is advisable that each spouse seek advice of separate counsel prior to signing a prenuptial agreement.

separate property: Property that is (1) acquired by a spouse prior to marriage, (2) income from property acquired by a spouse prior to marriage unless commingled in a manner that makes it community property, (3) acquired solely through separate funds, or (4) acquired by gift, will, or descent, unless the gift or will clearly indicates that the property is given to both husband and wife.

community property: All property, both real and personal, acquired during marriage by either spouse, in states that recognize this concept.

Absent a prenuptial or *postnuptial agreement* (an agreement made during the marriage; if made in contemplation of separation and divorce, it is called a *separation agreement*) to the contrary, community property is divided equally should a husband and wife divorce. Community property to be divided in this fashion is considered all property acquired during the marriage, and the time period of the marriage, for purposes of division of property, typically is calculated until the time the petitioner files a petition for dissolution of marriage with the court, not the time at which the divorce is granted. Once the spouses are divorced, they hold title to the property as tenants in common.

The intestacy laws of each state govern the manner in which community property passes upon the death of a spouse who dies intestate. In some community property states, the surviving spouse receives his or her one-half of the community property plus the deceased spouse's half and additionally, as an heir, may be entitled to all or a portion of the property the deceased spouse held as separate property. In others, the surviving spouse receives his or her one-half share and the deceased spouse's share passes to his or her heirs.

HOMESTEAD PROPERTY

Homestead property is defined as the primary dwelling house or residence of the head of household plus adjoining land. Although a person may own many properties, he or she may have only one domicile qualifying as homestead property. The concept of homestead property is important in three contexts: (1) the probate laws pertaining to homestead property, (2) the property tax exemption laws pertaining to homestead property, and (3) the homestead right of protection against claims of creditors. Some states limit statutory homestead by size restrictions (for example, a certain amount of acreage outside city limits and within city limits) while others limit it to a certain dollar amount (for example, $7,500 or some other figure).

Traditionally, one had to be head of a family in order to reap the benefits accorded to homestead property, which meant that one had to be the primary supporter of a spouse and minor children. In many states, the "head of family" has been broadened to include unmarried, divorced, legally separated, or widowed persons who provide support of a child or other dependent, and in certain contexts, a single person with no dependents may claim his or her primary residence as homestead for specified purposes, such as the property tax exemption.

Probate homestead refers to the right the surviving spouse and minor children have in homestead property. When a husband or wife dies leaving a surviving spouse and minor children, the homestead property passes automatically to the surviving spouse and children. This is the case even if the deed to the homestead property is solely in the name of the deceased spouse. Under state statutory law, the surviving spouse may receive a life estate with the minor children as vested remaindermen, or the surviving spouse may receive a fee simple in the homestead property. Because of this statutory right, homestead property cannot be sold or mortgaged without the signatures of both spouses on the deed or mortgage documents.

Many states provide *homestead property tax exemptions* on real property taxes levied. The term *exemption* is a misnomer, for most states do not exempt

homestead property: The primary dwelling house or residence of the head of household plus adjoining land.

homestead property entirely from real property taxes. Rather, the majority of states that provide these statutory exemptions allow a set dollar figure (for example, $25,000) to be subtracted from the assessed value of the homestead property before real property taxes are calculated. For example, in a state that allows a $25,000 tax exemption on homestead property, a homestead property that has an assessed value of $200,000 will be taxed on $175,000 of the property value.

In states that allow such exemptions, there is usually the prerequisite requirement that a formal homestead declaration be recorded, often in the property appraiser's office or in the clerk's office where the deed is recorded. Typically there are statutory deadlines for the recording of such declarations before one may take advantage of the exemption (for example, the declaration must be recorded by March 1st of the year in which the exemption on real property taxes is claimed). In some states, verification of this declaration must be made each year if the exemption is to remain in force, while in others, the exemption is automatic after the initial filing of the declaration.

Homestead property also is afforded certain protection against the claims of creditors under the doctrine of *homestead rights*. Homestead rights may prevent a forced sale of the primary residence to satisfy creditors or may protect a certain dollar amount of equity in the primary residence should the residence be sold. The rationale behind homestead rights is that of providing a struggling family with a roof over their heads or at least a minimum amount of capital to prevent them from living on the streets. A few states, such as Florida, have become known as a bankruptcy debtor's paradise because homestead property may not be sold to pay off creditors as long as any mortgage payments on the homestead property are current. Thus, in Florida, one may conceivably declare bankruptcy and still keep a million dollar homestead property out of the hands of creditors as long as the homestead property meets statutory size restrictions (in this case, 160 acres of contiguous land and improvements if located outside a municipality, one-half acre of contiguous land and improvements within a municipality). Federal bankruptcy exemptions allow protection of $7,500 for equity in the bankruptcy petitioner's homestead property. Some states allow a bankruptcy petitioner to choose between federal or state bankruptcy exemptions while others only permit the use of state exemptions.

CHAPTER SUMMARY

1. Property is a generic term used to describe anything that can be owned. Property can be divided into various classifications. For the purpose of the study of real property law, the two most important classifications are real property (land and any permanent attachment thereto) and personal property (everything else).
2. Surface rights in real property are divided into land rights and water rights. Land rights include rights to all land contained within specified boundaries and permanent attachments to that land, be they manmade or natural elements. Water rights pertain to the right to use water adjacent to one's land as well as the right to possess property covered by water adjacent to one's land. Air rights may be classified as public air rights, which

allow use for aerial transportation and communications technology, and private air rights owned by real property owners, which extend from the surface of an allotted parcel of land up to a statutorily specified height. Private air rights are valuable in congested metropolitan areas where they may be sold as air "lots" upon which buildings may be built. They also are of value on properties located in scenically desirable spots where they may be purchased to ensure an uninterrupted view. Subsurface rights also can be of considerable value should the subsurface contain hard minerals or oil and gas deposits.

3. A fixture is an item of personal property that, through the process of attachment, is transformed into real property. To determine whether an item is a fixture that must remain with the real property, the intention of the parties is of primary concern. Cautious parties include a carefully drafted fixtures provision in their real estate contract or lease. In the absence of this, the courts must decide the matter should a dispute arise. The courts have several tests at their disposal. First, they attempt to determine the intent of the parties. If this cannot be ascertained, they may look at the method of annexation, the adaptation of the item, and the relationship of the parties.

4. The basic ownership rights acquired when purchasing real property include the right of disposition (which allows one to freely transfer all or any portion of one's property by sale, lease, gift, or will), the right of use (which allows one to use one's property in any manner one chooses as long as such use is consistent with local laws), the right of possession (which allows one privacy on one's property), and the right of exclusion (which allows one to control entry upon the land).

5. Although the most common method of acquiring title to real property is by purchasing it, one may acquire it by other means. A real property owner's heirs may take title to property through the right of descent should the owner die intestate. If a real property owner dies leaving a will, the named beneficiaries in the will are the devisees and take title by devise. Property also may be acquired by a gift of real property by a donor to a donee. For the gift to be valid, a deed of conveyance must be executed by the donor and delivered to the donee. Absent such evidence of conveyance, an oral promise to convey real property usually will not be upheld, although some courts have upheld such a promise where the donee could show evidence of intent on the part of the donor, possession of the property in reliance on the promise, and improvements made upon the property.

6. The largest estate one may acquire is a fee simple absolute, the ownership of which confers all the legal rights to real property: the right of disposition, the right of use, the right of possession, and the right of exclusion. A fee simple absolute passes by descent to the property owner's heirs or by will to the owner's named beneficiaries. A life estate is a freehold estate that is conveyed for the lifetime of the grantee or the lifetime of some other person. The life estate holder may enjoy full use of the property and may keep any income derived from the property. While in possession, the life estate holder must do nothing to devalue the market value of the property. He or she must pay all real property taxes, insurance, and other maintenance costs.

7. Leasehold estates exist either for a definite period of time, as in the case of an estate for years, or for successive intervals, as in the case of a tenancy from period to period. Upon the expiration of a lease, a tenancy at will can be created if the tenant remains on the property by agreement with the landlord and continues to pay rent. Under common law, should the tenant continue in possession without agreement by the landlord, the tenant becomes a tenant at sufferance and may be evicted without notice.

8. There are three basic methods of concurrent ownership: a tenancy in common, a joint tenancy, and a tenancy by the entirety. Co-owners in a tenancy in common may dispose of their interest in the property in any manner they choose, and upon their death, their interest in the property will pass to their heirs or beneficiaries. Both a joint tenancy and a tenancy by the entirety share the characteristic of right of survivorship, with a co-owner's interest automatically passing to the surviving co-owner(s). Although any number of persons may be co-owners in a tenancy in common or a joint tenancy, only a husband and a wife may take title to property as tenants by the entirety.

REVIEW QUESTIONS

1. Distinguish between the following.
   a. Littoral rights and riparian rights
   b. Dower rights and curtesy rights
   c. Freehold estates and leasehold estates
2. Explain how one determines whether an item is a fixture.
3. List and explain the basic ownership rights acquired when purchasing real property.
4. Distinguish between (a) a tenancy in common, (b) a joint tenancy, and (c) a tenancy by the entirety.
5. List and explain the four basic leasehold estates.

ETHICAL QUESTIONS

Client Marjorie Greenway recently purchased a house and your supervising attorney handled the closing. Marjorie telephones to say that she wants to file for your state's homestead tax exemption. She asks you where she must go to file and the procedures she must follow to file for the exemption. You are thoroughly familiar with the procedure. May you answer her question?

PRACTICAL ASSIGNMENTS

Assignment 2:1. Research your state statutes regarding homestead. How is homestead defined? What special rights are granted the property owner in homestead property? Photocopy the relevant statutes and insert them under the "Residential Property" section of your resource portfolio.

Assignment 2:2. Your supervising attorney, Deborah Sanders, represents Russell and Janet Ward, who are selling their home to Gary and Monica Morgan. The Wards have agreed to sell certain personal property within the home as well, namely: a dining room set comprised of a mahogany dining table, eight matching chairs, and a breakfront; a tapestry sofa and matching loveseat in the family room; a 6' × 9' Oriental rug in the living room; and a mahogany four-poster bed with matching dresser and night tables in the master bedroom. Also included in the sale are all window treatments. The home is located at 38 Sudeley Terrace in your city, county, and state, and the real estate closing is to take place one week from today's date. Deborah has asked you to prepare a bill of sale. After review, insert it under the "Residential Property" section of your resource portfolio.

Assignment 2:3. Research your state statutes to determine whether your state recognizes dower or curtesy rights. Has your state substituted the concept of the spousal elective share for these rights?

Assignment 2:4. Research your state statutes regarding the applicable notice requirements to terminate residential and commercial leases. Photocopy the relevant statutes and insert them under the "Leases" section of your resource portfolio.

Assignment 2:5. Client Erskine Properties, Inc., owns a large tract of land located within your city, county, and state and has subdivided the tract into smaller parcels to sell to developers. CSN Development Corporation is interested in purchasing a parcel for the negotiated price of two million dollars. Three weeks ago from today's date, the board of directors of Erskine Properties met and approved the contract for sale and purchase. The parcel in question is described as follows:

Tract 7 of ARUNDELL ESTATES, 3rd Section, according to the plat thereof, recorded at Plat Book 105, Page 14 of the Public Records of (your county and state).

The president and secretary of the corporation are authorized to execute all necessary documents for the sale. Mitchell Cowling, secretary of Erskine Properties, has been very ill and has not prepared the resolution by the board ratifying the sale, so your supervising attorney, Deborah Sanders, has asked you to draft the necessary resolution for Mitchell's signature.

Assignment 2:6. Define the following key terms.

adverse possession	life estate
bill of sale	life estate pur autre vie
community property	littoral rights
curtesy	personal property
dower	real property
elective share	riparian rights
estate for years	separate property
fee simple absolute	tenancy at sufferance
fixture	tenancy at will
freehold estate	tenancy by the entirety
homestead property	tenancy from period to period
joint tenancy	tenancy in common
leasehold estate	

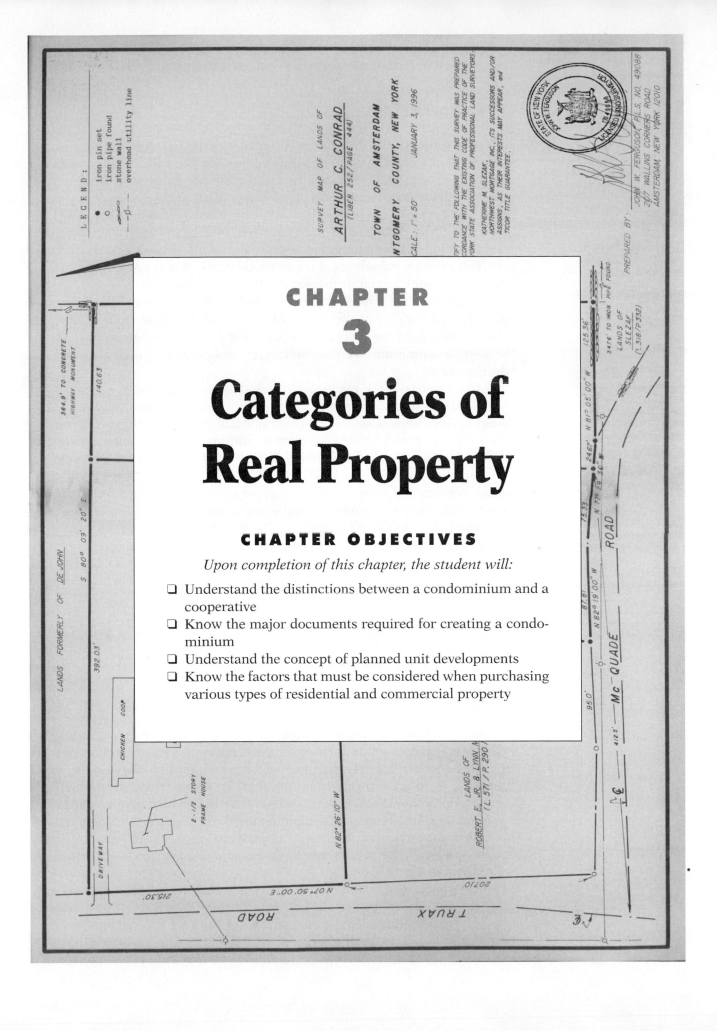

CHAPTER
3

Categories of
Real Property

CHAPTER OBJECTIVES

Upon completion of this chapter, the student will:

❑ Understand the distinctions between a condominium and a cooperative
❑ Know the major documents required for creating a condominium
❑ Understand the concept of planned unit developments
❑ Know the factors that must be considered when purchasing various types of residential and commercial property

INTRODUCTION

Real property may be purchased for residential use, for commercial use, or a combination of these. As a paralegal, you may be called upon to assist in a variety of real estate transactions that require the knowledge of the special factors influencing the sale and purchase of different categories of real property. The concerns of a prospective purchaser of a single-family home will differ from those of a prospective purchaser of a strip center. The sale of a condominium will require different procedures than the sale of a cooperative.

This chapter introduces you to various types of real property, both residential and commercial. It focuses on the factors that must be considered in each type of transaction, an understanding of which will aid you in the drafting or reviewing of the contract for sale and purchase. Additionally, this chapter discusses the mechanics of creating and operating certain types of residential communities: condominiums, cooperatives, and planned unit developments.

A knowledge of the manner in which these communities are created and operated is important for several reasons. Your law firm may represent a developer who is developing a condominium project, and your supervising attorney may require your assistance in drafting the documents used in creating and operating the condominium. Your law firm may represent a condominium association, the body of which oversees the operation of a condominium and enforces its rules, in which instance a knowledge of your state condominium statutes will enable you to assist your supervising attorney in addressing the client's objectives. On the other hand, your firm may be representing a purchaser who is planning on buying a condominium or home in a planned unit development. You may be asked by your supervising attorney to review the requisite documents to determine whether there are any restrictions that would impinge on his or her enjoyment and use of the property.

RESIDENTIAL PROPERTY

In General

American families are more transient than they were several decades ago. When considering the purchase of a residential property, purchasers must take into account not only their immediate personal needs but also the resale potential of the real property in question. Residential real estate includes single-family homes in traditional suburban neighborhoods, houses in planned unit developments, condominiums, and cooperatives. The purchase of each of these types of properties has distinct advantages and disadvantages. There are some general considerations, however, for the purchase of any type of residential property.

The purchase of a home is a major commitment and responsibility. The ability to obtain satisfactory financing for the purchase is a primary concern. No prospective purchaser should enter into a contract for sale and purchase without ensuring the inclusion of a provision that makes closing on the property contingent upon the obtaining of satisfactory financing. Prospective purchasers should take into account the purchase price of the property and other costs associated with it. For example, there is the cost for any renovations the purchaser plans on making to the property. Additionally, there are the costs of utilities, maintenance, and homeowners' insurance. A prospective purchaser will want to obtain copies of average utility bills from the seller as well as copies of any lawn care or other maintenance-related expenses.

When evaluating the costs of home ownership, the purchaser should also understand that certain tax benefits are associated with home ownership. The loan interest on mortgage loans is tax deductible, as are loan origination fees and real property taxes.

Further, the Taxpayer Relief Act of 1997 allows property owners to exclude up to $250,000 of gain ($500,000 for married couples filing a joint return) realized on the sale or exchange of a principal residence occurring after May 6, 1997. Prior to the enactment of this law, property owners had a one-time exclusion when selling or exchanging a principal residence. Under this new act, however, this exclusion is allowed each time a property owner sells or exchanges a principal residence (with the caveat that the exclusion may not be claimed more frequently than once every two years). Additionally, the property owner is not required to reinvest the sales proceeds in a new residence to claim this exclusion. In order to be eligible for the exclusion, the property owner must have owned and used the residence as his or her primary residence for a combined period of at least two years out of the five years prior to the sale or exchange.

Location impacts the present and resale value of the property. The prospective purchaser of a home should check to see how close to major roadways and shopping the subject property is located. How close is it to where the purchaser works? Is it located in a good school district? This is important even if the purchaser does not have school-age children because location within a good school district will be a marketing advantage for resale.

Is the property located within or without city limits? This will impact the real property taxes on the property, as each local governing authority may impose real property taxes. Thus, property located within city limits will have both city and county real property tax assessments imposed. The prospective purchaser will want to obtain copies of the real property tax assessments from the seller.

Is the property located within an area that is zoned strictly residential or is there mixed zoning? Zoning may be a major consideration for a purchaser who plans on using a portion of his or her home for business purposes. Conversely, if the property is located in a mixed zoning area, there may be commercial entities located nearby that adversely affect the noise and traffic conditions in the area. Additionally, the purchaser should consider whether the property is located in a flood-prone area, which would require the obtaining of flood insurance.

The prospective purchaser will be concerned about the condition of the premises. Are the plumbing, mechanical, and electrical systems in good condition? What is the condition of the roof? Has a termite inspection been done? What are the conditions of the interior and exterior walls?

The prospective purchaser should consider the resale prices of similar properties in the neighborhood. Is the subject property the most expensive property on the street or in the neighborhood? If so, he or she may find it more difficult to sell it down the road. Purchasers often are advised to "purchase" the best neighborhood or area they can afford rather than the best house.

Ownership of a condominium, a cooperative, or a residence located within a planned unit development entails living in a community environment in which there are certain trade-offs. A purchaser looking to own a residence who wants the accessibility of recreational amenities yet does not want the responsibility of maintaining the grounds surrounding his or her living quarters may opt for one of these types of residential housing. In doing so, however, the purchaser will be required to pay a proportionate share of the assessments for maintaining the grounds and recreational facilities. Additionally, he or she may face certain restrictions that run the gamut from the way in which he or she may decorate the exterior of the residence to the type of vehicle permitted in the parking lot. The following sections discuss the creation and operation of condominiums, cooperatives, and planned unit developments and explain the special factors inherent in these forms of ownership.

Condominiums

A **condominium** is a form of ownership in which the property owner owns the interior of his or her unit, plus an undivided interest, expressed as a percentage interest, in the common elements of the condominium complex. The unit owner is given a deed to the property upon closing and is responsible for his or her own real property taxes.

The **common elements** are those areas that all of the owners use in common, such as the grounds on which the condominium building is located, the roof, exterior walls and structural components, the parking lot, and any recreational facilities (for example, swimming pools, tennis courts, clubhouses). Areas that benefit less than all of the condominium unit owners are sometimes referred to as *limited common elements* (for example, assigned parking spaces or storage facilities). The payment for the upkeep of the common elements and the real estate taxes on them is assessed proportionately to each unit owner who pays the condominium association or its management agent condominium assessments monthly, quarterly, semiannually, or annually.

Because condominium ownership assumes living in a communal environment, rules and regulations promoting the general good for the condominium as a whole are upheld by a **condominium association,** comprised of members who are unit owners. Should a unit owner fail to abide by these rules, the association may fine the unit owner. Further, should a unit owner fail to pay any assessments, the association may place a lien on the delinquent owner's unit and foreclose on it in a manner similar to the foreclosure of a mortgage.

A condominium is more than just a structure; it is a creature of statute. Every state has statutes that govern both the creation and operation of condominiums. The first statutes to apply to condominiums were adopted by the state legislature of Puerto Rico. These statutes remained a model after which many states patterned their statutes until the Uniform Condominium Act was originally approved by the Commissioners on Uniform State Laws in 1977. This act was amended in 1980. A *uniform law* is a law in a specific subject area, in this instance condominium law, that is approved by the Commissioners on Uniform State Laws and is adopted in whole or in part by

condominium: A form of ownership in which the property owner owns the interior of a unit, plus an undivided interest, expressed as a percentage interest, in the common elements of the condominium complex.

common elements: Those areas of a condominium development that all of the owners use in common, such as the grounds on which the condominium building is located, the roof, the exterior walls and structural components, the parking lot, and any recreational facilities.

condominium association: An association comprised of unit owners that sets rules and manages the operation of the condominium.

individual states. At the time of this writing, the states that have adopted the Uniform Condominium Act are Maine, Minnesota, Missouri, Nebraska, New Hampshire, New Mexico, North Carolina, Pennsylvania, Rhode Island, Texas, Virginia, and Washington.

In addition to state laws, there are federal laws that can impact condominiums. If the condominium units are marketed in any state other than the state in which they are located, the sale of the condominiums must comply with the requirements of the Securities Act of 1933 and any other pertinent regulations promulgated by the Securities and Exchange Commission.

Creation. A condominium is legally created when a **declaration of condominium,** sometimes referred to as a *master deed,* is prepared, signed by the developer, and recorded in the land records for the county in which the condominium is located. Although the statutory requirements for the contents of a declaration vary from state to state, most states require that a declaration include the following:

1. The name of the condominium
2. The name of the county in which the condominium is located
3. The legal description of the condominium
4. A statement of the maximum number of units that will be included in the condominium
5. A description of the boundaries of each unit
6. A description of any limited common elements
7. A description of any development rights reserved by the developer of the condominium (this is particularly pertinent if the developer is building the condominium complex in stages or phases)
8. A statement indicating the allocation of percentage interests in the common elements to each unit
9. A statement indicating the voting rights of each unit
10. Any restrictions on use, occupancy, and transfer of units
11. A plat or plan of the condominium

The plat or plan that is attached as an exhibit to the declaration is a general schematic map of the entire condominium. It shows the location and dimensions of the vertical and horizontal boundaries of each condominium unit and each unit's identifying number, the location and dimensions of all common and limited common elements, and all easements burdening the property (for example, utility easements, cable easements). A sample declaration of condominium is provided in Figure 3–2, at the end of this chapter.

The next step is creating a condominium association to oversee the operation of the condominium. The condominium association generally is organized as a not-for-profit corporation and, therefore, similarly to other corporations, is not legally created until its articles of incorporation are filed with the state filing authority. The association must be organized no later than the date the first condominium unit is conveyed. If the developer is creating a multiphased condominium, the developer often creates a **master association,** sometimes referred to as an *umbrella association,* that provides management services and decision-making functions to smaller condominiums. The membership of the association consists of all of the unit owners, who elect an executive board of directors to oversee the condominium operations. The Uniform

declaration of condominium: The document that legally creates a condominium.

master association: An umbrella association that provides management services and decision-making functions to smaller condominiums.

Condominium Act and most state statutes recognize the necessity of allowing the developer, called the *declarant* or *sponsor,* to control the association during the developmental phases of a condominium project. The developer then relinquishes control after all or a certain percentage of the units have been sold.

Although the powers granted to condominium associations by state statute may vary, they usually include the powers set forth in section 3-102 of the Uniform Condominium Act, which provides associations with powers such as the power to adopt and amend bylaws and rules and regulations, to adopt and amend budgets, to hire and discharge employees, and to make contracts and incur liabilities, and with many other powers, including the right to exercise any powers necessary for the governance and operation of the association.

The third requirement is the preparation of condominium bylaws. The bylaws set forth the governing procedures of the condominium. Unlike the articles of incorporation, the bylaws are not recorded in the public records. Because the articles of incorporation become public knowledge when recorded, most attorneys drafting them prefer to keep them skeletal, containing only those provisions required by state statute. All other matters pertaining to the operation of the condominium are set forth in the bylaws. Generally, the bylaws of a condominium association include the following:

1. The number of directors on the executive board and the titles of the officers of the association
2. The election by the executive board of the officers of the association
3. The qualifications, powers, duties, and term of office of the directors on the executive board
4. The manner of electing and removing directors and officers and the manner of filling vacancies
5. Which, if any, of its powers the executive board or officers may delegate to others
6. Which of its officers may prepare, execute, certify, and record amendments to the declaration
7. The method of amending the bylaws
8. Any other matters the association deems necessary and appropriate

Operation. Once the condominium's executive board is elected, its primary duties are twofold: (1) to ensure that all unit owners abide by the association's rules and regulations that have been promulgated for the common good of the condominium community, and (2) to oversee the maintenance, repair, and replacement of the common elements. To perform this latter duty, the board must develop a budget that covers the normal, everyday expenses of maintaining the common areas and that also sets aside reserves for those repairs or replacements that occur less often, such as repaving the parking lots, painting the exterior of the buildings, or resurfacing the roof. The association must obtain property insurance on the common elements insuring against all risks of physical damage. Additionally, it must obtain liability insurance covering all occurrences commonly insured against for death, bodily injury, and property damage arising out of, or in connection with, the use, ownership, or maintenance of the common elements. The monies to cover all these expenses come from assessing each unit owner for his or her proportionate share. The budgets on which these assessments are based are devised annually and list each expense, both in terms of monthly cost and annual cost, such as the sample budget provided in Figure 3–1.

As noted previously, should a unit owner fail to make an assessment payment, the condominium association may file a lien against the unit and foreclose that lien in a manner similar to a lender foreclosing on a defaulted mortgage loan. The lien may cover not only the delinquent assessment amount but also fees, late charges, fines, and interest. Further, section 3.116(b) of the Uniform Condominium Act provides that the association's lien on a unit takes priority over all other liens and encumbrances except those recorded prior to the recordation of the declaration, those imposed for real estate taxes or other governmental assessments or charges against the unit, and first mortgages recorded before the date the assessment became delinquent. Interestingly, this section of the act includes a caveat regarding first mortgages. It states that in regard to a prior first mortgage (that is, one given by the unit owner to a lender when financing the purchase of the unit), the condominium association's lien has priority for six months' assessments based on the periodic budget. This means that in those states whose statutes parallel the Uniform Condominium Act, a lender holding a first mortgage on a condominium unit whose owner is delinquent in maintenance payments would have to pay the six months' assessments if it wanted to prevent the foreclosure on the unit by the condominium association. If it did not do so, the association would have priority over the lender to any monies realized from bringing a foreclosure action.

If the executive board finds there are surplus funds left over at the end of a fiscal year, the board, unless otherwise stated in the declaration, typically uses them for the prepayment of reserves and credits any remaining funds to the accounts of the unit owners to reduce their future assessments.

To aid the executive board in carrying out its activities, the board may create committees to oversee various functions, such as a screening committee to screen potential new owners, or a development committee to oversee the addition or expansion of the recreational facilities. To manage the daily operations of the condominium, the association may hire a real estate management company to collect the assessments and to hire the contractors and subcontractors to carry out the maintenance and repair work required. If the association hires employees directly to carry out these tasks, the association must take care of such matters as workers' compensation and unemployment insurance.

Purchase and Sale. Prior to purchasing a condominium unit, a prospective purchaser will be given a set of condominium documents to review, containing the declaration, the articles of incorporation of the association, and the bylaws. Most states have statutes providing a "cooling off" period that allows a prospective purchaser a statutorily specified number of days after receiving the documents to cancel a contract for sale and purchase without any penalty. During this period, it is advisable for the prospective purchaser also to obtain copies of minutes of the last few condominium association meetings and bring these and the condominium documents to an attorney for review. A review of the minutes will indicate whether any recent decisions have been made to increase assessments or to amend the condominium documents. The

FIGURE 3–1
Budget for
condominium
association

RIVERDALE CONDOMINIUM ASSOCIATION, INC.
A Corporation Not-for-Profit
1997 BUDGET

		Monthly	Annually
I.	**Expenses for the Association and condominium**		
A.	Administration of Association	$ 150.00	$ 1,800.00
B.	Management fees	800.00	9,600.00
C.	Building cleaning and maintenance	165.00	1,980.00
D.	Lawn and property maintenance	500.00	6,000.00
E.	Expenses on Association property		
	(1) Taxes	61.00	732.00
	(2) Cleaning and maintenance	60.00	720.00
F.	Electricity (common elements)	375.00	4,500.00
G.	Water, sewer and garbage service	900.00	10,800.00
H.	Insurance	625.00	7,500.00
I.	Miscellaneous		
	(1) Annual filing fee with Bureau of Condominiums	5.00	60.00
	(2) Professional services (legal and accounting)	200.00	2,400.00
J.	Security provisions	.00	.00
K.	Pest control	135.00	1,640.00
	TOTAL	$3,976.00	$47,732.00
II.	**Reserves**		
A.	Building painting	$ 396.00	$ 4,752.00
B.	Pavement resurfacing	80.00	960.00
C.	Roof replacement	300.00	3,600.00
D.	Miscellaneous reserves	75.00	900.00
	TOTAL	$ 851.00	$10,212.00

BUDGET NOTES

1. The expenses for individual units are as follows.
    (a)   A-type units $179.76
    (b)   B-type units   183.10
    (c)   C-type units   190.50
2. The balance in the reserve accounts of the Association at the beginning of the current budget year is as follows:
    (a)   Building painting $ 28,512.00
    (b)   Pavement resurfacing   8,640.00
    (c)   Roof replacement   28,800.00
    (d)   Miscellaneous reserves   4,500.00
3. The formula for each reserve category is based on the following estimates.
    (a)   Building painting to occur every eight years, and one-eighth of the total estimated cost is allocated to each fiscal year. Six of the eight years are currently on deposit.
    (b)   Pavement resurfacing to occur every fifteen years, and one-fifteenth of the total estimated cost is allocated to each fiscal year. Nine of the fifteen years are currently on deposit.
    (c)   Roof replacement to occur every twenty years, and one-twentieth of the total estimated cost is allocated to each fiscal year. Eight of the twenty years are currently on deposit.
    (d)   Miscellaneous items of deferred maintenance and capital expenditures are based upon the need for such expenditures as determined over the previous ten years of the association and to cover needs not specifically identified in paragraphs (a), (b) and (c).

attorney, in turn, may turn the documents over to you, the paralegal, to scrutinize and prepare a summary of use restrictions, the purchaser's voting rights as a unit owner, and his or her responsibilities for regular and special assessments, for the attorney to review with the purchaser.

The prospective purchaser will need to know of any restrictions imposed on his or her use of the property. For example, a unit owner often is prohibited from making any alterations to the exterior of the property, including the addition of porches and/or the addition of decorative elements, without first obtaining association approval. The purchaser may be buying the unit as an investment. In this situation, particular attention should be paid to those sections of the rules and regulations pertaining to rental of the unit. Many condominium associations, to prevent transiency, limit the number of times a unit may be rented each year and may require leases no shorter than a specified period. Further, they often require the submission of the lease to the association for approval. In some instances, to purchase the unit the purchaser must be approved by a screening committee, and should he or she later wish to sell the unit, the screening committee will have to approve any prospective buyer. A number of condominiums impose restrictions on pets or on the types of motor vehicles allowed on the property. These and other use restrictions should be pointed out to the purchaser.

The purchaser of a condominium unit has many of the same concerns as the purchaser of other residential property, including financing, location, and other costs associated with home ownership such as real estate taxes and utilities. The following checklist should aid you in reviewing the matters to be considered when the firm's client is purchasing a condominium.

CONDOMINIUM CHECKLIST

1. *Purchase price*
2. *Location*
3. *Financing*
4. *Condominium documents*
   a. *Receipt of all documents required by state statute*
   b. *Compliance of contents of documents with state statute*
5. *Condominium board approval through screening*
6. *Cost of real estate taxes (obtain prior tax bills from seller if not a new unit)*
7. *Cost of utilities (obtain prior utility bills from seller if not a new unit)*
8. *Cost of homeowners' and other insurance*
9. *Recreational facilities provided*
   a. *Clubhouse(s)*
   b. *Swimming pool(s)*
   c. *Tennis court(s)*
   d. *Golf course(s)*
   e. *Other*
10. *Control of condominium board*
    a. *Developer-controlled; if so, until when?*
    b. *Unit owner-controlled*
11. *Condominium assessments*
    a. *Current amount for regular assessments*

    b. Any anticipated raises in assessments; if so, when and by how much?

    c. Last time special assessments were assessed and whether any are projected in the near future; if so, how much?

    d. Timing of assessment payments (for example, monthly, quarterly)

    e. Any late fees charged for late payment; amount of fee; any grace period

    f. Lien rights of association for delinquent assessments

12. *Voting rights*
    a. Do all unit owners have an equal vote?
    b. Do unit owners vote on proposed budgets?
    c. Do unit owners vote on amendments to condominium documents?

13. *Use restrictions*
    a. Restrictions on use of unit (for example, cannot use for business purposes)
    b. Restrictions on pets
    c. Restrictions on parking
    d. Restrictions on vehicles
    e. Restrictions on visitors
    f. Restrictions on transfer of unit
    g. Restrictions on leasing of unit
    h. Restrictions on decorating exterior of unit; balcony or porch usage
    i. Restrictions on right to make improvements
    j. Other

14. *Responsibility for other contracts when purchasing, such as cable television contracts*

15. *Expansion by developer*
    a. Timing of additional phases
    b. Number of units in each additional phase
    c. Architecture and aesthetics of building(s) in additional phase(s)
    d. Impact on unit owner's assessments

16. *Fixtures included with the unit*

17. *Easements and other encumbrances*

Cooperatives

A **cooperative** is a multiunit building owned by a corporation. One does not purchase a unit within the building; rather, one purchases stock in the corporation. This entitles the purchaser of stock to enter into a long-term lease with the corporation. Acquiring a larger unit often entails purchasing a larger number of shares. The corporation owns not only the multiunit building but also the land on which it is built, together with all common elements shared by the shareholder-tenants. The law governing cooperatives generally is state corporate law.

As in the case of other corporations, the shareholders are the owners of the corporation. In this instance, the shareholders are owners of the cooperative rather than owners of individual units. Just as in other corporations, shareholders of a cooperative control the corporation indirectly by electing a board of directors to manage the cooperative. Similarly, the shares

cooperative: A multiunit building owned by a corporation. One purchases stock in the corporation, which entitles the purchaser of the stock to enter into a long-term lease with the corporation.

of stock in the cooperative are transferable, just as stock in any corporation is transferable. A shareholder in a cooperative can increase his or her share of ownership by acquiring additional shares of stock.

Because ownership in a cooperative pertains to the ownership of shares of stock, the cooperative owner is a purchaser of personal property rather than a purchaser of real property. His or her real property interest is a leasehold interest. Thus, the documents involved in this type of transaction differ from those in other real estate transactions. In most real estate transactions, the document evincing ownership is the deed. Here, the document allowing use of the premises is a long-term lease, and the documents evincing the ownership interest in the cooperative building are the stock certificates.

Individuals residing in the units are not taxed individually for real property assessments. The building as a whole is assessed and taxed. The shareholders each pay periodic assessments to the corporation to cover the maintenance of the property, the real property taxes, insurance, and the mortgage payments on the building. To purchase the property and construct the cooperative building, the corporation will have given a mortgage to a lending institution, which will be a first mortgage on the property. All shareholders are responsible for this first mortgage. If an individual purchaser of an interest in the cooperative needs to obtain additional financing to purchase his or her shares or to make improvements in his or her unit, the mortgage instrument he or she gives to a lender is considered a second mortgage. As security for this second mortgage, the purchaser pledges his or her long-term lease and shares of stock.

Mortgage liens (in the event of failure to pay by the individual with a second mortgage loan) are liens against the whole building. Therefore, financing is more complicated in this type of transaction. Failure of one or more individuals to pay assessments in a timely manner may cause the corporation to default on its obligations, and the result may be a foreclosure on the corporation that affects all shareholders, unless other shareholders pay additional sums to make up for the delinquency. Because the financial viability of the cooperative is so dependent on the communal responsibility of the shareholders, prospective cooperative owners typically face tougher screening committees than prospective condominium owners. As in the case of condominiums, cooperatives have strict rules and regulations by which each tenant must abide.

A client considering cooperative ownership should understand the distinctions between cooperatives and condominiums, particularly the fact that he or she will not own an individual unit and the collective responsibility for mortgage and tax payments. Just as in the case of a prospective purchaser of a condominium, the rules and regulations of the cooperative must be scrutinized. The attorney for the prospective purchaser will want to inspect the original prospectus and all amendments to it as well as the corporation's records and financial statements. Inspection of the records includes the inspection of the corporation's minutes. The minutes may reveal plans to undertake repairs or refurbishment that translate into increased costs for each member of the corporation. Further, they may reveal delinquencies in assessment payments. These should be thoroughly investigated prior to purchasing shares and signing a lease.

Time Shares

Time share ownership is the purchase of the right to use real property for a limited, specified period of time each year. Other time share owners purchase the right to use the same property for varying time segments during the year. Each time share owner becomes a tenant in common with the other time share owners.

Time share owners usually purchase time shares because they are located in resort areas and the purchasers want assurance of regular, prepaid vacation spots. Should the owner of a time share choose not to use his or her allotted time spot, he or she may lease the property to another for the time period or partake in a time share exchange. For example, Ann might own a time share in Florida, while Roger owns one in Aspen for the same time period. Ann and Roger might swap their time shares for the year so Roger can get a suntan and Ann can have a ski holiday.

Although one may purchase a time share in a cooperative or a home, most time shares involve condominiums. Many state statutes do not include provisions pertaining to time share ownership. The Uniform Condominium Act, however, provides that if the declaration of condominium states that ownership or occupancy of any units is or may be in time shares, the condominium documents must include the following information:

1. The number and identity of units in which time shares may be created
2. The total number of time shares that may be created
3. The minimum duration of any time shares that may be created
4. The extent to which the creation of time shares will or may affect the enforceability of the association's lien for assessments

Just as in the case of the purchase of a condominium, the prospective time share purchaser is given a statutorily prescribed period of time in which to review the relevant documents and rescind a contract for sale and purchase.

Planned Unit Developments

A **planned unit development (PUD)** is also referred to as a *planned community* or a *cluster development*. It is a subdivision containing individual lots with common areas controlled by a homeowners' association. Although the association usually takes the form of a nonprofit corporation, it may be organized as a for-profit entity. The association is comprised of members who are homeowners within the subdivision. The common areas are owned not by the property owners, but rather by the association as a distinct entity. Statutes pertaining to planned unit developments have been adopted in many states.

The homes within a planned unit development may be uniform or mixed. For example, one might find attached town houses and large detached homes within the same development. The shared common areas may include some of the same recreational facilities found in condominium developments, such as shared swimming pools, tennis courts, and clubhouses.

A planned unit development is created by the recordation of a subdivision plat in the county in which the subdivision property is located. The subdivision map is a plat map (discussed in detail in Chapter 5) that indicates the

time share: The purchase of the right to use real property for a limited, specified period of time each year.

planned unit development (PUD): A subdivision containing individual lots with common areas controlled by a homeowners' association.

property set aside to be dedicated for public use, the location of each lot, with the demarcation of lot size, the location and description of all common areas, and the location and description of all easements and other encumbrances.

In addition to the recording of a subdivision plat, a **declaration of covenants and restrictions** is recorded. This declaration is very similar to the declaration of condominium recorded to create a condominium because it covers such topics as property ownership, land use restrictions, membership and voting rights, and assessments for common expenses. Many homeowners' associations have architectural committees through which plans to renovate, expand, or construct on vacant lots must be submitted and approved. Therefore, the land use restrictions may be relaxed or stringent.

Membership in the homeowners' association usually is automatic upon purchasing a lot in the subdivision. Members are assessed their proportionate share of the expenses for the maintenance of the common areas. As with condominium ownership, should a homeowner within a planned unit development fall delinquent in his or her assessment payments, the homeowners' association may place a lien on his or her property and foreclose.

To limit the homeowners' liability in common areas, the homeowners' association is created as a separate legal entity by the filing of articles of incorporation with the state filing authority. The functions of the association are governed by its bylaws. Unless special state statutes exist, state corporate law governs the association.

The purchaser of a home or vacant lot within a planned unit development has to consider many factors prior to purchase. He or she may hire an attorney to review the declaration of covenants and restrictions to determine whether any of the land use restrictions imposed will be problematic. Figures and payment periods of assessments should be ascertained. If the purchaser is buying a vacant lot, local ordinances must be researched as well as the architectural standards set forth by the association's architectural committee. Further, if all the land is not yet developed within the subdivision, the purchaser will want information concerning future building projects within the community and how the future development will impact the resale value of his or her property as well as the cost of future assessments.

COMMERCIAL PROPERTY

A commercial real estate transaction often is a more complex procedure than a residential transaction. These transactions may require more complicated financing methods than the purchase of a single-family home. (These transactions are discussed in detail in Chapter 14.) Increased government controls such as zoning, environmental, and energy considerations tend to complicate matters. Items to be taken into consideration in a commercial real estate transaction are enumerated in the following checklist. Many of these items can be addressed as contingencies in the contract for sale and purchase.

declaration of covenants and restrictions: A document setting forth the rights and restrictions of property owners within a planned unit development.

COMMERCIAL PROPERTY CHECKLIST
1. *Zoning and local ordinances*
2. *Location for traffic*
3. *Traffic count*

4. *Visibility*
5. *Competition*
6. *Availability and cost of utilities*
7. *Water supply facilities*
8. *Sewage disposal facilities*
9. *Expansion capability*
10. *Availability of rail, water, air, and other freight shipping facilities*
11. *Availability of concomitant or contributing businesses*
12. *Access for pedestrian patronage*
13. *Access for vehicular traffic*
14. *Parking*
15. *Character of neighborhood as affecting particular businesses*
16. *Population type and density*
17. *Source of labor and labor laws*
18. *Load-bearing qualities of the land*
19. *Soil conditions of the land*
20. *Drainage*
21. *Financing*
22. *Licenses*
23. *Taxes*

Transportation; Demographics

Although not every one of the factors in the preceding checklist will pertain to every business, most of them are relevant to the purchase of commercial property. Certain factors may be of primary concern. For example, if the property is being sought as the location of an import-export business, transportation facilities will be of primary concern. In such a situation, the attorney for the prospective purchaser of the property should include a clause in the contract for sale and purchase that conditions the obligation to close on the obtaining of satisfactory agreements with railroad officials, port officials, and so forth. The cost of fuel, for instance, for water transportation can be a major factor if most of the acquisitions or sales are shipped by water transportation. For other businesses, local demographics may be of utmost concern. If this is the case, the closing on a contract for sale and purchase should be conditioned on a satisfactory report from a professional business survey firm.

Load-Bearing; Drainage

In some parts of the country, some of the factors to be considered in a commercial real estate transaction are of greater importance than others. For example, in parts of the country that contain much filled land, the load-bearing quality of the property is crucial. Commercial buildings generally are large, and the cost to fill in the area of land needed, or to construct the building on pilings, could be prohibitive. In these parts of the country, drainage also may be of greater concern. It is almost universal in contracts for sale and purchase of land for commercial property to include a provision that the contract is subject to positive results of engineering and soil tests.

Zoning; Local Ordinances

Although zoning and local ordinances play a role in the purchase of residential property, they often play an even greater role in the purchase of commercial property. If the zoning regulations are too restrictive, the plans of the purchaser may never see the light of day. Getting property rezoned is a lengthy and, at times, expensive procedure, as it may require the hiring of attorneys to aid in the process. Certainly, if rezoning would be necessary for the purposes of the purchaser, a contract for sale and purchase should make the sale conditional on the rezoning. Because rezoning can take so much time, the seller may not be willing to tie up a property for that length of time. On the other hand, if the property has been sitting for awhile without other prospects in sight, it is in the seller's best interests to help the purchaser obtain the rezoning required for the nature of the proposed business. A prospective purchaser also must consider local ordinances pertaining to setback requirements, advertising signage, and so forth.

Taxes

Real estate taxes are a consideration for purchasers of both residential and commercial properties, but because the value of the land and the improvements upon it is often greater with commercial properties, the taxes are also proportionately greater. Specialty use business taxes by state and local governmental authorities, such as hotel tax and airport area tax, may be imposed. If the property to be purchased is a lot upon which a structure will be built, the real estate tax assessment will indicate the tax only for the land itself and will not give the purchaser any idea about the tax assessment on the building to be constructed. Real property taxes are local taxes, assessed by the city and county and special taxing districts. All other factors remaining the same, a purchaser would be better off taxwise to purchase property that is located outside of city limits because then city taxes would not apply. In reality, this may not be feasible because, depending on the nature of the purchaser's business, the demographics might indicate that prospective customers are located within the city limits and prefer the convenience of shopping close to home. Even if the property desired is located outside of a city, an investigation should be made in regard to whether there is a probability that the unincorporated area will be annexed by the city or will be incorporated to form a new city. In addition to regular real property taxes, the purchaser must consider whether the city or county are planning any improvements in the area in which the property is located, requiring special assessments to be paid by local property owners.

Federal, State, and Local Laws

A thorough investigation prior to the purchase of commercial real estate must include researching state and federal environmental protection laws (discussed in detail in Chapter 4). This is of special concern for properties that will be used for industrial purposes. Further, labor laws must be checked to determine the cost of compliance with state and local laws affecting employees, such as unemployment compensation and workers' compensation.

Traffic Flow

Traffic flow is of greater concern to developers of shopping centers and office buildings than to developers of warehouses and industrial parks. A prospective purchaser who considers traffic flow of major importance should try to determine whether local or state authorities have any future plans that would alter the present traffic patterns surrounding and leading to the subject property. Those plans may include not only include a rerouting that would decrease traffic flow but also road improvements that would alter ingress and egress to the property due to the placing of medial strips. Often the best way to obtain this information is by contacting the state department of transportation. The department should have surveys available showing highway design, traffic flow, intersections, interchange patterns, breaks, and crossovers in road patterns. Local police and fire departments may be asked to review and comment on proposed designs regarding traffic flow.

Licensing

Licensing compliance is required. Purchasers planning on constructing restaurants, entertainment establishments, hotels, and motels must check local licensing laws to determine the requirements for obtaining liquor licenses. State statutes and local ordinances regarding the sale of liquor should be checked. If the laws are too restrictive, another site may be more appropriate. Other businesses also require special licenses, including, but not limited to, banks, insurance companies, and cemeteries.

Competition

A further consideration is the competition factor. The purchaser may be looking to purchase a parcel of land that is part of a larger tract. The purchaser needs to consider not only the existing businesses in the vicinity but also the prospective purchasers of the rest of the seller's tract. A purchaser seeking to limit competition may attempt to negotiate with the seller to include a clause in the contract for sale and purchase that the seller will not sell the remainder of the parcel to businesses in direct competition with the purchaser. Many sellers are reluctant to do this, not wanting to limit their future sales opportunities.

Expansion

The prospective purchaser must contract with an eye not only to present but also to future needs. Should the purchaser wish to expand in the future, the property under contract should be conducive to this. If the seller owns not only the subject property but also surrounding properties, the purchaser may wish to include an option in the contract for sale and purchase to lease or purchase one or more of the surrounding parcels, or a right of first refusal should the seller have prospects for the surrounding property.

Purchasing an Existing Business

Not all transactions involve the purchase of a tract of land for future development of a commercial enterprise. Many commercial transactions involve the purchase of an existing business or commercial structure. If the prospective purchaser is looking to purchase a retail or wholesale business as well as the property on which the business is located, the purchaser must investigate not only the matters discussed previously but also federal and state commercial law. For example, most states have **bulk transfer laws** that pertain to the sale and purchase of all or substantially all of the inventory of a business. These laws generally require that the seller provide the prospective purchaser with an affidavit (a sworn statement) setting forth the name and address of each of the seller's creditors and the amount owed to each. The purchaser must give notice of the sale of the business to all creditors within a statutorily prescribed time period before the closing of the sale. In some states, a notice must be published in a local newspaper of general circulation as well.

If the prospective purchaser is looking to buy an existing office building or shopping center, there is a great likelihood that there are existing leases for all or a portion of the space contained within the building or center. Before committing to the purchase, the prospective purchaser will want to examine the existing leases, noting the time period of each, the rent amount, and the security deposits paid. (A thorough discussion of commercial leases is found in Chapter 17.) The purchaser of a rented commercial property is purchasing that property for investment purposes. Therefore, in addition to inspecting the individual leases, the purchaser will need to make accurate income projections. In order to do this, the purchaser will need to obtain financial statements from the seller as well as access to inspect the seller's financial records, and copies of any management and service contracts.

Finally, the purchaser of an existing business or commercial structure will want to consider any fixtures and personal property located on the property. As noted in Chapter 2, all personalty and fixtures should be described in great detail on an addendum to be attached to the contract for sale and purchase. Care must be taken here. Whereas in a residential transaction the fixtures and personalty are owned by the seller, the seller in a commercial transaction may be leasing much of the equipment located on the premises. Leased items must be clearly separated from other items.

Special Considerations for Shopping Centers

A shopping center is distinct from a strip center or the groups of retail stores often found in downtown business areas of a city. A *shopping center* is an integrated merchandising unit. The developer of a future center or the purchaser of an existing one is very concerned with obtaining the optimal tenant mix of goods and services to create the maximum drawing power from the community.

A primary draw to any shopping center is an **anchor store.** An anchor store is a major lessee, typically a major department store or a supermarket. A prospective purchaser of land for the development of a shopping center should condition the purchase on obtaining a commitment for occupancy by one or more anchor stores.

Traffic considerations are of greater importance to developers of shopping centers, as well as city planners. The developer will be concerned with access to the site from major traffic arteries. City planners will not give site approval of a large shopping center until they are assured that surrounding traffic

bulk transfer laws: Laws that pertain to the sale and purchase of all or substantially all of the inventory of a business.

anchor store: A major lessee in a shopping center, typically a major department store or, in the case of a neighborhood center, a supermarket.

arteries will be able to absorb the traffic flowing into and out of the site. Additional traffic signals and turning lanes may need to be installed. The developer also must consider the location of interior drives of the shopping center tract. Because of the complexity of traffic concerns, a developer of a shopping center should have a traffic survey prepared by a qualified engineer and make closing on the tract of land contingent upon the approval of the survey by local governmental authorities.

Finally, the developer interested in building a shopping center and acting as lessor must consider the creation of a merchants' association. A purchaser of an existing shopping center must ascertain whether a merchants' association exists and obtain a copy of its bylaws (prior to contracting, if possible). A **merchants' association** is an organization consisting of the merchants of a shopping center whose primary purpose is the promotion of the common good of the center. It will work on joint advertising and special promotions. It will oversee the conduct of its members and ensure that all members are abiding by the policies set forth in its bylaws. The lessor of the center typically is expected to contribute a certain percentage of the annual contributions made each year. A lessee's contributions are often proportionate to the square footage rented.

ACREAGE

Acreage is a tract of undeveloped real property, often purchased for development purposes, but at times purchased for cultivation as farmlands, timberlands, groves, orchards, or grazing property. Large tracts are often sold at a specified price per acre rather than at a lump sum figure. A special problem occurs in areas in which large tracts of land include sections of inland water. The purchaser paying a price per acre does not want to pay for the area covered in water, yet he or she will want that area included in the deed conveying the property. The purchaser should negotiate a reduced price per acre for those acres that include inland water.

As in the case of commercial properties, zoning laws and local ordinances relating to the use of the property are of key concern to potential purchasers. A prospective purchaser with an eye toward development of acreage into a residential subdivision may find the ideal tract in an area zoned as agricultural. Having the area rezoned for residential purposes may be a time-consuming and laborious process. Further, land may not be subdivided without first obtaining the requisite subdivision approval from local governmental authorities. As in the case of a commercial purchaser, the purchaser of acreage with future plans for development should make the closing of the transaction contingent upon obtaining the necessary zoning and subdivision approvals.

The purchaser may require that the contract for sale and purchase include a provision whereby the seller must pay or share the costs incurred in preparing the documentation to be submitted to the local governing boards. As with any other real estate purchase, the prospective purchaser of acreage should also make closing on the property contingent on obtaining satisfactory financing. Additionally, the purchaser will need to have qualified personnel perform soil and other engineering tests to determine the condition of the property and

merchants' association: An organization consisting of the merchants of a shopping center whose primary purpose is the promotion of the common good of the center.

acreage: A tract of undeveloped real property.

suitability for the intended building plans and make the closing on the property contingent upon satisfactory engineering reports.

Because acreage tracts often are quite large in size, the question of access to public roads may become an issue. The purchaser will want to obtain assurances from the seller that direct access to public roads exists or will be provided. Finally, the purchaser will need to consider water supply facilities, sewage disposal facilities, and utility hookups. Even if water and sewage facilities presently exist, there is the question of whether they will be sufficient for the prospective purchaser's future needs, especially if the tract is to be used for the construction of large residential developments.

CHAPTER SUMMARY

1. The basic categories of residential property include single-family homes (located within or without a planned unit development), condominiums, and cooperatives. Prior to purchasing any of these properties, one should consider such factors as the cost of purchasing the property (the purchase price and all other associated costs), the feasibility of obtaining adequate financing, the location of the property, the condition of the property, and the projected resale value of the property.

2. A condominium is a form of ownership in which the property owner owns the interior of a unit plus an undivided interest in the common elements. A creature of statute, a condominium cannot legally be created until a declaration of condominium is recorded in the county in which the property is located. The overseeing body of the condominium is the condominium association, which elects an executive board to supervise daily operations. The board's primary duties are the policing of the condominium's rules and regulations, and the development of annual budgets for the maintenance, repair, and replacement of common elements.

3. Some of the factors to consider when purchasing a condominium are the amount of regular and special assessments, the voting rights of unit owners, the recreational facilities provided, use restrictions imposed upon unit owners, and any plans for expansion of the condominium development.

4. A cooperative is ownership by a corporation of a multiunit building, together with the property on which it is located. The purchase of a cooperative is the purchase of personal property rather than real property because one purchases shares in the building rather than an individual unit. Each shareholder owns a percentage of the building and holds a long-term lease to an individual unit.

5. A planned unit development (PUD) is a subdivision created by the recording of a subdivision plat and a declaration of covenants and restrictions in the county in which the subdivision is located. The homeowners within the subdivision are members of a homeowners' association, which assesses the members for the costs of maintaining common areas. Just as in the case of condominium ownership, use restrictions are enforced to promote the aesthetic sense of the community as well as the character of the community.

6. The purchase of commercial property for use as an office complex, shopping center, or industrial park is more complex than the purchase of residential property. In addition to many of the same concerns confronting a residential purchaser, the purchaser of commercial property must consider factors such as demographics, traffic count, visibility, competition, expansion capability, federal and state environmental laws, labor sources, and licensing procedures.

7. The purchaser of an existing business must investigate federal and state commercial law as well as obtain all relevant financial statements from the seller. The purchaser of an existing commercial structure must obtain and examine any existing leases and management and service contracts. The purchaser of an existing shopping center also must examine the bylaws of any existing merchants' association.

REVIEW QUESTIONS

1. What factors are of common concern to purchasers of any type of residential property?
2. Explain the purpose of each of the following.
   a. Declaration of condominium
   b. Articles of incorporation of a condominium association
   c. Condominium bylaws
3. Compare and contrast condominium and cooperative ownership.
4. How is a planned unit development created?
5. What factors should be considered when purchasing commercial property?

ETHICAL QUESTIONS

You were recently hired by your present law firm. Your supervising attorney concentrates on condominium law and represents many of the major condominium associations in your area. Carl Jackson, president of Shoreham Condominium Association, Inc., has been referred to your firm and has called to set up an appointment with your supervising attorney to discuss the possibility of your firm's representation of Shoreham in a construction defects suit it wants to bring against the developer, Skyline Development Co. After setting the appointment, you recall that when you were with your previous firm, one of the partners (not your then-supervising attorney) represented Skyline Development in several matters. What should you do?

PRACTICAL ASSIGNMENTS

Assignment 3:1. Research your state statutes to find the provisions relating to the following.
   a. Condominiums
   b. Time shares
   c. Planned unit developments

Photocopy the relevant statutes. Then read through the condominium statutes and make checklists listing your state's requirements for the contents of (1) the declaration of condominium, (2) the articles of incorporation of the condominium association, and (3) the condominium bylaws. If your state has statutes pertaining to planned unit developments, prepare the same sort of checklists for the declaration of covenants and restrictions, the association articles of incorporation, and the association bylaws. Insert the photocopied statutes and your prepared checklists under the "Residential Property" section of your resource portfolio.

Assignment 3:2. Review the declaration of condominium provided in Figure 3–2 and determine whether it meets all requirements under your state law.

Assignment 3:3. Assume that the Whitehaven Condominium, described in the declaration of condominium in Figure 3–2, is located in your state and complies with your state statutes. Marianne and Simon Grayson are prospective purchasers of a condominium unit in Whitehaven. They have signed a contract for sale and purchase, rescindable within fifteen days, and have received a copy of the condominium documents. They have retained your supervising attorney, Deborah Sanders, to represent them in the transaction. Marianne has been running a successful mail order business from her present home and plans on continuing with her home-run business from her unit in Whitehaven. Simon, a veterinarian, has a local practice. As an additional convenience to his clients, he provides transportation to and from the veterinarian clinic in his minivan for grooming, boarding, and emergency services for the animals. This minivan is his primary vehicle. Affixed to the van is the removable, magnetic sign "Grayson Mobile Veterinarian Unit." In addition, the Graysons own a cocker spaniel and a macaw.

Deborah Sanders asks you to review the condominium bylaws to determine whether there are any restrictions that will impact on the Graysons' lifestyle. Having reviewed the bylaws, you have found the following relevant provisions in Article 9:

9.2(a). The sidewalks, entrances, and all other Common Elements must not be obstructed, encumbered or used for any purpose other than ingress and egress to and from the premises. No carriages, bicycles, motorcycles, wagons, shopping carts, chairs, benches, tables, furniture, or any other object of a similar type and nature shall be stored thereon. No structure of a temporary character, trailer, shack, barn, or other building shall be moved to, erected on, or used on any part of the Condominium Property at any time for a residence, workshop, office, storage room, either permanently or temporarily. No business, service, repair or maintenance for the general public shall be allowed on the Condominium Property at any time.

9.2(e). The parking facilities shall be used in accordance with the regulations adopted by the Board of the Community Association. No vehicle which cannot operate on its own power shall remain on the Condominium Property for more than twelve hours, and no repair, except emergency repair, of vehicles shall be made on the Condominium Property. No commercial vehicle owned or driven by a condominium owner shall be parked on the Condominium Property. No boat, boat trailer, trailer, recreational vehicle, camper, truck, bus, mobile home, tractor, motor coach, commercial vehicle, lettered commercial vehicle or vehicle in excess of 6,000 pounds or gross weight or like vehicle shall be left or stored on the Condominium Property except with the prior, written approval of the Association. Bicycles shall be parked in the areas, if any, provided for that purpose.

(Assignment 3:3 continued on p. 83)

**DECLARATION OF CONDOMINIUM
OF
WHITEHAVEN, A CONDOMINIUM**

A Corporation Not for Profit
Under the Laws of the State of Any State

HORIZON CONSTRUCTION CORPORATION, an Any State corporation, being the owner of record of the fee simple title to the real property situated, lying and being in Any County, Any State, as more particularly described in the Survey Exhibit attached hereto as Exhibit 1, which is incorporated herein by reference, does hereby declare that the really described in Exhibit 1 under the legend "Whitehaven 1, A Condominium, Phase 1," together with improvements thereon, is submitted to condominium ownership pursuant to the Condominium Act of the State of Any State (Chapter 525 of the Any State Statutes) and does hereby file this Declaration of Condominium.

1. PURPOSE; NAME AND ADDRESS; LEGAL DESCRIPTION; EFFECT.
    1.1 PURPOSE. The purpose of this Declaration is to submit the lands and improvements herein described to condominium ownership and use in the manner prescribed by the Laws of the State of Any State.
    1.2 NAME AND ADDRESS. The name of this Condominium is as specified in the title of this document.
    1.3 THE LAND. The real property described in Exhibit 1 is the Condominium Property contemplated to be subject to condominium ownership as provided for herein. Such property is subject to such easements, restrictions, reservations and rights of way of record, together with those contained or provided for in this instrument and the exhibits attached hereto.
    1.4 EFFECT. All of the provisions of this Declaration of Condominium and all Exhibits attached hereto shall be binding upon all Unit Owners and are enforceable equitable servitudes running with the Condominium Property and existing in perpetuity until this Declaration is revoked and the Condominium is terminated as provided herein. In consideration of receiving, and by acceptance of a grant, devise or mortgage, all grantees, devisees or mortgagees, their heirs, personal representatives, successors and assigns, and all parties claiming by, through, or under such persons agree to be bound by the provisions hereof. Both the burdens imposed and the benefits granted by this instrument shall run with each Unit as herein defined.

2. SURVEY AND DESCRIPTION OF IMPROVEMENTS.
    2.1 SURVEY. On Exhibit 1 is a survey of the land, graphic description, and plot plans of the improvements constituting the Condominium, identifying the Units, Common Elements and Limited Common Elements, and their respective locations and approximate dimensions.
    2.2 PHASING. This Condominium is a phase condominium as provided for in Section 525.301 of the Any State Statutes. On Exhibit 1, Sheets two (2) through eight (8), there are representations and descriptions of the land which may become part of the Condominium and upon which each phase is to be built. There

FIGURE 3–2
Declaration of
condominium

FIGURE 3–2
(continued)

are three types of units to be constructed in the Condominium: Type A, approximately 1,025 square feet; Type B, approximately 1,195 square feet; and Type C, approximately 1,500 square feet. Such size is the maximum per unit type.

The proposed arrangement of the three unit types for each phase of the Condominium appears on Sheets eight (8) and nine (9) of Exhibit 1. The Declarant reserves the right to alter the mix and size of unit types so long as there will be no material or adverse change in the approximate size of the units. The maximum and minimum number of units to be included in each phase is twenty (20) units.

2.3   AMENDMENT. No amendment, notwithstanding anything in the Declaration to the contrary, adding phases to the Condominium shall require the execution of such amendment or any form of consent thereto by Unit Owners, the Association or by any party other than the Declarant. The form of such amendment is attached hereto as Exhibit 2.

2.4   EFFECT OF PHASING. The general effect of phasing a condominium is the submission of a parcel of property to condominium ownership as the initial condominium phase and the addition(s) of subsequent parcels to condominium ownership with such subsequent parcels being part and parcel of the same condominium and governed by the same condominium association. It is not anticipated that the submission of additional phases to the Condominium will have significant impact upon the individual Unit Owner's rights except as set forth in this Declaration. The adding of a subsequent phase to this Condominium, thereby adding additional Units, will reduce the fraction of common elements attributable to each previously created Unit, as specifically set forth in Exhibit 3. The adding of a subsequent phase to this Condominium will not affect the vote of any Unit Owner as a member of the Association. Each Unit Owner shall continue to have one vote for each Unit in the Condominium owned by such Unit Owner, provided, however, that the total number of votes entitled to be cast will increase by the number of Units contained in the phase so added. If Declarant decides not to add any or all of the additional phases to this Condominium, the number of Units in this Condominium will be as created by this Declaration and the Owners thereof shall comprise the complete membership of the Association and thereby be entitled to cast 100% of the votes of the Association. No time shares may be created with respect to Units in any phase. There are no recreation areas and facilities owned as common elements of the Condominium, and therefore, phasing will have no effect on such areas and facilities.

The phases of the Condominium will be completed by the following schedule.

Phase	Completion date	Phase	Completion date
1	June 30, 1997	3	August 31, 1997
2	June 30, 1997	4	August 31, 1997

3.   THE UNIT AND COMMON ELEMENTS.

3.1   INTEREST IN COMMON ELEMENTS. Each Unit Owner shall own, as an appurtenance to his or her Unit, an undivided interest in the Common Elements as assigned thereto in Exhibit 3 (subject to the

FIGURE 3–2
(continued)

provisions of Paragraph 2.4). The percentage of undivided inter-est of each Unit shall not be changed without the unanimous con-sent of all owners of all of the Units except as otherwise provided herein.

3.2   BOUNDARIES. The boundaries of each Unit shall be the horizon-tal plane of the undecorated finished ceiling, the horizontal plane of the undecorated finished floor, and the vertical planes of the undecorated finished interior walls.

3.3   AUTOMOBILE PARKING AREAS. After the filing of this Declaration, there shall be assigned to each Unit the exclusive right to use at least one automobile parking space. Such assigned parking spaces shall be used only by the owner of such Unit or such owner's guests and invitees. The assignment of such parking spaces shall be made by the Declarant and may be amended by the Community Association at its discretion. Parking spaces shall be assigned by a Designation of Parking Space to be conveyed to each Unit Owner at closing. Said designations shall be retained in the Community Association's files but will not be recorded.

4.   EASEMENTS.

4.1   PERPETUAL NONEXCLUSIVE EASEMENT. The Common Elements are hereby declared to be subject to a perpetual nonexclusive easement in favor of all of the Unit Owners in the Condominium for their use and the use of their immediate families, guests, and invitees, for all proper and normal purposes, including the provid-ing of services for the benefit of all Units.

4.2   UTILITY EASEMENTS. Utility easements are reserved and/or granted through the Condominium Property as may be required for utility service (including construction and maintenance) in order to adequately serve the Condominium.

4.3   INGRESS AND EGRESS. A nonexclusive easement for ingress and egress is hereby created for pedestrian traffic over, through and across sidewalks, paths, walks, driveways, passageways and lanes as the same, from time to time, may exist upon the Common Elements; and for vehicular traffic over, through and across such portions of the Common Elements as, from time to time, may be paved and intended for such purposes.

4.4   ADDITIONAL EASEMENTS. Declarant reserves unto itself, or its designee, the unequivocal right to create additional easements over, upon, or through the Condominium Property, at any time, for any purpose without the joinder of the Association or any Unit Owners whomsoever, provided that said easements so created shall not cause a diminution of parking spaces or cause a taking of part or all of the actual building. However, if requested, the Association and Unit Owners shall join in the creation thereof.

5.   COMMON EXPENSE; COMMON SURPLUS.

5.1   LIABILITY AND METHOD OF SHARING. Each Unit shall share in the Common Surplus and be liable for the Common Expenses in the same percentage as the percentage representing the undi-vided interest of each Unit in the Common Elements as it may exist at any time. The right to share in the Common Surplus does not include the right to withdraw, or to require payment or distribution thereof, except upon termination and dissolution of the Condominium.

FIGURE 3–2
(continued)

5.2   DECLARANT'S OBLIGATION. The Declarant shall be excused from payment of the share of Common Expenses in respect to those units owned by Declarant which have not been leased and which are offered for sale during such period of time that Declarant shall have guaranteed that the assessment for Common Expenses of the Condominium imposed upon the Unit Owners other than Declarant shall not increase over a stated dollar amount, and for which period Declarant shall have obligated itself to pay any amount of Common Expenses not produced by the assessments at the guaranteed level receivable from other Unit Owners. Declarant guarantees that monthly assessments shall not exceed the amount per year for each Unit listed on Exhibit 4 during the year of the guarantee period. The time period during which assessments shall be guaranteed at the stated rate shall be in effect for a period for one year from the date of recordation of this Declaration.

6.   ADMINISTRATION OF THE CONDOMINIUM.
6.1   THE ASSOCIATION. The Association shall administer the operation and management of the Condominium Property and undertake and perform all acts and duties incident thereto in accordance with this Declaration, its exhibits and the Condominium Act and join with other corporations or entities in becoming a member of the Community Association to assist same in promoting the health, safety and welfare of the residents of the Whitehaven Community.

As phases are added to, and become a part of, this Condominium, the Association shall administer the operation and management of the Condominium as it then exists.
6.2   MEMBERSHIP. Each Unit Owner shall automatically become a member of the Association with full voting rights. No person holding any lien, mortgage or other encumbrance upon any Unit shall be entitled, by virtue thereof, to membership in the Association or Community Association or to any of the rights or privileges of such membership.
6.3   POWERS OF ASSOCIATION. In the administration of the Condominium, the Association shall have, and is hereby granted, the authority and power to enforce the provisions of this Declaration, to levy and collect assessments in the manner hereinafter provided, and to adopt, promulgate and enforce such Rules and Regulations governing the use of the Units, Common Elements and Limited Common Elements as the Board of the Association may deem to be in the best interest of the Condominium. The Association shall have all of the powers and duties set forth in the Condominium Act except where limited herein or where the exercise of such powers and duties will impair the rights of other parties.
6.4   VOTING. Each Unit Owner or Owners, including the Declarant, shall be entitled to only one (1) vote for each Unit owned. The vote of each Unit Owner shall be governed by the provisions of the Bylaws.
6.5   MANAGEMENT AGREEMENT. The Association may enter into an agreement with any person, firm or corporation for the administration, maintenance and repair of the Condominium Property

FIGURE 3–2
(continued)

and may delegate to such contractor or manager such of the powers and duties of the Association as the Association and such person, firm or corporation shall agree.

7. USE AND OCCUPANCY.

    7.1 RESIDENTIAL USE. Each Unit is hereby restricted to residential use as a single-family residence by the owner or owners thereof, their immediate families, guests and invitees but in no event shall there be more than two (2) natural person owners of any Unit or more than one non-natural person owner of any Unit. Guests and invitees may visit and temporarily reside in a Unit no more than twice in any calendar year for a period of time not to exceed thirty (30) days for each visit unless otherwise approved by the Association in cases of extreme personal need or hardship.

    7.2 ALTERATIONS AND ADDITIONS. No Unit Owner shall make or permit to be made any internal material alteration, addition or modification to his or her Unit without the prior written consent of the Association and Declarant. No Unit Owner shall cause the balcony or terrace which is abutting, or part of, his or her Unit to be enclosed or cause any improvements or changes to be made therein or to the exterior of the Unit without the written permission of the Association, Declarant and the Architectural Control Committee of the Community Association for so long as at least one (1) unit in the Whitehaven Community remains for sale in the ordinary course of business by Declarant. All improvements or changes which may be permitted shall be uniform in appearance. No Unit Owner shall cause to be made any modification or installation of electrical wiring, satellite dishes, television antenna systems or connections whether inside or outside the Unit or in any manner change the appearance of any portion of the Condominium Property. No Unit Owner may cause any material puncture or break in the boundaries of his or her Unit. No Unit Owner shall grow or plant any type of plant, shrub, flower, etc. outside his or her Unit or in his or her Privacy Area without the prior, written consent of the Association and Declarant. The Declarant's consent shall not be unreasonably withheld. All units above ground level shall maintain fully carpeted floors in said units at all times (except in bathrooms and kitchens).

    7.3 LEASING. No lease may be made for less than a ninety (90) day period nor shall any transient accommodations be provided. No Owner may lease his or her Unit more than twice a calendar year. A Unit Owner intending to lease his or her Unit shall furnish the Association a copy of said lease. No part of a unit may be leased. All leases of a unit shall be subject to the provisions of the Condominium Documents. Failure of any lessee to comply with the provisions of said documents shall constitute a default under the terms of the lease.

    7.4 RULES AND REGULATIONS. All Unit Owners and other persons shall use the Condominium Property in accordance with the Rules and Regulations promulgated by the entity in control thereof and the provisions of this Declaration and the Bylaws of the Association, as applicable.

FIGURE 3–2
(continued)

8. MAINTENANCE, ALTERATION AND REPAIR OF THE CONDOMINIUM PROPERTY.

8.1 MAINTENANCE BY ASSOCIATION. The Association, at its expense, shall be responsible for and shall maintain, repair and replace all of the Common and Limited Common Elements, except for lawn maintenance which shall be the responsibility of the Community Association. Any exterior painting, repair or replacement requires the prior approval of the Architectural Control Committee of the Community Association.

8.2 MAINTENANCE BY UNIT OWNER. The Unit Owner shall, subject to the other provisions of this Declaration, maintain, repair and replace, at his or her expense, all portions of his or her Unit including, but not limited to, all doors, windows, glass, screens, porch, balcony, screening, electric panels, electric wiring, electric outlets and fixtures, heaters, hot water heaters, refrigerators, dishwashers and other appliances, drains, plumbing fixtures and connection, interior surfaces of all walls, floors and ceilings, and all other portions of his or her Unit. The Unit Owner shall maintain and repair the air-conditioning compressor, refrigerant and electrical line appurtenant to his or her Unit.

8.3 LIABILITY OF UNIT OWNER. Should a Unit Owner undertake additions and modifications to his or her Unit or to his or her Privacy Area(s) without the prior written consent of the Board of Directors and Declarant, or refuse to make repairs as required, or should a Unit Owner cause any damage to the Common Elements, the Association may make such removals, repairs or replacements and have the right to levy a special assessment for the cost thereof against the said Unit Owner. In the event a Unit Owner threatens to or violates the provisions hereof, the Association shall also have the right to proceed in a court of equity for an injunction to seek compliance with the provisions hereof.

8.4 RIGHT OF ENTRY BY ASSOCIATION. Whenever it is necessary to enter any Unit for the purpose of inspection, including inspection to ascertain a Unit Owner's compliance with the provisions of this Declaration, or for performing any maintenance, alteration or repair to any portion of the Common Elements or Unit, the Unit Owner shall permit an authorized agent of the Association and Management Firm to enter such Unit, to go upon the Limited Common Elements, or to go upon the Common Elements, provided that such entry shall be made only at reasonable times and with reasonable advance notice. In the case of emergency such as, but not limited to, fire, flood or hurricane, entry may be made without notice or permission. The Unit Owners acknowledge that the Association has retained a master pass key to all the Units in the Condominium. Each Unit Owner does hereby appoint the Association as his or her agent for the purposes herein provided and agrees that the Association shall not be liable for any alleged property damage or theft caused or occurring on account of any entry.

9. TAX OR SPECIAL ASSESSMENT ASSESSED AGAINST THE CONDOMINIUM PROPERTY. If any taxing authority levies or assesses any Tax or Special Assessment against the Condominium Property as a whole, and not the individual Units, the same shall be paid as a Common Expense

FIGURE 3–2
(continued)

by the Association and assessed to the Unit Owners. In such event, the amount due shall constitute a lien prior to all mortgages and encumbrances upon any parcel to the same extent as though such Tax or Special Assessment had been separately levied by the taxing authority upon each unit.

10. INSURANCE PROVISIONS. The insurance which shall be purchased and maintained for the benefit of the Condominium shall be governed by the following provisions.

   10.1 PURCHASE OF INSURANCE. All insurance purchased pursuant to this Paragraph shall be purchased by the Association for the benefit of the Association, the Unit Owners and their respective mortgagees, as their interest may appear, and shall provide for the issuance of certificates of insurance and mortgagee endorsements to any or all of the holders of institutional first mortgages. Said policies and endorsements shall be deposited with the Insurance Trustee who must first acknowledge that the policies and any proceeds thereof will be held in accordance with the terms and conditions hereof.

   10.2 COST AND PAYMENT OF PREMIUMS. The cost of obtaining all insurance hereunder, excluding only the insurance as may be purchased by individual Unit Owners, is declared to be a Common Expense, as are any other fees or expenses incurred which may be necessary or incidental to carry out the provisions hereof.

   10.3 UNIT OWNERS' RESPONSIBILITY. Each Unit Owner may obtain insurance, at his or her own expense, affording coverage upon his or her own property and for his or her own liability and living expenses as he or she deems advisable. All such insurance shall contain the same waiver of subrogation that is referred to herein and shall waive any right to contribution.

   10.4 DETERMINATION TO RECONSTRUCT. If any part of the Condominium Property shall be damaged by casualty, the determination as to whether or not it shall be reconstructed shall be made in the following manner.

      10.4.1 COMMON ELEMENTS. If the damage is only to Common Elements, the damaged property shall be reconstructed unless it is determined in the manner elsewhere provided that the Condominium shall be terminated.

      10.4.2 DAMAGE TO UNITS

        (a) If the damage is to Units to which more than 70% of the Common Elements are appurtenant and the Units are found by the Board of Directors to be untenantable, then the damaged property will not be reconstructed and the Condominium will be terminated without agreement as elsewhere provided, unless within sixty (60) days after the casualty Unit Owners owning 75% or more of the Common Elements agree in writing to such reconstruction.

        (b) If the damage is to Units to which more than 30% of the Common Elements are appurtenant and the Units are found by the Board of Directors to be tenantable, then reconstruction shall be determined on a building-by-building basis.

FIGURE 3–2
(continued)

11. ASSESSMENTS.

11.1 GENERAL AUTHORITY. The Association, through its Board, shall have the power to make, levy and collect regular and special assessments for Common Expenses and such other assessments as are provided for by the Condominium Act and the provisions of this Declaration and all other expenses declared by the Directors of the Association to be Common Expenses from time to time.

11.2 UNIT OWNERS' GENERAL LIABILITY. All Common Expenses levied against Unit Owners and Units shall be on a uniform basis in the same proportion as the percentages of the undivided shares in the ownership of the Common Elements unless specifically otherwise provided for herein, without increase or diminution for the existence, or lack of existence, of any exclusive right to use a part of the Limited Common Elements. Should the Association be the owner of any Unit(s), the assessment, which would otherwise be due and payable to the Association or others by the owner of such Unit(s), shall be a Common Expense as the same relates to the collection of such sums from the Unit Owners to pay the Association's obligations.

11.3 PAYMENT. The assessments of the Association levied against the Unit Owner and his or her Unit shall be payable in such installments, and at such times, as may be determined by the Board of Directors of the Association and for which the Unit Owner and his or her Unit shall be responsible and liable.

11.4 EMERGENCIES. If statements levied are, or may prove to be, insufficient to pay the costs of operation and management of the Condominium, or in the event of emergencies, the Board of Directors shall have the authority to levy such additional assessment or assessments as it shall deem necessary.

11.5 LIEN. The Association is hereby granted a lien upon each Condominium Unit, together with a lien on all tangible personal property located within said Unit (except that such lien upon the aforesaid tangible personal property shall be subordinate to prior bona fide liens of record), which lien shall secure the payment of all monies from each Unit Owner for which he or she is liable to the Association, including all assessments, interest and expenses provided for in the Declaration and reasonable attorneys' fees incurred as an incident to the enforcement of said lien. The lien granted to the Association may be foreclosed as provided in the Condominium Act. The lien granted to the Association shall further secure such advances for taxes and payments on account of Institutional Mortgages, liens or encumbrances which may be advanced by the Association in order to preserve and protect its lien. The lien shall be effective, have priority and be collected as provided by the Condominium Act, unless by the provisions of this Declaration, such liens would have a greater priority or dignity, in which event, the lien rights in favor of the Association having the highest priority and dignity shall be the lien of the Association. Notwithstanding anything herein to the contrary, any such lien shall be subordinate to any mortgage guaranteed by the Veterans Administration and any first mortgage on the Condominium Unit.

12. TERMINATION. The Condominium may be terminated in the following manner:

FIGURE 3–2
(continued)

12.1 DESTRUCTION. If it is determined in the manner provided above that the Condominium Property as a whole shall not be reconstructed, the Condominium will be terminated.

12.2 AGREEMENT. As provided in Section 525.201 of the Any State Statutes, the Condominium may be terminated at any time by the approval in writing of all Unit Owners and all record owners of mortgages on Units.

12.3 CERTIFICATE. The termination of the Condominium shall be evidenced by a certificate of the Association executed by its President and Secretary certifying the fact of the termination, which shall become effective upon the certificate being recorded in the Public Records.

13. AMENDMENTS. Except as herein or elsewhere provided, this Declaration may be amended in the following manner:

13.1 NOTICE. Notice of the subject matter of a proposed amendment shall be included in the notice of any meeting at which a proposed amendment is to be considered in the form prescribed by Section 525.104 of the Any State Statutes.

13.2 PROPOSAL OF AMENDMENT. An amendment may be proposed by either the unanimous vote of the Board of Directors of the Association, or by fifteen percent (15%) of the members of the Association. Directors and members not present in person or by proxy at the meeting considering the amendment may express their approval in writing, provided such approval is delivered to the Secretary within ten (10) days after the meeting. Except as elsewhere provided, a proposed amendment must be approved by either:

13.2.1 Not less than seventy-five percent (75%) of the entire membership of the Board of Directors and by not less than seventy-five percent (75%) of the votes of the entire membership of the Association. Provided however, in the event said amendments relate to leasing of units, or provisions which are for the express benefit of Institutional Mortgagees, the Association shall furnish said Mortgagees with notice of proposed amendments and must procure fifty-one percent (51%) approval of said Mortgagees to the proposals in addition to the percentage unit owner approval provided for herein.

13.2.2 Until the first election of a majority of the directors by the membership as provided for in Article VII of the Articles of Incorporation, only by all of the directors.

13.3 EXECUTION AND RECORDING. Except as otherwise provided in this Declaration, a copy of each amendment shall be attached to a certificate, executed by the officers of the Association, certifying that the amendment was duly adopted. The amendment shall be effective when the certificate and copy of the amendment are recorded in the Public Records.

14. CONDEMNATION PROCEEDINGS. If condemnation proceedings are successfully litigated against all or any part of the Condominium Property, the entire Association shall secure the condemnation award in accordance with the ratio of ownership herein provided as it pertains to the Common Elements and disburse same to Unit Owners and their mortgagees as their interests appear of record. The Association shall

FIGURE 3–2
(continued)

give prompt written notice to each holder of a mortgage of record of any such condemnation procedures, and shall take no action in any such proceedings that will disturb any mortgagee's first lien priority.

The Association shall represent the Unit Owners in any condemnation proceedings or in negotiations, settlements and agreements with the condemning authority for acquisition of the Common Elements or part thereof. Each Unit Owner hereby appoints the Association as its attorney-in-fact for the purposes described herein.

15. CONSTRUCTION. All of the provisions of this Declaration shall be construed in accordance with the Law of the State of Any State. This construction shall govern in all matters, including matters of substantive and procedural law.

16. CAPTIONS. The captions to the paragraphs of this Declaration are intended for convenience only and are not deemed to be all inclusive as to the matters contained in such paragraphs or considered in connection with the construction of any of the provisions of this Declaration.

17. SEVERABILITY. If any terms or provision of this Declaration, or the application thereof to any person or circumstance, shall, to any extent, be determined to be invalid or unenforceable, the remainder of this Declaration, or the application of such term or provision to persons or circumstances other than those to which such term may be held invalid or unenforceable, shall not be affected thereby and each term and provision of this Declaration shall be valid and enforceable to the fullest extent permitted by law.

IN WITNESS WHEREOF, the Declarant has executed this Declaration on this
_____ day of _____.

Signed, sealed and delivered   HORIZON CONSTRUCTION CORP.,
in the presence of: an Any State corporation

_____By:_____ (Seal)
_____ President
    Corporate Seal

STATE OF ANY STATE
COUNTY OF ANY COUNTY

BEFORE ME, the undersigned authority, personally appeared _____ to me well known to be the person described in and who executed the foregoing instrument as President of Horizon Construction Corporation, an Any State corporation, and he acknowledged before me that he executed such instrument as such Officer of said Corporation, and that the Seal affixed thereto is the Corporate Seal of said Corporation, and that it was affixed to said instrument by due and regular Corporate authority, and that said instrument is the free act and deed of said Corporation.

WITNESS my hand and official seal, at the State and County aforesaid, this
_____ day of _____.

_____
Notary Public, State of Any State
My commission expires:_____

9.2(j). Only one (1) walking animal with a weight of not more than forty (40) pounds shall be kept or harbored in a Unit at any time. Walking animals shall be permitted only within a Unit or Privacy Area. No other pets may be kept without the written consent of the Board. Such consent may be given upon such conditions as the Board may prescribe and shall be deemed provisional and subject to revocation at any time. No animal or pet shall be maintained or harbored within a Unit that would create a nuisance to any other Unit Owner. A determination by the Board that an animal or pet maintained or harbored in a Unit creates a nuisance shall be conclusive and binding upon all parties. In no event shall a Unit Owner or any other person allow a walking animal anywhere on the Condominium Property unless carried or held on a leash not to exceed six (6) feet. Each Unit Owner and any other person so walking an animal shall be responsible for the immediate, appropriate and complete removal of all animal excrement.

Write a memorandum to Deborah Sanders addressing these issues.

Assignment 3:4. Gregory Wilkenson purchased a lot in Crystal Waters subdivision two years ago. He is now planning to build a large home on the lot and has had an architect draw up plans that he has submitted to the Crystal Waters architectural committee for approval. Prior to the submission of the plans, the architectural committee told Gregory that the development does not allow structures in excess of 6,000 square feet nor in excess of 40 feet in height. Gregory originally wanted to construct a house containing 6,050 feet, but told his architect to readjust the dimensions so that the house will be exactly 6,000 square feet.

The architectural committee was divided on whether or not to approve the plans. The structure would fit the requisite dimensions, but some members on the committee believe the house would be overbearing on the lot in question and do not find the aesthetics of the structure in keeping with the "feel" of the development. During the thirty-day period within which the committee reviewed the plans, one committee member orally told Gregory that he believed the plans would be approved. At the end of the thirty-day period, the plans were rejected. Gregory has come to Deborah Sanders to find out whether he has grounds to sue the homeowners' association and/or the individual committee members. Deborah has obtained the declaration of covenants and restrictions of Crystal Waters. She has asked you to review it and prepare a memorandum to her addressing this issue.

Having reviewed the declaration, you have found the following relevant provisions in Article V.

Section 2: Review of Proposed Construction. No fence, wall, or other structure or improvement (including landscaping) shall be commenced, painted, erected or maintained upon the Property, nor shall any addition, change or alteration visible from the exterior be made, nor shall any awning, canopy or shutter be attached to or placed upon the outside walls or roofs of any Residence or Improvement constructed on the Common Area until the plans and specifications showing the nature, kind, shape, height, color, materials, location and cost of the same shall have been submitted to and approved in writing by the Committee. The Committee shall approve proposals or plans and specifications submitted for its approval only if it deems that the construction, alterations or additions contemplated thereby in the locations indicated will not be detrimental to the appearance of the surrounding area in the Property as a whole, and that the appearance of any structure affected will be in harmony with the surrounding structures and is otherwise desirable. The Committee may condition its approval of proposals and plans and specifications as it deems appropriate and may require submission of additional plans and specifications or other information prior to approving or disapproving material submitted. The Committee may also issue rules or guidelines setting forth procedures for the submission of plans for approval. The Committee may require such detail in plans and specifications submitted for its review as it deems proper, including, without limitation, floor plans, site plans, drainage plans, elevation drawings and descriptions or samples of exterior materials and colors. Until receipt by the Committee of any required plans and specifications, the Committee may postpone review of any plans submitted for approval. The Committee shall have thirty days after delivery of all required materials to approve or reject any such plans.

Section 7: Nonliability of Committee Members. Neither the Committee nor any member thereof, nor its duly authorized Committee representative, shall be liable to the Association, or to any Owner or any other person or entity for any loss, damage or injury arising out of or in any way connected with the performance of the Committee's duties hereunder, unless due to the willful misconduct or bad faith of a member, and then only that member shall have any liability. The Committee shall review and approve or disapprove all plans submitted to it for any proposed improvement, alteration or addition solely on the basis of aesthetic considerations and the overall benefit or detriment which would result to the immediate vicinity and to the Property. The Committee shall take into consideration the aesthetic aspects of the architectural designs, placement of buildings, landscaping, color schemes, exterior finishes and materials and similar features, but shall not be responsible for reviewing, nor shall its approval of any plan or design be deemed approval of, any plan or design from the standpoint of structural safety or conformance with building or other codes.

Section 8: Variance. The Committee may authorize variances from compliance with any of the architectural provisions of this Declaration when circumstances such as topography, natural obstructions, hardship, aesthetic or environmental considerations require. Such variance must be evidenced in writing, which must be signed by at least two (2) members of the Committee. If such variances are granted, no violation of the covenants, conditions and restrictions contained in this Declaration shall be deemed to have occurred with respect to the matter for which the variance was granted. The granting of such a variance shall not, however, operate to waive any of the terms and provisions of this Declaration for any purpose except as to the particular property and particular provisions hereof covered by the variance, nor shall it affect in any way the Owner's obligation to comply with all governmental laws and regulations affecting his or her use of the premises, including, but not limited to, zoning ordinances and setback lines or requirements imposed by any governmental or municipal authority.

Assignment 3:5. Define the following key terms.

acreage	declaration of condominium
anchor store	declaration of covenants and restrictions
bulk transfer laws	master association
common elements	merchants' association
condominium	planned unit development (**PUD**)
condominium association	time share
cooperative	

CHAPTER
4
Ownership Restrictions

CHAPTER OBJECTIVES

Upon completion of this chapter, the student will:

- ❑ Understand the concept of police power and the various ways the exercise of this power by federal, state, and local governments can impact the private property owner
- ❑ Know the different types of zoning and the methods by which a private property owner can be relieved from zoning restrictions
- ❑ Understand the obligations placed upon property owners by environmental protection and fair housing laws
- ❑ Know the steps taken in assessing property for real property tax purposes
- ❑ Know the different types of easements, how they are created, and how they may be terminated

INTRODUCTION

Earlier in this text, the basic ownership rights of property owners were discussed. Recall that these rights include the right of disposition, the right of possession, the right of exclusion, and the right of use. The property owner, however, is not allowed complete freedom in the exercise of these rights. The truth is that each of these rights may be restricted in some manner by governmental or private restrictions on ownership.

The right of disposition is granted to the holder of a fee simple estate. In theory, this right seems to allow the property owner to choose to whom he or she sells or leases the property. In practice, this right is restricted by state and federal fair housing laws that prohibit certain discriminatory practices in the sale or leasing of private property. The rights of possession and exclusion, in theory, allow the property owner to occupy his or her premises in privacy and allow for total control over entry onto the property. In practice, the property owner may be forced to permit access to others, as is the case with appurtenant easements, or may be forced to surrender the property to the government through the government's exercise of eminent domain. The right of use implies the right of a property owner to utilize his or her property in any manner in which he or she sees fit. However, zoning laws, environmental protection laws, and restrictive covenants each place limitations on that use.

As a real estate paralegal, you may be asked to assist your supervising attorney with a zoning matter, the drafting of an easement, or the finding of an expert to perform an environmental audit in compliance with environmental regulations. This chapter begins with a discussion of zoning and situations in which permission to deviate from zoning ordinances might be obtained. It then moves into a discussion of environmental protection and fair housing laws, followed by a discussion of tax assessments and exemptions, and a look at situations in which a local, state, or federal government may take private property. The chapter concludes with a discussion of private restrictions on ownership, including but not limited to restrictive covenants and easements.

GOVERNMENTAL RESTRICTIONS ON OWNERSHIP

Federal, state, and local governments impose restrictions on the rights of owners of real property through the implementation of their police powers. **Police powers** are those powers given to the federal government and to the states by their constitutions to create laws necessary for the protection of public health, safety, and welfare. State governments may, in turn, vest local governmental bodies with the power to create and enforce local regulations that do not conflict with state statutes. Laws fitting this category include, but are not limited to, those designed to curtail noise, water, and air pollution, and to control population density, as well as those to prevent the use of discriminatory practices in the sale or rental of real property. Real property can be regulated through various means, such as zoning, subdivision regulations, building codes, and environmental and fair housing legislation. Police powers include the power of taxation as a method of raising revenue for the public welfare.

police powers: Those powers given to the federal government and to the states by their constitutions to create laws necessary for the protection of public health, safety, and welfare.

Zoning

Zoning and land use planning are fundamental methods of government control over real estate development. Local governments are given the authority by state enabling acts to formulate comprehensive plans that are subsequently implemented and enforced through local government zoning ordinances that control density of population as well as intensity of use, and help to stabilize and protect property values in a given area.

Local governmental authorities have the responsibility of identifying and prioritizing the economic, social, and ecological needs within their jurisdiction and then formulating a plan that best meets these needs. A planning commission may be appointed to create a **master plan,** sometimes referred to as a *general plan*. Based on information gleaned from physical, demographic, and economic surveys, a master plan serves two objectives. The first is to present a comprehensive policy statement outlining the goals of the local authorities based on the perceived needs of the community. The second is to present a working plan of how those goals are to be met.

Although master plans vary significantly, most include provisions for land use, conservation, circulation, noise regulation, and public facilities. *Land use* includes the creation of standards for economic and residential development. *Conservation* includes the preservation of natural and historical resources. *Circulation* includes the routing of public roads to prevent traffic congestion and the accessibility of public transportation systems. *Noise regulation* includes the imposition of regulations specifying permissible noise decibel limits and the routing of air and railroad traffic to less populated areas. For example, the Concord jet is a marvel of aerodynamics, but it is a particularly noisy aircraft. Because of the noise factor, the jet is prohibited from landing at Washington National Airport, which is located close to densely populated areas, and instead is routed to Dulles Airport, which is located in a more sparsely populated area. Planning for *public facilities* includes planning for libraries, courthouses, schools, utility plants, and the like.

Zoning is the primary mechanism for implementing the master plan. In so doing, zoning necessarily places restrictions on land use for the sake of the common good. Without the creation and enforcement of zoning ordinances, nothing would prevent a property owner from building a textile factory next to a single-family residence. Zoning can regulate the size and height of physical structures, the purposes for which such structures may be used, the number of persons permitted to occupy the structures, the setback requirements for the structures, and even the appearance of the structures. The zoning specifications of a given area can be found on a *zoning map*. These maps usually use various colors to differentiate different zoning categories.

Because zoning is one of the several police powers afforded to local governments, zoning ordinances must be reasonably related to the promotion of the public welfare in order to be deemed valid. In most states, not only must the ordinance be reasonably related to public welfare, but it also must be exercised in a reasonable and nondiscriminatory manner.

Prior to the passage of any zoning regulation, due process dictates that the public receive notice of the proposed ordinance and be given an opportunity to voice their approval or objections at a public hearing. Notice typically is given through publication in general and legal newspapers. Often the notice

master plan: A plan created by a local planning commission that provides for land use, conservation, circulation, noise regulation, and public facilities in a given area.

will provide the text of the proposed ordinance as well as the time and date upon which the hearing will take place. Affected property owners may demand that the zoning board present evidence that the ordinance is valid. Most ordinances provide certain procedures to be followed should a property owner wish to appeal the enforcement of a zoning decision. An example of a notice of public hearing is found in Figure 4–1.

Once adopted, zoning ordinances usually are enforced through the issuance of *building permits*. Most cities and counties require permits to be obtained before any construction can be done on real property. This can include not only new construction but remodeling and additions as well. Compliance with all zoning and *building code* regulations is implied in the issuance of a permit. Building inspectors are sent out to the site at various stages of construction to assure compliance, and no one is allowed to occupy a constructed premises until a *certificate of occupancy* is issued.

Should a property owner decide to defy a zoning ordinance, compliance can be enforced through the imposition of fines and the issuance of an *injunction*, which is a court order demanding that a party stop certain activities or be held in contempt of court. For example, if a seamstress operates a clothing alteration business out of her home that is located in a residential zoning district, she can be prevented from continuing operations and may be subject to fines. If, however, the district was zoned for mixed use, residential and commercial, the seamstress may be permitted to continue her business.

FIGURE 4–1
Notice of public hearing

CITY OF ANY CITY
936 MAIN STREET
ANY CITY, ANY STATE

**NOTICE OF PUBLIC HEARING
ON PETITION TO AMEND MASTER PLAN**

The City Council of the City of Any City will hold a public hearing in the meeting room of the City Hall, 936 Main Street, at 7:00 p.m. or as soon thereafter as practicable, on the dates hereinafter specified. Comments of any interested parties relative to this matter may be submitted in writing and/or presented at the hearing.

PETITIONER/OWNER: Orange Blossom Estates, Inc.

DATE OF CITY COUNCIL HEARING: August 6, 1997

LOCATION DESCRIPTION: Generally located within Orange Blossom Estates

ADDRESS OF SUBJECT PROPERTY: 2500 block of Orange Blossom Drive

REQUEST: Reconsideration of request to amend the PRD Master Plan associated with Ordinance 92-44.

THIS MATTER SHOULD BE REFERRED TO AS ZB 30-3-97. FOR FURTHER INFORMATION, CALL GAIL GRANT IN THE PLANNING AND ZONING DIVISION AT 444-0000. ANY PERSON WISHING TO APPEAL ANY DECISION MADE BY THIS BOARD OR COMMITTEE WITH RESPECT TO ANY MATTER CONSIDERED AT SUCH MEETINGS OR HEARINGS WILL NEED A RECORD OF THE PROCEEDINGS AND, FOR SUCH PURPOSES, MAY NEED TO ENSURE THAT A VERBATIM RECORD OF THE PROCEEDINGS IS MADE, WHICH RECORD INCLUDES THE TESTIMONY AND EVIDENCE UPON WHICH THE APPEAL IS MADE.

July 31, 1997

Injunctions and fines also are imposed for failure to obtain a building permit. In some instances, fines are accrued on a daily basis for each day on which noncompliance occurs. For example, suppose Frank Dawson decides to enclose his patio. The city of Any City requires that plans and architectural drawings be submitted for approval and a building permit obtained before work can proceed. Frank does not submit drawings nor obtain a permit, instead he simply proceeds with the construction of the enclosure. A building inspector inspecting other construction in the area passes by Frank's house and notices that work is proceeding without a permit. The city issues Frank a citation, requiring that all work cease and informing him that a fine of $50 per day is imposed for each day work is done in violation of the citation. Ten days have passed since Frank began work on the enclosure. To date, his fines total $500. Depending on the wording of the citation, the fines may continue to accrue even if work is stopped until such time as Frank obtains a permit.

Types of Zoning.   Zoning ordinances divide land use into a number of classifications. These can include the following.

1. *Residential:* permitting single-family or multifamily dwellings or a combination of the two. Residential zoning is designed to regulate population density by limiting the number of dwellings per acre.
2. *Commercial:* permitting office buildings, shopping centers, and other commercial development. Commercial zoning is not as concerned with population density as it is with use intensity. By regulating the commercial enterprises permitted in a particular locality, zoning can indirectly regulate the flow of traffic patterns.
3. *Industrial:* permitting factories and other industrial enterprises that bring employment opportunities into a particular locality. Industrial zoning is similar to commercial zoning in that it is concerned with use intensity. It is additionally concerned with industrial wastes and emissions that can impact the quality of life for the general public.
4. *Agricultural:* permitting crop production and animal farming.
5. *Public:* permitting public facilities such as post office buildings, libraries, recreation centers, and so forth. The placement of these facilities takes into consideration both population density and use intensity. For example, the placement of a large convention center must take into consideration public access to the center, traffic flow to and from the center, and noise levels emanating from the crowds entering and exiting the center.

Some zoning ordinances divide these categories further. For example, a residential zone may be subdivided into areas that permit only certain types of residences, such as detached single-family homes or duplexes, and disallow high-rise buildings. This is sometimes referred to as *exclusive zoning.* Another example would be an industrial zone that permits only one type of industrial activity, such as a paper mill or a textile mill. Conversely, zoning ordinances may provide for *multiple-use zoning,* sometimes referred to as *cumulative zoning* or *cluster zoning.* This zoning facilitates the growth of planned unit developments. The advantages of multiple-use zoning are apparent with the expansion of suburban areas into small cities. An area that is sparsely populated does not require numerous shopping centers or hospitals. As demographics change and certain areas become more densely populated, however, the need for support services in those areas increases. Multiple-use zoning allows residential and commercial growth to complement each other.

Periodically the need to rezone occurs, as when a formerly agricultural area undergoes economic changes and farming diminishes. The once-productive farmland can be put to better use, for example, by encouraging light industry to build plants in the area. Before this can be done, the area must be rezoned. Additionally, zoning officials are increasingly implementing the use of *buffer zones* to ease the transition between one zoning area and another. For example, a park may be placed as a buffer zone between a commercial and residential area.

In addition to zoning ordinances that classify areas into designated uses, there are ordinances that are primarily concerned with aesthetics. For example, an ordinance may forbid modern-looking office buildings in a historical district or may prohibit billboards in certain areas.

Variances. Property owners desiring to deviate from strict compliance with all or part of a zoning ordinance may apply for a **variance** to the zoning board or other applicable board. In order to be granted a variance, a property owner typically has to show that compliance with the ordinance will create an undue hardship that will either prevent the anticipated benefits to the property or prevent best usage of the property. Additionally, the property owner must show that the variance will not adversely affect the surrounding properties nor change the character of the community.

For example, suppose that plans have been approved and a house has been constructed on a lot. If an engineering team comes out to the property to conduct a final survey before the certificate of occupancy can be issued and during the survey discovers that the house has exceeded the back setback by three inches, the property owner will have to apply for a variance from the board. In this case, the variance will most likely be granted, as it would be unconscionable to require that a house in its final stages of construction be torn down for a three-inch variance from the setback requirements. Further, the property owner can show that the three-inch difference will not change the character of the community nor adversely affect surrounding properties. Another example would be one in which a developer is planning to build a high-rise luxury apartment building on beachfront property. The area in which the apartment building is to be constructed has a height variance of forty feet. If the developer can show that the best usage of the property would be to add an additional story to the building, although this addition may be over the forty-foot limit, the board may be willing to grant a variance.

If the board will not grant a variance, one possible recourse is to attempt to change the zoning ordinance by amendment. The proposed amendment will then be noticed and debated at a public hearing. If successful, the property owner's efforts will change the zoning regulations for the entire area. If neither a variance nor an amendment to the ordinance is granted, the final recourse available to the property owner is the court system.

Special Exceptions. A property owner may seek a **special exception,** also referred to as a *conditional-use permit,* if the property owner wishes to use property for a use undesignated in that area. For example, suppose there is a

variance: Permission given to a property owner to deviate from strict compliance with all or part of a zoning ordinance.

special exception: Permission given to a property owner to use property for a use undesignated in that area.

large orthodox Jewish population living in a particular residential area. There may be several synagogues in the city; however, building an orthodox synagogue within walking distance in the neighborhood would be beneficial because orthodox Jews are not allowed to drive on the Sabbath. If the residential area is zoned exclusively for residential use, the prospective purchaser who wishes to build the synagogue would have to apply for a special exception.

Nonconforming Use. A different problem confronts the property owner who has built an improvement on land prior to the enactment of a zoning ordinance and now finds that the improvement is in conflict with the ordinance. For example, suppose a property owner built a gasoline station in an area many years ago when the area was relatively undeveloped. Over the years as the population grew, the zoning map was redrawn and the area is now zoned exclusively residential. The zoning authorities will have to "grandfather" the property in and declare it a permissible **nonconforming use,** in some areas referred to as *preexisting use*. In some jurisdictions, the permitted nonconforming use is phased out over a specified period of time.

If the nonconforming use is permitted, the property owner may not make alterations to the property or change from one type of nonconforming use to another. For example, the gasoline station owner could not add a car wash to the property or tear the station down and replace it with a car dealership. Further, once an owner discontinues a nonconforming use, the owner may not subsequently revive it. If the owner sells the property, the new owner purchases the property with the understanding that he or she must comply with the zoning ordinance and the permission for nonconforming use will be discontinued.

Environmental Protection Laws

The federal government understood a century ago the need for federal regulation of real estate development to curtail damage to the nation's natural resources when it enacted the Rivers and Harbors Act of 1899, which prohibited unauthorized construction in navigable waters. Nonetheless, most of the major legislation in the area of environmental protection did not begin until the late 1960s, growing in range and complexity in recent years. Environmental legislation imposes restrictions on the development and use of real property, as well as imposing affirmative obligations such as waste management and cleanup. Although the greatest initial impact on environmental legislation was on industrial and commercial developers, today all real property owners are impacted to some extent by federal, state, and local environmental protection laws.

In 1969, Congress passed the National Environmental Policy Act (NEPA), which established the Environmental Protection Agency (EPA) for the purpose of creating environmental standards. In conjunction with the EPA, a Council on Environmental Quality was created, and environmental impact studies became a prerequisite for approval of large federal government projects as well as for federal decisions regarding large private projects. (The council was replaced in the 1990s by the White House Office on Environmental Policy.) The NEPA was shortly followed by the passage of the Clean Air Act in 1970 (amended in 1975, 1977, and 1990), which established national primary and

nonconforming use: Also referred to as *preexisting use*. Permission given to a property owner who has built an improvement on land prior to the enactment of a zoning ordinance to continue to use the land in the same manner as before.

secondary air quality standards—the former for protection of public health, and the latter for the protection of plant and animal life. Further, this act made it a requirement for states to comply with these standards in two ways: (1) by reviewing preconstruction plans to determine direct (for example, industrial plant emissions) and indirect (for example, traffic congestion) sources of potential air pollution, and (2) by developing programs to maintain air quality standards (for example, vehicle emissions inspections).

In 1972, the Clean Water Act gave the United States Army Corps of Engineers control over dredge and fill activities. Section 404 of the act requires that any party wishing to engage in dredge and fill activities in any body of water, whether publicly or privately owned, first obtain a permit from the Army Corps of Engineers.

Environmental legislation continued its expansion a few years later with the passage of the Solid Waste Disposal Act in 1976 (amended in 1988) and the Federal Water Pollution Control Act in 1977. The Solid Waste Disposal Act was enacted to improve the methods for disposal of solid and hazardous waste by prohibiting open dumping and imposing severe civil and criminal penalties for violations. It also mandates various guidelines for solid waste management upon state governments. The Federal Water Pollution Control Act has two objectives: (1) to establish a comprehensive plan to eliminate pollution from navigable waters, making them safe for public recreation, and (2) to provide federal assistance for public waste treatment facilities and waste management programs.

The biggest advance in federal environmental legislation in the 1980s was brought about by the 1980 Comprehensive Environmental Response, Compensation and Liability Act (CERCLA). This legislation imposes liability for hazardous waste cleanup of toxic sites, regardless of cost or degree of responsibility for the presence of hazardous waste on the property. Those parties who may be held responsible for the cleanup of property polluted by hazardous waste include the current owner or operator of a facility on the property, the party that owned or operated a facility when the hazardous wastes were dumped on the property, and the party that selected the site or arranged for disposal of hazardous waste. Thus, the liability originally imposed under the CERCLA was strict and could be applied retroactively.

To temper this harsh result, the CERCLA was amended in 1986 by the Superfund Amendments and Reauthorization Act (SARA), which allows purchasers a defense to liability if they can prove that proper inquiry into the property's prior ownership and usage was made. To clarify its intentions further, the federal government later issued policy statements indicating that the CERCLA was not meant to impose liability on residential property owners who did not directly contribute to the toxic pollution of the property. Consequently, the SARA encourages prospective property owners, other than residential owners, to research the environmental compliance of previous owners prior to purchase or potentially suffer the consequences for their failure to do so. As a result of the SARA, it has become common for buyers to make a sales contract contingent upon the results of an environmental audit and to demand inclusion in the contract of a hazardous waste indemnification provision.

There are tens of thousands of abandoned hazardous waste disposal sites around the country. Recognizing the urgency for cleanup of these sites and the potential hindrance of cleanup operations due to the great cost, the CERCLA created the Superfund, a congressional appropriation of over a billion dollars to clean up the most badly polluted sites. Even in instances in which private parties are held liable, they may not have adequate funds to cover the total cost of cleanup; therefore, the Superfund may be used for partial government subsidizing of private cleanup efforts.

The increase of public awareness of the interdependency of ecological systems has led to concern in recent years for the preservation of wetlands. Correspondingly, there has been an increase of federal and state legislation to control development in these ecologically fragile areas. The definition of *wetland* can vary, depending on the federal or state agency reviewing a particular development project. The United States Army Corps of Engineers' definition of *wetlands* is found in section 328.3(b), Title 33 of the *Code of Federal Regulations*, defining *wetlands* as those areas that are inundated or saturated by surface groundwater at a frequency and duration sufficient to support, and under normal circumstances which do support, a prevalence of vegetation typically adapted for life in saturated soil conditions.

Whether development will be permitted and what types of assurances will be required in order to proceed with development will depend on the role of a particular parcel of land in the structure of the ecosystem. For example, some wetlands play an integral role by providing plant and wildlife habitats, by aiding in the control of erosion and flooding, or by serving as a buffer for upland areas in the event of a hurricane. Section 320.4(b)(2) of Title 33 of the *Code of Federal Regulations* requires an assessment of the effect of development on the following categories of wetlands before development is permitted.

1. Wetlands that serve significant biological functions, including food chain production, general habitat and nesting, spawning, rearing, and nesting sites for aquatic and land species
2. Wetlands set aside for study of the aquatic environment or as sanctuaries or refuges
3. Wetlands the destructions or alteration of which would affect detrimentally natural drainage characteristics, sedimentation patterns, salinity, distribution, flushing characteristics, current patterns, or other environmental characteristics
4. Wetlands that are significant in shielding other areas from wave action, erosion, or storm drainage. Such wetlands are often associated with barrier beaches, islands, reefs, and bars
5. Wetlands that serve as valuable storage areas for storm and flood waters
6. Wetlands that are groundwater discharge areas that maintain minimum baseflows important to aquatic resources and those which are prime natural recharge areas
7. Wetlands that serve significant water purification functions
8. Wetlands that are unique in nature or scarce in quantity to the region or local area

A summary of the major federal environmental laws impacting land use is found in Figure 4–2.

FIGURE 4–2
Federal environmental
laws impacting land use

FEDERAL ENVIRONMENTAL LAWS IMPACTING LAND USE

Act	Purpose
Clean Air Act	Establishes national primary and secondary air quality standards. Requires compliance through review of preconstruction plans to determine direct and indirect sources of air pollution.
Clean Water Act	Requires property owners to obtain permit from Army Corps of Engineers prior to dredge and fill activities in any body of water.
Solid Waste Disposal Act	Prohibits open dumping of solid and hazardous waste and imposes civil and criminal penalties for such activities.
Federal Water Pollution Control Act	Establishes comprehensive plan to eliminate pollution from navigable water and provides federal assistance for public waste treatment facilities and waste management.
Comprehensive Environmental Response, Compensation and Liability Act (CERCLA)	Imposes liability for hazardous waste cleanup of toxic sites.
Superfund Amendments and Reauthorization Act (SARA)	Amends CERCLA. Limits liability of residential property owners to those who directly contribute to toxic polution of the property and encourages others to research environmental compliance of prior owners. Sets up federal fund to clean up the most badly polluted sites.

In addition to federal restrictions on land use, state and local governments have implemented their own conservation regulations. Some states carve out areas designated as Areas of Critical State Concern (ACSC) due to environmental, historical, natural, or archaeological resources located in these areas (for example, the Green Swamp Area in Florida). These areas must meet state land use guidelines.

From the preceding discussion, it is clear that a prospective developer of real property should commission a full environmental audit to identify and resolve any environmental problems prior to closing. Legal counsel should exercise great care in drafting an environmental audit provision for a sales contract. Prior to drafting the provision, legal counsel should identify and review all applicable federal, state, and local environmental laws. The provision should detail all steps to be taken in the environmental audit. These steps may include a public records search, site inspection, and historical review of operations on the property. Additionally, the audit may include a sampling and analysis of soil, air, and groundwater. The prospective buyer should retain all audit records and property appraisals to evince the actions taken in his or her preacquisition inquiry.

Fair Housing Laws

In addition to placing restrictions on how a real property owner may use his or her property, federal and state governments also place certain restrictions on how he or she may dispose of real property. Ironically, although these laws may be interpreted as restrictive of an owner's right to dispose of property freely, the legislative intent was, and continues to be, to make real property available to greater numbers by preventing discriminatory practices.

The first move by the federal government in this direction directly followed the Civil War. The federal Civil Rights Act of 1866 was enacted to prohibit racial discrimination, declaring that "[a]ll citizens of the United States shall have the same right in every state and territory as is enjoyed by white citizens thereof to inherit, purchase, lease, sell, hold and convey real and personal property." Still in force, this act pertains to the sale or leasing of any real property, whether it be transacted by the owner of the property or through the use of a real estate broker.

One hundred years passed before the next significant federal measure occurred, again a result of civil struggle—this time, the civil rights movement of the 1960s. The Kennedy administration in 1962, noting that little effort had been made to date to enforce the Civil Rights Act of 1866, decided to impose an executive order, No. 11063, designed to prevent discrimination in all housing financed by FHA and VA loans. This measure was followed by the congressional enactment of the Civil Rights Act of 1964, which prohibited discrimination in any housing program that received whole or partial federal funding.

Shortly thereafter, Congress passed the Civil Rights Act of 1968. Title VIII of the act, devoted to fair housing legislation, has come to be known as the Federal Fair Housing Act. With it, Congress was attempting to reach out even further by broadening both the type of discriminatory practices prohibited and the type of housing covered by federal antidiscrimination statutes. The Federal Fair Housing Act of 1968 prohibits discrimination not only on the basis of race but also on the basis of color, religion, and national origin. While broadening its range to include housing other than government-subsidized housing, the act does not pertain to all housing, but only to the following.

1. With regard to single-family dwellings:
   a. All houses not privately owned
   b. All privately owned houses if a real estate broker or salesperson is employed to sell or rent the premises
   c. All houses owned by a person who owns three or more houses
   d. Any house owned by a person who, during any two-year period, sells two or more houses belonging to other persons
2. With regard to multifamily dwellings:
   a. All multifamily dwellings with five or more units
   b. All multifamily dwellings of four or less units if none of the units are owner-occupied

The Federal Fair Housing Act of 1968 does not preempt the Civil Rights Act of 1866. Thus, racial discrimination is prohibited regardless of whether the real property owner's premises fits into one of the above housing categories. These categories are relevant with regard to the added protected classes.

The Federal Fair Housing Act of 1968 specifies certain prohibited practices that include, but are not limited to, the refusal to sell or rent to persons in the protected classes. Additionally, quoting different terms or conditions to different people for the rental or sale of real property and discriminatory advertising are both prohibited. Real estate brokers and salespersons may not use blockbusting or steering practices. **Blockbusting** is the attempt to get homeowners to list their property for sale by stating or implying that minority groups may be moving into the neighborhood. **Steering** is the attempt to guide prospective homeowners into one neighborhood as opposed to another based on the racial, religious, or ethnic composition of a particular neighborhood. Lending institutions are prohibited from **redlining,** which is denying a loan or presenting different terms or conditions for a loan based upon the composition of a neighborhood or other discriminatory reasons. Further, denying membership to a member of a protected class in any real estate–related organization or service is prohibited.

The scope of protected classes was expanded to include sex when the Housing and Community Development Act of 1974 was enacted. The Fair Housing Amendments Act of 1988 extended protection to handicapped persons and to familial status. The term *handicapped* refers to persons with physical and mental impairments, including recovering alcoholics and recovering drug addicts, although current drug addicts are excluded from protection. The amendment also protects persons with AIDS. In reference to blind or deaf persons, the amendment prohibits a landlord from refusing to rent, evicting, or charging an increased security deposit because the tenant owns a guide dog. The amendment additionally prohibits refusal to permit reasonable modifications of the premises if the modifications are necessary to allow the handicapped person full enjoyment of the premises and are paid for at his or her expense.

The familial status designation in the amendment refers to children under the age of eighteen residing with either a parent or another person having legal custody of the child. It also prohibits discrimination against pregnant women and persons seeking custody of a child. In enacting this section of the amendment, Congress carved out the following three exceptions in which seniors-only housing is permitted.

1. Housing provided under any federal or state program that is specifically designed and operated to assist elderly persons
2. Housing intended for and occupied solely by persons sixty-two years of age or older, if existing prior to the amendment
3. Housing in which eighty percent or more of the units are occupied by persons fifty-five years of age or older and to which additional facilities have been provided to meet the needs of older persons (for example, congregate dining facilities, emergency care). In addition, there must be publication of, and adherence to, procedures that evince an intention to house persons fifty-five years of age or older

All real estate brokers must have an equal housing opportunity poster placed conspicuously in their offices. This poster is available from the United

blockbusting: The attempt to get homeowners to list their property for sale by stating or implying that minority groups may be moving into the neighborhood.

steering: The attempt to guide prospective homeowners into one neighborhood as opposed to another based on the racial, religious, or ethnic composition of a particular neighborhood.

redlining: Denying a loan or presenting different terms or conditions for a loan based upon the composition of the neighborhood or other discriminatory reasons.

States Department of Housing and Urban Development and contains the equal housing opportunity logo and a statement supporting the Fair Housing Act. Failure to display the poster may be considered in an investigation of a broker for discriminatory practices.

Due to continuing confusion over what wording in advertisements would be considered discriminatory and in violation of the amendment, in 1995, the United States Department of Housing and Urban Development issued some guidelines in a memorandum in an attempt to clarify prohibited versus acceptable advertising. The use of words describing a neighborhood or its residents in ethnic, racial, or religious terms is prohibited. Thus, an advertisement stating "four-bedroom home in Jewish neighborhood" or "no Haitians" is in violation of the amendment.

A tricky situation occurs when the premises is owned by a religious organization, for example, the Hebrew Home for the Aged. Can an advertisement use the name of the premises without violating the amendment? The guidelines indicate that it may, as long as a disclaimer is included stating that "This home does not discriminate on the basis of race, color, religion, national origin, sex, handicap or familial status." Advertisements are not allowed to contain words indicating an explicit preference based on sex; however, certain terms that have become common usage, such as *bachelor apartment*, are not considered discriminatory in and of themselves and may be used without violation. Additionally, advertisements cannot contain limitations on the ages or number of children, although a landlord is allowed to deny rental to a family whose numbers exceed any local ordinances regulating the number of persons per unit.

The most recent significant federal legislation in this area is the Americans with Disabilities Act of 1990 (ADA). Although its primary intention is to prevent discrimination in the employment of qualified individuals with disabilities, Title III of the ADA spills over into the area of real estate by requiring the removal of physical barriers in buildings of public accommodation (for example, restaurants, hotels) that impede the disabled. In structures already existing prior to the enactment of the ADA, installation of ramps, handicapped toilet stalls, and the like must be added if this can be easily accomplished. In new or remodeled structures, installation of these facilities is required.

Many states have enacted state laws similar to the federal laws concerning fair housing. States are permitted to include additional protected classes, and local ordinances generally may be more restrictive than federal and state law (for example, adding age as a protected class), but are not allowed to be less so.

Taxation

County and city governments are permitted to impose ad valorem taxes on real property located within their jurisdictions as well as **special assessments** for shared improvements that enhance the value of real property, such as the installation of sewer lines or sidewalks. State and federal governments do not levy direct property taxes. Income or losses realized in real property taxes, however, must be included in state and federal income tax returns.

special assessment: An assessment for shared improvements that enhance the value of real property.

Recall from the discussion of homestead property in Chapter 2 that *ad valorem taxes* are taxes imposed on the value of the real property and any improvements thereon. Certain designated *tax districts* are permitted to impose ad valorem taxes as well. These districts may include school districts, drainage districts, water districts, and sanitary districts.

County or city taxing authorities have the responsibility of assessing the value of real property for taxation purposes. They also have the authority to establish a tax rate, called a **millage rate,** to be used in computing ad valorem taxes. A mill equals one-tenth of a penny and is written .001. Some state legislatures impose tax rate ceilings, for example, a ten-mill cap. The taxable value of the property is multiplied by the millage rate to determine the taxes owed. For example, if the taxable value of the real property is $200,000 and the millage rate is .0115000, the taxes owed would be $2,300.

State statutes dictate the tax year for real property taxes. In many states, property taxes are levied on a calendar-year basis. This means that real property taxes are paid in arrears for the period January 1 through December 31 each year. After assessment is completed and the taxes computed, these taxes become a lien against the subject real property until such time as they are paid in full. A real property owner receives a tax bill informing him or her of taxes owed and the due date, sometimes referred to as the penalty date, for payment of the taxes. Some areas encourage prompt payment by offering discounts. Conversely, penalties may be imposed for late payment. In other areas, taxes may be paid in monthly, quarterly, or semiannual installments. Failure to pay real estate taxes can subject the real property to a tax foreclosure or tax sale. (For a detailed discussion of tax liens, see Chapter 9.)

Budgets and Tax Levies. As noted, there may be many different taxing authorities: counties, cities, school boards, or special tax districts. Each of these taxing authorities must prepare operating budgets each year that provide for all anticipated expenditures for the upcoming fiscal year. To complicate the task, each taxing authority's budget is really a composite of several departmental budgets. For example, the fire department will submit its budget, which will include the estimated cost of operating every phase of the fire department in the upcoming fiscal year (for example, new fire trucks, additional staff), and that budget will be reviewed and combined with the budgets submitted by other departments, such as the sheriff's department, social services, and so forth.

Once each taxing authority has put together an operating budget based on the information provided from each subordinate department, it has to estimate the revenue that can be anticipated from sources other than real property taxes. This revenue may come from a variety of sources, such as occupational license fees, building permit fees, fines for parking and speeding tickets, and state and federal funding for specified programs. Once this figure has been calculated, each taxing authority is in a position to determine how much revenue must be raised through real property taxes. The amount of property taxes received by each taxing authority must come from a **tax base,** which is the total assessed value of all taxable property in that taxing authority's jurisdiction.

Assessments. All real property undergoes the process of *assessment*. Property taxes are levied against land and all permanent improvements to the land.

millage rate: A rate used in computing ad valorem real property taxes.

tax base: The total assessed value of all taxable real property in a taxing authority's jurisdiction.

Often the assessed value of the land and the value of its improvements are arrived at separately and then combined in a single tax statement. The assessment is done by a county property appraiser or similar official. The appraiser determines the ownership and value of each parcel of real property placed on an *assessment roll*, sometimes referred to as a *tax list*. Real property is required by law to be assessed at *just value*. Staff members from the property appraiser's office typically go out to assess real property using forms and specific recording procedures. The information obtained through the property inspection is processed through a computer by utilizing applicable formulas to arrive at the assessment value. Depending on state statute, appraisers are to take into consideration numerous factors in calculating just value, such as the following.

1. The present value of the property
2. The location of the property
3. The quantity or size of the property
4. The condition of the property
5. The highest and best use to which the property can be expected to be put in the immediate future, and the present use of the property (the most profitable use of the land only, *not* the land and improvements)
6. The cost of the property and the replacement value of any improvements thereon
7. The income from the property
8. The net proceeds of the sale of the property, as received by the seller, after deduction of all usual and reasonable fees and costs and allowance for atypical financing

If real property is sold during the year, the sale price of the property may become a factor for consideration in assessing its value, but generally it is not the controlling factor.

In many parts of the country, residential areas are divided into subdivisions. It is common in community developments within subdivisions to find standard-size lots. In these developments, appraisers often carry out their inspections by making a thorough inspection of a single lot that is selected as a standard lot. Its assessed value can then be applied to all other lots in the subdivision that correspond to that standard lot. Corner lots or lots with unusual features are exceptions and must be inspected individually. While the majority of lots in a subdivision may be similar, the houses or other improvements built on them are different and are assessed on an individual basis.

Once an assessment has been made, the owner is informed of the taxes owed through receipt of a tax statement. Tax statements are mailed to the property owner at the last address of record, and it is the responsibility of the property owner to ensure that a current address is on file in those counties in which he or she owns real property.

Should a real property owner wish to dispute the assessment, he or she must follow statutorily prescribed procedures. In some states, the first step is to seek an *adjustment* by contacting the property appraiser's office within a prescribed time period. The appraiser will then review the request for adjustment. If the appraiser finds that the property owner's arguments are valid, the appraiser is authorized to make an adjustment to the tax statement. Should the appraiser reject the property owner's argument, the next step is often to go before a *board of assessment*, sometimes referred to as an *adjustment board*, and request a review. In some states, the appraiser is not contacted as a first step and the board review process is the appropriate procedure for filing an assessment protest or complaint. In many states, the members of the board of assessment are elected officials. This allows taxpayers to change the composition of the board should they believe certain members to be biased or unfair. Some states use a *board of equalization*, whose purpose is to determine whether a taxing authority's assessments are in line with those of neighboring areas. Should the board reject the property owner's arguments, the last resort typically is litigation. The property owner may choose to file suit against the appraiser and the tax collector if the real property tax is paid under protest. Most courts, however, are not in a position to make assessments; rather, they can specify the procedures to be used in reassessing the property if they believe the assessment to be improper.

Exemptions. State statutes dictate the categories of real property not included in the tax base as well as the categories and dollar amounts of permissible deductions that may be taken when calculating the amount of real property taxes owed. Although it is a misnomer, all of these categories are commonly classified as *exemptions*. Certain properties are immune from real property taxation. These properties include city, county, state, and federal government properties, which are not taxed unless they are leased or sold to private parties. Other properties may be subject to taxation but wholly or partially released from the obligation. These properties include religious properties, homestead properties, and properties owned by disabled persons.

The concept of homestead was discussed at length in Chapter 2. There it was noted that many states allow a statutorily prescribed dollar amount to be deducted from the assessed value of real property before the real property taxes are calculated. In this manner, homestead property is granted a partial tax exemption. Thus, the assessed value of real property is not always the taxable value of the property.

Some states grant partial tax exemptions to widows and widowers. In these states, a widow or widower who is a bona fide resident of the state may claim a specified dollar amount as a partial exemption that will be deducted from the assessed property value before the real property tax is calculated, just as is done with the homestead exemption. For example, if state law permits a $1,000 exemption for widows and widowers, $1,000 will be deducted from the assessed value of the property to get the taxable value. This taxable value will then be multiplied by the tax rate (the millage rate) to ascertain the taxes owed. In states that allow this exemption, the exemption eligibility expires when the widow or widower remarries.

Many states permit a disability tax exemption. In some states, the tax exemption may be partial, while others allow for a total tax exemption for the homestead property of a disabled person. The definition of *disabled* varies from state to state. Quadriplegics, paraplegics, hemiplegics, persons whose disabilities necessitate the use of a wheelchair, and persons who are legally blind are often included in statutory definitions. Proof of disability is required before the exemption will be allowed. For those disabled in an armed services–related activity, the proof commonly required is a certificate from the Veterans Administration or the United States government. Some states permit a certificate from state-licensed physicians.

Whole or partial tax exemptions are not automatic but, rather, must be applied for to the taxing authority, and often the initial application must be made in person at the office of the property appraiser or other designated official. In many localities, once the initial application is made and approved, subsequent renewals may be made by mail or, in some instances, are automatic. Because the procedure varies widely, local law must be checked.

Tax Rates. From the discussion thus far, it is clear that the assessed value and taxable value of real property are often different. It is the taxable value and the tax rate that ultimately determine the amount of taxes. Taxing authorities determine the applicable tax rate through the application of formulae. The following is one commonly used formula.

$$Tax\ rate = \frac{Approved\ budget\ minus\ nonproperty\ tax\ revenue}{Total\ assessed\ valuation\ minus\ exemptions}$$

The following example should provide some clarification. Assume that the operating budget of Any County has been approved. This budget projects expenditures of $20,000,000 for the next fiscal year. Based on past experience, it is estimated that $5,000,000 in revenue can be culled from sources other than real property taxes. The assessed value of all real property in Any County is $1,750,000,000. The homestead tax exemption in Any County is $10,000, and ten thousand properties are eligible and have applied for this exemption, so the total exemptions amount to $100,000,000. With these figures and the above formula, the officials of Any County can calculate the required tax rate as follows.

$$Tax\ rate = \frac{\$20,000,000 - \$5,000,000}{\$1,750,000,000 - \$100,000,000}$$

This becomes

$$\frac{\$15,000,000}{\$1,650,000,000} = .009$$

Thus, the tax rate to be applied in Any County is nine mills.

Suppose that Angela and Andrew Aronson own a home in Any County. The assessed value of the property is $150,000, and they have applied for a homestead exemption. The calculation of their annual county property taxes is as follows.

Assessed value	$150,000
Homestead exemption	– $ 10,000
Taxable value	$140,000
County tax rate	× .009
County property taxes	$ 1,260

If Angela and Andrew lived within city limits, they would be subject to any city property taxes as well, plus the taxes imposed by any other taxing authorities.

Special Assessments. Finally, taxing authorities may impose *special assessment taxes*. These taxes are not paid annually. Rather, they are paid once, when some improvement in the area or neighborhood is planned that increases the property value of the properties to be assessed. These improvements may include sewer hookup, installation of septic tanks, street lighting, sidewalk paving, and so forth. Special assessment taxes are not ad valorem taxes and, therefore, are not calculated based upon the value of the property. Typically, these taxes are levied based upon the front footage of the property. Each property benefiting from the improvement will be taxed its pro rata share. An example will help illustrate this concept.

Suppose the City of Any City is installing sewer hookups in a neighborhood that has previously been dependent on septic tanks. Veronica Jackson lives in this neighborhood. Any City is slated to pay forty percent of the costs involved, and the residents of the neighborhood are to be taxed a special assessment for the remaining sixty percent of the costs. The city officials have calculated that the costs should run $30 per foot. Veronica's lot frontage is 115 feet. Because there is property on both sides of the street, once an initial calculation is made based on the frontage, Veronica will be responsible for only half of that amount.

Lot frontage	115 feet
Cost per foot	× $30
Total cost for 115 feet	$3,450
City's percentage	× .40
City's share of cost	$1,380
Total cost for 115 feet	$3,450
City's share of cost	– $1,380
Property owners' share	$2,070

Dividing $2,070 by two shows that Veronica's assessment will be $1,035.

In addition to ad valorem taxes and special assessments, other taxes have an impact on real property ownership. Although it is beyond the scope of this chapter, please note that many people and businesses purchase real property for investment purposes. Property owners will be responsible for federal and, when applicable, state income taxes on income received from these properties. Additionally, property owners are allowed certain deductions for expenses when computing taxable income from the operation of investment properties. As the laws in this area are continually revised, it is advisable to consult a tax adviser before acquiring income-producing real estate.

Eminent Domain

eminent domain: The right of federal, state, and local governments and certain public and quasi-public corporations and utilities to take private property for public use.

The greatest governmental intrusion on private property ownership is the governmental taking of private real property for public use. This is done under the power of **eminent domain,** granted the federal government by the Fifth Amendment of the United States Constitution, and applied to the states under the Fourteenth Amendment. Eminent domain is the right of federal, state, and local governments and certain public and quasi-public corporations and utilities, such as railroads and electric companies, to take private property for public use. The process through which the private property is taken is called **condemnation.** Property may be taken by condemnation only after a legislative enactment for public use, payment of *just compensation,* and due process. Therefore, affected property owners receive notice of *suit for condemnation* and are given an opportunity to make objections at a hearing.

At the hearing, a property owner may attempt to argue that the governmental agency does not need the property for public use or, more often, that the compensation offered is not a fair price for the property. Courts are reluctant to rule on whether the taking of private property is necessary to serve public interests, preferring to leave that determination to government agencies. Rather, a court will consider whether the taking is for public use. In evaluating whether the compensation paid to the property is just compensation, a court will determine whether the price paid reflects the value of the property if put to its best usage. For evaluation purposes, it is irrelevant if the property, at the time of suit, is indeed being put to this best usage. If only a portion of the property is condemned, then just compensation is calculated by determining the decrease in value of the entire property by the taking of the portion.

A more difficult situation occurs when governmental authorities rezone areas for conservation or other public welfare purposes. For example, an area that was originally zoned residential may be rezoned into a special conservation area to protect endangered wildlife. This rezoning will dramatically affect the market value of the property in that area. The question becomes whether the rezoning is equivalent to the exercise of eminent domain. If so, the government may be required to pay just compensation to property owners in the area for the difference in the value of their property under the original zoning versus the value of their property under the rezoning. If it is determined that the rezoning does not constitute a "taking," then the property owners will have to live with the newly imposed restrictions without receiving any compensation.

Escheat to the State

Perhaps the most encompassing power of the state, and sometimes local, governments is the right of reversion of title to private property in their jurisdiction. This right of reversion is exercised when a property owner dies intestate leaving no heirs. In that circumstance, his or her real property will **escheat** to the state. The probate laws of each state determine the point at which real property reverts to the state or, in certain instances, to the city or county in which the property is located. For example, the intestacy laws of some states require that there must be no heirs not only of the decedent but also of the decedent's spouse to claim the property before the property escheats.

condemnation: The process by which private property is taken by federal, state, and local governments for public use.

escheat: The right of reversion of title to private property in their jurisdictions, given to state and local governments.

PRIVATE RESTRICTIONS ON OWNERSHIP

Restrictive Covenants

Restrictive covenants are private restrictions imposed on the use of private property, which may take the form of *subdivision regulations*, restrictions imposed by a developer or a condominium or homeowners' association, or **deed restrictions,** which are restrictive covenants contained in the deed transferring property from seller to buyer. In each of these situations, the restrictions upon which title to the property is taken are recorded in the public records. As is the case with zoning regulations, most restrictive covenants attempt to preserve or increase the value of the subject parcel and surrounding properties. They may restrict the size of the homes constructed on the property, may require committee approvals for alterations, or may impose setback requirements. Restrictive covenants are binding on present and future owners of the property.

Similarly, as noted in the previous chapter, a condominium owner takes title to a condominium unit subject to the restrictions contained in the declaration of condominium, which is recorded when the condominium is created. The declaration may include several use restrictions, such as those pertaining to pets, those which regulate trucks and commercial vehicles, and those which regulate the sale or lease of a condominium unit. The condominium association is invested with the authority to enforce these restrictions.

Other restrictive covenants arise when restrictions are placed in a deed transferring title from one party to another. These restrictions limit the use of the real property described in the deed. The restrictions imposed may be perpetual or for a specified period of time. While in effect, the restrictions are binding on the present owner and all subsequent owners. The courts, however, will not enforce any deed restriction that is discriminatory as to race, ethnicity, sex, or religion. For example, a deed restriction contained in a deed from the 1930s that states "No sale to member of African descent," enforceable at the time, is now considered illegal and would not be binding on a present-day owner.

Easements

An **easement** is the enforceable right to use the real property of another for a particular purpose. Because an easement is considered an encumbrance on the real property on which it is located, it can be considered a nonexclusive limitation of the property owner's full use and enjoyment of his or her property.

Types of Easements. An **easement in gross** is an easement given to benefit a particular individual or entity rather than one given to confer a benefit to real property. Although some easements in gross may be noncommercial, the most common are commercial in nature, such as those granted to utility or cable companies. The granting of the easement permits a company to come onto the grantor's real property to install and repair transmission lines. These easements usually are created by the execution of a *grant of easement*, which contains the names of the grantor and grantee, the date upon which the easement is created, the legal description of the property on which the easement is

restrictive covenants: Private restrictions imposed on the use of private property.

deed restrictions: Restrictive covenants contained in a deed transferring property from seller to buyer.

easement: The enforceable right to use the real property of another for a particular purpose.

easement in gross: An easement given to benefit a particular individual or entity rather than one given to confer a benefit to real property.

conferred, and the specific rights of usage conveyed by the easement. The grant of easement is signed by the parties, witnessed and notarized, and recorded in the public records in the county in which the property is located. Because this easement is personal to the easement holder, it is not considered a right that runs with the land. Traditionally, easements in gross were non-transferable for this reason. Today, however, many courts permit the assignment or sale of commercial easements in gross.

An **appurtenant easement** is an easement given to confer a benefit to adjacent real property. This easement typically is created to permit ingress and egress to landlocked property. For example, suppose Sarah Bostwick purchases acreage in an area that has one main access road on the north end of the property. She then decides to keep a parcel (Parcel A) and to sell a parcel located on the south end of the property (Parcel B) to Eric Winters. Prior to purchasing the property, Eric wants assurance of access to the main access road. In granting this access across her property, Sarah's property has become the *servient estate,* sometimes referred to as the *servient tenement.* In other words, Sarah's property "serves" Eric's by providing access. Eric's property becomes the *dominant estate,* sometimes referred to as the *dominant tenement.* Eric's property is "dominant" because it receives the benefit conferred, as illustrated in Figure 4–3.

An appurtenant easement runs with the land and thus is transferred to the new owner when the dominant estate is transferred. This is the case even if the deed transferring the real property does not specifically mention the easement. An appurtenant easement may be created by an express grant, such as a grant of easement, but is customarily created by operation of law inasmuch as egress and ingress is considered a necessity.

Another type of appurtenant easement is a **party wall easement.** A party wall is a shared partition wall separating two properties. Each property owner owns that portion of the party wall that is located on his or her property and has an appurtenant easement on the remaining portion. Unlike other

appurtenant easement: An easement given to confer a benefit to adjacent real property.

party wall easement: An easement on the part of a shared partition wall between two properties.

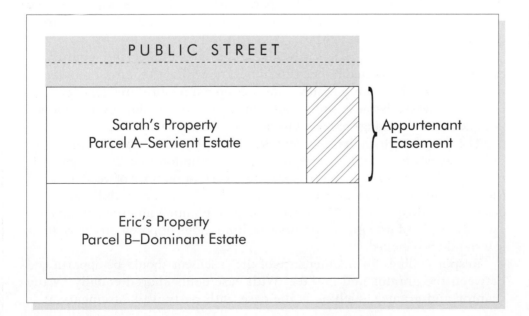

FIGURE 4–3
Illustration of an appurtenant easement

appurtenant easements, a party wall easement is not created by operation of law and must be created by an express grant.

A **prescriptive easement,** sometimes referred to as an *easement by prescription,* is created when a person adversely uses the property of another for a statutorily specified time period. Thus, the acquiring of a prescriptive easement is similar to adverse possession, discussed at length in Chapter 2. In most states, the use must be continuous, uninterrupted, hostile, open, and notorious. Periods of occupation by successive users may be tacked on to meet the statutory time requirements if the successive users are successors in interest, that is, legally related by blood or contract.

Sometimes easements are granted to permit an encroachment on the property. An **encroachment** is an illegal intrusion of a building or appurtenance onto the property of another. For example, suppose Malcolm Gallagher decides to redesign and resurface his driveway. Engineers come out and survey and the design is approved. After the driveway is completed, it is found that the new driveway extends a few inches over Malcolm's boundary line and onto that of his neighbor, Gwendolyn Stewart. Legally, if Gwendolyn does nothing and the prescriptive time period passes, Malcolm will acquire a prescriptive easement over those few inches. Before this happens, Gwendolyn can force Malcolm to realign his driveway so that it fits within his boundary lines, but that may be unreasonable and cause hard feelings between neighbors. A third alternative is for Gwendolyn to grant an easement to Malcolm for a specified duration.

Drafting Easements. The drafting of the document that grants an easement is similar to the drafting of other formal real estate documents in that attention to detail is crucial. Prior to drafting, certain matters should be addressed. First, a boundary survey should be done of the easement area. Second, any third-party approvals should be obtained. For example, if the servient estate is mortgaged, the consent of all mortgagees must be obtained. Next, it is important to verify the legal names of both the grantor and grantee. The grantor must be of legal age and of sound mind. There is no reciprocal requirement of the grantee. The legal names of the parties and the legal description of the easement area must be included in the document, the latter to be copied from the boundary survey.

An easement is not necessarily a contract. For example, an appurtenant easement may be granted by the servient estate without requiring remuneration in return. Therefore, a number of states do not require a recital of consideration. However, because some states do require this recital, even if money does not actually change hands, state statutes should be checked.

The term for which the easement is granted should be stated. If the document does not include this, there is a legal assumption that the easement is meant to be perpetual. It can be stated in a certain number of years or until the happening of a certain event. The right of use conveyed should be described with specificity. The grantor may be granting an exclusive or nonexclusive right of use. Any restrictions or limitations imposed on the right of use should be detailed.

Responsibilities for maintenance of the easement should be apportioned between the grantor and grantee. With easements shared equally by the grantor and grantee, such as is the case with party wall easements, it is

prescriptive easement: An easement created when a person adversely uses the property of another for a statutorily specified time period.

encroachment: An illegal intrusion of a building or appurtenance onto the property of another.

common for these responsibilities to be apportioned equally. Additionally, the grantor may desire that an indemnification provision be included in the document whereby the grantee indemnifies the grantor from any liability for injury to persons or property arising out of the use of the easement and may require, as a condition of granting the easement, that the grantee carry appropriate liability coverage and provide the grantor with a copy of the policy.

Once these provisions are reviewed by the grantor and grantee, both must sign the grant of easement in front of the statutorily prescribed number of witnesses and notary public, each of whom in turn will sign the document. Finally, the easement is recorded with the appropriate recording clerk in the county in which the property is located. A sample easement is found in Figure 4–4.

FIGURE 4–4
Utility easement

THIS UTILITY EASEMENT is made this 6th day of August, 1997, by and between Tresham Development Corporation, an Any State corporation ("Grantor"), and Any City Electric Company ("Grantee").

In consideration of Three Thousand Dollars ($3,000.00) paid by Grantee to Grantor, the receipt and sufficiency of which is hereby acknowledged, Grantor does hereby grant and convey to Grantee, its successors and assigns, a thirty (30) foot permanent easement across and along the tract of land described as Tract 8, Tresham Estates No. 5, as recorded in Plat Book 518, Page 20, of the Public Records of Any County, Any State, the location of said easement is as set forth on the attached survey. By conveyance of this easement, Grantor gives Grantee the right to install, operate, inspect, repair, alter, and extend utility lines upon said land. Further, Grantor gives Grantee the right to trim and clear limbs from any trees that may obstruct or interfere with the operation of said utility lines.

Grantee indemnifies Grantor from any liability for injury to persons or property arising out of the use of this easement.

The granting of this easement conveys only those rights and privileges set forth above and does not convey any further rights or interests in the real property herein described.

IN WITNESS WHEREOF, Grantor has set forth its hand and seal, this 6th day of August, 1997.

Signed, sealed and delivered   TRESHAM DEVELOPMENT
in the presence of: CORPORATION, an Any State corporation

Robin Hobart   By: _Francis Tresham_
                                            President
Terrence Lowell   Attest: _Candace Darcy_
                                            Secretary
                                            [Corporate Seal]

Subscribed and sworn to before me this 6th day of August, 1997, by Francis Tresham, President, and Candace Darcy, Secretary, of Tresham Development Corporation, a corporation organized under the laws of the State of Any State.

Gillian Furniss
Notary Public, State of Any State
My commission expires:_____

Termination of Easements. Easements may be terminated in various ways. An appurtenant easement will terminate should the dominant estate and the servient estate merge into one property. This is called *termination by merger.* For example, suppose the area in which Sarah Bostwick and Eric Winters live is zoned for mixed use, residential and commercial. Recall that Sarah originally owned all the acreage encompassing both properties prior to selling a portion to Eric. Eric was granted an appurtenant easement over Sarah's property for right of ingress and egress to the main access road. Now XYZ Corporation, a developer of shopping malls, wants to purchase both properties, and Eric and Sarah agree to sell. When title to their properties is transferred to XYZ Corporation, the easement granted to Eric by Sarah will terminate by merger.

If a grant of easement provides that an easement shall last for a specified duration of time or until a specified event occurs, when that time period expires or that event occurs, the easement naturally is terminated. In addition, an easement may be terminated by a written release in which the grantee expressly releases the easement right to the grantor. Easements also may be terminated through physical abandonment by the grantee. The intention of the parties is decisive in determining whether an easement has, in fact, been abandoned. For example, suppose The Repertory Theatre Company is located in a seasonal area, and although it has adequate parking for most of the year, during "season," its patrons complain of lack of parking space. George Goodwin owns the vacant lot next to the theatre and grants an easement to The Repertory Theatre Company, permitting the parking overflow onto his lot during specified months of the year. Should The Repertory Theatre Company move across town to a larger location with increased parking, the move would indicate the theatre's intention of abandoning the easement. Additionally, an easement may be terminated by foreclosure on the servient estate by a prior lienholder. Finally, an easement may be terminated by a court in a suit to quiet title against a person claiming an easement.

Licenses

A **license** is the personal right to perform specified activities on the real property of another. A license is often difficult to distinguish from an easement in gross. Perhaps the best way to make the distinction is to say the emphasis with a license is on the right to perform activities, whereas the emphasis with an easement in gross is on the right to use the land. Some licenses are implied. For example, the owner of a supermarket impliedly gives customers a license to enter the premises to shop. However, the owner does not give an implied license to persons to come onto the premises to hand out political flyers, and if they do so without express permission, they may be required to leave. A license can also be express, either oral or written. For example, an owner of property may grant an express license permitting a charitable organization to hold a weekend carnival on the property to raise money for that particular charity. The charitable organization (the *licensee)* may or may not pay for this right, depending on the agreement it made with the property owner (the *licensor).* Generally speaking, unless consideration is paid for the license privilege, the privilege may be revoked at will by the licensor.

license: A personal right to perform specified activities on the real property of another.

Somewhat similar to a license or easement is **profit à prendre,** sometimes referred to as *profit. Profit à prendre* is the right to remove certain items from another's land or to remove a portion of the land. What generally is removed is a natural resource, such as lumber, minerals, or crops.

Leases

When a buyer purchases income-producing property, that buyer typically takes title to the property subject to the leases executed by the seller/landlord and the tenants. In so doing, the new owner of the income-producing property is restricted in his or her disposal of the rental space by the terms of the leases. Because of this, a prospective buyer will request, prior to closing, *estoppel certificates* from each of the tenants, which state the names of the tenants; their addresses; the terms of their leases; their rental payments and rental due dates; the amounts of any security deposits, other deposits, and advance rents; the condition of any fixtures and/or furniture if rented furnished; statements regarding any options to purchase; and statements pertaining to monies owed by or claims made against the landlord. (Leases are covered in depth in Part III of this text.)

Liens

A **lien** is a claim or charge against property for payment of a debt. The property acts as security for the debt. Should the property owner fail to satisfy the debt, the lienholder may foreclose on the property. If not removed prior to sale of the real property, the buyer takes title to the property subject to the liens and risks foreclosure.

Some liens are *general liens,* that is, they affect any and all property of the debtor, both real and personal. For a general lien to attach against a particular parcel of real property, that lien must be recorded against the property with the records clerk in the county in which the property is located. An example of a general lien is a *judgment lien,* a charge on property owing as the result of a court-awarded judgment, such as a personal injury award by a civil court. Other liens are *specific liens,* attaching only to specific real property. An example of a specific lien is a *mortgage lien,* which attaches only to the mortgaged real property.

Certain liens have priority over others. Therefore, if a junior lienholder wants to foreclose on real property, the junior lienholder must first search the title to the property to determine whether there are any lienholders in senior position who have priority. If there are such lienholders and the junior lienholder forecloses, these senior lienholders must be paid with the proceeds from the foreclosure sale before the junior lienholder receives any money to partially or wholly satisfy the outstanding debt. (For a detailed discussion of liens, see Chapter 9.)

profit à prendre: The right to remove certain items from another's land or to remove a portion of the land.

lien: A claim or charge against property for payment of a debt.

CHAPTER SUMMARY

1. The federal and state constitutions grant police powers to governmental agencies that allow them to place restrictions on private property owners

when deemed necessary for the protection of public health, safety, and welfare. Police power is exercised through the right of taxation given to city and county taxing authorities to levy ad valorem taxes. Further, it is exercised through the creation and enforcement of zoning regulations, the adoption of environmental protection and fair housing laws, and the ultimate power to take possession of private property through eminent domain and escheat to the state.

2. Zoning regulations are imposed to implement the goals set forth in the master plans devised by planning commissions. A master plan prioritizes perceived needs in the area of land use, conservation, circulation, noise regulation, and public facilities. Through examination of this plan, zoning maps are designed to delineate zoning areas that best accomplish the plan's objectives. A zoning map divides areas into land use classifications. The typical classifications are residential, commercial, industrial, agricultural, and public use. Some areas may be designated for multiple use.

3. When property owners desire to deviate from strict compliance with zoning regulations, they may request a variance or permission to be treated as a special exception or nonconforming use. A property owner requests a variance if he or she believes that undue hardship will occur unless he or she is allowed to vary from the requirements of the regulation. A property owner seeks classification as a special exception if he or she wishes to use the property for a use undesignated in that area. Finally, a property owner may seek to be "grandfathered" in as a nonconforming use if the zoning regulations change after the property owner has constructed improvements on the property.

4. The late 1960s marked a significant stride in the area of environmental protection legislation with the passage of the National Environmental Policy Act (NEPA) and the establishment of the Environmental Protection Agency (EPA). In the years that have followed, Congress has placed increasing emphasis on legislation designed to preserve air and water quality and improve methods for disposal of solid and hazardous wastes. In 1980, Congress established a Superfund to aid in toxic waste cleanup.

5. The Fair Housing Act of 1968 and its amendments prohibit discrimination in the sale or rental of certain properties on the basis of race, color, religion, gender, national origin, handicap, or familial status. The act prohibits the refusal to sell or lease to members of these protected classes. Further, it prohibits such practices as blockbusting, steering, and redlining.

6. For the purpose of levying ad valorem property taxes, a designated appraiser and staff must assess the value of each parcel of land and any permanent improvements to the land. The assessment process must establish the just value of the property. Factors aiding in determining just value include the present value, location, size, and condition of the property as well as the highest and best use to which the property may be put.

7. An easement is the enforceable right to use the real property of another for a particular purpose. The two major types of easements are easements in gross and appurtenant easements. An easement in gross is considered a personal right given to benefit a particular individual or entity, whereas

an appurtenant easement is conferred to benefit real property. An appurtenant easement runs with the land, but an easement in gross does not. Both may be created by execution of a grant of easement. An appurtenant easement also may be created by operation of law. In addition, a prescriptive easement may be created if a claimant adversely uses the property of another for a statutorily prescribed time period. Easements may be terminated by merger, abandonment, foreclosure, expiration of a term, execution of a release, or by suit to quiet title.

REVIEW QUESTIONS

1. Explain the concept and purpose behind "police powers" given to federal, state, and local governments, and explain the various methods of exercising these powers.
2. Explain the process by which real property tax assessments are made.
3. Distinguish between (a) blockbusting, (b) redlining, and (c) steering.
4. What provisions should be included when drafting an easement?
5. Distinguish between (a) an appurtenant easement, (b) a prescriptive easement, and (c) an encroachment.

ETHICAL QUESTIONS

Your cousin is a real estate developer and needs an attorney to represent him in a zoning matter. Your supervising attorney is out of town, but you know she handles zoning matters for several clients, so you tell your cousin she will handle his case. He asks you what her fees are, and you go over the typical fee arrangement she has with regard to handling such matters. Have you acted within your scope of authority?

PRACTICAL ASSIGNMENTS

Assignment 4:1. Find out where and how building permits are issued in your city and/or county.

Assignment 4:2. Locate an expert who performs environmental audits in your area, and draft a list of steps to be taken during an environmental audit. Insert the list under the "General Information" section of your resource portfolio.

Assignment 4:3. Research your state fair housing statutes. Photocopy them and insert them under the "General Information" section of your resource portfolio.

Assignment 4:4. Research your state statutes regarding (a) the tax year for real property taxes, (b) the factors appraisers must take into consideration when calculating just value for taxation purposes, (c) the procedures a property owner must follow if he or she wishes to dispute the assessment, (d) the categories of real property not included in the tax base, and (e) permissible deductions that may be taken and how to apply for them. Photocopy the relevant statutes and insert them under the "General Information" section of your resource portfolio.

Assignment 4:5. Deborah Sanders, your supervising attorney, has asked you to draft an easement for a client, Wintour Properties, Inc. Wintour Properties is in the completion stages of a planned unit development called Wintour Estates, located in your city, county, and state. Basic cable service will be included in the maintenance assessments charged to homeowners, and Wintour Properties wants to grant an easement to Campion Cable Company so that cable lines can be installed and maintained. The easement is to be a twenty-five-foot easement running across Tract 2, Wintour Estates No. 7, as recorded in Plat Book 601, Page 11 (your county and state). The location of the easement is set forth on a survey that will be attached to the easement document. The easement given to Campion Cable Company will be perpetual and nonexclusive. Campion will be paying Wintour Properties two thousand dollars for the right to the easement. The rights conveyed by the easement document are the rights to install, operate, and maintain cable lines, which include the right to inspect, repair, alter, and extend lines. The client wants an indemnification provision included. The easement will benefit the named parties and their respective heirs, successors, and assigns. Wintour Properties, Inc.'s president, Veronica Wintour, will be signing on behalf of the corporation, and Kyle Bates will be attesting as secretary of the corporation.

Assignment 4:6. Define the following key terms.

appurtenant easement

blockbusting

condemnation

deed restrictions

easement

easement in gross

eminent domain

encroachment

escheat

license

lien

master plan

millage rate

nonconforming use

party wall easement

police powers

prescriptive easement

profit à prendre

redlining

restrictive covenants

special assessment

special exception

steering

tax base

variance

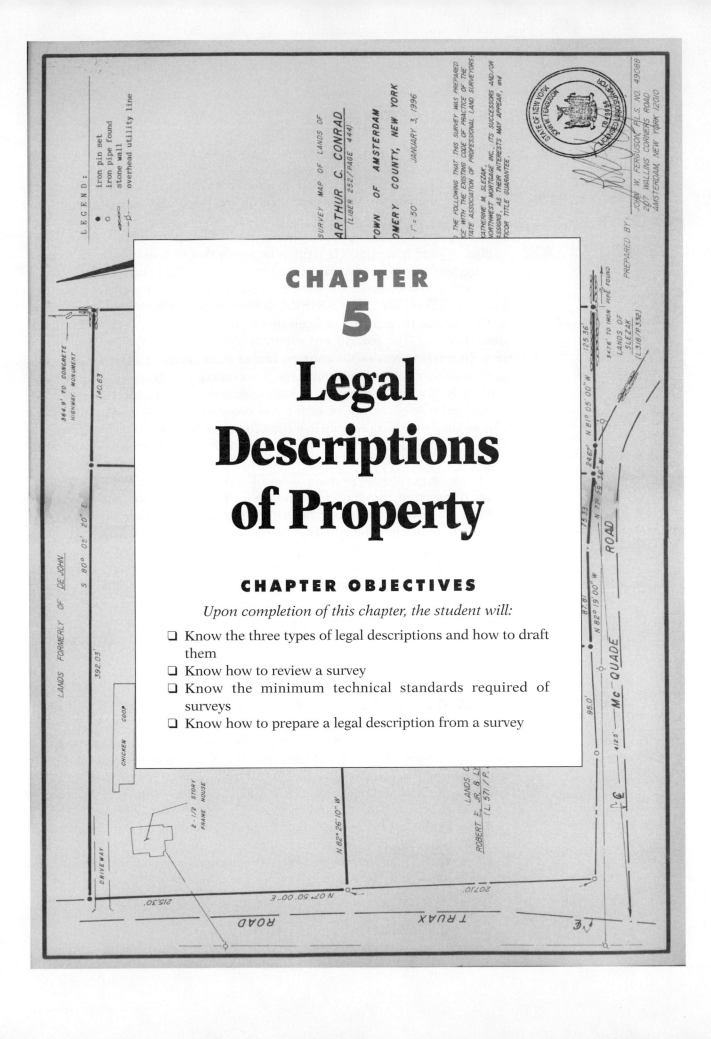

CHAPTER
5

Legal Descriptions of Property

CHAPTER OBJECTIVES

Upon completion of this chapter, the student will:

❏ Know the three types of legal descriptions and how to draft them
❏ Know how to review a survey
❏ Know the minimum technical standards required of surveys
❏ Know how to prepare a legal description from a survey

INTRODUCTION

Every major document pertaining to a real estate transaction contains a legal description of the subject real property. The **legal description** provides the parties with a precise delineation of the specific property involved that sets the property apart from all other parcels of real estate. A legal description is more technical than a street address and sets forth the exact boundaries of the real property, indicating where one parcel of property ends and another begins. A legal description is written in words that also may be used to map out a graphic form on a survey map. Surveys show the boundary lines of the property, improvements on the property, and encroachments or encumbrances. Surveys are discussed in detail later in the chapter.

There are three types of legal descriptions: (1) the metes and bounds description, (2) the government survey description, and (3) the plat description. In certain areas of the country, one of these methods may be in greater use than the others. For example, the government survey method is not used uniformly across the country. In some instances, one method may be precluded because of the nature of the real property involved. For example, the plat method may be used only in a situation in which the parcel of property is located within a subdivision for which a plat map has been drawn and recorded.

Because paralegals prepare most of the documents involved in a real estate transaction, they have to be able to read and understand the three types of legal descriptions utilized in describing property. A paralegal may be asked simply to proofread a lengthy legal description for mistakes, comparing it to previous descriptions. Alternatively, a paralegal may be asked to prepare a written description from a survey map provided. This chapter outlines the three types of legal descriptions, explaining the components of each and the most common situations in which each type of description is used. The chapter then discusses surveys—the parties who may require a survey, the standards that must be met for an acceptable survey, and the process of reviewing a survey.

TYPES OF LEGAL DESCRIPTIONS

In many contexts, the use of a street address is sufficient to describe real property. However, in many legal documents and in real estate transactions in which property is being sold, leased, or mortgaged, a more precise identification is required that indicates the exact boundary lines of the real property. A prospective buyer wants to know the exact size of the parcel of property being bought as well as the line at which the property ends and another parcel begins. The boundary lines are important not only to describe size but also to indicate whether any improvements to the property are within the boundary lines or encroaching on another's property, and likewise, to indicate whether any improvements to the neighboring properties are encroaching on the subject property. Further, boundary lines provide a starting point for measuring setback requirements when building on real property.

To meet the needs for a precise description, one of three methods may be used. The first is the **metes and bounds method,** which is the oldest of the

legal description: A precise delineation of a specific parcel of real property that sets the property apart from other parcels of real estate.

metes and bounds method: A method of legal description that outlines the boundary lines of a parcel of real property by establishing a starting point called the point of beginning, describing the course and distance each boundary line travels from that point around the perimeters of the property and back again, returning to the point of beginning.

three methods and which many consider the most detailed method of describing real property. An alternative method, commonly used in a majority of states in the country, is the **government survey method.** Figure 5–1 indicates which states are government survey states and which are not. The third method, undeniably the simplest and only pertinent to certain types of real property, is the **plat method.**

Metes and Bounds Method

A metes and bounds legal description is one that outlines the boundary lines of a parcel of real property by establishing a starting point called the **point of beginning,** describing the *course* (direction) and *distance* each boundary line travels from that point around the perimeters of the property and back again, returning to the point of beginning. The point of beginning must be a readily identifiable point. It may be a street intersection, a lot corner, a monument, or a described course and distance from a monument. A **monument** is a natural or manmade object that is permanent and fixed, such as a boulder, a large tree, a statue, or a building. The term *metes* refers to the distance of a line, and the term *bounds* refers to the direction of a line. The course and distance of each line is broken down into short segments, referred to as **calls.** "South 30° East, a distance of 45.15 feet" is an example of a call. This same call can be written as follows: S30°00'00"E45.15'. Thus, the legal description is comprised of a series of calls. By drawing out the series of calls, the resulting diagram should display a parcel of property with closed borders. If the lines do not result in the description ending at the precise place at which it started, there is a problem with the legal description.

Notice the first half of the sample call in the preceding paragraph. The first half of the call provides the the direction, or course, of the boundary line. This portion of the call is referred to as the **bearing,** or the *course bearing.* Notice that in the sample bearing, the direction is given as south 30 degrees. This is the case because a bearing is determined by a compass reading, a compass dividing measurements into 360 degrees to make a full circle. A surveyor takes the 360-degree circle and divides it into four quadrants, each comprised of 90 degrees. The bearing S30°E is thus located in the southeast quadrant. For more exact measurements, each degree can be divided into 60 minutes. The symbol for minutes is ('). Each minute can be further divided into 60 seconds. The symbol for seconds is ("). Therefore, the bearing N48°27'42" reads as north 48 degrees, 27 minutes, 42 seconds.

The second portion of the call, providing the distance traveled, typically measures distance in feet or in hundredths of a foot. In the sample call S30°00'00"E45.15', the distance this segment of the boundary line travels is 45 and 15/100ths of a foot. In some areas, other forms of measurements are used, such as rods, chains, and yards. Figure 5–2 provides a chart setting forth the equivalencies of feet, yards, rods, and chains.

If you are required to draw out a written metes and bounds legal description, you need a compass and ruler at hand. The first step is to break the legal description into a series of calls so that you are working with only one call at a time. Then locate the point of beginning and place the center of the compass circle over the point of beginning so that the compass lines up in a north-south direction. Next, read the first call, for example, South 30°E, a

government survey method: A method of legal description, established by the United States Congress, that works on a grid system.

plat method: A method of legal description that describes real property by making reference to its location on a plat map recorded in the land records in the county in which the property is located.

point of beginning: A readily identifiable point that is the starting point of a metes and bounds legal description of the subject real property.

monument: A natural or manmade object that is permanent and fixed.

call: A short segment providing the course and distance of a line of a metes and bounds legal description.

bearing: That part of a call which provides the direction or course of a boundary line.

State	Metes and Bounds	Government Survey	State	Metes and Bounds	Government Survey
Alabama		X	Missouri		X
Alaska		X	Montana		X
Arizona		X	Nebraska		X
Arkansas		X	Nevada		X
California		X	New Hampshire	X	
Colorado		X	New Jersey	X	
Connecticut	X		New Mexico		X
Delaware	X		New York	X	
District of Columbia	X		North Carolina	X	
			North Dakota		X
Florida		X	Ohio		X
Georgia	X		Oklahoma		X
Hawaii	X		Oregon		X
Idaho		X	Pennsylvania	X	
Illinois		X	Rhode Island	X	
Indiana		X	South Carolina	X	
Iowa		X	South Dakota		X
Kansas		X	Tennessee	X	
Kentucky	X		Texas	X	
Louisiana		X	Utah		X
Maine	X		Vermont	X	
Maryland	X		Virginia	X	
Massachusetts	X		Washington		X
Michigan		X	West Virginia	X	
Minnesota		X	Wisconsin		X
Mississippi		X	Wyoming		X

FIGURE 5–1 Methods used to describe real property in various states

distance of 45.15 feet. Find the southeast quadrant and locate 30 degrees east of the north-south line. Make a mark at the 30-degree point. Then read the rest of the call, which in this example states a distance of 45.15 feet. Taking a ruler, from the point of beginning draw a line to the mark you made at the 30-degree point, and then measure along that angle a straight line equivalent to 45.15 feet.

The term *equivalent* is used here because you are drawing to scale. When drawing to scale, you are making sure that the measurements of the boundary lines in your diagram relate in size to the measurements of the actual boundary lines of the particular parcel of real property. For example, the scale might indicate that 1 mile equals 8 inches. Once this line is drawn, you have drawn your first call. To continue, take the compass and place the center of the compass in a north-south direction at the end of the line just drawn and repeat the procedure with the next call. Once you have drawn each call, the diagram should close at the point of beginning.

The measurements described thus far work well enough when the property in question is perfectly square or rectangular. Many parcels of property, however, contain curved boundary lines. To demarcate curved lines, a

	Measurement Equivalencies		
Feet	Yards	Rods	Chains
66	22	4	1
132	44	8	2
198	66	12	3
264	88	16	4
330	110	20	5
396	132	24	6
462	154	28	7
528	176	32	8
594	198	36	9
660	220	40	10
726	242	44	11
792	264	48	12
838	286	52	13
924	308	56	14
990	330	60	15
1,056	352	64	16
1,122	374	68	17
1,188	396	72	18
1,254	418	76	19
1,320	440	80	20

FIGURE 5–2
Measurement
equivalencies

surveyor makes reference to the arc distance of the curve, the radius distance of the curve, and the course and distance of the chord. The term **arc** refers to the length of a curved line that makes up a segment of the boundary of the real property. The **radius** refers to the distance between any point on that curved line and the center of an imaginary circle that could be drawn if that curved line was extended to form a full circle. A **chord** is a straight line drawn from the starting point of an arc to the end point of the arc. A sample call demarcating a curved boundary line reads as follows: "thence run along said curve to the right having a chord bearing of S32°01'E, a radius of 47 feet, and a central angle of 46°50' for an arc distance of 35.17 feet to a point of tangency." This example illustrates the complexity of some metes and bounds descriptions. Figure 5–3 provides a sample metes and bounds description, first in paragraph form, and then broken down into a list of calls. Figure 5–4 provides a diagram of this metes and bounds description.

If you are asked to prepare a written metes and bounds description from a provided survey, the first thing you must do is find the point of beginning and describe it. If you were asked to provide the legal description for the property diagramed in Figure 5–4, for example, you would notice that the point of beginning does not start at the exact northwest corner of Section X. It starts 21 feet south and 10 feet east of the corner. Therefore, the description would begin: "Begin at the NW corner of Section X, thence south 21 feet, thence east 10 feet to a Point of Beginning." Then find the first call, in this instance, due east 34 feet, and describe each call in turn until you come back to the point of beginning.

arc: The length of a curved line that makes up a segment of the boundary of the real property.

radius: The distance between any point on a curved line and the center of an imaginary circle that could be drawn if that curved line was extended to form a full circle.

chord: A straight line drawn from the starting point of an arc to the end point of an arc.

FIGURE 5–3
Metes and bounds
description

SAMPLE METES AND BOUNDS
DESCRIPTION IN PARAGRAPH FORM

Begin at the NW corner of Section X, Thence South along section line 21 feet, Thence east 10 feet to a Point of Beginning, Thence due east a distance of 34 feet, Thence south 62°50′ east a distance of 32 feet, Thence southeasterly along a line forming an angle of 8° to the right with a prolongation of the last described course a distance of 30 feet, Thence south 13° to the left of a prolongation of the last described line a distance of 50 feet, Thence due east a distance of 40 feet, Thence due south a distance of 30 feet to a point of curvature of a curve to the right concave to the northwest having a radius of 20 feet and a central angle of 90°, Thence along the arc of said curve a distance of 31.4 feet to a point of tangency, Thence run due west a distance of 100 feet to a point of curvature of a curve to the right concave to the northeast having a radius of 60 feet and a central angle of 15°, Thence along the arc of said curve a distance of 15.7 feet to a point of tangency, Thence north 30° west a distance of 40 feet, Thence north 40° east a distance of 30 feet, Thence north 42°04′ west a distance of 55.3 feet to the Point of Beginning.

SAMPLE METES AND BOUNDS
LEGAL DESCRIPTION IN LIST FORM

1. Begin at the NW corner of Section X
2. Thence south along the section line 21 feet
3. Thence east 10 feet to a Point of Beginning
4. Thence due east a distance of 34 feet
5. Thence south 62°50′ east a distance of 32 feet
6. Thence southeasterly along a line forming an angle of 8° to the right with a prolongation of the last described course a distance of 30 feet
7. Thence south 13° to the left of a prolongation of the last described line a distance of 50 feet
8. Thence due east a distance of 40 feet
9. Thence due south a distance of 30 feet to a point of curvature of a curve to the right concave to the northwest having a radius of 20 feet and a central angle of 90°
10. Thence along the arc of said curve a distance of 31.4 feet to a point of tangency
11. Thence run due west a distance of 100 feet to a point of curvature of a curve to the right concave to the northeast having a radius of 60 feet and a central angle of 15°
12. Thence along the arc of said curve a distance of 15.7 feet to a point of tangency
13. Thence north 30° west a distance of 40 feet
14. Thence north 40° east a distance of 30 feet
15. Thence north 42°04′ west a distance of 55.3 feet to the Point of Beginning

Reproduced through the courtesy of Attorneys' Title Insurance Fund, Inc.

Government Survey Method

The second oldest method of legal description is the government survey method, also referred to as the *rectangular survey method*. This is the most widely used method in this country. It was established by the United States

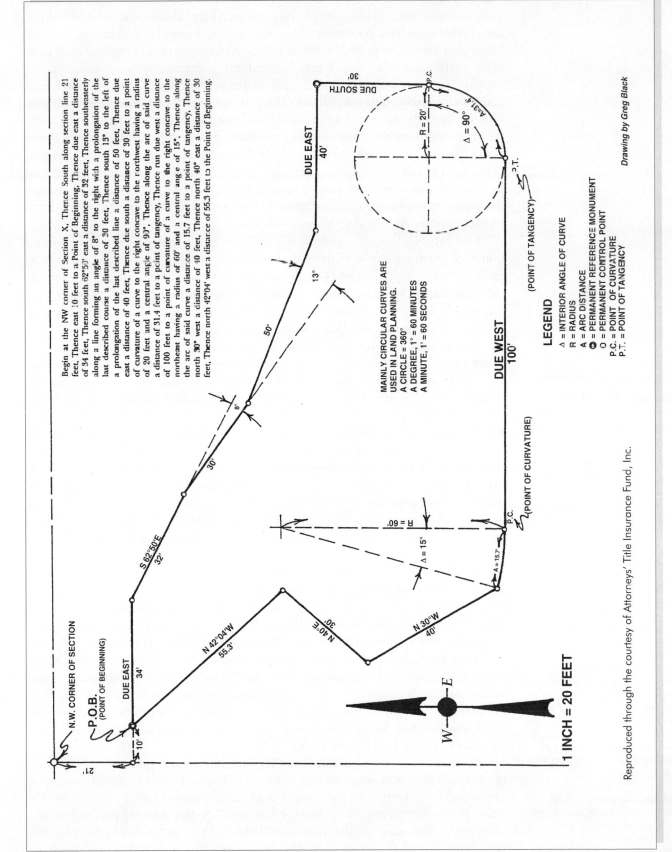

Begin at the NW corner of Section X, Thence South along section line 21 feet, Thence east 10 feet to a Point of Beginning, Thence due east a distance of 34 feet, Thence south 62°50′ east a distance of 32 feet, Thence southeasterly along a line forming an angle of 8° to the right with a prolongation of the last described course a distance of 30 feet, Thence south 13° to the left of a prolongation of the last described line a distance of 50 feet, Thence due east a distance of 40 feet, Thence due south a distance of 30 feet to a point of curvature of a curve to the right concave to the northwest having a radius of 20 feet and a central angle of 90°, Thence along the arc of said curve a distance of 31.4 feet to a point of tangency, Thence run due west a distance of 100 feet to a point of curvature of a curve concave to the right concave to the northeast having a radius of 60′ and a central angle of 15°, Thence along the arc of said curve a distance of 15.7 feet to a point of tangency, Thence north 30° west a distance of 40 feet, Thence north 40° east a distance of 30 feet, Thence north 42°04′ west a distance of 55.3 feet to the Point of Beginning.

MAINLY CIRCULAR CURVES ARE USED IN LAND PLANNING.
A CIRCLE = 360°
A DEGREE, 1° = 60 MINUTES
A MINUTE, 1′ = 60 SECONDS

LEGEND

Δ = INTERIOR ANGLE OF CURVE
R = RADIUS
A = ARC DISTANCE
● = PERMANENT REFERENCE MONUMENT
○ = PERMANENT CONTROL POINT
P.C. = POINT OF CURVATURE
P.T. = POINT OF TANGENCY

DUE SOUTH 30′
DUE EAST 40′
P.C.
R = 20′
Δ = 90°
A = 31.4′
P.T.
(POINT OF TANGENCY)

13°
50′
8°
30′
S 62°50′E 32′
DUE WEST 100′
(POINT OF CURVATURE)
R = 60′
Δ = 15°
P.C.
A = 15.7′
N 30°W 40′
N 40°E 30′
N 42°04′W 55.3′
N.W. CORNER OF SECTION
P.O.B. (POINT OF BEGINNING)
DUE EAST 34′
10′
21′

1 INCH = 20 FEET

Drawing by Greg Black

FIGURE 5-4 Metes and bounds drawing

Congress in 1785 to provide the federal government with a standard method of describing and dividing large tracts of territory west of the original established colonies. The government survey method works on a grid system. The basic grid structure is built around intersecting government survey lines running north-south and east-west. The federal government has established at various points throughout the United States vertical lines running north and south called **principal meridians.** The principal meridians intersect with designated lines running east and west called **base lines.** For example, in Florida, the principal meridian and baseline intersect at a point in Tallahassee. There are thirty-five principal meridians in the United States, each of which is identified by a name or a number. Principal meridians and base lines are located by referring to degrees of longitude and latitude. These intersecting lines are the reference point for dividing areas of land into a grid of squares to enable a particular parcel of land to be readily located.

The intersection of a principal meridian and a base line is the starting point for forming a grid. Surveyors have established lines running parallel to each principal meridian at 24-mile intervals both east and west of each principal meridian. They also have established lines running parallel to each base line at 24-mile intervals both north and south of each base line. This forms a grid pattern of squares called **checks.** Each check is 24 miles square.

The grid can be further refined by the addition of survey lines every six miles in both directions. These additional survey lines are referred to as *range lines* and *township lines.* **Range lines** are located at each six-mile interval running in a north-south direction parallel to the principal meridian. Each range line is identified as being east or west of the principal meridian and each is numbered sequentially. For example, the third range line from the principal meridian located east of the principal meridian is referred to as Range 3 East, or shortened to R3E. **Township lines** are located at each six-mile interval running in an east-west direction parallel to the base line. Each township line is identified as being north or south of the base line, and like range lines, each is numbered sequentially. Thus, the fourth township line from the base line located south of the base line is referred to as Township 4 South, or shortened to T4S.

The intersection of these lines divides each check into sixteen smaller squares called **townships.** Each township is six miles square (thirty-six square miles). The location of a township is described by making reference first to the township line number and direction and then to the range line number and direction—for example, Township 2 North, Range 3 East (see Figure 5–5).

Each township is divided into thirty-six smaller squares, each measuring one mile square and containing 640 acres. These one-mile squares are called **sections.** Each section is given a consecutive number from 1 to 36, with Section 1 always in the northeast corner of the township, Section 6 in the northwest corner, Section 31 in the southwest corner, and Section 36 in the southeast corner (see Figure 5–6).

Each section can be divided further into halves and quarters until a particular parcel of real property can be located. Each division of a section can be identified by referring to the direction of the division (that is, North, South, East, West, Northeast, Northwest, Southeast, or Southwest) and a fraction indicating the size of the division (that is, 1/2, 1/4)—for example, the Northeast 1/4 of the Northeast 1/4 of Section 8, Township 5 South, Range 3

principal meridian: An imaginary line running north and south used in a government survey method of legal description.

base line: An imaginary line running east and west used in the government survey method of legal descriptions.

check: A measurement of land that is twenty-four miles square.

range lines: Imaginary lines located at each six-mile interval, running in a north and south direction parallel to a principal meridian.

township lines: Imaginary lines that are located at each six-mile interval running in an east-west direction parallel to a baseline.

township: A measurement of land that is six miles square, or thirty-six miles.

section: A measurement of land that is one mile square and contains 640 acres.

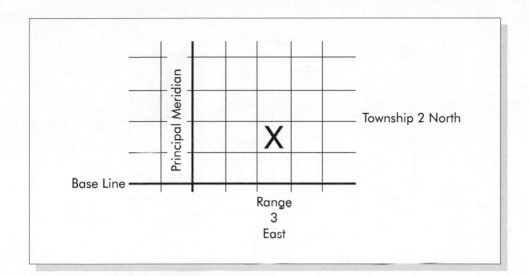

FIGURE 5–5
Location of a township

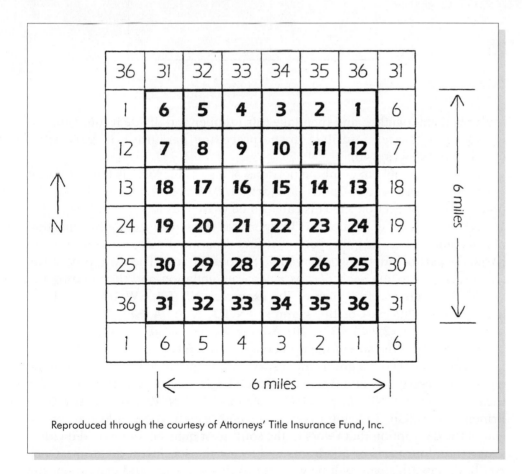

Reproduced through the courtesy of Attorneys' Title Insurance Fund, Inc.

FIGURE 5–6
Section location diagram

West of the Any State Principal Meridian. This description also can be written as NE 1/4, NE 1/4 of Section 8, T5S, R3W, of the Any State Principal Meridian. Notice the commas between each division. These commas are synonymous with the word *of*. The location of this property is diagrammed in Figure 5–7.

Recall that each section equals 640 acres. To figure out the size of a parcel, you can take the denominators of each fraction in the legal description,

FIGURE 5–7
Identifying property
within a section

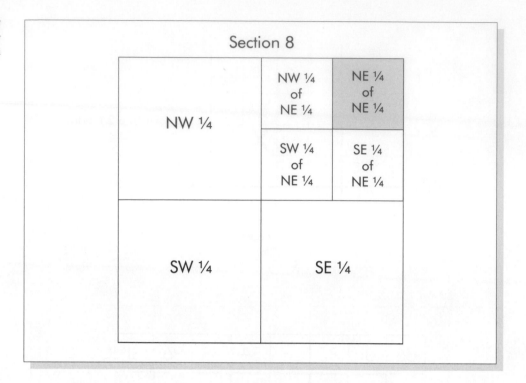

multiply them together, and then take this number and divide it into 640. For example, the parcel described in the preceding paragraph is forty acres (4 × 4 = 16; 640 ÷ 16 = 40).

It is also possible to combine portions of a section, such as the Northeast 1/4 of the Southwest 1/4 and the North 1/2 of the Northwest 1/4 of the Southeast 1/4 of Section 11. This can also be written as NE 1/4, SW 1/4 and N 1/2, NW 1/4, SE 1/4 of Section 11. To figure out the size of a combined portion of a section such as this one, you must first separate the description into two parts: the part before the word *and,* and the part after it. Then you proceed as stated above, treating each part as a separate equation and then adding the results together. The first part of the example—NE 1/4, SW 1/4—equals 40 acres. The second part of the example—N 1/2, NW 1/4, SE 1/4—equals 20 acres (2 × 4 × 4 = 32; 640 ÷ 32 = 20). Adding the first 40 acres with the second 20 acres provides the size of the property, which is 60 acres.

When drawing out a government survey description, always start from the end of the description and work toward the beginning. To illustrate, consider the example N 1/2, NE 1/4, SW 1/4 of Section 29, T8N, R6E of the Any State Principal Meridian. To begin to draw this description, you would start at the end of the description that refers to the southwest quarter. You would divide a square into four parts or quadrants and locate the southwest quadrant. Once you have done this, you will be working in this quadrant and can ignore the others. Next, reading back to front, the description refers to the northeast quarter. Again, you have to divide this quadrant into four parts and find the northeast portion. Finally, you have to take this portion and divide it into halves, as the last part of the description refers to the north half. This description is illustrated in Figure 5–8.

Thus far, the discussion of the government survey method has assumed that land masses fit perfectly within a grid system. This assumes a flat earth.

STEP ONE

NW ¼	NE ¼
SW ¼	SE ¼

STEP TWO

NW ¼		NE ¼
NW ¼ of SW ¼	NE ¼ of SW ¼	SE ¼
SW ¼ of SW ¼	SE ¼ of SW ¼	

STEP THREE

NW ¼		NE ¼
NW ¼ of SW ¼	N ½ of NE ¼ of SW ¼	SE ¼
SW ¼ of SW ¼	SE ¼ of SW ¼	

FIGURE 5–8 Drawing a description

The curvature of lines produced by the roundness of the earth means that the range lines (running north-south) would converge. To compensate for this, the government survey method utilizes **correction lines** and **guide meridians.** Every fourth township line above and below the base line has been designated a correction line, and at each correction line, the range lines are remeasured to a distance of six miles apart. Further, every fourth range line east and west of the principal meridian has been designated a guide meridian.

Even with correction lines and guide meridians, the accuracy of the government survey method would be questionable without compensating for irregular tracts of land. These irregularities may be created, for example, by bodies of water such as rivers, lakes, and oceans. Because of these irregularities, sections may end up being undersized or oversized. These sections are referred to as fractional sections and cannot be properly divided by using the customary quartering system. Government surveyors have compensated for these irregular tracts by designating them **government lots** and giving each a number within a section—for example, "Government Lot 1 in the northwest quarter of fractional section 6, Township 9 South, Range 7 West of the Any State Principal Meridian."

Plat Method

The plat method is also commonly referred to as the *lot and block method* and has its basis in the government survey system. This is the simplest of the three types of legal descriptions, describing a particular parcel of real property by making reference to its location on a plat map recorded in the land records in the county in which the property is located. When a real estate developer purchases a large tract of land with the intention to divide that land into smaller parcels, the real estate developer creates a subdivision. To do this, the real estate developer must get approval from local authorities by submitting a survey called a **plat map,** or *survey plat,* which breaks the tract down into blocks referenced by letter or number.

correction lines: Every fourth township line above and below a baseline. At each correction line, the range lines are remeasured to a distance of six miles.

guide meridians: Every fourth range line east and west of the principal meridian.

government lot: An irregular-sized tract of land labeled by government surveyors.

plat map: A survey that breaks down a tract of land into blocks referenced by letter or number.

These blocks are further subdivided into individual lots referenced by sequential number. Lot sizes are indicated and details filled in, such as the locations and names of streets within the subdivision, the location of sewer lines and utility lines, and any land within the subdivision that is to be used as recreation areas or for other community use. The subdivision name also appears on the plat map. Additionally, the plat map includes the legal description for the entire tract. This description may be a metes and bounds description or a government survey description. Once a plat map is approved, it is recorded in a plat book or official records book in the public records in the county in which the tract is located. A sample recorded plat map is found in Figure 5–9.

A proper plat method legal description includes: (1) the name of the subdivision, (2) the lot number, (3) the block number or letter, (4) the plat book number or official records book number, (5) the page number in the plat book or official records book, and (6) the county and state in which the plat was recorded. Sometimes a developer divides a tract into sections (not to be confused with the term *section* as it is used in a government survey description). This is particularly common if the subdivision is to be developed in stages. If the subdivision is divided into more than one section, the number of the section also should be included in the legal description. The following is an example of a plat method legal description.

Lot 3, Block 5, of EMERALD ISLES ESTATES, 2ND SECTION according to the plat thereof, recorded in Plat Book 69, Page 16, of the Public Records of Any County, Any State.

The plat method is used for single-family homes within a subdivision, industrial parks, and condominiums. When a prospective condominium owner seeks to purchase a condominium, one of the documents he or she will receive is a declaration of condominium (see Chapter 3 for a detailed discussion). The declaration will include a map showing the location of the condominium units. The declaration is recorded in the county in which the condominium is located. Therefore, a plat method description of a condominium unit differs from a regular plat method description by (1) making reference to a unit number rather than a lot and block number, (2) making reference to the name of the condominium rather than to the name of a subdivision, and (3) making reference to a declaration of condominium rather than to a plat map, such as in the following example.

Unit 205, of LYNTON PLACE, a Condominium according to the Declaration of Condominium recorded at Official Records Book 1130, Page 42 of the Public Records of Any County, Any State

SURVEYS

A *survey* is an investigation or examination that determines the boundaries of a parcel of land or locates all improvements on the parcel. Once the examination is completed, the surveyor sets forth the results in a map or *plat of survey*. A surveyor may be a private individual or a local government official, depending on state law. There are many types of surveys. A

FIGURE 5-9 Plat map

Reproduced through the courtesy of Attorneys' Title Insurance Fund, Inc.

survey that simply sets forth the boundaries of a parcel is referred to as a *boundary survey*. A survey that sets forth the location of improvements on the parcel, such as buildings, driveways, and fences, is referred to as an *as-built survey, record survey,* or *loan survey*. Other surveys include, but are not limited to, condominium, topographic, and special purpose surveys. Surveys often are required by lending institutions prior to closing a mortgage loan. Title insurance companies may require a current survey prior to issuing a title policy.

Minimum Technical Standards

State statutes, administrative codes, or professional standards prescribe the minimum technical standards for surveys. Although these standards vary from state to state, minimum technical standards typically include the following.

1. A statement of the type of survey depicted in the survey map
2. The name, address, and certificate of authorization number of the surveying firm
3. The surveyor's name and license number
4. The date of the field survey and the date(s) of any revisions
5. A graphic scale of the map (for example, 1" equals 40')
6. Plotted features supported by accurate survey measurements (distance expressed to nearest hundredths of a foot)
7. Clearly referenced bearings, if applicable (for example, "Bearings are referenced to the South right-of-way line of Route 88, which bears N75°05'30"W as shown on the right-of-way maps for Route 88")
8. A showing of any inconsistencies between the legal description and the map (for example, overlapping descriptions)
9. A description of all monuments
10. A showing of all fences, walls, and other open, notorious evidence of boundary lines
11. Indications of any encroachments from or onto neighboring property
12. The location of recorded private and public rights-of-way and easements
13. The location of fixed improvements in reference to the boundaries

In addition to minimum technical standards mandated by state law, the American Land Title Association (ALTA) and the American Congress on Surveying and Mapping (ACSM) have adopted Minimum Standard Detail Requirements for ALTA/ACSM Land Title Surveys. The person ordering a survey, therefore, should be clear in his or her request as to which standards (local or ALTA/ASCM) the survey should meet.

Obtaining a Survey

In a real estate transaction, it is the buyer who typically asks for a survey and pays for it, although this is negotiable. If a survey was done recently (for example, during the past five to ten years), the existing survey may suffice and a new one need not be ordered. Therefore, before ordering a survey, it is good practice to check with the seller to ascertain whether an existing survey is in his or her possession, how old the survey is, and if additions have been made since the survey date, as well as checking with the lender and/or title company to determine whether the existing survey will meet their requirements.

If a new survey is to be ordered, it is common practice for the title insurance company or the buyer's attorney to order the survey. The person ordering the survey should contact the surveyor as soon as the contract for sale and purchase is signed to find out how much time it will take to complete the survey. Once this is determined, several days should be tacked on to this time period to take into account unforeseen interruptions, such as inclement weather. The client should be informed of the survey fee prior to ordering the survey, and unless the client has provided the attorney with a retainer to be used for this type of transaction-related expense, the surveyor should be informed that the client, not the law firm, is to be billed for the survey.

Contracts for sale and purchase of real property include clauses pertaining to an inspection period during which the buyer may inspect the property and report any defects or problems to the seller. It is advisable to include in the contract for sale and purchase a stipulation that the seller shall provide the buyer with all existing surveys within a specified time frame and that the buyer shall be granted an extended inspection period (and depending upon the length of delay, an extension of the closing date) should the surveys not be delivered within this time frame.

If a new survey is required, most attorneys representing buyers want to have a *title commitment* in hand prior to the receipt of the survey so that they can give the surveyor a copy of the commitment to enable the surveyor to demarcate all easements and other encumbrances set forth in the commitment on the survey map. A title commitment is a document from a title insurance company indicating the terms and conditions under which it will issue a title insurance policy. (Title commitments and title examination are discussed in detail in Chapter 11.) When reviewing a contract for sale and purchase, it is imperative to make sure that all deadlines relating to inspection periods, delivery of title documents, and delivery of surveys work with one another.

As a paralegal, should you be asked by your supervising attorney to order the survey for the buyer-client, you should provide the surveyor with the following.

1. A legal description of the real property
2. A copy of the title commitment
3. A list of all permitted exceptions included in the contract for sale and purchase (for example, restrictive covenants, utility easements)
4. Specific instructions regarding the minimum technical standards that must be met, together with any other specific instructions of the lending institution or title insurance company that will be requesting a copy of the survey

The cover letter should reconfirm the type of survey ordered (a survey providing both boundaries and location of improvements is typically desired), the date the survey will be delivered, and the survey fee, as well as indicate the number of copies requested.

Reviewing Surveys

Paralegals may be asked to verify information to ascertain whether any problems exist that must be sorted out prior to the closing of a real estate transaction. In order to do a thorough job, you should have these additional documents at hand: (1) the cover letter requesting the survey, (2) the contract for sale and purchase, and (3) the title commitment. The following checklist is a helpful guide in reviewing a survey.

SURVEY REVIEW CHECKLIST

1. *Cover letter*
   a. *Check the type of survey ordered with the survey received*
   b. *Check the delivery date stated in the letter with the date the survey is received*
   c. *Check the minimum technical standards specified with the survey to ensure they have been met*
   d. *Check any special instructions set forth in the cover letter with the survey to ensure they have been met*
2. *Contract for sale and purchase*
   a. *Check to ensure the survey meets the contract's requirements*
   b. *Check the time period within which to make objections to survey defects and the time period within which the seller has to cure defects*
   c. *Check the exceptions set forth in the contract (for example, home-owners' association restrictions, utility easement)*
3. *Title commitment*
   a. *Check the legal description in the survey with the legal description in the title commitment for discrepancies*
   b. *Check the legal description against the drawing shown on the survey for discrepancies*
   c. *Check the list of exceptions in the title commitment with the drawing, noting whether all are included and noting any encumbrances shown that do not appear on the commitment*

There will be some exceptions listed in the title policy that will not show up on the survey, such as a current outstanding mortgage. (An explanation of exceptions found in title commitments and policies is provided in Chapter 11.)

Defects Revealed in a Survey

If a prospective seller is hesitant to provide a survey, this may be an indication that there are problems the survey will reveal that the seller does not want to bring up. If a prospective seller knows of problems indicated on an existing survey (for example, an unrecorded easement or encroachment), the seller should bring these problems to the attention of his or her attorney prior to negotiating a contract for sale and purchase. If the problems are ones that can be cured, they should be cured prior to contracting, if possible. If they can be cured but curing will take time and the seller is anxious to go to contract, the seller may choose to include a clause in the contract that the defect will be cured within a specified period of time. The buyer may choose to include a clause in the contract that if the survey reveals defects that the seller is unable to cure, resulting in a failure to close the sale on the property, the seller is responsible for reimbursing the buyer for all expenses incurred by the buyer associated with the transaction (for example, survey fees, inspection fees). In no event should a seller with knowledge of a defect opt to forego informing the buyer, hoping the buyer will neglect to find out on his or her own.

What problems might be revealed by a survey? The most common ones include easements that are not listed as permitted exceptions under the contract of sale and purchase, encroachments, and violations of zoning or land use ordinances or statutes. Another possible problem is the existence of a variation in the legal description in the contract or the existing deed and the actual boundary measurements provided in the survey map. How much of a problem this poses depends on the magnitide of the variation between the description and the survey map. If the variation is slight, the problem can be remedied by having the title company issuing title insurance issue a survey endorsement as well, acknowledging that the real property described in the policy is the same as the property set forth on the survey map. One of the main reasons for requesting a survey is to determine whether there are any defects on the property that would make the title to the property unmarketable. A survey endorsement from a title company in this situation stipulates that any variation between the description and the survey does not affect the quality of the title to the property.

CHAPTER SUMMARY

1. The purpose of a legal description is to provide the exact boundary lines of a specific parcel of real property, indicating where one property ends and another begins. A legal description, rather than simply a street address, is required on many closing documents, such as deeds, title policies, and mortgage loan documents.

2. There are three basic types of legal descriptions: (1) the metes and bounds method, (2) the government survey method, and (3) the plat method. The oldest and most complicated is the metes and bounds method. The government survey method is utilized in a majority of states and is based on government survey lines running north-south and east-west, forming a grid pattern over large areas of the country. The plat method is the newest and simplest type of legal description. It pertains only to real property located within a subdivision for which a plat map has been recorded.

3. A metes and bounds legal description begins at a point certain, referred to as the point of beginning, and proceeds to describe a parcel's boundaries through a series of calls. The calls describe the direction and distance of each boundary line. A proper metes and bounds description must end back at the point of beginning.

4. In a metes and bounds description, the direction of each segment of a boundary line is measured in degrees, minutes, and seconds. The distance of each segment of a boundary line is typically measured in feet and in hundredths of a foot.

5. The government survey method, also known as the rectangular survey method, describes a particular parcel of property by its location within a grid system. The grid's infrastructure is built around government survey

lines called principal meridians and base lines. Range lines radiate every six miles to the east and west of a principal meridian and township lines radiate every six miles to the north and south of a base line, forming squares called townships. Each township is divided into thirty-six sections, each section measuring one mile square. Sections can further be divided into halves and quarters until the precise location of a parcel of property is identified.

6. The plat method of legal description describes a parcel of property within a subdivision by referring to the parcel's location on a plat map recorded in the county records. The plat map shows the location of blocks of land and the division of each block into individual lots, numbering each lot and providing its dimensions. A proper plat method description includes the name of the subdivision, the lot and block numbers, the plat book number and page number, and the county and state in which the plat was recorded.

7. A survey is an examination of a parcel of land to establish its exact boundaries and/or the location of any improvements and encumbrances on it. The results are set forth in a survey map. State law prescribes the minimum technical standards a surveyor must observe when preparing a survey. These most often include, but are not limited to, a statement of the type of survey depicted; the name, address, and certificate of authorization number of the surveying firm; the surveyor's name and license number; the date of the field survey; a graphic scale of the map; accurate and clearly referenced survey measurements; the location of all improvements; and the location of any encumbrances. In addition to state statutory standards, ALTA/ASCM minimum technical standards exist that surveyors may be requested to follow.

8. When reviewing a survey, a legal assistant should refer not only to the survey map but also to the cover letter sent when ordering the survey, the contract for sale and purchase, and the title commitment. The survey should meet the instructions set forth in the cover letter and the requirements set forth in the contract. It should match the legal description provided in the title commitment and include the exceptions listed in the title commitment as well as any encumbrances that do not appear in the commitment.

REVIEW QUESTIONS

1. Which type of legal description should be used to describe the following real property?
   a. A plot of acreage in Vermont
   b. A plot of acreage in California
   c. A condominium in Florida
2. Explain the procedure that should be used in drafting a written metes and bounds description from a survey map.
3. What is the size of each of the following parcels of real property?
   a. The W 1/2 of the SW 1/4 of Section 2
   b. The S 1/2 of the N 1/4 of the NE 1/4 of Section 4
   c. The SE 1/4 of the SE 1/4 of the SW 1/4 of Section 8
4. Referring to the plat map provided in Figure 5–9, write out the legal description for Lot 1 located in the top left corner of the map.
5. List the steps that should be taken when reviewing a survey map.

ETHICAL QUESTIONS

Two months ago, two of the paralegals in your law firm left, one moving out of state, and the other leaving due to a serious illness. Neither has been replaced, and the real estate files that they handled have become your responsibility. Your office is crowded with current client files requiring immediate attention. Although you are usually very organized and on top of things, your present caseload has you juggling too many real estate closings, and you are afraid that the pressure will cause you to forget important deadlines. You have been coming in early and leaving late for the last three weeks, and you still do not feel like you are catching up. Your supervising attorney has told you that the situation is temporary and that you were given the extra caseload because you are the most experienced real estate paralegal in the firm. What should you do?

PRACTICAL ASSIGNMENTS

Assignment 5:1. Working with the diagram provided in Figure 5–10, write out a metes and bounds description of this parcel of real property.

Assignment 5:2. Working with the metes and bounds legal description that follows, write out a list of all the calls contained in the description. Once you have done this, draw a diagram of this legal description.

Begin at the Northwest corner of Section 20; thence East a distance of 895.75 feet; thence Southerly, a distance of 335.30 feet; thence S89°52'56"E, a distance of 50.45 feet to the Point of Beginning; thence continuing S89°52'56"E a distance of 451.40 feet; thence S01°52'06"E, a distance of 829.72 feet; thence S87°59'36"W, a distance of 506.88 feet; thence N74°17'43"W, a distance of 86.60 feet; thence N07°42'04"E, a distance of 832.02 feet to the Point of Beginning.

Assignment 5:3. Research your state statutes and/or administrative code to find the minimum technical standards required for surveys in your state.

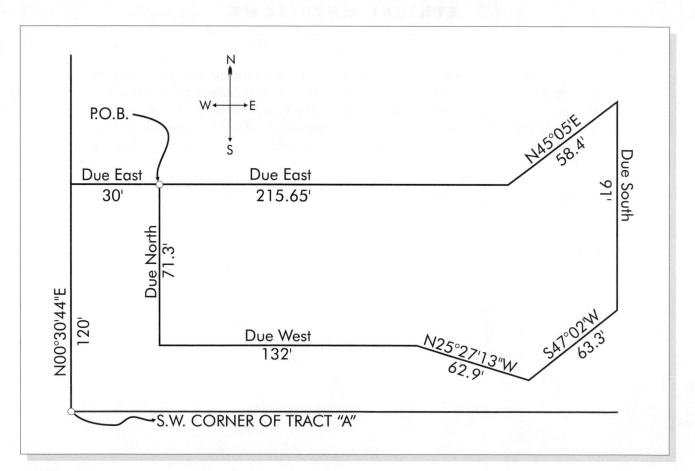

FIGURE 5–10 Practice metes and bounds diagram

Photocopy the relevant statutory or code provisions and insert them under the "Title Work" section of your resource portfolio.

Assignment 5:4. Define the following key terms.

arc	metes and bounds method
base line	monument
bearing	plat map
call	plat method
check	point of beginning
chord	principal meridian
correction lines	radius
government lot	range lines
government survey method	section
guide meridians	township
legal description	township lines

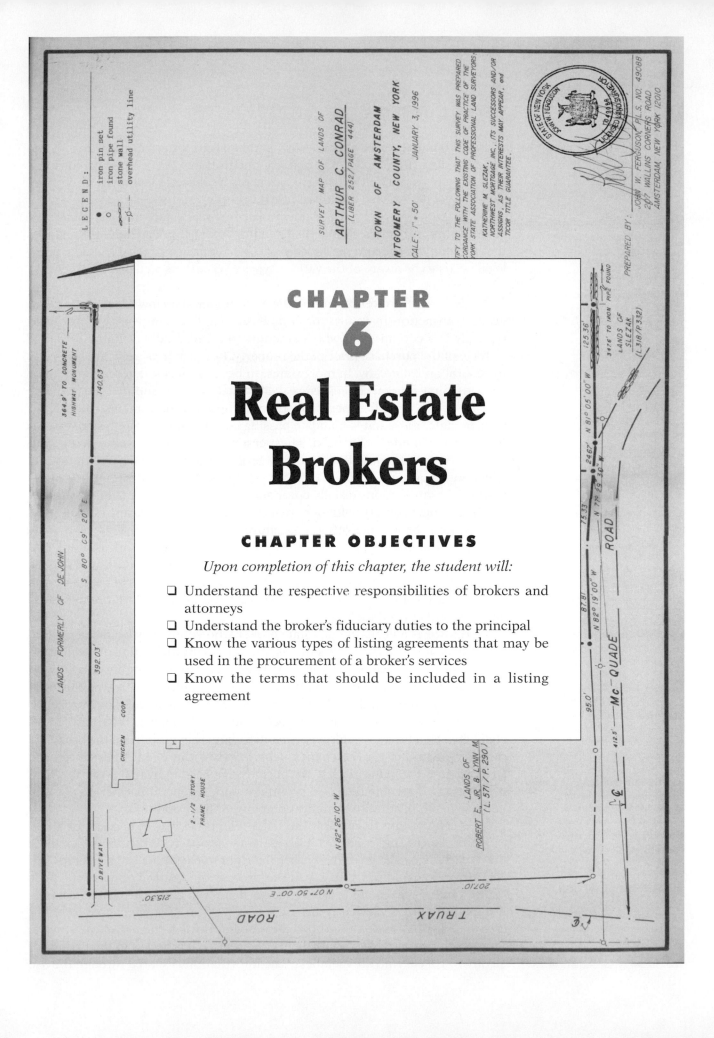

CHAPTER
6

Real Estate Brokers

CHAPTER OBJECTIVES

Upon completion of this chapter, the student will:

❏ Understand the respective responsibilities of brokers and attorneys
❏ Understand the broker's fiduciary duties to the principal
❏ Know the various types of listing agreements that may be used in the procurement of a broker's services
❏ Know the terms that should be included in a listing agreement

INTRODUCTION

Working in the area of real estate, paralegals may have as the firm's clients buyers, sellers, developers, and financial institutions. While these persons and entities may comprise the majority of clients, real estate law firms also represent real estate brokers, and therefore, it is important for a paralegal to understand the function of the real estate broker in a real estate transaction as well as the rights and duties of brokers. Even if a broker is not a client, the chances that a client will procure the services of a broker are considerable, and a paralegal needs to be aware of the various types of contracts a client can enter into with a broker.

A real estate **broker** is a person licensed under state law to facilitate a real estate transaction in return for compensation. The compensation received typically is a commission, which amounts to a certain dollar figure or a percentage of the purchase price of the property. Real estate brokers are governed by federal and state law. In most states, to become licensed, a real estate broker must first become a licensed real estate salesperson and then work under a broker for a specified period of time. Although requirements differ from state to state, most states mandate passing certain courses and a state examination to become a licensed salesperson. Additional course work and examinations are required to become a broker. Many states have a continuing education requirement for real estate salespersons and brokers. The course work and examinations usually cover such topics as residential and commercial financing, property valuation, real estate investment, leasing of real property, zoning, brokerage office procedures, ethics, the handling of escrow accounts, and state and federal laws impacting the sale and leasing of real property. Further, salespersons and brokers are instructed in the law of agency relationships (discussed in detail in the following text) because of the agency relationships created between brokers and their salespersons as well as between brokers and their clients.

A **realtor** is a licensed real estate broker who voluntarily becomes a member of a local board of realtors that is affiliated with the National Association of Realtors®. Neither brokers nor salespersons may use the term *realtor* in their advertisements, stationery, or business cards unless they are members of their local board of realtors. A **real estate agent** may be a real estate broker or a real estate salesperson. The term *agent* refers to the agency relationship created between a broker or salesperson and a client that authorizes the broker or salesperson to act on the client's behalf and in the client's best interests. **Brokerage** is the name given to the business engaged in by real estate brokers. A brokerage firm may be a sole proprietorship, a general partnership, a limited partnership, a limited liability company, or a corporation.

In most circumstances, it is the seller who procures the services of a real estate broker to find a buyer for a particular property. When the seller hires the broker, he or she gives the broker the right to *list* his or her property. This is referred to as a *listing*. To aid in the process of procuring buyers for their listings, many real estate brokerage firms belong to a multiple listing service. A **multiple listing service** is an organization of brokers who agree to publicize their listings to all other broker members through the use of the service. Thus, each broker who is a member of the service has access to the listings of all other brokers who are members. The information is shared through the use

---

broker: A person licensed under state law to facilitate a real estate transaction in return for compensation.

realtor: A licensed real estate broker who voluntarily becomes a member of a local board of realtors that is affiliated with the National Association of Realtors®.

real estate agent: A real estate salesperson or real estate broker.

brokerage: The name given to the business engaged in by real estate brokers.

multiple listing service: An organization of brokers who agree to publicize their listings to all other broker members through the use of the service.

of multiple listing directories and also may be accessed by computer. The sharing of this information helps brokers to build up an "inventory" of listings and increases the chances of finding a buyer for the property through the assistance of other brokers who will then share in the commission. Before a property can be listed with a multiple listing service, the broker must procure the consent of the seller. Many broker's agreements contain a multiple listing clause in which the seller gives his or her consent both to the listing of the property with such a service and to the authority of other broker members to assist in selling the listed property.

This chapter will explore the role of brokers in the real estate transaction, the agency relationship that is created between brokers and their clients as well as brokers and their subagents, the compensation paid for their services, their ethical duties as fiduciaries, and the various types of contractual relationships that can be created between brokers and their clients.

THE ROLE OF THE BROKER

Responsibilities of the Broker Versus the Attorney

Attorneys and real estate brokers each have responsibilities to their clients in that they occupy positions of trust and confidence with regard to their clients; in addition, each has certain responsibilities to third parties and the general public. Nonetheless, each has their own area of expertise, and if the client cannot distinguish between the responsibilities of the broker versus those of the attorney, it is the obligation of both the broker and the attorney to do so.

Real estate brokers are hired for their expertise in marketing real property, which includes knowledge of such areas as real estate valuation, financing, and investment. Brokers are allowed by law to make representations regarding the value of a particular property, although it is the seller who must ultimately determine the purchase price of the property. The average seller is less knowledgeable of the property's true value than the broker and, therefore, relies on the broker to assist in formulating the purchase price. A broker often makes a valuation of a particular property by conducting a **competitive market analysis,** which is a comparison of prices of properties similar to that of the seller's property that have recently been sold. Properties are compared that are similar in size, style, location, and amenities to determine the estimated market value of the seller's property.

Brokers are allowed by law to partake in the preliminary negotiations and the drafting of documents leading to an agreement between the parties to a real estate transaction. Therefore, a broker may draft memoranda, deposit receipts, or even, in some states, contracts for sale and purchase as long as, in so doing, the broker does not engage in the unauthorized practice of law by giving legal advice. No matter how experienced the broker, he or she must not give opinions of title or prepare documents effecting the transfer of title from one party to the other.

In the optimum situation, the attorney and broker will work hand-in-hand to ensure a smooth transaction for their mutual client. This can happen only if both the attorney and the broker respect each other's spheres of expertise and

competitive market analysis: A comparison of prices of properties similar to the seller's property that have recently been sold.

communicate that respect to the client. Neither should assume responsibility in a transaction that is beyond the scope of his or her employment. Further, neither should evaluate the services of the other or quote to the client what he or she thinks is reasonable compensation of the other.

The Broker as Agent and Fiduciary

The relationship between a real estate broker (or real estate salesperson) and the persons the broker represents in a real estate transaction is governed by the *law of agency.* An **agent** is a person authorized to act on behalf of another (the **principal).** The law of agency governs not only the rights and duties of principals and agents to each other, but also the obligations of each with respect to third parties.

As soon as a broker's services are procured, the agency relationship is created. Although the use of a written contract is customary, there is no requirement that a written contract exist in order for the agency relationship to be formed. This is because the contract between the broker and seller is a services contract (hiring of the broker's services to market the property and procure a buyer), not a contract for the transfer of an interest in real property. As such, it does not fall under the statute of frauds (discussed in the next chapter). However, state law does require that real estate brokers and salespersons meet state licensing requirements before a legal agency relationship can occur.

A real estate broker is the agent of the persons the broker is representing in a real estate transaction, regardless of which party pays the broker's commission. In addition, an agency relationship exists between a real estate broker and the broker's salespersons because a broker is a principal to the salespersons (his or her employees) and these employees are the broker's agents. With regard to this latter relationship, the common law principle of respondeat superior controls. **Respondeat superior** is a Latin term meaning "let the superior respond." This legal doctrine holds the principal (here, the broker) legally responsible for the actions of the agent (here, the salesperson).

Types of Agents. There are several types of agents. A *universal agent* is an agent who is authorized to conduct any and all transactions of every nature that may be lawfully delegated by a principal. Real estate brokers are not universal agents. A *general agent* is an agent who is authorized to act by a principal in all matters related to a particular business. A *special agent* is an agent who is authorized to conduct a single transaction, or a finite series of transactions not anticipated to be of an ongoing nature, for a principal. For example, when a broker is hired by a seller to sell the seller's primary residence, a special agency is formed. A **subagent** is someone who is authorized by an agent to aid in a transaction for a principal, if authorized under the original agency agreement. For example, a real estate salesperson is a subagent of a broker. A seller or buyer procures the services of a real estate brokerage firm. The firm thereby becomes the agent. The seller or buyer works with a salesperson of the firm to complete the transaction. The salesperson is the subagent. A subagent is under the control and authority of both the agent (here, the broker) and the principal (here, the seller or buyer).

A subagent may also be another brokerage firm. For example, a seller procures the services of Broker 1. Broker 1 lists the seller's house with a multiple

agent: A person authorized to act on behalf of another.

principal: The person upon whose behalf an agent is authorized to work.

respondeat superior: "Let the master answer." A legal doctrine that holds the principal legally responsible for the actions of the agent.

subagent: Someone who is authorized by an agent to aid in a transaction for a principal, if authorized under the original agency agreement.

listing service. Broker 2 is a member of the multiple listing service, sees the listing of the seller's house, and finds potential buyers for that house. Broker 2 has become a subagent in this transaction and must interact with the potential buyers on behalf of the seller as an agent of the seller. Should Broker 2's efforts result in the sale of the house, the commission due to Broker 1 will be divided between Broker 1 and Broker 2.

In the area of real estate, the special agency relationship is the one most commonly created. This relationship can be divided into two major categories: single agency and dual agency. A **single agency** occurs when a broker represents only one principal in a transaction, either the buyer or the seller. Brokers have a **fiduciary duty** (hold a special position of trust) to their principals. In a single agency, the broker's fiduciary duty is to one party only. Thus, a broker can be either a seller agent or a buyer agent. Even though brokers work closely with buyers, they are generally seller agents and their allegiance, therefore, is to the seller. If a broker is a seller agent, the broker works for the seller, but with the buyer. The distinction can often appear blurred in the course of a transaction. Agency policies must be clear and should require the disclosure of the agency relationship to all parties in the transaction at the first available opportunity as well as require written documentation evidencing the disclosure. Even in the absence of an official firm policy, most state statutes address the issue of agency disclosure. Typically, a broker must disclose his or her agency relationship before showing the property, eliciting confidential information, or executing an offer on the property.

A **dual agency** occurs when a broker represents both the seller and the buyer in a transaction. While disclosed dual agencies are permissible, an undisclosed dual agency (one in which the parties do not know and acknowledge that the broker is working for both parties) is illegal. Because there is a potential conflict of interest in dual agency relationships, most state statutes have strict laws governing them and require the written, informed consent of all parties to the transaction. Figure 6–1 provides an example of a consent form.

A distinction must be made between a dual agent and a transaction broker. A **transaction broker** is a broker who acts as a "middleman" between the parties by simply bringing the parties together, but who does not actively represent either party. Remember that a dual agent actively represents both parties. A transaction broker, therefore, is not an agent of either party and owes no fiduciary duties to either party except for the duties of care and accounting (discussed later). A transaction broker must give written notice to both parties at first contact of the broker's status as a transaction broker; otherwise, the broker may appear to be representing one or both parties to the transaction. In the situation where property is not for sale but rather is to be exchanged for like property, it is often unclear whether the broker is a transaction broker, a dual agent, or a single agent. The broker has the obligation to clarify his or her status at the outset and cannot assume that he or she is employed by and entitled to receive compensation from both parties.

The Fiduciary Duties of the Broker. A real estate broker owes his or her principal the duties of care, obedience, loyalty, confidentiality, disclosure, and accounting. The duty of *care* requires a real estate broker (and salesperson) to exercise reasonable skill and knowledge in representing the principal in a real

single agency: A broker who represents only one principal in a transaction.

fiduciary duty: A duty held by a person in a special position of trust (for example, the duty of care, obedience, diligence, loyalty).

dual agency: An agency situation in which a broker represents both the seller and the buyer in the same transaction.

transaction broker: A broker who acts as a "middleman" between the parties by simply bringing the parties together, but does not actively represent either party.

DUAL AGENCY DISCLOSURE AND CONSENT FORM

This Dual Agency disclosure and consent is an addendum to and made part of the contract dated August 9, 1997, between Seller and Buyer for the purchase and sale of the property described below:

Lot 5, Block 3 of CHURCHILL ESTATES, 3RD SECTION, according to the plat thereof recorded in Plat Book 44, Page 22, of the Public Records of Any County, Any State.

We, the undersigned, acknowledge that we have been informed that the broker listed below is a disclosed dual agent who, with the informed consent of the Seller and Buyer, is employed as an agent for both Seller and Buyer and may not represent the interests of one party at the exclusion or to the detriment of the other party. As a disclosed dual agent, the broker listed below owes all fiduciary duties to both Seller and Buyer, except the duty of full disclosure. This means that the broker may not disclose the motivations of the respective parties, nor disclose that the Seller will accept less or the Buyer pay more than the asking price for the above-described property unless the broker receives written instructions to disclose this information by the respective parties.

We hereby confirm that we give our informed consent to the disclosed dual agency of Atlantis Realty Company and Karen Wilson as its representative to represent both Seller and Buyer in this transaction.

August 9, 1997	*Ian Green*
Date	Seller
	Louise Green
	Seller
August 9, 1997	*Dennis Jackson*
Date	Buyer
	Ruth Jackson
	Buyer

estate transaction. Although a broker is not expected to, and indeed cannot, give legal advice, a broker is expected to be more knowledgeable than a layperson in the area of real estate and must be acquainted with such areas as financing, zoning, escrow accounts, and certain federal and state laws, such as those relating to fair housing, environmental protection, equal credit, and landlord-tenant rights and obligations. A broker must utilize this knowledge to properly represent the interests of his or her principal. As part of a broker's duty of care, the broker must not bind the principal to actions not specifically authorized by the principal. Thus, the broker must refrain from making unauthorized promises or representations on behalf of the principal. For example, the broker should not tell a prospective buyer that the seller will allow the buyer to move in before closing or that the seller will be willing to partially finance the sale unless the seller authorizes the broker to do so.

The duty of *obedience* requires a broker to follow all instructions given by the principal as long as those instructions are legal. This means that a broker must carry out a legal instruction, even if the broker believes the instruction is not in the best interest of the principal. For example, a broker is required to submit all counteroffers to the seller. If the broker is a seller agent and the seller tells the broker to accept a counteroffer that the broker believes to be unreasonably low, the broker must inform the seller accordingly, but then if the seller insists on accepting, the broker must accept the counteroffer on the seller's behalf.

If a broker finds that he or she is unable to carry out a legal instruction, the broker must withdraw from the transaction. A broker must never obey an illegal instruction and if asked to do so, must withdraw. For example, a broker may never engage in discriminatory practices in showing a house for a seller. If the seller insists, the broker has no choice but to withdraw as the seller's agent. The National Association of Realtors® has adopted a Code of Ethics and Standards of Practice that must be followed by all members of their association. Included in this code are certain prohibited practices. Federal law requires, and Article 10 of the Code states that:

> REALTORS® *shall not deny equal professional services to any person for reasons of race, color, religion, sex, handicap, familial status, or national origin. REALTORS®* *shall not be parties to any plan or agreement to discriminate against a person or persons on the basis of race, color, religion, sex, handicap, familial status, or national origin.*

See Figure 6–4 for a verbatim reproduction of the Code of Ethics and Standards of Practice.

Discriminatory practices are not the only area in which a broker may be asked to follow an illegal instruction. For example, a broker may be asked to put a false purchase price on a document. Note that there is a difference in naming nominal consideration, such as ten dollars, on a deed, which is a common practice, and naming a false purchase price.

The duty of *loyalty* requires the broker always to act in the best interest of the principal, to the exclusion of all other interests, including those of the broker. Thus, a broker may not act in self-interest without the informed consent of the principal. For example, as per federal law, a broker may not receive a secret commission. Further, a broker may not purchase a property listed with the broker for himself or herself directly or for an entity in which the broker has an interest without disclosing the interest to the seller and receiving the consent of the seller. Disclosure in this instance means not only informing the seller of the broker's interest but also informing the seller of every fact that he or she has knowledge of regarding the property in question that might influence the seller's decision. A broker who fails to do so will be subject to strict disciplinary action that may include suspension or revocation of his or her license.

Similarly, a broker may not sell real property he or she owns without disclosing his or her interest in the property and the fact that he or she is a broker to the prospective buyer. Article 4 of the Code of Ethics and Standards of Practice of the National Association of Realtors® states:

> REALTORS® *shall not acquire an interest in or buy or present offers from themselves, any member of their immediate families, their firms or any member thereof, or any entities in which they have any ownership interest, any real property without making their true position known to the owner or the owner's agent. In selling property they own, or in which they*

have any interest, REALTORS® shall reveal their ownership or interest in writing to the purchaser or the purchaser's representative.

See Figure 6–4 for a verbatim reproduction of the Code of Ethics and Standards of Practice.

The duty of *confidentiality* requires that a broker preserve the confidences of the principal, as long as it is ethically correct to do so. This duty exists both during and after the termination of the agency relationship. Thus, a broker cannot reveal a principal's underlying motives for selling (or purchasing) a particular property, the financial status of the principal, the principal's willingness to accept a lower price, or any other information without the consent of the principal. However, the broker must disclose any intent by the principal to commit a crime, such as intentional falsification of documents to procure a loan. In this respect, a broker's duties regarding confidentiality are quite similar to those of the legal profession. Standard of Practice 1-9 of the Code of Ethics and Standards of Practice of the National Association of Realtors® provides:

> *The obligation of REALTORS® to preserve confidential information provided by their clients continues after the termination of the agency relationship. REALTORS® shall not knowingly, during or following the termination of a professional relationship with their client:*
>   1) *reveal confidential information of the client; or*
>   2) *use confidential information of the client to the disadvantage of the client; or*
>   3) *use confidential information of the client for the REALTOR®'s advantage or the advantage of a third party unless:*
>   a) *the client consents after full disclosure; or*
>   b) *the REALTOR® is required by court order; or*
>   c) *it is the intention of the client to commit a crime and the information is necessary to prevent the crime; or*
>   d) *it is necessary to defend the REALTOR® or the REALTOR®'s employees or associates against an accusation of wrongful conduct.*

See Figure 6–4 for a verbatim reproduction of the Code of Ethics and Standards of Practice.

The duty of *disclosure*, sometimes referred to as *notice*, requires that the broker disclose all material facts, reports, and even rumors that have a bearing on the real estate transaction. In an effort to enable the principal to secure the best price and terms in the transaction, the broker should disclose any information that may be pertinent. Obviously, a broker is obligated to disclose any offers made on the property, regardless of whether the broker believes the offer to be reasonable, but disclosure is not limited to offers. Disclosure includes such subjects as the tax consequences of the sale (the broker may advise the seller or buyer to seek the counsel of a tax expert), rumors of zoning changes (even if the passing of such changes seems unlikely), and financing issues (such as the fact that the buyer may have a problem in making the down payment, if the broker is a seller agent).

The duty of disclosure includes the prohibition of both negligent and intentional misrepresentation to either party in a real estate transaction.

Prospective buyers are allowed to rely on any representations made by a broker through the mail, as well as any representations regarding construction that are not visibly apparent. Misrepresentation includes misrepresentation by both commission and omission.

Fraudulent misrepresentation is made with an intent to mislead or deceive. To prove a case of fraudulent misrepresentation, a party must show that (1) the statements made by the broker were misrepresentations, (2) the statements were material to the transaction, and (3) the party reasonably relied on the statements to his or her detriment. If a real estate contract was procured through fraudulent misrepresentation, the contract can be rescinded or canceled. Not only will the broker lose a commission in such an instance, but the broker also may be sued by the parties to the transaction for any damages incurred as a result of the broker's actions. A broker may not, however, be required to make independent investigations of all material facts presented to the broker by the seller. Thus, if the seller misrepresented a fact to the broker who, unaware of the misrepresentation, passed this information on to the buyer, the buyer would be able to rescind the contract, but the seller would still be liable to the broker for the sales commission.

Article 2 of the Code of Ethics and Standards of Practice of the National Association of Realtors® and its corollary Standard of Practice 2-1 state:

Article 2. REALTORS® shall avoid exaggeration, misrepresentation, or concealment of pertinent facts relating to the property or the transaction. REALTORS® shall not, however, be obligated to discover latent defects in the property, to advise on matters outside the scope of their real estate license, or to disclose facts which are confidential under the scope of agency duties owed to their clients.

Standard of Practice 2-1. REALTORS® shall only be obligated to discover and disclose adverse factors reasonably apparent to someone with expertise in those areas required by their real estate licensing authority. Article 2 does not impose upon the REALTOR® the obligation of expertise in other professional or technical disciplines.

See Figure 6–4 for a verbatim reproduction of the Code of Ethics and Standards of Practice.

The broker's responsibilities regarding disclosure go beyond the principal and include third parties when the disclosures have a bearing on public protection in the purchase of real property. In addition to the fiduciary duty of disclosure, both brokers and sellers have an affirmative legal duty to make certain disclosures to prospective buyers regarding real property. Although the common law doctrine of *caveat emptor* ("let the buyer beware") is often quoted in common parlance, it does not apply to real estate transactions.

For example, state statutes require brokers and sellers to disclose structural defects concerning the property and to provide inspection reports or allow buyers to have termite, roof, and other inspections made prior to closing on the property. Although the broker may not be required to inspect for latent defects, the broker and seller must both inform a prospective buyer of any known latent defects. If the property is in violation of building codes or city or county ordinances, even if the violation does not result in a structural defect

fraudulent misrepresentation: Misrepresentation made with an intent to mislead or deceive.

(for example, inadequate smoke detectors, utilization of the property in contravention of zoning ordinances), the prospective buyer must be informed.

In addition to structural concerns, notice must be made regarding the environmental integrity of the property. Because of CERCLA (see Chapter 4 for a detailed discussion), subsequent owners may be liable for cleanup costs of environmentally contaminated property. Therefore, investigations should be made and all details disclosed. Further, brokers and sellers should investigate any federal, state, or local environmental regulations that may impact the marketability of the property. For example, a commercial buyer may be attracted to the seller's property as a site upon which to build a textile factory. The zoning may be appropriate for such a use, but state or local regulations may prohibit the factory because of the noxious fumes that would emanate from it.

A more difficult call is that concerning disclosures that do not relate to the physical condition of the property but do have a bearing on the desirability of the property because of stigmatizing events that have taken place on the property. For example, a suicide, homicide, or other criminally related event may have occurred on the property. To some people, this is of little concern. Others, however, may prefer not to live in a house in which a murder took place. Whether such facts must be investigated and disclosed is a matter of state law and is largely unanswered.

The duty of **accounting** refers to the broker's duty in safeguarding any monies, documents, or property held by the broker on behalf of the principal. This includes all deposit monies, deeds, title commitments or abstracts, mortgage instruments, keys to the property, and so forth. All deposits and other monies retained on behalf of a principal must be strictly accounted for and kept in escrow accounts in accordance with state statutory law, as discussed in the next section of this chapter.

Thus far, a broker's duties to his or her principal have been detailed, but note that a principal also owes certain duties to his or her agent/broker. A broker is an agent with limited authority to act on the principal's behalf. Because this authority is limited to the carrying out of the principal's specific instructions, the principal has the duty to make himself or herself available to the agent for consultation. The inaccessibility of a principal prevents the agent from carrying out his or her job. Further, the principal has a duty to supply all necessary information to the agent concerning the property, the principal's requirements, and any other information that has an impact on the transaction.

The principal has the duty to compensate the agent in accordance with the agency agreement entered into by the principal and agent. If the principal is the seller, the agreement will often state that the seller is to pay the agent a specified commission upon the agent's procurement of a ready, willing, and able buyer. *Able* in this context refers both to the buyer's capacity to contract as well as the buyer's financial ability to meet the seller's price and terms (for example, ability to come up with the purchase price or to procure financing to meet the purchase price). If the agent finds a buyer willing and able to meet the seller's price and terms, the seller cannot then change the price or terms to back out of the deal and refuse to pay the commission. Finally, the principal has the duty to indemnify the agent if the principal's actions result in financial harm to the agent.

accounting: A broker's duty in safeguarding any monies, documents, or property held by the broker on behalf of the principal.

Broker's Responsibility for Earnest Money Deposits

A broker will often be the person to first receive an earnest money deposit. **Earnest money** is a sum of money paid by a buyer at the time of entering into a contract to indicate the buyer's intention of carrying out the terms of the contract. These deposits and fees must be placed in an escrow account. An **escrow account** is an account in a bank, savings and loan, credit union, or similar financial institution that is held by a third party called an *escrow agent* (such as a broker, attorney, or title company), in which funds are deposited to be held until the happening of a certain event (for example, the closing on the real property). Escrow agents are not required to open separate escrow accounts for each client. Escrow accounts can be interest-bearing or non-interest-bearing accounts. Prior to monies being placed in an interest-bearing account, a written agreement should be made by the parties to the real estate transaction as to who is entitled to the earned interest and when the interest must be disbursed. State law may specify a time period (such as twenty-four or forty-eight hours) within which a broker must deposit monies into an escrow account. Commingling of escrow deposits with other business funds is prohibited. An exception generally is made for small personal sums used in opening an escrow account or in keeping the account open or paying service charges on the account.

In addition to earnest money deposits, an agency agreement between the broker and principal may call for the collection of brokerage fees before the real estate transaction closes. Some states have laws regulating the collection of advance fees. State law may require that advance fees be deposited in the common escrow account or in a special escrow account called an **advance fee trust account.** Because the purpose of collecting advance fees usually is to provide the broker with coverage of advertising and other expenses incurred in marketing the property, the broker typically is entitled to use a certain percentage of the advance fees prior to closing. Before withdrawing the allowable sum from the account, the broker must provide the principal with an itemized statement showing the amount of the advance fee and how it is to be spent. Advance fees are not to be used to cover the broker's normal overhead expenses in running the brokerage office. If the property in question has not been sold or a contract for sale and purchase signed within the term of the agency agreement, the broker is required to return all advance fees to the principal.

Brokers are required by state law to keep records of monthly statements comparing the broker's trust liability with the reconciled bank balances of all escrow and trust accounts. The trust liability is the total of all deposits that are received, being held by the broker, or pending at any given time. The statement should include such items as the name of the financial institution, the account(s) and the account number(s); the date the reconciliation was done; the account balance(s); outstanding checks; and deposits in transit. The monthly statement should be signed by the broker. In some states, these statements must be sent to the state real estate commission or other similar governmental authority. A sample monthly reconciliation statement is found in Figure 6–2.

There are occasions when a real estate broker is faced with conflicting demands for the escrow deposits. Paralegals should be aware of the fact that

earnest money: A sum of money paid by a buyer at the time of entering a contract to indicate the buyer's intention of carrying out the terms of the contract.

escrow account: An account in a bank, savings and loan, credit union, or similar financial institution that is held by a third party and into which funds are deposited to be held until the happening of a stated event.

advance fee trust account: A special escrow account in which advance fees paid to a broker are deposited. These fees may be used for advertising and other expenses incurred in marketing real property.

FIGURE 6–2
Monthly reconciliation
statement

MONTHLY STATEMENT RECONCILIATION
ESCROW ACCOUNT OF ATLANTIS REALTY COMPANY
FOR THE MONTH ENDING JULY 31, 1997

I.   BANK RECONCILIATION
      Patriot Bank, Atlantis Realty Escrow Account
      Account Number 100009-000-3356
      Reconciliation performed August 31, 1997
      A.   Balance as per August 31, 1997: $110,500.00
      B.   Escrow Deposits in Transit

Date	Amount
August 31, 1997	$20,000.00
August 31, 1997	$15,000.00
Total deposits in transit:	$35,000.00

      C.   Total of A plus B: $145,500.00
      D.   Escrow Outstanding Checks Not Included in Bank Statement

Date	Check Number	Amount
August 28, 1997	6102	$10,000.00
August 29, 1997	6103	$12,000.00
Total escrow outstanding checks:		$22,000.00

      E.   Reconciled Bank Balance (C minus D): $123,500.00
II.   BROKER'S TRUST LIABILITY RECONCILIATION
      Comparison of Reconciled Bank Balance with Broker's Trust Liability:
      A.   Reconciled Bank Balance: $123,500.00
      B.   Broker's Trust Liability: $123,500.00
      I, the undersigned, hereby state that the Reconciled Bank Balance and the Trust
Liability _____ agree _____ do not agree. (If they do not agree, state the amount of
shortage or overage and the reason(s) for same below.)

                              ATLANTIS REALTY COMPANY

                    BY: _____
                         Broker

in most states there are statutes in place that outline the steps to be taken by a broker in the event of such a dispute. In such an instance, the attorneys for the parties may each make an argument to the broker regarding the deposits. These arguments may be based on the interpretation of the terms of the contract for sale and purchase. Nonetheless, the broker must abide by state statutes, not the contract terms, with regard to the settling of escrow disputes.

State statutes usually outline the notification procedures and deadlines as well as the settlement procedures to be followed in the event of escrow disputes. Often, the state real estate commission or other applicable governmental authority must be notified of the dispute. State statutes may call for mandatory mediation or arbitration within a specified time period from the date the broker notifies the appropriate governmental authority of the dispute. Similarly, if the broker has his or her own good faith doubt as to whether a party is entitled to escrow funds in a given situation (for example, a situation in which one party has indicated its intentions not to close and the broker has not received instructions, or has received conflicting instructions, with regard to the disbursement of the escrowed funds), the broker must follow state statutes governing the handling of escrow disputes. Should the broker's commission be in dispute, the broker may be allowed to retain the amount of commission in escrow until the dispute is settled through the use of statutorily mandated settlement procedures.

If a buyer makes an earnest money deposit at the time of making an offer to purchase, and the buyer then revokes the offer prior to its acceptance by the seller, the buyer is entitled to return of the deposit. Similarly, if a buyer makes an earnest money deposit at the time of making an offer to purchase and that offer is subsequently rejected by the seller, the buyer is entitled to return of the deposit. A contract may also state that if there is a default by the seller or buyer, the broker may be able to enforce commission against the defaulting party out of the earnest money deposit.

Broker's Compensation

A real estate broker is compensated for his or her services by the payment of a commission. Only licensed real estate brokers (and salespersons) are entitled to commissions. Further, most state statutes provide that a broker can only share commissions with other licensed brokers and salespersons. The amount to be paid is negotiated between the broker and the principal and usually is reduced to writing in an agency agreement. If the principal is the seller, the agency agreement is called a **listing agreement.** In most transactions, the commission is computed as an agreed-upon percentage of the purchase price of the property and is paid customarily to the broker at closing. *Antitrust laws* (laws protecting against unlawful restraints in trade and commerce such as monopolies and price fixing) prohibit the imposition by brokerage firms of uniform rates of commission.

Not only is price fixing prohibited, but so is the allocation of markets. The *allocation of markets* occurs when two or more brokers agree to allocate different market sectors, based on such criteria as geographic location or property price ranges. For example, Broker 1 may be allocated the northern half of the city, while Broker 2 is allocated the southern half of the city, the brokers agreeing not to infiltrate each other's market. Under the **Sherman Act** (a federal antitrust law), brokers engaged in price fixing or allocation of markets are guilty of a felony punishable by both a fine and a prison sentence.

The date the commission is earned may be different from the date upon which it is paid. The date upon which the commission is earned is crucial to both the principal and the broker because once the commission is earned, the principal is obligated to pay it. In order to earn a commission, a real estate broker (or salesperson) must be the procuring cause of the purchase and sale. The interpretation of "procuring cause" may be found in the wording of the listing agreement. In the case of a seller agent, the seller agent usually is the procuring cause of the purchase and sale of the real property when he or she (or one of his or her subagents) finds a buyer who is ready, willing, and able to purchase the property. A ready, willing, and able buyer is one who is agreeable and capable of purchasing the property on the seller's terms. If, however, the listing agreement stipulates that the broker must "effect a sale," the broker has not earned his or her commission until there is a written contract executed by both the buyer and the seller.

listing agreement: A contract between a seller and a broker.

Sherman Act: A federal antitrust law protecting against unlawful restraints in trade and commerce, such as monopolies and price-fixing.

Once a broker finds a ready, willing, and able buyer or, alternatively, effects a sale by obtaining a contract signed by both parties, the broker has earned the commission regardless of whether the transaction ever gets to closing. A number of obstacles may appear after the contract is signed that may prevent a closing from taking place. Such obstacles can include, but need not be limited to, title defects that cannot be corrected, inspection reports calling for repairs beyond the amount agreed to be paid by the seller, or simply a change of heart by one of the parties. Although a broker normally will make every effort to see that a transaction is consummated, once the broker's responsibilities under the listing agreement have been met, the principal must honor the agreement.

TYPES OF LISTING AGREEMENTS

Paralegals should be aware of the fact that there are several types of listing agreements that may be negotiated between a broker and a seller (recall that a seller, when hiring a broker, "lists" his or her property with that broker). Paralegals may be called upon by their supervising attorneys to draft listing agreements for broker clients or to review such agreements should a dispute arise between the broker and the seller. As noted earlier, there is no requirement for a written contract to establish an agency relationship because the relationship is established the moment the principal confers authority on the agent by delegating responsibilities to the agent. Further, a contract between broker and principal is a contract for services, not a contract for an interest in real property, and therefore, some jurisdictions hold that it does not have to be in writing to be legally valid. Nonetheless, written listing agreements are standard practice. The most common types of listing agreements are the open listing, the exclusive listing, and the exclusive-right-to-sell listing.

Open Listing

An **open listing,** sometimes referred to as a *general listing* or a *nonexclusive listing*, is the granting of the right to solicit and receive offers on the seller's property. This is a nonexclusive right given to a broker, and the broker shares this right with all other brokers with whom the seller decides to list the property. The broker is entitled to a commission only if he or she (or one of his or her salespeople) finds the buyer or effects the sale. Thus, an open listing can be characterized as a unilateral contract that only becomes binding if and when the broker procures the sale. The broker is not entitled to a commission if another broker procures the sale or if the seller finds a buyer for the property. Although at first glimpse this arrangement may seem advantageous to the seller, the truth is that most brokers expend very little time or energy on open listings and are unwilling to expend considerable expense in advertising the property when the chances of procuring a commission are risky. Therefore, an open listing will receive less of a broker's attention than an exclusive or exclusive-right-to-sell listing, and the seller may be stuck with the property for a longer period of time.

open listing: The granting of a nonexclusive right to solicit and receive offers on the seller's real property.

Exclusive Listing

An **exclusive listing** is one in which the seller agrees to list the property with no broker other than the listing broker for the term of the listing agreement. As an exclusive agent of the seller, the listing broker is entitled to receive compensation if the listing broker or any other person procures a buyer for the property. However, the seller reserves the right to find his or her own buyer, and if he or she is successful in so doing, no commission is owed to the listing broker.

For example, the seller gives Broker 1 an exclusive listing. Broker 1 proceeds to put the listing in the multiple listing service directory. Broker 2, a member of the multiple listing service, finds a buyer for the property. Broker 1 is called the listing broker or listing agent because the listing agreement was signed with him or her. Broker 2 is called the selling broker or selling agent because he or she procured the sale. Recall the prior discussion of subagency. Broker 2 will be considered a subagent of Broker 1 in this instance, and the commission will be split between the two brokers. If Broker 1 puts the listed property in the multiple service directory but ends up procuring a buyer with his or her own leads and efforts, Broker 1 keeps the entire commission. The only way Broker 1 will not receive a commission is if the seller finds the buyer.

A word of caution is in order here. The wording of an exclusive listing agreement often is very similar to the wording of an exclusive-right-to-sell listing agreement (discussed in the following text), although the rights that are conferred differ. If there is any ambiguity in the language of the contract, contract law dictates that the ambiguity must be construed against the drafter of the contract and in favor of the other party. Because the broker (or the broker's attorney) is usually the person responsible for drafting the contract, if there is any ambiguity leading one to question whether the contract is an exclusive listing agreement or an exclusive-right-to-sell listing agreement, the courts most likely will construe the contract to be the former rather than the latter.

Exclusive-Right-to-Sell Listing

All brokers want an **exclusive-right-to-sell listing.** Under this type of listing agreement, the listing broker is entitled to a commission if anyone procures a buyer for the property within the listing term. This means that even if the seller procures his or her own buyer, the listing broker is entitled to a commission. Because the seller is parting with his or her rights to sell the property, some jurisdictions require that an exclusive-right-to-sell listing agreement be in writing, even if the jurisdiction allows for other verbal listing agreements. Brokers are more willing to expend money for advertising and other costs associated with the marketing of real property if they have the property listed under this type of agreement.

Other Listing Arrangements

Net Listing. A **net listing** agreement is one in which the seller specifies the net amount of money he or she must receive in order to sell the property. Under the terms of the agreement, the listing broker receives any monies in excess of this specified amount as commission. Therefore, the broker sets

exclusive listing: A listing agreement in which the seller agrees to list the property with no broker other than the listing broker for the term of the agreement. As an exclusive agent, the listing broker is entitled to receive compensation if the listing broker or any person other than the seller procures a buyer within the listing term.

exclusive-right-to-sell listing: A listing agreement in which the listing broker is entitled to a commission if anyone procures a buyer within the listing term.

net listing: A listing agreement in which the seller specifies the net amount of money he or she must receive in order to sell the property. Under the terms of the agreement, the broker receives any monies in excess of this specified amount as commission.

the purchase price, keeping the seller's requirements in mind. Net listing agreements are illegal in a number of states because of the potential for fraud. In those states in which net listing agreements are allowed, however, brokers receive compensation only if the property is sold. Thus, if the broker sets the purchase price prohibitively high in an effort to glean greater compensation, the chances of the property selling are minimal, so it is in the broker's best interests to allocate a reasonable purchase price.

Flat Fee Sales. The **flat fee sale** has become a popular method of selling property for those sellers who do not mind putting some effort into selling their own property. A flat fee sales arrangement is one in which, for a flat fee (which is considerably smaller than the average commission), a broker will evaluate and photograph the seller's property, write a description sheet of the property that will be placed in a special directory made available at the broker's office, and provide the seller with For Sale signs. The seller is responsible for holding open houses and showing the property to prospective buyers who find out about the property by looking through the directories in the broker's office or by driving by the property.

BROKER'S AGREEMENT CHECKLIST AND SAMPLE AGREEMENT

As noted earlier, a paralegal may be called upon to draft an agreement for a broker client or to review such an agreement to determine the rights and obligations of a client who is a principal under such an agreement. Just as with any other aspect of real estate practice, a paralegal should obtain as much detailed information as possible to aid with the task. The following checklist will aid in the drafting or reviewing of a broker's agreement.

BROKER'S AGREEMENT CHECKLIST

1. *Parties*
   a. *Names of all parties and marital status of the principal(s)*
2. *Commencement date of agreement*
3. *Termination date of agreement*
4. *Type of agreement established*
   a. *Open listing*
   b. *Exclusive listing*
   c. *Exclusive-right-to-sell listing*
   d. *Net listing*
   e. *Flat fee sales*
   f. *Other (specify)*
5. *Listing price of the property*
6. *Amount of commission*
   a. *Dollar figure*
   b. *Percentage of purchase price*
7. *Property description*
   a. *Street address*
   b. *Legal description, if available*
   c. *Size of the lot*

flat fee sale: An arrangement in which, for a flat fee, a broker evaluates and photographs a property, inserts a property description in a special directory, and provides For Sale signs to the seller.

    d. Size and description of the improvements (for example, house, apartment building, shopping center), including the following:
      i. Square footage of the total structure (indicating whether the derived figure is air-conditioned/heated space or includes space that is not air-conditioned/heated)
      ii. A room count
      iii. Square footage of each room within the structure, if possible
      iv. The age of the improvements
      v. The method of construction used
    e. Zoning classification of the property
    f. Fixtures to be sold with the premises
    g. Any personal property to be sold with the premises
8. *Seller's warranties with regard to the property*
9. *Broker's authority*
    a. Rights given to broker, including:
      i. Permissible types of advertising
      ii. Holding of open houses
      iii. Placement of signs on the property
      iv. Acceptance of earnest money deposits
10. *Multiple listing service provision*
11. *Broker's responsibilities*
    a. For procuring buyer (if seller agent)
      i. Finding ready, willing, and able buyer
      ii. Effecting a sale
    b. Disclosure of agency relationship
    c. Accounting
12. *Renewal of agreement*
    a. Automatic renewal
    b. Conditions for renewal
13. *Indemnification of broker*
14. *Termination of the agreement*
    a. Circumstances under which agreement terminates
    b. Broker protection clause (a clause that states that the broker is entitled to commission within a specified time frame after the expiration of the agreement if the property is sold to a party originally in contact with the broker)
15. *Signatures of the parties*

Figure 6–3 is a sample exclusive-right-to-sell listing agreement.

CHAPTER SUMMARY

1. A real estate broker is a person who is duly licensed by the state to negotiate the sale and purchase of real property for compensation. A broker may become a realtor by becoming a member of a local board of realtors that is affiliated with the National Association of Realtors®. Brokers may employ real estate salespersons to act as their subagents in providing services for the broker's principal. All earned commissions must be paid

EXCLUSIVE-RIGHT-TO-SELL LISTING AGREEMENT

THIS AGREEMENT is entered into this 9th day of August, 1997 by and between Carl Andrews, a duly licensed real estate broker as representative of Atlantis Realty Company, a real estate brokerage firm duly licensed under the laws of the State of Any State ("Broker"), and Grant Daniels, a single man ("Owner").

I. EXCLUSIVE RIGHT TO SELL. Owner agrees to give Broker an exclusive and irrevocable right to sell the property described below for a period commencing on the date above listed and terminating at midnight on February 9, 1998. There shall be no automatic renewal of this Agreement. Broker agrees to use his best efforts to effect a sale of the property described below, plus all fixtures therein as set forth in Exhibit B attached to and made a part of this Agreement.

II. PROPERTY DESCRIPTION. The Property for which the Broker's services have been procured to effect a sale is described as follows:

Lot 10, Block 7 of THE PALLADIUM according to the plat thereof, recorded in Plat Book 60, Page 7 of the Public Records of Any County, Any State.

The improvements on said Property contain 2,500 square feet under air. A floor plan of said improvements is set forth in Exhibit A attached to and made a part of this Agreement.

III. PRICE. The listing price of the Property shall be $200,000.00 to be paid on terms acceptable to the Owner.

IV. COMMISSION. In effecting a sale during the term of this Agreement, the Broker shall be entitled to a commission equal to Six (6%) Percent of the Purchase Price of the Property. Should the Property be sold within six months from the expiration date of this Agreement to a person or persons who were in contact with Broker prior to the expiration of this Agreement, Broker shall be entitled to the full commission set forth in this paragraph.

V. BROKER'S ACCESS TO THE PROPERTY. Owner hereby grants Broker and Broker's subagents, together with potential buyers, access to the Property through the installation of a lockbox containing a key to the Property. Broker shall not be held responsible for any loss due to theft, loss or vandalism resulting from any such access, and the Owner shall be solely responsible for obtaining appropriate insurance.

VI. DEPOSITS. Owner authorizes Broker to accept earnest deposits on behalf of Owner and to issue receipts for such deposits.

VII. SIGNAGE. Owner authorizes Broker to place appropriate signage on the Property during the term of this Agreement.

VIII. MULTIPLE LISTING SERVICE. Broker is a member of a local Board of Realtors®. Broker is authorized to disseminate information concerning the Property through a multiple listing service and utilize the assistance of cooperating brokers to effect a sale of the Property.

IX. AGENCY RELATIONSHIP. Broker and Owner hereby acknowledge that an agency relationship is created upon execution of this Agreement and that Broker has the right to inform all prospective buyers of the existence of said agency relationship upon Broker's first contact with the potential buyers.

X. OWNER'S WARRANTIES. Owner represents and warrants that Owner is the owner of record of the Property. Owner further represents and warrants that the

FIGURE 6–3
(continued)

roof is in good repair and that the heating, cooling, plumbing and electrical systems and built-in appliances are in good working condition.

XI. INDEMNIFICATION. Owner agrees to indemnify and hold Broker and all other cooperating brokers harmless against any and all claims, liability, damage or loss arising from any misrepresentation or breach of warranty by Owner in this Agreement. Owner further agrees to indemnify and hold Broker and all other cooperating brokers harmless against any incorrect information supplied by Owner relating to adverse conditions or latent defects.

XII. ATTORNEY'S FEES. In connection with any litigation arising out of this Agreement, the prevailing party shall be entitled to recover reasonable attorney's fees and costs.

XIII. ENTIRE AGREEMENT. This Agreement, including all attached Exhibits, shall constitute the entire agreement between Owner and Broker and supersede any other written or oral agreements between them. This Agreement may be modified only by a writing signed by Owner and Broker.

OWNER: BROKER: ATLANTIS REALTY COMPANY

Grant Daniels   BY: _Carl Andrews_
                                            Representative

directly to the broker who, in turn, may pay a certain portion of the commission to a salesperson.

2. Attorneys and brokers are both professionals who provide valuable services for their clients. A broker's expertise is in the area of marketing properties and negotiating sales. An attorney's expertise is in the area of examining title and drafting the documents necessary to consummate the transaction. Neither the broker nor the attorney should assume responsibility beyond the scope of his or her employment.

3. A broker may be a single agent or a dual agent. Because there is an inherent conflict of interest in dual representation, a broker's role as dual agent must be disclosed to all parties, and the broker must receive their written consent.

4. A broker is a fiduciary and owes his or her principal the duties of care, obedience, loyalty, confidentiality, disclosure, and accounting. A broker is expected to exercise his or her knowledge and skill in the diligent service of his or her principal. A broker must obey all legal instructions of the principal and always act in the principal's best interests. This includes keeping confidences and making full disclosure to the principal of all matters material to the real estate transaction.

5. Brokers may act as escrow agents. Any deposits and advance fees received must not be commingled with other business funds but, rather, must be placed in special accounts. Brokers must make an accounting to their principals regarding the keeping of these accounts and any disbursements made from them.

6. A broker and seller may enter into one of several types of listing agreements. An open listing provides the seller with the most flexibility because

the seller gives no one broker the exclusive right to sell the property. However, this type of listing is least favored by brokers, and therefore, brokers are not likely to expend much time on an open listing. An exclusive listing makes the listing broker the seller's exclusive agent while allowing the seller to retain the right to procure a buyer on his or her own. An exclusive-right-to-sell listing guarantees the listing broker a commission regardless of who procures a buyer as long as a buyer is procured within the listing period.

7. A listing agreement should include, but need not be limited to, the following terms: the names of the parties, the commencement and termination dates of the agreement, a description of the property, a description of the type of listing established, the amount of commission, the listing price of the property, and the rights and responsibilities of the broker.

REVIEW QUESTIONS

1. Distinguish between (a) a real estate broker, (b) a realtor, and (c) a real estate agent.
2. Explain the fiduciary duties owed by a real estate broker to his or her principal.
3. Compare and contrast the following.
   a. A dual agent and a transaction broker
   b. An exclusive listing and an exclusive-right-to-sell listing
4. What are a broker's responsibilities regarding disclosure to (a) parties to the transaction and (b) third parties?
5. What terms should be included in a listing agreement?

ETHICAL QUESTIONS

You have been asked by your supervising attorney to research a matter for a client, Ed Reed. Ed had signed an exclusive-right-to-sell listing agreement for the sale of his home. The listing agreement expires in two months. The real estate bro ker just discovered through independent investigation that ten years prior to the client's purchase of the property, a multiple murder took place on the property. The broker telephoned Ed and informed him of this incident and told him that both he and Ed must disclose this information to all prospective buyers. Ed does not want to reveal this information because he believes it will deter prospects and has asked that state law be researched to determine whether such a disclosure is required. You have found only one case on point in your state. In that court opinion, the bro ker was required to return a deposit to a buyer who executed a contract for sale and purchase and later discovered that three years prior two children had been mur dered in the residence. The court said that not only structural defects, but all facts that might materially affect a buyer's decision to purchase a property must be dis closed and that a murder on the premises is a material fact. You have shown this case to your supervising attorney who, in turn, has just met with Ed and informed him of the legal obligations of both the broker and seller in such a situation.

As Ed is leaving the office, he asks to use a telephone. You usher him into the conference room where there is an available telephone. On your way to the recep tion area to greet another client, you pass by the conference room and overhear Ed telling his wife that he is going to wait two months, not renew the listing agreement, and find a buyer for the property on his own. He further states that he plans not to say a word about the murders on the property to any prospective buyer. What should you do?

Assignment 6:1. Research your state statutes to determine the prerequisites that must be met to become a duly licensed real estate salesperson and real estate broker in your state. Photocopy the relevant statutes and insert them under the "General Information" section of your resource portfolio.

Assignment 6:2. Contact your local or state real estate commission and find out whether special dual agency disclosure and confirmation forms are required to be used by brokers in your state. If so, obtain a copy of the forms and insert them under the "Contracts" section in your resource portfolio.

Assignment 6:3. Research your state statutes to determine the mandatory disclosure requirements in your state. Photocopy the relevant statutes and insert them under the "General Information" section of your resource portfolio.

Assignment 6:4. Contact a local real estate brokerage firm and request a copy of the questionnaire it uses to interview a client as well as copies of any listing agreements it uses. Insert these items under the "Contracts" section of your resource portfolio.

Assignment 6:5. Your supervising attorney has asked you to draft an exclusive-right-to-sell listing agreement for a client, Terra Firma Realty Company. Terra Firma's address is 555 Madison Road (insert your city, county, and state). The broker in the transaction is Paula Hinson. The sellers are Mitchell and Gloria Stewart, who are contracting to sell their home, the legal description of which is:

> Lot 17, Block 11, FOUR LEAF CLOVER ESTATES, 2ND SECTION according to the plat thereof as recorded in Plat Book 32, Page 45 in the Public Records of (insert your county and state).

The residence is 2,200 square feet under air. The property includes a heated swimming pool. The sellers want to sell the house completely furnished and have provided a listing of all fixtures and personal property that will be attached to the agreement as an exhibit. The listing price is $250,000. The commencement date of the agreement is today's date, and the agreement term is eight months. The broker is to receive a commission of seven percent upon producing a ready, willing, and able buyer.

The broker protection clause should allow the broker to receive a commission if the property is sold within four months of the expiration of the agreement to a party who was in contact with the broker. The broker is a member of a multiple listing service. The sellers authorize the broker to receive earnest money deposits on their behalf. The client wants to include a provision in the agreement that states that the sellers agree not to rent the property during the term of the agreement. Further, the client wants the agreement to include a provision that states that if the closing of the sale is prevented by the default of the sellers, the broker is entitled to the full commission, and if the closing of the sale is prevented for any other reason (apart from the fault of the broker), the sellers shall pay the broker one-half of any earnest money deposits as full compensation. Upon completion and review, insert the agreement under the "Contracts" section of your resource portfolio.

Assignment 6:6. Define the following key terms.

accounting	fraudulent misrepresentation
advance fee trust account	listing agreement
agent	multiple listing service
broker	net listing
brokerage	open listing
competitive market analysis	principal
dual agency	real estate agent
earnest money	realtor
escrow account	respondeat superior
exclusive listing	Sherman Act
exclusive-right-to-sell listing	single agency
fiduciary duty	subagent
flat fee sale	transaction broker

Code of Ethics and Standards of Practice of the NATIONAL ASSOCIATION OF REALTORS®

Effective January 1, 1998

Where the word REALTORS® is used in this Code and Preamble, it shall be deemed to include REALTOR-ASSOCIATE®S.

While the Code of Ethics establishes obligations that may be higher than those mandated by law, in any instance where the Code of Ethics and the law conflict, the obligations of the law must take precedence.

Preamble . . .

Under all is the land. Upon its wise utilization and widely allocated ownership depend the survival and growth of free institutions and of our civilization. REALTORS® should recognize that the interests of the nation and its citizens require the highest and best use of the land and the widest distribution of land ownership. They require the creation of adequate housing, the building of functioning cities, the development of productive industries and farms, and the preservation of a healthful environment.

Such interests impose obligations beyond those of ordinary commerce. They impose grave social responsibility and a patriotic duty to which REALTORS® should dedicate themselves, and for which they should be diligent in preparing themselves. REALTORS®, therefore, are zealous to maintain and improve the standards of their calling and share with their fellow REALTORS® a common responsibility for its integrity and honor.

In recognition and appreciation of their obligations to clients, customers, the public, and each other, REALTORS® continuously strive to become and remain informed on issues affecting real estate and, as knowledgeable professionals, they willingly share the fruit of their experience and study with others. They identify and take steps, through enforcement of the Code of Ethics and by assisting appropriate regulatory bodies, to eliminate practices which may damage the public or which might discredit or bring dishonor to the real estate profession.

Realizing that cooperation with other real estate professionals promotes the best interests of those who utilize their services, REALTORS® urge exclusive representation of clients; do not attempt to gain any unfair advantage over their competitors; and they refrain from making unsolicited comments about other practitioners. In instances where their opinion is sought, or where REALTORS® believe that comment is necessary, their opinion is offered in an objective, professional manner, uninfluenced by any personal motivation or potential advantage or gain.

The term REALTOR® has come to connote competency, fairness, and high integrity resulting from adherence to a lofty ideal of moral conduct in business relations. No inducement of profit and no instruction from clients ever can justify departure from this ideal.

In the interpretation of this obligation, REALTORS® can take no safer guide than that which has been handed down through the centuries, embodied in the Golden Rule, "Whatsoever ye would that others should do to you, do ye even so to them."

Accepting this standard as their own, REALTORS® pledge to observe its spirit in all of their activities and to conduct their business in accordance with the tenets set forth below.

Duties to Clients and Customers

Article 1
When representing a buyer, seller, landlord, tenant, or other client as an agent, REALTORS® pledge themselves to protect and promote the interests of their client. This obligation of absolute fidelity to the client's interests is primary, but it does not relieve REALTORS® of their obligation to treat all parties honestly. When serving a buyer, seller, landlord, tenant or other party in a non-agency capacity, REALTORS® remain obligated to treat all parties honestly. (Amended 1/93)

- **Standard of Practice 1-1**
  REALTORS®, when acting as principals in a real estate transaction, remain obligated by the duties imposed by the Code of Ethics. (Amended 1/93)

- **Standard of Practice 1-2**
  The duties the Code of Ethics imposes are applicable whether REALTORS® are acting as agents or in legally recognized non-agency capacities except that any duty imposed exclusively on agents by law or regulation shall not be imposed by this Code of Ethics on REALTORS® acting in non-agency capacities.

  As used in this Code of Ethics, "client" means the person(s) or entity(ies) with whom a REALTOR® or a

FIGURE 6–4 Code of Ethics and Standards of Practice of the National Association of Realtors®

REALTOR®'s firm has an agency or legally recognized non-agency relationship; "customer" means a party to a real estate transaction who receives information, services, or benefits but has no contractual relationship with the REALTOR® or the REALTOR®'s firm; and "agent" means a real estate licensee acting in an agency relationship as defined by state law or regulation. *(Adopted 1/95, Amended 1/98)*

- **Standard of Practice 1-3**
  REALTORS®, in attempting to secure a listing, shall not deliberately mislead the owner as to market value.

- **Standard of Practice 1-4**
  REALTORS®, when seeking to become a buyer/tenant representative, shall not mislead buyers or tenants as to savings or other benefits that might be realized through use of the REALTOR®'s services. *(Amended 1/93)*

- **Standard of Practice 1-5**
  REALTORS® may represent the seller/landlord and buyer/tenant in the same transaction only after full disclosure to and with informed consent of both parties. *(Adopted 1/93)*

- **Standard of Practice 1-6**
  REALTORS® shall submit offers and counter-offers objectively and as quickly as possible. *(Adopted 1/93, Amended 1/95)*

- **Standard of Practice 1-7**
  When acting as listing brokers, REALTORS® shall continue to submit to the seller/landlord all offers and counter-offers until closing or execution of a lease unless the seller/landlord has waived this obligation in writing. REALTORS® shall not be obligated to continue to market the property after an offer has been accepted by the seller/landlord. REALTORS® shall recommend that sellers/landlords obtain the advice of legal counsel prior to acceptance of a subsequent offer except where the acceptance is contingent on the termination of the pre-existing purchase contract or lease. *(Amended 1/93)*

- **Standard of Practice 1-8**
  REALTORS® acting as agents of buyers/tenants shall submit to buyers/tenants all offers and counter-offers until acceptance but have no obligation to continue to show properties to their clients after an offer has been accepted unless otherwise agreed in writing. REALTORS® acting as agents of buyers/tenants shall recommend that buyers/tenants obtain the advice of legal counsel if there is a question as to whether a pre-existing contract has been terminated. *(Adopted 1/93)*

- **Standard of Practice 1-9**
  The obligation of REALTORS® to preserve confidential information provided by their clients continues after the termination of the agency relationship. REALTORS® shall not knowingly, during or following the termination of a professional relationship with their client:
  1) reveal confidential information of the client; or
  2) use confidential information of the client to the disadvantage of the client; or
  3) use confidential information of the client for the REALTOR®'s advantage or the advantage of a third party unless:
     a) the client consents after full disclosure; or
     b) the REALTOR® is required by court order; or
     c) it is the intention of the client to commit a crime and the information is necessary to prevent the crime; or
     d) it is necessary to defend the REALTOR® or the REALTOR®'s employees or associates against an accusation of wrongful conduct. *(Adopted 1/93, Amended 1/97)*

- **Standard of Practice 1-10**
  REALTORS® shall, consistent with the terms and conditions of their property management agreement, competently manage the property of clients with due regard for the rights, responsibilities, benefits, safety and health of tenants and others lawfully on the premises. *(Adopted 1/95)*

- **Standard of Practice 1-11**
  REALTORS® who are employed to maintain or manage a client's property shall exercise due diligence and make reasonable efforts to protect it against reasonably foreseeable contingencies and losses. *(Adopted 1/95)*

- **Standard of Practice 1-12**
  When entering into listing contracts, REALTORS® must advise sellers/landlords of:
  1) the REALTOR®'s general company policies regarding cooperation with subagents, buyer/tenant agents, or both;
  2) the fact that buyer/tenant agents, even if compensated by the listing broker, or by the

FIGURE 6–4 (continued)

seller/landlord will represent the interests of buyers/tenants; and

3) any potential for the listing broker to act as a disclosed dual agent, e.g. buyer/tenant agent. *(Adopted 1/93, Renumbered 1/98)*

- **Standard of Practice 1-13**

  When entering into contracts to represent buyers/tenants, REALTORS® must advise potential clients of:

  1) the REALTOR®'s general company policies regarding cooperation with other firms; and

  2) any potential for the buyer/tenant representative to act as a disclosed dual agent, e.g. listing broker, subagent, landlord's agent, etc. *(Adopted 1/93, Renumbered 1/98)*

Article 2

REALTORS® shall avoid exaggeration, misrepresentation, or concealment of pertinent facts relating to the property or the transaction. REALTORS® shall not, however, be obligated to discover latent defects in the property, to advise on matters outside the scope of their real estate license, or to disclose facts which are confidential under the scope of agency duties owed to their clients. *(Amended 1/93)*

- **Standard of Practice 2-1**

  REALTORS® shall only be obligated to discover and disclose adverse factors reasonably apparent to someone with expertise in those areas required by their real estate licensing authority. Article 2 does not impose upon the REALTOR® the obligation of expertise in other professional or technical disciplines. *(Amended 1/96)*

- **Standard of Practice 2-2**

  (Renumbered as Standard of Practice 1-12 1/98)

- **Standard of Practice 2-3**

  (Renumbered as Standard of Practice 1-13 1/98)

- **Standard of Practice 2-4**

  REALTORS® shall not be parties to the naming of a false consideration in any document, unless it be the naming of an obviously nominal consideration.

- **Standard of Practice 2-5**

  Factors defined as "non-material" by law or regulation or which are expressly referenced in law or regulation as not being subject to disclosure are considered not "pertinent" for purposes of Article 2. *(Adopted 1/93)*

Article 3

REALTORS® shall cooperate with other brokers except when cooperation is not in the client's best interest. The obligation to cooperate does not include the obligation to share commissions, fees, or to otherwise compensate another broker. *(Amended 1/95)*

- **Standard of Practice 3-1**

  REALTORS®, acting as exclusive agents of sellers/landlords, establish the terms and conditions of offers to cooperate. Unless expressly indicated in offers to cooperate, cooperating brokers may not assume that the offer of cooperation includes an offer of compensation. Terms of compensation, if any, shall be ascertained by cooperating brokers before beginning efforts to accept the offer of cooperation. *(Amended 1/94)*

- **Standard of Practice 3-2**

  REALTORS® shall, with respect to offers of compensation to another REALTOR®, timely communicate any change of compensation for cooperative services to the other REALTOR® prior to the time such REALTOR® produces an offer to purchase/lease the property. *(Amended 1/94)*

- **Standard of Practice 3-3**

  Standard of Practice 3-2 does not preclude the listing broker and cooperating broker from entering into an agreement to change cooperative compensation. *(Adopted 1/94)*

- **Standard of Practice 3-4**

  REALTORS®, acting as listing brokers, have an affirmative obligation to disclose the existence of dual or variable rate commission arrangements (i.e., listings where one amount of commission is payable if the listing broker's firm is the procuring cause of sale/lease and a different amount of commission is payable if the sale/lease results through the efforts of the seller/landlord or a cooperating broker). The listing broker shall, as soon as practical, disclose the existence of such arrangements to potential cooperating brokers and shall, in response to inquiries from cooperating brokers, disclose the differential that would result in a cooperative transaction or in a sale/lease that results through the efforts of the seller/landlord. If the cooperating broker is a buyer/tenant representative, the buyer/tenant representative must disclose such information to their client. *(Amended 1/94)*

FIGURE 6–4 (continued)

- **Standard of Practice 3-5**

  It is the obligation of subagents to promptly disclose all pertinent facts to the principal's agent prior to as well as after a purchase or lease agreement is executed. *(Amended 1/93)*

- **Standard of Practice 3-6**

  REALTORS® shall disclose the existence of an accepted offer to any broker seeking cooperation. *(Adopted 5/86)*

- **Standard of Practice 3-7**

  When seeking information from another REALTOR® concerning property under a management or listing agreement, REALTORS® shall disclose their REALTOR® status and whether their interest is personal or on behalf of a client and, if on behalf of a client, their representational status. *(Amended 1/95)*

- **Standard of Practice 3-8**

  REALTORS® shall not misrepresent the availability of access to show or inspect a listed property. *(Amended 11/87)*

Article 4

REALTORS® shall not acquire an interest in or buy or present offers from themselves, any member of their immediate families, their firms or any member thereof, or any entities in which they have any ownership interest, any real property without making their true position known to the owner or the owner's agent. In selling property they own, or in which they have any interest, REALTORS® shall reveal their ownership or interest in writing to the purchaser or the purchaser's representative. *(Amended 1/91)*

- **Standard of Practice 4-1**

  For the protection of all parties, the disclosure required by Article 4 shall be in writing and provided by REALTORS® prior to the signing of any contract. *(Adopted 2/86)*

Article 5

REALTORS® shall not undertake to provide professional services concerning a property or its value where they have a present or contemplated interest unless such interest is specifically disclosed to all affected parties.

Article 6

When acting as agents, REALTORS® shall not accept any commission, rebate, or profit on expenditures made for their principal, without the principal's knowledge and consent. *(Amended 1/92)*

- **Standard of Practice 6-1**

  REALTORS® shall not recommend or suggest to a client or a customer the use of services of another organization or business entity in which they have a direct interest without disclosing such interest at the time of the recommendation or suggestion. *(Amended 5/88)*

- **Standard of Practice 6-2**

  When acting as agents or subagents, REALTORS® shall disclose to a client or customer if there is any financial benefit or fee the REALTOR® or the REALTOR®'s firm may receive as a direct result of having recommended real estate products or services (e.g., homeowner's insurance, warranty programs, mortgage financing, title insurance, etc.) other than real estate referral fees. *(Adopted 5/88)*

Article 7

In a transaction, REALTORS® shall not accept compensation from more than one party, even if permitted by law, without disclosure to all parties and the informed consent of the REALTOR®'s client or clients. *(Amended 1/93)*

Article 8

REALTORS® shall keep in a special account in an appropriate financial institution, separated from their own funds, monies coming into their possession in trust for other persons, such as escrows, trust funds, clients' monies, and other like items.

Article 9

REALTORS®, for the protection of all parties, shall assure whenever possible that agreements shall be in writing, and shall be in clear and understandable language expressing the specific terms, conditions, obligations and commitments of the parties. A copy of each agreement shall be furnished to each party upon their signing or initialing. *(Amended 1/95)*

- **Standard of Practice 9-1**

  For the protection of all parties, REALTORS® shall use reasonable care to ensure that documents pertaining to the purchase, sale, or lease of real estate are kept current through the use of written extensions or amendments. *(Amended 1/93)*

FIGURE 6–4 (continued)

Duties to the Public

Article 10

REALTORS® shall not deny equal professional services to any person for reasons of race, color, religion, sex, handicap, familial status, or national origin. REALTORS® shall not be parties to any plan or agreement to discriminate against a person or persons on the basis of race, color, religion, sex, handicap, familial status, or national origin. *(Amended 1/90)*

- **Standard of Practice 10-1**

  REALTORS® shall not volunteer information regarding the racial, religious or ethnic composition of any neighborhood and shall not engage in any activity which may result in panic selling. REALTORS® shall not print, display or circulate any statement or advertisement with respect to the selling or renting of a property that indicates any preference, limitations or discrimination based on race, color, religion, sex, handicap, familial status or national origin. *(Adopted 1/94)*

Article 11

The services which REALTORS® provide to their clients and customers shall conform to the standards of practice and competence which are reasonably expected in the specific real estate disciplines in which they engage; specifically, residential real estate brokerage, real property management, commercial and industrial real estate brokerage, real estate appraisal, real estate counseling, real estate syndication, real estate auction, and international real estate.

REALTORS® shall not undertake to provide specialized professional services concerning a type of property or service that is outside their field of competence unless they engage the assistance of one who is competent on such types of property or service, or unless the facts are fully disclosed to the client. Any persons engaged to provide such assistance shall be so identified to the client and their contribution to the assignment should be set forth. *(Amended 1/95)*

- **Standard of Practice 11-1**

  The obligations of the Code of Ethics shall be supplemented by and construed in a manner consistent with the Uniform Standards of Professional Appraisal Practice (USPAP) promulgated by the Appraisal Standards Board of the Appraisal Foundation.

  The obligations of the Code of Ethics shall not be supplemented by the USPAP where an opinion or recommendation of price or pricing is provided in pursuit of a listing, to assist a potential purchaser in formulating a purchase offer, or to provide a broker's price opinion, whether for a fee or not. *(Amended 1/96)*

- **Standard of Practice 11-2**

  The obligations of the Code of Ethics in respect of real estate disciplines other than appraisal shall be interpreted and applied in accordance with the standards of competence and practice which clients and the public reasonably require to protect their rights and interests considering the complexity of the transaction, the availability of expert assistance, and, where the REALTOR® is an agent or subagent, the obligations of a fiduciary. *(Adopted 1/95)*

- **Standard of Practice 11-3**

  When REALTORS® provide consultive services to clients which involve advice or counsel for a fee (not a commission), such advice shall be rendered in an objective manner and the fee shall not be contingent on the substance of the advice or counsel given. If brokerage or transaction services are to be provided in addition to consultive services, a separate compensation may be paid with prior agreement between the client and REALTOR®. *(Adopted 1/96)*

Article 12

REALTORS® shall be careful at all times to present a true picture in their advertising and representations to the public. REALTORS® shall also ensure that their professional status (e.g., broker, appraiser, property manager, etc.) or status as REALTORS® is clearly identifiable in any such advertising. *(Amended 1/93)*

- **Standard of Practice 12-1**

  REALTORS® may use the term "free" and similar terms in their advertising and in other representations provided that all terms governing availability of the offered product or service are clearly disclosed at the same time. *(Amended 1/97)*

- **Standard of Practice 12-2**

  REALTORS® may represent their services as "free" or without cost even if they expect to receive compensation from a source other than their client provided that the potential for the REALTOR® to obtain a benefit from a third party is clearly disclosed at the same time. *(Amended 1/97)*

- **Standard of Practice 12-3**

  The offering of premiums, prizes, merchandise discounts or other inducements to list, sell, purchase, or

FIGURE 6–4 (continued)

lease is not, in itself, unethical even if receipt of the benefit is contingent on listing, selling, purchasing, or leasing through the REALTOR® making the offer. However, REALTORS® must exercise care and candor in any such advertising or other public or private representations so that any party interested in receiving or otherwise benefiting from the REALTOR®'s offer will have clear, thorough, advance understanding of all the terms and conditions of the offer. The offering of any inducements to do business is subject to the limitations and restrictions of state law and the ethical obligations established by any applicable Standard of Practice. *(Amended 1/95)*

- **Standard of Practice 12-4**
  REALTORS® shall not offer for sale/lease or advertise property without authority. When acting as listing brokers or as subagents, REALTORS® shall not quote a price different from that agreed upon with the seller/landlord. *(Amended 1/93)*

- **Standard of Practice 12-5**
  REALTORS® shall not advertise nor permit any person employed by or affiliated with them to advertise listed property without disclosing the name of the firm. *(Adopted 11/86)*

- **Standard of Practice 12-6**
  REALTORS®, when advertising unlisted real property for sale/lease in which they have an ownership interest, shall disclose their status as both owners/landlords and as REALTORS® or real estate licensees. *(Amended 1/93)*

- **Standard of Practice 12-7**
  Only REALTORS® who participated in the transaction as the listing broker or cooperating broker (selling broker) may claim to have "sold" the property. Prior to closing, a cooperating broker may post a "sold" sign only with the consent of the listing broker. *(Amended 1/96)*

Article 13
REALTORS® shall not engage in activities that constitute the unauthorized practice of law and shall recommend that legal counsel be obtained when the interest of any party to the transaction requires it.

Article 14
If charged with unethical practice or asked to present evidence or to cooperate in any other way, in any disciplinary proceeding or investigation, REALTORS® shall place all pertinent facts before the proper tribunals of the Member Board or affiliated institute, society, or council in which membership is held and shall take no action or disrupt or obstruct such processes. *(Amended 1/90)*

- **Standard of Practice 14-1**
  REALTORS® shall not be subject to disciplinary proceedings in more than one Board of REALTORS® or affiliated institute, society or council in which they hold membership with respect to alleged violations of the Code of Ethics relating to the same transaction or event. *(Amended 1/95)*

- **Standard of Practice 14-2**
  REALTORS® shall not make any unauthorized disclosure or dissemination of the allegations, findings, or decision developed in connection with an ethics hearing or appeal or in connection with an arbitration hearing or procedural review. *(Amended 1/92)*

- **Standard of Practice 14-3**
  REALTORS® shall not obstruct the Board's investigative or disciplinary proceedings by instituting or threatening to institute actions for libel, slander or defamation against any party to a professional standards proceeding or their witnesses. *(Adopted 11/87)*

- **Standard of Practice 14-4**
  REALTORS® shall not intentionally impede the Board's investigative or disciplinary proceedings by filing multiple ethics complaints based on the same event or transaction. *(Adopted 11/88)*

Duties to REALTORS®

Article 15
REALTORS® shall not knowingly or recklessly make false or misleading statements about competitors, their businesses, or their business practices. *(Amended 1/92)*

Article 16
REALTORS® shall not engage in any practice or take any action inconsistent with the agency or other exclusive relationship recognized by law that other REALTORS® have with clients. *(Amended 1/98)*

- **Standard of Practice 16-1**
  Article 16 is not intended to prohibit aggressive or innovative business practices which are otherwise ethical and does not prohibit disagreements with other REALTORS® involving commission, fees, compensation

FIGURE 6–4 (continued)

or other forms of payment or expenses. *(Adopted 1/93, Amended 1/95)*

- **Standard of Practice 16-2**
  Article 16 does not preclude REALTORS® from making general announcements to prospective clients describing their services and the terms of their availability even though some recipients may have entered into agency agreements or other exclusive relationships with another REALTOR®. A general telephone canvass, general mailing or distribution addressed to all prospective clients in a given geographical area or in a given profession, business, club, or organization, or other classification or group is deemed "general" for purposes of this standard. *(Amended 1/98)*

  Article 16 is intended to recognize as unethical two basic types of solicitations:

  First, telephone or personal solicitations of property owners who have been identified by a real estate sign, multiple listing compilation, or other information service as having exclusively listed their property with another REALTOR®; and

  Second, mail or other forms of written solicitations of prospective clients whose properties are exclusively listed with another REALTOR® when such solicitations are not part of a general mailing but are directed specifically to property owners identified through compilations of current listings, "for sale" or "for rent" signs, or other sources of information required by Article 3 and Multiple Listing Service rules to be made available to other REALTORS® under offers of subagency or cooperation. *(Amended 1/93)*

- **Standard of Practice 16-3**
  Article 16 does not preclude REALTORS® from contacting the client of another broker for the purpose of offering to provide, or entering into a contract to provide, a different type of real estate service unrelated to the type of service currently being provided (e.g., property management as opposed to brokerage). However, information received through a Multiple Listing Service or any other offer of cooperation may not be used to target clients of other REALTORS® to whom such offers to provide services may be made. *(Amended 1/93)*

- **Standard of Practice 16-4**
  REALTORS® shall not solicit a listing which is currently listed exclusively with another broker. However, if the listing broker, when asked by the REALTOR®, refuses to disclose the expiration date and nature of such listing;

i.e., an exclusive right to sell, an exclusive agency, open listing, or other form of contractual agreement between the listing broker and the client, the REALTOR® may contact the owner to secure such information and may discuss the terms upon which the REALTOR® might take a future listing or, alternatively, may take a listing to become effective upon expiration of any existing exclusive listing. *(Amended 1/94)*

- **Standard of Practice 16-5**
  REALTORS® shall not solicit buyer/tenant agreements from buyers/tenants who are subject to exclusive buyer/tenant agreements. However, if asked by a REALTOR®, the broker refuses to disclose the expiration date of the exclusive buyer/tenant agreement, the REALTOR® may contact the buyer/tenant to secure such information and may discuss the terms upon which the REALTOR® might enter into a future buyer/tenant agreement, or, alternatively, may enter into a buyer/tenant agreement to become effective upon the expiration of any existing exclusive buyer/tenant agreement. *(Adopted 1/94, Amended 1/98)*

- **Standard of Practice 16-6**
  When REALTORS® are contacted by the client of another REALTOR® regarding the creation of an exclusive relationship to provide the same type of service, and REALTORS® have not directly or indirectly initiated such discussions, they may discuss the terms upon which they might enter into a future agreement or, alternatively, may enter into an agreement which becomes effective upon expiration of any existing exclusive agreement. *(Amended 1/98)*

- **Standard of Practice 16-7**
  The fact that a client has retained a REALTOR® as an agent or in another exclusive relationship in one or more past transactions does not preclude other REALTORS® from seeking such former client's future business. *(Amended 1/98)*

- **Standard of Practice 16-8**
  The fact that an exclusive agreement has been entered into with a REALTOR® shall not preclude or inhibit any other REALTOR® from entering into a similar agreement after the expiration of the prior agreement. *(Amended 1/98)*

- **Standard of Practice 16-9**
  REALTORS®, prior to entering into an agency agreement or other exclusive relationship, have an affirmative obligation to make reasonable efforts to determine

FIGURE 6–4 (continued)

whether the client is subject to a current, valid exclusive agreement to provide the same type of real estate service. *(Amended 1/98)*

- **Standard of Practice 16-10**
REALTORS®, acting as agents of, or in another relationship with, buyers or tenants, shall disclose that relationship to the seller/landlord's agent or broker at first contact and shall provide written confirmation of that disclosure to the seller/landlord's agent or broker not later than execution of a purchase agreement or lease. *(Amended 1/98)*

- **Standard of Practice 16-11**
On unlisted property, REALTORS® acting as buyer/tenant agents or brokers shall disclose that relationship to the seller/landlord at first contact for that client and shall provide written confirmation of such disclosure to the seller/landlord not later than execution of any purchase or lease agreement.

 REALTORS® shall make any request for anticipated compensation from the seller/landlord at first contact. *(Amended 1/98)*

- **Standard of Practice 16-12**
REALTORS®, acting as agents or brokers of sellers/landlords or as subagents of listing brokers, shall disclose that relationship to buyers/tenants as soon as practicable and shall provide written confirmation of such disclosure to buyers/tenants not later than execution of any purchase or lease agreement. *(Amended 1/98)*

- **Standard of Practice 16-13**
All dealings concerning property exclusively listed, or with buyer/tenants who are subject to an exclusive agreement shall be carried on with the client's agent or broker, and not with the client, except with the consent of the client's agent or broker or except where such dealings are initiated by the client. *(Adopted 1/93, Amended 1/98)*

- **Standard of Practice 16-14**
REALTORS® are free to enter into contractual relationships or to negotiate with sellers/landlords, buyers/tenants or others who are not subject to an exclusive agreement but shall not knowingly obligate them to pay more than one commission except with their informed consent. *(Amended 1/98)*

- **Standard of Practice 16-15**
In cooperative transactions REALTORS® shall compensate cooperating REALTORS® (principal brokers) and shall not compensate nor offer to compensate, directly or indirectly, any of the sales licensees employed by or affiliated with other REALTORS® without the prior express knowledge and consent of the cooperating broker.

- **Standard of Practice 16-16**
REALTORS®, acting as subagents or buyer/tenant agents or brokers, shall not use the terms of an offer to purchase/lease to attempt to modify the listing broker's offer of compensation to subagents or buyer's agents or brokers nor make the submission of an executed offer to purchase/lease contingent on the listing broker's agreement to modify the offer of compensation. *(Amended 1/98)*

- **Standard of Practice 16-17**
REALTORS® acting as subagents or as buyer/tenant agents or brokers, shall not attempt to extend a listing broker's offer of cooperation and/or compensation to other brokers without the consent of the listing broker. *(Amended 1/98)*

- **Standard of Practice 16-18**
REALTORS® shall not use information obtained by them from the listing broker, through offers to cooperate received through Multiple Listing Services or other sources authorized by the listing broker, for the purpose of creating a referral prospect to a third broker, or for creating a buyer/tenant prospect unless such use is authorized by the listing broker. *(Amended 1/93)*

- **Standard of Practice 16-19**
Signs giving notice of property for sale, rent, lease, or exchange shall not be placed on property without consent of the seller/landlord. *(Amended 1/93)*

- **Standard of Practice 16-20**
REALTORS®, prior to or after terminating their relationship with their current firm, shall not induce clients of their current firm to cancel exclusive contractual agreements between the client and that firm. This does not preclude REALTORS® (principals) from establishing agreements with their associated licensees governing assignability of exclusive agreements. *(Adopted 1/98)*

FIGURE 6–4 (continued)

Article 17

In the event of contractual disputes or specific non-contractual disputes as defined in Standard of Practice 17-4 between REALTORS® associated with different firms, arising out of their relationship as REALTORS®, the REALTORS® shall submit the dispute to arbitration in accordance with the regulations of their Board or Boards rather than litigate the matter.

In the event clients of REALTORS® wish to arbitrate contractual disputes arising out of real estate transactions, REALTORS® shall arbitrate those disputes in accordance with the regulations of their Board, provided the clients agree to be bound by the decision. *(Amended 1/97)*

- **Standard of Practice 17-1**
  The filing of litigation and refusal to withdraw from it by REALTORS® in an arbitrable matter constitutes a refusal to arbitrate. *(Adopted 2/86)*

- **Standard of Practice 17-2**
  Article 17 does not require REALTORS® to arbitrate in those circumstances when all parties to the dispute advise the Board in writing that they choose not to arbitrate before the Board. *(Amended 1/93)*

- **Standard of Practice 17-3**
  REALTORS®, when acting solely as principals in a real estate transaction, are not obligated to arbitrate disputes with other REALTORS® absent a specific written agreement to the contrary. *(Adopted 1/96)*

- **Standard of Practice 17-4**
  Specific non-contractual disputes that are subject to arbitration pursuant to Article 17 are:

  1) Where a listing broker has compensated a cooperating broker and another cooperating broker subsequently claims to be the procuring cause of the sale or lease. In such cases the complainant may name the first cooperating broker as respondent and arbitration may proceed without the listing broker being named as a respondent. Alternatively, if the complaint is brought against the listing broker, the listing broker may name the first cooperating broker as a third-party respondent. In either instance the decision of the hearing panel as to procuring cause shall be conclusive with respect to all current or subsequent claims of the parties for compensation arising out of the underlying cooperative transaction. *(Adopted 1/97)*

  2) Where a buyer or tenant representative is compensated by the seller or landlord, and not by the listing broker, and the listing broker, as a result, reduces the commission owed by the seller or landlord and, subsequent to such actions, another cooperating broker claims to be the procuring cause of sale or lease. In such cases the complainant may name the first cooperating broker as respondent and arbitration may proceed without the listing broker being named as a respondent. Alternatively, if the complaint is brought against the listing broker, the listing broker may name the first cooperating broker as a third-party respondent. In either instance the decision of the hearing panel as to procuring cause shall be conclusive with respect to all current or subsequent claims of the parties for compensation arising out of the underlying cooperative transaction. *(Adopted 1/97)*

  3) Where a buyer or tenant representative is compensated by the buyer or tenant and, as a result, the listing broker reduces the commission owed by the seller or landlord and, subsequent to such actions, another cooperating broker claims to be the procuring cause of sale or lease. In such cases the complainant may name the first cooperating broker as respondent and arbitration may proceed without the listing broker being named as a respondent. Alternatively, if the complaint is brought against the listing broker, the listing broker may name the first cooperating broker as a third-party respondent. In either instance the decision of the hearing panel as to procuring cause shall be conclusive with respect to all current or subsequent claims of the parties for compensation arising out of the underlying cooperative transaction. *(Adopted 1/97)*

  4) Where two or more listing brokers claim entitlement to compensation pursuant to open listings with a seller or landlord who agrees to participate in arbitration (or who requests arbitration) and who agrees to be bound by the decision. In cases where one of the listing brokers has been compensated by the seller or landlord, the other listing broker, as complainant, may name the first listing broker as respondent and arbitration may proceed between the brokers. *(Adopted 1/97)*

FIGURE 6–4 (continued)

The Code of Ethics was adopted in 1913. Amended at the Annual Convention in 1924, 1928, 1950, 1951, 1952, 1955, 1956, 1961, 1962, 1974, 1982, 1986, 1987, 1989, 1990, 1991, 1992, 1993, 1994, 1995, 1996 and 1997.

Explanatory Notes

The reader should be aware of the following policies which have been approved by the Board of Directors of the National Association:

In filing a charge of an alleged violation of the Code of Ethics by a REALTOR®, the charge must read as an alleged violation of one or more Articles of the Code. Standards of Practice may be cited in support of the charge.

The Standards of Practice serve to clarify the ethical obligations imposed by the various Articles and supplement, and do not substitute for, the Case Interpretations in *Interpretations of the Code of Ethics.*

Modifications to existing Standards of Practice and additional new Standards of Practice are approved from time to time. Readers are cautioned to ensure that the most recent publications are utilized.

©1998, NATIONAL ASSOCIATION OF REALTORS®, All Rights Reserved

Form No. 166-288 (12/97)

NATIONAL ASSOCIATION OF REALTORS®

430 North Michigan Avenue
Chicago, Illinois 60611

FIGURE 6–4 (continued)

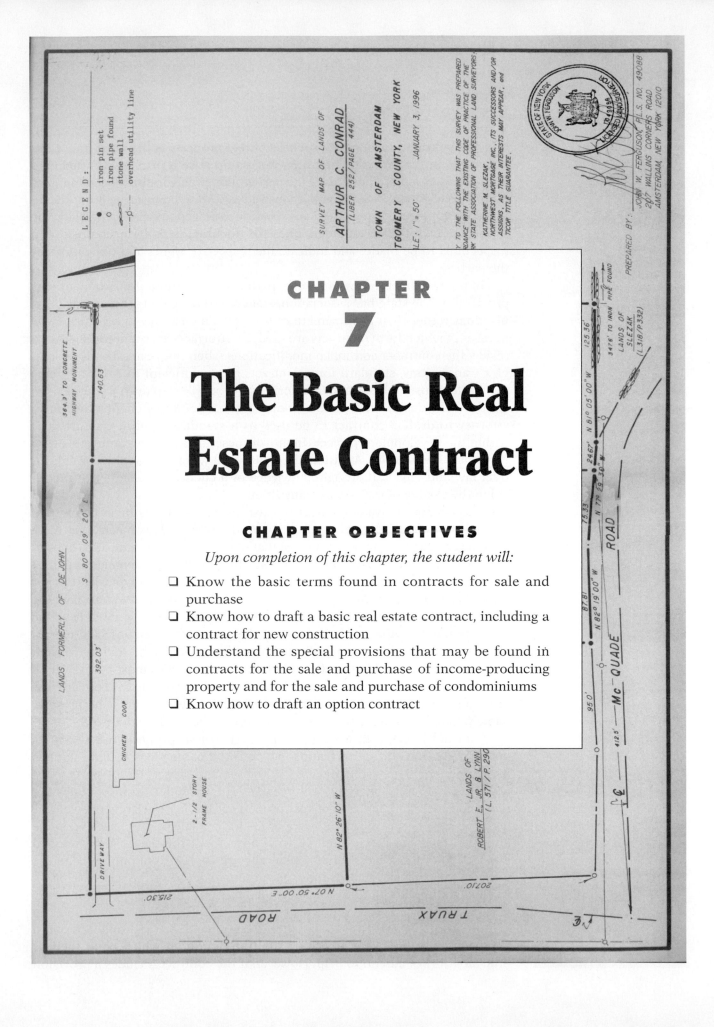

CHAPTER
7

The Basic Real Estate Contract

CHAPTER OBJECTIVES

Upon completion of this chapter, the student will:

❑ Know the basic terms found in contracts for sale and purchase

❑ Know how to draft a basic real estate contract, including a contract for new construction

❑ Understand the special provisions that may be found in contracts for the sale and purchase of income-producing property and for the sale and purchase of condominiums

❑ Know how to draft an option contract

INTRODUCTION

The contract for sale and purchase of real property is the most important document in the real estate closing process because a properly drafted contract serves as a map that guides the parties along the winding and sometimes bumpy road to closing. A comprehensive real estate contract will outline all agreements of the parties, detail any conditions placed upon the closing on the property, set forth various deadlines for documents to be exchanged and inspections to be made, and indicate the respective rights and obligations of the parties.

In many residential transactions, parties turn to standard form contracts provided by the state bar association, state board of realtors, or similar organizations rather than hiring an attorney to draft a customized contract. Even in cases in which form contracts are used, an attorney's assistance is needed to review the contracts and make modifications when necessary. In more complex transactions, standard form contracts are insufficient to cover all items the parties must address, and an attorney may be asked to draft a contract tailored to the transaction at hand. At other times, a developer client may hire an attorney to draft a contract to be used as a standard contract for all sales within the development project. In any of these instances, a paralegal's assistance may be required. Additionally, a paralegal will need to know basic contract law and have a thorough knowledge of a client's real estate contract to aid in the closing of the client's transaction.

In order for any valid contract to exist, certain elements must be present. First, there must be mutual assent between the parties. This means that there must be an offer and an acceptance of that offer. Second, there must be consideration. Consideration is something of value that the parties exchange as part of their bargain. In the case of a real estate contract, this would typically (but not always) be money in exchange for real property. Third, the parties must have the legal capacity to enter into the contract. This means that they must have the requisite mental capacity to understand the agreement. Persons held to lack capacity are minors, those adjudicated mentally incompetent, and intoxicated persons. Finally, the obligation(s) undertaken by the parties must be legal. If all of these elements are present, a valid contract ordinarily exists. There are certain contracts, however, in which an additional element must be present, namely, that the contract be in writing, in order to be legally enforceable.

Contracts for the transfer of an interest in real property are contracts falling under the **statute of frauds,** which is the name given to state statutes indicating which contracts must be in writing and signed by the party to be charged in order to be legally enforceable. The exception in most states are those contracts for the lease of real property if the lease term is one year or less. Parties entering into written contracts for the sale or purchase of a home are often entering into a binding legal agreement for the largest financial transaction of their lives, yet they generally are cognizant of only some of the terms of the contract, such as those pertaining to deposits, the purchase price, financing, and closing date; they become aware of the other provisions only when a problem arises. Often, a client caught up in the excitement of the sale or purchase of property will sign a real estate contract and only afterward approach an attorney for advice on the transaction, at which point there is little an attorney can do to help. However, if the contract includes a provision

statute of frauds: A state statute indicating which contracts must be in writing and signed by the party to be charged in order to be legally enforceable.

THE BASIC REAL ESTATE CONTRACT 175

making the terms of the contract contingent upon an attorney's approval, the attorney may make suggestions for modifications that can then be incorporated into the contract upon agreement by the parties. Should the parties desire to modify a standard form contract, the altered provisions should be crossed out and the new provisions typed in, either in the body of the contract itself or as an attachment. It is advisable to have each party initial the crossed-out provisions as well as the new provisions to evidence that no unilateral changes have been made.

This chapter shall explore the provisions found in most contracts for sale and purchase, whether those contracts are form contracts or contracts negotiated and drafted by the parties and their attorneys. This discussion shall be followed by a look at special types of real estate transactions, such as option contracts and installment contracts, that require particular care in drafting.

COMMON CONTRACTUAL TERMS

The Date

The date of the contract may be found at the beginning or the end of the contract. The date is often referred to as the **effective date,** meaning the date upon which the contract becomes legally binding on all parties. The frequent use of real estate brokers as "middlemen" between buyer and seller often means that sellers and buyers do not come together and sign a contract at the same time. The broker usually presents the prospective buyer with the seller's asking price, and the prospective buyer may accept the offer or make a counteroffer. Any counteroffers are submitted to the seller for acceptance or rejection. When a purchase price is agreed upon, the broker may then ask the prospective buyer to sign a standard contract for sale and purchase that is submitted to the seller for signature. If negotiations are handled in this manner, the effective date is the date upon which the last required party signs the contract.

The effective date is only one of many dates that may appear in a real estate contract. Other dates that may appear include the closing date, the date by which the buyer must obtain financing, the date by which evidence of title must be submitted by the seller to the buyer, the date by which inspections must be made, and so forth. A paralegal reviewing a real estate contract must be cognizant of all of these dates and their significance.

The Parties

The names and status of each party to the contract should be clearly identified. If, for example, the buyer's name is listed as John Winthrop, care must be taken to determine whether John Winthrop is indeed the buyer's proper legal name (for instance, his legal name may be Jonathan Winthrop or Michael Jonathan Winthrop and he prefers to be called John Winthrop), and the buyer's marital status must be determined. If John is a single man, that fact should be designated on the contract. If, on the other hand, John is a married man but is planning to purchase the property in question in his own

effective date: The date upon which a contract becomes legally binding on all parties.

name, his status as a married man should nonetheless be noted because many states require the joinder of a spouse on mortgage documents and closing documents. Further, if the seller is married, regardless of whether title is held jointly or singly, the seller's spouse should be included in the contract and in the signing of all closing documents, including the deed, to indicate the spouse's relinquishment of any contingent rights the spouse legally may have in the sold property. (For a detailed discussion of these contingent rights, see Chapter 2.)

Note that assumptions should not be made about spelling. For example, Frances Sterling may really be Francis Stirling. It is advisable to have the seller's name appear on the contract in precisely the manner in which it appears on the present deed to the property and to have the buyer's name appear on the contract precisely as it is to appear on the new deed transferring title.

If either party is not a natural person (for example, a party is a business entity, such as a corporation or a partnership), a determination must be made as to whether the entity legally exists and if the person signing the contract on behalf of the entity has the authority to do so. Additionally, care must be taken that the signatory's representative capacity be clearly indicated (for example, Marie Ellison, President, when signing on behalf of Ellison Enterprises, Inc.) or else the signatory may be found to be personally responsible for all contractual obligations. The sale or purchase of real property by a corporation typically requires a resolution of the board of directors or the shareholders to authorize the transaction, and a certified copy of this resolution should be obtained.

Property Description

An accurate description of the real property is required. A street address should be supplemented with a legal description of the property. This legal description may be a metes and bounds description, a governmental survey description, or a plat method description, each of which is discussed in detail in Chapter 5. The best way of ensuring that the property description is accurate is to look at the way the property is described on the current deed or title report and copy the description verbatim. Another method is to attach a copy of the survey of the property to the contract as an exhibit. Attachment of a survey may be particularly appropriate in the case of rural property. The fence lines surrounding a parcel of rural property may not be the true boundary lines of the property, and a prospective buyer reading the legal description may assume that the fence lines he or she inspected on the property match the legal description.

Any personal property to be sold together with the real property should be itemized with particularity, as outlined in Chapter 2. Often, standard form contracts provide inadequate space for a detailed listing of all personal property and fixtures. The natural tendency is to try to fit all items into the space provided. The better method is to refer in the contract to an attachment upon which all personal property and fixtures are listed.

Consideration

As noted earlier, every contract must indicate the true consideration to be provided by each party to the contract. In most real estate contracts, the consideration provided by the seller is the real property, and the consideration provided by the buyer is the payment of the negotiated purchase price. The purchase price, exclusive of closing costs, should be indicated, as well as the method of payment of the purchase price. The seller typically requires one or more deposits to be made prior to the closing, and the amount of the deposits will be deducted from the purchase price, the balance to be paid at closing. Although the seller may accept personal checks for the payment of deposits, the seller usually will require that the balance be paid in cash or by certified check or cashier's check. If this is the case, the type of check required should be stated in the real estate contract; otherwise, the buyer may present a personal check at closing, which is unacceptable to the seller, and the seller may then delay closing until the buyer can obtain a certified or cashier's check.

If the purchase price is contingent on any conditions, such as an appraisal of the property by the Federal Housing Administration or the United States Department of Veteran Affairs in the event the buyer is seeking FHA or VA financing, these conditions should be stated, as in the following example.

> The total purchase price (exclusive of prorations and closing costs as set forth in this Agreement) shall be $200,000.00. It is expressly agreed that, notwithstanding any other provisions of this Agreement, the Purchaser shall not incur any penalty by forfeiture of deposit or down payment or otherwise be obligated to complete the purchase of the property described herein, if the purchase price or cost exceeds the reasonable value of the property established by the Department of Veteran Affairs and/or the Federal Housing Administration. The appraised valuation is arrived at to determine the maximum mortgage the Department of Housing and Urban Development will insure. HUD does not warrant the value or the condition of the property. The Purchaser should satisfy himself/herself that the price and condition of the property are acceptable.

Deposits

The seller often will require an initial deposit from the buyer, usually upon execution of the contract. This initial deposit is referred to as an *earnest money deposit*, a deposit that indicates the earnestness of the buyer's intent to purchase the property. In some circumstances, the seller may require additional deposits on specified dates or within a specified time period from the execution of the contract. What happens to these deposits between the time they are paid by the buyer and the date of closing is a matter of state statute or negotiation between the parties. It is common practice for deposits to be held in escrow until the closing. The escrow agent may be an attorney, a bank, a title company, or a real estate broker.

The handling of escrow accounts is strictly regulated by state statute. Recall that monies placed in escrow accounts may not be commingled with other business accounts. An escrow agent need not open an individual account for each earnest money deposit; rather earnest money deposits from several buyers may be placed in a single escrow account. This system requires meticulous recordkeeping by the escrow agent. Statutory law may specify that deposits be placed in interest-bearing or in noninterest-bearing accounts, or the law may leave such decisions to negotiation between the parties.

As previously mentioned, state statutes often require that reports on escrow accounts be made to applicable authorities, such as the state bar association for escrow accounts held by attorneys or the state real estate commission for escrow accounts held by real estate brokers. Additionally, state statutes set forth the procedures to be taken by escrow agents in the event that a dispute arises between the parties to the contract over escrowed monies, including the time period for notification of the appropriate governing authorities and the settlement procedures to be taken. The real estate contract should outline the amount and due date of each deposit, the type of account in which the deposits will be placed, and the name and address of the escrow agent, as in the following provision.

Deposit to be paid upon signing of
this Agreement...$15,000.00
Deposit to be paid within fifteen (15)
days of signing this Agreement...$ 5,000.00
All deposits are to be held in escrow in a noninterest-bearing account with Terra Nova Title Company, 4500 Commercial Avenue, Any City, Any State, and shall be applied in accordance with the terms and conditions of this Agreement.

The Method of Payment

The method of payment provision spells out the method by which the buyer will pay the balance of the purchase price to the seller. The transaction may be a **cash sale** in which the buyer pays cash for the property and does not acquire financing from a lending institution. More often, the buyer will finance the purchase by acquiring a mortgage loan in return for executing a mortgage instrument and note. In this latter instance, the buyer will want the purchase of the property to be contingent upon obtaining loan approval. The seller, on the other hand, will want a strong commitment from the buyer to make diligent efforts to seek loan approval and will want to give a limited time frame within which to obtain it. If the purchase of the property is contingent upon loan approval, the contract should specify this contingency, as well as the type of loan sought and the time frame within which the loan must be approved.

There are four basic financing mechanisms available to the buyer: (1) a new loan from a lending institution, (2) assumption of the seller's existing mortgage, (3) taking the property subject to the seller's existing mortgage, and (4) a purchase money mortgage (for a detailed discussion of mortgages, see Chapter 10). The first financing mechanism is acquiring a new mortgage loan, the most common method of acquiring primary financing, in which the buyer procures a new loan and the seller's existing loan (if any) is paid off in full with the closing proceeds. A buyer will seek out new financing if the current interest rates and other conditions are more favorable than those existing under the terms of the seller's existing mortgage loan. An example of a method-of-payment clause for new financing follows.

If the purchase price or any part of it is to be financed by a third-party loan, this Agreement is conditioned on the Purchaser obtaining a written commitment within sixty (60) days after the Effective Date of this Agreement for a fixed or adjustable rate loan in the principal amount of

cash sale: A sale in which a buyer pays cash for the property and does not acquire financing from a lending institution.

One Hundred Twenty-Five Thousand Dollars ($125,000.00), at an initial interest rate not to exceed eight percent (8%) and a term of thirty (30) years. The Purchaser agrees to use best efforts to make prompt application and to execute diligently and in good faith all necessary papers for the loan set forth above.

If interest rates are currently high, the buyer may, alternatively, seek an **assumption of mortgage** in which the buyer assumes personal responsibility for payment of the seller's existing mortgage loan. Should the buyer default in any mortgage payments under the term of the loan and the lending institution initiate foreclosure on the property, the buyer will be primarily liable for any deficiency judgments. An assumption of mortgage may take place only if the existing mortgage is assumable. If the existing mortgage is assumable, the lending institution's approval will be required before an assumption may take place. The lending institution will most likely undertake a thorough financial investigation of the buyer before giving (or denying) its approval. If the lending institution agrees to the assumption, it may choose to release the seller from all responsibility for the loan, or may choose to make the buyer primarily liable and the seller secondarily liable for the loan.

A **sale subject to existing mortgage** is one in which the buyer becomes responsible for the seller's payments under the existing mortgage, but the seller remains primarily liable under the mortgage note. In this situation, if the buyer defaults in paying the mortgage payments, the lending institution may foreclose on the property (forcing the buyer out) but must seek out the seller for any deficiency judgment, not the buyer. The following is an example of a method-of-payment provision providing for the assumption of, or taking subject to, an existing mortgage loan.

This Agreement is conditioned upon the Purchaser's ability to ____ take title subject to or ____ assume the existing first mortgage loan of record with an approximate balance of One Hundred Twenty-Five Thousand Dollars ($125,000.00), payable over a remaining term of twenty-five years, three months, with a current fixed interest rate of eight percent (8%) per annum. If the Purchaser has agreed to assume a mortgage which requires approval of Purchaser by the Mortgagee for assumption, then Purchaser shall promptly obtain the necessary application and diligently complete it and return it to the Mortgagee. The Purchaser agrees to pay an assumption fee not to exceed two (2) points.

A **purchase money mortgage sale** is one in which the seller finances all or a portion of the purchase price of the property, the buyer executing a mortgage instrument and mortgage note in favor of the seller. A purchase money mortgage may be either a first or a second mortgage. Purchase money mortgages, especially if they are second mortgages, usually are of shorter duration than institutional mortgages. A sample provision for a purchase money mortgage loan as a second mortgage loan follows.

In addition to the third-party loan set forth above, the balance of the Purchase Price shall be financed by the Purchaser executing a note and mortgage in the amount of Fifty Thousand Dollars ($50,000.00) in favor of the Seller secured by the property payable over a term of five (5) years

assumption of mortgage: A situation in which a buyer assumes personal responsibility for payment of the seller's existing mortgage loan.

sale subject to existing mortgage: A situation in which a buyer becomes responsible for the seller's payments under an existing mortgage, but the seller remains primarily liable under the mortgage note.

purchase money mortgage sale: A sale in which the seller finances all or a portion of the purchase price of the property, the buyer executing a mortgage instrument and mortgage note in favor of the seller.

in monthly installments of $833.34, plus interest at a rate of nine percent (9%) per annum from date of closing.

In the case of new construction, in which the seller is a developer or builder who sells a lot and builds a house for the buyer, the seller may require that the purchase price be paid in a series of payments as construction progresses. The amount of each progress payment, together with the corresponding completion stage, should be set forth as exemplified in the following provision.

The balance of the purchase price shall be payable in accordance with the schedule of progress payments set forth below. Each progress payment shall be an amount equal to twenty percent (20%) of the balance of the purchase price and shall be payable as follows:
(A) Completion of floor slab; block walls up; the beam poured..$40,000.00
(B) Roof dry-in; interior partitions completed..$40,000.00
(C) Interior drywall taped and painted; stucco finish coat applied; windows installed..$40,000.00
(D) Cabinets and trim complete; painting finished; driveway finished.....................................$40,000.00
(E) Balance due at closing..$40,000.00

Another possibility in the case of new construction is that the seller obtains a construction loan to finance the construction of the house, and the buyer is made responsible for the balance of the purchase price at closing (said balance to be paid in cash or to be financed by a mortgage loan to the buyer by one of the financing mechanisms discussed earlier). In this instance, the seller may choose to include, under the method-of-payment provision, a statement in which the buyer's rights under the contract are subordinate to the rights of the construction lender. Additionally, the seller may provide that the buyer is responsible for all of the seller's closing costs in connection with the construction loan, such as in the following provision.

Seller may borrow construction money from lenders to construct the improvements on the property. Purchaser agrees that any lender advancing construction funds will have a first mortgage on the property until closing. At that time, Seller may use all closing proceeds to release the property from the lien of the construction mortgage. This Agreement and the deposits paid hereunder will not give Purchaser any lien or claim against the property, and Purchaser's rights hereunder will be subordinate to those of any lender holding a mortgage. At closing, Purchaser shall reimburse Seller any and all costs incurred by Seller in connection with the construction mortgage, as reflected on the loan closing statement.

Quality of Title

The buyer of real property wants to be assured that upon closing, the title to the property is free from all liens, restrictions, and other encumbrances, and will require that any unacceptable encumbrance be removed before title is transferred. As noted in Chapter 4, most real property is encumbered in some manner, and not all encumbrances will be unacceptable. For example, if the property in question is located within a large subdivision, it is likely that the property will be subject to utility easements that create a benefit to the property owner. Additionally, title may be subject to homeowners' association restrictions that exist for the benefit of all property owners within the development.

The prospective buyer must be made aware of these restrictions, but should be advised by his or her attorney of which encumbrances are benign and which are problematic. This typically is done by inspection of an abstract or title commitment by the buyer's attorney (discussed in detail in Chapter 11). Benign encumbrances do not diminish the marketability of title to the property.

The real estate contract should include a provision pertaining to the inspection of title. The provision should set forth the respective parties' responsibilities for obtaining evidence of title, the time period within which inspection of title must be made, the time within which the seller must cure any defects, the respective parties' responsibilities for procurement and payment of title insurance, and the type of deed to be delivered upon closing. A sample title provision is set forth below.

> *It is understood and agreed that title to the property shall be marketable and insurable. At least forty-five (45) days before the closing date, Seller shall, at Seller's expense, deliver to Purchaser or Purchaser's attorney, a title commitment and, after closing, an owner's policy of title insurance. Title shall be conveyed by General Warranty Deed. If at time of closing, Seller's title does not conform to the provisions hereof, Seller shall have ninety (90) days within which to satisfy its obligations hereunder. If, within such ninety-day period, Seller is unable to cure title so that title conforms to the provisions hereof, all deposits shall be refunded to the Purchaser and this Agreement shall be deemed terminated.*

Possession

The real estate contract should indicate the date, or events upon which, the buyer may take possession of the property. Typically the buyer takes possession on the closing date. There may be situations, however, in which the buyer desires to take possession prior to closing. For example, the buyer may have sold his or her home sooner than anticipated and want to move into the new property prior to closing date, or the buyer may wish to begin certain improvements (for example, new cabinetry or flooring) prior to the closing date. The seller, on the other hand, may not want to allow the buyer to move in (or have buyer's subcontractors on the site) and alter or potentially damage the property until the closing funds have cleared. Difficulties are compounded if the buyer takes possession prior to closing, and during the interval between buyer's taking possession and closing, fire or other casualty occurs on the property. An issue may arise as to which party suffers the risk of loss in such a situation. The possession provision should address such concerns, as does the provision that follows.

Seller shall deliver exclusive possession to Purchaser upon closing and clearance of all funds due Seller. Should the parties, subsequent to the signing of this Agreement, agree in writing that Purchaser be allowed to take occupancy prior to the closing date, it is hereby agreed by Purchaser that Purchaser assumes all risk of loss to property from date of occupancy, shall be responsible and liable for maintenance from that date, and shall be deemed to have accepted property in its existing condition as of time of taking occupancy.

Inspections and Warranties

Prior to the signing of the real estate contract, the seller and/or seller's real estate broker will have made full disclosure, as required by law, of all known defects on the property. Nonetheless, the buyer may be allowed to make inspection of the premises prior to closing, and the seller may be required to repair any defects revealed by these inspections. The most important inspections are roof and termite inspections, but other inspections may also be provided for. The seller will want a time limit within which the inspections must take place and adequate time within which to make any warranted repairs, and will want to make only those repairs considered "reasonable" and not be obligated to incur repair expenses exceeding a specified cost. Both the buyer and the seller will want to be able to cancel the contract without liability should the inspections show defects in the property. Further, the buyer will want the seller to warrant that full disclosure has been made to the buyer.

If the property in question is new construction, the buyer will want the seller to warranty the construction and the improvements, including all appliances and fixtures placed on the property. With regard to new construction built after November 30, 1979, the Federal Trade Commission has mandated in the *Federal Register*, sections 460.1 through 460.24, that builders include in the sales contract information pertaining to the type of insulation used in the home, its thickness, and its resulting R-value.

State statutes may require that other disclosure provisions be included as a matter of course, such as those pertaining to radon gas, special flood hazards, or hazardous waste. A combined inspection and warranty provision follows.

Seller warrants that all heating, cooling, electrical, and plumbing systems are in good working condition as of date of closing. The Purchaser may, within the time period allowed for delivery of evidence of title and examination thereof, have, at Purchaser's expense, roof and termite inspections conducted on the property. If, as a result of said inspections, repairs are deemed necessary, Seller agrees to pay up to three percent (3%) of the purchase price for said repairs, repairs to be undertaken by contractors duly licensed under the laws of the State of Any State.

Closing Time and Place

The real estate contract should specify the date, time, and location of the closing. In the case of new construction, the developer/builder will desire an estimated closing date and will want inclusion of a statement in this provision that the seller does not guarantee closing by the specified date. It is common in many real estate contracts to find a statement that "time is of the essence." This statement implies that a party delaying closing is in breach of contract. The inclusion of a "time is of the essence" statement, however, does not conclusively mean that time is of the essence.

Should a dispute arise, courts may look at several factors to determine whether a delay results in breach, including the reasonableness of the date set for performance. Additionally, courts may look at circumstances behind the transaction. For example, a union strike may have delayed construction materials or services due to no fault of the seller, or a bank may be undergoing a merger that delays the approval of the buyer's loan. Nonetheless, if time is indeed of the essence, a clause to this effect should be included in the contract, such as the provision that follows.

Closing shall be held on August 10, 1997 at 2:00 p.m. at the offices of Terra Nova Title Company. Both parties hereby acknowledge that time is of the essence of this Agreement and that delay in closing by either party shall be deemed a default under this Agreement.

Closing Documents

This provision sets forth each party's responsibility for producing certain documents at the closing. Although the parties themselves may find this provision less important than many of the others already discussed, the absence of such a provision, or ambiguous drafting of such a provision, can cause confusion and delays with the closing. A paralegal preparing or reviewing a real estate contract will want to pay special attention to this provision because it is the paralegal's responsibility to keep track of all documents that are necessary for the client's transaction, the persons responsible for preparation or obtaining of each document, and the dates of receipt of each document. A sample provision follows.

Seller shall furnish the deed, bill of sale, no-lien affidavit, mortgage estoppel letters and corrective instruments. Purchaser shall furnish the closing statement, mortgage, mortgage note, security agreement, and financing statements.

Broker's Fee

Although the person procuring a real estate broker will often sign a separate contract with the broker regarding payment of any broker's fee, some contracts include a provision pertaining to the payment of brokers' fees. These provisions should be drafted carefully and should include a statement regarding each party's obligation for payment of the broker fee should either the seller or buyer default. For example, the buyer may be obligated to forfeit all or a portion of the deposit as payment to the broker should the buyer fail to perform under the terms of the contract, and seller may be obligated to pay the broker the full commission earned should the seller fail to perform under the terms of the contract. A sample provision follows.

The parties agree that the broker named below is the procuring cause of the sale of the property. Seller agrees to pay, at time of closing, from the proceeds of the sale, the broker's commission set forth in the listing agreement between Seller and broker for broker's services in finding a Purchaser ready, willing, and able to purchase the property in accordance with the terms of this Agreement. In the event Purchaser defaults, it is agreed that Seller shall not be obligated to pay the commission and that the Purchaser shall be obligated to pay said commission to the broker. In the event the Seller defaults, the Seller shall pay said commission to broker on demand.

Closing Costs and Apportionments

Each party will be responsible for certain expenses relating to the transfer of the property. Certain expenses may be assigned to individual parties, while other expenses may be shared. These expenses are commonly referred to as *closing costs*. Closing costs can include, but are not limited to, such items as appraisal fees, attorneys' fees, title fees, recording fees, documentary stamps, and prorations.

Prorations are charges that are apportioned between the parties. For example, if the buyer is taking title to the property on June 1st, it is not fair for either the buyer or the seller to pay the entire tax bill for the year. Therefore, the amount of the tax bill each party must pay will be prorated. Other prorations include hazard and flood insurance, rents (for income-producing property), maintenance fees to condominium or homeowners' associations, and mortgage interest on loans that are taken subject to the existing mortgage or assumed. (Prorations are discussed in detail in Chapter 12.)

A closing cost provision is set forth below.

Seller shall pay the cost of recording the deed, documentary stamps affixed to the deed, and the cost of furnishing to the Purchaser an owner's policy of title insurance. Purchaser shall pay for all inspections and shall pay all loan fees, loan closing costs and all other related sums, including but not limited to escrows for taxes and insurance, recording fees, documentary stamps, intangible tax, and credit report. Each party shall be responsible for their respective attorneys' fees. In addition, taxes, insurance, and homeowners' association dues shall be prorated as of date of closing.

Risk of Loss

The risk of loss provision indicates which party bears the risk of loss should the property be damaged by fire or other casualty prior to closing. State statute may govern this provision. If state statutory law is silent on the matter, then the matter may be negotiated by the parties. Often the risk of loss is borne by the party in possession of the property at the time the loss occurred. A risk of loss provision may provide the seller with an option to restore the property and, if the seller fails to do so, allow the buyer to choose between terminating the contract or accepting the property as is and receiving any insurance proceeds paid out. Alternatively, the risk of loss provision may provide that the buyer is obligated under the contract if the damage to the property does not exceed a specified amount and that the purchase price will be adjusted accordingly or that the purchase price shall remain the same but

prorations: Charges that are apportioned between the parties.

the buyer shall receive applicable insurance proceeds. Another option is to allow the seller a specified time period within which to restore the premises to its original condition, such as in the following provision.

> *If the improvements are damaged by fire or other casualty, the Seller shall have the option of canceling this Agreement and returning all deposits to the Purchaser or, if the Seller so chooses, to extend the date of closing for a period not to exceed ninety (90) days and restore the property to substantially its original condition.*

Contract Assignability

If for some reason the buyer cannot perform under the contract, he or she will want the option of assigning his or her obligations under the real estate contract. The seller, however, may be concerned that the buyer will assign the contract to an unqualified individual or undercapitalized corporation to avoid personal liability. In some states, the matter of assignment may be dictated by statute with the statutory presumption that the contract is assignable unless the contract provides otherwise. A concerned seller may, if statutorily permissible, forbid assignment, or may make assignment contingent upon the seller's written consent, such as in the sample provision set forth below.

> *The Purchaser shall not assign this Agreement or any right, interest or obligation hereunder without the prior written consent of the Seller.*

Default and Remedies

If the buyer defaults, the buyer wants to risk as little as possible. The buyer will want to risk only the deposits paid to the seller prior to the default and will want to prevent the seller from bringing suit to recover damages or specific performance of the buyer's obligations under the contract. Conversely, the seller will want to have the election of as many options as possible should the buyer default. The seller will want the options of either retaining the deposits or bringing suit for damages (in which event the measure of damages usually is the difference between the purchase price under the contract and the amount the seller received from the sale of the property) or suit for specific performance (in which the seller asks the court to specifically enforce the contract and make the buyer pay the purchase price under the contract).

If the seller defaults, the seller wants to limit his or her damages to the return of any deposits. The buyer, on the other hand, wants the option of accepting the return of the deposits and payment of all expenses incurred by the buyer up to the date of default, or bringing suit against the seller for specific performance. A sample default and remedies provision follows.

> *If the Purchaser defaults under the terms of this Agreement, the Seller shall be entitled to retain all deposits paid as liquidated damages, and the Seller shall have no other recourse against the Purchaser. If the Seller defaults under the terms of this Agreement, the Purchaser shall be entitled to the return of all deposits paid as liquidated damages, and the Purchaser shall have no other recourse against the Seller.*

Attorneys' Fees

Under common law, no party to a contract is entitled to attorneys' fees unless the contract so provides. Real estate contracts usually provide either that the prevailing party in litigation shall be entitled to recovery of attorneys' fees and costs from the losing party or, alternatively, that each party shall be responsible for his or her own attorneys' fees. Sometimes a dispute arises that requires intervention of legal counsel but is settled before litigation occurs. In such an event, the party hiring counsel to settle the dispute will want the other party to pay his or her legal fees. A clause such as the following covers both litigation and prelitigation matters.

In the event the Purchaser needs to consult with legal counsel or resort to litigation (including any appellate proceedings) to enforce the terms of this Agreement, then the Purchaser shall be entitled to recover reasonable attorneys' fees and costs. In the event the Seller needs to consult with legal counsel or resort to litigation (including any appellate proceedings) to enforce the terms of this Agreement, then the Seller shall be entitled to recover reasonable attorneys' fees and costs.

Special Provisions

Income-Producing Property. In addition to the basic provisions discussed so far, the parties to a real estate contract may have special needs that must be addressed in the contract. The buyer of income-producing property, for example, will require clauses pertaining to inspection of the seller's books and records regarding the operating costs incurred and income produced by the property. The buyer also will want to examine current and pending lease agreements and will require estoppel certificates from all tenants verifying the terms and status of their leases (discussed in detail in Chapter 14) and an assignment of all lease rights. Sample provisions addressing these concerns are set forth below.

__Inspection of Books and Records.__ This Agreement is conditioned upon the Purchaser's inspection and approval of the Seller's books, records and tax returns pertaining to the subject property. Within ten (10) days from the execution of this Agreement, Seller shall deliver to Purchaser or to Purchaser's named accountant for approval, originals or conformed copies of all books, records, and tax returns pertaining to the subject property. Seller warrants that all books and records to be inspected by Purchaser are maintained by the Seller in the ordinary course of business. If the Purchaser does not, with fifteen (15) days of receipt of said books and records, indicate in writing Purchaser's disapproval of the information contained in said books and records, Purchaser shall be deemed to have waived this condition.

__Estoppel Certificates.__ Prior to closing, the Seller shall provide the Purchaser with estoppel certificates from all current tenants. Said certificates shall set forth the name of the tenant, a description of the leased premises, the term of the rental agreement, the total amount owed under the terms of the rental agreement, the amount of any deposits and *advance rents paid, any delinquent payments, and any claims the tenant may have against the Seller.*

Contract Subject to Sale of Other Property. Often a buyer must sell his or her current home in order to afford a new one. The buyer will want to make his or her obligations under the real estate contract contingent upon the buyer's sale of the current residence. The seller usually will be reluctant to tie up the property until the buyer sells the current residence. Therefore, if the seller agrees to the condition, the seller will want the inclusion of an "escape clause" allowing the seller to terminate the contract if the seller receives a bona fide offer from another party, such as the clause included in the following provision.

> *This Agreement is conditioned upon the sale by the Purchaser of the Purchaser's real property located at 125 Jasmine Lane, Any City, Any State, provided, however, that should Seller receive another offer in writing acceptable to Seller, the Purchaser shall have ten (10) days from written notice by Seller to remove this contingency. If the Purchaser fails to remove this contingency within the stated time period, this Agreement shall be terminated and all deposits paid to date shall be returned to the Purchaser.*

Condominiums. If the property in question is a condominium, the buyer will want an opportunity to inspect the condominium documents before committing to the purchase of the property. In some states, statutory law dictates a specified period within which the buyer may cancel a real estate contract after inspection of these documents. Further, the buyer's obligations under the contract may be contingent upon approval of the buyer by the condominium association. If so, a provision stating this condition should be included. Set forth below are sample provisions covering these areas.

> **Cancellation by Purchaser.** *This Agreement is voidable by Purchaser by delivering written notice of the Purchaser's intention to cancel within fifteen (15) days after the date of execution of this Agreement by the Purchaser and receipt by Purchaser of all condominium documents. In the event the Purchaser voids this Agreement, s/he must return all condominium documents furnished by Seller.*

> **Association Approval.** *This Agreement is contingent upon approval of the Purchaser by the condominium association. The Purchaser shall make application for approval within ten (10) days of execution of this Agreement. Any association fees charged in connection with approval shall be paid by the Purchaser.*

Vacant Land. A buyer may purchase a parcel of vacant land with the objective of building a particular project. The buyer will want the contract to be contingent on zoning permitting the building of the proposed project. Further, the buyer will want the contract to be contingent upon the land's physical suitability for the proposed project and may require satisfactory engineering reports as a condition of the purchase. A provision combining these contingencies is set forth below.

Conditions of Sale. This Agreement is contingent upon zoning permitting the construction of an industrial park. Further, this Agreement is contingent upon receipt of engineering reports on the subject property satisfactory to Purchaser's designated contractor.

From the discussion thus far, it is apparent that a paralegal assigned to draft a real estate contract must employ the aid of a comprehensive checklist or worksheet to ensure that all requisite provisions are included. Such a checklist or worksheet can also aid a paralegal in reviewing a prepared contract. A sample completed worksheet can be found in the Hypothetical Client Matter at the end of the chapter.

SPECIAL TYPES OF REAL ESTATE CONTRACTS

Installment Contracts

Traditionally, an **installment contract** was one in which the buyer made a down payment and the balance of the purchase price was payable in monthly installments over a period of years. At closing, the buyer received possession of the property and became responsible for the payment of real property taxes and all other expenses associated with real property ownership, but the seller retained legal title to the property. This method of sale was sometimes referred to as a *contract for deed* because the buyer received the deed to the property either when all installments had been paid or when the unpaid balance had been reduced to a previously agreed upon figure. In the latter instance, when the specified figure had been reached and the buyer had built up a certain percentage of equity in the property, the seller would transfer the deed to the buyer who, in turn, would provide the seller with a purchase money mortgage and note covering the balance of the purchase price.

This situation worked well for the buyer who had little money to put down as a down payment and/or had trouble with financing. The seller obtained favorable tax treatment by being able to spread the gain and the income tax on the gain over the period of time in which the payments were being made by the buyer. In order to obtain this favorable tax treatment, however, the sale had to comply with the federal tax laws governing installment sales that allowed installment sale treatment of gains only if thirty percent or less of the purchase price was received by the seller in the year of the sale.

Changes occurred in 1980 with the implementation of the federal Installment Sales Revision Act of 1980, which deleted the thirty-percent-down rule and now treats all sales as installment sales (unless the seller elects otherwise) if at least one payment under the contract is made after the close of the taxable year of sale. Under the act, the seller pays tax in any taxable year on the gain received in that year. This means that installment sales contracts can now be structured with as many or as few payments as the parties negotiate between themselves as long as there is at least a single deferred payment after the year of sale. Note that some states have statutes governing installment contracts, and these statutes should be researched thoroughly before drafting an installment contract.

installment contract: A contract in which at least one payment under the contract is made after the close of the taxable year of sale.

Option Contracts

An **option contract** is one in which the seller *(optionor)* gives a potential buyer *(optionee)* the exclusive right within a specified, limited time period to purchase real property. The potential buyer pays the seller for this exclusive right. The money that the potential buyer pays is not considered a deposit because the buyer is not committing himself or herself to the purchase of the property. The potential buyer is paying for time within which to decide whether or not to purchase the property. The consideration paid by the potential buyer is irrevocable. The parties may agree that if the option is exercised, the consideration paid under the option will be applied toward the purchase price of the property. If the seller accepts another offer within the specified time period, then the seller is in breach of the option contract.

Although option contracts can be used in many situations, they are most often used in land development transactions (for example, where the developer is working on getting additional investors) and in transactions in which the potential buyer is looking at the property as an investment and is speculating on the increase in value of the property without committing to the purchase of the property (for example, the outcome of a voting referendum on gambling for a potential hotel/casino site or a vote on highway expansion bringing larger populations to the site).

The use of an option contract is a relatively safe way to speculate with real property because the purchase price and terms for the contract of sale are all negotiated and made a part of the option contract. If the potential buyer exercises the option, he or she has "locked in" the purchase price and other terms at the originally negotiated price, regardless of the increase in value of the property. If the value does not increase as the potential buyer anticipated, then he or she has forfeited only the money paid for the option and can walk away from the deal. A checklist for an option contract is provided below, and a sample option contract is shown in Figure 7–1.

OPTION CONTRACT CHECKLIST

1. *The effective date*
2. *The legal names and addresses of the parties*
3. *Property description*
4. *The consideration paid for the option and the method of payment*
5. *The time period of the option, with commencement and termination dates*
6. *Extension of the option period, if any, and the consideration to be paid for the extension*
7. *Whether or not the consideration paid for the option is to be applied to the purchase price*
8. *Manner in which the option is to be exercised*
9. *Purchase price and terms of payment*
10. *Right of entry by optionee on the option property to conduct tests, inspections, and surveys*
11. *Optionor's warranty not to encumber the property during the option period*
12. *Risk of loss during the option period (if there are improvements on the real property)*

option contract: A contract in which the seller gives a potential buyer the exclusive right, within a specified limited time period, to purchase real property. The potential buyer pays the seller for this exclusive right.

13.   *Assignability of the option*
14.   *Date of closing upon exercise of option*
15.   *Other applicable basic contract provisions (for example, title, method of payment, prorations)*

FIGURE 7–1
Option contract for
purchase of real property

OPTION CONTRACT FOR PURCHASE OF REAL PROPERTY

THIS AGREEMENT is made and entered into this 10th day of August, 1997 by and between PBD Properties, Inc., an Any State corporation having its principal office at 446 S.W. 10th Avenue, Suite 112, Any City, Any State (hereinafter referred to as "Optionor"), and Shangri-La Land Investments Corp., an Any State corporation having its principal office at 800 Revere Road, Suite 405, Any City, Any State (hereinafter referred to as "Optionee").

I. OPTION PERIOD AND CONSIDERATION. The Optionee hereby agrees to pay to the Optionor the sum of Fifty Thousand Dollars ($50,000.00) evidenced by personal check, receipt of which is hereby acknowledged, for an option to purchase the real property described below, the option period beginning August 10, 1997 and terminating at midnight on October 9, 1997.

II. EXTENSION OF OPTION. Optionor agrees to grant the Optionee the right to extend the original option period set forth above to midnight on November 9, 1997, upon payment by the Optionee of the sum of Twenty Thousand Dollars ($20,000.00) before the expiration of the original option period.

III. PROPERTY DESCRIPTION. The Optionor agrees, upon proper exercise of the option by the Optionee, to sell to the Optionee the real property described as:

SW 1/4 of the NE 1/4 of the SW 1/4, Sec 4, T32S, R23E, Any County, Any State

IV. CREDIT OF OPTION PAYMENT. Upon proper exercise of the option, the total consideration paid for the option (including the consideration paid for any extension of the option period) shall be applied to the purchase price.

V. PURCHASE PRICE AND METHOD OF PAYMENT. Upon proper exercise of the option by the Optionee, the Optionor agrees to sell the above-described property for the purchase price of Two Million Dollars ($2,000,000.00). The Optionee agrees to use best efforts to secure a Mortgage Loan in the principal amount of One Million Four Hundred Thousand Dollars ($1,400,000.00). Purchase of the property is contingent upon loan approval within ninety (90) days from the exercise of the option by the Optionee, otherwise either party may terminate the Agreement. Should the Agreement be terminated due to failure of the Optionee to secure financing, the Optionor shall retain the total consideration paid by the Optionee for the option period (including any extensions thereof).

VI. OPTIONOR'S WARRANTY. The Optionor hereby agrees not to encumber the above-described property in any manner nor grant any contractual or other property rights in the above-described property during the option period.

VII. RIGHT OF ENTRY. During the option period or any extension thereof, the Optionee shall have the right to enter upon the above-described property for the purpose of conducting a survey of said property and to conduct engineering tests. The costs of the survey and the engineering tests shall be borne by the Optionee.

VIII. EXERCISE OF OPTION. The Optionee may exercise this option by delivering notice of said exercise of option to the Optionor during the option period (or any permitted extensions thereof). Notice shall be in writing addressed to the Optionor at the address set forth in this Agreement and shall be (i) hand delivered, (ii) sent

FIGURE 7–1
(continued)

by certified or registered mail, postage prepaid, return receipt requested, (iii) sent by Federal Express or similar overnight courier service, or (iv) by telecopy. Notice shall be deemed given when received by the Optionor.

IX. FAILURE TO EXERCISE OPTION. If the Optionee fails to exercise this option in accordance with its terms and within the option period (including any extensions thereof), then this option shall automatically terminate, and Optionor shall retain all consideration paid by the Optionee for the option period (including any extensions thereof).

X. CLOSING DATE. Upon proper exercise of this option, the parties agree that the closing shall take place within thirty (30) days from the date the Optionee receives loan approval.

XI. TITLE. The Optionor shall deliver to the Optionee at the Optionor's expense a preliminary title report within twenty (20) days from the proper exercise of the option and shall deliver, at Optionor's expense, a standard owner's title policy upon closing. The parties agree that title is to be free of liens, easements, and restrictions other than: (i) current property taxes and (ii) covenants, conditions, restrictions, and public utility easements of record, if any. Title shall be transferred upon closing by General Warranty Deed.

XII. CLOSING COSTS, PRORATIONS, AND CLOSING DOCUMENTS. The Optionor shall pay for documentary stamps and recording of deed and recording of corrective instruments. The Optionee shall pay for documentary stamps and any intangible tax on mortgage and all costs associated with the closing of the mortgage loan. The Optionor shall provide, at closing, the General Warranty Deed, no-lien affidavit, mortgage estoppel letter, and corrective instruments. The Optionee shall provide, at closing, the closing statement, mortgage, mortgage note, security agreement and financing statements.

XIII. BROKER'S FEE. Upon execution of this option, the Optionor agrees to pay to Broker the amount agreed upon in the broker's agreement, a copy of which is attached as an exhibit to this Agreement. In the event the Optionee exercises the option, then the Broker shall receive from the Optionor the additional sum indicated in the broker's agreement.

XIV. ASSIGNABILITY. This option is not assignable by Optionee.

XV. ATTORNEYS' FEES. In any action between Optionor and Optionee arising out of this Agreement, the prevailing party shall be entitled to reasonable attorneys' fees and costs.

IN WITNESS WHEREOF, the parties have hereunto set their hands and seals the day and the year first above written.

Signed, Sealed and Delivered
in the presence of:

OPTIONOR: PBD PROPERTIES, INC.,
an Any State corporation

_____

BY: _____
    Paul Davidson, President

_____

OPTIONEE: SHANGRI-LA LAND
INVESTMENTS CORP.,
an Any State corporation

_____

BY: _____
    Kenneth Colby, President

HYPOTHETICAL CLIENT MATTER

Barbara Hammond is a real estate paralegal who has worked for the law firm of Fisher, Ross, and Simon, P.A. for the past three years. Barbara works most closely with attorney Ava Ross, and over the years, Ava, impressed with Barbara's competency, has provided Barbara with the opportunity to assist in a variety of real estate–related matters. This morning Ava asked Barbara to sit in on a meeting with a client.

The client is a real estate development company, Lyndale Properties, Inc., headed by its president, Craig Newfield. Approximately six months ago, Craig's company purchased a tract of land within a subdivision for the purpose of building a luxury single-family community called Orange Walk Estates. Ava assisted Craig with the closing on the property, as well as with other real estate matters. Orange Walk Estates will be offering prospective purchasers five model homes from which to choose. Construction on the first two models has already begun, and Craig's company is in the process of installing a trailer to be used as a temporary sales office on the property.

Craig has asked to meet with Ava to discuss the drafting of a real estate contract that his company can use in negotiations with prospective purchasers. The standard form real estate contract approved by the state bar association and the state association of realtors does not meet the particular needs of parties negotiating a contract for new construction.

The prospective purchaser of a home in Orange Walk Estates must select a lot within the subdivision tract upon which the home will be built. A lot deposit reservation will be required to secure the lot prior to the signing of a sale and purchase contract. The purchaser must then pick one of the models offered. Each model will have a base purchase price, and numerous optional extras will be made available to the prospective purchaser, the cost of each extra to be added to the base price. The prospective purchaser will be given certain choices in color selection of cabinets, countertops, appliances, carpeting, and similar items. Some of these decisions will be made by the prospective purchaser at the time of contracting. Should the purchaser change his or her mind about selections or wish to add other extras not specifically listed in the contract, Craig requires that all change orders and requests for additional extras be made in writing and that payment for them be made at the time they are ordered. Further, Craig requires final decisions to be made within a certain period of time and wants a contract that will allow the developer to make choice selections for the purchaser if the purchaser does not reply within that time frame.

Some purchasers may not like the selections offered and may choose to install their own flooring, appliances, or other fixtures and receive a "credit" for the items not selected. The credit amount will be deducted from the purchase price. If this is done, however, Craig wants to prevent the purchaser from bringing his or her own subcontractors to the construction site to begin the installation of fixtures or make other improvements to the property until after the closing.

Because each home in Orange Walk Estates will be built as deposits are received and contracts signed, Craig does not want to guarantee a closing date, only to find his company in breach of contract if construction is not completed by that date. Instead, he suggests that the contract provide an estimated closing date but allow some leeway if that date needs to be adjusted. Also, as an experienced builder and developer, Craig realizes that certain modifications may need to be made from the original plans as work progresses. For example, building code specifications may change or a particular material may no longer be available. Craig wants to be able to make such modifications without first obtaining the purchaser's approval. Further, if such modifications are required by a governmental authority and increase the costs of construction, Craig wants the increased costs to be paid by the purchaser.

It is customary in the building industry in Any State for builders to provide a one-year warranty on new construction and to present the purchaser with a builder's warranty at the closing. Such a warranty usually provides that the builder has completed the construction in substantial conformity with the approved plans and specifications. In addition, most sellers (builders included) provide a no-lien affidavit at closing, stating under oath that no liens have been placed on the property within a specified time period other than those listed in the affidavit, or else that those liens placed on the property have been paid off and removed. This document is of great importance to the purchaser, especially in the matter of new construction inasmuch as numerous subcontractors have provided services or materials to the property. Craig will provide both a builder's warranty and a no-lien affidavit at the closing. Apart from providing a general warranty deed upon closing, however, Craig does not want to provide evidence of title or title policies to purchasers unless these items are specifically requested, and then only at the purchasers' expense.

The majority of prospective purchasers will be financing the purchase of their homes. To prevent a lengthy tie-up of a particular lot, Craig wants to give the purchasers a time limit within which they must secure financing. Further, even if a married person is purchasing a home in his or her name only, Craig knows that most lenders require the signatures of spouses on mortgage instruments. Craig wants a financing provision that requires the signatures of spouses on all mortgages and other closing documents.

All deposits are to be kept in a noninterest-bearing escrow account Craig has set up with Patriot Bank. Should his company default under the contract, Craig wants to limit the purchasers' remedies to the return of deposits. Conversely, should the purchasers default, Craig wants the option of retaining the deposits or litigating the matter.

These matters and several others are discussed at length between Craig and Ava, after which Ava suggests that Barbara escort Craig to the conference room to complete a worksheet in which these and other contractual provisions will be detailed. Craig plans on beginning a large advertising campaign for Orange Walk Estates in two weeks and, therefore, would like to review the drafted contract as soon as possible. Upon completion of her session with Craig, Barbara's worksheet reads as shown in Figure 7–2.

From the information provided in this worksheet, Barbara is able to draft a contract tailored to meet her client's needs. In addition to the provisions indicated above, Barbara will include certain boilerplate provisions. A boilerplate provision is a provision found in most standard contracts, such as a provision indicating the applicable law governing the interpretation of the contract, or a provision indicating that any section of the contract that may be found to be invalid or illegal will be severed from the contract and the remainder of the contract will remain in full force and effect. Note that even when including such standard provisions, care must be taken that these provisions meet the client's needs and do not contradict other provisions in the contract. With her worksheet as a guide, Barbara drafts the contract shown in Figure 7–3 for Ava's review.

FIGURE 7–2
Real estate contract worksheet

REAL ESTATE CONTRACT WORKSHEET

DATE OF INTAKE: August 11, 1997
ATTORNEY: Ava Ross
PARALEGAL: Barbara Hammond
CLIENT NUMBER: 2007
MATTER NUMBER: 0004
PERSON RESPONSIBLE
FOR INTAKE: Barbara Hammond

1. SELLER(S) (Provide name(s) as appear on deed):
   Lyndale Properties, Inc.
2. ADDRESS(ES):   1800 Coolidge Street, Suite 400
   Any City, Any State
3. PHONE NUMBER(S): (000) 233-4991 FAX NUMBER: (000) 233-4909
4. SOCIAL SECURITY NUMBER(S):
   EIN #81-9082
5. DESCRIBE MANNER IN WHICH TITLE TO PROPERTY IS
   PRESENTLY HELD: Held in name of Lyndale Properties, Inc., an
   Any State corporation.
6. BUYER(S) (Provide name(s) as to appear on new deed):
   To be filled in at a later date.
7. ADDRESS(ES):   To be filled in at a later date.
8. PHONE NUMBER(S): N/A   FAX NUMBER: N/A
9. SOCIAL SECURITY NUMBER(S):
   To be filled in at a later date.
10. DESCRIBE MANNER IN WHICH TITLE TO PROPERTY WILL BE HELD:
    To be filled in at a later date
11. ATTORNEY FOR OTHER PARTY:
    To be filled in at a later date.
12. ADDRESS: To be filled in at a later date.
13. PHONE NUMBER: N/A   FAX NUMBER: N/A
14. REAL ESTATE BROKER:
    Seller has sales office on location; any cobrokers
    to be specified at a later date.
15. ADDRESS: To be filled in at a later date.
16. PHONE NUMBER: N/A   FAX NUMBER: N/A

FIGURE 7–2
(continued)

17. COMMISSION: Amount of seller's commission to sales office
                   not to be included in this contract.

18. COMMISSION TO BE PAID BY:
                   Sales office commission (and cobrokers
                   registering therewith) to be paid by seller.

19. ESCROW AGENT: Patriot Bank

20. ADDRESS: 2000 Truman Avenue, Any City, Any State

21. PHONE NUMBER: (000) 445-6677   FAX NUMBER: (000) 445-6688

22. TYPE OF CONTRACT: ___VACANT LAND ___ RESIDENTIAL RESALE
                         _X_RESIDENTIAL NEW CONSTRUCTION
                         ___CONDOMINIUM/COOPERATIVE
                         ___COMMERCIAL PROPERTY
                         ___OTHER (SPECIFY): _____

23. STREET ADDRESS OF PROPERTY:
                   To be filled in at a later date.

24. LEGAL DESCRIPTION OF PROPERTY:
    Lot   , of ORANGE WALK ESTATES, according to the plat thereof,
    recorded in Plat Book 71, Page 117, Public Records of Any County,
    Any State; together with the single-family residence to be constructed
    thereon; and together with all appurtenances thereto.

25. PERSONAL PROPERTY TO BE INCLUDED WITH SALE (Describe with
    specificity):   To be filled in at a later date.

26. CLOSING:
    (A) DATE: Estimated closing date to be filled in at a later date.
    Estimated closing date is not guaranteed. Time is not of the essence as
    to the estimated date. Seller shall give buyer not less than 10 days'
    notice of closing. Permanent Certificate of Occupancy shall evidence
    unit is ready for delivery and shall be the sole condition of closing.
    (B) TIME: To be filled in at a later date.
    (C) PLACE: To be filled in at a later date.

27. PURCHASE PRICE: To be filled in at a later date.

28. DEPOSITS:
    (A) LOT RESERVATION DEPOSIT (Applicable for new construction):
         1. AMOUNT OF DEPOSIT: To be filled in at a later date.
         2. DUE DATE: Prior to signing of contract.
         3. METHOD OF PAYMENT: Cash or check subject to collection.
         4. ___INTEREST-BEARING ACCOUNT
             _X_NONINTEREST-BEARING ACCOUNT
         5. IF PLACED IN INTEREST-BEARING ACCOUNT, PROVIDE
             DETAILS: _____
    (B) INITIAL DEPOSIT:
         1. AMOUNT OF DEPOSIT: To be filled in at a later date.
         2. DUE DATE: Upon execution of contract.
         3. METHOD OF PAYMENT: Cash or check subject to collection.
         4. ___INTEREST-BEARING ACCOUNT
             _X_NONINTEREST-BEARING ACCOUNT
         5. IF PLACED IN INTEREST-BEARING ACCOUNT, PROVIDE
             DETAILS: _____

FIGURE 7–2
(continued)

(C)   ADDITIONAL DEPOSIT(S):
    1.   AMOUNT OF DEPOSIT(S): <u>To be filled in at a later date.</u>
    2.   DUE DATE(S): <u>To be filled in at a later date.</u>
    3.   METHOD OF PAYMENT(S): <u>Cash or check subject to</u>
        <u>collection.</u>
    4.   ___INTEREST-BEARING ACCOUNT
       X NONINTEREST-BEARING ACCOUNT
    5.   IF PLACED IN INTEREST-BEARING ACCOUNT, PROVIDE
       DETAILS: _____

29.   PAYMENT:
    (A)   SOURCE OF PAYMENT: ___ CASH
                           ___ FINANCING
                           ___ LENDING INSTITUTION
                           ___ SELLER
                           ___ OTHER (SPECIFY): <u>Either cash</u>
                               <u>or financing.</u>

    (B)   IF FINANCED, SPECIFY: ___ NEW CONVENTIONAL
                                  MORTGAGE
                           ___ NEW FHA MORTGAGE
                           ___ NEW VA MORTGAGE
                           ___ ASSUMPTION OF EXISTING
                                  MORTGAGE
                           ___ TAKING SUBJECT TO
                                  EXISTING MORTGAGE
                           ___ PURCHASE MONEY
                                  MORTGAGE

       [Note: To be filled in at a later date.]

    (C)   IF FINANCED, SPECIFY:
       1.   TIME PERIOD WITHIN WHICH TO OBTAIN FINANCING:
          <u>60 days.</u>
       2.   TERM OF LOAN: <u>To be filled in at a later date.</u>
       3.   AMOUNT OF LOAN: <u>To be filled in at a later date.</u>
       4.   INTEREST RATE: <u>To be filled in at a later date.</u>
       5.   TERMS AND CONDITIONS: <u>To be filled in at a later date.</u>

30.   IF NEW CONSTRUCTION, ARE PROGRESS PAYMENTS REQUIRED?
                  _____ YES ___X___ NO
IF YES, SUPPLY AMOUNT AND DUE DATE OF EACH PAYMENT.

_____

31.   CONSTRUCTION SPECIFICATIONS (Applicable for new construction):
<u>Seller agrees that construction shall be substantially in accordance with</u>
<u>the plans and specifications attached to contract. Seller reserves right</u>
<u>to make minor modifications in plans and to make substitution of</u>
<u>materials, fixtures, appliances and equipment, provided substitutions</u>
<u>are of substantially the same or better quality. If changes are required</u>
<u>by any governmental or quasi-governmental authority, buyer shall, at</u>
<u>closing, pay any costs incurred by such changes.</u>

FIGURE 7–2
(continued)

32. CHANGE ORDERS AND COLOR SELECTIONS (Applicable for new construction):   All change orders must be in writing and paid for at time change is ordered. Seller reserves right to refuse or accept change orders. If extras are ordered, other than those set forth in contract, they shall be paid for by buyer at the time ordered. Buyer shall submit to seller in writing selections of color, materials, and extras, other than those set forth in contract, not later than 15 days from seller's request. If buyer does not comply, seller may make selection in seller's sole discretion, declare buyer in default, or delay closing without seller incurring liability for delay.

33. EVIDENCE OF TITLE: ____ ABSTRACT _X_ TITLE COMMITMENT
    (A) DUE DATE: To be supplied only at request of buyer.
    (B) PAYMENT OBLIGATION: Buyer, if buyer requests evidence of title.
    (C) INSPECTION PERIOD: Within 10 days of closing.
    (D) CURE PERIOD: Seller to use reasonable diligence within reasonable time period.
    (E) ADDITIONAL INFORMATION: If cannot be cured within reasonable time, seller to return all deposits to buyer and contract is terminated. However, buyer can choose to accept title in existing condition. If buyer does so, buyer waives any and all obligations and claims with respect to title.

34. TITLE POLICY:
    (A) TITLE COMPANY: To be determined at a later date.
    (B) AGENT: To be determined at a later date.
    (C) TYPE(S) OF POLICY(IES) TO BE PROVIDED:
        Title commitment or owner's policy only upon request of buyer.
    (D) PAYMENT OBLIGATION: Buyer, if buyer requests policy.
    (E) SPECIAL PROVISIONS: N/A

35. INSPECTIONS:
    (A) TERMITE:
        1. TIME WITHIN WHICH TO MAKE INSPECTION: N/A
        2. TIME WITHIN WHICH TO MAKE OBJECTIONS: N/A
    (B) ROOF:
        1. TIME WITHIN WHICH TO MAKE INSPECTION: N/A
        2. TIME WITHIN WHICH TO MAKE OBJECTIONS: N/A
    (C) APPLIANCES:
        1. TIME WITHIN WHICH TO MAKE INSPECTION: See (E) below.
        2. TIME WITHIN WHICH TO MAKE OBJECTIONS: See (E) below.
    (D) HEATING/COOLING/ELECTRICAL/PLUMBING SYSTEMS:
        1. TIME WITHIN WHICH TO MAKE INSPECTION: See (E) below.
        2. TIME WITHIN WHICH TO MAKE OBJECTIONS: See (E) below.
    (E) OTHER INSPECTIONS (Specify):
        Buyer will be given a reasonable opportunity to examine unit with seller's representative prior to closing and at that time will pre-

FIGURE 7–2
(continued)

sent seller with an inspection statement setting forth any defects. Seller will be obligated to correct any defects within a reasonable period of time, but neither seller's obligation to correct nor buyer's failure to inspect shall be grounds for deferring closing.

36. WARRANTIES: Seller warrants its workmanship and materials for one year from date the improvements are completed. If manufacturers' warranties exceed one year, these warranties inure to the buyer's bene-fit. Buyer will receive a builder's warranty at closing that construction is in substantial compliance with approved plans and specifications. Seller will not be obligated to correct, and will not be liable to buyer as a result of, any insubstantial variations from filed building plans or those which are necessitated by site conditions or job requirements provided that (i) the approval of any governmental authority having jurisdiction is obtained, if required, and (ii) the market value of the unit is not substantially diminished.

37. REPAIRS: New construction, so not applicable except as pro-vided under inspection provision.

38. SURVEY: Seller shall provide if requested by buyer, at buyer's expense.

39. ZONING: Residential, single-family homes.

40. EASEMENTS AND DEED RESTRICTIONS:
      Zoning and regulatory ordinances; restrictions and limitations of record including but not limited to those common to the subdivision; all easements of record; ad valorem real property taxes for the current year; encumbrances assumed or created by buyer.

41. LIENS: At closing seller shall give buyer a no-lien affidavit.

42. OCCUPANCY: Buyer shall not enter into possession of property or onto construction site until after closing and all funds have cleared. Buyer cannot make any improvements or modifications until closing is completed.

43. RISK OF LOSS: If property is damaged by fire or other casualty before closing and cost of restoration does not exceed 3% of assessed valuation of property, seller shall restore property. If cost of restoration exceeds 3%, buyer can take property as is, together with the 3% or any insurance proceeds, or buyer may terminate contract.

44. TYPE OF DEED TO BE GRANTED: _X_ GENERAL WARRANTY DEED
                                                                __ SPECIAL WARRANTY DEED
                                                                __ QUITCLAIM DEED
                                                                __ OTHER (Specify):

45. CLOSING DOCUMENTS:
      (A) SELLER WILL PROVIDE:
            Deed, no-lien affidavit, builder's warranty, and any corrective instruments.
      (B) BUYER WILL PROVIDE:
            Closing statement, mortgage instrument, mortgage note, security agreement and financing statements.

46. PRORATIONS:
      (A) PRORATED THROUGH THIS DATE: Closing date.

FIGURE 7–2
(continued)

(B)   PRORATION FORMULA: __ 360-DAY YEAR _X_ 365-DAY YEAR

(C)   TO BE PRORATED:

_X_ CITY TAXES	__ SPECIAL ASSESSMENTS
_X_ COUNTY TAXES	__ RENT
__ OTHER TAXES	__ INTEREST
__ INSURANCE	__ OTHER (Specify):

47. CLOSING EXPENSES:

(A)   EXPENSES TO BE PAID BY SELLER:

Documentary stamps on deed and recording of corrective instruments. Also, sales office commissions.

(B)   EXPENSES TO BE PAID BY BUYER:

Documentary stamps and intangible tax on mortgage and all costs incurred with buyer's mortgage loan.

48. ASSIGNMENT OF CONTRACT: Contract may not be assigned without prior written consent of seller. Seller, in its sole discretion, can withhold consent and contract will remain in full force and effect, or can terminate contract and return buyer's deposits.

49. DEFAULT AND REMEDIES:

(A)   SELLER'S DEFAULT/BUYER'S REMEDIES: If seller defaults, buyer may elect to void contract and all deposits will be returned to buyer within a reasonable period of time upon written demand, allowing for the clearance of any deposits. Upon return of deposits, contract is terminated. Failure by buyer to give notice in writing to seller of any alleged default before seller tenders performance of any omitted act shall constitute a waiver of seller's default.

(B)   BUYER'S DEFAULT/SELLER'S REMEDIES: If buyer fails or refuses to perform any contractual obligation, seller, at its sole option, may terminate contract and retain all deposits as liquidated damages. In lieu of termination, seller may elect to institute legal proceedings to specifically enforce the contract.

50. ATTORNEYS' FEES/COSTS: In connection with any litigation, including appellate proceedings, prevailing party shall be entitled to reasonable attorneys' fees and costs. In the event of a dispute or litigation in connection with any alleged default of buyer in which seller deems it advisable to retain counsel, and which is settled prior to litigation by buyer's compliance, seller shall be entitled to recovery of costs and reasonable attorneys' fees incurred in connection therewith at closing.

51. NOTICE:

(A)   TO SELLER: At address provided in contract.

(B)   TO BUYER: At address provided in contract.

52. ADDITIONAL PROVISIONS: Contract not recordable. Buyer subordinate to any construction loan mortgage. Costs of all construction loan financing to be paid by seller. Insulation disclosure to be included as attachment.

FIGURE 7–3
Purchase and sale
agreement

PURCHASE AND SALE AGREEMENT

THIS AGREEMENT, made and entered into this ____ day of_____,19__, by and between LYNDALE PROPERTIES, INC., an Any State corporation ("Seller"), having its principal office located at 1800 Coolidge Street, Suite 400, Any City, Any State, and the Purchaser(s) named below ("Purchaser").

Purchaser: _____

Address:_____

City: _____

Home Phone Number: _____   Business Phone Number: _____

Fax Number: _____   Social Security Number(s): _____

I. DESCRIPTION OF PROPERTY. Seller agrees to sell to Purchaser, on terms contained in this Agreement, Lot ____, of ORANGE WALK ESTATES according to the plat thereof, recorded in Plat Book 71, Page 117, Public Records of Any County, Any State; together with the single-family residence to be constructed thereon; and together with all appurtenances thereto. The above-described Lot and improvements thereon ("Dwelling Unit") are referred to in this Agreement as the "Property." The Property address shall be _____, Any City, Any State.

II. PURCHASE PRICE. The type of Dwelling Unit and sale price listed below are followed by a list of changes and extras to be added to this new Dwelling Unit. Purchaser acknowledges that Purchaser understands that the models on view at Orange Walk Estates contain certain optional extra changes which are not included in the total adjusted price unless specifically listed below.

A. Model Type (Base Price) .... _____ $ _____
                                    (Name of Model)

B. Add................................_____ $ _____
C. Add................................_____ $ _____
D. Add................................_____ $ _____
E. Add................................_____ $ _____
F. Add................................_____ $ _____

                            TOTAL PURCHASE PRICE $ _____

The purchase price for the Property, exclusive of any closing costs described in this Agreement, shall be as follows.

A. Lot Reservation Deposit (previously received): $ _____
B. Deposit of ten percent (10%) of the Purchase
    Price less Lot Reservation Deposit, if any
    (received this date): $ _____
C. Additional Deposit to be paid on or
    before _____ $ _____
D. Balance due at closing in cash or certified check
                                                           $ _____

All monies receipted herein are held in escrow in a noninteresting-bearing account, to be applied in accordance with the terms and conditions of this Agreement.

III. FINANCING. The Purchaser agrees to use his or her best efforts to make prompt application and to execute diligently and in good faith all necessary papers for a ____ Mortgage Loan ("Loan") for the principal amount of _____. If the Purchaser is married, and the Purchaser's spouse is not named as a Purchaser herein, Purchaser shall be responsible and liable for such spouse executing the mortgage and other closing documents as required by lender and Seller. Failure of said spouse to do so shall be considered a default of this Agreement and Seller shall be entitled to such remedies as are provided in this Agreement. The Agreement is contingent upon loan approval within sixty (60)

FIGURE 7–3
(continued)

days from the execution of this Agreement, otherwise at Seller's option, this Purchase Agreement will be null and void and Seller shall refund all payments made by the Purchaser.

IV. COMPLETION OF CONSTRUCTION AND CLOSING DATE. Completion of the proposed construction, in substantial accordance with plans and specifications approved by appropriate governmental authorities, is estimated, but not guaranteed, on or about _____. The estimated time of delivery set forth in the preceding sentence is made as an accommodation to Purchaser to assist Purchaser in formulating future plans, but such estimated time of delivery shall not be considered as time which is of the essence of this Agreement. Seller shall not be liable to Purchaser for any expense or inconvenience which may directly arise from delay of completion or from delay of delivery of possession. Closing shall be held at such place and on such day and hour as Seller may designate, but not less than ten (10) days from the giving of notice of closing by the Seller to Purchaser. The issuance of a Permanent Certificate of Occupancy as to Purchaser's Dwelling Unit by the Building Department of Any County, Any State, or its equivalent shall evidence that the Dwelling Unit is ready for delivery and shall be the sole condition of closing.

V. CONSTRUCTION SPECIFICATIONS. Seller agrees that the construction of the Dwelling Unit shall be substantially in accordance with the Plans and Specifications attached hereto and incorporated by reference herein. Seller specifically reserves the right to make minor modifications in said Plans and Specifications and to make substitutions of materials, fixtures, appliances and equipment, provided same are of substantially the same or better quality. In the event changes in said Plans, building materials or other items for the Dwelling Unit are required by any governmental or quasi-governmental rule, regulation, code, order, statute or ordinance, Purchaser shall pay Seller at closing any and all costs incurred by Seller in effectuating such changes.

VI. WARRANTIES. Seller shall warrant its workmanship and materials furnished under this Agreement for a period of one (1) year from the date the improvements are completed; provided, however, that manufacturer's warranties which exceed one year shall inure to the Purchaser's benefit. The Purchaser will receive at closing a warranty from Seller of completion of construction in substantial conformity with the approved plans and specifications. Seller will not be obligated to correct, and will not be liable to the Purchaser as a result of, any insubstantial variations from filed Plans or which are necessitated by site conditions or job requirements, provided only that (i) the approval of any governmental authority having jurisdiction thereof is obtained, if required, and (ii) the market value of the Property is not substantially diminished. Further, Seller warrants that the insulation used in the construction of the Dwelling Unit is in conformity with the information provided in the Insulation Exhibit attached to this Agreement.

VII. CHANGE ORDERS AND COLOR SELECTIONS. All change orders must be in writing and paid for at the time the changes are ordered. Seller reserves the right to refuse to accept any change orders after the date hereof. In the event Purchaser orders an option or extra other than those set forth in this Agreement, same shall be paid for at the time such option or extra is ordered. Such order shall not be subject to cancellation by Purchaser, nor shall Purchaser be entitled to a credit or refund therefor.

Purchaser shall submit to Seller in writing selections of color, materials and extras, other than those set forth in this Agreement, not later than fifteen (15) days of Seller's request therefor, which request may be made by telephone, regular mail or other reasonable means of communication. In the event Purchaser fails to comply herewith, Seller may at its option (i) make such selections in its sole discretion, (ii) declare Purchaser in default and exercise any and all remedies set forth in this Agreement, or (iii) delay closing without liability therefor.

VIII. SURVEY. Seller will not furnish a survey to Purchaser except upon request of Purchaser and at Purchaser's expense.

FIGURE 7–3
(continued)

IX. TITLE. Seller will not furnish an owner's title insurance policy or commitment except upon request of Purchaser and at Purchaser's expense. Seller shall convey to Purchaser a good and marketable title by General Warranty Deed subject only to (i) zoning and regulatory ordinances of governmental agencies having jurisdiction; (ii) conditions, restrictions and limitations of record including but not limited to those common to the subdivision in which the Property is located; (iii) all easements of record; (iv) ad valorem real property taxes for the current year which shall be prorated as of date of closing; and (iv) encumbrances assumed or created by the Purchaser.

In the event that title shall not be found marketable within ten (10) days of closing, Seller agrees to use reasonable diligence to make the title good and marketable, and shall have a reasonable time to do so. If after reasonable diligence and reasonable time Seller is unable to make said title good and marketable, this Agreement shall be deemed canceled and Seller shall return to Purchaser all deposits paid by Purchaser under this Agreement. Thereupon, each of the parties shall be relieved from any further obligations under this Agreement. Upon request of Purchaser, however, Seller shall deliver the title in its existing condition, whereupon Purchaser shall be deemed to have waived any and all objections and claims with respect to title.

X. LIENS. At closing, Seller shall deliver to Purchaser a Seller's form No-Lien Affidavit in the form attached hereto.

XI. INSPECTION. Purchaser shall be given a reasonable opportunity to examine the Dwelling Unit with Seller's representative prior to closing, and at that time shall present to Seller an Inspection Statement signed by Purchaser setting forth any defects in workmanship or materials. As to any items therein described which are truly defects in workmanship and materials (keeping in mind the construction standards prevalent in Any County relative to the type and price of the subject Dwelling Unit), Seller shall be obligated to correct the same at its cost within a reasonable period of time, but Seller's obligation to correct shall not be a ground for deferring the closing nor the imposition of any condition upon closing. Failure of Purchaser to examine the Dwelling Unit prior to the date established by Seller for closing shall not be a ground for deferring closing or for the imposition of any condition upon closing.

XII. OCCUPANCY. Purchaser shall not enter into possession of the Property or onto the construction site (with the exception of inspection of the Dwelling Unit as provided in paragraph XI) until this transaction has been fully closed and all funds due Seller have cleared. Purchaser shall be prohibited from commencement of any construction, improvement, modification or work with respect to the Property until closing has been completed.

XIII. RISK OF LOSS. If the Property is damaged by fire or other casualty prior to closing and the cost of restoration does not exceed three percent (3%) of the assessed valuation of the Property as damaged, the cost of restoration shall be the obligation of the Seller and the closing shall proceed pursuant to this Agreement, with said restoration costs escrowed at closing. Should the restoration costs exceed three (3%) percent of the assessed valuation of the Property as damaged, Purchaser shall have the option of either taking the Property as is, together with either the three (3%) percent or any applicable insurance proceeds payable for said damage, or of canceling this Agreement. Should Purchaser choose the latter option, all received deposits shall be returned to Purchaser.

XIV. CLOSING DOCUMENTS. Seller shall deliver to Purchaser at closing a General Warranty Deed, Seller's form No-Lien Affidavit, Builder's Warranty and any corrective instruments. Buyer shall furnish the closing statement, mortgage, mortgage note, security agreement and financing statements.

XV. PRORATIONS. Proration of real estate taxes shall be made at the date of closing as of the date of closing. Real property taxes will be prorated on the latest information available. If the taxes for the year of closing are not precisely ascertainable, such taxes will be prorated based on estimates and will be adjusted later

FIGURE 7–3
(continued)

based on the exact amount of taxes with allowance for full discount. Proration of any and all other proratable items shall be made at the date of closing as of the date of closing.

XVI. CLOSING EXPENSES. Documentary stamps on the General Warranty Deed, recording of any corrective instruments, and commissions owed to the sales office (and any cobroker registered therewith) shall be paid by the Seller. Documentary stamps and intangible tax on mortgage, loan fees, loan closing costs and all other related sums (including but not limited to attorneys' fees, escrows for taxes and insurance, recording fees and credit report) shall be paid by Purchaser. In addition, Purchaser shall be responsible for payment of commission owed to any Buyer's real estate broker(s) according to the terms of such broker agreement.

XVII. ASSIGNMENT. This Agreement is binding on the parties hereto and their heirs, legal representatives, successors and assigns, and this Agreement may not be assigned by the Purchaser without the prior written consent of Seller. A transfer of a legal, equitable or beneficial interest in Purchaser shall be deemed an assignment hereunder. Seller, in its sole discretion, may withhold consent to any attempted assignment of this Agreement and the Agreement shall remain in full force and effect, or may terminate this Agreement and refund all deposits to Purchaser, in which event the parties shall be relieved of further liability hereunder. No assignment of this Agreement shall be effective unless in writing upon such form as Seller shall provide, with the written consent of Seller as noted thereon.

XVIII. DEFAULT AND REMEDIES. If Purchaser fails or refuses to perform any of his or her obligations under this Agreement, Seller, at its sole option, may notify Purchaser in writing that this Agreement is terminated. In the event of such termination, Seller may retain all payments theretofore made by Purchaser as agreed upon liquidated damages which shall not be construed as a penalty; and all further rights and obligations of the parties under this Agreement shall thereupon be terminated. In lieu of such termination, the Seller may elect to institute legal proceedings to specifically enforce this Agreement between the parties and collect damage owing to Purchaser's failure or refusal to perform.

If Seller defaults in the performance of this Agreement, Purchaser may elect to void this Agreement, in which event all sums paid by Purchaser under this Agreement shall be returned to Purchaser within a reasonable period of time upon written demand, allowing for, without limitation, the clearance of any deposits made hereunder, and upon such refund being made to Purchaser, this Agreement shall be terminated and Seller shall be under no obligation or liability whatsoever to Purchaser for any damages that Purchaser may have sustained and neither party will have any claim as against the other under the terms of the Agreement. Failure by Purchaser to give notice in writing to Seller of any alleged default before Seller tenders performance of any omitted act shall constitute a waiver of Seller's default.

XIX. ATTORNEYS' FEES AND COSTS. In connection with any litigation including appellate proceedings arising out of this Agreement, the prevailing party shall be entitled to recover reasonable attorneys' fees and costs. In the event of any dispute or litigation between Seller and Purchaser in connection with any alleged breach or default upon the part of the Purchaser wherein Seller deems it advisable or necessary to retain the services of an attorney, and which is settled prior to litigation by Purchaser otherwise complying with the demands of Seller as to Purchaser's duties and obligations hereunder, Seller shall be entitled to the recovery of costs and reasonable attorneys' fees incurred in connection therewith at closing.

XX. ESCROW AGENT. The escrow agent for all deposits paid hereunder shall be Patriot Bank, 2000 Truman Avenue, Any City, Any State. Purchaser may obtain a receipt for deposits from the escrow agent upon written request.

XXI. AGREEMENT NOT RECORDABLE. This Agreement shall not be recorded and execution hereof shall not create any lien or lien right in favor of the Purchaser, the Purchaser hereby expressly waiving and relinquishing any such lien or lien rights. The Purchaser agrees that all terms and provisions of this

FIGURE 7–3
(continued)

Agreement are and shall be subject and subordinate to the lien of any building loan mortgage heretofore or hereafter made, and advances heretofore or hereafter made thereon to the full extent thereof without the execution of any further legal documents by the Purchaser. The costs of all construction loan financing are to be paid by the Seller.

XXII. NOTICES. Except as otherwise provided, whenever a notice is required to be sent, the same shall be in writing addressed to the parties at the addresses set forth in this Agreement and shall be (i) hand delivered; (ii) sent by certified or registered mail, postage prepaid, return receipt requested; (iii) sent by Federal Express or similar overnight courier service; or (iv) by telecopy. Notice given by or to the attorney representing either party shall be effective as if given by or to said party. All notices shall be deemed and considered given upon mailing or telecopying.

XXIII. JOINT AND SEVERAL LIABILITY. Purchasers, if more than one, shall be jointly and severally liable for full performance of all obligations of Purchaser hereunder.

XXIV. SEVERABILITY. If any part, clause, provision or condition of this Agreement is held to be void, invalid or inoperative, the parties agree that such invalidity shall not affect any other part, clause, provision or condition hereof, but that the remainder of this Agreement shall be effective as though such void part, clause, provision or condition had not been contained herein.

XXV. APPLICABLE LAW. This Agreement shall be construed under the laws of the State of Any State.

XXVI. EFFECTIVE DATE. The effective date of this Agreement shall be the date when the last one of the Seller and Purchaser has executed this Agreement.

IN WITNESS WHEREOF, the parties have hereunto set their hands and seals the day and year first above written.

Signed, Sealed and Delivered
in the presence of:

SELLER: LYNDALE PROPERTIES, INC., an Any State corporation

BY: _____
       Craig Newfield, President

_____

PURCHASER(S):

_____

_____

_____

Social Security or Federal I.D. Number(s) of Purchaser(s):

_____

_____

CHAPTER SUMMARY

1. A well-drafted real estate contract is key to achieving the client's goals in the closing of a real estate transaction. The contract will address the responsibilities not only of the parties to the contract but also of the lenders, brokers, escrow agents, title companies, and attorneys. All elements important to the closing of the transaction should be set forth in adequate detail in the real estate contract.

2. To prepare a properly drafted contract, all pertinent information must be gathered, preferably with the aid of a worksheet. Legal names and marital

status of the parties should be verified by checking official documents, legal descriptions copied from current deeds, zoning restrictions verified with governmental authorities or zoning maps, and profits and expenses of income-producing property verified by inspection of operating statements.

3. The basic provisions found in a real estate contract for sale and purchase include, but need not be limited to, the naming of the parties, the legal description, the effective date, the closing date, the purchase price, deposits, the method of payment, inspections and warranties, evidence and quality of title, closing costs and apportionments, brokers' fees, defaults and remedies, and attorneys' fees.

4. The purchase of real property may be financed in a number of ways. The buyer may pay cash and take title clear of all mortgage liens. Alternatively, the buyer may seek out a new conventional, FHA, or VA loan; may take the property subject to the existing mortgage; may assume the existing mortgage; or may receive a purchase money mortgage loan from the seller.

5. Most buyers want to make minimum deposits, want ample contingencies included in the contract to provide a means of escape should they wish to back out (for example, contingencies pertaining to attorney approval, financing, zoning, inspection), want as many warranties from the seller as possible, want the right to assign the contract, want to limit the seller's remedies in case of the buyer's default to the retaining of deposits, and want a choice of options in the event the seller defaults.

6. Most sellers want to receive large deposits, want no buyer contingencies, want to give minimum warranties, want to retain deposits as well as seek specific performance or damages should the buyer default, and want to limit the buyer's remedies to the return of deposits in the event the seller defaults. A well-negotiated contract gives neither party everything it wants, yet addresses each party's primary concerns.

7. The contract for purchase and sale of a condominium may be governed by statutory law setting forth a time period within which the buyer may inspect the condominium documents and, upon inspection, cancel the contract. The purchase of a condominium may be subject to approval of the buyer by the condominium association.

8. An option contract is one in which the optionee pays the optionor an agreed-upon price for the privilege of keeping the property off the market for a specified period of time. During this time period, the optionee has the exclusive right to purchase the property. The option price paid is irrevocable. If the optionee chooses to exercise the option, the transaction proceeds in like manner to a regular real estate transaction.

REVIEW QUESTIONS

1. What are the elements of a valid contract?
2. Why is the contract for sale and purchase considered the most important document in the real estate closing?
3. Distinguish between (a) a sale subject to an existing mortgage and (b) a sale with an assumption of mortgage.
4. What are the basic provisions found in a real estate contract for sale and purchase?
5. What special provisions should be included in the following contracts?
   a. An option contract
   b. A contract for the sale and purchase of income-producing property
   c. A contract for the sale and purchase of a condominium

ETHICAL QUESTIONS

Attorney Michael Hogan is acting as escrow agent in several real estate transactions. Michael has been particularly busy with an inordinate number of real estate closings during the past two months, and you have been asked by your supervising attorney to assist him. State law dictates that all earnest money deposits be deposited in escrow accounts within forty-eight hours of receipt. In reviewing a number of files Michael has assigned to you, you come across several earnest money deposit checks dated several weeks ago that have yet to be deposited. What should you do?

PRACTICAL ASSIGNMENTS

Assignment 7:1. Research your state statutes to find your state's statute of frauds. Photocopy the statute and insert it under the "Contracts" section of your resource portfolio.

Assignment 7:2. Contact your local or state board of realtors and find out whether there is a standard contract for sale and purchase form that is used in real estate transactions in your county or state. If so, obtain a copy and insert it under the "Contracts" section of your resource portfolio. If not, obtain a copy of the form contract used by a major real estate brokerage firm in your area and insert it under this section.

Assignment 7:3. In the last chapter, you were asked to research your state statutes to determine what disclosures are mandatory for brokers and sellers in your state. Place a note in the "Contracts" section of your resource portfolio indicating a cross-reference to the applicable statutes pertaining to mandatory disclosures in the "General Information" section of your resource portfolio.

Assignment 7:4. Research your state statutes to determine whether prospective buyers of condominiums are afforded a specified time period within which to cancel a contract for sale and purchase of a condominium unit. If such a statute exists, photocopy it and insert in under the "Contracts" section of your resource portfolio.

Assignment 7:5. Research your state statutes to determine whether your state has statutory law governing installment contracts. If so, photocopy the relevant statutes and insert them under the "Contracts" section of your resource portfolio.

Assignment 7:6. Examine the standard contract for purchase and sale used for residential sales in your county (or state). Make note of those provisions that are drafted in favor of the seller. Take a separate sheet of paper and label it "Provisions in Favor of Buyer," and on this sheet redraft those provisions in favor of the buyer. Take another sheet of paper and label it "Neutral Provisions," and redraft those provisions to read as neutral provisions. Next, make note of those provisions in the standard contract that are drafted in favor of the buyer. Take a third sheet of paper and label it "Provisions in Favor of Seller," and redraft those provisions in favor of the seller. On the sheet labeled "Neutral Provisions," redraft these provisions to read as neutral provisions. Insert these sheets under the "Contracts" section of your resource portfolio. If you are asked to use the standard contract form to prepare a contract for a client, you can refer to these sheets and modify the standard contract accordingly (for example, in favor of a buyer client or a seller client or, if the client so desires, with neutral provisions.)

Assignment 7:7. Assume your client is Lyndale Properties and you have drafted the new construction contract set forth in Figure 7–3. Further, assume that both Lyndale Properties, Orange Walk Estates, and the escrow agent Patriot Bank are located in your city, county, and state. Alan and Laura Newman want to buy a home in Orange Walk Estates and have put down a lot reservation deposit of $10,000 on lot 4. The street address of the lot is 100 Orange Grove Circle (your city, county, and state). They are interested in the Valencia model, which has a base purchase price of $275,000. In addition, they want a tile upgrade ($3,500) and an appliance upgrade ($1,000). An additional ten percent deposit will be required upon signing the contract. To finance the purchase, they are interested in obtaining a fixed rate mortgage loan in the amount of $225,000. Craig Newfield estimates the closing date to be ten months from the signing of the contract. The Newmans' present address is 261 Azalea Drive (your city and state). Their home telephone number is 111-2222 (your area code). Alan works out of their home. Laura's telephone number at work is 111-3333 (your area code), and her fax number is 111-4444 (your area code). Alan's social security number is 000-11-2222, and Laura's social security number is 000-11-3333. Take this information and customize the new construction contract set forth in Figure 7–3 accordingly. After review, insert the contract under the "Contracts" section of your resource portfolio.

Assignment 7:8. Define the following key terms.

assumption of mortgage	prorations
cash sale	purchase money mortgage sale
effective date	sale subject to existing mortgage
installment contract	statute of frauds
option contract	

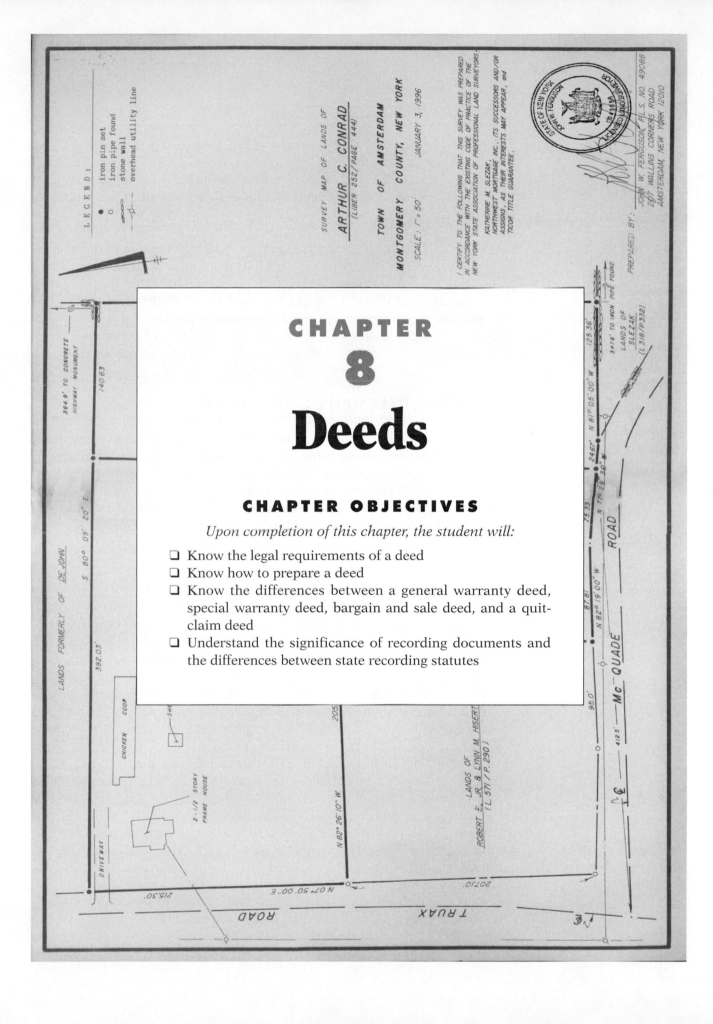

CHAPTER
8

Deeds

CHAPTER OBJECTIVES

Upon completion of this chapter, the student will:

❑ Know the legal requirements of a deed
❑ Know how to prepare a deed
❑ Know the differences between a general warranty deed, special warranty deed, bargain and sale deed, and a quit-claim deed
❑ Understand the significance of recording documents and the differences between state recording statutes

SURVEY MAP OF LANDS OF

ARTHUR C. CONRAD
(LIBER 252/PAGE 444)

TOWN OF AMSTERDAM

MONTGOMERY COUNTY, NEW YORK

SCALE : 1" = 50'   JANUARY 3, 1996

I CERTIFY TO THE FOLLOWING THAT THIS SURVEY WAS PREPARED
IN ACCORDANCE WITH THE EXISTING CODE OF PRACTICE OF THE
NEW YORK STATE ASSOCIATION OF PROFESSIONAL LAND SURVEYORS.

KATHERINE M. SLEZAK,
NORTHWEST MORTGAGE INC., ITS SUCCESSORS AND/OR
ASSIGNS, AS THEIR INTERESTS MAY APPEAR, and
TICOR TITLE GUARANTEE.

JOHN W. FERGUSON, P.L.S. NO. 49088
207 WALLINS CORNERS ROAD
AMSTERDAM, NEW YORK 12010

PREPARED BY :

LEGEND :
● iron pin set
○ iron pipe found
stone wall
overhead utility line

INTRODUCTION

A **deed** is a formal written instrument that conveys title to real property from one party to another. Unlike a contract, which is signed by both parties to a transaction, a deed is signed only by the person(s) conveying the property. It serves as documentary evidence of the transfer, describes the quality of title transferred, and outlines any restrictions regarding the transfer of the property.

Paralegals are often asked to prepare deeds at the direction of their supervising attorney. Therefore, this chapter focuses on the legal requirements for a valid deed, the clauses typically included in a deed, and the drafting of deeds. The most commonly used deeds are discussed, together with a number of special purpose deeds a paralegal may have occasion to draft. The chapter concludes with a discussion of the recording of deeds and other real estate documents.

LEGAL REQUIREMENTS OF A DEED

The basic requirements for a valid deed are (1) a written instrument (2) signed by a competent grantor, (3) identifying the grantee(s), (4) indicating the date of conveyance, (5) containing a recital of consideration, (6) words of conveyance of (7) real property described with specificity, which is (8) witnessed (if required by state statute) and (9) acknowledged (if required by state statute) and which is (10) delivered by the grantor to the grantee.

Grantor

A valid deed requires a competent grantor. The **grantor** is the person (or entity) that transfers ownership of the real property. Grantors may be individuals, corporations, partnerships, limited liability companies, trustees, guardians, personal representatives, or governmental authorities or agents. For an individual, competence means being of legal age (in most states, eighteen years of age or older) and being of sound mind (capable of understanding the nature and consequence of the transaction). For a business entity, such as a corporation, competence means being in legal existence (organized and operating in full accordance with the laws of the state of domicile) and having proper authorization to convey the real property in question (in the case of a corporation, this means a resolution by the board of directors or shareholders authorizing the president of the corporation to enter the transaction on behalf of the corporation).

If the grantor is an unmarried individual, the deed should so indicate (for example, "Gail Bryce, a single woman" or "Gail Bryce, an unmarried woman"). If the grantor is married, his or her spouse should also be named as grantor, even if title to the property is held in only one name (for example, "Martin Compton and Allison Compton, his wife" or "Martin Compton and Allison Compton, husband and wife"). It is necessary to name both spouses and to have both spouses execute the deed to remove any question concerning dower, curtesy, or homestead rights in the property in states that recognize these rights.

deed: A formal written instrument that conveys title to real property from one party to another.

grantor: The person or entity conveying title of real property to another.

If the grantor is a business entity, the legal name of the business entity should be designated, followed by its state of domicile (for example, "Grantham Properties, Inc., a Nebraska corporation" or "Crowley Associates, a California general partnership"). If the grantor is a fiduciary acting on behalf of a minor or a personal representative acting on behalf of an estate, this should be so indicated (for example, "Millicent Linton, Legal Guardian of Justin Pearce, a minor" or "Brian Tyson, Executor of the Estate of Vernon Tyson, deceased").

It is important that the grantor's name appear precisely the way it was written in the deed by which he or she acquired the property. For example, if Nicole Branston is the owner of the property in question and her present deed reads "Nicole D. Branston, a single woman," her middle initial should be included when entering her name in the new deed as grantor. If she has not married since acquiring the property, the designation "a single woman" should be included as well. If she has married since acquiring the property and has taken the surname "Dickenson," her name on the deed should read "Nicole D. Dickenson, a married woman (formerly known as Nicole D. Branston)," and her husband's name should be included on the deed. It is good practice to obtain the prior deed before drafting a new deed. The prior deed will not only provide the proper spelling of names but will also provide the legal description of the property and, usually, any restrictions that should be noted.

Finally, the grantor's name on the signature line of the deed should conform to the grantor's name as it appears in the opening paragraph. If the grantor is a corporation, statutory law should be followed. Typically, the president of the corporation executes the deed, his or her signature is attested to by the secretary of the corporation, and the corporate seal is embossed on the deed. If the grantor is a general partnership, all partners should execute the deed. If the grantor is a limited partnership, all general partners should sign the deed. If the grantor is a limited liability company, depending on state law, either the members or the managers must sign the deed (state law varies, so it should be carefully checked). Statutory law provides authority for fiduciaries to sign deeds on behalf of a trust, guardian, or estate. A court order may be required, so refer to state statutes.

Grantee

The next requirement for a valid deed is the inclusion of the name of the grantee. The **grantee** is the person to whom the real property is to be conveyed and, therefore, does not sign the deed. There is no requirement that the grantee be of sound mind or of the age of majority. The marital status of the grantee should be indicated. In the case of a business entity, the type of entity and its state of domicile should be noted. If there is more than one grantee, the manner by which the grantees take joint title should be clearly indicated. For example, in some states, the designation "Frank Potter and Hilda Potter, husband and wife" would raise the legal presumption that the Potters are taking title as tenants by the entirety, while in other states, this designation would indicate that the Potters are taking title as tenants in common (recall the detailed discussion of joint tenancies in Chapter 2). In some states, the words "with right of survivorship" must follow a designation of the parties

grantee: The person or entity to whom title to real property is conveyed.

as joint tenants or a tenancy in common will be presumed. Nothing should be presumed; the manner in which title is to be held should be discussed with the client and spelled out on the deed.

Date

The date of execution of the deed should appear in the opening paragraph or clause, or near the signature. A transfer of ownership is completed when a deed is delivered by the grantor to the grantee. Unless there is contrary evidence, the delivery date is presumed to be the date appearing on the face of the deed.

Consideration

A deed must include a recital of consideration. In most instances, a recital of nominal consideration (for example, Ten Dollars) is sufficient. The actual consideration paid for the real property must be disclosed to local and/or state tax departments for tax purposes. Real property may be conveyed as a gift, in which case no actual monetary consideration is being exchanged for the real property. There are special circumstances in which the actual sales price must be inserted, as in the case of a deed in which the grantor is acting in a fiduciary capacity on behalf of the owner of the real property (see the discussion that follows).

Words of Conveyance

A deed must include words of conveyance by which the grantor expresses his or her intention to make a present conveyance of title to the property to the grantee. The exact words used vary from state to state and vary depending upon the type of deed used in the conveyance. The words of conveyance also indicate the type of estate being conveyed (for example, a fee simple, a life estate). In some states, the words "and his/her heirs" are used to indicate the conveyance of a fee simple estate. In many states, a fee simple estate will be presumed if there are no words of limitation indicating otherwise.

Legal Description

An accurate description of the real property to be transferred must be included in the deed. If personal property is to be sold as well, the listing of personal property should not be included in the deed; rather, it should be listed in a bill of sale (for a discussion of bills of sale, see Chapter 2). The description should meet the requirements for one of the three major types of land descriptions: the metes and bounds description, the government rectangular survey description, or the plat description. In most cases, it is good practice to copy the legal description from the prior deed or title policy. However, situations arise in which a grantor may not be granting the entirety of the land owned, or all rights owned, so this information must be checked before drafting the deed.

Witnesses and Acknowledgment

The rules pertaining to the witnessing and acknowledgment of the execution of a deed vary from state to state. In some states, two disinterested witnesses are required to sign the deed. In others, such as New York, the acknowledgment before a notary public is sufficient. In still other states, witnesses are required only if the deed is to be recorded. Thus, state law should be consulted prior to execution of the deed.

Delivery

The legal transfer of ownership of real property is not complete until the deed is physically delivered by the grantor (or his or her agents) to the grantee and the deed is accepted by the grantee. As long as the deed remains in the possession of the grantor, there is a rebuttable presumption that the transfer of ownership has not taken place. If the deed is physically delivered to the grantee, the grantee's acceptance is presumed. Further, if the deed is recorded in the public records, it is presumed to have been delivered and accepted.

Other Requirements

In addition to the requirements already discussed, some states require other information to appear in a deed, such as social security numbers, the property appraiser's identification number, or the preparer's name and address. Further, state law typically imposes a tax on the transfer of real property. Evidence of payment of this tax is made through the placing of **documentary stamps** on the deed, and the deed cannot be recorded unless the proper amount of documentary stamps are affixed to the deed or the proper statutory exemption noted on the deed. The documentary stamp tax is based on the purchase price of the property and is usually calculated on each $100 or fraction thereof of this purchase price (for example, $.70 per each $100 or fraction thereof).

For example, if the purchase price of the property is $200,000 and the tax imposed is $.50 per each $100 or fraction thereof, the documentary stamp tax would be $1,000. To arrive at this amount, one takes the purchase price of $200,000 and divides it by 100 to arrive at 2,000. This number is then multiplied by the amount of the tax, in this instance, $.50, to arrive at a tax of $1,000.

DEED CLAUSES

Premises Clause

The **premises clause** is the opening paragraph of a deed. This clause sets forth the date of execution of the deed, the parties to the deed (together with their designation, either "grantor" and "grantee," or "party of the first part" and "party of the second part"), and in states that so require, the addresses of the parties. It is common for the opening words of this clause to read, "This Indenture made this . . . day of . . .," "Know all men by these presents that . . .,"

documentary stamps: A tax imposed on the transfer of real property.

premises clause: The opening paragraph of a deed, setting forth the date of execution of the deed, the parties to the deed, and, in states that so require, the addresses of the parties.

"This deed is made on . . .," or similar wording. An example of a premises clause follows.

> THIS INDENTURE, Made this 12th day of August, 1997, between CLAIRE MASTERSON, an unmarried woman, of the County of Any County, State of Any State, Grantor, and VICTOR DRAPER and DENISE DRAPER, husband and wife, of the County of Any County, State of Any State, Grantees.

Granting Clause

The premises clause is followed by the **granting clause,** which contains the words of conveyance expressing the grantor's intention of transferring the real property. As noted earlier, the precise wording varies from state to state and depending upon the type of deed used. Words of conveyance may include any of the following: *grant, bargain, sell, release, convey,* or *remise.* Besides the words of conveyance, the granting clause also includes the recital of consideration and the legal description of the real property to be conveyed, such as in the following example.

> WITNESSETH, that the said Grantor, for and in consideration of the sum of Ten Dollars ($10.00), and other good and valuable consideration to said Grantor in hand paid by said Grantee, the receipt of which is hereby acknowledged, has granted, bargained and sold to the said Grantee, real property in Any County, Any State, described as follows:
>
> Lot 5 in Block 14 of PINE TREE ESTATES, 1ST SECTION, according to the plat thereof, recorded in Plat Book 61, Page 3, of the Public Records of Any County, Any State.

Encumbrance Clause

When the grantor conveys title, he or she may be conveying title to property that is encumbered by existing mortgages or other liens, leases, easements, or restrictions. These encumbrances should be set forth in the deed in the **encumbrance clause,** sometimes referred to as the *"subject to" clause.* This clause directly follows the legal description of the property. Some attorneys believe the best practice is to list all known encumbrances separately. The encumbrances that are on record should be obtained through a title search. A number of attorneys prefer to use a catchall clause, like the one that follows, to put the grantee on notice that he or she is taking the property subject to all encumbrances on record.

> SUBJECT TO all valid and subsisting restrictions, reservations, covenants, conditions, rights-of-way, and easements properly of record, if any, affecting the above described property, and taxes for the current year and subsequent years.

Please note the reference to taxes in this example. This reference is included because a grantee searching the title of the real property will not come across a written lien filed against the property for currently owed property taxes, and therefore, these taxes will not be "of record."

granting clause: A deed clause that contains the words of conveyance expressing the grantor's intention of transferring the real property. It also includes the recital of consideration and description of the property to be conveyed.

encumbrance clause: A deed clause setting forth any encumbrances on the real property conveyed, such as mortgages, leases, liens, easements, or restrictions.

If the grantee is agreeing to take over the grantor's mortgage rather than obtain a new mortgage to purchase the property, the mortgage lien created when the grantor obtained the mortgage loan will remain on the property and should be noted in the encumbrance clause as follows.

SUBJECT TO a first mortgage in the original amount of $100,000.00 given by Malcolm Johnson to Patriot Bank, dated March 5, 1991 and recorded on March 5, 1991 in Official Records Book 1213, Page 57 of the Public Records of Any County, Any State, now in the unpaid amount of $88,000.00, which mortgage debt with interest and other lawful charges thereon, from the date hereof, the grantee hereby assumes and agrees to pay in accordance with the terms of the said note and mortgage.

Perhaps the seller is helping to finance the purchase of the subject property through a purchase money mortgage as a second mortgage that is secured by a mortgage note and mortgage lien given to the seller by the buyer. In this case, many states require that this mortgage be included in the encumbrance clause, as in the following example.

SUBJECT TO a purchase money second mortgage in the amount of $30,000.00, which said mortgage is to be executed and delivered by the grantee to the grantor as security for a portion of the purchase price of the premises, and which said mortgage is intended to be recorded simultaneously herewith.

Reddendum Clause

The **reddendum clause,** sometimes referred to as the *reserving clause,* reserves some right in the real property for the grantor or imposes a restriction on the use of the property by the grantee. This clause often runs together with the encumbrance clause. The most common use of this clause is to restrict the size or type of structure that can be built on the property to have conformity within a subdivision, such as in the following clause.

Only one single-family residence of not less than 2,000 square feet of living space may be erected, altered, or placed on the above described property.

Habendum Clause

The **habendum clause** describes the type of estate being conveyed to the grantee(s). In most instances, the estate conveyed will be a fee simple estate. As noted earlier, the words "in fee simple" may be expressly used, or the words "to said Grantee, his heirs and assigns forever" will indicate that a fee simple estate is being conveyed. In circumstances of joint ownership, the type of joint tenancy in which the property will be held may be included in the granting clause or the habendum clause, or sometimes is found in both. A sample habendum clause follows.

TO HAVE AND TO HOLD the premises herein granted unto the party of the second part, the heirs or successors and assigns of the party of the second part, forever, in fee simple.

reddendum clause: A deed clause reserving some right in the real property for the grantor or imposing a restriction on the use of the property by the grantee.

habendum clause: A deed clause describing the type of estate being conveyed to the grantee(s).

Tenendum Clause

The **tenendum clause** indicates the improvements that are being conveyed together with the land, such as the buildings built on the land. This clause begins with the words *together with* and may appear as a separate clause or as part of the habendum clause. The following wording is commonly found in a tenendum clause.

TOGETHER with all the tenements, hereditaments and appurtenances thereto belonging or in anywise appertaining.

Warranty Clause

Some deeds will include a **seisin clause** (sometimes spelled *seizin)* whereby the grantor warrants that he or she is the rightful owner of the property in question and thereby has the right and power to convey the property to the grantee. To be "seized" of real property means to own or to have legal and equitable title to real property. This clause may be found in general warranty deeds and special warranty deeds, both of which are discussed later. The following is an example of a seisin clause.

The said Grantor does covenant, grant, and agree to and with the Grantee that the Grantor, at the time of the sealing and delivery of this deed, is lawfully seized in his own right of a good, absolute, and infeasible estate of inheritance, in fee simple, of the above-granted premises, with the appurtenances.

General warranty deeds include other warranties as well, such as the promise that the property is unencumbered by liens, easements, and restrictions (other than those expressly listed), or the promise that the grantee may enjoy ownership of the property undisturbed by claims of others. These and other warranties, discussed in the following text, may be implied or may be expressly stated, such as in the following clause.

Said Grantor covenants that the said Grantee, her heirs and assigns, may forever hereafter have, hold, possess and enjoy the said premises without any suit, molestation or interruption, by any person whatever, lawfully claiming any right therein.

Testimonium Clause

The final deed clause is the **testimonium clause,** in which the deed is executed, witnessed, and acknowledged. The typical language of this deed is "In Witness Whereof, the Grantor has signed and sealed this deed, the day and year first above written."

COMMON TYPES OF DEEDS

The most common types of deeds are (1) the general warranty deed, (2) the special warranty deed, (3) the bargain and sale deed, and (4) the

tenendum clause: A deed clause indicating the improvements that are being conveyed together with the land, such as the buildings built on the land.

seisin clause: A deed clause whereby the grantor warrants that he or she is the rightful owner of the property in question and thereby has the right and power to convey the property to the grantee.

testimonium clause: A deed clause in which the deed is executed, witnessed, and acknowledged.

quitclaim deed. In states that have statutory forms of these deeds, the statutory forms should be used.

General Warranty Deeds

A **general warranty deed** is sometimes called a *full covenant and warranty deed,* or simply a *warranty deed.* This type of deed provides the greatest degree of protection for the buyer (grantee). With a general warranty deed, the seller (grantor) is stating that the seller has valid title and will defend that title against any defect arising from the actions of the seller or the actions of any of the seller's predecessors. Further, the seller is stating that he or she will defend the buyer's title against any claim made against that title. In essence, when the seller conveys real property through a general warranty deed, the seller is making a number of promises or guarantees, called **covenants,** to the buyer.

The first covenant contained in a general warranty deed is the *covenant of seisin.* Through this covenant the seller is guaranteeing the buyer that he or she has good title to convey. A second covenant contained in a general warranty deed is the *covenant against encumbrances,* which guarantees that the title being conveyed is not encumbered by easements, liens, restrictions, dower or curtesy rights, or other encumbrances with the exception of those set forth in the deed instrument. A third covenant contained in a general warranty deed is a *covenant of quiet enjoyment.* This covenant guarantees that the buyer may enjoy ownership of the real property undisturbed by claims against his or her title to the property by third parties. Additionally, a general warranty deed contains a *covenant of further assurances,* by which the seller guarantees that if necessary the seller will obtain any and all legal instruments to cure a defective title. Lastly, a general warranty deed contains a *covenant of warranty forever,* by which the seller guarantees that he or she will defend the buyer's good title to the property forever. If any of these covenants are breached by the seller, the buyer may bring suit for damages against the grantor or former grantors.

In some states, these covenants are set forth explicitly, while in other states, the use of certain words implies the existence of these covenants. For example, in many states, the use of the words "grants, bargains, and sells" indicates that the instrument conveying title is a general warranty deed. In other states, other words may be used to indicate the same, such as "convey and warrant" or "grants, sells, and conveys." In some states, such as Texas, a general warranty deed will include the formulaic words "grants, sells, and conveys" and will also include a statement that "Grantor binds Grantor and Grantor's heirs, executors, administrators, and successors to warrant and forever defend all and singular the property to Grantee and Grantee's heirs, executors, administrators, successors, and assigns against every person whomsoever lawfully claiming or to claim the same or any part thereof, except as to the reservations from and exceptions to conveyance and warranty." A sample general warranty deed is provided in Figure 8–1.

Special Warranty Deeds

From its name, one may be tempted to draw the implication that a **special warranty deed** is somehow superior to a general warranty deed. Just the

general warranty deed: A deed by which the grantor states that he or she has valid title and will defend that title against any defect arising from the actions of the grantor or those of the grantor's predecessors. This type of deed provides the greatest degree of protection for the grantee.

covenant: A promise or guarantee.

special warranty deed: Also known as a *limited warranty deed.* A deed by which the grantor, in conveying title to real property, only warrants that he or she has done nothing to encumber the property, but does not provide further assurances with regard to the grantor's predecessors.

FIGURE 8–1
General warranty deed

GENERAL WARRANTY DEED

THIS INDENTURE, Made this 12th day of August, 1997, Between
HAROLD NICHOLSON and PAULA NICHOLSON, Husband and Wife of the County of Any County, State of Any State, grantors, and
MATTHEW BROMLEY and VICTORIA BROMLEY, Husband and Wife of the County of Any County, State of Any State, grantees;
WITNESSETH, That said grantors, for and in consideration of the sum of Ten Dollars ($10.00), and other good and valuable considerations to said grantors in hand paid by said grantees, the receipt whereof is hereby acknowledged, have granted, bargained, and sold to the said grantees, and grantees' heirs and assigns forever, the following described land, situate, lying and being in Any County, Any State, to-wit:

Lot 9 in Block 10 of ROOKWOOD ESTATES, 1ST SECTION according to the plat thereof, recorded in Plat Book 211, Page 3, of the Public Records of Any County, Any State.

SUBJECT TO taxes for the year 1997 and subsequent years, and the Declaration of Restrictions and Covenants of Rookwood Estates Subdivision as appear of record in Official Records Book 366, Page 28, of the Public Records of Any County, Any State.

and said grantors do hereby fully warrant the title to said land, and will defend the same against the lawful claims of all persons whomsoever.
IN WITNESS WHEREOF, Grantors have hereunto set their hands and seals the day and year first above written.
Signed, sealed and delivered in our presence:

Kelly Kirkland

Claire Haggerty

Harold Nicholson
Harold Nicholson
Paula Nicholson
Paula Nicholson

STATE OF ANY STATE
COUNTY OF ANY COUNTY

I HEREBY CERTIFY that on this day before me, an officer duly qualified to take acknowledgments, personally appeared HAROLD NICHOLSON and PAULA NICHOLSON, Husband and Wife, to me known to be the persons described in and who executed the foregoing instrument, and acknowledged before me that they executed the same.
WITNESS my hand and official seal in the County and State last aforesaid this 12th day of August, 1997.

Rebecca Barclay
Notary Public, State of Any State
My commission expires:_____

opposite is the case. A special warranty deed is also known as a *limited warranty deed.* Thus, the guarantees that the seller is making to the buyer and all subsequent purchasers are limited in scope. By using this deed instrument to convey title, the seller is warranting only that he or she has done nothing to encumber the title to the property (with the exception of any encumbrances set forth in the deed itself), but does not provide further assurances or guarantees with regard to the seller's predecessors and therefore will only be responsible to the buyer for any defects caused by his or her own actions.

For example, if the seller had made improvements to the property and failed to pay certain contractors in full, resulting in a construction lien being placed on the property after closing (in many states, contractors have a statutorily prescribed period of time within which to record a lien after completing work on the property, as discussed in detail in the next chapter), the seller would be responsible to the buyer for removing that lien. If the seller's predecessor, however, had encumbered the property in some manner, such as obtaining a second mortgage and failing to secure a release of mortgage evidencing the extinguishment of the debt, that second mortgage would remain an encumbrance on the property, but the buyer would not be able to sue the seller for defective title because that encumbrance was not caused by the seller. Although conveyance by special warranty deed may seem precarious to the buyer, note that in current practice, the process of searching title and the acquisition of title insurance considerably reduces the risk of this method of conveyancing.

The wording that indicates this limited warranty is "by and through the grantor" or "by, through, or under the grantor" in the following covenant: "And the grantor hereby covenants with said grantee that the grantor is lawfully seized of said land in fee simple; that it has good, right and lawful authority to sell and convey said land; that it hereby fully warrants the title to said land and will defend the same against the lawful claims of all persons claiming by, through, or under the said grantor." A special warranty deed commonly is used when real property is sold at public auction, such as in the case of foreclosure on a mortgage or a tax lien, or when property is conveyed by a personal representative of an estate. However, it may be used in other circumstances, especially in instances when property has changed hands frequently. A sample special warranty deed is found in Figure 8–2.

Bargain and Sale Deeds

A **bargain and sale deed** is also sometimes referred to as a *deed of bargain*. When this instrument is used, the seller simply is transferring the real property itself, together with any structures on the property, rather than transferring any particular interest in the property. This deed generally contains no warranties, although the words "grants and conveys" or "grants, bargains, and sells" may be used. The words "conveys and warrants" cannot be used with this deed because the seller is not making any warranties about the title to the property. (Note that in New York, however, there are two types of bargain and sale deeds, those with and those without covenants). In some states, the words "grants and releases" are used, which are the most accurate in describing the conveyance made. Figure 8–3 provides an example of a bargain and sale deed.

bargain and sale deed: A deed that transfers the real property itself rather than transferring any particular interest in the property.

quitclaim deed: A deed in which the grantor transfers whatever interest he or she may have without making any warranties regarding the quality of the title.

Quitclaim Deeds

More commonly used than the bargain and sale deed to transfer property when the seller does not wish to make any guarantees to the buyer is the **quitclaim deed,** sometimes referred to as a *release deed*. There is a technical distinction that should be made between a bargain and sale deed and a quitclaim

FIGURE 8–2
Special warranty deed

SPECIAL WARRANTY DEED

THIS SPECIAL WARRANTY DEED, Made and executed the 12th day of August, 1997, by WOODARD PROPERTIES, INC., a corporation existing under the laws of Any State, and having its principal place of business at 1539 N.E. 4th Avenue, Any City, Any State, hereinafter called the grantor, to DAVID BOSWORTH, a single man, whose post office address is 135 Union Drive, Any City, Any State, hereinafter called the grantee:

WITNESSETH, That the grantor, for and in consideration of the sum of Ten Dollars ($10.00) and other valuable considerations, receipt whereof is hereby acknowledged, by these presents does grant, bargain, sell, alien, remise, release, convey and confirm unto the grantee, all that certain land situate in Any County, State of Any State, to-wit:

The Southeast one-quarter of the Southeast one-quarter of the Northwest one-quarter of Section 2, Township 32 South, Range 12 West, Any County, Any State.

SUBJECT TO easements, restrictions and limitations of record and taxes for the year 1997 and subsequent years.

TOGETHER, with all the tenements, hereditaments and appurtenances thereto belonging or in anywise appertaining.

TO HAVE AND TO HOLD, the same in fee simple forever.

AND the grantor hereby covenants with said grantee that the grantor is lawfully seized of said land in fee simple; that it has good, right and lawful authority to sell and convey said land; that it hereby fully warrants the title to said land and will defend the same against the lawful claims of all persons claiming by, through, or under the said grantor.

IN WITNESS WHEREOF, the grantor has caused these presents to be executed in its name, and its corporate seal to be hereunto affixed, by its proper officers thereunto duly authorized, the day and year first above written.

[Corporate seal]

ATTEST: *Frances Wheeler*
      Secretary

Signed, sealed and delivered in the presence of:

Ruth Barton
Norman Portman

WOODARD PROPERTIES, INC.

By: *George Woodard*
    President

STATE OF ANY STATE
COUNTY OF ANY COUNTY

I HEREBY CERTIFY that on this day before me, an officer duly authorized to administer oaths and take acknowledgments, personally appeared GEORGE WOODARD and FRANCES WHEELER, known to me to be the President and Secretary respectively of WOODARD PROPERTIES, INC., the corporation in whose name the foregoing instrument was executed, and that they severally acknowledged executing the same for such corporation, freely and voluntarily, under authority duly vested in them by said corporation.

WITNESS my hand and official seal in the County and State last aforesaid this 12th day of August, 1997.

Rebecca Barclay
Notary Public, State of Any State
My commission expires: _____

FIGURE 8–3
Bargain and sale deed

BARGAIN AND SALE DEED

THIS INDENTURE, Made this 12th day of August, 1997, Between
           CARY KNOWLES, a single man,
whose post office address is 220 S.E. 9th Terrace, Any City, Any State, referred to as the grantor, and
           NICOLE QUINN, a single woman,
whose post office address is 980 Chastleton Avenue, Any City, Any State, referred to as the grantee.

WITNESSETH, that said grantor, for and in consideration of the sum of Ten Dollars ($10.00), and other good and valuable considerations, the receipt of which is hereby acknowledged, grants and releases to the said grantee, in fee simple, the following described property, consisting of the land and all the buildings and structures on the land, to-wit:

Lot 5 in Block 5 of HEWELL GRANGE, according to to the plat thereof, recorded in Plat Book 1100, Page 13, of the Public Records of Any County, Any State.

SUBJECT TO taxes for the year 1997 and subsequent years, and certain conditions and restrictions of record in Official Records Book 1204, Page 44, of the Public Records of Any County, Any State.

IN WITNESS WHEREOF, grantor has hereunto set his hand and seal the day and year first above written.

Signed, sealed and delivered in our presence:

Sally Griffin   _Cary Knowles_
                                            Cary Knowles

Gene Powell
STATE OF ANY STATE
COUNTY OF ANY COUNTY

I HEREBY CERTIFY that on this day before me, an officer duly qualified to take acknowledgments, personally appeared CARY KNOWLES, a single man, to me known to be the person described in and who executed the foregoing instrument and acknowledged before me that he executed the same.

WITNESS my hand and seal in the County and State last aforementioned this 12th day of August, 1997.

Rebecca Barclay
Notary Public, State of Any State
My commission expires: _____

deed. A bargain and sale deed transfers land only, not interest in the land. With a quitclaim deed, the grantor is transferring whatever interest he or she may have, without making any warranties regarding the quality of his or her interest. If the title is defective, the grantee has no recourse whatsoever against the grantor. Indeed, the grantor may be uncertain as to whether he or she even has a legitimate interest in the real property in question. What the grantor does, in effect, with the use of a quitclaim deed, is convey to the grantee any interest he or she has or *may* have, and no more.

The term *grantor* or *releasor* is used here intentionally rather than *seller* because the transferor of the real property is usually not a "seller" when a quitclaim deed is used. In a sales transaction, a buyer will rarely accept a quit-claim deed. These deeds often are used in intrafamily transfers of title, in divorce proceedings when one spouse transfers his or her interest to the other, in probate proceedings when an heir wishes to give up a claim (present or future) to real property, and to clear any present or potential cloud on the title to real property, or the transfer of less than fee simple title.

Because no warranties are provided by the grantor, in a quitclaim deed, the word *warrant* will be omitted, and the words *remise, release, and quitclaim* will be found. In some states, such as in New Jersey, the conveyance language may be "neutral" (for example, "grant and convey"), but a clause will be inserted to indicate that the deed is a quitclaim deed. A sample quitclaim deed is found in Figure 8–4.

FIGURE 8–4
Quitclaim deed

QUITCLAIM DEED

THIS INDENTURE, Made this 12th day of August, 1997, between AGNES PERKINS, Widow, of the County of Any County, State of Any State, hereinafter referred to as grantor, and PETER PERKINS, a single man, of the County of Any County, State of Any State, hereinafter referred to as grantee.

WITNESSETH that grantor, for and in consideration of the sum of Ten Dollars ($10.00) and other good and valuable considerations, the receipt of which is hereby acknowledged, by these presents does remise, release, and forever quit-claim unto the said grantee the following property:

Condominium Unit No. 201, in HUDDINGTON COURT CONDO-MINIUM, according to the Declaration of Condominium thereof, recorded in Official Records Book 3210, Page 88, of the Public Records of Any County, Any State.

TO HAVE AND TO HOLD the said described premises to grantee, so that nei-ther grantor nor any person or persons claiming under grantor shall at any time have, claim, or demand any right or title to said premises or appurtenances, or any rights thereof.

IN WITNESS WHEREOF, grantor has signed and sealed this deed the day and year first above written.

Signed, sealed and delivered in the presence of:

Jessica McDonnell

Jason Long

Agnes Perkins
Agnes Perkins

STATE OF ANY STATE
COUNTY OF ANY COUNTY

I HEREBY CERTIFY that on this day before me, an officer duly qualified to take acknowledgments, personally appeared AGNES PERKINS, a widow, to me known to be the person described in and who executed the foregoing instrument, and acknowledged before me that she executed the same.

WITNESS my hand and official seal in the County and State last aforesaid this 12th day of August, 1997.

Rebecca Barclay
Notary Public, State of Any State
My commission expires: _____

SPECIAL PURPOSE DEEDS

Corrective Deeds

In most circumstances, conveyance of real property will be done through the use of one of the four deed instruments discussed previously. There are times, however, when special circumstances require the use of a particular special purpose deed. For example, suppose the deed used to transfer title from seller to buyer is later found to contain an error in the spelling of a name, in the marital status of a party, in the legal description, or in the omission of a restriction. To correct such an error, a corrective deed must be prepared, signed, and recorded. Note that documentary stamp taxes need not be paid on corrective deeds because this deed does not represent another conveyance of the property. An example of a corrective deed is found in Figure 8–5, in this case to correct an error of transposing the numbers of an Official Records Book in which a mortgage has been recorded. The buyer (grantee), rather than applying for a new mortgage, has agreed to take over the existing mortgage on the property.

Deeds Conveying Government-Owned Property

Sometimes the grantor of real property is not a private individual or corporation but is a city, county, or state. Prior to the conveyance of government-owned real property, certain procedures must take place. The conveyance must be approved by the appropriate legislative body. This legislative body must, in turn, confer authority upon an official to act on behalf of the city, county, or state in the transaction. If the land is state-owned, the governor, a state agency, or committee must approve the actions of the state legislature in making the decision to sell the property. The deed must recite the date and number of the bill approving the conveyance, must be signed by the official authorized to act on behalf of the state and by the governor, and must be attested to by the secretary of state (if state-owned property). At times, a legislative body may vote to auction off government-owned land to increase revenue. If this is the case, as it is in the sample deed provided in Figure 8–6, the property is sold to the highest bidder.

Fiduciary Deeds

There are circumstances under which the grantor may not be able to sign a deed. For example, the grantor may be under age, the grantor may not have the legal mental capacity because the grantor has been adjudicated incompetent, or the grantor may be deceased. In these and similar circumstances, an appointed fiduciary is given the authority to sign the deed on the grantor's behalf. A fiduciary, such as a personal representative of an estate, a guardian of a minor, or a trustee, ordinarily will not convey property through the use of a general warranty deed but, rather, through the use of a special warranty deed, guaranteeing that he or she did nothing to encumber the property but not making guarantees to defend the title against liens, claims, or defects arising from the actions of others.

FIGURE 8–5
Corrective deed

CORRECTIVE DEED

THIS INDENTURE, made this 12th day of August, 1997, between MARK ROSWELL and DONNA ROSWELL, his wife, of the County of Any County, State of Any State, Grantors, and EMILY STRATFORD, a single woman, of the County of Any County, State of Any State, Grantee,

Whereas, by a warranty deed dated the 30th day of July, 1997 and recorded on the 31st day of July, 1997 in Official Records Book 720, Page 23, of the Public Records of Any County, Any State, the Grantors conveyed to the grantee certain lands therein and hereinafter described; and

Whereas, in the said deed by mistake the words "SUBJECT TO the lien of that certain mortgage to Patriot Bank, dated February 11, 1992, filed of record February 18, 1992 in Official Records Book 689, Page 112 of the Public Records of Any County, Any State, which the Grantee herein assumes and agrees to pay" were written instead of the words "SUBJECT TO the lien of that certain mortgage to Patriot Bank, dated February 11, 1992, filed of record February 18, 1992 in Official Records Book 698, Page 112 of the Public Records of Any County, Any State, which the Grantee herein assumes and agrees to pay," and this deed is executed for the purpose of correcting the said mistake.

WITNESSETH, that the Grantors, for and in consideration of the sum of Ten Dollars ($10.00) and other good and valuable considerations, the receipt whereof is hereby acknowledged, have granted, bargained, and sold to Grantee, and Grantee's heirs and assigns forever, the following described land, situate, lying and being in the County of Any County, State of Any State:

Lot 9 in Block 5 of MAPLE TREE ESTATE, 2ND SECTION, according to the plat thereof, recorded in Plat Book 102, Page 33, of the Public Records of Any County, Any State.

SUBJECT TO the lien of that certain mortgage to Patriot Bank, dated February 11, 1992, filed of record February 18, 1992 in Official Records Book 698, Page 112 of the Public Records of Any County, Any State, which the Grantee herein assumes and agrees to pay.

SUBJECT TO easements, restrictions, and limitations of record and taxes for the year 1997 and subsequent years.

together with all the tenements, hereditaments, and appurtenances thereto belonging or in any wise appertaining.

TO HAVE AND TO HOLD the same in fee simple forever.

AND said Grantors do hereby fully warrant the title to said land, and will defend the same against the lawful claims of all persons whomsoever.

IN WITNESS WHEREOF, Grantors have hereunto set their hands and seals the day and year first above written.

Signed, sealed and delivered in our presence:

Michael Watson _____   _Mark Roswell_ _____
                                     Mark Roswell
Eric Brown _____   _Donna Roswell_ _____
                                     Donna Roswell

STATE OF ANY STATE
COUNTY OF ANY COUNTY

FIGURE 8–5
(continued)

I HEREBY CERTIFY that on this day before me, an officer duly qualified to take acknowledgments, personally appeared MARK ROSWELL and DONNA ROSWELL, his wife, to me known to be the persons described in and who executed the foregoing instrument, and acknowledged before me that they executed the same.

WITNESS my hand and official seal in the County and State aforesaid this 12th day of August, 1997.

Rebecca Barclay
Notary Public, State of Any State
My commission expires: _____

Personal Representatives' Deeds. A personal representative is a person (or entity) who administers the estate of a deceased person. The personal representative operates under the auspices of the probate court. A decedent may have left explicit instructions in a will about how he or she would like to dispose of his or her real property. Unless the will is contested, the probate court by court order normally authorizes the personal representative to make the conveyance(s) in accordance with the decedent's express wishes. If the decedent died intestate, the real property of the decedent is passed on according to the intestate statutes of the state in which the real property is located.

Sometimes a will may direct that a personal representative sell certain real property and deliver the proceeds of the sale to named persons in the will. In these circumstances, the recital of nominal consideration is insufficient, and a recital of the actual consideration paid for the real property must be included in the deed to safeguard the interests of the beneficiaries named in the will. If a conveyance is to be made to a named beneficiary in a will and not to a bona fide purchaser, money does not change hands in the transaction and, therefore, a recital of nominal consideration is appropriate.

Figure 8–7 provides an example of a personal representative's deed conveying real property to a beneficiary named in a will. The real property in question here is a condominium unit. Note that in some states, such as Connecticut, a probate court Certificate of Descent/Devise is used to convey title to heirs or devisees, while a personal representative's deed is used to convey real property to others.

Guardians' Deeds. Not as frequently, a minor may be the owner of real property. As noted earlier, a person must be legally competent to convey real property as a grantor but need not be legally competent to receive real property as a grantee. Infancy (minority) makes a party incapable of conveying real property. However, a minor's real property may be sold on the minor's behalf by the minor's guardian acting as the minor's fiduciary.

As in the case of a personal representative, when a guardian sells real property on behalf of a minor, full disclosure must be made in the deed regarding the actual consideration paid for the property. In most states, the minor, through his or her guardian, must petition the court for permission to

FIGURE 8–6
Deed

DEED

BY VIRTUE OF the authority conferred upon me by Senate Bill No. 97-108 introduced on June 27, 1997 and approved by the state legislature of Any State on July 3, 1997, I, WILLIAM ELLIS, Director of the Department of Agriculture, duly authorized and acting for and on behalf of the State of Any State, Grantor, do hereby grant, sell, and convey to LFR CORPORATION, Grantee, a corporation duly organized and operating under the laws of the State of Any State, having its principal office in the City of Any City, State of Any State, the following described real property:

ALL THAT TRACT of land lying and being in the Southeast quarter of the Northeast quarter of the Northwest quarter of Section 10, Township 50 South, Range 41 East, Any County, Any State.

TO HAVE AND TO HOLD the same unto the said Grantee, and Grantee's successors and assigns, in fee simple, together with all appurtenances thereunto belonging, said Grantee having been the highest bidder at public auction held at the location of the above-described real property on the 5th day of August, 1997, at 10:00 A.M., pursuant to notice duly published as required by law.

Given under my hand and official seal, and of the seal of the State of Any State, this 12th day of August, 1997.

State of Any State

By *William Ellis*
Director of the Department of Agriculture

[Seal]

Approved this 12th day of August, 1997.

Rosemary Maxwell
Governor

Attest:

Alfred Creighton
Secretary of State
[State Seal]

STATE OF ANY STATE
COUNTY OF ANY COUNTY

I HEREBY CERTIFY on this day that an officer duly authorized in the state and county aforesaid, WILLIAM ELLIS, Director of the Department of Agriculture of the State of Any State, personally known to me to be the same person and official who executed the above and foregoing instrument, appeared before me this day in person and acknowledged that, as such official, he signed, sealed and delivered the above and foregoing instrument on behalf of the Grantor, State of Any State, pursuant to authority conferred on him by law.

IN WITNESS WHEREOF I hereunto set my hand and official seal in the County and State last aforesaid this 12th day of August, 1997.

Gregory Nicholls
Notary Public, State of Any State
My commission expires: _____

sell the real property, the court then overseeing the transaction. The court may require that the guardian post a bond and may appoint an individual to act as referee during the transaction as an added protection of the minor's interests.

PERSONAL REPRESENTATIVE'S DEED

THIS INDENTURE, made this 13th day of August,1997, between HENRY MARSHALL, personal representative of the last will and testament of JUDITH STEVENSON, late of the County of Any County, Any State, deceased, as Grantor, and BETH STEVENSON, a single woman, residing at 45 Cotswald Lane, Any City, Any County, Any State, as Grantee.

Whereas, by her last will and testament, dated the 30th day of September 1990, the said JUDITH STEVENSON appointed HENRY MARSHALL as personal representative thereof; and

Whereas, the said JUDITH STEVENSON died on the 11th day of January,1997, and her last will and testament was duly proved and allowed by the probate court of the County of Any County and State of Any State on the 19th of January, 1997;

WITNESSETH, that in the exercise of the powers to him given by the said last will and testament, and in consideration of the sum of Ten Dollars ($10.00) to him in hand paid by the Grantee, the receipt whereof is hereby acknowledged, the Grantor, personal representative as aforesaid, does hereby grant and convey unto the said Grantee all that real property herein described, to wit:

Unit 202, in BRAMBLEWOOD CONDOMINIUM, according to the Declaration of Condominium thereof, recorded in Official Records Book 4907, Page 78 of the public records of Any County, Any State.

SUBJECT TO all valid and existing restrictions, reservations, covenants, conditions, and easements of record.

together with the appurtenances, and also all the estate which the said decedent had at the time of decedent's death in said premises, and also the estate therein, which the Grantor has power to convey;

TO HAVE AND TO HOLD the premises herein granted unto the Grantee in fee simple forever.

AND Grantor covenants that the Grantor has not done or suffered anything whereby the said premises have been encumbered in any way whatever, except as aforesaid.

IN WITNESS WHEREOF, the Grantor has duly executed this deed the day and year first above written.

In presence of:

Jane Harley

Henry Marshall
Henry Marshall as Personal Representative
of the Last Will and Testament of
Christina Owens
Judith Stevenson, Deceased

STATE OF ANY STATE
COUNTY OF ANY COUNTY

I HEREBY CERTIFY that on this day before me, an officer duly authorized in the state and county aforesaid to take acknowledgments, personally appeared HENRY MARSHALL, personal representative of the last will and testament of JUDITH STEVENSON, to me known to be the person described in and who executed the foregoing instrument, and acknowledged before me that he executed the same for the purposes herein expressed.

IN WITNESS WHEREOF I hereunto set my hand and official seal in the County and State last aforesaid this 13th day of August, 1997.

James O'Connell
Notary Public, State of Any State
My commission expires: _____

FIGURE 8–7
Personal representative's deed

Sheriffs' or Referees' Deeds

When real property is foreclosed upon, statutorily prescribed procedures are followed by which title to the real property is passed from the property owner to the highest bidder at a foreclosure sale. Although these procedures differ from state to state, most commonly a court entering judgment on behalf of the creditor (for example, the lender in a mortgage foreclosure, the city or county in a tax sale) will direct a sheriff or court-appointed referee to oversee the public auction of the real property, after which the real property is conveyed to the highest bidder by a deed called a *sheriff's deed* or a *referee's deed*, which is similar to a special warranty deed. The owner of the property does not sign the deed as grantor; rather, the sheriff or referee signs the deed as grantor. Although the sheriff or referee is not considered a fiduciary, a sheriff's or referee's deed is similar to a fiduciary deed in that the grantor makes no guarantees to the grantee(s) concerning title except for the guarantee that he or she has not encumbered the title. A sheriff's or referee's deed is also similar to a fiduciary deed in that the deed must fully disclose the consideration paid for the real property.

Mention must be made here of other circumstances under which a sheriff's or referee's deed may be used to convey real property. In a situation in which real property is jointly owned, the owners may request the court to partition the real property. This commonly occurs in divorce proceedings where the spouses own real property as tenants by the entireties and wish to have the property sold and the proceeds distributed accordingly. A court may order that the property be partitioned and sold at public auction by a sheriff or referee. Figure 8–8 provides an example of a sheriff's deed.

PREPARATION OF DEEDS

As a paralegal, you will often be assigned the task of preparing deeds by your supervising attorney. The first step to take, prior to drafting, is to determine whether your state law prescribes a statutory form that must be utilized. Your office may have blank statutory deed forms on file or on computer that are ready to be customized to the needs of the parties involved in the transaction. The next step is to determine which form of deed is appropriate for the particular transaction. The contract for sale and purchase often specifies the type of deed that will be conveyed upon closing. If the contract is silent, consult the client file notes or ask your supervising attorney. Generally, if the contract for sale and purchase does not otherwise specify, a general warranty deed is used; however, you should not make any assumptions in this regard.

Once the type of deed to be used is determined, the next step is to ascertain the correct, legal names of the parties and their status. As noted earlier, the grantor's current deed or title policy may be consulted to ascertain the correct name of the grantor. Check on whether the grantor's marital status has changed since he or she acquired the property in question. If the grantor was single and is now married, or if the grantor took title to the property in his or her sole name although married, ascertain the name of the grantor's spouse. It may be necessary to have the spouse sign the deed as well. The grantee's name

SHERIFF'S DEED

THIS INDENTURE, made this 14th day of August, 1997, between ROBERT HANDLER, sheriff of the County of Any County, State of Any State, as Grantor, and MONICA JONES, a single woman, residing at 88 Foxtail Lane, Any City, Any County, Any State, as Grantee.

Whereas, at a hearing of the Circuit Court of the County of Any County held on the 8th day of July, 1997, it was ordered by said court, in a certain action then pending therein between plaintiff and defendant, that the mortgaged premises mentioned in the complaint in said action and in said judgment and hereinafter described be sold at public auction according to statute by or under the direction of the sheriff of the County of Any County; that the sale be made in the county where the premises are situated; that said sheriff give public notice of the time of the sale according to statute; that the sheriff execute to the purchaser or purchasers of said mortgaged premises a good and sufficient deed of conveyance for the same; and

Whereas, the sheriff, pursuant to said judgment, did on the 6th day of August, 1997, sell at public auction the premises, due notice of the time and place of such sale being first given, to the Grantee for the sum of One Hundred and Forty-Eight Thousand Dollars ($148,000.00), that being the highest sum bid for the sale.

WITNESSETH, that the Grantor, sheriff as aforesaid, pursuant to the order and judgment of said court and in consideration of the sum of money aforesaid being first duly paid by the Grantee, the receipt whereof is hereby acknowledged, has bargained and sold and by these presents doth grant and convey unto the Grantee the following described land, situate, lying and being in Any County, Any State, to-wit:

Lot 5 in Block 18 of CRESTWOOD ESTATES, 1ST SECTION, according to the plat thereof, recorded in Plat Book 88, Page 41, of the Public Records of Any County, Any State.

To have and to hold the same unto the Grantee, her heirs and assigns forever.

IN WITNESS WHEREOF, the Grantor, sheriff as aforesaid, has hereunto set Grantor's hand and seal the day and year first above written.

Signed, sealed and delivered in our presence:

Faith Freemont   _Robert Handler_
                        Robert Handler, Sheriff of
Gregory Evans   Any County

STATE OF ANY STATE
COUNTY OF ANY COUNTY

I HEREBY CERTIFY that on this day before me, an officer duly qualified to take acknowledgments, personally appeared ROBERT HANDLER, Sheriff of Any County, to me known to be the person described in and who executed the foregoing instrument, and acknowledged before me that he executed the same.

WITNESS my hand and official seal in the County and State last aforesaid this 14th day of August, 1997.

Maria Perez
Notary Public, State of Any State
My commission expires: _____

FIGURE 8–8
Sheriff's deed

will appear on the contract for sale and purchase; however, it is good practice to double-check the spelling, use of middle initials, and so forth.

In states that require the inclusion of the grantee's social security number, obtain this either from the contract for sale and purchase (it is sometimes included under the signature line) or from the grantee directly. Inquiry also must be made about the manner in which title is to be held (for example, tenants by the entirety, tenants in common). The contract for sale and purchase should provide the current addresses of the parties, information that should be included in the deed if required by state statute. If your state requires inclusion of the property appraiser's parcel identification number, this can be copied from the grantor's current deed.

Once this information is obtained, you will be able to draft the premises clause of the deed. The date of execution typically is the date set for closing, but last minute complications often arise, so it is advisable to leave the date blank and fill it in at or directly before closing. A deed should be double-spaced, with the exception of the legal description and any encumbrance or reserving clauses, which are single-spaced and block-indented.

Next, insert a nominal consideration in the granting clause unless your supervising attorney instructs otherwise or unless the deed is a fiduciary deed. Then the grantor's current deed or an updated survey should be reviewed to verify the proper legal description of the real property. If a standard form is used and inadequate space is given for the legal description, make reference in the deed to an attached exhibit and type the description on the exhibit. After typing a legal description, it is always good practice to have someone else review it with you by reading the description from the current deed aloud to the other person and having that person check your typed description for any discrepancies. This is imperative with lengthy metes and bounds legal descriptions.

Unless your supervising attorney prefers you to use a catchall encumbrance clause, such as the one discussed earlier, make sure to list all "subject to" provisions. The encumbrances of record should appear on the title examination. Remember that there may be other encumbrances, such as a second mortgage, that may need to be included, so also review the contract, any addendums, and all other papers in the client's file. Some attorneys, as an extra precaution, list all encumbrances and also include a catchall clause.

Having reviewed state statutes to determine the proper number of witnesses and the required form of acknowledgment, you can draft the testimonium clause, making sure that the grantor's name under the signature line conforms with the grantor's name in the premises clause. If the grantor is a corporation, the name of the corporation should appear above the signature line, the word "By" should appear in front of the signature line, and the name of the signing corporate officer and his or her representative capacity should appear under the signature line (for example, Mildred White, President). Further, be sure to include the attestation of the corporate secretary and the affixation of the corporate seal. The witnesses' names generally do not have to be typed under the signature lines for the witnesses. When typing the acknowledgment, you must include the name and status of the grantor as his or her name appears in the premises clause. If your state statutes require the inclusion of the name and address of the preparer, this appears either at the top or the bottom of the deed. Your supervising attorney's name should be inserted, together with the law firm's address.

After your attorney reviews the deed, calculate the documentary stamps that will be affixed to the deed after signing and prior to recording. To do this, check the contract for sale and purchase for the actual purchase price and the state statutes for the current documentary stamp tax rate. Check compliance with local and state taxing departments. After recordation, the original deed is returned to the grantee. The deed preparation checklist below will provide a helpful review.

DEED PREPARATION CHECKLIST

1. Review state statutes to determine:
   a. Statutory deed forms.
   b. If no statutory forms, state requirements regarding number of witnesses, form of acknowledgment, inclusion of parties' addresses, and so on.
   c. Documentary stamp tax.
2. Review grantor's current deed for:
   a. Correct spelling of grantor's name and grantor's marital status.
   b. Legal description of the property.
   c. Listing of any encumbrances.
   d. Property appraiser's tax identification number (if required).
3. Review updated title examination for a listing of any encumbrances (check against the grantor's current deed).
4. Review contract for sale and purchase for:
   a. Type of deed required by contract.
   b. Correct spelling of grantee's name and marital status (double-check against other documents or directly with the grantee).
   c. Closing date.
   d. Social security numbers (if required).
5. Determine manner in which title is to be held by grantee(s).
6. Determine whether additional encumbrances (other than those of record) exist or will be created (for example, a second mortgage). These must be included in the deed.
7. Using the information supplied above, draft:
   a. Premises clause.
      i. Leave date of execution blank.
      ii. Insert appropriate county and state, names and statuses of the parties, manner in which title will be held (this may be included additionally or alternatively in the granting clause), and the addresses of the parties, if applicable.
   b. Granting clause.
      i. Insert the recital of consideration and the manner in which title is to be held by the grantees, if this was not included in the premises clause.
      ii. Insert legal description (either type legal description in the body of the deed or include as an exhibit).
   c. Encumbrance and reddendum clauses. Insert all "subject to" provisions and any reserving clauses.
   d. Testimonium clause.
      i. Prepare signature lines for grantor(s) and witnesses.
      ii. Prepare acknowledgment.

8. *Before the deed is signed:*
    a. *Have supervising attorney review it.*
    b. *Once date of closing is confirmed, insert date, and then make copies for grantor, lending institution, and office file.*
9. *After the deed is signed:*
    a. *Conform copies to the original.*
    b. *Affix documentary stamps.*
    c. *Record deed and comply with local and state taxing departments.*
    d. *Return original deed to the grantee.*

RECORDING DEEDS AND OTHER REAL ESTATE DOCUMENTS

In the preceding discussion, mention was made a number of times of documents in the public record. Documents are placed in the public record through a process called **recording.** When a document is recorded, it is delivered to the appropriate government official for transcription into a plat book, deed book, mortgage book, or official records book. The document may then be perused by anyone who knows the book number and page number. An inquiring person who does not know the book and page number may locate them through one of several indexes, such as a grantor-grantee index or a mortgage index. Many types of documents may be recorded, including but not limited to deeds, mortgages, satisfactions of mortgages, liens, easements, releases of liens, plat maps, and declarations of condominium.

The purpose of recording documents is to put the public on notice regarding the information contained in the document. If the document in question is a deed, the recording of the deed puts the public on notice regarding the contents of the deed, including the identification of the current owner of the real property, the legal description of the property, and the encumbrances on the property. This notice is referred to as **constructive notice,** meaning that the information recorded has been made available to anyone who searches the public records. **Actual notice** refers to direct knowledge a person has about the ownership and condition of title of real property. For example, title to property is conveyed by deed to Janet Ingram. The deed is recorded. Michael Holt drives by the property in question and decides he would like to buy it if it is available. Michael has constructive notice of the owner of the subject property because the deed is recorded in the public records. If Michael visits the registry office and inspects the deed, he then has actual notice of the owner of the property and of the encumbrances on the property.

Recording Statutes

Each state has statutory law referred to as **recording statutes** that prescribes the requirements for recording a document and determines the priority of rights to real property if there are conflicting claims. There are three types of recording statutes: (1) race statutes, (2) notice statutes, and (3) race-notice statutes. To understand the differences between these statutes, imagine a situation in which more than one party is making a claim to a particular parcel of real property, and both parties acquired the property from the same

recording: Delivering a document to the appropriate government official for transcription into a plat book, deed book, mortgage book, or official records book.

constructive notice: Notice legally presumed because of the recording of documents in the public records.

actual notice: Direct knowledge a person has about the ownership and condition of title of real property.

recording statute: A statute that prescribes the requirements for recording a document and that determines the priority of rights to real property if there are conflicting claims.

grantor. Further, imagine that both parties are bona fide purchasers for value. A **bona fide purchaser for value** is someone who purchases property in good faith and for valid consideration.

Race Statutes. Assuming the above scenario, in a state with a **race statute,** priority of claim to title of the property is determined literally by a race to the recording office. The first person to record his or her deed to the property is deemed to have superior title. For example, suppose Stanley is the owner of the subject property and he conveys the property to Karen by a deed on the 4th of January, 1998. Karen plans on recording the deed but does not get around to doing so until the 20th of January. In the interim, Stanley conveys the same property to Nicholas by a deed dated the 7th of January, 1998. Nicholas records the deed that same day. If both Karen and Nicholas are bona fide purchasers for value in a race statute state, Nicholas would have a superior claim to the property. This is true even if Nicholas knew of Stanley's prior conveyance to Karen. The first to record the deed wins.

Notice Statutes. In a state with a **notice statute,** the notice a subsequent purchaser has of a previous purchaser's deed is controlling. Assume the same scenario with Stanley, Karen, and Nicholas, but add the fact that Nicholas had actual knowledge of Stanley's prior conveyance to Karen at the time Nicholas accepted delivery of his deed on the 7th of January. Because Nicholas had actual knowledge, in a state with a notice statute, he is deemed to have been put on notice of Karen's claim, and Karen's claim is therefore considered superior to that of Nicholas.

Race-Notice Statutes. A **race-notice statute** is the most common form of notice statute, combining aspects of both theories. In a race-notice state, the premise is to protect a bona fide purchaser for value without notice if he or she is the first to record the deed. Thus, if the subsequent purchaser has no notice of a prior purchaser's claim and is the first to record his or her deed, this subsequent purchaser has priority.

The Torrens System

The **Torrens system** was invented by Sir Robert Torrens in the late nineteenth century and provides a unique method for determining title to real property through the institution of a lawsuit. The procedure commences when an applicant files an application with the court in which he or she makes a claim to title of the property and lists any other parties who have any interest in the property. A suit is brought in which all those listed are defendants and must defend their claims to title. If they fail to appear in court to defend their claims or if their claims are found to be inferior, the applicant is considered the proper titleholder, and the court orders the registrar of title to issue a certificate of title called a **Torrens certificate,** presenting title to the applicant. The Torrens certificate is the actual legal title to the property in states that still use this system. This certificate is then registered in the public records. When the property is transferred, the certificate is canceled and a new certificate is issued to the transferee. Because this system is laborious and time-consuming, it is not widely used.

bona fide purchaser for value: Someone who purchases property in good faith and for valid consideration.

race statute: A recording statute whereby priority of claim to title of real property is determined literally by a race to the recording office.

notice statute: A recording statute whereby the notice a subsequent purchaser has of a previous purchaser's deed is imperative in determining the priority of title to the real property.

race-notice statute: A recording statute premised on protecting a bona fide purchaser for value without notice if he or she is the first to record the deed to real property.

Torrens system: A method for determining title to real property through the institution of a lawsuit.

Torrens certificate: In states that utilize the Torrens system, a certificate, issued by the registrar of title, that is the actual legal title to the real property.

HYPOTHETICAL CLIENT MATTER

Scott and Theresa Reed are selling their condominium in Fair Isles Village to Warren and Melissa Sloane. The Sloanes have been screened by the condominium association and have been approved. The Reeds have hired attorney Ava Ross to handle the real estate closing. According to the client file, the closing is to take place at the end of the week. Since everything seems to be on schedule, Ava has asked her paralegal, Barbara, to prepare the deed for review. Ava will be out of the office for the next two days and, therefore, would like to review the deed as soon as possible. Barbara consults the contract for sale and purchase, which indicates that the property is to be conveyed by general warranty deed. She checks the signatures of the grantees for proper spelling. She then consults a copy of the Reeds' current deed in the client file and notices that Scott's name includes the middle initial "P." She continues to review the deed for the legal description of the property as well as any encumbrances on the property. She notes an easement in favor of the Any State Power and Light Company as well as a reference to the Declaration of Condominium of Fair Isles Village. She then checks the title examination and notes a mortgage in favor of Hamilton Savings and Loan Association that will be paid off at closing because the Sloanes have opted for a new mortgage loan rather than assuming the outstanding one. Her file notes indicate that the Sloanes are taking title as tenants by the entirety.

With this information in hand, Barbara locates her state's statutory general warranty deed on her computer. The signatures of two witnesses are required. Besides being a paralegal, Barbara is also a notary public, and she will notarize the deed. Her completed deed reads as shown in Figure 8–9.

Barbara next refers back to the contract for sale and purchase to determine the purchase price of the condominium, which is stated in the contract as $150,000. The current documentary stamp tax rate in Any County is $.60 per each $100 or fraction thereof. Barbara divides the purchase price by one hundred and then multplies the resulting sum by .60, arriving at a documentary stamp tax of $900. After the deed is signed at closing, Barbara will affix the appropriate stamps to the deed. Finally, she pulls up on her computer screen the state department of revenue form and completes it as shown in Figure 8–10.

As a final touch, Barbara places stickers on the sections of the form that must be filled in on the day of closing.

FIGURE 8–9
Warranty deed

This instrument prepared by:

Ava Ross, Esquire
Fisher, Ross, and Simon, P.A.
1900 N.W. 3rd Avenue
Any City, Any State

WARRANTY DEED

THIS INDENTURE, Made this _____ day of _____, 1997, by and between SCOTT P. REED and THERESA REED, husband and wife, hereinafter called Grantors, and WARREN SLOANE and MELISSA SLOANE, husband and wife, as tenants by the entirety, hereinafter called Grantees.

WITNESSETH, That said Grantors, for and in consideration of the sum of Ten Dollars ($10.00), and other good and valuable considerations to said Grantors in hand paid by said Grantees, the receipt whereof is hereby acknowledged, hereby grant, bargain, and sell to said Grantees the following described land, situate, lying and being in Any County, Any State, to-wit:

Unit 301, of FAIR ISLES VILLAGE, a Condominium according to the Declaration of Condominium recorded in Official Records Book 2238, Page 170, of the Public Records of Any County, Any State.

SUBJECT TO an easement to Any State Power and Light Company dated September 6, 1981, recorded September 6, 1981 in Official Records Book 2030, Page 11, of the Public Records of Any County, Any State.

SUBJECT TO the Declaration of Condominium of Fair Isles Village, a Condominium, and Exhibits thereto recorded January 9, 1987 in Official Records Book 3065, Page 40, of the Public Records of Any County, Any State.

SUBJECT TO taxes for the year 1997 and subsequent years.

TO HAVE AND TO HOLD the above described premises, unto the Grantees in fee simple forever, together with all the tenements, hereditaments, and appurtenances thereto belonging or in any wise appertaining.

AND the Grantors hereby covenant with the said Grantees that the Grantors are lawfully seized of said premises in fee simple; that the Grantors have good right and lawful authority to sell and convey said premises; that the Grantors fully warrant the title to said premises and will defend the same against the lawful claims of all persons whomsoever; and that said premises is free of all encumbrances, except those expressly stated herein.

IN WITNESS WHEREOF, the Grantors have signed and sealed these presents the day and year first above written.

Signed, sealed and delivered in our presence:

_____   _____
                                     SCOTT P. REED

_____   _____
                                     THERESA REED

STATE OF ANY STATE
COUNTY OF ANY COUNTY

FIGURE 8–9
(continued)

I HEREBY CERTIFY that on this day before me, an officer duly qualified to take acknowledgments, personally appeared SCOTT P. REED and THERESA REED, husband and wife, to me known to be the persons described in and who executed the foregoing instrument, and they acknowledged before me that they executed the same.

WITNESS my hand and official seal in the County and State last aforesaid this ____ day of _____, 19__.

_____
Notary Public, State of Any State
My commission expires: _____

FIGURE 8–10
State department of revenue form

DEPARTMENT OF REVENUE OF ANY STATE RETURN FOR TRANSFERS OF INTEREST IN ANY STATE REAL PROPERTY

PART I:
A.   Grantor (Seller): Scott P. Reed and Theresa Reed, husband and wife
B.   Mailing Address: 27 Windsor Court, Any City, Any State
C.   Grantee (Buyer): Warren Sloane and Melissa Sloane, husband and wife
D.   Mailing Address: 350 Fair Isles Lane, # 301, Any City, Any State
E.   Description of Property: Unit 301 of FAIR ISLES VILLAGE, a Condominium according to the Declaration of Condominium recorded in Official Records Book 2238, Page 170 of the Public Records of Any County, Any State
F.   Date of Sale: _____
G.   Type of Document: General warranty deed
H.   Recorded in: Any County, Any State
I.   Total Consideration Paid or to Be Paid: $150,000.00

I HEREBY CERTIFY that this return has been examined by me and to the best of my knowledge and belief is a true and complete return.

_____   _____
Signature of Grantee   Date

_____   _____
Signature of Grantee   Date
PART II: (To be completed by the Clerk of the Circuit Court's Office):

File Number: _____ or O.R. Book _____ Page _____
Clerk's Date Stamp: _____ Date Recorded: _____

CHAPTER SUMMARY

1. A valid deed includes the names and current statuses of the grantor and grantee, the date of execution, a recital of consideration, words of conveyance, a legal description of the property, the signatures of the grantor and witnesses, and an acknowledgment. In addition, some states require the inclusion of other items such as the grantee's social security number, the property appraiser's parcel identification number, and/or the addresses of one or both parties.

2. Extra care should be taken in the spelling of the parties' names, the typing of the legal description, and the inclusion of all pertinent restrictions.

Should an error come to light after a deed is signed and recorded, a corrective deed must be prepared indicating and correcting the error.

3. Documentary stamps must be affixed to a deed prior to recording. These stamps evidence the payment of a transfer tax on the transfer of the real property. The tax is based on the purchase price of the property.

4. All deeds contain a premises clause, a granting clause, a habendum clause, and a testimonium clause. These first three clauses specify the parties, the date of execution, the words of conveyance, and the type of estate being conveyed. The testimonium clause includes the signatures of the grantor and the witnesses as well as the acknowledgment. Depending on the type of deed used and the nature of the transaction, other clauses may be added.

5. A general warranty deed provides the greatest protection for the grantee. It includes the covenant of seisin, the covenant against encumbrances, the covenant of quiet enjoyment, the covenant of further assurances, and the covenant of warranty forever. Through conveyance of property by a general warranty deed, the grantor is promising to forever defend the grantee's title against any and all claims.

6. A special warranty deed is limited in the number of covenants made by the grantor to the grantee. The grantor of a special warranty deed is warranting only that he or she has done nothing to encumber the property, but makes no statements of warranty regarding the actions of prior titleholders.

7. Neither a bargain and sale deed nor a quitclaim deed contains convenants guaranteeing good title. A bargain and sale deed simply transfers property, not any particular interest in the property. A quitclaim deed only transfers whatever interest the grantor has in the property, if any, and thus makes no representations regarding the quality of title.

8. There are a number of preliminary steps that should be taken prior to drafting a deed. State statutes should be consulted to determine state requirements for the content of the deed and to determine whether the use of statutory deed forms is mandated. The grantor's current deed should be examined for correct spelling of the grantor's name, for the legal description, and for the listing of any encumbrances. An updated title examination should be consulted for a listing of encumbrances not listed with particularity in the current deed. Finally, the contract for sale and purchase should be reviewed to ascertain the type of deed required, the closing date, and the correct spelling of the grantee's name.

9. The recording of documents such as deeds, mortgages, and other liens puts the public on constructive notice of the existence of these documents. Each state has its own recording statutes prescribing the requirements for recording documents and determining the priority of adverse claims. State recording statutes are either race statutes, notice statutes, or race-notice statutes, each of which has its own method of determining the priority of rights to real property.

REVIEW QUESTIONS

1. Distinguish between the following.
   a. A general warranty deed and a special warranty deed
   b. A bargain and sale deed and a quitclaim deed
2. Name and explain each of the covenants contained in a general warranty deed.
3. Outline the steps to be taken:
   a. Prior to the actual drafting of a deed
   b. During the actual drafting of a deed
   c. After the drafting of a deed
4. Compare and contrast a race statute, a notice statute, and a race-notice statute.

ETHICAL QUESTIONS

You have just assisted in a closing on a large commercially zoned tract of land purchased by your firm's client, Talbott Industries, Inc. Talbott Industries is a large pharmaceutical company and is planning on moving its headquarters from its present location to your city. Approximately seven thousand employees will be employed at this new location once Talbott constructs its plant on the acquired property. Thus far, the only people with knowledge of these plans are the parties directly involved in the real estate closing transaction. Talbott is planning on making a public announcement after its annual meeting of its shareholders at the beginning of next month.

This afternoon, another client, Jim Campbell, president of Campbell Construction Company, has an appointment with your supervising attorney to discuss a possible land acquisition. Campbell Construction Company specializes in moderately priced residential developments and, at the present time, is considering the acquisition of one of three land tracts for a new development project, each in a different area of the city. One of the tracts being considered is very close to the future Talbott headquarters. You know that a moderately priced residential development would be a great success in that location because of the number of new families that will be transferring from the present Talbott headquarters to its new location. Jim Campbell tells your supervising attorney that he is coming close to signing a contract on one of the other tracts of land, and he wants her to review the seller's proposed contract. What should you do?

PRACTICAL ASSIGNMENTS

Assignment 8:1. Research your state statutes regarding the following.
a. Statutory deed forms used in your state
b. Requirements pertaining to deed contents, number of witnesses, and form of acknowledgment
c. Current documentary stamp tax rate
d. Your state's recording statute(s)

Photocopy the relevant statutes and insert them under the "General Information" section of your resource portfolio.

Assignment 8:2. Obtain a copy of your local and state tax department's requirements for reporting the sale of real property and insert them under the "General Information" section of your resource portfolio.

Assignment 8:3. Recall the contract you drafted under Assignment 7:7 in the preceding chapter. Assume the parties signed the contract on the date it was drafted, and as estimated, the closing is to take place exactly ten months from that date. The property will be conveyed by general warranty deed. The legal description of the property is as follows:

> Lot 4 in Block 4 of ORANGE WALK ESTATES according to the plat thereof, recorded in Plat Book 71, Page 117 of the Public Records of (your county and state).

Assume that Lyndale Properties, Inc., is incorporated in your state and that Craig Newfield will be signing the deed as president of Lyndale Properties, with Margaret Spencer attesting as secretary. Alan and Laura Newman are taking title as tenants by the entirety (if your state does not recognize this form of joint tenancy, substitute joint tenants with right of survivorship). They are taking title to the property subject to all easements, restrictions, and limitations of record and taxes for the current year and subsequent years. The property appraiser's property identification number (if required by your state) is 5716-901. If your state requires the preparer's name and address, indicate that the deed was prepared by your supervising attorney, Deborah Sanders, Esq., Hernandez, Sanders, and Norris, P.A., 263 Republic Avenue (your city, your state). With this information, prepare a general warranty deed that meets your state's requirements. Any other information that might be required may be found in the contract. Upon review, insert the deed under the "Residential Property" section of your resource portfolio.

Assignment 8:4. After completing the deed, calculate the documentary stamp tax that will be imposed on the transfer of the property. Obtain a copy of your state's department of revenue form (if applicable), photocopy it, and complete one copy according to instructions. Insert the original blank revenue form under the "General Information" section of your resource portfolio. Upon review of the completed form, insert it under the "Residential Property" section of your resource portfolio.

Assignment 8:5. Define the following key terms.

actual notice

bargain and sale deed

bona fide purchaser for value

constructive notice

covenant

deed

documentary stamps

encumbrance clause

general warranty deed

grantee

granting clause

grantor

habendum clause

notice statute

premises clause

quitclaim deed

race-notice statute

race statute

recording

recording statute

reddendum clause

seisin clause

special warranty deed

tenendum clause

testimonium clause

Torrens certificate

Torrens system

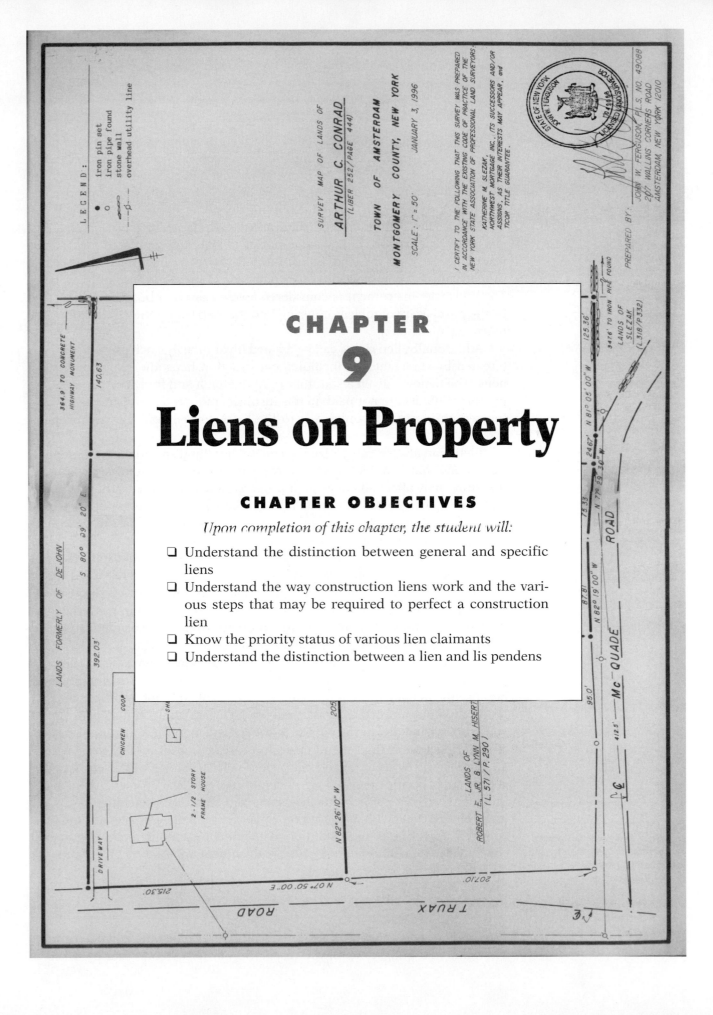

CHAPTER
9

Liens on Property

CHAPTER OBJECTIVES

Upon completion of this chapter, the student will:

❑ Understand the distinction between general and specific liens
❑ Understand the way construction liens work and the various steps that may be required to perfect a construction lien
❑ Know the priority status of various lien claimants
❑ Understand the distinction between a lien and lis pendens

INTRODUCTION

A *lien* is a claim against property that secures a debt incurred by the property owner. A lien acts as an *encumbrance* on property because it is an interest in property that diminishes the property's value. A lien allows a *lienholder*, also referred to as a *lienor*, to request a court order to force the sale of property to satisfy, or partially satisfy, the outstanding debt.

Lien rights can be created voluntarily, such as when a prospective purchaser of real property takes out a mortgage loan and, in return for the borrowed money, gives the lending institution a *mortgage* that attaches to the real property until the borrowed monies plus agreed-upon interest are paid back. The mortgage instrument is considered a voluntary lien because it is created by the purchaser voluntarily entering into the loan transaction and signing the mortgage instrument.

Additionally, lien rights can be created involuntarily, such as *statutory liens* (created by state statute), including construction liens and real property tax liens. The lienor is given a statutory right to attach and foreclose upon certain property if debts are not paid, in this instance, monies due to persons improving real property or monies due to the local government for real property taxes.

Liens can also be categorized as general liens and specific liens. A **general lien** is one that is not secured by any particular parcel of real property and, therefore, may affect all nonexempt property of a debtor. An example of a general lien is a lien for federal estate taxes. If these taxes are not paid, the United States government may go after any nonexempt property of the decedent's estate, wherever it is located, as full or partial satisfaction of the debt. Thus, the government may force the sale of a home, a car, a boat, and so forth.

A **specific lien** is one that is secured by a particular parcel of real property. An example of a specific lien is a special assessment lien. As discussed in detail in Chapter 4, property owners are charged for special improvements in their neighborhood that enhance their property value, such as the installation of sidewalks or sewer hookups. If the charges are not paid, a real property owner may have a special assessment lien recorded against his or her real property. The lienholder cannot go after other property of the debtor, however, because the lien attaches to the real property itself, and not to the debtor.

As a paralegal working in the area of real estate law, you may be asked by your supervising attorney to assist in the enforcement of a judgment or construction lien for a firm client, to draft a satisfaction of mortgage or writ or attachment, or to file a notice of lis pendens. This chapter will discuss various general and specific liens that are encumbrances on real property, the manner in which each type of lien attaches, and each lien's priority status in the lien hierarchy. Special focus is placed on construction liens, for they are the most complex of liens in terms of statutory regulation and enforcement. The chapter concludes with a discussion of writs of attachment and notices of lis pendens.

general lien: A lien that is not secured by any particular parcel of real property and, therefore, may affect all nonexempt property of a debtor.

specific lien: A lien that is secured by a particular parcel of real property.

JUDGMENT LIENS

A *judgment* is a final decree of a court resolving a dispute and determining the rights and obligations of the respective parties. A court can be asked to award a monetary judgment or a declaratory judgment. A **monetary judgment** is an award of monies to a plaintiff if he or she wins the lawsuit. A **declaratory judgment** is one that is sought when the parties want a judicial decree on their status and rights with regard to a particular matter.

When a money judgment is issued in favor of a plaintiff in a lawsuit, the plaintiff becomes a *judgment creditor* of the defendant (debtor) who is now indebted to the plaintiff for the amount stated in the judgment award. If the defendant fails to pay the plaintiff according to the terms of the court award, the plaintiff, as creditor, may have legal recourse to force the sale of the plaintiff's property to satisfy the debt. Because the amount of debt, if any, owed by the defendant to the plaintiff is undetermined prior to a court determination, the plaintiff has no collateral for the alleged debt. Once a judgment has been awarded in the plaintiff's favor, the plaintiff can look to both the real and personal property of the defendant. Thus, a judgment lien is a general lien.

A judgment award in and of itself is not the lien. For a judgment to become a lien and attach to real property, a certified copy of the judgment must be recorded in a *judgment docket, register,* or in some counties, the *official records book,* in the county in which the real property is located. This is true even if the county in which the property is located is the same county as the one in which the judgment was rendered by the court.

For example, suppose David Holmes brought suit against Jack Alexander in a personal injury action in the County of Any County and was successful. The jury returned a judgment in David's favor in the amount of $100,000. The judgment is recorded in the public records by the clerk of the civil court. Jack has some income property located in Any County. If David wants to proceed against this property to satisfy the $100,000 award, David must obtain a certified copy of the judgment from the clerk and record it as a judgment lien in the judgment docket or register. If a plaintiff wishes to proceed against property located outside the court's jurisdiction, the plaintiff must obtain a certified copy of the judgment and have it recorded in the other counties in which the defendant has property.

State statutes determine what property is exempt by law from forced sale. In some states, homestead property is exempted totally from forced sale to satisfy a judgment. In other states, a statutorily specified dollar amount of the value of the homestead property, or of the debtor's equity in the homestead property, is exempt from creditors. Therefore, if homestead property was totally exempt in Jack's state, David would be prevented from proceeding against Jack's home, but he would not be prevented from proceeding against other property, such as the income property owned by Jack.

To enforce a judgment lien, the plaintiff must have the court issue a **writ of execution,** which directs the sheriff to levy upon the property and sell it at a sheriff's sale. The proceeds of the sale are used to pay the plaintiff the monies owed to him or her and to pay for the expenses incurred in the execution process. Any surplus from the sale is returned to the defendant.

State statutes dictate the priority date of judgment liens. In most states, a judgment lien's priority in regard to a particular parcel of real property is established by the date of the recording of the lien in the county in which the parcel is located. In some states, priority status is determined not by the date of recording, but rather by the date the court entered the judgment. In still other states, priority status is determined by the date of issuance of the writ of

monetary judgment: An award of monies to a plaintiff if he or she wins a lawsuit.

declaratory judgment: A judgment sought when the parties to a lawsuit want a judicial decree on their status and rights with regard to a particular matter.

writ of execution: A court order that directs the sheriff to levy upon real property and sell it at a sheriff's sale.

execution. Once a judgment lien is recorded, it remains a lien against real property until the debt is paid or the statute of limitations expires. If the defendant pays the court award, plus any accrued interest, a **satisfaction of judgment** must be recorded to evidence the satisfaction of the debt and the removal of the encumbrance from the property.

In the earlier example, if David records a judgment lien against Jack's income property and Jack then sells the property to Oscar Addison, Oscar takes title to the property subject to the lien. Thus, Oscar must pay off the lien or take the risk of having a writ of execution issued and the property levied against. If Oscar had researched, or had his attorney or a title company research, the title to the property prior to closing on it, he would have been aware of the judgment lien, and he would have elected either to have Jack clear the title by satisfying the debt and recording a satisfaction of judgment, or he would have chosen not to proceed with the closing. A sample judgment and satisfaction of judgment are provided in Figures 9–1 and 9–2, respectively.

satisfaction of judgment: A document recorded to evidence the satisfaction of a debt and the removal of an encumbrance from real property.

FIGURE 9–1
Final judgment

IN THE CIRCUIT COURT OF THE NINTH JUDICIAL CIRCUIT, IN AND FOR ANY COUNTY, ANY STATE

DAVID HOLMES,   CASE NO. 97-12345 GORDON
    Plaintiff,
vs.
JACK ALEXANDER,
    Defendant.
_____/

FINAL JUDGMENT

THIS CAUSE coming on to be heard before the Honorable Christine Gordon and a jury who, having been first duly sworn according to law, returned in open Court the following verdict, to-wit:

"WE, THE JURY, find in favor of the Plaintiff, DAVID HOLMES, and against the Defendant, JACK ALEXANDER, and assess the damages of the Plaintiff, DAVID HOLMES, in the amount of One Hundred Thousand Dollars ($100,000.00).

SO SAY WE ALL.

/s/ James McGee
Foreman

DATE: May 17, 1997"

IT IS, THEREFORE, ORDERED AND ADJUDGED that Final Judgment be, and it is hereby entered, in said cause in favor of the Plaintiff, DAVID HOLMES, and against the Defendant, JACK ALEXANDER; and the Plaintiff, DAVID HOLMES, shall have and recover from said Defendant the sum of ONE HUNDRED THOUSAND DOLLARS ($100,000.00), lawful money of the United States of America, for which sum let execution issue; each party to bear their own costs.

DONE AND ORDERED in Chambers at Any City, Any County, Any State, this 17th day of May, 1997.

Christine Gordon
Circuit Judge

FIGURE 9–2
Satisfaction of judgment

IN THE CIRCUIT COURT OF THE NINTH JUDICIAL CIRCUIT,
IN AND FOR ANY COUNTY, ANY STATE

DAVID HOLMES,   CASE NO. 97-12345 GORDON
  Plaintiff,

vs.

JACK ALEXANDER,
  Defendant.

_____/

SATISFACTION OF JUDGMENT

KNOW ALL MEN BY THESE PRESENTS: That I, DAVID HOLMES, the Plaintiff in the above-styled cause, wherein a judgment was rendered on the 17th day of May, 1997 in the above-named court for ONE HUNDRED THOUSAND DOLLARS ($100,000.00) against JACK ALEXANDER, the Defendant therein, and judgment being duly recorded in the minutes of said Court and a copy thereof having been recorded in Official Records Book number 147157, Page 288, of the public records of Any County, Any State, do hereby acknowledge full payment and satisfaction thereof and hereby consent that the same shall be satisfied of record.

WITNESS my hand and seal this 15th day of August, 1997.

Signed, sealed, and delivered in the presence of:

_____   _____
Jean Karney   David Holmes

_____
Deborah Portman

STATE OF ANY STATE
COUNTY OF ANY COUNTY

On this 15th day of August, 1997, personally appeared before me David Holmes and acknowledged that he executed the foregoing Satisfaction of Judgment for the purposes therein expressed.

WITNESS my hand and seal the day and year last above written.

_____
Notary Public, State of Any State
My commission expires: _____

TAX LIENS

Federal, state, and local governments can attach liens to private property if a taxpayer fails to pay taxes in a timely manner. These tax liens can include liens for failure to pay federal and state income taxes, federal and state estate and inheritance taxes, intangible taxes, corporate franchise taxes, business-related taxes, and real property taxes. All of these taxes except the last one, real property taxes, are general liens.

Federal tax liens attach to all property of the debtor, including property that may be exempt from judgment liens, such as homestead property. A federal tax lien's priority is based on the date of its recording. According to federal statute, federal tax liens are valid for ten years and thirty days from the date of assessment unless the lien is refiled during that time period. Please note that the date of assessment is different than the date of recording of the lien.

A federal tax lien will indicate the name and address of the delinquent tax-payer, the kind(s) of taxes owing, the pertinent tax period(s), the date(s) of assessment, identifying number(s), and the unpaid balance of the assessment(s). A *tax sale* is held after a notice of tax sale is published in a newspaper of general circulation in the county in which the real property to be sold is located. The purchaser of the property must pay, at a minimum, the amount of the delinquent tax, any accrued penalties, and court costs. The delinquent tax-payer is given the **equitable right of redemption,** which is the right to buy back the property at any time prior to the tax sale by paying the full amount of the tax owed and all additional charges. In some states, the delinquent tax-payer may redeem the property even after a tax sale by paying the amount paid at the tax sale, plus any additional interest and charges. This right, if granted, is a statutory right and is known as the *statutory right of redemption.*

State tax liens, such as those for state estate and inheritance taxes, intangible taxes, corporate franchise taxes, and business-related taxes, are governed by state statute. *Estate and inheritance tax liens* are encumbrances on a decedent's real and personal property and are normally satisfied as part of the probate proceedings of a decedent's estate. **Intangible taxes** are taxes imposed in certain states for the right to issue, execute, sell, assign, trade in, or receive income from intangible property, such as stocks and bonds. *Corporate franchise taxes* are taxes imposed for the right to exist and do business as a corporation in a certain state.

Real property tax liens may be enforced only against the real property that is the subject of the tax. They have priority over all other liens and need not be recorded to be enforced. Real property tax liens may be imposed for failure to pay ad valorem real property taxes or special assessment taxes. As with other tax liens, the real property can be sold at a tax sale to satisfy the outstanding tax bill, penalties, and costs. The owner of the real property must be given notice of the proposed sale, and notice is also published in a newspaper of general circulation in the county in which the real property is located. (See Figure 9–3 for a sample notice of sale.) In some states, prior to giving public notice of the sale, the taxing authority must file a *bill of complaint* in the appropriate court in the county in which the property is located, naming itself as complainant and the property as defendant. After a tax sale, the purchaser of the property receives a *tax deed.* If the real property is not sold at a tax sale because of lack of interest, the real property may be forfeited to the state.

MORTGAGE LIENS

equitable right of redemption: The right to buy back real property at any time prior to a forced sale by paying the full amount of the debt owed and all additional charges.

intangible tax: A tax imposed for the right to issue, execute, sell, assign, trade in, or receive income from intangible property.

A *mortgage* instrument is one of two documents given by the *mortgagor* (the person or entity receiving the loan) to the *mortgagee* (the lender). Although financing instruments, including mortgage instruments, are discussed in great detail in the next chapter, a word concerning mortgage instruments is necessary here to illustrate how one works as a lien on real property.

When an individual or business entity takes out a loan to purchase real property, the lender requires a promissory note and a mortgage. The *promissory note* is a document in which an individual or business entity, called the *maker,* promises to repay a loan to the lender. If a default on the loan occurs,

FIGURE 9–3
Notice of sale

**IN THE CIRCUIT COURT OF THE SEVENTH JUDICIAL CIRCUIT,
IN AND FOR ANY COUNTY, ANY STATE**

CITY OF ANY CITY,   CASE NO. 6000830
    Complainant,   Phase III, Parcel 65B
vs.
CERTAIN LANDS UPON WHICH SPECIAL ASSESSMENTS ARE DELINQUENT,
    Defendants.

NOTICE

TO ALL PERSONS AND CORPORATIONS INTERESTED IN OR HAVING ANY LIEN OR CLAIM UPON ANY OF THE LANDS DESCRIBED HEREIN:

You are hereby notified that the CITY OF ANY CITY has filed its Bill of Complaint in the above-named court to foreclose delinquent special assessments, with interest and penalties, upon the parcel of land set forth below. The aggregate amounts of such special assessments, including accelerated principal balance, with interest and penalties through August 15, 1997, against said parcel of land, as set forth in said Bill of Complaint, are set forth below:

DESCRIPTION OF LAND
Phase III, Parcel 65B

A portion of Section 18, Township 49 South, Range 41 East, more particularly described as follows:

The South 112.00 feet of the Northeast one-quarter of the Southwest one-quarter of the Southeast one-quarter of said Section 18, less therefrom the East 332.90 feet thereof, together with:

The Southeast one-quarter of the Southwest one-quarter of the Southeast one-quarter of said Section 18, less therefrom the South 577.00 feet and the East 332.90 feet thereof.

Said lands situate, lying and being in the City of Any City, Any County, Any State, and contain 1.0424 acres, more or less. Said parcel being a portion of PINERIDGE INDUSTRIAL PARK, PARCEL 65, as recorded in Plat Book 126, Page 28, of the Public Records of Any County, Any State.

Amount Due: $49,922.18 (plus per diem interest and penalty after 8/15/97).

In addition to the amount set forth herein, interest and penalties, as provided by law, on such delinquent special assessments, together with the costs and expenses of this suit are sought to be enforced and foreclosed in this suit. You are hereby notified to appear and make your defenses to said Bill of Complaint on or before the date of August 26, 1997, and if you fail to do so on or before said date, the bill will be taken as confessed by you, and you will be barred from thereafter contesting said suit, and said respective parcel of land will be sold by decree and said Court for nonpayment of said assessment lien, interest and penalties thereon, and the costs of this suit.

IN WITNESS WHEREOF, I have hereunto set my hand and affixed the official seal of said Court, this date of August 15, 1997.

NINA HORNSBY
Clerk of said Court
By: Steven Lockridge
Deputy Clerk
A True Copy
Circuit Court Seal

Helen Douglas
Assistant City Attorney
Attorney for Complainant
CITY OF ANY CITY
1500 N.W. 10th Street
Any City, Any State
(000) 444-1111

the promissory note permits the lender to proceed against the maker personally and any property, real or personal, owned by the mortgagee. The mortgage instrument is a specific lien, attaching only to the particular real property that is purchased with the loan proceeds. A mortgage becomes a lien against the real property when recorded in the public records in the county in which the real property is located.

A mortgage lien's priority status is determined by the date of its recording. As noted, real property tax liens are superior to all other liens, including mortgage liens. Because of this, many lenders include in their calculation of monthly mortgage payments the amount of annual real property taxes and escrow this sum until the tax bill is issued. The original tax bill is then forwarded to the lender rather than the property owner, and the lender pays the taxes due with the escrowed sum. Most lenders want to maintain priority status over all other liens. To accomplish this, they may require subordination agreements to be executed by other lienors. A **subordination agreement** is one in which a party agrees that his or her interest in real property should have a lower priority than the interest to which it is being subordinated.

Should a mortgagor default on a loan, the mortgagee may foreclose on the property. Mortgage foreclosures are discussed in detail in Chapter 20. Once a mortgage loan is paid in full, either when the real property is sold, when the term expires, or at some earlier date, a **satisfaction of mortgage** must be recorded to remove the lien as an encumbrance on the real property, such as the one provided in Figure 9–4.

CONSTRUCTION LIENS

In General

A **construction lien,** often referred to as a *mechanic's lien* or *materialman's lien,* is a *statutory lien.* It allows certain persons and entities who provide labor or materials for the improvement of real property and who are not paid the statutory right to place a claim of lien on and ultimately foreclose on specific real property and any improvements thereon. Construction liens are based on the principle of *unjust enrichment,* preventing a party from being unjustly enriched by receiving the services, labor, or materials of another without full reimbursement. Construction liens can be placed on both commercial and residential properties, although some states prohibit the placement of construction liens on owner-occupied residential real property.

Because a construction lien is statutory in nature, there generally is no requirement that the lien claimant be in privity of contract with the property owner. The persons or entities entitled to a construction lien are specified by state statute and typically include general contractors, subcontractors (and in some states, more remote subcontractors, such as subsubcontractors), laborers, and suppliers of materials. Many state statutes include lessors of equipment, architects, interior designers and decorators, professional engineers, and land surveyors as parties entitled to construction liens. In states that do require an express or implied contract with the property owner or an authorized representative of the owner in order for a person to be entitled to place a construction lien on property, a general contractor who has a contract with

subordination agreement: An agreement by which one party agrees that his or her interest in real property should have lower priority than the interest to which it is being subordinated.

satisfaction of mortgage: A document recorded to evidence the payment in full of a mortgage loan.

construction lien: A statutory lien placed on real property by persons or entities providing labor or materials for the improvement of real property.

LOAN NO. 1302-762724 33

This instrument was prepared by:

AMERICAN SECURITY BANK
6008 South Commercial Avenue
Any City, Any State

SATISFACTION OF MORTGAGE

KNOW ALL MEN BY THESE PRESENTS:

That AMERICAN SECURITY BANK, a corporation organized and existing under the laws of the United States of America, the owner and holder of a certain mortgage executed by

EDWARD S. TURNER and EVELYN C. TURNER, his wife

to AMERICAN SECURITY BANK, bearing date of the 12th day of October, 1995, and recorded in Official Records Book 14501, Page 306, of the Public Records of Any County, Any State, given to secure the sum of

------- TWO HUNDRED TWENTY-FIVE THOUSAND AND NO/100 -------

Dollars evidenced by a certain promissory note, has received full payment of said indebtedness and does hereby acknowledge satisfaction of said mortgage, and hereby directs the Clerk of the Circuit Court of Any County, Any State, to cancel the same record.

IN WITNESS WHEREOF, AMERICAN SECURITY BANK has caused these presents to be executed in its name this 15th day of August, 1997.

SIGNED, SEALED AND DELIVERED
IN THE PRESENCE OF:

AMERICAN SECURITY BANK

By _____

Tamara St. James

Ann Marcus, Vice President

Gerald Randall

STATE OF ANY STATE
COUNTY OF ANY COUNTY

I HEREBY CERTIFY that on this day before me, an officer duly authorized in the state and county aforesaid to take acknowledgements, personally appeared Ann Marcus, well known to me to be the Vice President of American Security Bank, and that she acknowledged executing the same in the presence of two subscribing witnesses freely and voluntarily under the authority duly vested in them.

WITNESS my hand and official seal in the county and state last aforesaid this 15th day of August, 1997.

Notary Public, State of Any State
My commission expires: _____

FIGURE 9–4
Satisfaction of mortgage

the owner may be considered the owner's authorized representative, carrying the authority to hire anyone necessary to complete the construction job, including subcontractors, laborers, and material suppliers.

In a number of states, a claimant, in order to be entitled to file a construction lien, must supply services, labor, or material that result in a fixture or "permanent benefit" to the real property. Although state statutes may be vague in defining this term, court cases seem to indicate that the improvement must be one that prepares the structure for occupancy, including site preparation such as excavation and grading, or incorporates materials in the structure or land (for example, planting of landscaping materials, installation of flooring).

This requirement is not difficult for certain lien claimants, such as a plumber or electrician, to meet, but it may be tricky for certain suppliers who sell materials to subcontractors or to owners over-the-counter without knowing the particular job site in which the materials are to be incorporated. If the materials are delivered to a particular construction site, most courts hold that there is a presumption that they are to be used at that site. Nonetheless, it is advisable for the supplier to have a delivery receipt signed by the person ordering the materials to evidence the drop-off location. If the materials are sold over-the-counter, it is advisable that the supplier have the buyer fill out a form indicating the location of the site at which the materials will be used, the name and address of the owner of the site, and other relevant information.

If the materials furnished are customized, the supplier generally has a right to file a construction lien, even if the materials are not ultimately used on the site. For example, if a supplier is asked to customize a tub to meet specified size requirements not found in standard tubs, the supplier, if not paid, may file a claim of lien against the property on which the tub was supposed to be installed, even if the owner does not install the tub.

In states that require an express or implied contract with the owner or the owner's authorized representative, the owner may avoid responsibility for unauthorized work done or unauthorized materials furnished by completing a **notice of nonresponsibility,** which then is posted on the construction site and recorded in the public records in the county in which the property is located.

A lien claimant is only entitled to his or her claim once work is done or materials are furnished to the real property. To establish a claim of lien, a lien claimant must record a claim of lien within a statutorily specified time period with the recording clerk in the county in which the real property is located. In some states, the lien claimant, upon first beginning work or furnishing materials, must send a notice to the owner of the property indicating that the claimant is providing goods or services to improve the property (see the discussion of notice to owner later in this chapter). This notice makes the owner aware of all parties involved with the improvements to the real property. This is important to the owner because often the owner only contracts with the general contractor and leaves it to the general contractor to hire the necessary subcontractors, laborers, and suppliers for the job. In states requiring a notice to owner, failure to provide one will negate the lien rights of the claimant.

The amount of monies a lien claimant is entitled to is determined by state statute. In some states, a lien claimant is entitled to the entire amount owed and outstanding regardless of whether the owner of the real property has made payment to the general contractor. In these states, it is especially important for the owner to know how many subcontractors, laborers, and suppliers are involved with the job and the amounts owing to each at each stage of the construction.

To ensure that the monies paid to the general contractor are being paid, in turn, to parties hired by the general contractor, the owner may insist that the general contractor supply the owner with **lien waivers,** or *lien releases,* from the subcontractors and others at various stages before further payment is made. These waivers show that the subcontractors have been paid and will not

notice of nonresponsibility:
A notice posted on a construction site by the owner of the property to avoid legal responsibility for unauthorized work done or unauthorized materials furnished.

lien waiver: A document indicating that a subcontractor has been paid and will not be subjecting real property to liens.

be subjecting the property to liens. Some states require that lien waivers be witnessed and notarized. The signatory of a lien waiver should be an agent of the company duly authorized to sign. A president of a company typically is authorized to bind a company and, therefore, may sign a lien waiver, while a secretary of a company may or may not be so authorized. A lien waiver absent a duly authorized signature will not bind the company, so authorization must be checked. A right to claim a lien may not be waived in advance. A lien right may be waived only to the extent of labor, services, or material furnished.

In some states, a lien claimant is limited by the contract price as set forth in a contract between the general contractor and the owner, and thus the owner will not be held liable beyond that amount. For example, suppose the owner and general contractor enter into a contract for a patio enclosure to be constructed on an already existing house. The contract price is $30,000, to be paid in three installments of $10,000 each; the first installment to be paid upon the signing of the contract, the second to be paid halfway through the job, and the third to be paid at the completion of the job. The general contractor hires a drywall company to put up walls for the enclosure for $15,000. At the time of completion of the work, the owner has paid $20,000 to the general contractor, and the general contractor has not paid the drywall company.

In states that limit the construction lien to the contract price between the owner and the general contractor, the drywall company can claim only $10,000 against the property of the owner, which is the difference between the contract price of $30,000 and the amount owed on the contract, namely, $10,000. In states imposing no such limitation, the drywall company can record a claim of lien for the entire $15,000.

Construction liens generally attach to property retroactively, their priority established not by the date upon which the lien was recorded but, rather, by the date work is first performed or supplies furnished by the lien claimant. In some states, priority of the lien dates back to the date upon which the claimant completed work on the premises; in other states, it dates back to the first date the lien claimant entered the property; and in still other states, the lien, once recorded, dates back to the first date work began on the property. In the latter instance, state statute requires that the owner of the real property record a **notice of commencement** indicating the first date upon which construction began. In applicable states, once this notice is filed and recorded, all construction liens properly filed and recorded date back to the date of the notice.

For example, suppose an owner files a notice of commencement dated February 1, 1997. A roofing company hired by the general contractor will not come onto the premises for the first time until a good portion of the construction is completed, for example, on May 1, 1997, completing work on May 18, 1997. If the roofing company is not paid and files a claim of lien against the property on July 1, 1997, in states that require owners to record a notice of commencement, the roofing company's lien will date back to February 1, 1997. Suppose further that the paving company installing the driveway begins work on June 1, 1997, completes work on June 6, 1997, and files a claim of lien on August 1, 1997. Although the two lien claimants, the roofing company and the paving company, commenced work and completed work on different dates, neither is superior to the other in lien priority in this instance because both liens date back to February 1, 1997.

notice of commencement: A document recorded by a property owner indicating the date upon which construction began on the property.

In states with statutes that date construction liens back to the date upon which the claimant first furnished labor or services, the roofing company's lien would date back to May 1, 1997, and the paving company's lien would date back to June 1, 1997; therefore, the roofing company's lien would be superior. In states with statutes that date construction liens back to the date the claimant completed work or the last date materials were supplied, the roofing company's lien would again be superior inasmuch as the roofing company completed work on May 18, 1997, whereas the paving company completed work on June 6, 1997. Many states treat liens recorded by architects, engineers, land surveyors, and other hired professionals differently than other construction liens, establishing their lien priority by the date upon which the lien was recorded rather than the date upon which work was first furnished.

A construction lien is similar to the other liens previously discussed in the manner of its enforcement. Construction liens are enforced through foreclosure suits. Although state statutes vary in setting a statute of limitations for bringing a foreclosure action on a construction lien, the statute of limitations typically is of short duration (for example, one year). In some states, the statute of limitations may run from the date of the recording of the claim of lien, whereas in other states, it may run from the last furnishing of labor or materials to the construction site. If the lien claimant fails to file a foreclosure suit within this time period, he or she cannot thereafter recover on the claim of lien. At that point, the lien claimant's best alternative would be to file a breach of contract action against the party with whom he or she was in privity of contract.

If full payment is made, either after the recording of a claim of lien or the filing of a foreclosure action, a release of lien must be recorded to remove the lien as an encumbrance on the property. Some states permit an owner to file a *notice of contest of lien* in which the owner states that he or she disputes the lien claim. The filing of a notice of contest of lien may statutorily shorten the time period within which a lien claimant may file suit to enforce the lien. In most states, should a foreclosure action accrue, the owner of the real property has a right of redemption in the same manner as is provided for mortgage foreclosures.

Notice of Commencement

In states that make a notice of commencement a statutory requirement, the recording of such a notice serves as notification to third parties that the owner of the specified real property has authorized certain improvements to be undertaken on the property. In these states, a notice of commencement is executed and recorded by the owner after a building permit is issued allowing construction on the property.

Recall from the earlier discussion that construction liens in some states date back to the recording of the notice of commencement. Lending institutions providing construction loans typically require that the notice of commencement be recorded after their mortgage deed is recorded in order to preserve their lien priority. Often, to ensure that documents are recorded in a certain order, the lending institution will have the owner execute a notice of commencement and give it to the lending institution to record after the mortgage deed is recorded. State statute may mandate that a notice of commencement automatically expires after a specified time period (for example, one year) unless the notice of commencement provides otherwise.

In addition to providing notice that improvements to real property are to commence, a notice of commencement contains information helpful to potential lien claimants. Although the contents may vary from state to state, a notice of commencement usually contains the following information:

1. The legal description of the real property
2. A description of improvements to be made
3. The owner's name and address
4. The owner's interest in the real property
5. The general contractor's name and address
6. If the project is bonded, the name and address of the surety company and the amount of the bond
7. The lending institution's name and address
8. The name and address of all persons other than the owner who are designated to receive notices
9. The expiration date for the notice of commencement if the project completion date is expected to be after the statutorily prescribed expiration date
10. The signature of the owner
11. Notarization

Once the notice of commencement is signed by the owner and notarized, it is recorded in the clerk's office in the county in which the property is located. In some states, recording alone is insufficient, and there is the additional requirement of posting a certified copy of the notice of commencement in a conspicuous place on the real property. In these states, the posting of the notice may be a prerequisite to obtain a first inspection approval for work on the property. Once recorded, the improvements described in the notice of commencement must begin within a specified time period (for example, ninety days) or else the notice becomes void and a new notice must be recorded.

Suppose Austin Moore purchased a parcel of land and hired a general contractor, Prestige Builders, Inc., to build a custom home on the property. All applicable plans are approved and the building permit has been issued. According to state statute, Austin must record a notice of commencement and post a certified copy on the property. His notice of commencement may read like that provided in Figure 9–5.

Notice to Owner

In many states, a potential lien claimant must comply with the state's **notice to owner** requirements in order to enforce a construction lien. Some states do not require that parties in privity of contract with the owner, such as the general contractor, file a notice to owner as a prerequisite to the later filing of a claim of lien; rather, they require this step only from subcontractors, laborers, and material suppliers who are not in privity of contract with the owner.

A notice to owner puts an owner on notice of those parties expecting payment for work or materials incorporated into the owner's property. Without this requirement, the owner may not be aware of all parties providing services, labor, and materials because the owner typically does not enter into individual

notice to owner: A document that puts a property owner on notice of those parties expecting payment for work or materials incorporated into the owner's real property.

FIGURE 9–5
Notice of commencement

NOTICE OF COMMENCEMENT

STATE OF ANY STATE
COUNTY OF ANY COUNTY

THE UNDERSIGNED hereby gives notice that improvement will be made to certain real property, and in accordance with Section 893.07 of the Statutes of Any State, the following information is provided in this Notice of Commencement.

1. Description of property: <u>Lot 56 in Block 18, according to the plat thereof, recorded in Plat Book 12, Page 27, of the Public Records of Any County, Any State.</u>
2. General description of improvement: <u>Construction of a two-story, single-family residence.</u>
3. Owner information:
   (a) Name and address: <u>Austin Moore</u>
   <u>127 Palliser Drive, Any City, Any State</u>
   (b) Interest in property: <u>Fee simple</u>
4. Contractor's name and address: <u>Prestige Builders, Inc.</u>
   <u>633 Kennedy Avenue, Any City,</u>
   <u>Any State</u>
5. Surety information:
   (a) Name and address: <u>Not applicable</u>
   (b) Amount of bond: $<u>   </u>
6. Lender's name and address: <u>American Security Bank</u>
   <u>6008 South Commercial Avenue, Any City, Any State</u>
7. Expiration date of Notice of Commencement: <u>April 10, 1998</u>

<u>   </u>
Austin Moore, Owner

Sworn to and subscribed before me by Austin Moore on this 10th day of April, 1997.

<u>   </u>
Notary Public, State of Any State
My commission expires: <u>   </u>

contracts with each of these parties. As noted earlier, once the owner has knowledge of these parties, the owner can demand that the general contractor provide lien waivers indicating payment of each subcontractor, laborer, or supplier as work progresses.

State statutes may specify the time period within which a notice to owner must be served on the owner and any other indicated parties (for example, within forty-five days from first furnishing services, labor, or materials). In states requiring a *contractor's final affidavit* at completion of a construction project, a notice to owner should be served prior to the presentation of the affidavit. In most states, a notice to owner is considered properly served when hand delivered or mailed to the owner's address provided on the notice of commencement. It is advisable to mail the notice to owner by certified mail, return receipt requested. If service cannot be made by either mail or hand delivery, it may be permissible to post the notice to owner at the project site. If there is more than one owner of the real property, serving a notice to owner on one owner may legally suffice as service on all.

In some states, the notice to owner must be served not only upon the owner, but also upon everyone higher up in the construction chain, such as the general contractor, the surety company posting bond on the property, if applicable, and the lending institution. The potential lien claimant often is not required to serve a notice to owner on the party with whom he or she is in privity of contract. Thus, for example, a supplier of sod and planting materials providing these materials under contract with a landscape architect would not have to serve a notice to owner on the landscape architect because the landscape architect is well aware of the supplies to be furnished and the amount owed under the terms of the contract.

Continuing the example above, suppose the general contractor hired by Austin Moore in turn hires various subcontractors, including a plumbing contractor, S & G Plumbing, Inc. S & G Plumbing, Inc., enters into a contract with Ellison Plumbing Supplies, Inc., to provide plumbing fixtures for the residence under construction. Ellison Plumbing Supplies, Inc., furnishes most of the plumbing fixtures on May 25, 1997; however, some plumbing fixtures are on special order and will not be available for several weeks. Nonetheless, Ellison Plumbing Supplies, Inc., wants to serve a notice to owner as soon as the first materials are furnished. It may serve a notice to owner such as the one provided in Figure 9–6.

FIGURE 9–6
Notice to owner

NOTICE TO OWNER

DATE: May 25, 1997

TO: Austin Moore
         127 Palliser Drive
         Any City, Any State

The undersigned hereby informs you that he/she has furnished, or is furnishing, service of materials as follows:

plumbing fixtures

for the improvement of the real property identified as:

Lot 56 in Block 18, according to the plat thereof recorded in Plat Book 12, Page 27, of the Public Records of Any County, Any State.

under an order given by:

S & G Plumbing, Inc.
310 N.E. 10th Street
Any City, Any State

Ellison Plumbing Supplies, Inc.

By _____
Noel Ellison, President

Copies furnished to:

Prestige Builders, Inc.
633 Kennedy Avenue
Any City, Any State

American Security Bank
6008 South Commercial Avenue
Any City, Any State

Claim of Lien

If full payment is not received for services, labor, or materials furnished for the improvement of real property, a lien claimant may, after following all statutorily mandated prerequisites, such as serving a notice to owner, record a claim of lien against the real property. This lien will remain an encumbrance on the property until full payment is made, settlement is reached, or the time period for bringing suit has expired. State statute specifies the time period within which a claim of lien must be recorded.

A claim of lien must be executed under oath, and it usually contains the following information:

1. The state and county in which the lien is executed
2. The name and position of the lienor
3. The address of the lienor
4. The name of the person or entity with whom the lienor contracted
5. The name of the owner of the real property
6. The legal description of the real property
7. The total value of labor, services, or materials
8. The amount owing
9. The date of service of notice to owner (including return receipt certified mail numbers, if applicable)
10. The names of witnesses (if required by state statute)
11. Signature of the lienor
12. Notarization

Some states require that the lienor serve a copy of the recorded claim of lien on the owner and all others listed on the notice of commencement and notice to owner within a specified time period (for example, within fifteen days after recording). Again, if served by mail, it is advisable to send the copies by certified mail, return receipt requested.

Suppose Ellison Plumbing Supplies, Inc., delivered the last of the plumbing fixtures on special order to the project site on June 18, 1997, and the fixtures were accepted by S & G Plumbing, Inc. Although its contract states that payment in full is due within ten business days after the last of the plumbing fixtures are furnished, by July 2, 1997, only half of the monies owed to Ellison Plumbing Supplies, Inc., have been paid. State statute requires that a construction lien be recorded within ninety days from the date of last furnishing services, labor, or supplies. Noel Ellison waits until July 30th before recording a claim of lien, having decided that the sooner the lien is recorded, the better are the chances of being paid. The lien he files is found in Figure 9–7.

If Ellison Plumbing Supplies, Inc., is paid in full prior to filing a foreclosure action on the property, a Release and Satisfaction of Recorded Claim of Lien must be recorded with the clerk's office in the county in which the property is located to remove the lien as an encumbrance on the property. Thus, if Noel Ellison receives the remaining $5,000 owed from whatever source, be it S & G Plumbing, Inc., Austin Moore, or Prestige Builders, Inc., a release, such as the one provided in Figure 9–8, must be recorded.

FIGURE 9–7
Claim of lien

CLAIM OF LIEN

STATE OF ANY STATE
COUNTY OF ANY COUNTY

BEFORE ME, the undersigned authority, personally appeared Noel Ellison who, being duly sworn, says that he is the President of Ellison Plumbing Supplies, Inc., whose address is 675 S.W. Parkway Avenue, Any City, and that pursuant to a contract with S & G Plumbing, Inc., Lienor furnished labor, services or materials consisting of plumbing fixtures on the following described real property in Any County, Any State:

Lot 56 in Block 18, according to the plat thereof recorded in Plat Book 12, Page 27, of the Public Records of Any County, Any State.

owned by Austin Moore for a total of $10,000.00, of which there remains unpaid $5,000.00 and furnished the first of the same on May 25, 1997, and the last of the same on June 18, 1997, and that Lienor served its Notice to Owner on May 25, 1997, by U.S. Certified Mail, Return Receipt No. P244 615 899, on the general contractor by U.S. Certified Mail, Return Receipt P244 615 900, and on the lender by U.S. Certified Mail, Return Receipt P244 615 901.

Signed, sealed and delivered   Ellison Plumbing Supplies, Inc.
in the presence of:

_____   By_____
Lisa Gray   Noel Ellison, President

_____
Simon Larkin

Sworn to and subscribed before me by Noel Ellison on this 30th day of July, 1997.

_____
Notary Public, State of Any State
My commission expires: _____

Copies furnished to:

Austin Moore
127 Palliser Drive
Any City, Any State

Prestige Builders, Inc.
633 Kennedy Avenue
Any City, Any State

American Security Bank
6008 South Commercial Avenue
Any City, Any State

OTHER LIENS

In addition to the most common liens already discussed, there are several other liens that can attach to real property. One such lien is a *vendor's lien*. A vendor is a seller, and more specifically in this instance, a seller of real property. Often a mortgage loan will not cover the full purchase price of real property. The buyer then must make up the difference between the loan

RELEASE AND SATISFACTION OF RECORDED CLAIM OF LIEN

STATE OF ANY STATE
COUNTY OF ANY COUNTY

The undersigned, having filed a Claim of Lien in the amount of $5,000.00 against the property of Austin Moore, on the 1st day of July, 1997, in Official Record Book 1720, at Page 743, in the Office of the Clerk of the Circuit Court of Any County, State of Any State, against the following described real property in Any County, Any State:

Lot 56 in Block 18, according to the plat thereof recorded in Plat Book 12, Page 27, of the Public Records of Any County, Any State.

NOW, THEREFORE, the Lienor, for TEN DOLLARS ($10.00) and other good and valuable consideration, does hereby acknowledge having received full payment and satisfaction of the Claim of Lien and does direct the Clerk of the Circuit Court to cancel and discharge the Claim of Lien in accordance with Section 893.12 of the Statutes of Any State.

Signed, sealed and delivered this 15th day of August, 1997.

Signed, sealed and delivered   Ellison Plumbing Supplies, Inc.
in the presence of:

_____   By_____
Lisa Gray   Noel Ellison, President

_____
Simon Larkin

Before me personally appeared Noel Ellison, the President of Ellison Plumbing Supplies, Inc., who did take an oath and acknowledged to and before me that he executed this instrument for the purposes therein expressed on behalf of said company, this 15th day of August, 1997.

_____
Notary Public, State of Any State
My commission expires: _____

amount and the purchase price. The buyer may do this with accumulated savings, by taking out a second mortgage loan, or by owing the difference to the seller. In the latter instance, the difference between the purchase price and the mortgage loan is seller-financed by a *purchase money mortgage*, through which the seller obtains a specific lien on the real property. Unless a written mortgage deed is properly executed and recorded, a vendor's lien is enforceable only against the original purchaser, not subsequent purchasers.

Other specific liens are *condominium liens* and *homeowners' association liens*. As discussed in the Chapter 3, property owners living in condominiums and developments run by condominium and homeowners' associations are required to make regular maintenance payments (for example, monthly, quarterly, semi-annually) to meet the common expenses, such as maintenance of common areas, security guard services, and the like. Condominium associations and homeowners' associations are required annually to prepare a budget of common expenses covering their financial affairs. From these budgets, each condominium owner's or homeowner's share of expenses is determined. Additionally, these associations occasionally require special assessments to be paid for certain expenses that do not occur on a regular basis, such as the repaving of parking lots or roof repairs. The right to impose liens on the condominium units or homes of individuals failing to make their required payments is found in the declaration of condominium or the declaration of restrictions and covenants for the subdivision that is governed by a homeowners' association. The priority of these liens is determined by date of recording.

LIEN PRIORITY

As can be gleaned from the discussion so far, the priority of most liens (except real property tax liens) typically is established by date of recording under the principle of first in time, first in right. As also observed, exceptions to this rule do exist. Priority becomes important in the case of foreclosure on real property. Recall that when foreclosure occurs, the real property is sold under court order to pay debts. The proceeds from the sale are taken to pay all lienors if the sale procures enough money to go around. However, this is not always the case.

Suppose Warren Masterson purchases real property with the proceeds of a mortgage loan from American Security Bank, and a mortgage deed is recorded on February 4, 1997. Warren then takes out a second mortgage loan from Roosevelt Bank to finance certain home improvements; the second mortgage deed is recorded on April 2, 1997. Next, Warren hires a contractor to add an extra bathroom onto the house. Warren records a notice of commencement on May 5, 1997. Warren then has the misfortune of being named a defendant in a lawsuit and loses the case, the court awarding the plaintiff, Rosemary Wright, a judgment award. Rosemary records a certified copy of the judgment in the county in which Warren's property is located on May 25, 1997. Unable to meet his cash flow problems, Warren fails to pay the tile installer, who records a construction lien on June 28, 1997, having served a notice to owner on May 11, 1997, and completed work on May 13, 1997. Finally, Warren fails to pay his monthly maintenance payments to the homeowners' association, which records a lien against his property on August 6, 1997.

In order of priority, American Security Bank is first, followed by Roosevelt Bank. If Warren's property is located in a state in which construction liens date back to the date of the notice of commencement or the date the lienor completed work on the property, then the tile installer is third in line because, although he did not record his lien until June 28th (after the recording of Rosemary's judgment lien on May 25th), the notice of commencement is dated May 5th and work was completed on May 13th. However, if Warren's property is located in a state in which the priority of construction liens is based on the date of recording, then Rosemary is third in line, followed by the tile installer. The homeowners' association, having recorded its lien on August 6th, is last.

If Warren defaults on his first mortgage with American Security Bank, American Security Bank, which in this example is in a superior position to that of the other lienors, can foreclose on the property by suing Warren and all subordinate lienors (that is, Rosemary, Roosevelt Bank, the tile installer, and the homeowners' association). If there are insufficient proceeds from the foreclosure sale to pay all lienors, American Security Bank must be paid in full (that is, the total amount of the loan, plus any penalties, additional charges, and costs) before any of the other lienors are paid. If there are proceeds remaining to pay some but not all of the remaining lienors, the lienor next in priority must be fully paid before any subordinate lienor can receive anything. In this instance, the next in line is Roosevelt Bank because it recorded its lien prior to the recording of the judgment lien or homeowners' assessment lien. Thus, lienors are not paid off on a pro rata basis.

If, instead of defaulting on his first mortgage, Warren defaulted on his second mortgage, Roosevelt Bank could bring action to foreclose, but any proceeds from the sale would first go to pay off American Security Bank, because of its superior position, before Roosevelt Bank would receive anything from the sale. In both examples, before either American Security Bank or Roosevelt Bank are paid, all real property taxes must be paid because they are superior to any other liens. Recall from an earlier discussion that real property tax liens do not have to be recorded to be enforced.

ATTACHMENT

A **writ of attachment** prevents a party to a lawsuit from conveying title to property, real or personal, while the suit is pending. The property need not be the subject matter of the suit. Litigation attorneys adhere to the adage that a lawsuit is only as good as its collectibility. Prior to commencing suit, a plaintiff's attorney will seek to determine if the defendant has any nonexempt assets. If not, the plaintiff may choose to reconsider bringing suit, for even if the court awards judgment in the plaintiff's favor, the plaintiff may never be able to collect on the judgment. If, however, the defendant owns sufficient nonexempt property, the plaintiff may seek a writ of attachment to ensure that the defendant does not transfer title to that property to someone else prior to the conclusion of the suit. In most instances, a court will require that a plaintiff post a surety bond or deposit with the court a sum of money to cover any possible loss in value of the attached property the defendant may sustain pending the outcome of the suit. An example of a writ of attachment is found in Figure 9–9.

LIS PENDENS

writ of attachment: A court order that prevents a party to a lawsuit from conveying title to property, real or personal, while the suit is pending.

lis pendens: A notice recorded when a lawsuit affects title to a particular parcel of real property.

Unlike a writ of attachment, a notice of **lis pendens** (Latin for "litigation pending") is a notice recorded when a lawsuit affects title to a particular parcel of real property. The lawsuit can be a suit to foreclose on the property, a suit to quiet title to the property, a suit to partition the property, a bankruptcy proceeding, or any other suit in which a court judgment can affect the property. The notice is recorded in the public records in the county in which the property is located. A notice of lis pendens is not a lien. Its purpose is to put third parties on notice that the property is the subject matter of litigation. The notice of lis pendens cuts off the rights of any party whose interest in the real

FIGURE 9–9
Writ of attachment

IN THE CIRCUIT COURT OF THE FIFTH JUDICIAL CIRCUIT,
IN AND FOR ANY COUNTY, ANY STATE

THOMAS JOHNSON,   CASE NO. 97-22018 WOLF
   Plaintiff,

vs.

ELEANOR FISHER,
   Defendant.
_____/

WRIT OF ATTACHMENT

THE STATE OF ANY STATE:

To Each Sheriff of the State:

   YOU ARE COMMANDED to attach and take into custody so much of the lands, tenements, goods and chattels of Defendant, ELEANOR FISHER, as is sufficient to satisfy the sum of Fifty Thousand Dollars ($50,000.00) and costs.

   ORDERED in Any County, Any State, on August 16, 1997.

                          Franklin Wolf
                          CIRCUIT COURT JUDGE

Ava Ross
_____
Attorney for the Plaintiff
Any State Bar No. 123456

Fisher, Ross, and Simon, P.A.
1900 N.W. 3rd Avenue
Any City, Any State
(000) 232-7000

property arises after the notice is filed. State statutes dictate the expiration date of the notice. The court may require that a bond be posted to maintain the lis pendens or to renew it after the expiration date. Should a lien later result as an outcome of the litigation, the lien's priority is established by the date the notice of lis pendens is recorded.

To illustrate a situation in which the recording of a notice of lis pendens would be appropriate, suppose Neil and Annette Adams are having marital problems and Neil decides to file for a divorce. If Neil and Annette do not reach an amicable agreement about the division of property, that matter will have to be determined by the judge presiding in the divorce action.

If Neil moves out of the house and Annette decides to put the house on the market, there is nothing in the public records to indicate that title to the house may be affected by the judgment of the divorce court. The court may award the house to one party or the other, or may order it sold and the proceeds split. However, if a notice of lis pendens is recorded by either Neil's attorney or Annette's attorney, a prospective purchaser will have fair warning that title may be affected by court proceedings. If instead of selling the house, Annette wants to take out a home equity loan, the notice of lis pendens warns the potential lender that its lien may be inferior to any lien arising out of the lawsuit for which the notice has been recorded. A sample notice of lis pendens is provided in Figure 9–10.

IN THE CIRCUIT COURT OF THE FOURTH JUDICIAL CIRCUIT,
IN AND FOR ANY COUNTY, ANY STATE

NEIL ADAMS,   CASE NO. 97-22019 MURPHY
  Petitioner,   FAMILY DIVISION
vs.
ANNETTE ADAMS,
  Respondent.
_____/

NOTICE OF LIS PENDENS

TO RESPONDENT ANNETTE ADAMS, AND ALL OTHERS WHOM IT MAY
CONCERN:

  YOU ARE NOTIFIED of the institution of this action by the petitioner against you
seeking a divorce and relief concerning the following property in Any County, Any
State:

> Lot 22 in Block 4, VINTAGE ESTATES, a subdivision according to the plat
> thereof as recorded in Plat Book 78, Page 11, of the Public Records of
> Any County, Any State.

DATED on August 16, 1997.

Ava Ross
_____
Attorney for the Petitioner
Any State Bar No. 123456

Fisher, Ross, and Simon, P.A.
921 Warwick Drive, Suite 604
Any City, Any State
(000) 232-7000

CHAPTER SUMMARY

1. Liens are encumbrances on the title to real property. General liens, such as judgment liens and federal income tax liens, are not secured by any particular parcel of real property. Therefore, the lienholder of a general lien is free to proceed against all nonexempt property of the debtor, both real and personal, wherever located. A specific lien, on the other hand, is one that attaches only to specific real property. Specific liens include mortgage liens, construction liens, real property tax liens, condominium association liens, and homeowners' association liens.

2. Tax liens include liens for federal and state income taxes, estate and inheritance taxes, intangible taxes, corporate franchise taxes, and real property taxes. Although the priority of most liens (including most tax liens) is established by date of recording, real property tax liens have a superpriority and thus are superior to all other liens.

3. Construction liens are specific liens that attach to a particular property on which improvements are made by contractors, subcontractors, laborers, suppliers of materials, and certain professionals. Construction liens typically attach retroactively. In this regard, they are distinct from any other lien.

4. The statutory procedures for establishing and enforcing construction liens vary considerably from state to state. Depending on state statute, a property owner may be required to record a notice of commencement to begin construction on real property. As each potential lienor commences work on the property, he or she serves a notice to owner on the property owner and persons in positions superior to the potential lienor in the construction chain. If a potential lienor is not paid, or is not paid in full, he or she may record a claim of lien against the real property. The lienor then must file suit to foreclose before the statute of limitations expires.

5. A notice of lis pendens is recorded when a lawsuit is pending that affects the title of real property. The notice is not a lien; rather, it puts third parties on notice of pending litigation and cuts off the rights of any party whose interest in the real property arises after the notice is recorded.

REVIEW QUESTIONS

1. Explain the distinction between the following liens.
   a. General liens and specific liens
   b. Voluntary liens and statutory liens
2. Once a plaintiff is awarded a judgment in a lawsuit, what steps must be taken before he or she can enforce the judgment and have the defendant's real property sold to pay off the debt?
3. How is lien priority typically established? What are the exceptions to the rule?
4. Explain the steps that may be required to perfect a construction lien.
5. Explain the difference between a lien and a notice of lis pendens.

ETHICAL QUESTIONS

You are the paralegal in your law firm with the most experience in the area of construction lien law. You have assisted your supervising attorney with numerous client matters in this area and have kept up-to-date on changes in state statutory law regarding construction liens. Your firm has just hired some new associates, and your supervising attorney has asked you to prepare a procedure manual on the steps to take to perfect a construction lien that is intended for use by the new associates and other paralegals in the firm. May you prepare the manual?

PRACTICAL ASSIGNMENTS

Assignment 9:1. Research your state statutes regarding the priority date of the liens discussed in this chapter. Then make a chart illustrating the lien priority.

Assignment 9:2. Research your state statutes regarding the procedure for enforcing real property tax liens. Photocopy the relevant statutes and insert them under the "General Information" section of your resource portfolio.

Assignment 9:3. Research your state construction lien statutes and outline the steps that must be taken to perfect a construction lien in your state. If your state has statutory forms to be used (for example, for notice to owner, claim of lien, and so on), photocopy them and insert them under the "General Information" section of your resource portfolio.

Assignment 9:4. Interior decorator Natalie Henrickson has telephoned your supervising attorney, Deborah Sanders, for legal advice. Natalie completed a decorating job for Mr. and Mrs. Brandt over six weeks ago and has yet to receive final payment from them. She has left several messages for them, and they do not return her calls. She wants to know if she can place a construction lien on the Brandts' home, which is the location of the decorating project. Deborah asks you to check your state statutes to determine whether interior decorators are included among those persons permitted to file construction liens in your state. Can Natalie record a claim of lien against the Brandt property?

Assignment 9:5. Client Ferguson Drywall, Inc., recorded a claim of lien against the property of Bernard Adkins three weeks ago from today's date in the amount of $7,500. The property against which the lien was placed is described as follows:

> Lot 16 in Block 3, according to the plat thereof recorded in Plat Book 44, Page 38, of the Public Records of (your county and state).

The lien was recorded in Official Record Book 1900, at Page 57, in the public records of your county and state. Bernard has since sent a check to Ferguson Drywall for the full amount owed, and Deirdre Ferguson, president of the company, has asked your firm to prepare a release and satisfaction of recorded claim of lien to be filed. In preparing the release, check your state statutes to determine the number of witnesses needed, if any, and to determine whether the release must be notarized.

Assignment 9:6. Define the following key terms.

construction lien	notice of nonresponsibility
declaratory judgment	notice to owner
equitable right of redemption	satisfaction of judgment
general lien	satisfaction of mortgage
intangible tax	specific lien
lien waiver	subordination agreement
lis pendens	writ of attachment
monetary judgment	writ of execution
notice of commencement	

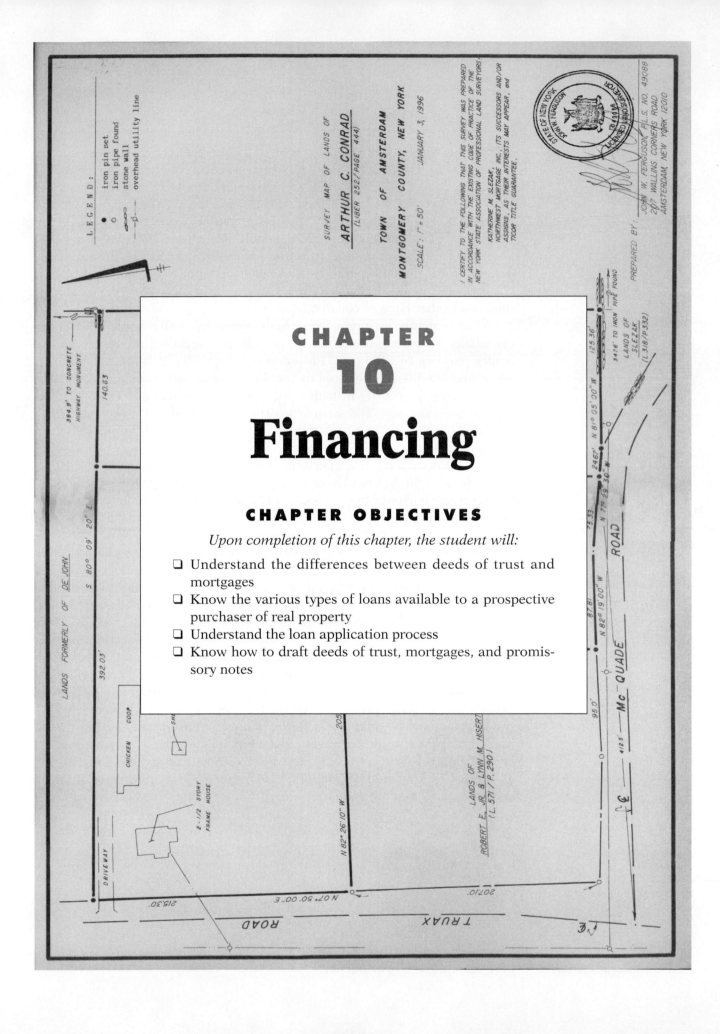

CHAPTER
10

Financing

CHAPTER OBJECTIVES

Upon completion of this chapter, the student will:

❑ Understand the differences between deeds of trust and mortgages
❑ Know the various types of loans available to a prospective purchaser of real property
❑ Understand the loan application process
❑ Know how to draft deeds of trust, mortgages, and promissory notes

INTRODUCTION

The purchase of real property is often the largest financial expenditure in a person's life. The purchaser looks at the real property both as a form of security and stability, and also as a major investment. Similarly, lenders look at the financing of real property as a stable investment. A loan to purchase real property will be collateralized by the real property that is to be purchased. Real property is choice collateral because it is physically fixed in terms of location and thus cannot be removed from the lender's reach should the purchaser default on the loan payments. It is also considered choice collateral because, with proper upkeep, it is more likely to increase in value over the loan term than most other types of collateral.

When a purchaser enters into a loan agreement with a lender, the lender essentially is "selling" the purchaser money at a specified interest rate. The lender requires two things: (1) a promise to repay the debt on agreed-upon terms and conditions evidenced in a written **promissory note,** and (2) a written financing or security instrument that pledges the real property as collateral for the loan debt. The security instrument generally will take one of two forms: (1) a mortgage, or (2) a deed of trust, both of which are discussed in detail in this chapter. The note is the legal evidence of the borrower's intentions to repay the debt. It is a personal obligation, which means that if the borrower defaults on the loan, the lender may come after the borrower personally wherever the borrower may be located and seek a court judgment against the borrower. The judgment allows the lender to seize, through legal measures, any of the borrower's assets for repayment of the debt.

Most often, the lender will choose, rather than going after the borrower personally, to go after the real property that is the collateral for the loan, which is the borrower's greatest asset. In some states, the lender must initiate a court action to foreclose on the real property, sell it at public auction, and use the proceeds as repayment for the debt. In other states, the lender does not have to bring a court action and the foreclosure procedures are simplified. In either situation, if the proceeds from the sale of the real property are insufficient to cover the total outstanding loan obligation, plus fees and costs associated with the foreclosure, the lender may seek a **deficiency judgment** against the borrower personally, on the basis of the note, looking to the borrower personally to make up the difference between the sales price and the outstanding debt. If the borrower cannot pay the deficiency judgment and it is forgiven, the borrower is considered to have incurred income for that taxable year (the amount of the debt that is forgiven). Some states have antideficiency statutes that preclude the lender from looking to the borrower for the deficiency.

This chapter discusses the primary sources for financing, the types of loans available, the lending process, and the governmental regulations surrounding it. If you, as a paralegal, are working with the in-house counsel of a lender, you may be asked to monitor and review loan files, which will require knowledge of the loan application process. Further, whether working for a lender or in a real estate law firm, you may be asked to prepare promissory notes and security instruments. This chapter discusses the differences between a deed of trust and a mortgage and outlines the steps to take to prepare each of these instruments.

promissory note: A written promise to repay a debt on agreed-upon terms and conditions. The note is the legal evidence of the borrower's intentions to repay the debt.

deficiency judgment: A court judgment for the difference between the sale of real property in a foreclosure action and the outstanding loan debt.

LEGAL THEORIES OF FINANCING INSTRUMENTS

As in most other aspects of American law, imported English practices have had an impact in the development of the law relating to financing instruments. Two separate legal theories pertaining to financing instruments developed in England: the **title theory** and the **lien theory.** The theories differ regarding whether a financing instrument transfers conditional title in the secured real property to the lender, as the title theory claims, or whether a financing instrument simply serves as a lien on the real property, similar to other types of liens, as the lien theory maintains. Some states have adopted the title theory, while other states have adopted the lien theory.

In states that have adopted the title theory, when a borrower gives the lender a financing instrument as security for the promise to repay the loan obligation outlined in the promissory note, the title to the real property vests in the lender or in a third party acting as an escrow agent. That third party may be a title company, an escrow company, or a trust company. The borrower retains possession of the real property and remains in possession as long as the borrower conforms to the terms of the loan agreement. When the loan is paid off, the legal title to the property then transfers to the borrower. In some title theory states, this arrangement allows the lender, in the event of a default by the borrower, to take possession and sell the property to satisfy the outstanding debt obligation without commencing a foreclosure lawsuit.

In states that have adopted the lien theory, when the borrower gives the lender a financing instrument, such as a mortgage, as security for the promise to repay the loan obligation, the borrower is only giving the lender a lien on the real property. The borrower obtains legal title to the property. The lender perfects its lien by recording it in the recording office in the county in which the real property is located. The lender, as a lienholder, has the right to enforce this lien by bringing a foreclosure action should the borrower default. The lender may not take possession of the property until the foreclosure action is completed. A detailed discussion of foreclosure is found in Chapter 20.

FINANCING SOURCES

A prospective purchaser of real property has a variety of sources with which to finance the acquisition. As noted in Chapter 7, the purchaser may pay all cash, although this is rare. If the seller has an outstanding loan, the purchaser may attempt to assume that loan or take the property subject to that loan.

Recall that an *assumption of a loan* occurs when the purchaser takes over the seller's loan. A purchaser may want to do this if the current interest rates are high and the seller has a low-interest loan. In order to assume the loan, the seller's existing loan documents must not contain a nonassumption clause. Further, the lender must approve the assumption. The lender typically will check out the purchaser's financial situation as thoroughly as if the purchaser were applying for a new loan. Should the assumption be approved, the purchaser becomes primarily liable for the loan obligation. Additionally, lenders have the right to charge an assumption fee, and if the original loan documents have a due-on-sale clause, the lender has the right to raise the

title theory: A legal theory pertaining to financing instruments which maintains that a financing instrument transfers conditional title in the secured real property to the lender.

lien theory: A legal theory pertaining to financing instruments maintaining that a financing instrument serves as a lien on the secured real property.

due-on-sale clause: A clause in a loan document which states that should the real property securing the loan obligation be sold, the total amount outstanding on the loan becomes immediately due.

fiduciary lender: A lender that has a fiduciary duty to its principals.

commercial bank: A lender that is a major source of construction loans, short-term loans, and home improvement loans.

demand deposit: An account in which the depositor may take out his or her money on demand; a checking account.

Federal Deposit Insurance Corporation (FDIC): An institution that insures depositors' accounts.

Bank Insurance Fund (BIF): A fund that insures depositors' accounts.

savings and loan association: A lending institution that primarily makes residential, conventional loans but, on occasion, makes FHA and VA loans.

Financial Institutions Reform, Recovery and Enforcement Act (FIRREA): A federal law that restructured the savings and loan regulatory and insurance systems, giving management of insurance funds for savings and loans to the FDIC.

Savings Association Insurance Fund (SAIF): A fund that insures savings and loan deposits.

interest rate, which may defeat the purchaser's objective in assuming the loan. A **due-on-sale clause** is a clause that states that should the real property securing the loan obligation be sold, the total amount outstanding on the loan becomes immediately due.

As noted in Chapter 7, when a purchaser buys real property *"subject to" an existing loan*, the seller remains primarily liable for the debt obligation. The loan remains in the seller's name. The purchaser makes the loan payments, and if the purchaser defaults, the lender can move to foreclose on the property. However, the purchaser is not personally liable for the debt and, therefore, cannot be personally sued. Should the value of the real property prove to be less than the amount of the outstanding debt obligation, the lender may sue for a deficiency judgment against the seller, who still is primarily liable for the loan.

More commonly, a prospective purchaser will seek to obtain new financing. The source of the new financing may be a fiduciary lender. A **fiduciary lender** is a lender that has a fiduciary duty to its principals. A fiduciary lender's principals may be its depositors, as in the case of commercial banks and savings and loan institutions, or its premium payers, as in the case of insurance companies. In safeguarding their principals' monies, fiduciary lenders have the responsibility of making careful and prudent choices in accepting loan applications through scrupulous screening of loan applicants.

Commercial Banks

Commercial banks are a major source of construction loans, short-term loans, and home improvement loans. They generally choose not to tie up their resources in long-term loans because a large portion of their deposits are demand deposits rather than savings deposits. A **demand deposit** is exactly what the term suggests, an account in which the depositor may take out his or her money on demand, for example, a checking account. Depositors' accounts are insured by the **Federal Deposit Insurance Corporation (FDIC)** through the **Bank Insurance Fund (BIF).** Commercial banks are either state chartered or federally chartered. Commercial banks may make conventional loans or governmentally backed loans, such as FHA and VA loans, which are discussed later in this chapter.

Savings and Loan Associations

Like commercial banks, **savings and loan associations** are either federally or state chartered. They primarily make conventional loans but on occasion make FHA or VA loans. Unlike commercial banks, however, savings and loan associations specialize in residential, long-term loans. In the 1980s, many savings and loan associations closed as a result of defaults on high-risk loans. In response to the perceived crisis in the savings and loan industry, the federal government enacted the **Financial Institutions Reform, Recovery and Enforcement Act of 1989 (FIRREA).** Under the FIRREA, the savings and loan regulatory and insurance systems were restructured. Now, insurance funds for savings and loan associations are managed, like commercial banks, by the FDIC, which insures savings and loan deposits through the **Savings Association Insurance Fund (SAIF).**

Mutual Savings Banks

Mutual savings banks are found primarily in the Northeast. They are owned by their depositors, who are their investors. Their depositor-investors receive a return on their investments through the payment of interest on their savings accounts. Mutual savings banks operate similarly to savings and loan associations in that they offer only limited checking account services. They differ from savings and loan institutions, however, in the types of loans they make. Unlike savings and loan associations, which focus on residential loans, mutual savings banks make loans for both residential and income-producing properties. Mutual savings banks also gravitate to FHA and VA loans more than do savings and loan associations.

Insurance Companies

Insurance companies invest a large portion of the premiums paid to them by policyholders in real estate loans. They invest primarily in large commercial and industrial loans. Additionally, they often purchase blocks of residential FHA and VA loans from secondary markets, such as the Federal National Mortgage Association, which is discussed later in the chapter. Some insurance companies become partners or joint venturers in commercial real estate projects and thereby not only receive interest on the monies loaned for these projects, but also share in the appreciation of value of the properties.

Other Financing Sources

Other financing sources are also available to prospective borrowers. One such source is a **credit union.** Credit unions are cooperative associations in which members make savings deposits. Credit unions pay interest on the savings accounts and permit members to borrow money for both short-term loans, such as home improvement loans, and long-term residential loans.

Retirement and pension plans accumulate large sums that are invested on behalf of the plan participants. A portion of these sums are invested in real estate financing activities. Retirement and pension plan funds typically are invested in both residential and commercial loans, often through the services of mortgage brokers.

Mortgage banking companies are private corporations that originate loans for other lenders and investors, such as those mentioned above, for which they receive a servicing fee. They make a variety of loans, rather than specializing in a particular type of loan. Some mortgage banking companies borrow money to make loans. These loans are then sold to investors. **Mortgage brokers,** on the other hand, act as middlemen in a financing transaction, bringing lenders and borrowers together, similar to the manner in which a real estate broker brings sellers and buyers together. As a matter of fact, many mortgage brokers are also real estate brokers. Mortgage brokers are agents of their principals, be the principal the lender or the borrower. They differ from mortgage bankers in two respects. First, they do not service a loan. Rather, they locate potential borrowers (if their principal is the lender) or potential lenders (if their principal is the borrower) and process the initial loan application. In return, they receive a placement fee. Second, they are not lenders themselves; they simply act as intermediaries.

mutual savings bank: A lending institution found primarily in the Northeast that is owned by the depositors, who are the investors. The depositor-investors receive a return on their investment through the payment of interest on their savings accounts. Mutual savings banks make loans for both residential and income-producing properties.

credit union: A cooperative association in which members make savings deposits. Credit unions pay interest on the savings accounts and permit members to borrow money for both short-term and long-term residential loans.

mortgage banking company: A private corporation that originates loans for other lenders and investors for which it receives a servicing fee.

mortgage broker: A licensed individual who acts as a middleman in a financing transaction, bringing lenders and borrowers together in return for a placement fee.

Title insurance companies recently have become active in the real estate investment market. Title companies prefer to invest in subdivision developments. In addition to receiving interest on the loan, the title company becomes the exclusive title insurer on the subdivision project and, therefore, also makes money on the title policies written for each lot. Further, the title company may act as closing agent for all real estate closings within the subdivision and receive a closing agent's fee.

Real Estate Investment Trusts (REITs) provide another source of funds for borrowers. REITs accumulate funds by selling beneficial interests in the trusts to members of the public. Through the utilization of mortgage bankers, the trusts invest in various types of loans, typically construction loans and loans for larger real estate projects.

Finally, individuals may provide a source of financing. A seller may agree to accept a certain percentage of the sale price in cash and finance the remainder by accepting a purchase money mortgage and accompanying note from the buyer. Alternatively, the buyer may take out a first mortgage loan with a financial institution and still need another loan in order to meet the purchase price. The seller may be agreeable to taking a second mortgage and accompanying note to make up the difference. Purchase money mortgages generally are short-term loans (for example, five, ten years) as opposed to long-term loans (for example, twenty-five, thirty years).

TYPES OF FINANCING INSTRUMENTS

Mortgages

Some states in this country utilize mortgages as their primary security device, while others utilize deeds of trust. A **mortgage** is a two-party instrument. The parties to a mortgage are the **mortgagor** (the borrower) and the **mortgagee** (the lender). The mortgage instrument includes a description of the real property that serves as collateral for the loan, as well as all pertinent information included in the promissory note, such as the loan amount, the interest rate, the monthly payments, and so forth. The mortgage sets forth the rights of the mortgagee should the mortgagor default on the loan payments. The **acceleration clause** permits the mortgagee, at its option, upon default by the mortgagor, to accelerate the entire loan amount, making the full outstanding balance, plus interest and penalties, immediately due. Should the mortgagor fail to cure his or her default, the mortgagee may bring a court action to foreclose on the real property and sell it at public auction. An example of a short form of mortgage instrument is found in the Hypothetical Client Matter section at the end of the chapter. Mortgage instruments and deeds of trust are similar in most of their provisions, and therefore, most of the provisions found in the sample deed of trust in Figure 10–2 would be applicable to mortgage instruments as well.

Deeds of Trust

A **deed of trust,** unlike a mortgage, is a three-party instrument. The three parties to this instrument are: (1) the trustor (the borrower), (2) the

---

Real Estate Investment Trust (REIT): A trust that accumulates funds by selling beneficial interests in the trust to members of the public. The trust then invests in various types of loans, typically construction loans and loans for larger real estate projects.

mortgage: A two-party security instrument between the mortgagor/borrower and the mortgagee/lender that describes the property serving as collateral for the loan and sets forth the rights of the lender should the borrower default.

mortgagor: The borrower.

mortgagee: The lender.

acceleration clause: A clause in a financing instrument that permits the lender, at its option, upon default by the borrower, to accelerate the entire loan amount, making the full outstanding balance, plus interest and penalties, immediately due.

deed of trust: A three-party financing instrument between the trustor/borrower, beneficiary/lender, and trustee. The borrower, as trustor, signs legal title to the real property in question to the trustee as collateral for the loan, while the borrower remains in physical possession of the property.

beneficiary (the lender), and (3) the trustee (an escrow or a title or trust company). The borrower, as trustor, signs legal title to the real property in question to the trustee as collateral for the loan, while the borrower remains in physical possession of the property. The trustee holds legal title to the property on behalf of the lender-beneficiary. The lender is the holder of the promissory note that outlines the loan terms. Upon payment in full of the loan obligation, the trustee reconveys the real property to the borrower. By deeding over legal title through the execution of a deed of trust, the borrower gives the trustee, through a **power-of-sale clause,** the power to sell the property at public auction if the borrower defaults on his or her loan obligation. State statute dictates who can serve as trustee, as well as the procedures to be followed in the foreclosure of the real property. Generally, the foreclosure procedures under a deed of trust are faster and less complex than the foreclosure procedures under a mortgage instrument.

Figure 10–1 provides a chart indicating which states use deeds of trust, which states use mortgages, and which states use both.

Figure 10–2 provides an example of a deed of trust instrument.

power-of-sale clause: A clause in a deed of trust that gives the trustee the power to sell the real property serving as collateral for a loan at public auction if the borrower defaults on his or her loan obligation.

DEED OF TRUST AND MORTGAGE STATES

State	Deed of Trust	Mortgage	Both	State	Deed of Trust	Mortgage	Both
Alabama		X		Missouri	X		
Alaska	X			Montana	X		
Arizona	X			Nebraska	X		
Arkansas			X	Nevada	X		
California	X			New Hampshire		X	
Colorado	X			New Jersey		X	
Connecticut		X		New Mexico	X		
Delaware		X		New York		X	
District of Columbia	X			North Carolina	X		
Florida		X		North Dakota		X	
Georgia			X	Ohio		X	
Hawaii		X		Oklahoma		X	
Idaho	X			Oregon	X		
Illinois	X			Pennsylvania		X	
Indiana		X		Rhode Island		X	
Iowa		X		South Carolina		X	
Kansas		X		South Dakota		X	
Kentucky			X	Tennessee	X		
Louisiana		X		Texas	X		
Maine		X		Utah	X		
Maryland			X	Vermont		X	
Massachusetts		X		Virginia	X		
Michigan		X		Washington	X		
Minnesota		X		West Virginia	X		
Mississippi	X			Wisconsin		X	
				Wyoming		X	

FIGURE 10–1 Deed of trust and mortgage states

FIGURE 10-2
Deed of trust

DEED OF TRUST

THIS DEED OF TRUST ("Security Instrument") is made on August 17, 1997. The Grantor is SARAH MORGAN ("Borrower"). The Trustee is ANY CITY TRUST COMPANY of Any City, Any State. The Beneficiary is COMMERCE BANK, which is organized and existing under the laws of Any State, and whose address is 500 Commercial Avenue, Any City, Any State ("Lender"). Borrower owes Lender the principal sum of Sixty-Eight Thousand Dollars ($68,000.00). This debt is evidenced by Borrower's note dated the same date as this Security Instrument ("Note"), which provides for monthly payments, with the full debt, if not paid earlier, due and payable on September 17, 2027. This Security Instrument secures to Lender: (a) the repayment of the debt evidenced by the Note, with interest, and all renewals, extensions and modifications; (b) the payment of all other sums, with interest, advanced under paragraph 7 to protect the security of this Security Instrument; and (c) the performance of Borrower's covenants and agreements under this Security Instrument and the Note. For this purpose, Borrower irrevocably grants and conveys to Trustee, in trust, with power of sale, the following described property located in Any County, Any State:

> Lot 12 in Block 4 of CUMBERLAND ESTATES, a subdivision, according to the plat thereof, as recorded in Plat Book 101, Page 14, of the Public Records of Any County, Any State.

which has the address of 725 St. Ives Road, Any City, Any State ("Property Address");

TOGETHER WITH all the improvements now or hereafter erected on the property, and all easements, rights, appurtenances, rents, royalties, mineral, oil and gas rights and profits, water rights and stock and all fixtures now or hereafter a part of the property. All replacements and additions shall also be covered by this Security Instrument. All of the foregoing is referred to in this Security Instrument as the "Property."

BORROWER COVENANTS that Borrower is lawfully seized of the estate hereby conveyed and has the right to grant and convey the Property and that the Property is unencumbered, except for encumbrances of record. Borrower warrants and will defend generally the title to the Property against all claims and demands, subject to any encumbrances of record.

THIS SECURITY INSTRUMENT combines uniform covenants for national use and nonuniform covenants with limited variations by jurisdiction to constitute a uniform security instrument covering real property.

UNIFORM COVENANTS. Borrower and Lender covenant and agree as follows:

1. **Payment of Principal and Interest; Prepayment and Late Charges.** Borrower shall promptly pay when due the principal of and interest on the debt evidenced by the Note and any prepayment and late charges due under the Note.

2. **Funds for Taxes and Insurance.** Subject to applicable law or to a written waiver by Lender, Borrower shall pay to Lender on the day monthly payments are due under the Note, until the Note is paid in full, a sum ("Funds") equal to one-twelfth of: (a) yearly taxes and assessments which may attain priority over this Security Instrument; (b) yearly leasehold payments or ground rents on the Property, if any; (c) yearly hazard insurance premiums; and (d) yearly mortgage insurance premiums, if any. These items are called "escrow items." Lender may estimate the Funds due on the basis of current data and reasonable estimates of future escrow items.

FIGURE 10–2
(continued)

The Funds shall be held in an institution the deposits or accounts of which are insured or guaranteed by a federal or state agency (including Lender if Lender is such an institution). Lender shall apply the Funds to pay the escrow items. Lender may not charge for holding and applying the Funds, analyzing the account or verifying the escrow items, unless Lender pays Borrower interest on the Funds and applicable law permits Lender to make such a charge. Borrower and Lender may agree in writing that interest shall be paid on the Funds. Unless an agreement is made or applicable law requires interest to be paid, Lender shall not be required to pay Borrower any interest or earnings on the Funds. Lender shall give to Borrower, without charge, an annual accounting of the Funds showing credits and debits to the Funds and the purpose for which each debit to the Funds was made. The Funds are pledged as additional security for the sums secured by this Security Instrument.

If the amount of the Funds held by Lender, together with the future monthly payments of Funds payable prior to the due dates of the escrow items, shall exceed the amount required to pay the escrow items when due, the excess shall be, at Borrower's option, either promptly repaid to Borrower or credited to Borrower on monthly payments of Funds. If the amount of the Funds held by Lender is not sufficient to pay the escrow items when due, Borrower shall pay to Lender any amount necessary to make up the deficiency in one or more payments as required by Lender.

Upon payment in full of all sums secured by this Security Instrument, Lender shall promptly refund to Borrower any Funds held by Lender. If under paragraph 19 the Property is sold or acquired by Lender, Lender shall apply, no later than immediately prior to the sale of the Property or its acquisition by Lender, any Funds held by Lender at the time of application as a credit against the sums secured by this Security Instrument.

3. **Application of Payments.** Unless applicable law provides otherwise, all payments received by Lender under paragraphs 1 and 2 shall be applied: first, to late charges due under the Note; second, to prepayment charges due under the Note; third, to amounts payable under paragraph 2; fourth, to interest due; and last, to principal due.

4. **Charges; Liens.** Borrower shall pay all taxes, assessments, charges, fines and impositions attributable to the Property which may attain priority over this Security Instrument, and leasehold payments or ground rents, if any. Borrower shall pay these obligations in the manner provided in paragraph 2, or if not paid in that manner, Borrower shall pay them on time directly to the person owed payment. Borrower shall promptly furnish to Lender all notices of amounts to be paid under this paragraph. If Borrower makes these payments directly, Borrower shall promptly furnish to Lender receipts evidencing the payments.

Borrower shall promptly discharge any lien which has priority over this Security Instrument unless Borrower: (a) agrees in writing to the payment of the obligation secured by the lien in a manner acceptable to Lender; (b) contests in good faith the lien by, or defends against enforcement of the lien in, legal proceedings which in the Lender's opinion operate to prevent the enforcement of the lien or forfeiture of any part of the Property; or (c) secures from the holder of the lien an agreement satisfactory to Lender subordinating the lien to this Security Instrument. If Lender determines that any part of the Property is subject to a lien which may attain priority over this Security Instrument, Lender may give Borrower a notice identifying the lien. Borrower shall satisfy the lien or take one or more of the actions set forth above within 10 days of the giving of notice.

5. **Hazard Insurance.** Borrower shall keep the improvements now existing or hereafter erected on the Property insured against loss by fire, hazards

FIGURE 10–2
(continued)

included within the term "extended coverage" and any other hazards for which Lender requires insurance. This insurance shall be maintained in the amounts and for the periods that Lender requires. The insurance carrier providing the insurance shall be chosen by Borrower subject to Lender's approval which shall not be unreasonably withheld.

All insurance policies and renewals shall be acceptable to Lender and shall include a standard mortgage clause. Lender shall have the right to hold the policies and renewals. If Lender requires, Borrower shall promptly give to Lender all receipts of paid premiums and renewal notices. In the event of loss, Borrower shall give prompt notice to the insurance carrier and Lender. Lender may make proof of loss if not made promptly by Borrower.

Unless Lender and Borrower otherwise agree in writing, insurance proceeds shall be applied to restoration or repair of the Property damaged, if the restoration or repair is economically feasible and Lender's security is not lessened. If the restoration or repair is not economically feasible or Lender's security would be lessened, the insurance proceeds shall be applied to the sums secured by this Security Instrument, whether or not then due, with any excess paid to Borrower. If Borrower abandons the Property, or does not answer within 30 days a notice from Lender that the insurance carrier has offered to settle a claim, then Lender may collect the insurance proceeds. Lender may use the proceeds to repair or restore the Property or to pay sums secured by this Security Instrument, whether or not then due. The 30-day period will begin when the notice is given.

Unless Lender and Borrower otherwise agree in writing, any application of proceeds to principal shall not extend or postpone the due date of the monthly payments referred to in paragraphs 1 and 2 or change the amount of the payments. If under paragraph 19 the Property is acquired by Lender, Borrower's right to any insurance policies and proceeds resulting from damage to the Property prior to the acquisition shall pass to Lender to the extent of the sums secured by this Security Instrument immediately prior to the acquisition.

6. **Preservation and Maintenance of Property; Leaseholds.** Borrower shall not destroy, damage or substantially change the Property, allow the Property to deteriorate or commit waste. If this Security Instrument is on a leasehold, Borrower shall comply with the provisions of the lease, and if Borrower acquires fee title to the Property, the leasehold and fee title shall not merge unless Lender agrees to the merger in writing.

7. **Protection of Lender's Rights in the Property; Mortgage Insurance.** If Borrower fails to perform the covenants and agreements contained in this Security Instrument, or there is a legal proceeding that may significantly affect Lender's rights in the Property (such as a proceeding in bankruptcy, probate, for condemnation or to enforce laws or regulations), then Lender may do and pay for whatever is necessary to protect the value of the Property and Lender's rights in the Property. Lender's actions may include paying any sums secured by a lien which has priority over this Security Instrument, appearing in court, paying reasonable attorneys' fees and entering on the Property to make repairs. Although Lender may take action under this paragraph 7, Lender does not have to do so.

Any amounts disbursed by Lender under this paragraph 7 shall become additional debt of Borrower secured by this Security Instrument. Unless Borrower and Lender agree to other terms of payment, these amounts shall bear interest from the date of disbursement at the Note rate and shall be payable, with interest, upon notice from Lender to Borrower requesting payment.

FIGURE 10–2
(continued)

If Lender required mortgage insurance as a condition of making the loan secured by this Security Instrument, Borrower shall pay the premiums required to maintain the insurance in effect until such time as the requirement for the insurance terminates in accordance with Borrower's and Lender's written agreement or applicable law.

8. **Inspection.** Lender or its agent may make reasonable entries upon and inspections of the Property. Lender shall give Borrower notice at the time of or prior to an inspection specifying reasonable cause for the inspection.

9. **Condemnation.** The proceeds of any award or claim for damages, direct or consequential, in connection with any condemnation or other taking of any part of the Property, or for conveyance in lieu of condemnation, are hereby assigned and shall be paid to Lender.

In the event of a total taking of the Property, the proceeds shall be applied to the sums secured by this Security Instrument, whether or not then due, with any excess paid to Borrower. In the event of a partial taking of the Property, unless Borrower and Lender otherwise agree in writing, the sums secured by this Security Instrument shall be reduced by the amount of the proceeds multiplied by the following fraction: (a) the total amount of the sums secured immediately before the taking, divided by (b) the fair market value of the Property immediately before the taking. Any balance shall be paid to Borrower.

If the Property is abandoned by Borrower, or if, after notice by Lender to Borrower that the condemnor offers to make an award or settle a claim for damages, Borrower fails to respond to Lender within 30 days after the date the notice is given, Lender is authorized to collect and apply the proceeds, at its option, either to restoration or repair of the Property or to the sums secured by this Security Instrument, whether or not then due.

Unless Lender and Borrower otherwise agree in writing, any application of proceeds to principal shall not extend or postpone the due date of the monthly payments referred to in paragraphs 1 and 2 or change the amount of such payments.

10. **Borrower Not Released; Forbearance by Lender Not a Waiver.** Extension of the time for payment or modification of amortization of the sums secured by this Security Instrument granted by Lender to any successor in interest of Borrower shall not operate to release the liability of the original Borrower or Borrower's successors in interest. Lender shall not be required to commence proceedings against any successor in interest or refuse to extend time for payment or otherwise modify amortization of the sums secured by this Security Instrument by reason of any demand made by the original Borrower or Borrower's successors in interest. Any forbearance by Lender in exercising any right or remedy shall not be a waiver of or preclude the exercise of any right or remedy.

11. **Successors and Assigns Bound; Joint and Several Liability; Cosigners.** The covenants and agreements of this Security Instrument shall bind and benefit the successors and assigns of Lender and Borrower, subject to the provisions of paragraph 17. Borrower's covenants and agreements shall be joint and several. Any Borrower who cosigns this Security Instrument but does not execute the Note: (a) is cosigning this Security Instrument only to mortgage, grant and convey that Borrower's interest in the Property under the terms of this Security Instrument; (b) is not personally obligated to pay the sums secured by this Security Instrument; and (c) agrees that Lender and any other Borrower may agree to extend, modify, forbear or make any accommodations with regard to the terms of this Security Instrument or the Note without that Borrower's consent.

FIGURE 10–2
(continued)

12. **Loan Charges.** If the loan secured by this Security Instrument is subject to a law which sets maximum loan charges, and that law is finally interpreted so that the interest or other loan charges collected or to be collected in connection with the loan exceed the permitted limits, then: (a) any such loan charge shall be reduced by the amount necessary to reduce the charge to the permitted limit; and (b) any sums already collected from Borrower which exceeded permitted limits will be refunded to Borrower. Lender may choose to make this refund by reducing the principal owed under the Note or by making a direct payment to Borrower. If a refund reduces principal, the reduction will be treated as a partial prepayment without any prepayment charge under the Note.

13. **Legislation Affecting Lender's Rights.** If enactment or expiration of applicable laws has the effect of rendering any provision of the Note or this Security Instrument unenforceable according to its terms, Lender, at its option, may require immediate payment in full of all sums secured by this Security Instrument and may invoke any remedies permitted by paragraph 19. If Lender exercises this option, Lender shall take the steps specified in the second paragraph of paragraph 17.

14. **Notices.** Any notice to Borrower provided for in this Security Instrument shall be given by delivering it or by mailing it first-class mail unless applicable law requires use of another method. The notice shall be directed to the Property Address or any other address Borrower designates by notice to Lender. Any notice to Lender shall be given by first-class mail to Lender's address stated herein or any other address Lender designates by notice to Borrower. Any notice provided for in this Security Instrument shall be deemed to have been given to Borrower or Lender when given as provided in this paragraph.

15. **Governing Law; Severability.** This Security Instrument shall be governed by federal law and the law of the jurisdiction in which the Property is located. In the event that any provision or clause of this Security Instrument or the Note conflicts with applicable law, such conflict shall not affect other provisions of this Security Instrument or the Note which can be given effect without the conflicting provision. To this end the provisions of this Security Instrument and the Note are declared to be severable.

16. **Borrower's Copy.** Borrower shall be given one conformed copy of the Note and of this Security Instrument.

17. **Transfer of the Property or a Beneficial Interest in Borrower.** If all or any part of the Property or any interest in it is sold or transferred (or if a beneficial interest in Borrower is sold or transferred and Borrower is not a natural person) without Lender's prior written consent, Lender may, at its option, require immediate payment in full of all sums secured by this Security Instrument. However, this option shall not be exercised by Lender if exercise is prohibited by federal law as of the date of this Security Instrument.

If Lender exercises this option, Lender shall give Borrower notice of acceleration. The notice shall provide a period of not less than 30 days from the date the notice is delivered or mailed within which Borrower must pay all sums secured by this Security Instrument. If Borrower fails to pay these sums prior to the expiration of this period, Lender may invoke any remedies permitted by this Security Instrument without further notice or demand on Borrower.

18. **Borrower's Right to Reinstate.** If Borrower meets certain conditions, Borrower shall have the right to have enforcement of this Security Instrument discontinued at any time prior to the earlier of: (a) 5 days (or

FIGURE 10–2
(continued)

such other period as applicable law may specify for reinstatement) before sale of the Property pursuant to any power of sale contained in this Security Instrument; or (b) entry of a judgment enforcing this Security Instrument. Those conditions are that Borrower: (a) pays Lender all sums which then would be due under this Security Instrument and the Note had no acceleration occurred; (b) cures any default of any other covenants or agreements; (c) pays all expenses incurred in enforcing this Security Instrument, including, but not limited to, reasonable attorneys' fees; and (d) takes such action as Lender may reasonably require to assure that the lien of this Security Instrument shall continue unchanged. Upon reinstatement by Borrower, this Security Instrument and the obligations secured hereby shall remain fully effective as if no acceleration had occurred. However, this right to reinstate shall not apply in the case of acceleration under paragraphs 13 or 17.

NONUNIFORM COVENANTS. Borrower and Lender further covenant and agree as follows:

19. **Acceleration Remedies.** Lender shall give notice to Borrower prior to acceleration following Borrower's breach of any covenant or agreement in this Security Instrument (but not prior to acceleration under paragraphs 13 and 17 unless applicable law provides otherwise). The notice shall specify: (a) the default; (b) the action required to cure the default; (c) a date, not less than 30 days from the date of the notice given to Borrower, by which the default must be cured; and (d) that failure to cure the default on or before the date specified in the notice may result in acceleration of the sums secured by this Security Instrument and sale of the Property. The notice shall further inform Borrower of the right to reinstate after acceleration and the right to bring a court action to assert the nonexistence of a default or any other defense of Borrower to acceleration and sale. If the default is not cured on or before the date specified in the notice, Lender at its option may require immediate payment in full of all sums secured by this Security Instrument, without further demand, and may invoke the power of sale and any other remedies permitted by applicable law. Lender shall be entitled to collect all expenses incurred in pursuing the remedies provided in this paragraph 19, including, but not limited to, reasonable attorneys' fees and costs of title evidence.

If Lender invokes the power of sale, Lender or Trustee shall give to Borrower (and the owner of the Property, if a different person) notice of sale in the manner prescribed by applicable law. Trustee shall give public notice of sale by advertising, in accordance with applicable law, once a week for two successive weeks in a newspaper having general circulation in the county or city in which any part of the Property is located, and by such additional or any different form of advertisement the Trustee deems advisable. Trustee may sell the Property on the eighth day after the first advertisement or any day thereafter, but not later than 30 days following the last advertisement. Trustee, without demand on Borrower, shall sell the Property at public auction to the highest bidder at the time and place and under the terms designated in the notice of sale in one or more parcels and in any order Trustee determines. Trustee may postpone sale of all or any parcel of the Property by advertising in accordance with applicable law. Lender or its designee may purchase the Property at any sale.

Trustee shall deliver to the purchaser Trustee's deed conveying the Property with special warranty of title. The recitals in the Trustee's deed shall be prima facie evidence of the truth of the statements made therein. Trustee shall apply the proceeds

FIGURE 10–2
(continued)

of the sale in the following order: (a) to all expenses of the sale, including, but not limited to, Trustee's fee of 10% of the gross sale price and reasonable attorneys' fees; (b) to the discharge of all taxes, levies and assessments on the Property, if any, as provided by applicable law; (c) to all sums secured by this Security Instrument; and (d) any excess to the person or persons legally entitled to it. Trustee shall not be required to take possession of the Property prior to the sale thereof or to deliver possession of the Property to the purchaser at the sale.

20. **Lender in Possession.** Upon acceleration under paragraph 19 or abandonment of the Property, Lender (in person, by agent or by judicially appointed receiver) shall be entitled to enter upon, take possession of and manage the Property and to collect the rents of the Property including those past due. Any rents collected by Lender or the receiver shall be applied first to payment of the costs of management of the Property and collection of rents, including, but not limited to, receiver's fees, premiums on receiver's bonds and reasonable attorneys' fees, and then to the sums secured by this Security Instrument.

21. **Release.** Upon payment of all sums secured by this Security Instrument, Lender shall request Trustee to release this Security Instrument and shall surrender all notes evidencing debt secured by this Security Instrument to Trustee. Trustee shall release this Security Instrument without charge to Borrower. Borrower shall pay any recordation costs.

22. **Substitute Trustee.** Lender, at its option, may from time to time remove Trustee and appoint a successor trustee to any Trustee appointed hereunder. Without conveyance of the Property, the successor trustee shall succeed to all the title, power and duties conferred upon Trustee herein and by applicable law.

23. **Identification of Note.** The Note is identified by a certificate on the Note executed by any Notary Public who certifies an acknowledgment hereto.

24. **Riders to This Security Instrument.** If one or more riders are executed by Borrower and recorded together with this Security Instrument, the covenants and agreements of each such rider shall be incorporated into and shall amend and supplement the covenants and agreements of this Security Instrument as if the rider(s) were a part of this Security Instrument.

___ Adjustable Rate Rider   ___ Condominium Rider
___ Graduated Payment Rider   ___ Planned Unit Development Rider
___ 2-4 Family Rider   ___ Other(s) [Specify]

NOTICE: THE DEBT SECURED HEREBY IS SUBJECT TO CALL IN FULL OR THE TERMS THEREOF BEING MODIFIED IN THE EVENT OF SALE OR CONVEYANCE OF THE PROPERTY CONVEYED.

BY SIGNING BELOW, Borrower accepts and agrees to the terms and covenants contained in this Security Instrument and in any rider(s) executed by Borrower and recorded with it.

_____
Sarah Morgan

STATE OF ANY STATE
COUNTY OF ANY COUNTY

The foregoing instrument was acknowledged before me this 17th day of August, 1997, by SARAH MORGAN.

_____
Notary Public, State of Any State
My commission expires: _____

TYPES OF LOANS

Overview of Conventional Loans

A **conventional loan** is a loan made by a private lender in which the lender usually does not have any insurance or guarantee from a third party, such as a government agency, backing the loan should the borrower fail to meet his or her loan obligations. Traditionally, this meant that a lower percentage of the property value was loaned to correspondingly lower the risk to the lender, so that if the borrower defaulted and the lender had to foreclose and sell the property, the value of the property would meet or exceed the amount of the outstanding debt obligation.

The correspondence between the value of the property to serve as collateral for a loan and the amount of the loan is called the **loan-to-value ratio** (sometimes symbolized as L/V). Commonly, the loan-to-value ratio for a conventional loan is 80/20. For example, if the real property value is $100,000, the lender will provide an 80% loan, in this instance, $80,000, requiring the borrower to contribute $20,000. Thus, when considering a loan, a conventional lender not only qualifies the borrower and the property to serve as collateral for the loan, but also commonly wants to see the borrower put down a sizeable amount of cash, evidencing the borrower's equity in the property. The lower the loan-to-value ratio, the higher the down payment required of the borrower.

The loan-to-value ratio of conventional loans generally is lower than that of FHA and VA loans. In order to make conventional loans more competitive, however, the Mortgage Guaranty Insurance Corporation, in 1951, introduced the concept of **private mortgage insurance (PMI).** Private mortgage insurance is available from private insurance providers. The purpose of the private mortgage insurance is to insure the portion of the loan that exceeds the typical conventional loan-to-value ratio. Thus, if a conventional lender were to provide a 90% or 95% loan to a borrower, the private mortgage insurance would insure the top 20% or 25% of the loan. If the borrower defaults, the insurer buys the loan from the lender and then proceeds to enforce the debt obligation against the borrower. A borrower may pay the total private mortgage insurance premium at closing or, alternatively, a certain percentage with the rest factored into the balance of the loan.

Historically, conventional loans were all straight loans. A **straight loan** is one in which the borrower makes periodic interest payments, with the entire principal paid at the end of the loan term. Today, one sees a similar payment structure in a **balloon mortgage,** which is a loan calling for periodic payments that are less than the amount required to pay off the loan completely at the end of the loan term. The remaining balance of the principal thus "balloons" into a single, large payment at the end of the loan term. Balloon mortgages generally are used for short-term, second mortgage loans.

Most conventional loans are now fully amortized loans. An **amortized loan** is one in which level payments are made throughout the life of the loan. In the early years of the loan, the greater portion of each payment goes to pay off the interest on the loan. As years go by, although the monthly payments remain level, the portion of the payment applied to interest decreases and the portion of the payment applied to principal increases until, at the end of the loan term, all of the interest and principal are paid off.

conventional loan: A loan made by a private lender in which the lender usually does not have any insurance or guarantee from a third party, such as a government agency, backing the loan should the borrower fail to meet his or her loan obligations.

loan-to-value ratio: The correspondence between the value of the real property to serve as collateral for a loan and the amount of the loan.

private mortgage insurance (PMI): Insurance from private insurance providers that insures the portion of a loan which exceeds the typical conventional loan-to-value ratio.

straight loan: A loan in which the borrower makes periodic interest payments, with the entire principal paid at the end of the loan term.

balloon mortgage: A loan calling for periodic payments that are less than the amount required to pay off the loan completely at the end of the loan term. The remaining balance of the principal "balloons" into a single, large payment at the end of the loan term.

amortized loan: A loan in which level payments are made throughout the life of the loan.

Conventional loans often take less time to process than governmentally backed loans. There is less paperwork involved and fewer federal restrictions. Additionally, there are no set maximum amounts that may be borrowed, and conventional loans are available to the widest range of borrowers and properties.

Conventional lenders usually charge a **loan origination fee** to process the loan application, normally 1% of the loan amount. They may also charge **points** (sometimes referred to as *discount points*). Each point is equal to 1% of the loan amount. Thus, if the loan amount is $80,000 and the lender is charging 2 points, the points equal $1,600. The charging of points is a method of increasing the lender's yield while not increasing the interest rate. Remember that lenders are in the money business and are making money by lending it. The lender will make a certain amount on a loan, be it by charging points, increasing the interest rate, by charging prepayment penalties, or a combination of these methods.

FHA Loans

In the aftermath of the great stock market crash and subsequent Depression, the federal government sought a means for stimulating the national economy, particularly the real estate sector. In 1934, the Federal Housing Administration (FHA) was established to entice reluctant lenders to finance residential loans. The FHA operates under the Department of Housing and Urban Development (HUD) and does not make loans itself; rather, it insures loans made by approved lenders. Lenders that are members of the Federal Reserve System or the FDIC are automatically approved to make FHA-insured loans.

The FHA insures loans for owner-occupied one-to-four family dwellings. Before the FHA will insure a loan, both the borrower and the property to serve as collateral for the loan must qualify. The subject real property must be appraised. The borrower is provided with a notice stating that the purpose of the appraisal is to estimate the value of the property and not to serve as a warranty of its condition. With regard to homes constructed before 1978, borrowers must be given a notice pertaining to lead-based poisoning.

In addition to the lender's own loan application, an a HUD/VA addendum and a mortgage credit analysis worksheet is completed for the borrower of an **FHA loan.** The lender takes all of the loan application documents and forwards them to the FHA for approval. The FHA looks at many of the same factors that influence conventional lenders in accepting or rejecting loan applications. It looks at both the quality and the quantity of the borrower's income. While quantity is self-explanatory, quality refers to the stability of the income source (for example, long-term employment, stocks and bonds). It also looks at the other demands on the borrower's income (for example, car loan payments, credit card debt). If the results of the examination indicate that the borrower is a good prospect, the FHA will insure the loan.

The FHA sets maximum loan amounts, which vary from area to area. The FHA also strictly sets the minimum down payment to be made by the borrower. One of two methods are used in determining the minimum down payment: the traditional method and the Omnibus Budget Reconciliation Act

loan origination fee: A fee charged by lenders to process a loan application.

points: A lending charge, sometimes referred to as *discount points*. Each point is equal to one percent of the loan amount.

FHA loan: A loan insured by the Federal Housing Administration. The FHA insures loans for owner-occupied one-to-four family dwellings.

(OBRA) method. Both methods are based on the lesser of either the appraised value or the sales price. The difference is that under the traditional method, closing costs are added to both the appraised value and the sales price before calculating the minimum down payment, whereas under the OBRA method, closing costs are excluded.

Under the traditional method, if the lesser of the appraised value or sales price (plus closing costs) equals $25,000 or less, the maximum FHA loan amount is 97%, with the borrower putting down the remaining 3% as the minimum down payment. If the lesser of the appraised value or sales price (plus closing costs) falls between $25,001 and $125,000, the maximum FHA loan amount is calculated by taking 97% of the first $25,000 and 95% of the remainder. For example, if the lesser of the appraised value or sales price, plus closing costs, is $100,000, one would take 97% of the first $25,000, which is $24,250; then one would take 95% of the remaining amount ($75,000), which is $71,250, and add these figures together, totaling $95,500 for the maximum loan amount. The borrower would have to contribute $4,500 as the minimum down payment. If the lesser of the appraised value or sales price (plus closing costs) exceeds $125,000, then the maximum FHA loan amount is calculated by taking 95% of the first $100,000 and 90% of the remainder.

Under the OBRA method, closing costs are not included in the calculations. Under the OBRA method, if the lesser of the appraised value or sales price is $25,000 or less, the maximum FHA loan is 98.75%. If the lesser of the appraised value or sales price exceeds $25,000, the maximum FHA loan is 97.75%. Thus, if the lesser of the appraised value or the sales price, excluding closing costs, is $100,000, then the maximum FHA loan under the OBRA method is $97,750, and the borrower would have to contribute $2,250 as the minimum down payment.

Lenders always make FHA loans in even $50 increments, and if the loan amount does not come out evenly, the amount is rounded down rather than rounded up. Thus, if the permissible maximum loan amount is $100,343.25, the actual amount loaned would be $100,300.

FHA loans may be written for a term period of up to thirty years. The FHA does not set interest rates, the lenders do. The FHA does require that borrowers pay **mortgage insurance premiums,** which are collected into the FHA's Mutual Mortgage Insurance Fund. The FHA uses this fund to insure lenders against bad loans. The borrower pays a portion of the mortgage insurance premium at closing, and then pays an annual premium based on the unpaid principal balance of the loan. In addition to mortgage insurance premiums, lenders of FHA loans are allowed to charge a 1% loan origination fee and may charge points as well. Further, included in each monthly payment is one-twelfth of the annual real property taxes on the property and hazard insurance premiums. This type of loan payment is often referred to as **PITI** (principal, interest, taxes, insurance).

FHA loans allow prepayment privileges. They generally are assumable. Varying rules apply, based on the date of loan origination. If the FHA loan originated before December 1, 1986, there are no restrictions regarding assumption. If the FHA loan originated after this date, the FHA must perform a creditworthiness check on the person(s) wanting to assume the loan.

mortgage insurance premium: An insurance premium charged on FHA loans. These premiums are collected into the FHA's Mutual Mortgage Insurance Fund to insure lenders against bad loans.

PITI: A loan payment that is comprised of principal, interest, taxes, and insurance.

VA Loans

Ten years after the Federal Housing Administration was established, the Servicemen's Readjustment Act (commonly referred to as the GI Bill of Rights) was passed to help returning World War II veterans purchase homes. This act gave birth to the **VA loan.** "VA" stands for the Veterans Administration. The VA guarantees loans made to veterans by approved lenders. Unlike conventional loans and FHA loans, there is no requirement that an eligible veteran make a down payment. The VA does collect a funding fee of 1.25% of the loan amount, which may be paid by the borrower at closing or added into the total loan amount. As is the case with FHA loans, VA loans require PITI payments, the maximum loan term is thirty years, residential property must be owner-occupied, and the borrower is allowed to prepay the loan without suffering a penalty. The same HUD/VA addendum is added to the loan package of both FHA and VA loans. Unlike the FHA, the VA does not establish maximum loan amounts; however, it does set a limit on the amount it will guarantee, or pay the lender should the veteran default on the loan. (At the time of this writing, the maximum guarantee is 60%.)

A veteran applying for a VA loan must first complete a Request Pertaining to Military Records and a Request for Certificate of Veteran Status, which allows the lender to receive a copy of the veteran's military records. Next, the veteran must apply for a **certificate of eligibility.** The certificate states the maximum available loan guaranty entitlement for the veteran. Additionally, application must be made for a *certificate of reasonable value* for the property to be purchased. The certificate sets forth the current market value of the property based on a VA-approved appraisal and thus establishes the maximum allowable loan on the property. In addition to these forms and the lender's customary loan application forms, the VA requires the completion of its own loan analysis, a debt questionnaire, and a verification of VA benefit–related indebtedness. Further, the VA requires that the borrower sign two disclosure statements. The first is the Federal Collection Policy Notice, which sets forth the actions that may be taken if a veteran defaults on a loan. The second is an interest rate and discount disclosure statement, the signing of which indicates that the borrower understands the interest rate and points charged in the loan transaction.

Veterans who are eligible for a VA loan are those who have served a minimum of 181 days' active service since September 16, 1940; 90 days for veterans of World War II, the Korean War, and the Viet Nam War; 2 years for those enlisting for the first time after September 7, 1980. Unmarried widows and widowers of veterans are also eligible for VA loans. VA loans can be assumed by nonveterans; however, the veteran originating the loan will remain primarily liable on the loan unless the VA issues a release from liability.

Adjustable Rate Loans

A loan can either be a fixed rate loan or an **adjustable rate loan** (referred to as an *adjustable rate mortgage* or ARM). Which type of loan is preferable to a borrower depends on the prevailing interest rates at the time the loan is made. Under an adjustable rate loan, the interest rate typically starts lower than that under a fixed rate loan, and then periodically changes in relation to

VA loan: A loan made to veterans by approved lenders for residential, owner-occupied property and guaranteed by the Veterans Administration.

certificate of eligibility: A certificate that states the maximum available loan guaranty entitlement for a veteran.

adjustable rate loan: A loan in which the interest rate typically starts lower than that of a fixed rate loan, and then periodically changes in relation to an index rate, such as the rate on Treasury securities.

an index rate, such as the rate on Treasury securities or the national average of cost of funds to savings and loan associations. The period between one rate change and the next is called the **adjustment period.** Thus, a loan with a one-year adjustment period is often referred to as a one-year ARM.

The **margin** is the amount of percentage points the lender adds to the index rate to come up with the ARM interest rate (for example, 2 or 3 percentage points). The margin usually remains constant for the duration of the loan term.

ARMs have **interest rate caps** that limit the amount the interest rate can increase. Interest rate caps may take the form of periodic caps, which limit the interest rate increase from one adjustment period to the next, or they may take the form of overall caps, which limit the interest rate increase over the life of the loan. Federal law requires that lenders provide borrowers with a disclosure statement when a borrower applies for an adjustable rate loan.

Wraparound Loans

A **wraparound loan** is one that allows a borrower to pay off an existing loan to obtain additional financing from a second lender. The second lender provides the borrower with a new loan, charging a higher interest rate than the first lender. The second lender then assumes payment of the existing mortgage loan. The first lender still has priority should the borrower default on the loan payments made to the second lender. The new loan covers both the existing first loan and the additional loan amount required by the borrower. A wraparound loan is most frequently used when an existing loan cannot be prepaid without incurring hefty prepayment penalties. It is also used by cooperative corporations on buildings they own.

Graduated Payment Mortgages

A **graduated payment mortgage** is a loan in which the borrower's monthly payments during the first years of the loan term are reduced and the deferred portions of the payments are added on to the monthly payments made in later years. This type of loan was set up to attract young, first-time home buyers who could not ordinarily meet the monthly payment obligations under a standard loan. The rationale behind this loan is that both the property value and the borrower's income level will increase over the life of the loan.

A consequence of this type of loan arrangement is **negative amortization.** Negative amortization occurs when the monthly payments are not large enough to pay the interest costs on the loan. The interest cost that is not covered by the monthly payments is added to the unpaid principal balance, leaving the borrower owing the lender more than the borrower did at the beginning of the loan.

Shared Appreciation Mortgages

A **shared appreciation mortgage** (sometimes referred to as SAM, or as an *equity participation loan)* is a loan in which the lender lends money at a lower interest rate in return for a share in the appreciated value of the property when the property is sold. These loans originally were devised as financing devices for developers of large construction projects, but they have also

---

adjustment period: The period between one rate change and the next for an adjustable rate loan.

margin: The amount of percentage points a lender adds to the index rate to come up with an ARM interest rate.

interest rate cap: A limitation on the amount an interest rate can increase on an adjustable rate loan.

wraparound loan: A loan that allows a borrower to pay off an existing loan to obtain additional financing from a second lender. The second lender provides the borrower with a new loan, charging a higher interest rate than the first lender. The second lender then assumes payment of the existing first mortgage loan.

graduated payment mortgage: A loan in which the borrower's monthly payments during the first years of the loan term are reduced and the deferred portions of the payments are added onto the monthly payments made in later years.

negative amortization: A situation in which the interest cost that is not covered by the monthly payments is added to the unpaid principal balance, leaving the borrower owing the lender more than the borrower did at the beginning of the loan.

shared appreciation mortgage: A loan in which the lender lends money at a lower interest rate in return for a share in the appreciated value of the real property when the property is sold.

been offered to the residential home buyer. More popular in the 1970s and 1980s, their popularity has diminished in recent years.

Growing Equity Mortgages

A **growing equity mortgage** (often referred to as a GEM) is a loan in which the borrower quickly increases his or her equity in the real property by increasing the amount of the monthly payments by a certain percentage each year according to a schedule. This increase is applied to the principal in order to pay off the loan by an earlier maturity date than would be applicable in a standard loan. Because the purpose of the loan structure is to pay off the loan quickly, these loans are fixed rate loans. Thus, although the payments increase steadily, the interest rate remains the same.

Reverse Annuity Mortgages

A **reverse annuity mortgage** (commonly referred to as a RAM) is not a loan designed to help a borrower purchase real estate. With a reverse annuity mortgage, the borrower, a senior citizen, has 100% equity in his or her home. However, the senior citizen may be equity-rich but cash-poor and looking to the lender for a loan to cover his or her living expenses. The lender will lend the borrower up to 80% of the appraised value of the property. The borrower is thus borrowing against his or her equity in the home. He or she receives monthly payments from the lender over a period of years, and upon his or her death, the property is sold and the loan repaid from the proceeds.

Buy-Downs

A **buy-down** is not a type of loan. Rather, it is a financing arrangement that enables the borrower to afford a loan at the prevailing interest rate. A buy-down occurs when a seller is eager to sell his or her property. To finalize the sale, the seller will "buy down" the interest rate of the borrower's loan for a certain period of time. For example, the prevailing interest rate may be 10%. The seller may buy down the interest rate to 8% for a period of two years by paying the lender a lump sum covering the difference in the interest in advance. Thus, for the first two years of the loan term, the borrower makes monthly payments based on 8% interest. After the two-year period expires, the borrower makes monthly payments based on 10% interest. Unlike a graduated payment loan, negative amortization does not occur because the seller pays the difference between the amount of the loan payment made by the borrower and the amount of the requisite loan payment in order to fully amortize the loan by paying the difference in the interest in advance.

THE LENDING PROCESS

The Loan Application and Related Documents

The lending process begins with a loan application and an interview between the prospective borrower and a loan officer. A prospective borrower

---

growing equity mortgage: A loan in which the borrower quickly increases his or her equity in the real property by increasing the amount of the monthly payments by a certain percentage each year according to a schedule. This increase is applied to the principal in order to pay the loan off by an earlier maturity date than would be applicable in a standard loan.

reverse annuity mortgage: A situation in which a real property owner who has one hundred percent equity in his or her home borrows against that equity and receives monthly payments from the lender over a period of years. Upon the owner's death, the property is sold, and the loan is repaid from the proceeds.

buy-down: A financing arrangement whereby the seller will "buy down" the interest rate of the borrower's loan for a certain period of time.

should realize that he or she should bring certain documents to the initial interview to assist the loan officer in finalizing the loan application documents. The borrower should have ready at the initial interview:

1. Borrower's social security number
2. The contract for sale and purchase with closing date or a construction contract
3. The names and addresses of all financial institutions in which the borrower has accounts, together with the account numbers
4. If divorced, a copy of the divorce decree and separation agreement, including evidence of income or payment resulting from the divorce action
5. The names and addresses of all employers for the past two years; if self-employed, copies of federal income tax returns for the past two years
6. Borrower's annual gross salary, together with last year's W-2 form. If overtime or bonuses were paid, these should be listed separately.
7. List of all assets, together with their current market value (including monthly or quarterly statements, if applicable)
8. Name of life insurance company and policy number of life insurance policy
9. A complete list of all outstanding debt obligations, including the names and addresses of creditors and the amount owed to each (for example, department stores, student loans, car loans; each credit card creditor should be listed separately). If borrower has an outstanding mortgage loan, the name and address of the lending institution, the original loan amount, the current balance, and the account number.

With this information in hand, the borrower can effectively complete a standard loan application. A uniform residential loan application form is provided in Figure 10–3. The loan officer will also ask the borrower to sign certain request forms, such as a request for credit reports, a request for verification of employment, a request for verification of deposits (to verify monies in bank accounts), and, if the borrower presently is a renter, a request for verification of rent. The borrower may also be asked to sign a general certification and authorization form, certifying that the information provided to the lender is accurate and complete and authorizing the release of pertinent information to the lender.

The loan officer can determine the amount of a loan the borrower qualifies for from the loan application information. The first step is determining the borrower's monthly income. The gross monthly income generally is multiplied by a percentage up to 28% to arrive at the borrower's allowable monthly payment for principal and interest. There will be additional payments that must be figured, such as monthly real estate taxes (one-twelfth the annual real property tax) and monthly homeowners' insurance.

Before completing the loan application forms, the loan officer will discuss with the borrower the types of loans available. The loan officer will also order an appraisal to be done on the real property to verify its value and request a credit report verifying the borrower's credit. After the loan officer receives

Uniform Residential Loan Application

This application is designed to be completed by the applicant(s) with the lender's assistance. Applicants should complete this form as "Borrower" or "Co-Borrower", as applicable. Co-Borrower information must also be provided (and the appropriate box checked) when ☐ the income or assets of a person other than the "Borrower" (including the Borrower's spouse) will be used as a basis for loan qualification or ☐ the income or assets of the Borrower's spouse will not be used as a basis for loan qualification, but his or her liabilities must be considered because the Borrower resides in a community property state, the security property is located in a community property state, or the Borrower is relying on other property located in a community property state as a basis for repayment of the loan.

I. TYPE OF MORTGAGE AND TERMS OF LOAN

Mortgage Applied for:	☐ VA ☐ Conventional ☐ Other: ☐ FHA ☐ FmHA		Agency Case Number	Lender Case No.
Amount $	Interest Rate ___%	No. of Months	Amortization Type:	☐ Fixed Rate ☐ Other (explain): ☐ GPM ☐ ARM (type):

II. PROPERTY INFORMATION AND PURPOSE OF LOAN

Subject Property Address (street, city, state, & zip code)	No. of Units

Legal Description of Subject Property (attach description if necessary)	Year Built

Purpose of Loan	☐ Purchase ☐ Construction ☐ Refinance ☐ Construction-Permanent	☐ Other (explain):	Property will be: ☐ Primary Residence ☐ Secondary Residence ☐ Investment

Complete this line if construction or construction-permanent loan.

Year Lot Acquired	Original Cost $	Amount Existing Liens $	(a) Present Value of Lot $	(b) Cost of Improvements $	Total (a + b) $

Complete this line if this is a refinance loan.

Year Acquired	Original Cost $	Amount Existing Liens $	Purpose of Refinance	Describe Improvements ☐ made ☐ to be made Cost: $

Title will be held in what Name(s)	Manner in which Title will be held	Estate will be held in: ☐ Fee Simple ☐ Leasehold (show expiration date)
Source of Down Payment, Settlement Charges and/or Subordinate Financing (explain)		

III. BORROWER INFORMATION

Borrower | **Co-Borrower**

Borrower's Name (include Jr. or Sr. if applicable)	Co-Borrower's Name (include Jr. or Sr. if applicable)

Social Security Number	Home Phone (incl. area code)	Age	Yrs. School	Social Security Number	Home Phone (incl. area code)	Age	Yrs. School

☐ Married ☐ Unmarried (include single, divorced, widowed) ☐ Separated	Dependents (not listed by Co-Borrower) no. ___ ages ___	☐ Married ☐ Unmarried (include single, divorced, widowed) ☐ Separated	Dependents (not listed by Borrower) no. ___ ages ___
Present Address (street, city, state, zip code) ☐ Own ☐ Rent ___ No. Yrs.		Present Address (street, city, state, zip code) ☐ Own ☐ Rent ___ No. Yrs.	

If residing at present address for less than two years, complete the following:

Former Address (street, city, state, zip code) ☐ Own ☐ Rent ___ No. Yrs.	Former Address (street, city, state, zip code) ☐ Own ☐ Rent ___ No. Yrs.

Former Address (street, city, state, zip code) ☐ Own ☐ Rent ___ No. Yrs.	Former Address (street, city, state, zip code) ☐ Own ☐ Rent ___ No. Yrs.

IV. EMPLOYMENT INFORMATION

Borrower | **Co-Borrower**

Name & Address of Employer ☐ Self Employed	Yrs. on this job	Name & Address of Employer ☐ Self Employed	Yrs. on this job
	Yrs. employed in this line of work/profession		Yrs. employed in this line of work/profession
Position/Title/Type of Business	Business Phone (incl. area code)	Position/Title/Type of Business	Business Phone (incl. area code)

If employed in current position for less than two years or if currently employed in more than one position, complete the following:

Name & Address of Employer ☐ Self Employed	Dates (from - to)	Name & Address of Employer ☐ Self Employed	Dates (from - to)
	Monthly Income $		Monthly Income $
Position/Title/Type of Business	Business Phone (incl. area code)	Position/Title/Type of Business	Business Phone (incl. area code)

Name & Address of Employer ☐ Self Employed	Dates (from - to)	Name & Address of Employer ☐ Self Employed	Dates (from - to)
	Monthly Income $		Monthly Income $
Position/Title/Type of Business	Business Phone (incl. area code)	Position/Title/Type of Business	Business Phone (incl. area code)

Freddie Mac Form 65/Rev. 10/92   Page 1 of 4   Fannie Mae Form 1003/Rev. 10/92

Bankers Systems, Inc., St. Cloud, MN (1-800-397-2341) Form URLA 5/3/94

FIGURE 10–3 Uniform residential loan application

V. MONTHLY INCOME AND COMBINED HOUSING EXPENSE INFORMATION

Gross Monthly Income	Borrower	Co-Borrower	Total	Combined Monthly Housing Expense	Present	Proposed
Base Empl. Income*	$	$	$	Rent	$	
Overtime				First Mortgage (P&I)		$
Bonuses				Other Financing (P&I)		
Commissions				Hazard Insurance		
Dividends/Interest				Real Estate Taxes		
Net Rental Income				Mortgage Insurance		
Other (before completing, see the notice in "describe other income" below)				Homeowner Assn. Dues		
				Other:		
Total	$	$	$	**Total**	$	$

* Self Employed Borrower(s) may be required to provide additional documentation such as tax returns and financial statements.

Describe Other Income *Notice:* Alimony, child support, or separate maintenance income need not be revealed if the Borrower (B) or Co-Borrower (C) does not choose to have it considered for repaying this loan.

B/C		Monthly Amount
		$

VI. ASSETS AND LIABILITIES

This Statement and any applicable supporting schedules may be completed jointly by both married and unmarried Co-Borrowers if their assets and liabilities are sufficiently joined so that the Statement can be meaningfully and fairly presented on a combined basis; otherwise separate Statements and Schedules are required. If the Co-Borrower section was completed about a spouse, this Statement and supporting schedules must be completed about that spouse also.

Completed ☐ Jointly ☐ Not Jointly

ASSETS Description	Cash or Market Value	Liabilities and Pledged Assets. List the creditor's name, address and account number for all outstanding debts, including automobile loans, revolving charge accounts, real estate loans, alimony, child support, stock pledges, etc. Use continuation sheet, if necessary. Indicate by (*) those liabilities which will be satisfied upon sale of real estate owned or upon refinancing of the subject property.	Monthly Payt. & Mos. Left to Pay	Unpaid Balance
Cash deposit toward purchase held by:	$	**LIABILITIES**		
		Name and address of Company	$ Payt./Mos.	$
List checking and savings accounts below				
Name and address of Bank, S&L, or Credit Union				
		Acct. no.		
		Name and address of Company	$ Payt./Mos.	$
Acct. no.	$			
Name and address of Bank, S&L, or Credit Union				
		Acct. no.		
		Name and address of Company	$ Payt./Mos.	$
Acct. no.	$			
Name and address of Bank, S&L, or Credit Union				
		Acct. no.		
		Name and address of Company	$ Payt./Mos.	$
Acct. no.	$			
Name and address of Bank, S&L, or Credit Union				
		Acct. no.		
		Name and address of Company	$ Payt./Mos.	$
Acct. no.	$			
Stocks & Bonds (Company name/number & description)	$			
		Acct. no.		
		Name and address of Company	$ Payt./Mos.	$
Life insurance net cash value	$			
Face amount: $				
Subtotal Liquid Assets	$			
Real estate owned (enter market value from schedule of real estate owned)	$	Acct. no.		
Vested interest in retirement fund	$	Name and address of Company	$ Payt./Mos.	$
Net worth of business(es) owned (attach financial statement)	$			
Automobiles owned (make and year)	$			
		Acct. no.		
		Alimony/Child Support/Separate Maintenance Payments Owed to:	$	
Other Assets (itemize)	$	Job Related Expense (child care, union dues, etc.)	$	
		Total Monthly Payments	$	
Total Assets a.	$	**Net Worth** (a minus b) ➡ $	**Total Liabilities b.**	$

Freddie Mac Form 65/Rev. 10/92   Page 2 of 4   Fannie Mae Form 1003/Rev. 10/92

Bankers Systems, Inc., St. Cloud, MN (1-800-397-2341) Form URLA 5/3/94

FIGURE 10–3 (continued)

VI. ASSETS AND LIABILITIES (cont.)

Schedule of Real Estate Owned (If additional properties are owned, use continuation sheet.)

Property Address (enter S if sold, PS if pending sale or R if rental being held for income)	Type of Property	Present Market Value	Amount of Mortgages & Liens	Gross Rental Income	Mortgage Payments	Insurance, Maintenance, Taxes & Misc.	Net Rental Income
		$	$	$	$	$	$
Totals		$	$	$	$	$	$

List any additional names under which credit has previously been received and indicate appropriate creditor name(s) and account number(s):

Alternate Name	Creditor Name	Account Number

VII. DETAILS OF TRANSACTION	VIII. DECLARATIONS

VII. DETAILS OF TRANSACTION

a. Purchase price	$
b. Alterations, improvements, repairs	
c. Land (if acquired separately)	
d. Refinance (incl. debts to be paid off)	
e. Estimated prepaid items	
f. Estimated closing costs	
g. PMI, MIP, Funding Fee	
h. Discount (if Borrower will pay)	
i. Total costs (add items a through h)	
j. Subordinate financing	
k. Borrower's closing costs paid by Seller	
l. Other Credits (explain)	
m. Loan amount (exclude PMI, MIP, Funding Fee financed)	
n. PMI, MIP, Funding Fee financed	
o. Loan amount (add m & n)	
p. Cash from/to Borrower (subtract j, k, l & o from i)	

VIII. DECLARATIONS

If you answer "yes" to any questions a through i, please use continuation sheet for explanation.

Borrower (Yes/No)   Co-Borrower (Yes/No)

a. Are there any outstanding judgments against you?

b. Have you been declared bankrupt within the past 7 years?

c. Have you had property foreclosed upon or given title or deed in lieu thereof in the last 7 years?

d. Are you a party to a law suit?

e. Have you directly or indirectly been obligated on any loan which resulted in foreclosure, transfer of title in lieu of foreclosure, or judgment? (This would include such loans as home mortgage loans, SBA loans, home improvement loans, educational loans, manufactured (mobile) home loans, any mortgage, financial obligation, bond, or loan guarantee. If "Yes," provide details, including date, name and address of Lender, FHA or VA case number, if any, and reasons for the action.)

f. Are you presently delinquent or in default on any Federal debt or any other loan, mortgage, financial obligation, bond, or loan guarantee? If "Yes," give details as described in the preceding question.

g. Are you obligated to pay alimony, child support, or separate maintenance?

h. Is any part of the down payment borrowed?

i. Are you a co-maker or endorser on a note?

j. Are you a U.S. citizen?

k. Are you a permanent resident alien?

l. Do you intend to occupy the property as your primary residence? If "Yes," complete question m below.

m. Have you had an ownership interest in a property in the last three years?

(1) What type of property did you own--principal residence (PR), second home (SH), or investment property (IP)?

(2) How did you hold title to the home--solely by yourself (S), jointly with your spouse (SP), or jointly with another person (O)?

IX. ACKNOWLEDGMENT AND AGREEMENT

The undersigned specifically acknowledge(s) and agree(s) that: (1) the loan requested by this application will be secured by a first mortgage or deed of trust on the property described herein; (2) the property will not be used for any illegal or prohibited purpose or use; (3) all statements made in this application are made for the purpose of obtaining the loan indicated herein; (4) occupation of the property will be as indicated above; (5) verification or reverification of any information contained in the application may be made at any time by the Lender, its agents, successors and assigns, either directly or through a credit reporting agency, from any source named in this application, and the original copy of this application will be retained by the Lender, even if the loan is not approved; (6) the Lender, its agents, successors and assigns will rely on the information contained in the application and I/we have a continuing obligation to amend and/or supplement the information provided in this application if any of the material facts which I/we have represented herein should change prior to closing; (7) in the event my/our payments on the loan indicated in this application become delinquent, the Lender, its agents, successors and assigns, may, in addition to all their other rights and remedies, report my/our name(s) and account information to a credit reporting agency; (8) ownership of the loan may be transferred to successor or assign of the Lender without notice to me and/or the administration of the loan account may be transferred to an agent, successor or assign of the Lender with prior notice to me; (9) the Lender, its agents, successors and assigns make no representations or warranties, express or implied, to the Borrower(s) regarding the property, the condition of the property, or the value of the property.

Certification: I/We certify that the information provided in this application is true and correct as of the date set forth opposite my/our signature(s) on this application and acknowledge my/our understanding that any intentional or negligent misrepresentation(s) of the information contained in this application may result in civil liability and/or criminal penalties including, but not limited to, fine or imprisonment or both under the provisions of Title 18, United States Code, Section 1001, et seq. and liability for monetary damages to the Lender, its agents, successors and assigns, insurers and any other person who may suffer any loss due to reliance upon any misrepresentation which I/we have made on this application.

Borrower's Signature	Date	Co-Borrower's Signature	Date
X		X	

X. INFORMATION FOR GOVERNMENT MONITORING PURPOSES

The following information is requested by the Federal Government for certain types of loans related to a dwelling, in order to monitor the Lender's compliance with equal credit opportunity, fair housing and home mortgage disclosure laws. You are not required to furnish this information, but are encouraged to do so. The law provides that a Lender may neither discriminate on the basis of this information, nor on whether you choose to furnish it. However, if you choose not to furnish it, under Federal regulations this Lender is required to note race and sex on the basis of visual observation or surname. If you do not wish to furnish the above information, please check the box below. (Lender must review the above material to assure that the disclosures satisfy all requirements to which the Lender is subject under applicable state law for the particular type of loan applied for.)

BORROWER
☐ I do not wish to furnish this information

Race/National Origin:
☐ American Indian or Alaskan Native ☐ Asian or Pacific Islander
☐ Black, not of Hispanic origin ☐ Hispanic ☐ White, not of Hispanic origin
☐ Other (specify) _____

Sex: ☐ Female ☐ Male

CO-BORROWER
☐ I do not wish to furnish this information

Race/National Origin:
☐ American Indian or Alaskan Native ☐ Asian or Pacific Islander
☐ Black, not of Hispanic origin ☐ Hispanic ☐ White, not of Hispanic origin
☐ Other (specify) _____

Sex: ☐ Female ☐ Male

To be Completed by Interviewer This application was taken by: ☐ face-to-face interview ☐ by mail ☐ by telephone	Interviewer's Name (print or type) Interviewer's Signature Date Interviewer's Phone Number (incl. area code)	Name and Address of Interviewer's Employer

Freddie Mac Form 65/Rev. 10/92   Page 3 of 4   Fannie Mae Form 1003/Rev. 10/92

Bankers Systems, Inc., St. Cloud, MN (1-800-397-2341) Form URLA 5/3/94

FIGURE 10–3 (continued)

Continuation Sheet/Residential Loan Application

Use this continuation sheet if you need more space to complete the Residential Loan Application. Mark **B** for Borrower or **C** for Co-Borrower.	Borrower:	Agency Case Number:
	Co-Borrower:	Lender Case Number:

☐ **NOTICE OF RIGHT TO APPRAISAL COPY**
You have the right to a copy of the appraisal report used in connection with your application for credit. If you wish a copy, please write to us at the mailing address we have provided. We must hear from you no later than 90 days after we notify you about the action taken on your credit application or you withdraw your application. In your letter, give us the following information: Loan or application number (if known), date of application, name(s) of loan applicant(s), property address, and current mailing address.

I/We fully understand that it is a Federal crime punishable by fine or imprisonment, or both, to knowingly make any false statements concerning any of the above facts as applicable under the provisions of Title 18, United States Code, Section 1001, et seq.

Borrower's Signature	Date	Co-Borrower's Signature	Date
X		X	

Freddie Mac Form 65/Rev. 10/92   Page 4 of 4   Fannie Mae Form 1003/Rev. 10/92

Bankers Systems, Inc., St. Cloud, MN (1-800-397-2341) Form URLA 5/3/94

FIGURE 10–3 (continued)

verification on all these information requests, a determination will be made on the loan application package.

If the borrower's loan application is accepted, the borrower will receive a **loan commitment,** which is a document outlining the terms under which the lender will loan the specified amount to the borrower. The loan commitment is an offer by the lender; when it is accepted by the borrower, it becomes a contract between the parties.

In this tangle of information, what are lenders truly looking for? First, they are looking for a favorable income ratio, one which shows that the majority of the borrower's income will not be devoted to the payment of principal, interest, taxes, and insurance. Second, lenders are looking at the borrower's overall debt load. They will set a ceiling on what percentage of the borrower's income can acceptably be apportioned to the payment of ongoing expenses. Third, lenders will be looking at the borrower's employment history, preferring steady employment and a consistent pattern of upward income growth over a particular salary amount. Fourth, lenders will be looking at the borrower's overall net worth. Fifth, lenders will be looking at the borrower's credit history.

The most common reasons for refusal of loan applications are lack of financial earning ability, lack of financial resources, frequent changes in employment, and excessive installment purchases. Lenders also are wary of unstable domestic relations in which the borrowers may soon divorce, which can radically alter the borrowers' financial situations. Marital status, however, is not a basis for denying a loan.

Government Regulation

Federal Truth in Lending Act. The **Federal Truth in Lending Act** and Regulation Z went into effect in 1969. The purpose of these laws is to inform consumers of the exact costs incurred when obtaining a loan. Lenders must make full disclosure of all costs incurred in obtaining credit. Further, lenders are required to disclose to borrowers the annual percentage rate applied to the loan. The **annual percentage rate (APR)** is the true interest rate, which includes charges added such as points and mortgage insurance. The Federal Truth in Lending Act was revised in 1987 to require complete disclosures regarding ARMs. Violation of the act can result in both civil and criminal penalties. A sample Truth in Lending Disclosure Statement is provided in Figure 10–4.

Real Estate Settlement Procedures Act. The **Real Estate Settlement Procedures Act** (commonly referred to as RESPA) complements the Truth in Lending Act. The RESPA was enacted to prevent kickbacks and to ensure that borrowers receive full disclosure of all charges they are to pay at closing. The RESPA requires the use of a uniform settlement statement called a HUD statement in all nonexempt loan transactions. (The HUD statement is discussed in detail in later chapters.) The RESPA also requires that lenders provide all prospective borrowers with an information booklet entitled *Settlement Costs: A HUD Guide.* Further, lenders are to provide borrowers with a good faith estimate of the closing costs within three days from the date the loan application is submitted. Figure 10–5 provides an example of a blank good faith estimate of settlements costs form.

loan commitment: A document outlining the terms under which the lender will loan a specified amount to the borrower. Once accepted by the borrower, it becomes a contract.

Federal Truth in Lending Act: A federal law requiring lenders to make full disclosure of all costs incurred in obtaining credit.

annual percentage rate (APR): The true interest rate on a loan, which includes charges added such as points and mortgage insurance.

Real Estate Settlement Procedures Act (RESPA): A federal law requiring the lender to provide the borrower with a good faith estimate of closing costs within three days from the date the loan application is submitted. It also requires the use of a uniform settlement statement for all nonexempt transactions.

TRUTH IN LENDING DISCLOSURE STATEMENT

REAL PROPERTY TRANSACTION   LOAN NO. _____
SECURED BY FIRST LIEN ON A DWELLING

The interest rate on this mortgage loan is _____.
The FINANCE CHARGE on this transaction will begin to accrue on _____.
The institution's security in this transaction is a _____ mortgage on property
located at _____,
also specifically described in the documents furnished for this loan. The documents executed in connection with this transaction cover all after-acquired property and also stand as security for future advances, the terms for which are described in the documents.

I.   The AMOUNT OF THE LOAN in this transaction is   _____
       Less PREPAID FINANCE CHARGE
       Interest from _____ to _____   _____
       Closing costs   _____

       Total PREPAID FINANCE CHARGE   _____
       AMOUNT FINANCED   _____

II.   OTHER NONFINANCE CHARGES
     _____ Not included   _____ Included in AMOUNT FINANCED
     Title charges   _____
     Appraisal   _____
     Preparation of documents   _____
     Credit report   _____
     Recording mortgage   _____
     Notary fee   _____
     First year mortgage insurance premiums   _____
     Title insurance   _____
           _____
           _____

     Total NONFINANCE CHARGES   _____
     NET PROCEEDS   _____

    FINANCE CHARGE—Required on ADDITIONAL ADVANCE and REFINANCE only.
    The finance charge on this transaction totals $_____. This amount includes all items represented in Part I shown above.
    The TOTAL OF PAYMENTS on this transaction will be $_____.
    ANNUAL PERCENTAGE RATE _____%
    PAYMENT TERMS. Payments for principal and interest on this transaction shall be monthly installments of $_____ beginning on _____ and due on the _____ day of each month thereafter.

    LATE CHARGE. In the event of default of any payment, the contract interest rate may be increased up to 1% during the period of default.
    MISCELLANEOUS CLAUSE.

    PREPAYMENT CHARGES
_____ Conventional—Association shall be entitled to a minimum of 90 days interest on the original amount of the Loan.
_____ Additional
INSURANCE

    PROPERTY INSURANCE. Property insurance, if written in connection with this loan, may be obtained by borrower through any person of borrower's choice,

FIGURE 10–4
Truth in lending disclosure statement

FIGURE 10–4
(continued)

provided however, the creditor reserves the right to refuse, for reasonable cause, to accept an insurer offered by the borrower.

OTHER INSURANCE. Credit life, accident, health or loss of income insurance is not required to obtain this loan. No charge is made for such insurance, and no such insurance is provided unless the borrower signs the appropriate statement below.

_____ is available at cost of $_____ per month for the ____ year term of the initial policy.

_____ is available at cost of $_____ estimated per month for the ____ year term of the initial policy.

_____ I desire coverage.

_____ I DO NOT desire such insurance coverage.

DATE	SIGNATURE	DATE	SIGNATURE

INSTITUTION
I do hereby acknowledge receipt of the disclosure made in this notice.

Equal Credit Opportunity Act. The **Equal Credit Opportunity Act (ECOA)** of 1974 was enacted to prevent discrimination in making credit available to consumers. Under the ECOA, no lender may discriminate against a borrower on any of the following bases: race, color, religion, national origin, sex, marital status, age, or receipt of income from public assistance programs. Lenders have borrowers sign an Equal Credit Opportunity Notice, verifying that the borrower is aware of the discrimination prohibition. A sample Equal Credit Opportunity Notice is provided in Figure 10–6.

PREPARATION OF FINANCING INSTRUMENTS

Promissory Notes

As noted in the introduction to this chapter, a promissory note is a document evidencing a promise to pay a specified amount of money over a specified period of time. The parties to the note are the borrower, referred to as the **maker,** and the lender, referred to as the **payee.** A promissory note is signed only by the maker and usually is not witnessed, notarized, or recorded. There are some exceptions, however, such as in New York where promissory notes are witnessed and sometimes notarized. In certain situations, the lender may require additional assurance that the loan will be paid and may require a guarantor. This is especially true when a corporation or limited liability company is the borrower. The owners of these businesses are not personally responsible under ordinary circumstances for business debts. Thus, if a corporation obtains a loan and then defaults, the lender cannot look to the individual shareholders to repay the debt. When the maker is a corporation or limited liability company, the lender will almost always require a key individual in the business, such as the president of the corporation, to personally guarantee

Equal Credit Opportunity Act (ECOA): A federal law enacted to prevent discrimination in making credit available to consumers.

maker: The borrower signing a promissory note.

payee: The lender as receiver of a promissory note.

GOOD FAITH ESTIMATE OF SETTLEMENT COSTS

PROPOSED MORTGAGOR(S) _____ DATE _____
PROPERTY ADDRESS _____
SALES PRICE $_____ MORTGAGE REQUESTED $_____ TYPE _____

In connection with your mortgage application for the above premises, we are submitting, for your information, the following HUD Good Faith Estimates for the SETTLEMENT CHARGES AND SERVICES, required by HUD pursuant to the Real Estate Settlement Procedures Act (RESPA). The figures listed below are only estimates, and the actual charges due at settlement may be different.

Loan Origination Fee...$ _____
Discount Fee (Points) ....$ _____
Appraisal Fee ....$ _____
Credit Report Fee...$ _____
Interest $ ___ Per Day ....$ _____
Mortgage Insurance Premium (PMI or MIP)...............................$ _____
Lender's Attorney Fee..$ _____
Title Insurance (Mortgage Policy)..$ _____
Recording Fees (Deed and Mortgage) ....$ _____
Instrument Survey ....$ _____
Pest Inspection...$ _____
State Mortgage Tax ....$ _____
Buyer's Attorney Fee ....$ _____
Fuel Adjustment..$ _____
Water Tests ....$ _____
Septic Certification...$ _____
VA Funding Fee (1%)...$ _____
Tax Service Charge (Conventional)..$ _____
_____$ _____
_____$ _____
One-year Property Taxes for Escrows and Adjustments ....$ _____
One-year Paid-in-full Homeowners' Insurance ....$ _____
(Policy NOT a binder is required at closing) ....$ _____
Total Estimated Funds Needed to Close.......................................$ _____

This form does not cover all items you will be required to pay in cash at settlement; for example: Deposits in escrow for real estate taxes and insurance; mortgage insurance premiums, if applicable; prepaid interest; and water and sewer adjustments. You may wish to inquire about the amounts of such other items, as you may be required to pay other additional amounts at settlement.
I/We acknowledge receipt of the Good Faith Estimate of Settlement Costs.

DATE_____   DATE _____

FIGURE 10–5
Good faith estimate of settlement costs form

the repayment of the loan by signing personally, not as the maker, but as a guarantor. This may be accomplished in a separate document. If this is done and the corporation defaults, the lender may look to the president personally to repay the debt obligation.

As a real estate paralegal, there may be many occasions on which you will be asked to prepare a promissory note. In order to prepare a note, you must know the names of the parties, the date, the place at which the note is made, the amount of the loan, the interest rate, the payment terms, the rights of the

FIGURE 10–6
Equal credit
opportunity notice

EQUAL CREDIT OPPORTUNITY NOTICE

E.C.O.A. NOTICE

THE FEDERAL EQUAL CREDIT OPPORTUNITY ACT PROHIBITS CREDITORS FROM DISCRIMINATING AGAINST CREDIT APPLICANTS ON THE BASIS OF RACE, COLOR, RELIGION, NATIONAL ORIGIN, SEX, MARITAL STATUS, AGE (PROVIDED THE APPLICANT HAS THE CAPACITY TO ENTER A BINDING CONTRACT); BECAUSE ALL OR PART OF THE APPLICANT'S INCOME DERIVES FROM ANY PUBLIC ASSISTANCE PROGRAM; OR BECAUSE THE APPLICANT HAS IN GOOD FAITH EXERCISED ANY RIGHT UNDER THE CONSUMER CREDIT PROTECTION ACT. THE FEDERAL AGENCY THAT ADMINISTERS COMPLIANCE WITH THIS LAW CONCERNING THIS CREDITOR IS THE FEDERAL TRADE COMMISSION, EQUAL OPPORTUNITY, WASHINGTON, D.C. 20588.

_____
SIGNATURE OF APPLICANT

parties upon default, and the prepayment provisions. Some lenders allow prepayment without penalty. Recall that in both FHA and VA loans, for example, the borrower is allowed to prepay without paying any penalty charges. Some lenders institute a lock-in period, such as the first two or three years of the loan, during which time prepayment is prohibited. Other lenders may prohibit all prepayment unless stiff prepayment penalties are paid. In preparing a promissory note, the checklist found below may prove helpful. A sample note is provided in the Hypothetical Client Matter section at the end of the chapter.

NOTE PREPARATION CHECKLIST

1. Date
2. City and state in which note is made
3. Parties
   a. Name of maker
   b. Name of payee
   c. Name of guarantor(s), if any
4. Amount of loan
5. Interest rate, fixed or adjustable. If adjustable, specify:
   a. Adjustment period
   b. Periodic cap
   c. Overall cap
   d. Index to which interest rate is tied
6. Total amount of payments
7. Maturity date
8. Amount of each payment and what is included in each payment
   a. Principal
   b. Interest
   c. Taxes
   d. Insurance
9. When payments are to be made
10. Where payments are to be made

11. *Late charges, if any*
12. *Security for note*
13. *Prepayment privileges or penalties*
14. *Parties' rights in event of default*
15. *Waiver of homestead or other debtor's rights*
16. *Signature(s) of maker and guarantor*

Mortgages and Deeds of Trust

Some attorneys use preprinted forms for mortgages and deeds of trust, while others prepare their own forms for the most common types of loans. Lenders may require their own printed forms, and FNMA and FHLMC documents are often used so that the loans can then be sold in secondary markets. (FNMA and FHLMC are discussed in the following text.)

There will be two or three parties to a financing instrument, depending on whether the instrument is a mortgage or a deed of trust. If the borrower is married, his or her spouse must also join as a party in order to relinquish all homestead and dower and curtesy rights in the property that is the collateral for the loan in states that recognize these rights. In addition to the names of the parties, a financing instrument must include the date, the social security number of the borrower, an accurate legal description of the property that is the security for the debt, a description of all personal property that is included as collateral for the loan, and a description of the debt terms (this should be taken directly from the note).

The financing instrument should include an agreement to pay the debt, a maintenance clause in which the borrower agrees to maintain the property in good condition and which allows the lender to take over maintenance and charge the borrower accordingly if the borrower defaults on this provision, a tax clause in which the borrower agrees to pay all real property taxes and which allows the lender to make the requisite tax payments and charge the borrower accordingly if the borrower defaults on this provision, an assignment of rents clause, if applicable, a receivership clause permitting the lender to have a receiver appointed to oversee income-producing property if it is necessary to preserve the income value of the property, and a clause permitting the lender to inspect the property. The name and address of the preparer of the instrument should be included, if state statute so requires. The signature of the borrower must be witnessed and notarized. State law specifies the number of witnesses and form of notarization.

After delivery to the lender or trustee, the financing instrument must be recorded in the county in which the real property securing the debt is located. The checklist found below should prove helpful in the preparation of deeds of trust and mortgages. A sample deed of trust can be found in Figure 10–2, while a sample short-form mortgage is provided in the Hypothetical Client Matter section at the end of the chapter.

FINANCING INSTRUMENT PREPARATION CHECKLIST
1. *Date*
2. *Parties*
   a. *If deed of trust:*
      i. *Trustor*

　　　　　ii.   *Trustee*
　　　　　iii. *Beneficiary*
　　　b. *If mortgage:*
　　　　　i.   *Mortgagor*
　　　　　ii. *Mortgagee*
　3. *Social security number of trustor/mortgagor*
　4. *Legal description of the real property*
　5. *Description of all personal property serving as additional collateral*
　6. *Description of the loan debt terms (take this from the note)*
　7. *Agreement by trustor/mortgagor to pay debt on above terms*
　8. *Tax clause*
　9. *Maintenance clause*
　10. *Inspection clause*
　11. *Assignment of rents clause, if applicable*
　12. *Receivership clause, if applicable*
　13. *Duties of trustor/mortgagor*
　14. *Due-on-sale clause, if applicable*
　15. *Rights of parties in event of default*
　16. *Signature of trustor/mortgagor*
　17. *Signatures of witnesses*
　18. *Notarization*
　19. *Name and address of preparer of instrument*

SECONDARY MARKETS

A **secondary market** is a market for the purchase and sale of existing mortgages. The lenders who originate loans comprise the primary market. Once a loan closing has been completed, that loan can be bought or sold in the secondary market. A loan is an investment. The return on the investment for a lender in the primary market is the interest paid on the loan. However, lenders can also profit by selling the loan to investors in the secondary market. Even after the loan is sold, the lender may continue to service the loan by collecting the loan payments from the borrower and passing them on to the investor. The lender receives a servicing fee for servicing the loan.

The secondary market takes all these purchased loans, "warehouses" them, and packages them to resell to investors. The three major secondary lenders are (1) the Federal National Mortgage Association (FNMA), referred to colloquially as Fannie Mae; (2) the Government National Mortgage Association (GNMA), referred to colloquially as Ginnie Mae; and (3) the Federal Home Loan Mortgage Corporation (FHLMC), referred to colloquially as Freddie Mac.

The **Federal National Mortgage Association (FNMA)** was established in 1938, originally as an agency of the federal government to create a secondary market for loans. In 1968, the FNMA became a private, though governmentally regulated, corporation. The FNMA buys and services conventional, FHA, and VA residential loans that meet its specified guidelines. The **Government National Mortgage Association (GNMA)** was established in 1968 as a division of HUD in order to provide special assistance for

---

secondary market: A market for the purchase and sale of existing mortgages.

Federal National Mortgage Association (FNMA): A governmentally regulated corporation that buys and services conventional, FHA, and VA residential loans that meet its specific guidelines.

Government National Mortgage Association (GNMA): A division of HUD that works in tandem with the FNMA in the secondary market assisting lending institutions with low-income housing projects.

disadvantaged residential borrowers as well as to manage a large portfolio of mortgages. The GNMA works in tandem with the FNMA in the secondary market assisting lending institutions with low-income housing projects. The GNMA provides these institutions with a commitment to purchase the low-income housing loans at a fixed rate. The GNMA then receives a commitment from the FNMA to buy these loans at the current market rate.

The **Federal Home Loan Mortgage Corporation (FHLMC)** was established in 1970 to provide a secondary market, primarily for conventional loans. Its main purpose is to provide liquidity to lenders, such as savings and loan associations, which can sell qualified loans for cash to the FHLMC and then use the cash proceeds to make new loans.

Federal Home Loan Mortgage Corporation (FHLMC): A corporation established to provide a secondary market, primarily for conventional loans.

HYPOTHETICAL CLIENT MATTER

In consulting her tickler file this morning, Barbara notices that she has scheduled the drafting of certain documents in preparation for an upcoming residential closing. The clients in question are Karen and Henry Lipton who have contracted to sell their house to Marilyn and Richard Olson. Reviewing the clients' file, Barbara reviews the financing arrangements for the purchase of the Lipton residence. Rather than taking out a loan with a lending institution, the Olsons pursued the option of seller financing. The Olsons are in the position to put down twenty percent of the $100,000 purchase price. The Liptons are willing to take a promissory note and mortgage deed securing the remainder of the purchase price. The interest to be charged on the $80,000 principal is nine percent, the note to be payable in monthly installments over a period of ten years. The monthly payments under this arrangement work out to be $1,013.14 for principal and interest.

Barbara prepares the note first, because a substantial portion of the note's contents must be repeated in the mortgage instrument. The closing is scheduled to take place on August 18th, so the monthly payments would begin September 18th (recall that loan payments are paid in arrears). When completed, the promissory note reads as shown in Figure 10–7.

Barbara next turns her attention to the mortgage instrument. The mortgage will be executed on the same day as the note and will be recorded when the deed transferring title is recorded. The mortgage must include the legal description of the property, which Barbara copies from the contract for sale and purchase. The mortgage will contain a recital of the major provisions of the note, as well as an acceleration clause, tax clause, and maintenance clause. Under state law, the mortgage must be witnessed by two witnesses for each signatory and must be notarized. Upon completion, the mortgage reads as shown in Figure 10–8.

FIGURE 10–7
Promissory note

PROMISSORY NOTE

$80,000.00   Any City, Any State
                                                      August 18, 1997

FOR VALUE RECEIVED, the undersigned, jointly and severally, promise to pay to HENRY LIPTON and KAREN LIPTON, his wife (hereinafter referred to as "Holders"), in the manner hereinafter specified, the principal sum of EIGHTY THOUSAND DOLLARS ($80,000.00) with interest from date at the rate of nine percent (9%) per annum on the unpaid balance, payable in lawful money of the United States of America at 55 Durham Lane, Any City, Any State, or at such place as may hereafter be designated by written notice from the Holders to the Makers hereof, on the date and in the manner following:

> Payable in equal monthly installments of One Thousand Thirteen and 41/100 Dollars ($1,013.41), principal and interest inclusive, for 120 months, commencing on the 18th day of September, 1997, and continuing on the 18th day of each month thereafter, until fully paid. Prepayment in full or a portion of the principal balance may be made at any time.

This note with interest is secured by a mortgage on real estate, of even date herewith, made by the Makers hereof in favor of the Holders, and shall be construed and enforced according to the laws of the State of Any State.

If default be made in the payment of any of the sums or interest herein mentioned or in said mortgage for a period of 30 days, the Holders may, at their option, declare the entire principal sum and interest at once due and collectible. Failure to exercise this option shall not constitute a waiver of the right to exercise the same in the event of any subsequent default.

In the event of default in the making of any payments herein provided and in the event the Holders exercise the option to declare the entire principal sum and interest at once due and collectible, said principal sum and accrued interest shall both bear interest from such time until paid at the highest rate allowable under the laws of the State of Any State. Makers hereby agree to pay all costs, including a reasonable attorney's fee, whether suit be brought or not if, after maturity of this note or default hereunder, or under said mortgage, counsel shall be employed to collect this note or to protect the security of said mortgage. Makers further waive demand, protest and notice of demand, protest and nonpayment.

GIVEN under the hand and seal of each party, the day and year first above written.

_____
Richard Olson

_____
Marilyn Olson

FIGURE 10–8
Mortgage

This instrument prepared by:
Ava Ross, Esquire
Fisher, Ross, and Simon, P.A.
1900 N.W. 3rd Avenue
Any City, Any State

MORTGAGE

Executed the 18th day of August, 1997, by RICHARD OLSON and MARILYN OLSON, his wife (hereinafter the "Mortgagors") to HENRY LIPTON and KAREN LIPTON, his wife (hereinafter the "Mortgagees"). In consideration of the principal sum specified in the promissory note hereafter described, the Mortgagors hereby mortgage to the Mortgagees the real property in Any County, Any State, described as follows:

Lot 7 in Block 3, DUMBARTON ESTATES, a subdivision according to the plat thereof, as recorded in Plat Book 206, Page 9, of the Public Records of Any County, Any State

as security for the payment of the promissory note herein substantially copied, to-wit:

$80,000.00   Any City, Any State
                                              August 18, 1997

FOR VALUE RECEIVED, the undersigned, jointly and severally, promise to pay to HENRY LIPTON and KAREN LIPTION, his wife (hereinafter referred to as "Holders"), in the manner hereinafter specified, the principal sum of EIGHTY THOUSAND DOLLARS ($80,000.00) with interest from date at the rate of nine percent (9%) per annum on the unpaid balance, payable in lawful money of the United States of America at 55 Durham Lane, Any City, Any State, or at such place as may hereafter be designated by written notice from the Holders to the Makers hereof, on the date and in the manner following:

Payable in equal monthly installments of One Thousand Thirteen and 41/100 Dollars ($1,013.41), principal and interest inclusive, for 120 months, commencing on the 18th day of September, 1997, and continuing on the 1st day of each month thereafter, until fully paid. Prepayment in full or a portion of the principal balance may be made at any time.

If default be made in the payment of any of the sums or interest herein mentioned or in said mortgage for a period of 30 days, the Holders may, at their option, declare the entire principal sum and interest at once due and collectible. Failure to exercise this option shall not constitute a waiver of the right to exercise the same in the event of any subsequent default.

In the event of default in the making of any payments herein provided and in the event the Holders exercise the option to declare the entire principal sum and interest at once due and collectible, said principal sum and accrued interest shall both bear interest from such time until paid at the highest rate allowable under the laws of the State of Any State. Makers hereby agree to pay all costs, including a reasonable attorney's fee, whether suit be brought or not if, after maturity of this note or default hereunder, or under said mortgage, counsel shall be employed to collect this note or to protect the security of said mortgage. Makers further waive demand, protest and notice of demand, protest and nonpayment.

FIGURE 10–8
(continued)

GIVEN under the hand and seal of each party, the day and year first above written.

/s/ Richard Olson
Richard Olson

/s/ Marilyn Olson
Marilyn Olson

The Mortgagors agree that this purchase money mortgage is given and intended to be recorded simultaneously with a deed executed and delivered by the Mortgagees to the Mortgagors, in order to secure a portion of the purchase price of the above-described real estate.

The Mortgagors further agree to pay promptly when due the principal and interest provided for in said note and this mortgage.

The Mortgagors agree to pay all taxes, assessments, liens and encumbrances on the above-described real estate promptly when due. Should the Mortgagors fail to pay them promptly, the Mortgagees may pay them, without waiving any rights of foreclosure, and such payments, with interest accruing from the date of payment at the same rate as specified in the note, shall also be secured by this mortgage.

The Mortgagors agree to permit no waste, impairment or deterioration of the above-described real property or the improvements thereon at any time, and to keep the building on said property insured in an amount of not less than eighty percent (80%) of full insurable value of the improvements, with a company acceptable to the Mortgagees, the policy or policies to be held by, and payable to, the Mortgagees. In the event any sum of money becomes payable by virtue of such insurance, the Mortgagees have the right to receive and apply the same to the indebtedness hereby secured, accounting to the Mortgagors for any surplus.

The Mortgagors agree to pay all expenses reasonably incurred by the Mortgagees because of Mortgagors' failure to comply with the agreements contained in the note or in this mortgage, including reasonable attorneys' fees. Such sums for expenses, with interest thereon from the date of payment at the same rate as specified in the note, shall also be secured by this mortgage.

If any sum of money herein referred to is not promptly paid within thirty (30) days after the same becomes due, or if any of the agreements, stipulations, conditions or covenants contained within the note or this mortgage are not fully complied with, the entire unpaid balance of the note shall, upon the option of the Mortgagees, become due and payable, and the Mortgagees may foreclose this mortgage in the manner provided by law and have the mortgaged property sold to satisfy the indebtedness hereby secured. Failure of the Mortgagees to exercise any of the rights or options herein provided shall not constitute a waiver of any rights or options under the note or this mortgage.

IN WITNESS WHEREOF, the said mortgage has been hereunto signed and sealed on the day and year first above written.

Signed, sealed and declared
in the presence of:

_____
_____   _____
                                            Richard Olson
_____

_____   _____
                                            Marilyn Olson

STATE OF ANY STATE
COUNTY OF ANY COUNTY

FIGURE 10–8
(continued)

I HEREBY CERTIFY that on this day before me, an officer duly authorized in the State aforesaid and in the County aforesaid to take acknowledgments, personally appeared RICHARD OLSON and MARILYN OLSON, his wife, to me known to be the persons described in and who executed the foregoing instrument, and they acknowledged before me that they executed the same.

WITNESS my hand and official seal in the County and State aforesaid this _____ day of _____, 19__.

_____
Notary Public, State of Any State
My commission expires: _____

CHAPTER SUMMARY

1. When a borrower enters into a loan transaction with a lender, the borrower, in return for the money loaned, gives the lender a promissory note, evidencing the borrower's pledge to repay the loan on specified terms. The borrower also gives the lender a security instrument in the form of either a deed of trust or a mortgage, which pledges the real property as collateral for the debt.

2. A mortgage is a two-party instrument. The parties are the borrower (mortgagor) and lender (mortgagee). The mortgage sets forth the legal description of the real property pledged as collateral, a description of the debt terms as provided in the note, various agreements by the borrower to maintain the property and pay all taxes and insurance, and the rights and remedies available should a default occur. In the latter instance, the lender is given the right to accelerate the loan. Should the borrower fail to pay the outstanding sum, the lender can initiate a foreclosure action.

3. A deed of trust is a three-party instrument. The parties are the borrower (trustor), the lender (beneficiary), and a third-party trustee. The terms of a deed of trust are similar to those found in a mortgage. In a deed of trust, however, the trustee is given a power of sale whereby, upon the borrower's default, the trustee can publish a notice of public sale of the property without bringing a court action.

4. There are a variety of financial sources from which a prospective borrower may seek financing. The two most common sources are commercial banks and savings and loan associations. Commercial banks generally provide construction loans, short-term loans, and home improvement loans. Savings and loan associations specialize in residential, long-term loans. Both commercial banks and savings and loan associations make conventional, FHA, and VA loans. Commercial banks, however, make a greater number of FHA and VA loans than do savings and loan associations. Other loan sources include insurance companies, mutual savings banks, credit unions, mortgage banking companies, REITs, and individuals.

5. A conventional loan typically has a lower loan-to-value ratio than an FHA or VA loan. The lender wants assurance that the borrower is committed to

repayment of the debt through the borrower's equity investment in the property. FHA loans require a minimum down payment from the borrower, while VA loans may require no down payment at all.

6. FHA and VA loans are made for owner-occupied residential dwellings. In applying for either an FHA or a VA loan, both the borrower and the property must qualify. FHA loans are available to all borrowers, whereas VA loans are available to eligible veterans and to their widows and widowers. The FHA insures loans made by approved lenders, whereas the VA guarantees loans made by approved lenders. The FHA charges the borrower a mortgage insurance premium. Both FHA and VA loans require the borrower to make PITI payments.

7. Loans can either be fixed rate loans or adjustable rate loans. Adjustable rate loans start out with a lower interest rate than fixed rate loans. The interest rate is tied to an index and is altered each adjustment period. Adjustable rate loans have both periodic and overall caps.

8. The lending process begins with an initial interview between the prospective borrower and a loan officer. The borrower provides the loan officer with the requisite information to complete the loan application forms. An appraisal is ordered on the real property to verify its value, and a credit report check is run on the borrower. Considerable time is spent on verifying the information supplied by the borrower. Should both the borrower and the property qualify, the lender provides the borrower with a loan commitment.

REVIEW QUESTIONS

1. What major differences exist between a deed of trust and a mortgage?
2. Explain the loan application process.
3. What are the primary reasons for refusal of a loan application?
4. Compare and contrast FHA and VA loans.
5. What information must be included in the following?
   a. A promissory note
   b. A deed of trust or mortgage

ETHICAL QUESTIONS

The law firm receptionist transfers a telephone call for your supervising attorney, Deborah Sanders, to your office. The caller is Mark Farnsworth, a prospective client. Mark is behind on his loan payments and has received a demand letter from his lender, Metropolitan Bank. He wants to meet with Deborah to discuss his options in responding to the letter. You set up an appointment for tomorrow morning. You then follow your usual routine of doing a conflict of interest check. Your law firm has offices in three counties of your state. Upon doing your search, you discover that Allen Mitchell, an attorney working out of another of your law firm's offices, represents Metropolitan Bank in several legal matters. May Deborah represent Mark? Why or why not?

PRACTICAL ASSIGNMENTS

Assignment 10:1. Research your state statutes regarding the required contents, witnessing, and notarization of a promissory note and deed of trust (or mortgage, whichever instrument is used in your state). Also research to determine whether your state has antideficiency statutes. Photocopy the relevant statutes and insert them under the "General Information" section of your resource portfolio.

Assignment 10:2. Contact a local mortgage company or bank and request copies of the loan application documents they use in processing a loan. Note the similarities and differences between these documents and the samples provided in the text. Insert these documents under the "General Information" section of your resource portfolio.

Assignment 10:3. Clients Jack and Eleanor Corbin are closing on the sale of their home next Friday. The sale price of the home is $150,000. The Corbins received a $15,000 escrow deposit upon contract signing and will receive another $15,000 in cash at closing. The remaining $120,000 will be financed by a purchase money mortgage (or deed of trust) and note made by the buyers, Gene and Joan Lawrence, on behalf of the Corbins.

Your supervising attorney, Deborah Sanders, has asked you to prepare the note and financing instrument (mortgage or deed of trust, whichever is prevalent in your state). Upon recording of the financing instrument, it is to be returned to Deborah at your office address [Hernandez, Sanders, and Norris, P.A., 263 Republic Avenue, (your city, your state)].

The loan term is ten years, and the interest rate is nine percent. The monthly loan payments are $1,520.12. The street address of the property is 135 Warminster Street (your city, your state), and the legal description of the property is as follows:

> Lot 2 in Block 9 of SWINDON ESTATES, a subdivision, according to the plat thereof, as recorded in Plat Book 75, Page 10, of the Public Records of (your county, your state).

The monthly payments will commence one month from the date of closing. Payment is to be made to the Corbins at 302 Sterling Road (your city, your state), or any other place the Corbins may designate in writing. After review, insert these documents under the "Residential Property" section of your resource portfolio.

Assignment 10:4. Define the following key terms.

acceleration clause
adjustable rate loan
adjustment period
amortized loan
annual percentage rate (APR)
balloon mortgage
Bank Insurance Fund (BIF)
buy-down
certificate of eligibility
commercial bank
conventional loan
credit union
deed of trust
deficiency judgment
demand deposit
due-on-sale clause
Equal Credit Opportunity Act (ECOA)
Federal Deposit Insurance
   Corporation (FDIC)
Federal Home Loan Mortgage
   Corporation (FHLMC)
Federal National Mortgage
   Association (FNMA)
Federal Truth in Lending Act
FHA loan
fiduciary lender

Financial Institutions Reform, Recovery
   and Enforcement Act (FIRREA)
Government National Mortgage
   Association (GNMA)
graduated payment mortgage
growing equity mortgage
interest rate cap
lien theory
loan commitment
loan origination fee
loan-to-value ratio
maker
margin
mortgage
mortgage banking company
mortgage broker
mortgagee
mortgage insurance premium
mortgagor
mutual savings bank
negative amortization
payee
PITI
points
power-of-sale clause
private mortgage insurance (PMI)

promissory note
Real Estate Investment Trust (REIT)
Real Estate Settlement Procedures
    Act (RESPA)
reverse annuity mortgage
savings and loan association
Savings Association Insurance
    Fund (SAIF)

secondary market
shared appreciation mortgage
straight loan
title theory
VA loan
wraparound loan

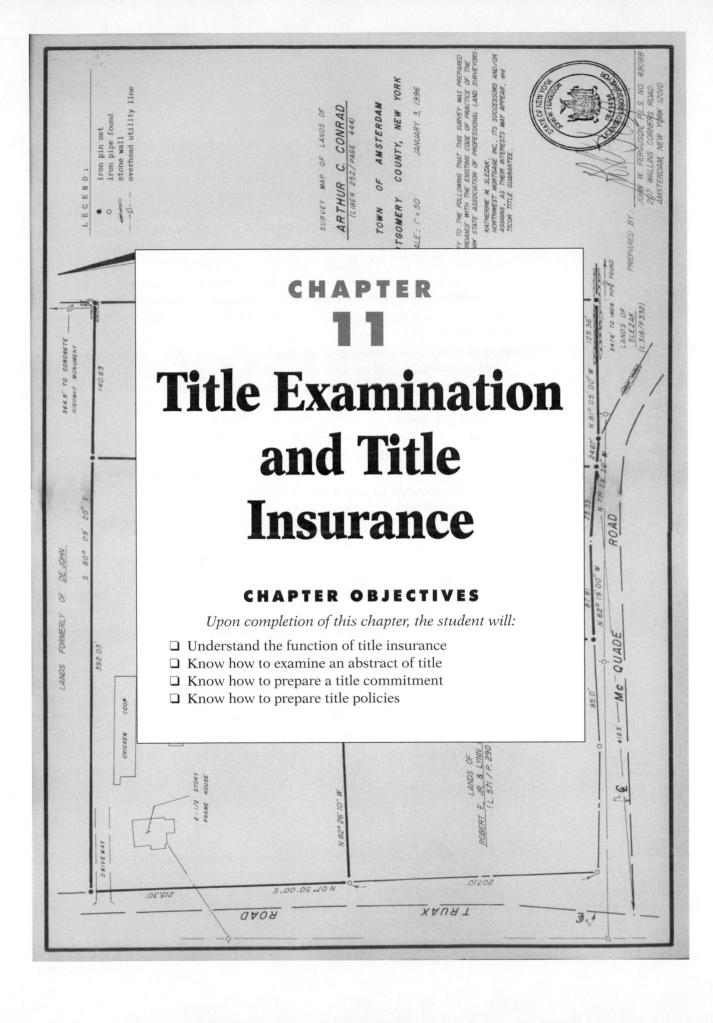

CHAPTER
11

Title Examination and Title Insurance

CHAPTER OBJECTIVES

Upon completion of this chapter, the student will:

❏ Understand the function of title insurance
❏ Know how to examine an abstract of title
❏ Know how to prepare a title commitment
❏ Know how to prepare title policies

INTRODUCTION

As noted in earlier chapters, when one purchases a parcel of land, one is purchasing not only the land itself but also the legal rights inherent in real property ownership. In addition to the individual rights held by the owner, others may have legal rights that have an impact on the owner's rights. These other rights may stem from the creation of easements on the property, liens recorded against the property, restrictions on usage imposed by homeowners' associations or condominium associations, or local, state, or federal regulations that affect the title of the owner of the property.

When purchasing real estate, the buyer wants assurance that the title to the property being conveyed is good and marketable. This does not necessarily mean that the property is free and clear of all encumbrances. For example, there may be an easement across a small portion of the property that was created to benefit the property, such as an utility easement. However, good and **marketable title** does mean a title that is free from encumbrances that would bring down the value of the property or threaten foreclosure against the property, such as an encroachment on the property or a construction lien filed against the property.

Prior to closing a real estate transaction, the purchaser must determine the quality of the title he or she will receive. In order to make this determination, a title search must be conducted. A **title search** is the search of the public records to determine if title to real property is marketable. All instruments that affect the title of the parcel of real property in question must be examined. The records must be searched first to determine what recorded instruments exist that affect the property. Instruments affecting title to real property include, but are not limited to, mortgage instruments; deeds; judgment, tax, and other liens; divorce decrees; declarations of condominiums; and homeowners' association declarations of covenants and restrictions.

Once the documents themselves are located, their legal sufficiency must be determined. For example, a deed recorded forty years ago conveying the property from a previous seller may not have been notarized. If notarization was required by state statute at the time the deed was recorded in the public records, this lack of notarization may be a defect in the title to the property unless statutory law presently exists that allows for correction of this defect. Similarly, if a mortgage instrument had been recorded but no satisfaction of mortgage was found canceling that obligation prior to or after the property passed to the grantee, that mortgage instrument remains on the record as a still-existing lien and thus is considered a defect in the title unless it can be removed.

From these illustrations, one can understand that title examination is a very detailed and scrupulous process that the average purchaser is not equipped to undertake on his or her own. Thus, the responsibility of title examination has fallen on attorneys who are in the position to provide a prospective purchaser with a written legal opinion of the condition of the title to the real property in question. When a client hires an attorney to represent him or her in a real estate transaction, the client is hiring the attorney to perform a myriad of tasks: (1) to prepare the necessary documents needed for the

marketable title: Title to real property that is free from encumbrances which would bring down the value of the real property or create reasonable doubt or controversy.

title search: The search of the public records to determine if title to real property is marketable.

real estate closing and ensure that they are properly recorded, (2) to examine the title to the property and prepare an opinion of the title, (3) to supervise the closing process, and (4) to provide title insurance to protect the purchaser and lender.

An attorney's legal opinion on the title of the property covers only those items that are contained in the public records. The attorney cannot give an opinion regarding matters that are not revealed by an examination of the records, such as a neighbor's encroachment, adverse possession, or forged signatures on crucial documents. Therefore, while an attorney's legal opinion letter regarding the title is important, it does not, and cannot, cover all matters that may affect the title. The purpose of title insurance is to cover those matters that are not readily identifiable.

Title insurance is insurance of an owner of real property or another having an interest in the real property (such as the lender-mortgagee) against loss brought about by encumbrances, defective titles, invalidity, or adverse claim to the title. While the attorney's role is to ascertain what the more obvious risks might be through an examination of the records, a title insurance policy is a contract to indemnify the property owner (or lender) against loss in value due to the more unlikely risks, such as forged deeds, recording mistakes, claims of undisclosed heirs, and so forth.

Title companies that issue title insurance are regulated by state statute and the insurance departments of their respective states. Their attorneys conduct title examinations and then issue a title report called a **title commitment,** or *title binder*. The title commitment sets forth the status of the title of a particular parcel of real property and states the terms under which a title policy for the property will be issued. The title commitment also may be used by the seller as evidence of marketable title prior to closing.

Because title companies issue title insurance policies based on attorneys' opinions, most title companies employ their own in-house counsel as title examiners. In some states, title insurers have been created specifically for attorneys. Attorneys become members by contributing a portion of the fee from real estate transactions to a statewide fund. The membership funding provides the monies to underwrite the title property.

The **American Land Title Association (ALTA)** is an organization that was created to meet the demands for uniform title insurance protection nationwide. The ALTA has devised title commitment and title policy forms that are used in many parts of the country. Most title insurers utilize the ALTA forms in their original form or in a modified form.

As a real estate paralegal, you may be working at a title insurance company that employs in-house counsel, at a law firm that utilizes the services of outside title insurance companies, or at a law firm that has attorney-members acting as title agents of an attorney-owned underwriter. In any of these situations, a knowledge of title examination and preparation is crucial. Your supervising attorney may call upon you to examine an abstract of title, to review or prepare a title commitment and/or title policies, or to conduct or update a title search. This chapter explains the function of title insurance and the process of title examination. It also details the procedures for writing title commitments and title policies, and explains the most commonly used endorsements attached to title policies.

title insurance: Insurance of an owner of real property or another having an interest in the real property against loss brought about by encumbrances, defective titles, invalidity, or adverse claim to the title.

title commitment: A document that sets forth the status of the title of a particular parcel of real property and the terms under which a title policy for the property will be issued.

American Land Title Association (ALTA): An organization that was created to meet the demands for uniform title insurance protection nationwide. It has devised title commitment and title policy forms that are used in many parts of the country.

THE FUNCTION OF TITLE INSURANCE

Title insurance, like other forms of insurance, is a contract in which the insurer agrees to pay for loss or damage arising from an event in return for the insured's payment of a premium. However, title insurance differs from other forms of insurance in several important aspects.

Most types of casualty insurance provide for coverage of loss arising from the occurrence of an event within a contractually prescribed time period beginning from the effective date of the policy, such as one year. The event covered must occur within this time period. Title insurance, on the other hand, provides coverage for loss in value to the real property from a defect in title that existed prior to the effective date of the policy. For example, suppose a title search mistakenly overlooks a mortgage lien placed on the property prior to the issuance of a title insurance policy. That mortgage lien is a defect that existed prior to the issuance of the policy. The title insurance company will cover the risk of such a happening.

Casualty insurance must be renewed continuously to keep the coverage effective. This is done through the periodic payment of premiums. At the end of each policy period, the insurer may reevaluate the cost of the insurance and adjust the premium payments accordingly. Title insurance, on the other hand, is purchased by the insured once through the payment of a single premium. The premium is based strictly on the amount of coverage provided. An owner's policy generally covers the purchase price of the real property. The insured is then covered against risks for as long as the insured retains title to the property. Note, however, that a title insurance policy may not be assigned from the existing property owner to a new purchaser.

Casualty insurers evaluate the risk they are taking by looking at the statistics showing the probability of a certain event (for example, a hurricane or flood) happening in a particular location within the contractual period. Title insurers evaluate marketable title determined from a search of the records of the subject property. Items affecting the quality of title must be either cleared up prior to the issuance of the policy (for example, the payment in full of the seller's existing mortgage on the property) or noted as exceptions to the coverage of the policy. By instituting these measures, the insurer greatly reduces its risk.

Title insurance provides coverage for risks of possible defects undiscovered because of an incomplete search, because of a misinterpretation by the title examiner, or because they cannot be ascertained by a regular examination of the documents (for example, forgery or lack of legal capacity of a party to an instrument). Although these risks seem unlikely to occur, they have occurred.

The cost of title insurance is modest compared to many of the other closing costs incurred in a real estate transaction. In addition to any owner's coverage that might be purchased, banking laws require lending institutions to obtain from a mortgagor title insurance covering the mortgagee's lien priority up to the loan amount. The mortgagee's coverage decreases as the loan balance is reduced. In some states, both the owner and the lender-mortgagee are covered on the same title policy. In other states, when title insurance is issued, two policies typically are issued: an owner's policy and a mortgagee's policy.

Who pays for title insurance is negotiated and is a matter of contract. Sellers must provide proof of marketable title. The contract for sale and purchase should indicate what proof is acceptable, who is required to do the title search, the date upon which the search must be completed and the results provided to the purchaser, who will issue the policy(ies), and who will pay for the policy(ies).

THE EXAMINATION PROCESS

In General

A title examination may be conducted by an attorney or delegated to the attorney's legal assistant. It may also be conducted by a title company or an abstract company. The examination process begins by a search of the public records to find all recorded documents pertaining to the subject real property. The public records books to be inspected often are located with the clerk of the court in the county in which the real property is located or in separate land records facilities. In some states and/or counties, recorded documents may be amassed in one set of books called official records books. In other states and/or counties, the documents are sorted and recorded according to type. In these places, several books must be inspected, such as deed books, mortgage books, and so forth.

When examining the public records, the title examiner attempts to establish a chain of title for the property in question. A **chain of title** is the genealogy of the property. It is a listing of all instruments affecting the property, from the first recorded instrument to the most recent, and indicates: (1) the kind of instrument, (2) the date recorded, (3) the place recorded, (4) the maker of the instrument, (5) the person for whose benefit the instrument was made, and (6) the interest(s) created by the instrument.

Initially, a title examiner may physically go to the courthouse and search the records or, when available, may utilize an abstract (discussed later). When manually searching the records, the title examiner begins with a set of indexes, commonly the *grantee index* and the *grantor index*, and begins with the present owner and works backward. For example, if the present owner of the property is Theodore Warner, the title examiner would start with the grantee index, because the last deed to the property was deeded to Theodore Warner. If Erica Lanson deeded the property to Theodore, then the grantee index for Erica Lanson must be consulted to determine who deeded the property to her. This process is repeated until the earliest public records have been found. After completing this procedure, the title examiner has a chronological list of grantors and grantees. Next, the title examiner must consult the grantor index, looking up the name of each grantor, to determine whether any of the grantors listed delivered more than one deed to the property or encumbered the property in any way during their periods of ownership.

Another way in which a title examiner may commence a search of the public records is by starting with a **tract index.** Whereas the grantor and grantee indices are compiled by the names of the parties in a real estate conveyance, the tract index is compiled by a description of parcels of property. Thus, rather than starting with the name of the present owner of the property in question, the examiner starts with the legal description of the property. The examiner first refers to that portion of the legal description that sets forth the record or

chain of title: The geneology of a particular parcel of real property.

tract index: An index compiled by a description of parcels of real property.

plat book number and page. Turning to that page, the plat or tract map to locate the parcel of real property is reviewed. The map should provide a parcel identification number for each parcel of property within the tract, which can then be used to find all other recorded documents directly pertaining to the property.

The search of the grantee and grantor indices, or the tract index, is just the start. There may be other matters affecting the title to the property in court records, such as a probate, divorce, or a mortgage foreclosure, that must be checked. Additionally, the current or previous owners of the property may have pledged personal property as well as the real property in question as security for a mortgage loan. To determine this, the examiner must research the Uniform Commercial Code financing statement index for recorded financing statements.

The examination of the indices is a laborious, time-consuming process. Therefore, title companies and abstract companies conveniently put together the "history" of properties in abstracts of title. An **abstract of title** is a copy or condensed version of each document pertaining to a particular parcel of property. Title examiners rely on the work of prior abstractors and update existing abstracts when the title to the property is to change hands. (Abstract examination is discussed in detail in the following text.)

Some states allow a title examiner to utilize the work of prior examiners to streamline the procedure by using a previous title policy issued on the subject property in place of a manual search of the records up to that date. The policy issuance date is the date until which the search is current. The title examiner must then do a search from that date until the present to bring the search up-to-date.

In addition to inspection of the records, a physical inspection of the property must be done to ascertain any encumbrances to the land that do not appear in the record. Many lending institutions require a survey be done as a condition of financing. (For a detailed discussion of surveys, see Chapter 5). The title examiner will want to review the survey for location of easements mentioned in the recorded documents to note where the easements are located in relation to the improvements on the property. The title examiner will also look for encroachments and any discrepancy between the legal description provided by the surveyor and the legal description in the previous title policy.

Examination of Documents

Once the title examiner finds all of the documents pertaining to the subject real property, each document must be examined in turn to ascertain its legal sufficiency. This process is called "chaining title." With each document, the examiner must make a notation of (1) the type of document (for example, a deed or mortgage), (2) the contents of the document, (3) the names of the parties to the document, (4) the date of the document, (5) the date of recording of the document, (6) the signatures and acknowledgments, and (7) any other information affecting interests or rights to the property mentioned in the document.

The type of the document will indicate the type of interest the document conveys (for example, a deed conveying ownership rights or a mortgage lien

abstract of title: A copy or condensed version of each document pertaining to a particular parcel of real property.

conveying lien rights). A deed may convey the entire property or a portion of it. It may convey a fee simple or a life estate. The deed may contain restrictions as to usage. It may refer to other encumbrances on the property. The type of deed may indicate what claims the grantor is making regarding the title (for example, a warranty deed, giving the greatest number of assurances, or a quitclaim deed, giving no assurances).

The names of the parties to each document must be examined to determine whether the granting party has the legal right to convey an interest in the real estate. For example, if a prior deed was granted by Marjory Williams to James M. Douglas and the next deed in chronological order was granted by Jim Douglas, Jr., to Alice Adams, there is a question about whether James M. Douglas and Jim Douglas, Jr., are the same person. The use of "Jr." indicates that there is more than one James Douglas, and the matter must be researched to determine whether the grantor in the second deed was indeed the grantee in the first. Examination of the parties to a document also includes examination of their marital status. As noted earlier in the text, spouses must be included as grantors in a deed to relinquish any dower, curtesy, or homestead rights the spouse may have in states that recognize these rights.

The date the document was signed and the date the document was recorded should be checked. The date the document was recorded establishes record title in the property. The date the document was signed may be relevant in determining the legal sufficiency of the instrument. For example, state statutes may require that all documents executed after a statutorily specified date be witnessed by two witnesses. If the document in question is signed by only one witness, the date of the document will determine whether or not it is defective.

Finally, the signatures on the document must be reviewed to determine legal sufficiency. The signatures must match the names of the granting parties. If a corporation is the grantor, the document must be signed by the officer(s) given the authority to act on behalf of the corporation by statute or by the corporation's board of directors. This information may be checked by looking at the corporate resolution giving the officer(s) the authority to sell the property on behalf of the corporation. If acknowledgments are required, make sure that they meet your state statute's requirements.

Abstract Examination

An abstract of title is a condensed history of each document affecting the title of a particular parcel of real property prepared by a licensed and bonded abstractor. The abstractor develops the chain of title and "abstracts" each document, which means that he or she writes out a synopsis of each document, setting forth only the information that directly pertains to the title of the subject property. In addition, most abstract or title companies now make a photocopy of every document in the public record pertaining to the property. Each document is marked by an entry number and compiled into one instrument, the abstract of title.

An abstract of title contains: (1) a caption setting forth the legal description of the real property and the name of the person or title company preparing the abstract, (2) each document in chronological order from the earliest to the most recent, and (3) an **abstractor's certificate** that states

abstractor's certificate: A certificate that states the records the abstractor has examined, any records not examined, and the dates covered by the search.

the records the abstractor has examined, any records not examined, and the dates covered by the search. The abstract is then updated each time ownership of the property is transferred.

As a real estate paralegal, you may be asked to review an abstract of title and report your findings to your supervising attorney. To begin, you should first compare the legal description in the caption of the abstract of title with the legal description of the property as set forth in the current owner's title policy or in the current deed. Next, keeping a pad next to you, you should write down at the top of the pad (1) the client file and matter number, (2) the name(s) of the purchaser(s), (3) the name(s) of the seller(s), (4) the legal description of the property, and (5) the abstract(s) reviewed, noting the number on the abstract(s), the name of the company preparing the abstract(s), the person from whom the abstract(s) was obtained, the dates covered by the abstract(s), and the number of entries in the abstract(s).

The next step is to divide your page into three columns. In one column, you will put your chain of title, commencing with the first entry in the abstract. In the middle column, you will put any encumbrances, such as mortgages or liens, as well as any satisfactions. In the third column, you will note any problems detected in a particular document entry, such as lack of witnesses, lack of spousal joinder, or lack of notarization. In the column in which you commence your chain of title, start by noting the entry number, and then indicate the following: (1) the grantor, (2) the type of document (you may use abbreviations, such as W.D. for warranty deed), (3) the date of the instrument, (4) the date of recording, and (5) the book and page number of the recorded document, such as is found in the example provided in Figure 11–1.

If, in your review of the entry, you find anything affecting the validity of the document or title, note it in the appropriate column. Mortgages should be noted in the encumbrance column. When noting a mortgage, set forth (1) the name of the mortgagee, (2) the date of execution, (3) the date of recording, and (4) the book and page number of the recorded instrument. Likewise, when a satisfaction of mortgage entry is found, put it in the encumbrance column, with a line connecting the mortgage and the satisfaction of mortgage. You can put an "X" through each, indicating that they cancel each other out.

For a better understanding of abstract examination, a small, sample abstract is provided in Figure 11–2, followed by a review of the contents of the abstract. Please note that most abstracts contain more entries than those provided in this sample.

FIGURE 11–1
Sample chain of title entry

Mark Hampton and Susan Hampton

Husband and Wife

W.D.
3-17-96
3-19-96
O.R.B. 107/25

FIGURE 11–2
Sample abstract

<u>SAMPLE ABSTRACT</u>

No. 2222

LOT 5, BLOCK 4 of

CEDARCREEK ESTATES

According to the plat thereof recorded in Plat Book 12, Page 50, of the Public Records of Any County, Any State

(Caption lies in the SE 1/4 of NW 1/4 of Section 9, Township 3 North, Range 5 West, Any County, Any State)

Compiled by

Any State Title Company

ENTRY 1

Edward Rodgers and 　Helen Rodgers, his wife	W.D.
to	Dated: March 1, 1929 Filed: March 9, 1929
Benjamin Adams	Deed Book 30, Page 40

Grant, bargain, sell and convey to party of second part the following property in Any County, Any State, to wit:

The SE 1/4 of NW 1/4 of Section 9, Township 3 North, Range 5 West.

Signed and sealed by Edward Rodgers and Helen Rodgers, his wife, in the presence of two witnesses.
Acknowledged by grantors March 1, 1929, before Notary Public, Any County, Any State. Notary's commission expired June 1, 1931—Notary's Seal.

ENTRY 2

Cynthia Adams, widow of Benjamin Adams	W.D. Dated: April 5, 1939
to	Filed: April 8, 1939
Jonathan Baker	Deed Book 60, Page 70

Grants, bargains, sells and conveys the SE 1/4 of NW 1/4 of Section 9, Township 3 North, Range 5 West.
Signed and sealed by grantor in presence of two witnesses. Acknowledged by grantor April 5, 1939, before Notary Public, Any County.
Notary's commission expired September 31, 1941—Notary's Seal.

ENTRY 3

Jonathan Baker and 　Louise Baker, his wife	Mortgage: $25,000.00
to	Dated: April 5, 1939 Filed: April 8, 1939
Cynthia Adams	Mortgage Book 20, Page 55

Encumbers property in Any County, Any State, the SE 1/4 of NW 1/4 of Section 9, Township 3 North, Range 5 West.
Secures one note of even date in amount of $25,000 bearing interest at 7% per annum, payable five years after date.
Signed and sealed by Jonathan Baker and Louise Baker, his wife, in presence of two witnesses. Acknowledged by mortgagors April 5, 1939. Notary's commission expired November 1, 1941—Notary's Seal.

FIGURE 11–2
(continued)

ENTRY 4

Cynthia Adams, widow	Satisfaction of Mortgage
to	Dated: March 2, 1944
	Filed: March 4, 1944
The Public	Mortgage Book 24, Page 13

Recites payment in full of mortgage indebtedness secured by mortgage executed by Jonathan Baker and Louise Baker, his wife, to Cynthia Adams dated April 5, 1939, recorded in Mortgage Book 20, page 55, Any County Records, and directs Clerk to cancel same of record.

Signed and sealed by Cynthia Adams. Acknowledged by Cynthia Adams, March 2, 1944. Notary's commission expired May 10, 1945—Notary's Seal.

ENTRY 5

Jonathan Baker and Louise Baker, his wife	W.D.
to	Dated: July 17, 1955
	Filed: July 20, 1955
Joan Grant, a single woman	Deed Book 70, Page 14

Grants, bargains, sells and conveys the SE 1/4 of the NW 1/4 of Section 9, Township 3 North, Range 5 West.

Signed and sealed by grantors in presence of only *one* witness, before Notary Public, Any County, Any State, July 17, 1955. Notary's commission expired October 1, 1957—Notary's seal.

ENTRY 6

Joan Grant, a single woman	W.D.
to	Dated: September 20, 1967
	Filed: September 25, 1967
Jay Davidson and Alice Davidson, his wife	Deed Book 80, Page 22

Grants, bargains, sells and conveys the SE 1/4 of the NW 1/4 of Section 9, Township 3 North, Range 5 West.

Signed and sealed by grantors in presence of two witnesses. Acknowledged by grantors September 20, 1967. Expiration of Notary's commission not stated—Notary's Seal.

ENTRY 7
IN THE CIRCUIT COURT OF THE 5TH JUDICIAL CIRCUIT, IN AND FOR ANY COUNTY, ANY STATE, CASE NO. 68-1000

Martha Kent	Dated: February 11, 1968
v.	Filed: February 11, 1968
	(Certified copy)
Jay Davidson	Official Records Book 902, Page 40

It is considered, ordered and adjudged that Plaintiff to have and recover from the Defendant, Jay Davidson, the sum of $11,000, together with interest at 8% per annum, from January 3, 1967, and costs of Court taxes at $45.00 for which let execution issue.

Done and ordered at Any City, Any County, Any State, this 11th day of February, 1968.

Gregory M. Hall
Circuit Judge

FIGURE 11–2
(continued)

ENTRY 8

IN RE:
  Estate of Jay Davidson,
    deceased

In Circuit Judge's Court
Any County, Any State Probate
No. 5555, Petition filed May 3, 1977

Petition for Letters of Administration filed by Alice Davidson recites that Jay Davidson died intestate April 20, 1977; that at the time of his death, he was domiciled in Any City, Any State; that the approximate value of his estate was $300,000; that the residence and post office address of the petitioner is 450 Cedarcreek Drive, Any City, Any State.

That the petitioner, aged 62, was the wife of the decedent and that the only other heir is Angela Davidson, daughter, aged 27, residing at 325 N.W. 16th Street, Any City, Any State. Prays for Letters of Administration to Petitioner.

Sworn by petitioner May 2, 1977. Orders for Letters of Administration entered May 3, 1977, no bond required. Oath of Administration filed May 3, 1977. Letters of Administration to Alice Davidson May 3, 1977. Administrator discharged November 10, 1979.

ENTRY 9

Angela Davidson, a single woman

  to

Alice Davidson

Q.C. Deed
Dated: November 15, 1979
Filed: November 18, 1979
Deed Book 90, Page 34

Remises, releases and quitclaims the SE 1/4 of the NW 1/4 of Section 9, Township 3 North, Range 5 West.

Signed and sealed by grantor in presence of two witnesses. Acknowledged by grantor November 15, 1979. Notary commission expired February 20, 1980—Notary's Seal.

ENTRY 10

Alice Davidson
  to
GEM Development Corp.
(an Any State corporation)

W.D.
Dated: June 6, 1985
Filed: June 8, 1985
Deed Book 97, Page 55

Grants, bargains, sells and conveys the SE 1/4 of the NW 1/4 of Section 9, Township 3 North, Range 5 West. Signed by grantor in presence of two witnesses.

Acknowledged by grantor June 6, 1985, before Notary, Any County, Any State. Notary's commission expired December 31, 1985—Notary's Seal.

ENTRY 11

GEM Development Corp.
(an Any State corporation)
  to
Lawrence Miller and
  Donna Miller, his wife

W.D.
Dated: August 14, 1994
Filed: August 15, 1994

Deed Book 105, Page 23

Grants, bargains, sells and conveys the SE 1/4 of the NW 1/4 of Section 9, Township 3 North, Range 5 West. Signed in the name of the corporation by Bruce Stewart as President. Corporate seal affixed and attested by Ann Evans as Secretary in the presence of two witnesses.

Acknowledged August 14, 1994, by Bruce Stewart as President and Ann Evans as Secretary of the corporation before a Notary Public, Any County. Notary's commission expired March 5, 1995.

FIGURE 11–2
(continued)

NO. 2222
CERTIFICATE
OF
ANY STATE TITLE COMPANY

Any State Title Company hereby certifies that the foregoing Abstract of Title comprising Entries numbered 1 to 11, inclusive, correctly exhibits or recites all matters affecting Title to, or encumbering the property described in the caption hereof (except zoning and other Governmental Regulations and matters expressly excepted therein), which were filed for Public Record during the period of time set out hereinbelow.

The period of time covered by this Abstract extends from the earliest public records to and including March 30, 1995, at 6:00 o'clock p.m.

IN WITNESS WHEREOF, Any State Title Company has caused this Certificate to be signed in its name and its corporate seal to be affixed this 31st day of March, 1995.

ANY STATE TITLE COMPANY
By: *Diane Barclay*
(Corporate Seal)   President

Working one's way through the abstract chronologically, the first entry appears to be in order. It sets forth that the conveyance was made by a warranty deed; it gives the pertinent information pertaining to date executed and recorded; it gives the deed book and page numbers. The legal description is correct. The deed was signed in the presence of two witnesses. Assuming that two witnesses are required in the state of Any State, the deed meets this specification. The deed was also notarized. The notary public's commission was still in force at the time of notarization, and the notary's seal appears on the deed.

In the second entry, the grantor is Cynthia Adams, the widow of Benjamin Adams. The title examiner would need to obtain proof of death for Benjamin Adams and to determine that Cynthia was the only heir, as her name did not appear on the prior deed, so she and Benjamin did not take title to the property together as tenants by the entirety. The title examiner would also have to ascertain that Cynthia was single at the time of the conveyance to Jonathan Baker. If she was not, then the joinder of her spouse was necessary to convey any curtesy rights and/or homestead rights in the property. (For a detailed discussion of homestead and dower and curtesy rights and a discussion of the various types of tenancies, see Chapter 2.)

The third entry is a mortgage lien securing a loan in the amount of $25,000. Because a mortgage lien is an encumbrance, a notation of this would be put in the encumbrance column rather than in the chain of title column when writing out a review of the abstract.

The fourth entry is a satisfaction of the mortgage loan in the third entry. A notation of the satisfaction would be put in the encumbrance column, with a line connecting it to the mortgage. An "X" can then be placed over each, indicating that one cancels out the other.

The fifth entry indicates that this deed was witnessed by only one witness. If the state of Any State required only one witness at the time, there is no problem here. The title examiner would have to research the relevant statute operating at the time of conveyance rather than the current statute. Thus, it is the statutory law of 1955 that controls. If it is found that two witnesses were indeed required, then the title examiner must research to determine whether there are any state corrective statutes that will cure the lack of witnesses.

In the sixth entry, there is a notation that the notary public's commission was not stated. This means that from looking at the information on the deed, one cannot determine whether the notary public's commission was still in force at the time the deed was notarized. The title examiner in this instance would have to research the relevant state statutes regarding notarizations to determine whether a statement of the expiration date of commission was required. If it was required, then the title examiner would have to research state statutes to determine the existence of a curative statute to correct this defect.

The seventh entry is a judgment lien against Jay Davidson, one of the grantees in the prior deed. Like the mortgage lien, the judgment lien is an encumbrance against the property and should be noted in the applicable column. Here, the question of tenancy is relevant. The prior deed indicates the grantees to be "Jay Davidson and Alice Davidson, his wife." The title examiner would need to determine whether this language would be sufficient in the state of Any State to create a tenancy by the entirety. If a tenancy by the entirety were created by the prior deed, the judgment would not create a lien on the property because a judgment against one spouse cannot encumber tenancy by the entirety property. Recall from earlier discussions that this form of tenancy gives a one hundred percent interest in the property to each spouse. Because the judgment is only against Jay, Alice's property interest cannot be affected, and she owns one hundred percent of the property, as does Jay.

If the language of the deed is found not to create a tenancy by the entirety, then the title examiner would have to see if any subsequent documents satisfy the judgment. If so, the lien is removed, as was the case with the mortgage lien noted earlier. If no satisfaction of judgment is recorded, the title examiner would research state statutes to determine how long a judgment lien remains a lien on the property. This lien was recorded in 1968. The abstract was completed in 1995. This is a span of twenty-seven years. It is likely that the statute of limitations pertaining to enforcement of the judgment lien has expired. If this is the case, the judgment lien is no longer an encumbrance.

If you are asked to review the abstract, you would continue to work through each entry in this fashion through the final entry. In each instance, you would note any concerns, such as those mentioned in the preceding text, and research your state's *curative statutes* (statutes designed to remedy legal defects in previous transactions), statute of limitations, and other relevant statutes to determine whether any title problems can be remedied.

Computerized Title Searches

In many states, title records can be obtained through computerized systems. An attorney-owned title insurance underwriter may have its own computerized system that it makes available to its agent-members. Figure 11–3 provides an example of one page of a printout from the Attorneys' Title Information Data System (ATIDS), a computer data system made available to

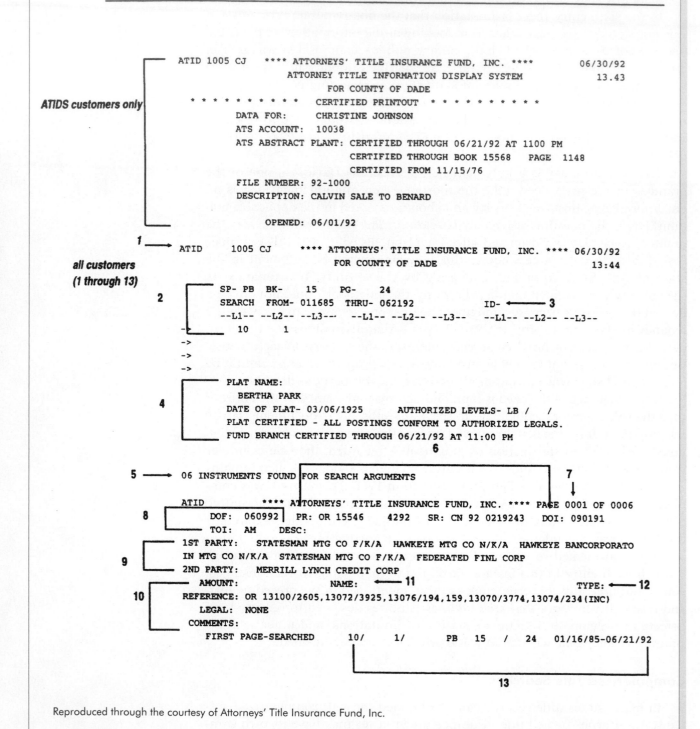

FIGURE 11–3 ATIDS printout

members of the Attorneys' Title Insurance Fund, Inc., a Florida title insurance underwriter. If an attorney wanted to update an abstract or obtain updated information since the last title policy was written for a particular property, he or she might utilize a similar system.

The information at the top of Figure 11–3 indicates that the printout information comes from an abstract certified from November 15, 1976, through June 21, 1992, at 11:00 P.M. The information contained in section 1 provides the date of the title search, the county in which the search was conducted, and the time the computer printout was produced. Section 2 provides a plat reference for the property searched. It gives the plat book number and page number on which the legal description of the property can be found. This section of the printout also provides the dates covered by the title search. This title search covers from January 16, 1985, through June 21, 1992. Section 3 pertains to restricted searches. If a special, restricted search was done, the ID code for the type of documents searched would be shown here.

Section 4 provides information concerning the plat. The name of the platted subdivision is Bertha Park. The plat was recorded in the public records on March 6, 1925. The "LB" following "authorized levels" indicates that the legal designation of the property is by lot and block number. The printout is certified through June 21, 1992, at 11:00 P.M. Section 5 indicates the number of instruments found for the search data provided (for example, for the property and dates indicated).

Section 6 refers to the primary and secondary references for the information. The primary reference (PR) for this first entry is the Official Records Book Number 15546, Page 4292. The secondary reference (SR) is to the clerk's file number, here 92 0219243. Section 7 provides the current page number of the printout and the total number of pages in the printout. Section 8 refers to the date of filing of the document (DOF); here, it is June 9, 1992. The type of instrument (TOI) is also referred to in section 8; here, the abbreviation "AM" appears, indicating an assignment of mortgage.

Section 9 names the parties to the instrument. The first party is Statesman Mortgage Company, which is assigning the mortgage to the second party, Merrill Lynch Credit Corporation. In section 10, the mortgage, lien, or documentary stamp amount would be provided, as well as a recording reference of the document. An abbreviated legal description would appear by "legal" if appropriate. The name of the instrument scrivener would appear in section 11. Section 12 provides a space to indicate the type of mortgage or UCC financing statement and section 13 provides the lot and block searched, which corresponds with the information set forth in section 3.

The proper reading of a computer printout title search necessarily requires familiarity with the format used by each particular data system. The example provided in Figure 11–3 is simply illustrative of one such system. A thorough reading also requires knowledge of the abbreviations used to refer to types of instruments (for example, BOS for Bill of Sale, TXD for Tax Deed, PRL for Partial Release of Lien), which also may vary considerably from one system to the next.

From this discussion, it should be clear that title examination is very detailed work. A paralegal should not attempt to perform a title examination without using a checklist to keep track of the various matters to consider. If your law firm has not developed a checklist for such use, the checklist provided below may be utilized.

TITLE EXAMINATION CHECKLIST

1. *Preliminary information obtained*
   a. *Legal description of the property*
   b. *Name of present owner of the property*
   c. *Copies of:*
      i. *Current deed and/or survey*
      ii. *Current title insurance policy*
2. *Period of search*
   a. *Full search (going back fifty years or whatever is required by statute)*
   b. *Limited search (going back to last search or last policy issued)*
3. *Title information reviewed*
   a. *Public records*
   b. *Abstract of title (note the dates covered)*
   c. *Prior policy*
   d. *Computer search printout*
4. *Items to be checked for each instrument*
   a. *Names of the parties to the instrument*
   b. *Type of instrument and interest in property provided*
   c. *Contents of the instrument, particularly those setting forth restrictions, conditions, and encumbrances on the property*
   d. *Date of the instrument*
   e. *Date of recording of the instrument*
   f. *Signatures and acknowledgments*
   g. *Other interests or rights*
5. *Title matters considered*
   a. *Ad valorem taxes*
   b. *Assessment liens*
   c. *Bankruptcy proceedings*
   d. *Construction liens*
   e. *Corporate status*
   f. *Creditors' rights issues*
   g. *Declaration of condominium*
   h. *Divorce proceedings*
   i. *Easements*
   j. *Encroachments*
   k. *Foreclosure proceedings*
   l. *Homestead*
   m. *Judgment liens*
   n. *Lis pendens*
   o. *Matters shown on plat map*
   p. *Mortgages*
   q. *Probate or guardianship proceedings*
   r. *Reservations*
   s. *Restrictions*
   t. *Tax liens*
   u. *UCC financing statements*
   v. *Other*

TITLE INSURANCE PREPARATION

Once a thorough title examination has been conducted, a title agent can prepare a document called a *title commitment*, sometimes referred to as a *title binder* or *title report*. As noted earlier, a title commitment assures the purchaser and the lending institution that the title to the subject real property has been examined to the date specified on the commitment and discloses the status of the title as of that date. It further creates an obligation on the insurer to write a title policy based on the stipulations set forth in the commitment. As a paralegal, you may be asked to review and/or draft title commitments, so a thorough knowledge of their components is necessary.

In the title insurance business, as in other insurance businesses, the use of standard forms is common practice. You must become familiar with those used most often in real estate transactions in your county. Most title insurance companies use ALTA forms, or modified versions of them. The sample forms provided in this section of the text are forms that use the ALTA format. They differ from the standard ALTA forms in two minor respects: (1) they contain a modified arbitration provision that is not included in the ALTA forms, and (2) they eliminate an ALTA form provision that requires an insured to become a coinsurer in certain situations.

The Commitment

Commitment Jacket. The cover, or jacket, of the title commitment stipulates the standard terms under which the title insurance company commits to issue a title policy (see Figure 11–4). The front of the commitment jacket will contain a serial number that represents the commitment number. The back of the commitment jacket lists the standard exceptions to insurance coverage. They are as follows:

1. Taxes for the year of the effective date of the commitment and taxes or special assessments that are not shown as existing liens by the public records
2. Rights or claims of parties in possession not shown by the public records
3. Encroachments, overlaps, boundary line disputes, and any other matters that would be disclosed by an accurate survey and inspection of the premises
4. Easements, or claims of easements, not shown by the public records
5. Any lien, or right to a lien, for services, labor, or material furnished, imposed by law and not shown by the public records

To understand the first exception, recall the manner in which real property owners are taxed. The ad valorem taxes are assessed upon a parcel of property as of January 1st of a particular year. However, they do not become due and payable until some later date, stipulated by statute. This exception for taxes may be waived by the insurer for the year in which the taxes are due if they have been paid and evidence of payment is provided to the insurer.

The second exception refers to the possibility of someone in possession of the real property other than the present owner who may have some claim to

(American Land Title Association Commitment — 1966 Rev.)

COMMITMENT

Attorneys' Title Insurance Fund, Inc.

ORLANDO, FLORIDA

Commitment To Insure or Guarantee Title

ATTORNEYS' TITLE INSURANCE FUND, INC., a Florida corporation, herein called The Fund, for a valuable consideration, hereby commits to issue its policy or policies of title insurance or guarantee of title, as identified in Schedule A, in favor of the proposed Insured named in Schedule A, as owner or mortgagee of the estate or interest covered hereby in the land described or referred to in Schedule A; subject to the provisions of Schedules A and B and to the Conditions and Stipulations hereof.

This Commitment shall be effective only when the identity of the proposed Insured and the amount of the policy or policies or guarantee committed for have been inserted in Schedule A hereof by The Fund, either at the time of the issuance of this Commitment or by subsequent endorsement.

This Commitment is preliminary to the issuance of such policy or policies of title insurance or guarantee of title and all liability and obligations hereunder shall cease and terminate six months after the effective date hereof or when the policy or policies or guarantee committed for shall issue, whichever first occurs, provided that the failure to issue such policy or policies or guarantee is not the fault of The Fund.

In Witness Whereof, ATTORNEYS' TITLE INSURANCE FUND, INC. has caused this Commitment to be signed and sealed as of the effective date of Commitment shown in Schedule A, the Commitment to become valid when countersigned by an authorized signatory.

Attorneys' Title Insurance Fund, Inc.

By *Charles J. Kovaleski*

Charles J. Kovaleski
President

SERIAL

C-

FUND FORM C/M08-049

Reproduced through the courtesy of Attorneys' Title Insurance Fund, Inc.

FIGURE 11–4 Title commitment jacket

Standard Exceptions

The owner policy or owner guarantee will be subject to the mortgage, if any, noted under item two of Section I of Schedule B hereof. All policies and guarantees will be subject to the following exceptions: (1) taxes for the year of the effective date of this Commitment and taxes or special assessments which are not shown as existing liens by the public records; (2) rights or claims of parties in possession not shown by the public records; (3) encroachments, overlaps, boundary line disputes, and any other matters which would be disclosed by an accurate survey and inspection of the premises; (4) easements, or claims of easements, not shown by the public records; (5) any lien, or right to a lien, for services, labor, or material heretofore or hereafter furnished, imposed by law and not shown by the public records.

Conditions and Stipulations

1. The term "mortgage," when used herein, shall include deed of trust, trust deed, or other security instrument.

2. If the proposed Insured has or acquires actual knowledge of any defect, lien, encumbrance, adverse claim or other matter affecting the estate or interest or mortgage thereon covered by this Commitment other than those shown in Schedule B hereof, and shall fail to disclose such knowledge to The Fund in writing, The Fund shall be relieved from liability for any loss or damage resulting from any act of reliance hereon to the extent The Fund is prejudiced by failure to so disclose such knowledge. If the proposed Insured shall disclose such knowledge to The Fund, or if The Fund otherwise acquires actual knowledge of any such defect, lien, encumbrance, adverse claim or other matter, The Fund at its option may amend Schedule B of this Commitment accordingly, but such amendment shall not relieve The Fund from liability previously incurred pursuant to paragraph 3 of these Conditions and Stipulations.

3. Liability of The Fund under this Commitment shall be only to the named proposed Insured and such parties included under the definition of Insured in the form of policy or policies or guarantee committed for and only for actual loss incurred in reliance hereon in undertaking in good faith (a) to comply with the requirements hereof, or (b) to eliminate exceptions shown in Schedule B, or (c) to acquire or create the estate or interest or mortgage thereon covered by this Commitment. In no event shall such liability exceed the amount stated in Schedule A for the policy or policies or guarantee committed for and such liability is subject to the insuring provisions, the Exclusions from Coverage and the Conditions and Stipulations of the form of policy or policies or guarantee committed for in favor of the proposed Insured which are hereby incorporated by reference and are made a part of this Commitment except as expressly modified herein.

4. Any action or actions or rights of action that the proposed Insured may have or may bring against The Fund arising out of the status of the title to the estate or interest or the status of the mortgage thereon covered by this Commitment must be based on and are subject to the provisions of this Commitment.

FIGURE 11–4 (continued)

an interest in the property. This exception may be waived by the insurer if the owner provides adequate evidence that there is no one physically on the property who may claim such an interest. To do this, the owner may have to provide a survey and allow a personal, physical inspection of the property. The insurer additionally may want an affidavit from the owner that no other person is in possession.

The third exception refers to possible encroachments and other matters that may be determined only by an actual survey of the real property. To waive this exception, the insurer will require that a survey be obtained and reviewed by one of its agents. The same is true of the fourth exception, pertaining to easements. With regard to this fourth exception, the insurer also may require an affidavit from the owner stating that no easements or claims to easements exists.

The fifth exception relates to construction liens. Recall from prior discussions that construction liens work retroactively in terms of date of priority. Thus, a construction lien may be placed on the property after the sale, yet attach as of the date the first work was done on the property. State statutes dictate the time period within which a construction lien must be filed. To waive this exception, the insurer will require that the owner provide an affidavit stating that no goods, services, or materials were provided within that statutory period. If, in fact, work has been done, the insurer will require a waiver of lien signed by all parties who performed services or provided materials. Additionally, the owner and general contractor may have to sign an affidavit indicating that all parties with potential claims have signed, and agreeing to indemnify the insurer.

Schedule A. Schedule A indicates (1) the effective date of the commitment, (2) the type(s) of policy(ies) to be issued, (3) the amount(s) of coverage, (4) the name(s) of the proposed insured(s), (5) the name(s) of the party(ies) in whom title to the property is presently vested, and (6) the legal description of the real property (see Figure 11–5).

In the top lefthand corner of Schedule A, one inserts the commitment number found on the front cover of the commitment jacket. Next to this, one inserts the effective date of the policy. The effective date is the month, day, year, and time through which the title of the property has been examined, *not* the date on which the commitment is prepared. The agent's file reference number is the client number and matter number the title agent has assigned to this transaction.

There are four basic types of title policies that may be issued: (1) an owner's policy, (2) an owner's policy leasehold, (3) a mortgagee's policy, and (4) a mortgagee's policy leasehold. The **owner's policy (OPM)** is a marketability policy, extending insurance coverage against loss or damage because of the inability to sell the property in the future because of title defects. The **owner's policy leasehold (OPL)** is used to insure the title that a purchaser of a leasehold is acquiring. This policy is most often issued when one purchases interest in a cooperative. The **mortgagee's policy (MP)** is issued to insure the mortgage lien that a lender is acquiring. The **mortgagee's policy leasehold (MPL)** is issued to insure the mortgage lien that a lender is acquiring in a leasehold estate and, again, is used most often when the mortgagor is acquiring interest in a cooperative.

If more than one policy will be issued simultaneously (that is, an owner's policy and a mortgagee's policy), both sections of part 1 are filled out. The proposed amount of insurance for an owner's policy is the full insurable value of the property. This most often is the purchase price. The proposed amount

owner's policy (OPM): A marketability policy, extending insurance coverage against loss or damage because of the inability to sell the property in the future because of title defects.

owner's policy leasehold (OPL): A title policy used to insure the title that the purchaser of a leasehold is acquiring.

mortgagee's policy (MP): A title policy issued to insure the mortgage lien that a lender is acquiring.

mortgagee's policy leasehold (MPL): A title policy issued to insure the mortgage lien that a lender is acquiring in a leasehold estate.

FUND COMMITMENT FORM

Schedule A

Commitment No.:   Effective Date: Agent's File Reference:

1.   Policy or Policies to be issued: Proposed Amount of Insurance

     OWNER'S: $

     Proposed Insured:

     MORTGAGEE: $

     Proposed Insured:

2.   The estate or interest in the land described or referred to in this commitment is a fee simple (if other, specify same) and title thereto is at the effective date hereof vested in:

3.   The land referred to in this commitment is described as follows:

ISSUED BY

NAME OF AGENT   AGENT NO.   AGENT'S SIGNATURE

MAILING ADDRESS   CITY   , Florida   ZIP

FUND Form C-SCH. A (rev. 1/90)

Reproduced through the courtesy of Attorneys' Title Insurance Fund, Inc.

FIGURE 11–5 Title commitment schedule A

of insurance for a mortgagee's policy most often is the full principal amount of the debt, although state statutes may allow a stipulated percentage in excess of this to cover interest and foreclosure costs.

The name(s) of the present owner(s) of the property and the legal description of the property are inserted in the spaces indicated. The name of the title agent issuing the policy is inserted at the bottom of the page, together with the agent's number (assigned by the title insurance company, *not* the attorney's bar number if the agent is an attorney) and address.

Schedule B. Schedule B contains two parts, Part I and Part II (see Figure 11–6). Part I specifies the requirements that must be complied with in order for the title insurer to issue the policy(ies). Above Part I, one inserts the commitment number. The first item under Part I requires that full payment be made for the property. Under the second item, one lists the items to be obtained and recorded before the issuance of the policy(ies), such as the deed from the seller to the purchaser and the mortgage instrument from the mortgagor to the mortgagee, and the satisfaction of mortgage for a mortgage loan that is in existence but that is not being assumed by the purchaser.

Part II of Schedule B is where the exceptions to the insurance coverage are listed. The standard exceptions are incorporated by reference here. The first paragraph under Part II excludes from coverage any defects in title that appear in the public records in the **gap period.** This refers to items appearing in the public record in the period between the effective date of the commitment and the recording date of the instruments giving rise to the interest being insured (for example, the recording of the deed and mortgage). The title insurer may delete the gap period exception if certain conditions are met. The title examination would need to be updated again just prior to the disbursement of funds at closing. Further, most title insurers require that the funds be disbursed through one of their agents in order to delete this exception.

In addition, one must insert in this section all liens, encumbrances, and other defects of record that have been discovered through inspection of the property. Items to be inserted here include, but are not limited to, deed restrictions, items contained in a declaration of condominium, and easements.

Owner's Policy

Policy Jacket. An owner's policy is not issued until the purchaser becomes the owner of the real property. Therefore, the policy generally is issued after the closing. The policy jacket sets forth the coverage provided (see Figure 11–7). It typically states that the policy insures the owner for any damages sustained by reason of the following:

1. Title to the estate or interest described in Schedule A being vested other than as stated therein
2. Any defect in or lien or encumbrance on the title
3. Unmarketability of the title
4. Lack of a right of access to and from the land

The first item indicates that the title insurer insures that the owner holds the type of interest in the property set forth in Schedule A of the policy. The second item states that apart from those items listed as exceptions to coverage

gap period: The period between the effective date of the commitment and the recording date of the instruments giving rise to the interest being insured.

FUND COMMITMENT FORM

Schedule B

Commitment No.:

I. The following are the requirements to be complied with:

1. Payment of the full consideration to, or for the account of, the grantors or mortgagors.

2. Instruments creating the estate or interest to be insured which must be executed, delivered and filed for record:

II. Schedule B of the policy or policies to be issued will contain exceptions to the following matters unless the same are disposed of to the satisfaction of The Fund:

1. Defects, liens, encumbrances, adverse claims or other matters, if any, created, first appearing in the public records or attaching subsequent to the effective date hereof but prior to the date the proposed Insured acquires for value of record the estate or interest or mortgage thereon covered by this commitment.

2. Any owner and mortgagee policies issued pursuant hereto will contain under Schedule B the standard exceptions set forth at the inside cover hereof unless an affidavit of possession and a satisfactory current survey are submitted, an inspection of the premises is made, it is determined the current year's taxes or special assessments have been paid, and it is determined there is nothing of record which would give rise to construction liens which could take priority over the interest(s) insured hereunder (where the liens would otherwise take priority, submission of waivers is necessary).

3. Any owner policy issued pursuant hereto will contain under Schedule B the following exception: *Any adverse ownership claim by the State of Florida by right of sovereignty to any portion of the lands insured hereunder, including submerged, filled and artificially exposed lands, and lands accreted to such lands.*

FUND Form C-SCH. B (rev. 5/94) [486]

FIGURE 11–6 Title commitment schedule B

OWNER'S TITLE INSURANCE POLICY

Attorneys' Title Insurance Fund, Inc.

ORLANDO, FLORIDA

SUBJECT TO THE EXCLUSIONS FROM COVERAGE, THE EXCEPTIONS FROM COVERAGE CONTAINED IN SCHEDULE B AND THE CONDITIONS AND STIPULATIONS, ATTORNEYS' TITLE INSURANCE FUND, INC., a Florida corporation, herein called The Fund, insures, as of Date of Policy shown in Schedule A, against loss or damage, not exceeding the Amount of Insurance stated in Schedule A, sustained or incurred by the insured by reason of:

1. Title to the estate or interest described in Schedule A being vested other than as stated therein;

2. Any defect in or lien or encumbrance on the title;

3. Unmarketability of the title;

4. Lack of a right of access to and from the land.

The Fund will also pay the costs, attorneys' fees and expenses incurred in defense of the title, as insured, but only to the extent provided in the Conditions and Stipulations.

In Witness Whereof, ATTORNEYS' TITLE INSURANCE FUND, INC. has caused this policy to be signed and sealed as of Date of Policy shown in Schedule A, the policy to become valid when countersigned by an authorized signatory.

Attorneys' Title Insurance Fund, Inc.

By

Charles J. Kovaleski
President

SERIAL

OPM -

FIGURE 11–7 Owner's policy jacket

in Schedule B, the title insurer insures against any other defects in title to the property. The third item insures against unmarketability of the title, meaning that the insurer insures that the owner holds superior title. The fourth item insures that the owner has access to the public roads from his or her property.

The back of the jacket itemizes the exclusions from coverage. In summary, these items usually include the following:

1. Governmental police power, laws, ordinances, or governmental regulations
2. Rights of eminent domain
3. Defects, liens, and encumbrances created by the insured, known to the insured but not to the insurer, created subsequent to the date of the policy, or which result in no damage to the insured
4. Bankruptcy

The last item listed indicates that the title insurer does not insure against a claim arising out of a postpolicy finding of the insolvency of the seller.

Schedule A. Schedule A of the owner's policy contains many similarities to Schedule A of the commitment (see Figure 11–8). In the top lefthand corner of the page, one inserts the policy number, which is taken from the front cover of the policy jacket. The effective date of the policy is the month, day, year, and time through which the title has been examined, which must be through the time of recording of the instrument that the policy insures, in this case, through the date of the recording of the deed conveying ownership. The agent's file number is inserted in the righthand corner.

Unlike the commitment schedule, Schedule A of the owner's policy only makes reference to the owner of the property as the insured. The amount of the insurance indicated in the commitment to cover the owner, usually the purchase price, is inserted on this schedule, as well as the name(s) of the insured(s). The name(s) of the insured(s) should appear in the manner in which they appear on the deed.

The second paragraph of the schedule refers to the recording information for the deed. The third paragraph is where the legal description of the property is inserted. The bottom of the form contains a certification statement in which the title agent certifies whether this transaction is covered by RESPA (the Real Estate Settlement Procedures Act, discussed in detail in the next chapter).

Schedule B. Schedule B of the owner's policy contains a listing of the specific exceptions to insurance coverage (see Figure 11–9). If the first exception is to be waived by the insurer, it should be crossed out and a notation should be inserted indicating that the taxes for the year in question have been paid as evidenced by a receipt dated and numbered as specified. Items 2 through 5 may be waived and deleted if the conditions discussed earlier have been satisfied. In addition to the preprinted exceptions, one must list on this schedule all matters discovered through title examination that are encumbrances on the title, such as easements, restrictions, and so forth. Note that if the purchasers have obtained a mortgage loan to finance the purchase of the property, the mortgage instrument securing the loan will be recorded against the property and may appear on this schedule.

FUND OWNER'S FORM

Schedule A

Policy No.:   Effective Date: Agent's File Reference:

Amount of Insurance: $

1.   Name of Insured:

2.   The estate or interest in the land described herein and which is covered by this policy is a fee simple (if other, specify same) and is at the effective date hereof vested in the named insured as shown by instrument recorded in Official Records Book _____ , Page _____ , of the Public Records of _____ County, Florida.

3.   The land referred to in this policy is described as follows:

I, the undersigned agent, hereby certify that
  • the transaction insured herein is governed by RESPA,   ☐ Yes   ☐ No
  • if Yes to the above, I have performed all "core title agent services."   ☐ Yes   ☐ No

_____   _____   _____
ISSUING AGENT - ATTORNEY OR FIRM OF ATTORNEYS   AGENT NO.   AGENT'S SIGNATURE

_____   _____ , Florida _____
MAILING ADDRESS   CITY   ZIP

FUND Form OPM-SCH. A (Rev. 12/92) [486]

Reproduced through the courtesy of Attorneys' Title Insurance Fund, Inc.

FIGURE 11–8 Owner's policy schedule A

FUND OWNER'S FORM
Schedule B

Policy No.:

This policy does not insure against loss or damage by reason of the following exceptions:

1. Taxes for the year of the effective date of this policy and taxes or special assessments which are not shown as existing liens by the public records.

2. Rights or claims of parties in possession not shown by the public records.

3. Encroachments, overlaps, boundary line disputes, and any other matters which would be disclosed by an accurate survey and inspection of the premises.

4. Easements or claims of easements not shown by the public records.

5. Any lien, or right to a lien, for services, labor, or material heretofore or hereafter furnished, imposed by law and not shown by the public records.

6. Any adverse ownership claim by the State of Florida by right of sovereignty to any portion of the lands insured hereunder, including submerged, filled and artificially exposed lands, and lands accreted to such lands.

FUND Form OPM-SCH. B (rev. 5/94) [486]

Reproduced through the courtesy of Attorneys' Title Insurance Fund, Inc.

FIGURE 11–9 Owner's policy schedule B

Mortgagee's Policy

Policy Jacket. Just as is the case with the owner's policy, the mortgagee's policy may not be issued until after the closing, when mortgage instruments have been executed and recorded. The cover page of the policy jacket sets forth the risks covered by the policy (see Figure 11–10). Some of these items will be the same as those appearing on the cover of the owner's policy. In addition, however, the mortgagee policy protects against items of specific interest to the lender. The policy protects against the unenforceability of the lien of the mortgagee. It also protects the priority of the insured mortgage over any other lien not shown on Schedule B of the policy, including construction liens for work begun prior to the date of the policy.

The back of the jacket sets forth the exclusions from coverage. Many of these exclusions are the same as those found in the owner's policy. In addition, the mortgagee's policy excludes from coverage any loss resulting from the unenforceability of the mortgagee's lien due to the mortgagee's failure to comply with the applicable "doing business" laws of the state in which the property is located. Further, the mortgagee's policy excludes from coverage construction liens arising from work commenced after the date of the policy.

Schedule A. Although Schedule A of the mortgagee policy is similar to Schedule A of the owner's policy, there are some differences (see Figure 11–11). The amount of the insurance listed on this schedule will be the amount of the insurance listed by the mortgagee's name on the commitment, typically the full amount of the loan. The name(s) of the owner(s) of the property are included, as well as the legal description of the property. Additionally, paragraph 4 requires the insertion of the mortgage record information; here, one indicates (1) who the mortgage is given by, (2) to whom it is given, (3) the date the mortgage instrument was executed, (4) the date the mortgage instrument was recorded, and (5) the record book and page numbers, and county and state of recording.

Schedule B. Schedule B contains a listing of all items the policy does not insure against (see Figure 11–12). Notice the difference in the preprinted form for the owner's policy and the mortgagee's policy. The mortgagee's policy does not include a listing of the standard exceptions found in the owner's policy. It does, however, include an item pertaining to real estate taxes, which may be deleted if the insurer waives this exception upon receipt of evidence that the current taxes have been paid. Unless the other standard exceptions have been waived (that is, easements not shown by the public records, encroachments that would be disclosed by a survey), one must insert them here. Additionally, one must list all restrictions and encumbrances that appear on record from the title examination.

Endorsements

endorsement: A form provided by the title insurer that is used for the amendment of any information that has appeared as part of a title commitment or title policy.

An **endorsement** is a form provided by the title insurer that is used for the amendment of any information that has appeared as part of a title commitment or title policy. The most commonly used endorsements pertain to a mortgagee's policy. An assignment of mortgage endorsement is used when the

MORTGAGEE TITLE INSURANCE POLICY

Attorneys' Title Insurance Fund, Inc.
ORLANDO, FLORIDA

SUBJECT TO THE EXCLUSIONS FROM COVERAGE, THE EXCEPTIONS FROM COVERAGE CONTAINED IN SCHEDULE B AND THE CONDITIONS AND STIPULATIONS, ATTORNEYS' TITLE INSURANCE FUND, INC., a Florida corporation, herein called The Fund, insures, as of Date of Policy shown in Schedule A, against loss or damage, not exceeding the Amount of Insurance stated in Schedule A, sustained or incurred by the insured by reason of:

1. Title to the estate or interest described in Schedule A being vested other than as stated therein;
2. Any defect in or lien or encumbrance on the title;
3. Unmarketability of the title;
4. Lack of a right of access to and from the land;
5. The invalidity or unenforceability of the lien of the insured mortgage upon the title;
6. The priority of any lien or encumbrance over the lien of the insured mortgage;
7. Lack of priority of the lien of the insured mortgage over any statutory lien for services, labor or material:
   (a) arising from an improvement or work related to the land which is contracted for or commenced prior to Date of Policy; or
   (b) arising from an improvement or work related to the land which is contracted for or commenced subsequent to Date of Policy and which is financed in whole or in part by proceeds of the indebtedness secured by the insured mortgage which at Date of Policy the insured has advanced or is obligated to advance;
8. The invalidity or unenforceability of any assignment of the insured mortgage, provided the assignment is shown in Schedule A, or the failure of the assignment shown in Schedule A to vest title to the insured mortgage in the named insured assignee free and clear of all liens.

The Fund will also pay the costs, attorneys' fees and expenses incurred in defense of the title or the lien of the insured mortgage, as insured, but only to the extent provided in the Conditions and Stipulations.

In Witness Whereof, ATTORNEYS' TITLE INSURANCE FUND, INC. has caused this policy to be signed and sealed as of Date of Policy shown in Schedule A, the policy to become valid when countersigned by an authorized signatory.

Attorneys' Title Insurance Fund, Inc.

By *Charles J. Kovaleski*

Charles J. Kovaleski
President

SERIAL

MP -

FIGURE 11–10 Mortgagee's policy jacket

FUND MORTGAGEE FORM

Schedule A

Policy No.:   Effective Date: Agent's File Reference:

Amount of Insurance: $

1.   Name of Insured:

2.   The estate or interest in the land described in this Schedule and which is encumbered by the insured mortgage is a fee simple (if other, specify same) and is at the effective date hereof vested in:

3.   The land referred to in this policy is described as follows:

4.   The mortgage, herein referred to as the insured mortgage, and the assignments thereof, if any, are described as follows:

I, the undersigned agent, hereby certify that
  • the transaction insured herein is governed by RESPA,   ☐ Yes   ☐ No
  • if Yes to the above, I have performed all "core title agent services."   ☐ Yes   ☐ No

_____   _____   _____
ISSUING AGENT - ATTORNEY OR FIRM OF ATTORNEYS   AGENT NO.   AGENT'S SIGNATURE

_____   _____, Florida _____
MAILING ADDRESS   CITY   ZIP

FUND Form MP-SCH. A (Rev. 12/92) [486]

Reproduced through the courtesy of Attorneys' Title Insurance Fund, Inc.

FIGURE 11–11 Mortgagee's policy schedule A

FUND MORTGAGEE FORM

Schedule B

Policy No.:

This policy does not insure against loss or damage by reason of the following:

1.   The lien of all taxes for the year 19____ and thereafter.

FUND Form MP-SCH. B (Rev. 4/91)

Reproduced through the courtesy of Attorneys' Title Insurance Fund, Inc.

FIGURE 11–12 Mortgagee's policy schedule B

note and the mortgage instrument are assigned by the holder to someone else, typically when an institutional mortgagee assigns a mortgage to the secondary market. A variable rate mortgage endorsement assures the mortgagee that the mortgagee's lien position will not be impaired in the event of negative amortization. (For a discussion of these mortgage terms, refer to Chapter 10).

A condominium endorsement is another commonly used endorsement. It provides affirmative coverage for matters specific to condominiums, such as the valid creation of the condominium. A PUD endorsement is used when the subject property is located in a planned unit development. A survey endorsement acknowledges that the property described in Schedule A is the same as that described in an identified survey. This endorsement comes into play when there are minor discrepancies between the legal description in the survey and that provided in the policy.

As a real estate paralegal, your supervising attorney may ask you to prepare title commitments and/or title policies. A checklist of those items to be included in the various schedules of title commitments and policies is provided below.

TITLE POLICY PREPARATION CHECKLIST

1. *Title commitment*
   a. *Schedule A*
      i. *Commitment number*
      ii. *Effective date (date through which title examination was conducted)*
      iii. *Agent's reference number*
      iv. *Type of policy(ies)*
      v. *Amount of coverage*
         (a) *Owner's policy—purchase price*
         (b) *Mortgagee's policy—loan amount*
      vi. *Name and estate or interest of current owner*
      vii. *Legal description of property*
      viii. *Agent's name, address, number, and signature*
   b. *Schedule B*
      i. *Part I—listing of all conditions that must be met prior to issuance of policy*
      ii. *Part II—listing of all liens, encumbrances, and defects to be exceptions from coverage*
2. *Owner's policy*
   a. *Schedule A*
      i. *Policy number*
      ii. *Effective date (date through which title examination was conducted)*
      iii. *Agent's reference number*
      iv. *Name(s) of insured(s)*
      v. *Amount of coverage —purchase price*
      vi. *Recording information for deed*
      vii. *Legal description of property*
      viii. *Agent's certification statement*
      ix. *Agent's name, address, number, and signature*

  b. *Schedule B—listing of all liens, encumbrances, and defects to be exceptions from coverage*
3. *Mortgagee's policy*
  a. *Schedule A*
    i. *Policy number*
    ii. *Effective date (date through which title examination was conducted)*
    iii. *Agent's reference number*
    iv. *Name(s) of insured(s)*
    v. *Amount of insurance—loan amount*
    vi. *Name and estate or interest of owner*
    vii. *Legal description of property*
    viii. *Mortgage recordation information*
    ix. *Agent certification statement*
    x. *Agent's name, address, number, and signature*
  b. *Schedule B—listing of all liens, encumbrances, and defects to be exceptions from coverage*
4. *Endorsements*
  a. *Condominium endorsement*
  b. *Planned unit development endorsement*
  c. *Variable rate mortgage endorsement*
  d. *Assignment of mortgage endorsement*
  e. *Survey endorsement*
  f. *Other*

HYPOTHETICAL CLIENT MATTER

Paralegal Barbara Hammond is assisting her supervising attorney, Ava Ross, with the Swanson real estate closing. Ava Ross is a title agent and a member of the Any State Title Insurance Fund. She is representing the sellers, Timothy and Karen Swanson, who have contracted with Charles and Erica Kelly. The closing took place last week, and all of the requisite documents have been recorded. Ava has asked Barbara to prepare the owner's and mortgagee's title policies.

Barbara first reviews the title commitment that has been issued to the Kellys (see Figure 11–13). Note that under Part I of Schedule B, the title insurer requires the recording of a warranty deed executed by the Swansons to the Kellys before it will issue an owner's title policy to the Kellys. Similarly, the title insurer requires the recording of a mortgage instrument executed by the Kellys in favor of Patriot Bank before it issues a mortgagee's policy to Patriot Bank. Finally, the satisfaction of the current outstanding loan given to the Swansons by their lender is listed as a condition prerequisite to the issuing of the policies. Some title agents choose not to include this, as it is not technically an instrument creating an estate or interest to be insured. (For an example of a title commitment that omits this requirement, see Chapter 13, Figure 13–13.)

Barbara notes the effective date of the commitment and conducts a computerized title search from that date to the present date. The only new encumbrance indicated on the printout is the mortgage given to Patriot Bank in the amount of $160,000. The mortgage loan given to the Swansons by Any State First National Bank has been satisfied, and a satisfaction of mortgage has been recorded. Using the printout and the title commitment, Barbara prepares the owner's and mortgagee's policy schedules for review by Ava (see Figures 11–14 and 11–15).

FUND COMMITMENT FORM

Schedule A

Commitment No.: 1111111   Effective Date: 07/28/97   Agent's File Reference: 1235.0001
5:00 p.m.

1.   Policy or Policies to be issued: Proposed Amount of Insurance
     OWNER'S: OPM $200,000.00

Proposed Insured:
              CHARLES KELLY and ERICA KELLY, his wife

MORTGAGEE: MP . $ 160,000.00

Proposed Insured:
              PATRIOT BANK

2.   The estate or interest in the land described or referred to in this commitment is a fee simple (if other, specify same) and title thereto is at the effective date hereof vested in:

              Timothy Swanson and Karen Swanson, his wife

3.   The land referred to in this commitment is described as follows:

              Lot 6 in Block 1 of PINEHURST ESTATES, according to the plat
              thereof recorded in Plat Book 70, Page 35, of the Public Records
              of Any County, Any State.

         ISSUED BY

         Fisher, Ross, and Simon, P.A.   2222_____   Ava Ross
                                                Agent's no.   Agent's signature

         1900 N.W. 3rd Avenue   Any City,   Any State

Form reproduced through the courtesy of Attorneys' Title Insurance Fund, Inc.

FIGURE 11–13 Kelly title commitment

FUND COMMITMENT FORM

Schedule B

Commitment No.:   1111111

I.   The following are the requirements to be complied with:

1.   Payment of the full consideration to or for the account of, the grantors or mortgagors.

1.   Instruments creating the estate or interest to be insured which must be executed, delivered and filed for record:

1.   Warranty Deed executed by Timothy Swanson and Karen Swanson, his wife, to Charles Kelly and Erica Kelly, his wife.

2.   Satisfaction of Mortgage in favor of Any State First National Bank dated November 8, 1991 and recorded November 9, 1991 at O.R. Book 5700, Page 81 of the Public Records of Any County, Any State.

3.   Mortgage in the principal amount of $160,000.00 in favor of Patriot Bank executed by Charles Kelly and Erica Kelly, his wife.

II. Schedule B of the policy or policies to be issued will contain exceptions to the following matters unless the same are disposed of to the satisfaction of The Fund:

1.   Defects, liens, encumbrances, adverse claims or other matters, if any, created, first appearing in the public records or attaching subsequent to the effective date hereof but prior to the date the proposed Insured acquires for value of record the estate or interest or mortgage thereon covered by this Commitment.

1.   Any owner policy issued pursuant hereto will contain under Schedule B the standard exceptions set forth at the inside cover hereof. Any mortgagee policy will contain under Schedule B the standard exceptions unless an affidavit of possession and a satisfactory current survey are submitted, an inspection of the premises is made, it is determined the current year's taxes or special assessments have been paid, and it is determined there is nothing of record which would give rise to mechanics' liens which could take priority over the mortgage (where the liens would otherwise take priority, submission of waivers is necessary).

1.   Easement from Any State Power and Light Company dated February 20, 1968 recorded March 2, 1968 at O.R. Book 4007, Page 48 of the Public Records of Any County, Any State.

1.   Restrictive covenants of Pinehurst Estates Subdivision, dated April 10, 1972, recorded April 12, 1972 at O.R. Book 4012, Page 90 of the Public Records of Any County, Any State.

Form reproduced through the courtesy of Attorneys' Title Insurance Fund, Inc.

FIGURE 11–13 (continued)

FUND OWNER'S FORM

Schedule A

Policy No.:   4444444   Effective Date: 09/15/97   Agent's File Reference: 1235.0001
                                              10:00 a.m.

              Amount of Insurance: $200,000.00

1.   Name of Insured:

                    CHARLES KELLY and ERICA KELLY, his wife

2.   The estate or interest in the land described herein and which is covered by this policy is a fee simple (if other, specify same) and is at the effective date hereof vested in the named insured as shown by instrument recorded in Official Records Book ___6200_____, Page ___103_____, of the Public Records of Any County, Any State.

3.   The land referred to in this policy is described as follows:

                    Lot 6 in Block 1 of PINEHURST ESTATES, according to the plat
                    thereof recorded in Plat Book 70, Page 35 of the Public Records of
                    Any County, Any State.

I, the undersigned agent, hereby certify that
   · the transaction insured herein is governed by RESPA,   [X] Yes [   ] No
   · if Yes to the above, I have performed all "core title agent services." [X] Yes [   ] No

Fisher, Ross, and Simon, P.A.   3333___   Ava Ross
ISSUING AGENT   AGENT NO.   AGENT'S SIGNATURE

1900 N.W. 3rd Avenue   Any City ,   Any State

Form reproduced through the courtesy of Attorneys' Title Insurance Fund, Inc.

FIGURE 11–14 Kelly owners' policy

FUND OWNER'S FORM

Schedule B

Policy No.: OPM - 4444444

This policy does not insure against loss or damage by reason of the following exceptions:

1. Taxes for the year of the effective date of this policy and taxes or special assessments which are not shown as existing liens by the public records.

2. Rights or claims of parties in possession not shown by the public records.

3. Encroachments, overlaps, boundary line disputes, and any other matters which would be disclosed by an accurate survey and inspection of the premises.

4. Easements or claims of easements not shown by the public records.

5. Any lien, or right to a lien, for services, labor, or material heretofore or hereafter furnished, imposed by law and not shown by the public records.

6. Any adverse ownership claim by the State of Any State by right of sovereignty to any portion of the lands insured hereunder, including submerged, filled and artificially exposed lands, and lands accreted to such lands.

7. Easement from Any State Power and Light Company dated February 20, 1968 recorded March 2, 1968 at O.R. Book 4007, Page 48 of the Public Records of Any County, Any State.

8. Restrictive covenants of Pinehurst Estates Subdivision, dated April 10, 1972, recorded April 12, 1972 at O.R. Book 4012, Page 90 of the Public Records of Any County, Any State.

9. Mortgage in the principal amount of $160,000.00 in favor of Patriot Bank dated September 9, 1997, and recorded in O.R. Book 6200, Page 104 of the Public Records of Any County, Any State.

Form reproduced through the courtesy of Attorneys' Title Insurance Fund, Inc.

FIGURE 11–14 (continued)

FUND MORTGAGEE FORM

Schedule A

Policy No.: MP -5555555   Effective Date: 09/15/97 Agent's File Reference: 1235.0001
                                                10:00 a.m.

        Amount of Insurance: $ 160, 000.00

1. Name of Insured: PATRIOT BANK

2. The estate or interest in the land described in this Schedule and which is encumbered by the insured
    mortgage is a fee simple (if other, specify same) and is at the effective date hereof vested in:

                CHARLES KELLY and ERICA KELLY, his wife

3. The land referred to in this policy is described as follows:

                Lot 6 in Block A of PINEHURST ESTATES, according to the plat
                thereof recorded in Plat Book 70, Page 35 of the Public Records of
                Any County, Any State.

4. The mortgage, herein referred to as the insured mortgage, and the assignments thereof, if any, are
    described as follows:

    Mortgage from Charles Kelly and Erica Kelly, his wife, to Patriot Bank, dated September 9, 1997,
    recorded September 9, 1997 in O.R. Book 6200, Page 104 of the Public Records of Any County, Any
    State.

I, the undersigned agent, hereby certify that
  · the transaction insured herein is governed by RESPA,   [X] Yes [   ] No
  · if Yes to the above, I have performed all "core title agent services." [X] Yes [   ] No

Fisher, Ross, and Simon, P.A.   3333   Ava Ross
ISSUING AGENT   AGENT NO.   AGENT'S SIGNATURE

1900 N.W. 3rd Avenue   Any City,   Any State

Form reproduced through the courtesy of Attorneys' Title Insurance Fund, Inc.

FIGURE 11–15 Patriot Bank's mortgagee's policy

FUND MORTGAGEE FORM

Schedule B

Policy No.: MP - 5555555

This policy does not insure against loss or damage by reason of the following:

1. The lien of all taxes for the year 1997 and thereafter.

2. Rights or claims of parties in possession not shown by the public records.

3. Encroachments, overlaps, boundary line disputes, and any other matters which would be disclosed by an accurate survey and inspection of the premises.

4. Easements or claims of easements not shown by the public records.

5. Easement from Any State Power and Light Company dated February 20, 1968 recorded March 2, 1968 at O.R. Book 4007, Page 48 of the Public Records of Any County, Any State.

6. Restrictive covenants of Pinehurst Estates Subdivision, dated April 10, 1972, recorded April 12, 1972 at O.R. Book 4012, Page 90 of the Public Records of Any County, Any State.

Form reproduced through the courtesy of Attorneys' Title Insurance Fund, Inc.

FIGURE 11–15 (continued)

CHAPTER SUMMARY

1. When a purchaser buys a parcel of real property, the purchaser wants to be assured that he or she is receiving marketable title, that is, a title free from encumbrances that would diminish its market value. To determine the marketability of title, a title examiner is hired to conduct a title examination. The title examination is composed of a search of all documents in the public records as well as a physical inspection of the property.

2. A manual title examination typically begins with a search through the grantor and grantee indices or the tract index. A thorough search of the public records will indicate whether there are any documents of record creating encumbrances or defects in the title. All recorded documents must be examined for both their contents and their legal sufficiency.

3. To examine documents thoroughly, a title examiner must note (1) the type of document, (2) the contents of the document, (3) the names of the parties to the document, (4) the date of the document, (5) the date of recording of the document, and (6) the signatures and acknowledgments. Should a problem with a document appear, the title examiner must research the state statutes to determine whether a curative statute exists that can negate the defect.

4. Numerous matters must be considered when conducting a title search. They include, but are not limited to, assessment liens; construction liens; judgment liens; divorce, probate, and bankruptcy proceedings; deed restrictions; easements; encroachments; and restrictive covenants.

5. An abstract of title is a condensed history of each document affecting the title of a particular parcel of real property. An abstractor creates a chain of title for the property as well as a synopsis of each recorded document pertaining to the property. The abstractor's certificate indicates the dates covered by the title search. The abstract is updated each time ownership of the property is transferred.

6. Title insurance is insurance provided to an owner or mortgagee against loss brought about by encumbrances or defects in the title. A title insurance policy insures against losses due to hidden defects such as recording errors, forged deeds, and undisclosed claims.

7. A title commitment sets forth the status of the title of a particular parcel of real property. It also states the condition under which a title policy will be issued. The commitment jacket sets forth the standard exceptions to insurance coverage. Schedule A sets forth the effective date of the commitment, the type(s) of policy(ies) to be issued, the amount(s) of coverage, the name(s) of the party(ies) in whom title is presently vested, and a legal description of the property. Schedule B indicates the conditions that must be complied with prior to issuance of the policy. It also sets forth all exclusions from coverage.

8. An owner's policy insures marketable title, while a mortgagee's policy insures the mortgage lien the lender is acquiring. An owner's policy covers the market value or purchase price of the property, whereas the mortgagee's policy covers the debt amount.

REVIEW QUESTIONS

1. Explain the ways in which title insurance differs from other forms of insurance.
2. List the records that should be searched when conducting a title examination.
3. Describe the four basic types of policies.
4. List the information contained in the following.
   a. Schedule A of a title commitment
   b. Schedule B of a title commitment
5. What are the most common exclusions from coverage under an owner's title policy?

ETHICAL QUESTIONS

Your firm has been hired to represent the buyer, Janet Monroe, in a real estate closing. You have been asked by your supervising attorney to examine the abstract sent to your office by the seller. It is a long document; you have reviewed most of it, but have not completed it. While your supervising attorney is out of the office, you receive a telephone call from Janet. She has heard that the seller was involved in major litigation a number of years ago, and she wants to know if there are any judgment liens recorded against the property that remain unpaid. She believes the litigation occurred about seven years ago. You have completed your review of abstract documents up to five years ago and have not come across any judgment liens, so you tell Janet that none appear that would correspond with the information she has received. Later in the afternoon, you resume your review and come across a judgment lien dated four years ago that has not been satisfied. What should you do?

PRACTICAL ASSIGNMENTS

Assignment 11:1. Research your state statutes to find provisions governing title insurance companies, agents, and the requirements for the issuance of title insurance. Photocopy the relevant statutes and insert them under the "Title Work" section of your resource portfolio.

Assignment 11:2. Assume that the property described in Figure 11–2 is located in your city, county, and state and that the abstract of title was performed by a local title company. Write out a review of the abstract of title, setting forth the relevant information in the three-column format specified in the text. Then insert it under the "Title Work" section of your resource portfolio.

Assignment 11:3. Research your state statutes to determine whether any of the noted problems pertaining to the title of the property described in Figure 11–2 (for example, only one witness, an unsatisfied judgment lien) can be cured. Note the appropriate statute number and a one- or two-line synopsis of the provision next to each problem on your abstract review.

Assignment 11:4. Assume the abstract of title set forth in Figure 11–2 pertains to property located in your state. Assume further that the grantees in the last entry, Lawrence and Donna Miller, have hired your supervising attorney, Deborah Sanders, to represent them in a real estate closing. The purchasers are Terrence and Christine Brown. Deborah is a title agent and will be preparing the commitment and policies. She has asked you to update the abstract. You have updated the title search. The only new entry is a home equity loan creating a mortgage from Lawrence Miller and Donna Miller, his wife, to Century Bank in the principal amount of $35,000, dated March 25, 1996, and recorded March 26, 1996, in Official Records Book 1212, Page 59, of the Public Records of your county and state. Your search is current as of 9:00 A.M. this morning.

Deborah has asked you to prepare a title commitment. The commitment number is 9999999. The agent's reference number is 54321. Use the plat method legal description provided in the caption of the abstract (making appropriate changes so that the property description indicates that the property is in your county and state). The proposed amount of insurance for the owner's policy is $250,000, and the proposed amount of insurance for the mortgagee's policy is $185,000. The mortgagee is Millennium Bank. Deborah's agent number is 0001. Your firm's title is Hernandez, Sanders, and Norris, P.A., located at 263 Republic Avenue (your city, your state). Photocopy the blank forms for Schedules A and B found in your student workbook and use them for this assignment (the originals are to be used for the workbook assignment). After review, insert the schedules under the "Title Work" section of your resource portfolio.

Assignment 11:5. Define the following key terms.

abstract of title	mortgagee's policy leasehold (MPL)
abstractor's certificate	owner's policy (OPM)
American Land Title Association (ALTA)	owner's policy leasehold (OPL)
chain of title	title commitment
endorsement	title insurance
gap period	title search
marketable title	tract index
mortgagee's policy (MP)	

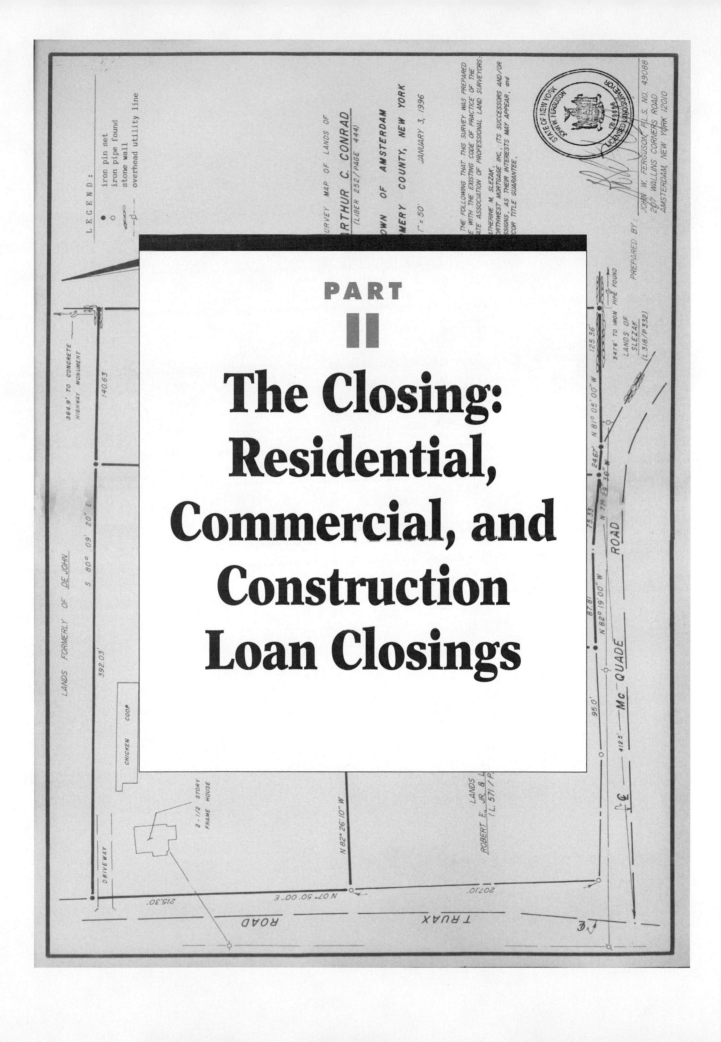

PART II

The Closing: Residential, Commercial, and Construction Loan Closings

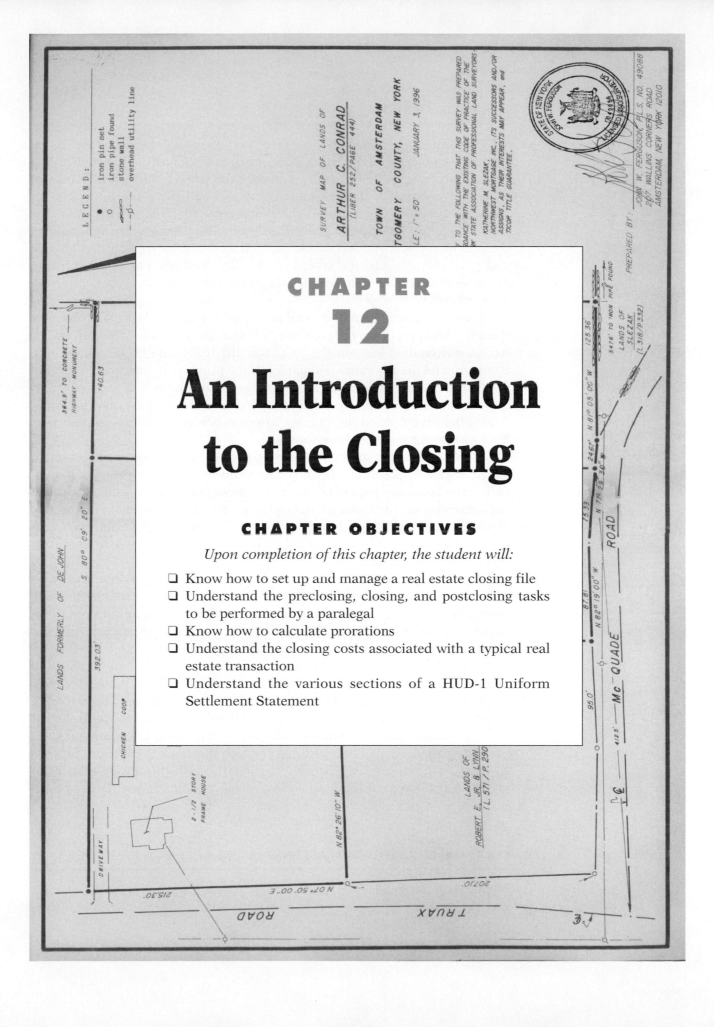

CHAPTER
12

An Introduction to the Closing

CHAPTER OBJECTIVES

Upon completion of this chapter, the student will:

❏ Know how to set up and manage a real estate closing file
❏ Understand the preclosing, closing, and postclosing tasks to be performed by a paralegal
❏ Know how to calculate prorations
❏ Understand the closing costs associated with a typical real estate transaction
❏ Understand the various sections of a HUD-1 Uniform Settlement Statement

INTRODUCTION

The terms *closing* or *settlement* refer to the process of transferring documents and monies to complete a real estate transaction in accordance with the contract for sale and purchase executed by the parties. Often, there are two types of closings occurring simultaneously. The first is the loan closing, whereby the purchaser executes the promissory note and related financing instruments in exchange for the lender's check to cover a certain amount of the purchase price. The second closing is the closing on the contract for sale and purchase, whereby the seller executes the deed and any other requisite documents to transfer marketable title to the purchaser in exchange for the sales proceeds.

There are a number of interested parties in any given closing. They include the seller and purchaser, the purchaser's lender, the seller's lender (if the seller has an outstanding loan on the property), the real estate broker(s), the title company, and the insurance companies. If the property in question is income-producing property, the tenants must be considered as well. If the property is a condominium or is located within a development that has a homeowners' association, the condominium association or homeowners' association may have to approve the prospective buyer.

The closing agent, sometimes referred to as the escrow agent or settlement agent, has the responsibility of pulling these diverse parties together and organizing the necessary paperwork to have a smooth-running closing. The closing agent may be a title company, law firm, attorney for the lender, or escrow agent. Similarly, a paralegal working on a real estate closing file may be working for the lender's in-house counsel, a title company, or a law firm that handles real estate transactions.

It is the paralegal's task to maintain control over a transaction that at times may seem to take on a life of its own. The paralegal must draft and organize correspondence and closing documentation, order surveys, and keep tabs on incoming inspection reports, information requests, expense receipts, or other documentation from third parties. The paralegal must keep track of all deadlines specified in the contract for sale and purchase, the loan commitment, and other relevant documents. Additionally, the paralegal must verify all computations on the closing statement for accuracy and make sure that all parties are able to close on the specified closing date so there is no breach of contract.

This chapter introduces the paralegal to the opening and managing of a real estate file. It walks the paralegal through the steps to be taken prior to closing, during closing, and after the closing. It details the closing costs associated with the typical residential closing and explains the HUD-1 Uniform Settlement Statement section by section.

OPENING AND MANAGING A REAL ESTATE FILE

Meticulous organization and attention to detail are the keys to managing a real estate file. The primary aid will be a closing worksheet. The following three chapters provide closing worksheets for residential, commercial, and construction loan closings. The worksheet should be kept at the front of the real estate file for easy access because it will give the paralegal quick reference to the names, addresses, and telephone numbers of the parties, the lenders, the real estate broker(s), the title company, and so forth. It will also contain the legal description of the property, the parcel identification number of the property, and a thorough list of items to be ordered, obtained, prepared, and reviewed. The worksheet will indicate which party has the responsibility for each item, the date by which item must be completed or obtained, and which party is to be charged. The worksheet therefore becomes an invaluable reference source and allows the paralegal quickly to surmise the status of the real estate file.

Your supervising attorney may have his or her own preference for the manner in which the file is to be organized, in which case you should follow those instructions accordingly. If the file organization is left to you, as is often the case, it is advisable to have separate folders for each document. This makes retrieval of a particular document effortless in a file that will be quickly expanding from the time the contract for sale and purchase is signed until the date of closing. Thus, you would set up a separate folder for the contract, for the deed, for the financing instrument, and so forth. All correspondence may be kept in the same folder. It is customary to arrange correspondence in reverse chronological order, with the most recent letter on top. The correspondence can be fastened to the righthand side of the folder, with each letter tabbed. The index to the correspondence can be placed on the lefthand side, with item numbers corresponding to the tabs.

Your client may be bringing in original documents, such as a deed or title policy if the client is a seller. Originals should never be hole-punched. One method is to affix a document-sized envelope to a folder and then insert the original document in the envelope. Another method is to staple an index card to the document, then hole-punch the index card and fasten it to a folder. Any original documents that you or your supervising attorney prepare should not be defaced by hole-punching. Copies of documents, such as a copy of the contract for sale and purchase, may be fastened directly to a folder.

As soon as you are assigned a file, you should set up a tickler system to keep track of all the various deadlines. Your worksheet can provide you with a rudimentary system, by noting the date items are due. From this, you will want to enter due dates in a computerized or manual tickler system, providing first, second, and third reminders. This gives you enough lead time to follow through. In manual systems, tickler cards that are similar to index cards are used. They have copies in various colors, with each color indicating a first, second, or third reminder. The appropriate dates are written on the cards, and the cards are placed in a tickler file. For example, suppose the contract for sale and purchase states that the seller is to provide a title commitment to the purchaser within fifteen days from the date of execution of the contract. Suppose further that your office is to prepare the title commitment. If the contract was executed on March 1st, the purchaser must receive the commitment by March 15th. You could put your first reminder about preparing the commitment under March 5th, the second under March 10th, and a final reminder under March 14th. Some of the real estate closing software discussed later in the chapter has tracking programs that work similarly to tickler systems to keep track of closing-related tasks.

When beginning to set up a tickler system and worksheet for a real estate file, the best place to start is with the contract for sale and purchase. A thorough contract acts as a blueprint for the future closing, providing not only the closing date but other due dates and specifying the parties responsible for preparing various documents. Go through the contract line by line and mark down on your worksheet the tasks or items and due dates as they appear for your tickler system.

Next, scrutinize the names of the parties and titles of the parties. Verify the correct spellings as they are to appear on the deed and other closing documents. If either the seller or purchaser is married, this information is important for the preparation of documents. A lender customarily will want both spouses to sign the note and financing instrument. Further, the marital status of the purchasers is important in preparing the deed, for the manner in which title is held has many legal ramifications, as noted in Chapter 8. Similarly, if the seller is married, even if the seller holds title to the property in his or her name only, the seller's spouse may be required to sign the deed conveying title. This is important as it relates to issues of homestead, dower, and curtesy rights in states that recognize these rights, as discussed in Chapter 2.

If either party is a corporation, verification of its corporate standing is required. This is done by requesting a certificate of good standing from the secretary of state's office. Some corporations keep up-to-date certificates in their corporate records book, in which case a copy can be obtained from the party itself. Additionally, the purchase or sale of real property is a matter that must be approved by a corporation's board of directors. Therefore, you will want to obtain a certified copy of the corporate resolution approving the purchase or sale. If a party is some other entity, such as a partnership, limited partnership, limited liability company, or trust, you will need to obtain copies of the relevant documents to ascertain whether the entity is in good standing (if applicable), whose authorization is necessary for the transaction, and who is to sign the closing documents on behalf of that party. With regard to any business entity, you should review the entity's organizational documents (for example, articles of incorporation and bylaws of a corporation) to determine that all requisite procedures required by these documents have been followed.

Although the contract will often provide the addresses of the parties, it will not always supply their telephone numbers. You can obtain this information from your client and from the real estate broker (if any) involved in the transaction. The contract will also specify the commission to be paid to the broker(s) or indicate that a separate listing brokerage agreement was signed. If the latter is the case, you will want to obtain a copy of the agreement and review it to ascertain not only the amount of the commission, but also the conditions precedent to be met by the broker before he or she is entitled to commission. (For a thorough discussion of this matter, refer to Chapter 6.) The contract will also indicate any earnest money deposits paid and whether there are subsequent deposits to be made.

The legal description of the subject property may appear on the contract. Sometimes an abbreviated description is used. It is important to obtain a full description from the seller's deed, current title policy, or survey. You will want to obtain these items as soon as possible. Make sure to copy the legal description accurately onto the worksheet. This will shortcut efforts later, when you can simply refer to the worksheet rather than sort through a pile of documents. If the description is lengthy, type it on a separate sheet of paper, make numerous copies, and put them in a file folder labeled "Legals" or "Legal Description." In this way, you can make an exhibit out of the legal description to be attached to various documents, such as the deed and seller's affidavit.

It is important to document everything. Although this may seem time-consuming initially, it will save time later in the closing process by preventing confusion. Confirm each party's responsibility by letter. The contract may not indicate who is to act as closing agent. This should be agreed upon by the parties as soon as possible and confirmed in writing. A letter should be sent to the other party or his or her attorney if legally represented to confirm the identity of the closing agent. If a lending institution is involved, a letter should be sent to the lender, confirming the documentation the lender is to prepare. A letter should be sent to your client as well, outlining the matters for which he or she is responsible.

As documentation comes in, review it thoroughly before checking it off on the worksheet as completed. There may be errors in a document, and you do not want to wait until the date of closing to make this discovery. Once documents are approved and/or tasks completed, be sure to put a check by the corresponding items on the worksheet. All closing documents should be in finalized form prior to the day of closing, as all parties to the transaction will want to review them in advance of closing. Never send originals for review. Keep them in your files and send photocopies. In the event it is imperative to send an original document, be sure to send it by certified mail, return receipt requested, or by overnight courier. Never let a document leave the file until a copy of it is made and inserted in its place.

PRECLOSING

The contract will indicate whether the purchaser is looking to obtain institutional financing as a condition for closing on the property. This is known as a financing contingency. If so, the contract will indicate how long the purchaser has to make a loan application as well as how long he or she has to obtain a loan commitment. The purchaser will be required to submit not only an application form, but various and sundry other items to the lender prior to obtaining loan approval, as noted in Chapter 10. Once a loan commitment is obtained, it generally will be valid only for a short duration. Therefore, it is important to review the loan commitment to determine its period of validity and make sure this period does not expire prior to the closing date. If there is a problem, the closing date may need to be changed, and this should be arranged by the parties as quickly as possible. An amendment to the contract may be required to change the closing date.

The loan commitment usually mandates that an appraisal of the property be done prior to the date of closing. The appraisal is the lending institution's assurance that the loan amount is not greater than the value of the property. This becomes important if the purchaser/borrower defaults and the lending institution has to foreclose on the property. The appraisal gives the lender assurance that it will most likely recoup the amount of the loan if it becomes necessary to foreclose on the property. The lender typically arranges for the appraisal, but the cost of the appraisal is charged to the purchaser.

If your firm is representing the seller, it may fall upon your party to provide an updated abstract or title commitment as stipulated in the contract with time periods. (Note that in some states, such as New York and New Jersey, the purchaser's attorney usually arranges for the title work.) You will want to find out from your client whether a current survey of the property exists. If your firm does not prepare title work in-house, make sure that the title company hired to prepare the commitment can do so within the contract deadlines. Notify the purchaser or his or her attorney as soon as the abstract or title commitment has been ordered. If there is a delay and the abstract or commitment cannot be completed within the contractually specified time frame, send the purchaser a copy of your client's current title policy for review in the interim period, as many of the exceptions to coverage on the current policy will appear in the upcoming commitment.

If your firm is representing the purchaser, once the title commitment is received, examine it to make sure that all information is set forth correctly. The current owner listed on the commitment should be the seller. Make sure the coverage amounts listed for the owner's policy and mortgagee's policy are correct. Check the legal description against the legal description in the contract for sale and purchase. Review the requirements to be satisfied prior to issuance of the policies and the exceptions to coverage. If any title problems exist, notify the seller immediately in writing. The contract for sale and purchase typically indicates the time period within which the seller must cure title defects. It also indicates the time period within which the purchaser must notify the seller of such defects, so review this portion of the contract carefully.

If the seller has one or more existing outstanding loans on the subject property, this loan must either be assumed by the purchaser or paid off at closing. Assuming the latter is the case, the firm representing the seller must send a written request to the appropriate lending institution asking for a **mortgage estoppel letter** (also referred to as a *payoff statement)* which specifies the amount to be paid to satisfy the debt. The mortgage estoppel letter will include (1) the outstanding balance of the loan as of a specified date, (2) the per diem interest on the loan from a specified date, (3) prepayment penalties, if any, (4) escrow amounts, if any, and (5) any other requirements to satisfy the loan. When writing to request a mortgage estoppel letter, include not only the seller's name and the property address but also the loan number. The seller should be able to provide you with this information.

If the purchaser is assuming the existing loan or taking title to the property subject to the existing loan, the seller's financing instruments must be reviewed to determine whether the loan may indeed be assumed or whether the instrument contains a due-on-sale clause. If assumption is permitted, the purchaser may still have to qualify with the lender, and the contract should indicate the time period within which this must be accomplished. Just as in the case of new financing, the lending institution will charge the purchaser certain processing and other fees. If there is an escrow account for interest reserves, escrowed taxes, and/or insurance, the seller must assign the escrow account to the purchaser. In turn, the purchaser must credit the seller on the closing statement for the amount the lender is holding in escrow.

The seller's most current tax bill for the property should be obtained, as the taxes must be apportioned between the seller and the purchaser. If the seller cannot find the bill, a copy should be obtained by making a written

mortgage estoppel letter: A letter specifying the amount to be paid to satisfy an outstanding loan debt.

request to the tax collector's office. Depending on the time of year, the seller may or may not have received the tax bill for the current year. If not, the current year's taxes will be estimated based on the most recent bill. Any adjustments can be made after the new bill is received. Additionally, the amounts of maintenance assessments paid to condominium associations or homeowners' associations must be confirmed by requesting this information in writing from the associations. If the property purchased is located within a condominium development or a development governed by a homeowners' association, it may be necessary to obtain approval by the association of the purchaser prior to closing. Check both state statutes and the governing condominium or homeowners' association documents to determine whether this is required.

The contract for sale and purchase will indicate the inspections to be made by the purchaser and the deadlines for these inspections. It will also indicate which party is to pay for the inspections. Should an inspection reveal a problem, such as termites or structural damage to the roof, the contract should be reviewed to determine the seller's responsibility to cure such problems. The contract usually will state that the seller has a specified time period within which to cure the defect. It may also state that the seller is only responsible for repairs up to a stated dollar amount or a percentage of the purchase price. The inspection dates should be monitored, and the purchaser should obtain inspection reports and receipts. Copies of these should be provided to the seller.

Lenders will have specific requirements for hazard and flood insurance to be effective on the day of closing. Some lenders will require that funds be escrowed for hazard and flood insurance premiums. If the property purchased is a condominium, it will be covered under a master policy held by the condominium association. A portion of the maintenance assessments pays for the unit owner's share of the master policy premiums. The lender will require a copy of the master policy. For other residential properties, a certificate of insurance should be obtained that specifies the amount of insurance, the type of coverage, and the dates of coverage.

If fixtures and/or personal property are included in the sale of the property, the UCC records must be searched to determine whether any financing statements have been filed that affect these items. Further, UCC-1 forms must be prepared to be filed for any fixtures and/or personal property that the lending institution has included in the financing instrument as security for the purchaser's loan. (Recall the example in Chapter 2.)

Schedule a final walk-through of the premises by the purchaser prior to closing so that if there is a problem, the seller can attempt to correct it prior to the scheduled closing date. If a cure cannot be accomplished prior to closing, a postclosing agreement and/or escrow may be established to address the problems identified at the walk-through. If the electricity has been turned off, arrange to have it turned on prior to the walk-through. When conducting the walk-through, the purchaser should have an itemized list of the fixtures and personal property (if any) that are to be transferred together with the real property. These items should be compared with the fixtures and personal property found on the property.

Most contracts for sale and purchase mandate that the purchaser pay the balance of the funds required to close and transfer title by cashier's check or wire transfer of funds. This means that the purchaser will need to obtain the check or arrange for the wire transfer before the date of closing. Therefore, the closing statement should be prepared in advance of closing so that the purchaser may be notified of his or her total costs.

Confirm the date of closing with all parties, the real estate broker(s), and the lending institution. The closing agent should arrange for checks to be disbursed or wire transfers to be made in accordance with the closing statement.

DOCUMENT PREPARATION AND EXECUTION

As noted, the contract for sale and purchase outlines the responsibilities of each party for document preparation. Although this, like most other items, is negotiable, in many states it is customary for the seller's attorney to prepare the majority of the closing documents, particularly those necessary for transferring marketable title to the purchaser. These documents would include the deed, the bill of sale (if personal property is transferred with the real property), the seller's affidavit (or no-lien affidavit), the continuous marriage affidavit if the seller is married, and the satisfaction of mortgage if the seller has an outstanding loan that is to be paid off at closing. Additionally, the contract may stipulate that the seller is to provide the title commitment and title policies. The seller's attorney may also prepare the closing statement.

The contract for sale and purchase should indicate the type of deed to be delivered by the seller upon closing. If no type of deed is specified, state law in most states indicates that a general warranty deed be used. If your state has statutorily prescribed forms for deeds, these should be used. As noted in Chapter 8, you should check your state statutes to determine the requirements for a valid deed in your state. The statutes should specify the number of witnesses necessary and the form of acknowledgment, if any, that is required. The marital status of the grantor(s) should be clearly stated on the deed as well as the manner in which title will be held by the grantee(s). Some state statutes require that the property parcel identification number be included on the deed as well as the social security number(s), or taxpayer's identification number(s), of the grantee(s) and the name and address of the person preparing the deed.

The legal description of the property must be inserted as well as the exceptions affecting title. Some attorneys prefer to list each exception separately, while others prefer to use a blanket statement such as "all easements, restrictions, and covenants of record." The deed restrictions should match the exceptions listed in the title commitment.

If the deed is to be executed by a corporation, you should check state statutes to determine the proper method of execution. Typically, deeds may be executed by the corporation's president or vice president in the presence of two subscribing witnesses. Alternatively, the deed may be signed by the president or vice president and embossed with the corporate seal.

As noted in Chapter 2, the bill of sale should include all items of personal property that are to be transferred with the real property with as much particularity as possible. The actual purchase price need not be indicated. It is customary to insert a nominal consideration, such as ten dollars. Some attorneys prepare a bill of sale even if only fixtures are to be transferred and no personal property is being sold. If the property is a condominium unit in which the fixtures transferred with the property are standard, then the description of the fixtures may be a general description.

The **seller's affidavit** (also referred to as a *no-lien affidavit*) is a sworn statement signed by the seller stating that there are no existing liens on the property that would encumber the purchaser's title. It includes (1) the legal description of the property; (2) a statement that the property is clear of all taxes, liens, encumbrances, and claims except those listed on the affidavit; (3) a statement that no improvements have been made on the property within the statutorily prescribed time frame (for example, thirty or ninety days) that could give rise to a statutory construction lien; (4) a statement that the seller is in exclusive possession of the property and that there are no leases or options pertaining to the property except those listed on the affidavit; and (5) a statement as to the purpose of executing the affidavit (for example, to induce the purchaser to purchase or the title company to issue a title policy).

If the seller(s) is/are married, a **continuous marriage affidavit** should be prepared, which is a sworn statement verifying the marital status of the seller(s). It includes (1) the legal description of the property, (2) the date of marriage, and (3) a statement that the affiants have lived together as husband and wife from that date, that the marriage was never dissolved, and that at the present time they are husband and wife.

The seller may also prepare a **nonforeign certification** (discussed later) to certify that the seller is not a *foreign person* as that term is defined in section 1445 of the Internal Revenue Code and that monies need not be withheld from the sale for tax purposes.

If the seller has an outstanding loan that is to be paid off, the seller should prepare a satisfaction and release of mortgage to be signed by the seller's lender. As discussed in Chapter 10, the satisfaction and release of mortgage nullifies the mortgage lien on the real property. It is recorded when the new deed and new financing instrument are recorded. The satisfaction sets forth (1) the name of the holder of the financing instrument, (2) the person who executed the financing instrument, (3) the principal amount of the loan, (4) the records book and page number in which the financing instrument was recorded, (5) the legal description of the real property securing the note, and (6) a statement that full payment and satisfaction of the note and financing instrument has been made. Check your state statutes to determine your state's particular requirements. It is a common requirement that the signator's signature be witnessed and acknowledged for recording purposes.

If your firm is acting as the closing agent, it will have to fill out a 1099 reporting form, which reports the transaction to the Internal Revenue Service (discussed later in the text). Additionally, many states require a state department of revenue form to be filed.

If your firm is representing the lender in the transaction, you will have to prepare the promissory note and financing instrument to be executed by the purchaser at closing. (These documents are discussed in detail in Chapter 10.) Once the note is drafted, it must be executed by the borrower exactly as the borrower's name appears on the deed. The note may be executed on the reverse side by the guarantors (if applicable). Alternatively, the guarantors may execute a separate guaranty document. The note should be drafted with

seller's affidavit: A sworn statement signed by the seller stating that there are no existing liens on the property that would encumber the purchaser's title.

continuous marriage affidavit: A sworn statement verifying the marital status of the sellers.

nonforeign certification: A statement certifying that the seller is not a foreign person as that term is defined in section 1445 of the Internal Revenue Code, and that monies need not be withheld from the sale for tax purposes.

care, as no markings for corrections or additions should appear on the face of the note.

The financing instrument, be it a deed of trust or a mortgage instrument, should include the name(s) of the borrower(s) exactly as they appear on the deed. If any riders are to be attached to the instrument (for example, a condominium rider or a PUD rider), these should be executed as well as the financing instrument. Witnessing and acknowledgment should be in compliance with your state statutes. Make sure that the date on the note and the date on the financing instrument are identical. It is common for lenders to require the signature of a spouse on the note and financing instrument even if that spouse is not included in the title to the deed.

The type of closing statement to be prepared will depend on the type of closing in question. Most residential transactions require that a HUD-1 Uniform Settlement Statement be used. (This type of closing statement is discussed in great detail later in the chapter.). A HUD-1 statement need not be used for commercial transactions. In addition to the closing statement, the parties may ask for separate buyer's and seller's statements, each detailing the debits and credits of the respective party. A HUD-1 statement must be signed by all parties. The buyer's and seller's statements are signed by each respective party.

CLOSING COSTS

In addition to the purchase price, the buyer will have to pay for a number of other items associated with closing on the loan and closing on the property as set forth in the contract. The seller also will have certain items deducted from the purchase price. Recording fees, brokerage charges, and attorneys' fees are some of the items considered closing costs associated with a real estate transaction. Items owed *by* a party will appear in the debit column of a closing statement; items owed *to* a party will appear in the credit column of a closing statement. Items that are paid in advance or arrears and are to be apportioned *between* the parties are referred to as *prorations*. The chart found in Figure 12–1 sets forth the common closing costs charged to the parties. Note that which party is charged for each item may vary depending on the terms of the contract, state law, or what is customary in a particular locale. For example, in some areas, it is more common for the seller to pay for such items as the title commitment, owner's title policy, and/or survey, while in other areas it is more common for the purchaser to bear these costs. To make the determination, always look to the contract for sale and purchase first, then to statutory law and custom.

Reviewing the chart, it is customary for the purchaser to pay all costs associated with the obtaining of a loan. Lenders may charge loan origination fees (a percentage of the loan amount, such as 1%) and discount points (a percentage of the loan amount, such as 1.5%). If the loan is a VA loan, however, the seller must pay for any discount points charged. Lenders may also charge appraisal fees, credit report fees, inspection fees for sending their own inspectors out to the property, fees for the processing of the mortgage insurance application, document preparation fees, assumption fees if the existing loan is to be assumed by the purchaser, and so forth. All or some of these fees may be paid at closing. If they are to be paid outside of closing, the closing statement

FIGURE 12-1
Common closing costs

COMMON CLOSING COSTS

Item	Purchaser's Cost	Seller's Cost	Prorated
Loan fees (e.g., discount points, loan origination fees)	X		
Attorneys' fees	X	X	
Hazard and flood insurance (new)	X		
Hazard and flood insurance (assigned to purchaser)			X
Title commitment	X		
Title insurance:			
(a) owner's policy	X		
(b) mortgagee's policy	X		
Termite inspection	X		
Roof inspection	X		
Survey	X		
Recording of financing instruments	X		
Recording of deed	X		
Recording of satisfaction of mortgage		X	
Documentary stamps on deed		X	
Documentary stamps on financing instruments	X		
Intangible tax on new financing	X		
Broker's commission		X	
Real property taxes			X
Utilities			X
Condo maintenance			X
HOA maintenance			X
Special assessments			X
Rent (if income-producing property)			X
Interest on loan (if loan assumed by purchaser)			X

typically will indicate this by the insertion of P.O.C. (Paid Outside Closing) next to the item.

If the seller is paying off an existing loan at closing, there may be certain charges accruing to the seller. For example, if the seller's financing instrument specifies that a prepayment penalty charge is to be paid if the loan is paid off before a specified time period, a penalty charge may be required of the seller. Therefore, it is important to review the seller's loan instruments prior to closing.

In addition to the items payable in connection with the loan, the lender may require that the purchaser pay certain items in advance, such as interest. Interest on loans is paid in arrears. This means that the mortgage interest payment made in April pays the interest owed for March. If the closing is to take place on the 15th of May, the purchaser would not be paying the interest for May until June. The lender may request that the interest owed from May 15th until the end of May be paid at closing. If a mortgage insurance premium is to be charged in connection with the loan, the lender may request that the premium for a specified number of months be paid in advance at closing. Hazard insurance and flood insurance are other items that the lender may require to be paid in advance upon closing.

The lender may require the purchaser to prepay hazard insurance and show proof of policy effective as of date of closing with the lender as a loss payee, or may require that the hazard, flood, or mortgage insurance premiums for a specified number of months be held in reserve by the lender. The same may be true with real property taxes. Many mortgage payments are PITI payments (principal, interest, taxes, and insurance), whereby each monthly mortgage payment includes not only a payment of interest and a portion of the principal, but also one-twelfth of the annual real property taxes and insurance on the property. In this manner, the lender guarantees that a real property tax lien will not accrue on the property with priority over the mortgage. The lender also is assured that the insurance coverage is paid to protect the collateral. In such a situation, when the tax bill is sent out, the original bill goes directly to the lender, who pays the real property taxes out of the escrow held in reserve for taxes. The same is true for the insurance.

The seller or purchaser may pay for the title examination. The party paying for the policies may differ from county to county, as noted earlier. In addition to the policy premiums, title agents usually charge extra for each endorsement attached to the policy. Thus, if the purchaser is buying a condominium, for example, a condominium endorsement may be attached to the title policy, and an additional charge will be added for this endorsement. (For a discussion of title endorsements, see Chapter 11.)

Each party is responsible for paying for his or her own attorneys' fees. Because the seller's attorney often is responsible for the majority of the document preparation, and the lender prepares the loan documentation, many purchasers choose not to be represented by an attorney in simple residential transactions. As noted, the closing agent may be a title company, a lender, an escrow agent, or a law firm. An additional charge may be added for serving as closing agent. This may be paid by one or the other of the parties, or it may be split between the two parties.

The seller is responsible for the broker's commission unless the broker is a buyer's broker (discussed in Chapter 6). The broker's fee may be a flat fee or may be a specified percentage of the sales price. If more than one broker is involved in the transaction, the commission is split between the brokers. Note that the commission is not always split evenly; therefore, the contract between the seller and listing broker must be consulted.

If the purchaser has put down an earnest money deposit that is being held in escrow by the broker, the broker's fee may be deducted from the escrowed amount, and any remaining monies from the deposit are credited to the seller. In some areas this is handled differently, however, with the broker giving the lender's attorney a check and the lender's attorney cutting the broker a check for the commission amount. If no deposit was made, or if the deposit is held in escrow with someone other than the broker, a check will have to be disbursed at closing to the broker(s) for the commission owed.

Governmental agencies charge fees for the recording of documents. The fees charged vary from county to county. They usually are a specified amount per page recorded (for example, $6.00 per page). The documents to be recorded include the deed, the satisfaction of mortgage for the seller's paid-off loan, and the new financing instruments.

City, county, and/or state authorities may also charge documentary stamp taxes on the deed and financing instrument. As noted in Chapter 8, the documentary stamp tax on the deed is calculated using the purchase price of the property. For example, the tax may be $.60 per each $100. If the purchase price is $100,000, you would divide this amount by 100, which would equal 1,000. You would then multiply 1,000 by .60 to arrive at the documentary stamp tax of $600.

The documentary stamp tax on the financing instrument is calculated using the principal amount of the loan. If the tax is $.32 per each $100, and the principal loan amount is $50,000, you would divide this amount by 100, which would equal 500. You would then multiply 500 by .32 to arrive at the documentary stamp tax of $160. In some jurisdictions, you are required to round up to the next increment of 100 before calculating the tax. For example, if the amount of the loan is $69,935, you would round up to $70,000 before dividing by 100 and then multiplying by the tax amount. Some governmental authorities charge an intangible tax on new loans (assumed loans would not be subject to the tax in this instance). The tax charged is multiplied by the principal amount of the loan. For example, if the loan amount is $30,000 and the intangible tax charged is two mills (.002), you would multiply 30,000 by .002 to arrive at the intangible tax of $60.

Certain items must be prorated between the purchaser and the seller. These items include, but are not limited to, real property taxes, rents paid or owed (if the property is rented to tenants), utility bills, loan interest if the existing loan is assumed by the purchaser, condominium maintenance fees, homeowners' association maintenance fees, special assessments, and hazard and flood insurance if the seller is assigning an existing policy to the purchaser. For example, if the closing is taking place on June 6th, it is not fair for either the purchaser or the seller to pay the tax bill for the entire year. Each must pay his or her share of the tax bill. To prorate an item, there are several steps involved, as noted in Figure 12–2.

Consider the following example. The closing is taking place on March 10th. The taxes for the year have not yet been paid. The tax bill is $2,000. The hazard insurance policy owned by the seller is to be assigned to the purchaser. It is a two-year policy. The premium is $1,000. The property is a condominium unit for which maintenance assessments are paid monthly. The monthly assessment is $200. Finally, the purchaser is assuming the seller's loan. The annual interest is $4,000. Each of these items will have to be prorated prior to closing. The parties are using a 365-day year (note that in a leap year, one would use a 366-day year). The actual days in the month are used to calculate monthly prorations. The day of closing is to be the proration date, and the day of closing is given to the purchaser.

To calculate the portion of the annual tax bill owed by each of the parties, you must first divide the bill by 365. The tax bill is $2,000, so dividing 2,000 by 365, you get 5.4794. You then determine how many days in the year belong to each of the parties. January has 31 days, February has 28 (except in a leap year), and the seller has 9 days in March, so the seller's days are 68. The remainder of the days, namely 297, belong to the purchaser. The taxes have not been paid in advance; the purchaser must pay for them when the bill comes. Therefore, the seller owes the purchaser. You take 68 (the number of seller's days) and multiply it by 5.4794 (the daily rate) to get $372.5992. This is

PRORATION STEPS

1. Determine the proration year used (365 or 360 days).
2. Determine the proration month used (actual days in the month or 30-day months).
3. Determine the proration date (for example, the date of closing, the day before closing, or some other date).
4. Determine to whom the day of closing belongs if the closing date is used as the proration date. (Does the closing day belong to the seller or the purchaser?)
5. Divide the amount of the bill accordingly (for example, by the number of days in the year for an annual bill such as taxes, by the number of days in the month for a monthly bill such as interest).
6. Determine how many days in the time frame (for example, month, year, quarter) belong to the seller and how many days belong to the purchaser.
7. Determine whether the amount is paid in arrears or in advance. If paid in advance, use the number of days of the year assigned to the purchaser to calculate and then credit the seller and debit the purchaser. If paid in arrears, use the number of days of the year assigned to the seller to calculate, and then credit the purchaser.

rounded up to $372.60. This is the amount of the bill owed by the seller. This amount would be debited the seller and credited to the purchaser at closing.

The next proration is the hazard insurance premium. The total amount of the policy is $1,000. The premium is for two years, so to break it down to a daily rate, you would divide not by 365, but by 730 to determine the daily cost. Thus, 1,000 divided by 730 equals 1.3698. If the policy was purchased at the beginning of this year, the purchaser owes for the remainder of the year, namely 297 days, and for the number of days in the second year, 365. Added together, the number of days owed by the purchaser is 662. This amount, 662, multiplied by the daily rate of 1.3698 equals 906.8076, which is rounded to $906.81. This is the amount that would be debited the purchaser and credited to the seller.

The third proration is for the monthly condominium maintenance fee, which is paid in advance. The monthly charge is $200. There are 31 days in March. The seller has 9 days in the month, and the purchaser has 22 days. The monthly charge is divided by 31 to arrive at a daily rate of 6.4516. Because the fee was paid in advance, the purchaser owes the seller, so you take 22 (the number of days allocated to the purchaser) and multiply it by 6.4516 to arrive at 141.9352, which is rounded to $141.94. This amount is debited the purchaser and credited to the seller.

The final proration is for the interest on the loan. Interest is paid in arrears. This means that the interest owed for the month of closing, March, will not be paid until April. Therefore, the seller owes the purchaser for the seller's portion of the March interest payment. The annual interest is $4,000. This is divided by 12 to arrive at a monthly interest of 333.333. This amount is then divided by the number of days in the month, in this case 31, to arrive at a daily rate of 10.7526. The seller owes the purchaser, so the seller's days are used in the calculation. Thus, 9 multiplied by 10.7526 equals 99.7734, which rounded equals $99.77. This amount is debited the seller and credited to the purchaser.

THE HUD UNIFORM SETTLEMENT STATEMENT

As noted in Chapter 10, the Real Estate Settlement Procedures Act of 1974 (RESPA) was enacted to ensure that residential borrowers receive full disclosure of all charges they are to pay at closing. This act requires that a uniform settlement statement, or closing statement, be utilized in all nonexempt closing transactions. This closing statement, the HUD-1 Uniform Settlement Statement, is often referred to as a "HUD statement." HUD stands for the Department of Housing and Urban Development.

The HUD-1 statement gives a detailed account of all charges connected with a residential transaction. The purchaser, seller, and lender each receive a copy of the statement at closing. The statement is signed and dated by both the seller and the purchaser. The purchaser is referred to as the "borrower" on the statement. A copy of a blank HUD-1 statement is provided in Figure 12–3. This statement is mandated when the transaction includes a federally related loan that is used, in whole or in part, to finance the purchase of residential properties, more particularly one-to-four-family dwellings. Condominiums and cooperatives are included in this definition. Transactions that are exempt from RESPA are all-cash transactions, transactions involving commercial loans, sales in which the existing loan is taken subject to or assumed (unless an assumption fee of more than $50 is charged), loans on vacant land, and loans to purchase property consisting of twenty-five acres or more. Although RESPA does not mandate the use of the HUD-1 statement for these exempt transactions, parties may want to use a HUD-1 statement in any transaction.

The HUD-1 statement is divided into alphabetical sections, from A through L. Section A is simply the title of the closing statement. Section B pertains to the specifics of the loan: the type of loan, the loan number, the mortgage insurance case number, and the file number are inserted in this section. Section C is a note pertaining to items paid outside of closing. Section D requires the name(s) and address(es) of the borrower(s). Section E requires the name(s) and address(es) of the seller(s) and also provides a space for the insertion of the seller's taxpayer identification number, which, if the seller is an individual, is the seller's social security number. Section F requires the name and address of the lender. Section G is where the property location is inserted. This is typically a street address, although one can insert a legal description. Section H is for the insertion of the name and address of the settlement agent; the agent's taxpayer identification number is inserted here as well. The closing date is inserted in section I.

Section J is a summary of the borrower's transaction, with the 100s relating to the borrower's debits and the 200s relating to the borrower's credits. Inserted in the 100s would be the contract price (line 101), the price of any personal property sold to the borrower (line 102), prorated items for which the seller has paid in advance (lines 106 through 112), and the closing costs to be paid by the borrower (inserted in line 103). (The closing costs are itemized in section L of the statement.) Line 120 totals the items to be debited the

A. SETTLEMENT STATEMENT

United States Department of Housing and Urban Development OMB No. 2502-0265

B. Type of Loan	Loan Number	Mortgage Ins. Case Number	File Number

C. Note: This form is furnished to give you a statement of actual settlement costs. Amounts paid to and by the settlement agent are shown. Items marked "p.o.c." were paid outside of closing, they are shown here for informational purposes and are not included in the totals.

D. Name and Address of Borrower:	E. Name and Address of Seller:
	TIN: _____

F. Name and Address of Lender:	G. Property Location:

H. Settlement Agent / Place of Settlement:	I. Settlement Date:
TIN: _____	

J. Summary of Borrower's Transaction		K. Summary of Seller's Transaction	
100 Gross amount due from borrower		**400 Gross amount due to seller**	
101 Contract sales price		401 Contract sales price	
102 Personal property		402 Personal property	
103 Settlement charges to borrower [1400]		403	
104		404	
105		405	
Adjustments for items paid by seller in advance		*Adjustments for items paid by seller in advance*	
106 City/town taxes / / to / /		406 City/town taxes / / to / /	
107 County taxes / / to / /		407 County taxes / / to / /	
108 Assessments / / to / /		408 Assessments / / to / /	
109		409	
110		410	
111		411	
112		412	
120 Gross Amount Due From borrower		**420 Gross Amount Due To Seller**	
200 Amounts paid by or on behalf of borrower		**500 Reductions in amount due to seller**	
201 Deposit or earnest money		501 Excess deposit (see instructions)	
202 Principal amount of new loan(s)		502 Settlement charges to seller [1400]	
203 Existing loan(s) taken subject to		503 Existing loan(s) taken subject to	
204		504 Payoff of first mortgage	
205		505 Payoff of second mortgage	
206		506 Deposit retained by	
207		507 (Deposit disbursed))	
208		508	
209 Mortgage in favor of seller		509 Mortgage in favor of seller	
Adjustments for items unpaid by seller		*Adjustments for items unpaid by seller*	
210 City/town taxes / / to / /		510 City/town taxes / / to / /	
211 County taxes / / to / /		511 County taxes / / to / /	
212 Assessments / / to / /		512 Assessments / / to / /	
213		513	
214		514	
215		515	
216		516	
217		517	
218		518	
219		519	
220 Total Paid By/For Borrower		**520 Total Reductions In Amount Due Seller**	
300 Cash At Settlement From/To Borrower		**600 Cash At Settlement To/From Seller**	
301 Gross amount due from borrower [120]		601 Gross amount due to seller [420]	
302 Less amount paid by/for borrower [220]		602 Less reductions in amount due seller [520]	
303 Cash From/(To) Borrower		**603 Cash To/(From) Seller**	

SUBSTITUTE FORM 1099-S SELLER'S STATEMENT: This is important tax information and is being furnished to the Internal Revenue Service. If you are required to file a return, a negligence penalty or other sanction may be imposed on you if this item is required to be reported and the IRS determines that it has not been reported. The information in Boxes E, G, H, and I, the amount on Line 401 and the amount(s) of any real estate tax adjustments appearing on Lines 406 through 412 are reported to the IRS on Form 1099-S.

REQUEST FOR SELLER'S TAXPAYER IDENTIFICATION AND CERTIFICATION: You, the Seller (see Box E) are required by law to provide the Settlement Agent (see Box H) with your correct taxpayer identification number. If you do not provide the Settlement Agent with your correct taxpayer identification number, you may be subject to civil or criminal penalties imposed by law. By signing the following page of this Settlement Statement, you, under penalties of perjury, certify that the number shown on this statement (see Box E - "TIN") is your correct taxpayer identification number.

Revis Closing System for Windows™

HUD-1 (Rev 3/86)

FIGURE 12–3 HUD-1 Uniform Settlement Statement

L. Settlement Charges

			Paid from borrower's funds at settlement	Paid from seller's funds at settlement
700	**Total Sales/Broker's Commission** Based on $ @ % =			
	Division of commission (line 700) as follows:			
701	to			
702	to			
703	Commission paid at settlement			
704	Commission retained by			
800	**Items Payable In Connection With Loan**			
801	Loan origination fee %			
802	Loan Discount %			
803	Appraisal fee to:			
804	Credit report to:			
805	Lender's inspection fee			
806	Mortgage insurance application fee to			
807	Assumption fee			
808				
809				
810				
811				
900	**Items Required By Lender To Be Paid In Advance**			
901	Interest from / / to / / / day			
902	Mortgage insurance premium for months to			
903	Hazard insurance premium for years to			
904	Flood insurance premium for years to			
905				
1000	**Reserves Deposited With Lender**			
1001	Hazard insurance months @ per month			
1002	Mortgage insurance months @ per month			
1003	City property taxes months @ per month			
1004	County property taxes months @ per month			
1005	Annual assessments months @ per month			
1006	Flood insurance months @ per month			
1007	months @ per month			
1008				
1100	**Title Charges**			
1101	Settlement or closing fee to			
1102	Abstract or title search to			
1103	Title examination to			
1104	Title insurance binder to			
1105	Document preparation to			
1106	Notary fees to			
1107	Attorney's fees to includes above items ( )			
1108	Title insurance fee to includes above items ( )			
1109	Lender's coverage premium			
1110	Owner's coverage premium			
1111				
1112				
1113				
1200	**Government Recording And Transfer Charges**			
1201	Recording fees: Deed Mortgage Release			
1202	City/county tax/stamps: Deed Mortgage			
1203	State tax/stamps: Deed Mortgage			
1204				
1205				
1300	**Additional Settlement Charges**			
1301	Survey to			
1302	Pest inspection to			
1303				
1304				
1305				
1306				
1307				
1400	**Total Settlement Charges**			

I have carefully reviewed the HUD-1 Settlement Statement and to the best of my knowledge and belief, it is a true and accurate statement of all receipts and disbursements made on my account or by me in this transaction. I further certify that I have received a copy of this HUD-1 Settlement Statement.

Borrower:_____ Date:_____   Seller:_____ Date:_____

Borrower:_____ Date:_____   Seller:_____ Date:_____

Borrower:_____ Date:_____   Seller:_____ Date:_____

Borrower:_____ Date:_____   Seller:_____ Date:_____

The HUD-1 Settlement Statement which I have prepared is a true and accurate account of this transaction. I have caused or will cause the funds to be disbursed in accordance with this statement.

Settlement Agent:_____ Date:_____

WARNING: It is a crime to knowingly make a false statement to the United States on this or any similar form. Penalties upon conviction include a fine and imprisonment. For details see Title 18 US Code Section 1001 and Section 1010.

HUD-1 (Rev 3/86)

Reproduced through the courtesy of Real Estate Expert Systems Associates, Inc.

FIGURE 12–3 (continued)

borrower. The 200s cover items paid by or on behalf of the borrower. This includes any earnest money deposit paid (line 201), the amount of the financing (lines 202 and 203), the amount of any purchase money mortgage to be held by the seller (line 209), and prorated items unpaid as yet by the seller (lines 210 through 219). The borrower's credits are totaled in line 220. The 300s subtract the borrower's credits from the borrower's debits to arrive at the amount of money owed by the borrower at closing.

Section K is a summary of the seller's transaction, with the 400s relating to the seller's credits and the 500s relating to the seller's debits. The seller's credits include the sales price of the property (line 401), the sales price for any personal property involved in the transaction (line 402), and prorated items paid in advance by the seller (lines 406 through 412). The seller's credits are totaled in line 420. The seller's debits include the payoff of the existing loan (line 504), the closing costs charged to the seller (line 502), which are itemized in section L, and any prorated items for which the seller has not yet paid (lines 510 through 519). If the seller is providing a purchase money mortgage loan to the borrower, this amount is debited the seller in line 509. The seller's debits are totaled in line 520. The 600s subtract the seller's debits from the seller's credits to arrive at the sum of money to be received by the seller at closing.

Section L itemizes the closing costs charged to each party. The 700s relate to brokerage commissions. The total commission is inserted in line 700. Lines 701 and 702 will show any commission split. Line 703 is where the commission is charged to the seller. This assumes that the earnest money deposit made by the borrower is held by someone other than the broker. If the deposit has been retained by the broker in escrow, the broker will subtract the commission amount from the deposit and give the seller a check for any excess. If there is any excess from the deposit, this amount should be inserted in line 501 with an indication that the excess is to be paid outside closing (P.O.C.), and the total amount of the commission is inserted in line 703.

The 800s pertain to items payable in connection with the loan. These include the loan origination fee (line 801), discount points (line 802), appraisal fees (line 803), credit report fees (line 804), lender's inspection fees (line 805), mortgage insurance application fees (line 806), assumption fees (line 807), and any other item charged by the lender, such as document preparation fees or courier fees. As stated earlier, most if not all of these items will be charged to the borrower.

The 900s pertain to items required by the lender to be paid in advance. These include interest on the loan (line 901) and various insurance premiums (lines 902 through 904). The 1000s pertain to reserves deposited with the lender for insurance, taxes, and assessments. The 1100s pertain to title charges. Notaries' fees and attorneys' fees are also found in this section (lines 1106 and 1107, respectively). If a separate settlement or closing fee is charged, this is inserted in line 1101.

Government-related fees, such as those charged for the recording of documents, documentary stamp taxes, and intangible taxes, are found in the 1200s. The 1300s are for miscellaneous charges, such as pest inspections, surveys, and so forth. The total closing cost charges for each party are inserted in line 1400. Each borrower and seller signs and dates the statement on the bottom of the second page. The settlement or closing agent who prepared the statement also signs and dates it.

REAL ESTATE CLOSING SOFTWARE

At times the paperwork involved in the average real estate closing may seem endless, and the task of putting together a final closing package may seem daunting. Fortunately, many real estate law firms, title companies, and lending institutions are taking advantage of an array of real estate closing software that simplifies the documentation process.

The software programs presently on the market differ in pricing, specialized features, and interfacing capabilities with other programs, but they have a number of common aspects. They all can print out the HUD-1 Uniform Settlement Statement and the basic closing documents, and they can automatically calculate prorations and recalculate should last-minute changes occur. The majority of the available programs work with either DOS or Windows applications (DoubleTime is available only in Windows and MacCLOZ is designed to work with MacIntosh systems). Most of the programs are used nationwide (Soft Design specializes in the Carolinas). While the primary function of these programs is to prepare the HUD-1 statement, they are capable of doing much more. They can print checks, loan amortization schedules, disbursement summaries, separate buyer's and seller's statements, and 1099 forms for filing with the Internal Revenue Service. (See a discussion of 1099 reporting requirements in the following text.) The key to these software programs is the single-entry concept, whereby in inputting information once, the relevant information appears in each document. For example, in typing the legal description of a property once, the legal description will appear in the deed, the seller's affidavit, the title commitment, and so forth. This is particularly useful because it can cut down not only on time but also on the possibility of error. If the legal description is checked for accuracy once, it will be reproduced accurately in all of the documents.

Most of the closing software can be customized to be state- and county-specific, which makes calculations effortless. Besides prorations, the systems can accurately and automatically calculate your county's recording fees, documentary stamp taxes, and intangible taxes. If the closing date changes, one need only input the new date once and it will appear on all corresponding documents. Additionally, the program will automatically recalculate all prorations on the closing statement.

Some of the software programs, for example Spencer Systems, DoubleTime, and SoftPro's ProTrax, have scheduling and calendar functions. They keep track of multiple closings on closing calendars, and they act as tickler files, tracking the parties responsible for various closing tasks.

Many of the programs have user-friendly main menus from which one can choose to enter or change closing data; print documents, checks, or amortization schedules; or prepare various reports. A number of programs use a look-alike HUD-1 statement for the initial inputting of data. DoubleTime uses a closing file concept whereby one inputs information based on tabs in the closing file. Some systems (such as Display Systems and DoubleTime) have their own word processing programs, while others (such as Reesa, Spencer Systems, SoftPro, Sulcus, TurboCLOSE, and MacCLOZ) interface with WordPerfect, Microsoft Word, or both. Landtech Real Estate Settlement System has its own word processing program, Landword, but also interfaces with WordPerfect and Microsoft Word. A number of the programs interface with Quicken for escrow accounting.

Each software program has its own special features. For example, DoubleTime provides closing file checklists and on-line access to Attorneys' Fund Title Notes and the Standard Commitment Clauses Handbook. It also provides electronic delivery of updates. SoftPro's ProScan allows one to scan documents into the program. Soft Design's Attorney's Deed Check software prepares an accurate professional graphic plot of a metes and bounds description with the bearings and distances printed directly on the lines of the map. This enables one to check a metes and bounds description for accuracy. Spencer Systems and SoftPro's ProIndex offer title plant programs for computerized posting, automatic indexing, and searching real property records.

Some of the real estate software programs are sold as complete systems (for example, Reesa, DoubleTime, Soft Design, Sulcus, and MacCLOZ), while others are sold in modules (for example, Spencer Systems, Display Systems, and SoftPro). One purchases the modules that one uses most often. Thus, if the firm never prepares title work, the firm would not purchase the module for preparing title policies. The licensing fee charged will depend on whether the system is to support single or multiple users. It may also vary depending on the number of closing files open at any one time. DoubleTime charges a minimal licensing fee and then charges on a per transaction basis, allowing the smaller firm or sole practitioner the opportunity to use the same software as a larger firm, but with less cost. All software companies charge an annual maintenance fee, although the amount of the fee varies.

Many attorneys have their paralegals research the available real estate closing software programs on the premise that the paralegal will be using the program on a daily basis. Besides the cost factor, both the paralegal and attorney should consider several other factors. They must check to see if the system is compatible with the firm's current computer hardware—its megabyte and RAM capabilities. The training and technical support provided by the software company is crucial. The length of time during which free technical support is offered varies considerably from company to company. Some companies will provide on-site training for no extra cost, while others charge for this service. Additionally, the system must be user-friendly and conducive to working with speed and accuracy. A busy real estate firm can have several closings scheduled daily, and the software system purchased should allow the paralegal to prepare the requisite documentation quickly enough to meet the needs of the firm.

It is advisable to obtain demonstration copies of the software programs prior to purchasing one of them. Some companies provide demonstration disks that can be used for a specified time period (for example, thirty days or six months). These disks may or may not limit the number of closing files that may be available at a given time. Reesa closing software has a demonstration program that can be downloaded by accessing www.reesa.com.

THE CLOSING

The closing date, time, and place must be confirmed with all parties, including the lender, in advance. Each party will want to review the closing documents and closing statement prior to the date of closing. Assuming all is in order, the paralegal should make a list of those parties signing original documents and those parties receiving original documents. For example, the seller signs the original deed, but once back from recording, the purchaser receives the original. Similarly, the purchaser signs the original note and financing instrument, but the lender receives the originals while the purchaser receives copies.

The paralegal must also make sure that a notary will be available to notarize documents at closing, that the requisite number of witnesses, if required, are available to sign necessary documents, and that the corporate secretary is available to attest signatures if a party to the transaction is a corporation. For example, grantees (purchasers) cannot be witnesses on deeds, so in jurisdictions requiring two witnesses for a valid deed, two nonparties must be available to witness the document. The paralegal should have a complete set of unexecuted copies of documents for the client file prior to closing.

If institutional financing is involved in the transaction, that portion of the closing often occurs first, with the purchaser executing the financing instruments before the other closing documents are executed. The parties should not be rushed through this process. Although the purchaser may have seen copies of the financing instruments prior to closing, the lender's representative (if present) should highlight the salient points once again prior to execution of the note and financing instrument. If the purchaser has any last-minute questions, the appropriate time to ask them is before, not after, signing the loan documentation. Once the loan portion of the closing has taken place, the lender's check for the loan amount may be deposited in the closing agent's trust account as part of the funds to be paid to the seller. Alternatively, the lender may wire the loan proceeds into the closing agent's trust account.

Next, the closing agent should review each closing document with the parties prior to execution and make certain that each document is executed, witnessed, and acknowledged (when applicable) in full before moving on to the next. For example, the purchaser should review the deed to determine whether the exceptions listed match those in the title commitment. The names of the parties should be rechecked for proper spellings and to ensure that they conform throughout the set of documents. The parties should bring along forms of identification, as the notary will require proper identification prior to notarization.

Once all documents are properly executed, the closing agent should retrieve them so that the appropriate documents may be recorded. If the seller's address is to change as a result of the transaction, the seller's new address must be obtained.

The parties may have prepared separate checks for disbursement to cover closing costs, or one cashier's check from the purchaser may be made out to the closing agent to be deposited into the escrow account for disbursal by the closing agent. In the latter situation, the paralegal must ensure that separate checks in the appropriate sums are cut from the account for brokerage commissions, title company fees, and so forth. A disbursement summary should be prepared and provided to the parties. In some states, all documents must be recorded prior to disbursing closing proceeds, so state law should be checked.

If the purchaser is providing a check other than a cashier's check (assuming the contract for sale and purchase does not specify payment in the form of a cashier's check), be aware that the Federal Reserve Board allows local checks to be held up to three business days and nonlocal checks to be held up to seven business days. Cashier's checks should clear immediately. If anything but a cashier's check, electronic transfer, or cash is provided by the purchaser, disbursement should not be made until the check has cleared.

Finally, the keys and any other pertinent items (for example, garage door openers or appliance warranties) must be given to the purchaser.

POSTCLOSING

The paralegal's responsibilities do not end with the closing. There are a number of postclosing matters that need attention. No documents should leave the office until copies have been made for the parties and the file. Certain disbursements will be made at the closing itself, while others will be made after closing. These latter disbursements include a check or wire transfer to pay off the seller's existing loan and checks for recording fees and documentary stamp taxes (depending upon the jurisdiction, some of these government-related charges may be combined in one check). Further, if your firm has acted as escrow agent, you must send interest statements to the party who received the interest on the deposit(s) at closing.

The original satisfaction of mortgage and payoff check or wire transfer must be sent immediately to the seller's lender. This is often done by courier service. The paralegal should prepare the satisfaction for signature by the lender as well as a cover letter and a self-addressed, postage-paid envelope for return of the executed satisfaction to the firm. Preferably, the envelope should be a Federal Express or similar delivery envelope. Examples of a satisfaction and corresponding cover letter are found in the next chapter.

Once the executed satisfaction is received, it should be sent, together with the original deed and original financing instrument, to the recording clerk's office, along with the appropriate fees. These documents should be sent by courier, if possible, with a cover letter explaining the items covered by the check. Again, a self-addressed, postage-paid envelope should be included with the package.

Once the original documents are returned from the recording office, the paralegal must provide the recording information to the title company so that the owner's and mortgagee's policies can be prepared. A photocopy of each recorded document should be kept in the client file for future reference to the recording information stamped on the document. If the paralegal's supervising attorney is a title agent, the paralegal may take part in the preparation of the policies. Prior to issuance of the policies, the title search must be updated.

Once the title policies are prepared, they should be reviewed for accuracy. The legal description should be checked, the coverage amounts should be checked, and the exceptions should be compared with a copy of the marked-up title commitment. If an abstract of title was used for the title examination, it should be sent to the purchaser or the purchaser's lender (whichever is indicated by the parties).

Next, closing packages must be organized for the purchaser, seller, and lender. The paralegal must organize the documents in chronological order, providing originals and copies as appropriate. The document packages should include a closing binder index. (Closing package organization and closing binder indices are discussed in detail in the next chapter.) In the interim between the recordation of the closing documents and the preparation of the final closing binders, the attorneys representing the respective parties may write letters to their clients describing the documents to be received. The clients can then check the closing binder packages against the attorneys' letters to make sure that all documentation has been provided. Once all these tasks are completed, the client file can be closed.

TAX-RELATED ITEMS

In 1985, an amendment to the Foreign Investment in Real Property Tax Act (FIRPTA) went into effect. Section 1445 of the Internal Revenue Code requires any individual or entity that purchases nonresidential property for more than $400,000 from a foreign person to withhold ten percent of the purchase price for the Internal Revenue Service. The code defines *foreign persons* as foreign nationals who do not hold permanent resident visas. This definition includes both individuals and business entities. If the stipulated ten percent is not withheld, real estate agents may be held liable to the extent of their commission, and purchasers are liable for the balance. The purchaser is responsible for determining the seller's citizenship status. Most attorneys prepare a nonforeign certification (sometimes referred to as a FIRPTA affidavit) to be signed by the seller, verifying that the seller is not a foreign person and, therefore, monies need not be withheld. The affidavit also includes the seller's address and federal taxpayer's identification number. A sample of this document is found in the hypothetical closings provided in the next three chapters.

In addition to the withholding requirements of section 1445 of the FIRPTA, the Tax Reform Act of 1986 mandates that all real estate transactions be reported to the Internal Revenue Service by the closing agent. As noted earlier in the chapter, the closing agent may be a title company, a lending institution, an escrow company, or an attorney. The person handling the closing has the legal responsibility for reporting. The transaction is reported on a **1099 form.** The form must be completed with the following information: (1) the closing agent's name, address, and taxpayer's identification number; (2) the seller's name, address, and taxpayer's identification number; (3) the closing date; (4) the sales price; (5) the type of transaction; (6) the property's address; and (7) the parcel identification number. A sample of this form is found in the hypothetical closing in the next chapter.

Certain real estate–related costs are tax deductible for income tax purposes. These items include interest paid on a promissory note, loan origination fees charged by the lender, and real property taxes. Other costs may be capitalized by adding them to the price paid for the property. By so doing, these costs become a part of the base for capital gains tax purposes when the property is later sold. Items that may be capitalized include attorneys' fees,

1099 form: A federal tax reporting form for the reporting of real property sales transactions.

appraisal fees, title insurance premiums, recording fees, notary fees, escrow fees, and transfer taxes.

ESCROW CLOSINGS

The description of the actual closing provided in the preceding text presumes that the parties are able to meet face-to-face at the closing agent's office. Sometimes this is not possible. A party may be out of town or too ill to attend. In such a situation, the absent party may have given someone a power of attorney to act in his or her stead, and the closing can still proceed as scheduled. Alternatively, instead of a face-to-face encounter, an **escrow closing** may be held (also referred to as a *closing in escrow)*. In some states, such as California, escrow closings are common practice. In an escrow closing, a third party, such as a title company, law firm, or escrow company, acts as the escrowee or escrow holder. Both parties deposit their closing documents with the escrowee, and the escrowee proceeds to close the transaction as an impartial agent, attending to the requirements of each party.

If the parties know at the time of contracting that an escrow closing will be required, the contract for sale and purchase may indicate the name of the person or firm to act as escrowee. The parties and the escrowee would then sign an escrow agreement. The escrow agreement stipulates the responsibilities of each signatory as well as the documents each party must prepare and deposit with the escrowee prior to the date of closing. The escrow agreement should also provide for interpleader in the event of a dispute and provide indemnification for the escrowee. Sometimes, instead of signing a separate escrow agreement, all of the terms for an escrow closing are included in the contract for sale and purchase, and the escrowee, as well as the purchaser and seller, signs the contract to indicate his or her agreement with the escrow terms.

The purchaser deposits any earnest money with the escrowee, and later the cash balance needed to close the transaction. The financing instruments are deposited with the escrowee by the lender to be sent to the purchaser for signature. The seller deposits with the escrowee the executed deed, the seller's affidavit, and any other documents required to transfer marketable title.

Once all the documentation is deposited, the escrowee examines it to ensure that it is in order. The escrowee checks to see that the documents are executed legally and that the necessary witnessing and acknowledgments are completed. The parties should provide the escrowee with copies of photo identification to compare with the signatures on the documents. The escrowee conducts a final title check to make sure that there are no encumbrances on the title to be transferred. If all is in order, the escrowee disburses the funds according to a set of escrow instructions signed by both parties, records the documents, and sends originals and copies to the respective parties.

escrow closing: A closing in which a third party acts as escrowee and receives closing documents deposited by each party, whereupon the escrowee proceeds to close the transaction.

CHAPTER SUMMARY

1. A closing is the process of transferring title documents and monies to complete a real estate transaction. The process requires the participation

not only of the seller and the purchaser, but of third parties as well. These third parties include, but are not limited to, real estate brokers, lenders, title companies, and insurance companies, each with their own set of criteria to be met.

2. The key to organization of a real estate file is attention to detail. The use of a closing worksheet puts information that is important and referred to repeatedly at ready access. The worksheet itemizes the tasks to be done, specifies the party responsible for each task, sets due dates, and indicates the party to be charged. A tickler system should be set up to work in conjunction with the worksheet.

3. Each closing document in a real estate file should have its own folder. All correspondence can be arranged in reverse chronological order in a single folder. Original documents should not be hole-punched or mutilated in any manner. It is important to document everything. Letters should be sent to all concerned parties confirming their respective responsibilities.

4. All closing documents should be prepared for final review prior to closing. Photocopies of these documents are sent to the other parties. Originals should not leave the office if at all possible. The closing statement figures must be made available to the purchaser at least two or three days prior to the closing date because the purchaser will have to pay all sums due with a cashier's check.

5. Prior to closing, a purchaser pursuing institutional financing will make a loan application and provide the prospective lender with all pertinent financial records. If accepted, a loan commitment will be issued that will be valid for a short duration. The closing must take place within this time frame, or an extension on the commitment must be sought. The commitment sets forth items that must be complied with to the lender's satisfaction prior to the closing of the loan. The fees for such items as appraisals, credit reports, and lender's inspections comprise part of the purchaser's closing costs.

6. Prior to closing, the seller must provide the purchaser with an updated abstract of title or title commitment. Any defects in title indicated by these instruments must be cured by the seller within the contractually stipulated time frame. If the seller has an outstanding loan encumbering the property, a mortgage estoppel letter must be obtained from the seller's lender providing the payoff amount. The seller must provide the most recent real property tax bill. Each party's share of the property taxes will be apportioned on the closing statement. Similarly, the seller must obtain official statements from his or her condominium or homeowners' association (if applicable) regarding regular and special assessments. These items will also be prorated on the closing statement.

7. The seller's attorney typically prepares the deed, seller's affidavit, bill of sale, nonforeign certification (if applicable), continuous marriage affidavit (if applicable), satisfaction of mortgage, and any other document necessary to transfer marketable title. The lender's attorney prepares the promissory note and financing instruments, including UCC-1 forms if personal property is to serve as part of the collateral for the loan.

8. Items owed *by* a party will appear in the debit column of a closing statement, and items owed *to* a party will appear in the credit column of a closing statement. Items that are paid in advance or arrears and are to be

apportioned *between* the parties are referred to as prorations. Items that may be prorated include, but are not limited to, hazard and flood insurance, property taxes, rent, utilities, maintenance fees, and interest on an assumed loan.

9. Certain disbursements, such as the payoff of the seller's loan, the documentary stamp and intangible taxes, and recording fees, are made after closing. Recorded documents include the deed, satisfaction of mortgage, and financing instruments. Once recorded documents are returned, title policies can be issued and closing binders be prepared for the seller, purchaser, and lender.

REVIEW QUESTIONS

1. What real estate–related costs are
   a. tax deductible for income tax purposes?
   b. capitalized?
2. What information is included in the following?
   a. Mortgage estoppel letter
   b. Seller's affidavit
   c. Satisfaction of mortgage
3. What closing costs are typically paid by (a) the seller and (b) the purchaser?
4. What items are prorated on a closing statement?
5. A closing is to take place on May 17th. The parties are using a 365-day year and an actual month for the calculations. The proration date is the day of closing, and the day of closing is given to the purchaser. Prorate the following items.
   a. Monthly homeowners' association assessment fee of $400 per month (already paid by the seller)
   b. Annual real property tax bill of $3,000 (not yet paid by the seller)
   c. Monthly utility bill of $500 (not yet paid by the seller)

ETHICAL QUESTIONS

Martha Patton and Audrey Edwards, two elderly sisters who are both widowed, have decided to purchase together a house listed with Hanson Realty. The sisters have not obtained an attorney to represent them. Brent Hanson, the real estate broker in charge of the listing, offers to complete the contract for sale and purchase by filling in the blanks on an approved, standardized contract form commonly used for residential transactions. If Brent completes the form, is he guilty of the unauthorized practice of law?

Brent has been a real estate broker for twenty years and has, over the course of the years, become familiar with the legal consequences attendant upon the manner in which title is held. He suggests to Martha and Audrey that they take title to the house as joint tenants with right of survivorship, since this would allow the unit to pass to the survivor upon the death of the other without the imposition of state death taxes. Is Brent engaging in the unauthorized practice of law by making this suggestion?

PRACTICAL ASSIGNMENTS

Assignment 12:1. Referring to the closing costs chart in Figure 12–1, research the customary allocation of each of these items in your county and create a county-customized chart for your jurisdiction. Insert the chart under the "Residential Closings" section of your resource portfolio.

Assignment 12:2. Copy the proration steps found in Figure 12–2. Insert them under the "Residential Closings" section of your resource portfolio.

Assignment 12:3. In a previous assignment you were asked to research your local documentary stamp tax rate and recording fee rates. To complete this research, find out whether intangible tax is charged on new loans and, if so, your local rate. If you have not already done so, find out to whom recording fees, documentary stamp fees, and intangible tax fees are to be made payable. Insert this information under the "General Information" section of your resource portfolio.

Assignment 12:4. Research your state laws to determine whether closing documents must be recorded prior to disbursement of closing proceeds.

Assignment 12:5. Outline the steps to be taken by a paralegal (a) preclosing, (b) during closing, and (c) postclosing. Insert this outline under the "Residential Closings" section of your resource portfolio.

Assignment 12:6. Contact some local real estate law firms to find out whether they utilize real estate closing software. Determine which software applications are most commonly used in your area. If possible, obtain a demonstration disk from a real estate software company or download the Reesa demonstration program. Use this software to prepare the closing statement and closing documents in the practical assignments at the end of Chapter 13.

Assignment 12:7. Define the following key terms.

continuous marriage affidavit   nonforeign certification
escrow closing   seller's affidavit
mortgage estoppel letter   1099 form

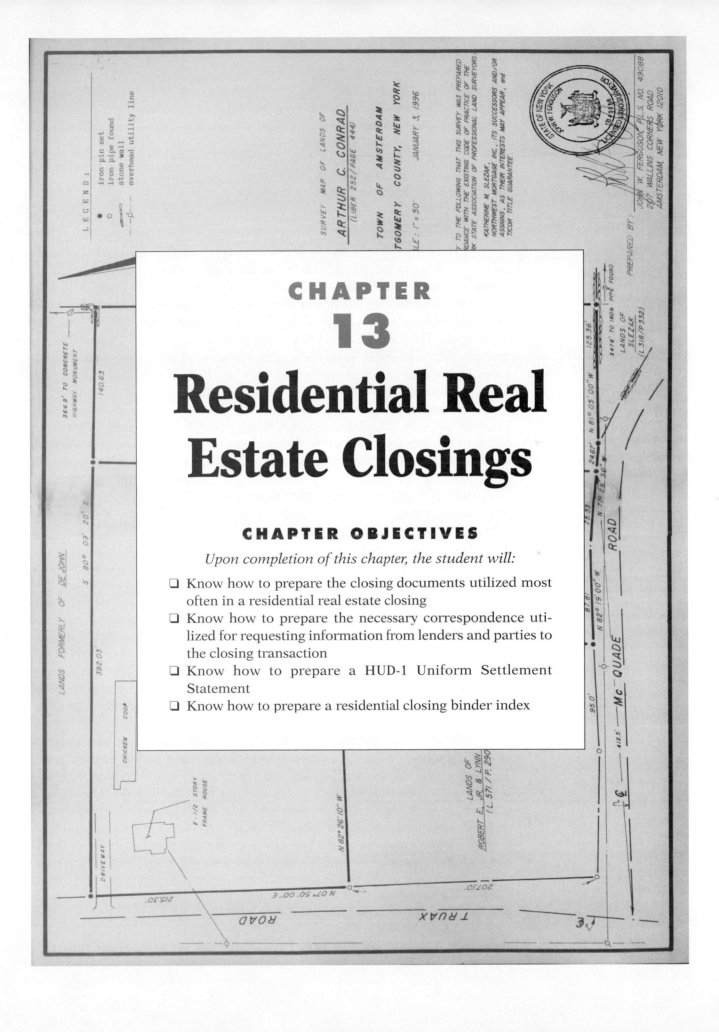

CHAPTER
13
Residential Real Estate Closings

CHAPTER OBJECTIVES

Upon completion of this chapter, the student will:

☐ Know how to prepare the closing documents utilized most often in a residential real estate closing

☐ Know how to prepare the necessary correspondence utilized for requesting information from lenders and parties to the closing transaction

☐ Know how to prepare a HUD-1 Uniform Settlement Statement

☐ Know how to prepare a residential closing binder index

INTRODUCTION

In the last chapter, we examined the procedures for opening a real estate closing file, the matters that must be attended to prior to closing, the types of documents that must be drafted, the items that must be prorated, and post-closing matters. In this chapter, we will focus on a sample residential real estate closing to illustrate how the procedures, looked at individually in the last chapter, come together.

As can be surmised from the previous chapter, there are a myriad of tasks and documents to keep track of between the time a contract for sale and purchase is signed and the time a closing actually occurs. It is imperative that each party understands his or her own obligations for performing such tasks as obtaining information, approvals, inspections, and preparing the requisite documents. The paralegal's task is to keep track of each party's responsibilities and due dates. In order to do so, a checklist or worksheet is crucial. A completed residential closing worksheet is found in the hypothetical closing in the following text.

The closing of a condominium unit was chosen for illustration purposes because virtually all of the documents required in the closing of a single-family home are also required in the closing of a condominium unit. Further, the closing of a condominium unit includes additional items *not* included in the closing of a single-family home, such as approval of the purchaser by the condominium association. Other items included in the purchase and sale of a condominium unit are similar to those encountered in the purchase and sale of a house located within a development controlled by a homeowners' association. These include such items as documents that must be provided to the purchaser for review, such as the declaration of condominium, bylaws, and related documents—or in the case of the homeowners' association, the declaration of restrictive covenants. Additionally, in both instances, there will be prorations of certain assessments, such as maintenance payments.

Besides organizing the file and drafting closing documents, paralegals must prepare the correspondence to their own clients, to the other party or his or her attorney if so represented, and to title companies, lenders, condominium associations, homeowners' associations, records clerks, and so forth. The sample closing provided here gives examples of some of the most commonly drafted letters.

Finally, the paralegal must present the parties with packets of the final documentation. Each party, including the lender, receives a packet of documents pertinent to the transaction. The paralegal must sort out who receives originals of certain items and who receives copies, and then put the documents in a coherent order for each recipient. One way to do this is through the preparation of a residential closing binder index for each party, which serves as a table of contents for the final closing package. Each document is tabbed and numbered according to the number indicated on the index for quick and easy reference.

HYPOTHETICAL CLIENT CLOSING

Barbara Hammond, Ava Ross's paralegal, has set aside some time this afternoon to prepare the last of the documents needed for an upcoming closing. The client is the seller, Parker Properties, Inc., the owner of a condominium development called Kingsfield Estates. Hugh Parker, president of Parker Properties, has hired Ava to handle all of its closings for units in Kingsfield Estates. Parker Properties is selling units directly from its sales office, so in many instances a real estate broker is not involved. The purchaser for the subject closing is Patricia Wallis, who is single. She has chosen not to hire an attorney to represent her in this matter. Parker Properties, according to the contract for sale and purchase, is responsible for preparing the requisite closing documents, including the closing statement.

When Hugh Parker called Ava's office to set up an appointment, Barbara advised him to bring along certain documents, such as the contract and survey. To reconfirm the meeting, she sent the letter found in Figure 13–1.

The client file was opened by Barbara on October 2, 1997, the date the client came into the office with the signed contract. In opening the file, Barbara reviewed the contract to assist her in completing the residential closing worksheet her firm utilizes for all of its residential real estate closings. From the contract, Barbara was able to ascertain such information as the names and addresses of the parties, the legal description of the property, the anticipated closing date, other due dates stipulated in the contract, and the responsibilities of each party. Unless otherwise stipulated, the effective date of the contract is the date upon which the parties signed the contract. If the parties sign on different dates, as is often the case, it is the date upon which the last of the parties signs. A copy of the contract, together with its exhibits, is found in Figures 13–2, 13–3, 13–4, and 13–5.

FIGURE 13–1
Confirmation of meeting letter

September 28, 1997

Mr. Hugh Parker
Parker Properties, Inc.
700 Commercial Blvd., Suite 360
Any City, Any State

Re: Parker Properties, Inc. to Patricia Wallis
     Unit 305, Bldg. 2550, Kingsfield Estates II

Dear Mr. Parker:

    This will confirm the meeting to be held in our office at 9:30 a.m. on October 2, 1997. Please bring the original signed contract for sale and purchase, together with either the original or a copy of the deed, survey, and other closing papers you received when you closed on the property now comprising Kingsfield Estates Condominium. This documentation will be of help to us in preparing the documentation for the above-referenced transaction.
    Should you have any questions, please feel free to call our office.

Sincerely,

Barbara Hammond
Legal Assistant to Ava Ross

FIGURE 13–2
Purchase and sale
agreement

PURCHASE AND SALE AGREEMENT

Seller: PARKER PROPERTIES, INC., an Any State corporation
700 Commercial Boulevard, Suite 360
Any City, Any State

Name: _Patricia Wallis, a single woman_
Address: _235 Crestview Drive, Apt. 205_
City: _Any City_   State: _Any State_
Phone: _(000) 010-0009_
(hereinafter called "Purchaser").

1. **DESCRIPTION.** Subject to the provisions of this Agreement, Seller agrees to sell and Purchaser agrees to purchase the condominium parcel known as:

    Unit 305, Building 2550, of KINGSFIELD ESTATES II, A CONDOMINIUM, according to the DECLARATION OF CONDOMINIUM thereof, recorded in Official Records Book 4676, Page 1342, of the Public Records of Any County, Any State; together with the undivided share of the Common Elements of the Condominium declared in the Declaration of Condominium to be appurtenant thereto; and use of Parking Space No. 300, which space shall be assigned to Purchaser at closing.

2. **PURCHASE PRICE AND TERMS OF PAYMENT.**

(a)	Base Purchase Price	$ 75,200.00
(b)	Additions to Purchase Price, if any	$ -0-
(c)	TOTAL PURCHASE PRICE	$ 75,200.00

    PAYMENT:

(d)	Deposit due to Seller upon execution of this Agreement	$ 4,000.00
(e)	Additional Deposit due _____	$ -0-
(f)	Institutional First Mortgage, if any	$ 67,600.00
(g)	Balance due at closing (subject to adjustments and prorations)	$ 3,600.00

3. **DEPOSITS.** All deposit monies shall be paid to Seller and shall be held by Seller in escrow in accordance with the terms of this Agreement. Purchaser shall not be entitled to any interest earned on the Deposit.

4. **TITLE INSURANCE.** Seller shall, at Purchaser's expense, cause a reputable title insurer or an agent thereof, designated by Seller, to issue to Purchaser a standard form of commitment for an Owner's Title Insurance Policy ("Title Policy"). The commitment shall show title in Seller subject to those exceptions customarily found in such commitments, and subject also to all matters affecting title to the Unit, none of which shall prohibit Purchaser's use of the Unit as a residence. Purchaser acknowledges that Seller may select, in Seller's sole discretion, the title company and the title insurance agent for the title company upon which the Title Policy shall be issued, and such agent may or may not be affiliated with Seller.

5. **FIXTURES.** Appliances, personal property, and/or fixtures displayed in models, if any, are not included in the Purchase Price unless they have been installed in the Unit as of the Effective Date of this Agreement. Models, if any, are for display purposes only and do not constitute a representation of items contained in the Purchase Price. All representations of dimensions are approximate.

FIGURE 13–2
(continued)

6. **FINANCING.** If the Purchase Price or any part of it is to be financed by an institutional third-party loan, this Agreement is conditioned upon the Purchaser obtaining a written commitment for (CHECK (1) or (2) or (3)): (1) _____ a fixed, (2) _____ an adjustable, or (3) _X_ a fixed or adjustable rate loan within _30_ days after the Effective Date at prevailing interest rates, for a term of _30_ years and for the principal amount of $67,600.00. Purchaser will make application within 10 days after Effective Date and use reasonable diligence to obtain the loan commitment and, thereafter, to meet the terms and conditions of the commitment and close the loan. Purchaser shall pay all loan expenses. If Purchaser fails to obtain the commitment or after diligent effort fails to meet the terms and conditions of the commitment, then either party thereafter by prompt written notice to the other may cancel this Agreement, and Purchaser shall be refunded the deposit(s).

7. **CONDOMINIUM ASSOCIATION.** Upon closing, Purchaser shall become a member of Kingsfield Estates Association, Inc. (hereinafter called the "Condominium Association") and will be bound by the terms and conditions of the Declaration of Condominium of this Condominium, the Articles and Bylaws of the Condominium Association, and any rules and regulations enacted pursuant thereto, including without limitation, the obligation to pay assessments and other exactions. Purchaser agrees to pay his/her proportionate share of the Common Expenses of the Condominium Association in accordance with the Association's documents. Purchaser acknowledges that the Condominium Association has a lien upon the Unit pursuant to its governing documents to secure payment by Purchaser of the applicable assessments and other exactions.

8. **CLOSING DATE AND POSSESSION.** The "Closing" is the conveyance of the Unit as evidenced by the delivery of the deed transferring title to Purchaser, which shall be at such office in Any County as designated by Seller. Closing shall take place (hereinafter called the "Closing Date") on or before November 24, 1997. Purchaser will be in default of this Agreement if he/she fails to close as scheduled. The Closing Date may be changed and rescheduled by mutual written agreement of the parties. Purchaser shall be given possession of his/her Unit as of the Closing Date. Until the Closing has been completed, Purchaser shall not be permitted to occupy the Unit or store any property therein.

   As of the Closing Date, Purchaser, when so requested by Seller, hereby agrees to execute a separate document as to the Unit wherein he/she acknowledges, assumes, and accepts the Condominium Documents and confirms the lien thereunder upon the Unit, acknowledges approval of same, and/or authorizes release to Seller of any escrowed deposits. The Closing of this transaction and acceptance of the deed by Purchaser shall be conclusive evidence of the compliance by Seller with Seller's obligations under this Agreement.

9. **EXPENSES OF CLOSING.** The following expenses will be paid by the Purchaser at time of closing: SEE RIDER ATTACHED HERETO AND MADE A PART HEREOF.

10. **TITLE AND CONVEYANCE.** Seller will convey insurable title by Warranty Deed, subject only to (1) the Declaration of Condominium and all Exhibits attached thereto; (2) utility easements, easements for vehicular rights-of-way and all other easements pertaining to the Condominium Property; (3) any mortgage executed by Purchaser

FIGURE 13–2
(continued)

encumbering the Condominium Unit; (4) taxes (including, but not limited to, those imposed by Any County) for the current year and subsequent years attributable to Purchaser's Unit; (5) zoning, restrictions, prohibitions and other requirements imposed by governmental authority; (6) matters shown on any recorded Plats of Condominium Property (as defined in the Declaration of Condominium); (7) such other easements, covenants, conditions and restrictions as Seller may reasonably consider necessary or expedient to hereafter impose on the Condominium Property, provided that the same do not prevent the use of the Condominium Property for residential purposes; (8) the standard printed exceptions contained in an Owner's Title Insurance Policy; and (9) all covenants, conditions and limitations, restrictions, reservations and easements of record.

If Seller is unable to deliver title as provided herein, Seller shall not be obligated to cure any objections or defects, but shall be afforded a reasonable time (not less than ninety [90] days) to do so if Seller so elects. If not cured within such period, or if Seller elects not to so cure, Purchaser may accept title in its then existing condition, but without any reduction in the Purchase Price, or may rescind this Agreement by providing written notice thereof to Seller, and thereafter receive a return of its Deposit, at which time this Agreement shall be null and void, and this shall be Purchaser's sole remedy at law and in equity.

11. **NO RIGHT TO PURCHASER'S LIEN.** Neither any rights of a Purchaser hereunder nor any deposits made hereunder shall constitute a lien upon the Condominium Property or any portion thereof, and in the event of a dispute between the parties involving this Agreement, Purchaser waives its right to file a Lis Pendens against the Unit.

12. **RECEIPT OF DOCUMENTATION.** Prior to the execution of this Agreement, Seller has provided to Purchaser copies of the documents described in Exhibit A attached to this Agreement, the receipt of which is acknowledged by Purchaser by the execution of this Agreement.

Notwithstanding anything to the contrary in this Agreement, Seller shall have the right to make such changes in the above documents as are necessary to meet the requirements of a lender, governmental entity, title insurer or for such other reasons as Seller, in its sole discretion, may determine. If Seller elects to exercise that right, Seller shall furnish to Purchaser a copy of the revised documents. If the modified documents materially alter or modify the documentation in a manner adverse to the Purchaser, Purchaser shall have the immediate right of cancellation of this Agreement on notice furnished to Seller within fifteen (15) days from Purchaser's receipt of said revised documents, and upon such cancellation, Seller shall return any deposit money paid to Seller or Escrow Agent under this Agreement. Failure to so notify the Seller of intent to cancel within the time provided shall be deemed a waiver of that right.

13. **BINDING EFFECT.** This Agreement is binding upon the parties hereto and their heirs, legal representatives, successors and assigns. This Agreement will supersede any and all understandings and agreements between the parties, and it is mutually understood and agreed that this Agreement represents the entire agreement between the parties. No amendment, supplement or rider to this Agreement shall be binding unless in writing and signed by both Purchaser and Seller. No employee, agent, broker, salesperson, officer or other representative of Seller has authority to make or has made any

FIGURE 13–2
(continued)

statement, representation, warranty, undertaking, agreement or promise (either oral, written, express or implied) in connection with this Agreement or the Unit, supplementing or amending the provisions of this Agreement.

14. <u>PURCHASER'S DEFAULT.</u> Purchaser shall be in default under this Agreement in the event that:

   (a) Purchaser fails or refuses to complete and execute all the instruments required of Purchaser under this Agreement promptly or when requested to do so by Seller or Purchaser's Mortgagee, if any; or

   (b) Purchaser fails or refuses to make timely payment of any payments required under this Agreement; or

   (c) Purchaser in any other manner fails or refuses to perform his/her obligations under this Agreement.

   In the event of any such default by Purchaser, Seller shall give Purchaser written notice of such default and allow five (5) calendar days from the date of such notice for Purchaser to cure such default. If Purchaser shall fail to cure such default with such five (5) day period, Seller shall, and does hereby have the unrestricted option to: (1) consider Purchaser in default under this Agreement; (2) retain all sums paid to it hereunder plus any interest accruing thereon, as agreed upon and liquidated damages, and (3) terminate all rights of Purchaser under this Agreement.

   Purchaser and Seller recognize the impossibility of measuring Seller's damages if Purchaser defaults. The provision herein contained for agreed upon and liquidated damages is a bona fide provision for such damages and is not a penalty. The Purchaser understands that by reason of the withdrawal of the Unit from sale to the general public at a time when other prospective purchasers would be interested in purchasing it, the Seller will have sustained damages if the Purchaser defaults, which damages will be substantial but not capable of being determined with mathematical precision. Purchaser agrees that if he/she defaults in this Agreement, he/she will not file any action against Seller seeking the return of any portion of said liquidated and agreed upon damages, nor seeking any reduction in the amount of liquidated and agreed upon damages.

15. <u>SELLER'S DEFAULT.</u> If Seller defaults in the performance of this Agreement, Purchaser shall give Seller written notice of such default, and Seller shall have seven (7) days from receipt of such written notice within which to begin to take such action as would cure the default within a reasonable period of time. In the event Seller fails to begin to take such action within such seven (7) day period, then Purchaser, upon having performed all of his/her obligations hereunder, shall have the right to either (1) seek specific performance, or (2) elect to receive a return of his/her Deposit, and/or right to seek damages from Seller by reason of such default.

16. <u>ATTORNEYS' FEES AND COSTS.</u> In connection with any litigation including, but not limited to, appellate proceedings, arising out of this Agreement, the prevailing party shall be entitled to recover reasonable attorneys' fees and costs.

17. <u>DELINQUENT PAYMENT.</u> If Purchaser is delinquent in the payment of any sums due under this Agreement, including the balance of the purchase money payable at the closing, and Seller has not elected to cancel this Agreement and declare a forfeiture of deposits pursuant

FIGURE 13–2
(continued)

to Paragraph 14 above, Purchaser shall pay to Seller interest on all delinquent sums at a rate of eighteen percent (18%) per annum or at the then highest rate allowed by law, whichever is less. Furthermore, if Purchaser is delinquent in closing the transaction, prorations for taxes, assessment charges, and other proratable items may, at the option of Seller, be calculated based on the scheduled Closing Date set forth above rather than the actual Closing Date.

18. **CLOSING DOCUMENTS.** Seller shall be responsible for providing the Warranty Deed, the Closing Statement, and any other documents necessary for transferring good and marketable title to Purchaser at Seller's expense. Seller shall, at Purchaser's expense, provide a Title Commitment in accordance with Paragraph 4 of this Agreement and, at Purchaser's expense, provide the Title Policy after closing.

19. **RECORDING.** Purchaser shall not record this Agreement nor any notice thereof in the Public Records of Any County, Any State, or in any other Public Records.

20. **NOTICES.** Any notice, request, demand, instruction or other communication to be given to either party, except where required by the terms of this Agreement to be delivered at the closing, shall be in writing and shall be sent by registered or certified mail, return receipt requested, or by express overnight courier, to the noticed party at the address herein set forth at the beginning of this Agreement or to such other address as either Seller or Purchaser shall designate by notice in accordance with this Paragraph. Notice shall be deemed given if forwarded by certified or registered mail through the facilities of the United States Post Office on the day following the date that the notice in question is deposited in the facilities of the United States Postal Service. If notice is forwarded by express overnight courier, it shall be deemed given on the day following the date that the notice in question is deposited in the facilities of an express overnight courier, but only if deposited in time for the courier to give next-day delivery service.

21. **CAPTIONS.** The captions contained herein are included solely for the convenience of the parties and do not, in any way, modify, amplify or give full notice of any of the terms, covenants or conditions of this Agreement.

22. **WAIVER.** Seller's waiver of any condition or provision of this Agreement shall not be construed as a waiver of any other application of that same condition or provision, nor as a waiver of any other condition or provision herein.

23. **GOVERNING LAW.** Purchaser certifies that Purchaser is executing this Agreement while in the State of Any State on Purchaser's own volition and that this purchase was not solicited either by telephone or mail in another state. The obligations under this Agreement shall be performed in the State of Any State and this Agreement shall be governed by Any State law. In the event any court of competent jurisdiction determines any provision of this Agreement to be invalid or unenforceable, no other provision shall be affected by such invalidity but shall remain in full force and effect according to its original terms.

24. **TIME OF ESSENCE.** Time is of the essence with respect to each provision of this Agreement which requires performance by either party upon a specified date or within a specified period, except where otherwise specifically provided for herein.

FIGURE 13–2
(continued)

25. <u>**REAL ESTATE BROKERS/SELLING AGENT.**</u> Seller and Purchaser represent and warrant that there is no real estate broker involved in this transaction who is entitled to a commission except _____N/A_____ (the "Broker"), who shall be paid a commission pursuant to a separate written agreement between Broker and Seller. If the name of the Broker is not written in the forgoing line and initialed by Seller, then it is absolutely presumed that there are no brokers involved in this transaction.

26. <u>**ASSIGNMENT.**</u> This Agreement may not be assigned by the Purchaser except with the express written permission of Seller which may be withheld at the sole discretion of Seller or which may be granted subject to those conditions specified by Seller, including but not limited to the payment to Seller of any assignment fee as assessed by Seller.

27. <u>**ADDENDUM TO AGREEMENT.**</u> The parties shall be bound by any addendum or addenda to this Agreement in the same manner as they are bound under this Agreement, provided that said addendum has been signed by all of the parties hereto.

28. <u>**EFFECTIVE DATE.**</u> The Effective Date of this Agreement shall be the date when the last of the Purchaser and Seller has signed this Agreement.

29. <u>**DISCLOSURE.**</u> THIS AGREEMENT IS VOIDABLE BY PURCHASER BY DELIVERING WRITTEN NOTICE OF THE PURCHASER'S INTENTION TO CANCEL WITHIN 15 DAYS AFTER THE DATE OF EXECUTION OF THIS AGREEMENT BY THE PURCHASER, AND RECEIPT BY PURCHASER OF ALL OF THE ITEMS REQUIRED TO BE DELIVERED TO HIM/HER BY THE SELLER UNDER SECTION 415.101, ANY STATE STATUTES. THIS AGREEMENT IS ALSO VOIDABLE BY PURCHASER BY DELIVERING WRITTEN NOTICE OF THE PURCHASER'S INTENTION TO CANCEL WITHIN 15 DAYS AFTER THE DATE OF RECEIPT FROM THE SELLER OF ANY AMENDMENT WHICH MATERIALLY ALTERS OR MODIFIES THE OFFERING IN A MANNER THAT IS ADVERSE TO THE PURCHASER. ANY PURPORTED WAIVER OF THESE VOIDABILITY RIGHTS SHALL BE OF NO EFFECT. PURCHASER MAY EXTEND THE TIME FOR CLOSING FOR A PERIOD OF NOT LESS THAN 15 DAYS AFTER THE PURCHASER HAS RECEIVED ALL OF THE ITEMS REQUIRED. PURCHASER'S RIGHTS TO VOID THIS AGREEMENT SHALL TERMINATE AT CLOSING.

30. There is no land or recreational lease associated with this Condominium.

31. This Unit is not being conveyed subject to a lease.

IN WITNESS WHEREOF, the undersigned have executed this Agreement on the dates below.

SELLER: PURCHASER:

PARKER PROPERTIES, INC.,   *Patricia Wallis*
an Any State corporation

By: *Hugh Parker*
    President

Date: September 28, 1997   Date: September 28, 1997

FIGURE 13–3
Receipts for condominium documents

EXHIBIT A
RECEIPTS FOR CONDOMINIUM DOCUMENTS

The undersigned acknowledges that the documents checked below have been received or, as to plans and specifications, made available for inspection.

Name of Condominium: KINGSFIELD ESTATES II, A CONDOMINIUM
Address of Condominium: 2500 Kingsfield Drive
                             Any City, Any State

Place an "X" in the column by each document received or, for the plans and specifications, made available for inspection. If an item does not apply, place "N/A" in the column.

DOCUMENT	RECEIVED
Prospectus Text	X
Declaration of Condominium	X
Articles of Incorporation	X
Bylaws	X
Current Operating Budget	X
Form of Agreement for Sale or Lease	X
Rules and Regulations	X
Ground Lease	N/A
Management and Maintenance Contracts for More than One Year	N/A
Renewable Management Contracts	X
Lease of Recreational and Other Facilities to Be Used Exclusively by Unit Owners of Subject Condominium	N/A
Phase Development Description	X
Plot Plan	X
Floor Plan	X
Survey of Land and Graphic Description of Improvements	X

THE PURCHASE AGREEMENT IS VOIDABLE BY PURCHASER BY DELIVERING WRITTEN NOTICE OF THE PURCHASER'S INTENTION TO CANCEL WITHIN FIFTEEN (15) DAYS AFTER THE DATE OF EXECUTION OF THE PURCHASE AGREEMENT BY THE PURCHASER AND RECEIPT BY THE PURCHASER OF ALL OF THE DOCUMENTS REQUIRED TO BE DELIVERED TO HIM/HER BY THE SELLER. THE AGREEMENT IS ALSO VOIDABLE BY THE PURCHASER BY DELIVERING WRITTEN NOTICE OF THE PURCHASER'S INTENTION TO CANCEL WITHIN FIFTEEN (15) DAYS AFTER THE DATE OF RECEIPT FROM THE SELLER OF ANY AMENDMENT WHICH MATERIALLY ALTERS OR MODIFIES THE OFFERING IN A MANNER THAT IS ADVERSE TO THE PURCHASER. PURCHASER MAY EXTEND THE TIME FOR CLOSING FOR A PERIOD OF NOT MORE THAN FIFTEEN (15) DAYS AFTER THE PURCHASER HAS RECEIVED ALL OF THE DOCUMENTS REQUIRED. PURCHASER'S RIGHT TO VOID THE PURCHASE AGREEMENT SHALL TERMINATE AT CLOSING.

Executed this ___28th___ day of ___September, 1997___.

Patricia Wallis
Purchaser

Because the sale in question is the sale of a condominium unit, the purchaser is entitled, by law, to receipt of all pertinent condominium documents for review. The documents provided are listed in Figure 13–3. Under the state statutes of Any State, a prospective purchaser of a condominium unit has fifteen days within which to inspect the documents. If within this time frame,

FIGURE 13–4
Notice to purchaser
of costs

EXHIBIT B
NOTICE TO PURCHASER OF COSTS

You are hereby notified that you, as Purchaser at KINGSFIELD ESTATES II, A CONDOMINIUM, may be required to pay additional costs in your purchase. The additional costs paid by the Purchaser at KINGSFIELD ESTATES II, A CONDO-MINIUM, include the following:

		Estimated Amount (not included if unknown)
1.	Prorated Association Assessments for the Month of Closing	$ 89.50
2.	Documentary Stamps Affixed to Deed	$ 526.40
3.	Cost of Recording Deed	$ 12.00
4.	Title Abstracting Charge	$ 125.00
5.	Title Insurance	$ 712.00
6.	Ad Valorem Real Estate Taxes	$ to be prorated
7.	Purchaser's Attorneys' Fees	$
8.	Assessments	$ to be prorated
9.	Solid Waste Authority	$ to be prorated
10.	Mortgage Closing Costs, if applicable (including discount points and escrow fees)	$ see Lender

I have read the above and understand it. I acknowledge receipt of a copy of this notice this __28th__ day of __September, 1997__, before signing the Purchase and Sale Agreement.

Purchaser: _Patricia Wallis_

---

the prospective purchaser decides not to go ahead with the purchase of the condominium, he or she is entitled to a full return of his or her deposit, and the contract is terminated. Purchasers in some states do not have such expansive rights. The other two exhibits to the contract explain the closing costs connected with the transaction.

Under the terms of the contract, the seller, at the purchaser's expense, provides a title commitment and subsequent title policies. Because Ava Ross is a title agent, Parker Properties has hired her to conduct the title search, examination, and preparation of the commitment and policies. These will show up as fees separate from the attorneys' fees charged for preparing the closing documents and acting as escrow/closing agent. Although the terms of this contract stipulate that the purchaser is responsible for the title work costs, who typically pays for these items is often a matter of custom in the county in which the property is located. In some instances, the seller pays for the owner's policy and the purchaser pays for the mortgagee's policy. To ensure the avoidance of a conflict of interest, Barbara prepared a letter pertaining to the title work and had both parties sign it. It may be found in Figure 13–6.

In a similar vein to the payment allocations made for the title work, this contract has the purchaser paying the documentary stamp tax on the deed, as well as on the mortgage instrument. Often the seller pays the documentary stamp tax on the deed. Custom notwithstanding, these matters, like so many others, are subject to negotiation between the parties.

FIGURE 13–5
Expense rider

EXPENSE RIDER

THIS EXPENSE RIDER ("Rider") is attached to and made a part of that certain Purchase and Sale Agreement ("Agreement") by and between PARKER PROPERTIES, INC., an Any State corporation ("Seller"), and Patricia Wallis ("Purchaser") under which Agreement Purchaser agrees to buy and Seller agrees to sell Unit _305_, Building _2550_, located in KINGSFIELD ESTATES II ("Property"). The Agreement and this Rider are sometimes collectively hereinafter referred to as the "Agreement."

1. In the event of any conflict between the terms and conditions of this Rider and the terms and conditions of the Agreement, the terms and conditions of this Rider shall control.

2. **EXPENSES OF CLOSING.** Purchaser shall pay, in addition to the Purchase Price, the following costs at the closing:

   A. The costs of recording the Deed, Any State Documentary Stamp Taxes required to be affixed to the Deed and the premium for an Owner's Policy of Title Insurance to be issued to Purchaser at closing by a title insurance agent to be selected by Seller, together with the abstracting fee charged by such title insurance agent, which abstracting fee shall not exceed $125.00.

   B. Purchaser's pro rata share of the maintenance assessments charged by the Condominium Association for the assessment period in which the closing occurs.

   C. An amount equal to any capital contribution that may from time to time be assessed by the Condominium Association, if any.

   D. In the event Purchaser chooses to obtain financing to complete this transaction, Purchaser shall pay to Lender all closing costs imposed by Lender, including, but not limited to, points, origination fees, prepaid loan interest, escrow account balances and private mortgage insurance premium, if required. The obligations of Purchaser under this Agreement are not contingent upon Purchaser qualifying for financing or obtaining a written loan commitment unless Paragraph 6 of this Agreement entitled "Financing" is completely filled in and initialed by the Seller.

   E. A pro rata share of real property taxes for the year of closing. Real property taxes will be prorated on the latest information available. If the taxes for the year of closing are not precisely ascertainable, such taxes will be prorated based upon estimates and will be later adjusted based upon the exact amount of taxes, with allowance for full discount. Certified special assessment liens as of the date of closing shall be paid by Seller. Pending special assessment liens as of the date of closing shall be assumed by Purchaser. Purchaser shall also pay all utility deposits or similar fees applicable to the Unit which may have been advanced by Seller on behalf of Purchaser.

IN WITNESS WHEREOF, the parties have hereunto set their hands and seals this _28th_ day of _September, 1997_.

SELLER: PURCHASER:

PARKER PROPERTIES, INC.,
an Any State corporation   _Patricia Wallis_

By: _Hugh Parker_
     President

October 2, 1997

Seller: Parker Properties, Inc.   Purchaser: Patricia Wallis

Property: Unit 305, Bldg. 2550, Kingsfield Estates II

Re: Services rendered to Seller and Purchaser

We, the undersigned Seller and Purchaser, hereby acknowledge that the law firm
of FISHER, SIMON, AND ROSS, P.A. represents the Seller in the above transaction.
We have prior knowledge of and consent to the firm also preparing and issuing a
title insurance policy for the Purchaser. This title policy shall be prepared and
issued for a fee as a convenience, and not as counsel for the Purchaser.

Seller: Parker Properties, Inc.   Purchaser: Patricia Wallis

            By: *Hugh Parker*   *Patricia Wallis*
                President

FIGURE 13–6
Letter pertaining to
title work

Barbara takes a moment to review the closing worksheet to determine what steps must be taken next. The closing worksheet is found in Figure 13–7.

The closing worksheet indicates several dates. According to the contract, Patricia has ten days from the signing of the contract to make a loan application, so the date indicated on the worksheet is October 8, 1997, ten days from the date of signing, September 28, 1997. In fact, Patricia filled out a loan application with Millennium Bank on October 2, 1997, well within the contractual requirements. A good faith estimate of costs associated with the loan procurement was provided to Patricia that same day, as evidenced in Figure 13–8.

The closing worksheet shows a due date for a loan commitment of October 28, 1997. Millennium Bank issued a loan commitment to Patricia on October 25, 1997, as shown in Figure 13–9. Note that the commitment expires on November 25, 1997, so if the closing is delayed for any reason and does not occur on November 24th, Patricia will need to obtain an extension of the commitment. It is the responsibility of the purchaser's attorney to review a loan commitment to make sure that the commitment truly binds the lender. Some loan commitments contain numerous contingencies that swallow up the commitment.

Certain condominium-related items are noted on the worksheet. The date of October 13, 1997, is indicated as the date by which Patricia must review the condominium documents she received upon signing the contract. In order to transfer title of the condominium unit to Patricia, certain condominium transfer information is required. This information includes information pertaining to maintenance payments, special assessments, transfer fees, and an interview of the prospective purchaser prior to obtaining condominium association approval. As stated in Chapter 3, condominium association approval of a sale is not always required, so this must be checked on a case-by-case basis. The worksheet indicates that Barbara sent a request for condominium transfer information on October 3, 1997. The request form, as completed by the condominium association, is found in Figure 13–10.

FIGURE 13-7
Residential closing
worksheet

RESIDENTIAL CLOSING WORKSHEET

DATE FILE OPENED: 10/02/97
ATTORNEY: Ava Ross
PARALEGAL: Barbara Hammond
CLIENT NUMBER: 15432
MATTER NUMBER: 001
CLIENT: _____ BUYER __X__ SELLER _____ LENDER

1. SELLER NAME(S): Parker Properties, Inc., an Any State corporation
2. ADDRESS(ES): 700 Commercial Boulevard, Suite 360
   Any City, Any State
3. PHONE NUMBER(S): (000) 012-3333
   FAX NUMBER(S): (000) 012-3335
4. SOCIAL SECURITY NUMBER(S) [IF A BUSINESS ENTITY, FEDERAL TAX
   I.D. NO.]: 000998888
5. BUYER NAME(S): Patricia Wallis, a single woman
6. ADDRESS(ES): 235 Crestview Drive, Apt. 205
   Any City, Any State
7. PHONE NUMBER(S): (000) 010-0009
   FAX NUMBER(S): N/A
8. SOCIAL SECURITY NUMBER(S) [IF A BUSINESS ENTITY, FEDERAL TAX
   I.D. NO.]: 000-50-5555
9. BUYER'S LENDER: Millennium Bank
10. ADDRESS: 1750 Wellington Avenue
    Any City, Any State
11. PHONE NUMBER: (000) 041-4000
    FAX NUMBER: (000) 041-4100
12. LOAN OFFICER ASSIGNED TO LOAN FILE: Derek Jamison
13. LOAN NUMBER: 677377
14. SELLER'S LENDER (IF SELLER HAS EXISTING MORTGAGE ON
    PROPERTY): Century Bank
15. ADDRESS: 1100 S. Main Street
    Any City, Any State
16. PHONE NUMBER: (000) 099-0020
    FAX NUMBER: (000) 099-0030
17. LOAN NUMBER: 540031
18. ATTORNEY FOR: __X__ BUYER _____ SELLER
19. ATTORNEY NAME: N/A
20. ADDRESS:

21. PHONE NUMBER:
    FAX NUMBER:
22. REAL ESTATE
    BROKER #1: N/A
23. ADDRESS:

24. PHONE NUMBER:
    FAX NUMBER:
25. REAL ESTATE
    BROKER #2: N/A
26. ADDRESS:

27. PHONE NUMBER:
    FAX NUMBER:

FIGURE 13–7
(continued)

28. COMMISSION: N/A
    HOW SPLIT: N/A
29. ESCROW AGENT: Fisher, Ross, and Simon, P.A.
30. ADDRESS: 1900 N.W. 3rd Avenue
    Any City, Any State
31. PHONE NUMBER: (000) 555-2000
    FAX NUMBER: (000) 555-2020
32. TITLE COMPANY: In-house
33. ADDRESS:

34. PHONE NUMBER:
    FAX NUMBER:
35. STREET ADDRESS OF PROPERTY:
    2550 Kingsfield Drive, Apt. 305
    Any City, Any State
36. LEGAL DESCRIPTION OF PROPERTY:
    Unit 305, Building 2550, of KINGSFIELD ESTATES II, A CONDO-
    MINIUM, according to the DECLARATION OF CONDOMINIUM
    thereof, recorded in Official Records Book 4676, Page 1342, of the
    Public Records of Any County, Any State; together with the undivided
    share of the Common Elements of the Condominium declared in the
    Declaration of Condominium to be appurtenant thereto.
37. PARCEL IDENTIFICATION
    NUMBER: 7989594939
38. CLOSING:
    (A) DATE: November 24, 1997
    (B) TIME: 10:00 a.m.
    (C) PLACE: our offices
39. PURCHASE PRICE: $75,200.00

40. DEPOSITS:

	AMOUNT	DATE DUE	DATE RECEIVED
(A) LOT:			
(B) INITIAL:	$4,000.00	9/28/97	9/28/97
(C) ADDITIONAL:			

41.

ITEM	DONE BY SELLER	DONE BY BUYER	DATE DUE	CHARGE TO
Title Search	X			Buyer
Order Survey				
Title Examination	X			Buyer
Title Commitment	X		10/26/97	Buyer
Remedy Defects				
Issue Policy(ies):				
(a) Owner's	X			Buyer
(b) Mortgagee's	X			Buyer
(c) Endorsements:				
ALTA 4.1	X			Buyer
Property Appraisal				
Loan Application		X	10/8/97	Buyer
Loan Commitment		Lender	10/28/97	Buyer
Promissory Note		Lender	11/24/97	Buyer
Mortgage/Deed of Trust		Lender	11/24/97	Buyer
UCC Forms				
Mortgage Estoppel Letter	X		11/10/97	Seller
Satisfaction of Mortgage/ Deed of Trust	X		11/24/97	Seller

FIGURE 13–7
(continued)

ITEM	DONE BY SELLER	DONE BY BUYER	DATE DUE	CHARGE TO
Insurance Coverage				
Request for Condo Transfer Information	X		10/3/97	Seller
Approval of Condo Documents		X	10/13/97	
Condo Ass'n Approval	X		10/28/97	Seller
HOA Approval				
Termite Inspection				
Roof Inspection				
Appliance Inspection				
Heating/Cooling/Elec./ Plumbing Inspection				
Verification of Corporate Status	X		10/15/97	Seller
Verification of Marital Status				
Corporate Resolution	X		8/14/97	Seller
Tax Receipts	X		11/5/97	
City Tax Prorated				
County Tax Prorated	X		11/22/97	Buyer
Special Assessments Prorated				
Maintenance Assessments Prorated	X		11/22/97	Buyer
Other Prorations:				
Solid Waste Authority	X		11/22/97	Buyer
Bill of Sale	X		11/24/97	Seller
Seller's Affidavit	X		11/24/97	Seller
Deed	X		11/24/97	Seller
Continuous Marriage Affidavit				
FIRPTA Affidavit				
Closing Statement	X		11/22/97	Seller
Final Walk-Through		X	11/24/97	
Keys	X		11/24/97	
Recordation of Deed	X			Buyer
Recordation of Financing Instrument	X			Buyer
Recordation of UCC Forms				
Recordation of Satisfaction of Mortgage/Deed of Trust	X			Seller
Doc. Stamps on Deed	X			Buyer
Doc. Stamps on Financing Instrument	X			Buyer
Intangible Tax on New Financing Instrument	X			Buyer
1099S Filed	X			
State Revenue Form Filed	X			
Disbursement to Seller			11/24/97	
Disbursement to Seller's Lender			11/24/97	
Disbursement to Brokers				
Disbursement to Title Company			11/24/97	
Residential Closing Binder Index Prepared	X			
Documents Mailed to Buyer	X			
Other:				

File Closed _____

FIGURE 13–8
Good faith estimate

Date: October 2, 1997

MILLENNIUM BANK

GOOD FAITH ESTIMATE

This document gives you an estimate of most of the charges you will have to pay at the settlement of your loan. The figures shown are estimates, based on sales price and proposed mortgage amount as stated on your loan application, and are subject to change.

PROPOSED LOAN TYPE: FIXED RATE LOAN		ESTIMATED SETTLEMENT CHARGES		
SALES PRICE OF		801	Orig. Fee	$338.00*
PROPERTY:	75,200.00	803	Appraisal	275.00
PROPOSED MORTGAGE		804	Credit Report	50.00
AMT.:	67,600.00	809	Courier Fee	35.00
		1102	Title Ins. Fees	815.80
PROPOSED INTEREST RATE:	8.000	1105	Doc. Prep. Fee/Bank	150.00*
TERM OF MORTGAGE:	30 YEAR	1111	Underwriting Fee	75.00
		1112	Tax Regist. Fee	69.00*
ESTIMATED PAYMENT		1201	Recording Fees/ Public Offls.	404.80
Principal and/or Interest	$496.02	TOTAL ESTIMATED SETTLEMENT		
Mortgage Insurance	0.00	CHARGES:		$2,212.60
Taxes	94.00			
Insurance	0.00			
Other	0.00			
TOTAL ESTIMATED PAYMENT	$590.02			

THIS FORM MAY NOT COVER ALL ITEMS YOU WILL BE REQUIRED TO PAY IN CASH AT SETTLEMENT, FOR EXAMPLE, DEPOSIT IN ESCROW FOR ACTUAL REAL ESTATE TAXES AND INSURANCE. YOU MAY WISH TO INQUIRE AS TO THE AMOUNT OF SUCH OTHER ITEMS. YOU MAY BE REQUIRED TO PAY OTHER ADDITIONAL AMOUNTS AT SETTLEMENT.

NOTE: Settlement Charges marked with an (*) are shown on the Disclosure as FINANCE CHARGES.

ESTIMATED PREPAID CHARGES

901	Interest for 30 days	$444.49
1004	County tax reserves, 2 payments at 94.00/pmt.	188.00
TOTAL ESTIMATED PREPAID CHARGES		$632.49

A.	Amount of this Mortgage	$67,600.00	H.	Purchase Price	$75,200.00
B.	Other Financing	0.00	I.	Total Est. Settlement Charges	2,212.60
C.	Other Equity	0.00	J.	Total Est. Prepaid Charges	632.49
D.	Amount of Cash Deposit	0.00			
E.	Closing Costs pd by Seller	0.00	K.	TOTAL (H + I + J)	$78,045.09
F.	Other Credits	0.00			
G.	TOTAL (A + B + C + D + E + F)	$67,600.00		Cash required for closing (K – G)	$10,445.09

This interest calculation represents our estimate of the amount of interest you could be required to pay at settlement. The actual amount will be determined by which day of the month your settlement is conducted. To determine the amount you will have to pay, multiply the number of days remaining in the month in which you close times $14.8164.

FIGURE 13–9
Conventional mortgage
loan commitment

CONVENTIONAL MORTGAGE LOAN COMMITMENT

BORROWER: Patricia Wallis
DATE: October 25, 1997
MORTGAGE COMMITMENT NUMBER: 677377

WE ARE PLEASED TO OFFER YOU A LOAN COMMITMENT WITH THE FOLLOW-
ING TERMS AND CONDITIONS:

LOAN TYPE: __X__ Fixed Rate
                                       _____ Adjustable Rate
                                              ( ) 1 Year ARM
                                              ( ) 3 Year ARM
                                              ( ) Other

LOAN AMOUNT: $ 67,600.00
POINTS: 0.500% OF LOAN AMOUNT: $338.00
TERM OF LOAN: 30 years
CURRENT INTEREST RATE: 8.000%
PRINCIPAL & INTEREST PAYMENT: $ 496.02
Payable on the first day of each month,
plus Taxes and Insurance

PURPOSE OF LOAN: Purchase
CLOSING AGENT: Fisher, Ross, and Simon, P.A.

PROPERTY ADDRESS: 2550 Kingsfield Drive, #305
                                       Any City, Any State

CLOSING COSTS: You will be responsible for all out-of-pocket expenses incurred
                by the Bank in processing your request including, but not lim-
                ited to, credit report(s), appraisal fees, abstract continuations,
                surveys, and the designated closing agent's fees. It is under-
                stood that any costs arising out of the proposed transaction
                shall be borne by you whether or not the loan is closed.

LOAN APPROVAL: Final loan approval is contingent upon items required for
                your loan in accordance with the following additional
                requirements.

CONTINGENCIES: Applicable if the following is checked including the attached
                "additional closing contingencies."

_____ Tax returns: Tax returns to be signed with original signatures at closing.
       Those pages requiring signatures will be sent to the designated closing
       agent for execution at closing.

_____ Private mortgage insurance: Approved by _____. You shall pay the
       cost of all subsequent private mortgage insurance policies which shall be
       included in your monthly escrow payments.

__X__ Condominium: This commitment is subject to approval by our designated
       closing agent of the Declaration of Condominium and related documents
       and approval by the condominium association if required.

__X__ Payoff(s): Subject to paying off existing mortgage with Century Bank.
       Payment of any outstanding taxes, liens or other outstanding obligations
       on the property.

_____ Sale of real estate: Prior to closing, evidence must be presented that your
       property located at _____ has been sold and closed.

_____ Completion of construction: This loan is subject to satisfactory completion
       of construction. Certificate of occupancy and soil treatment certificate are
       required at or prior to closing.

_____ Other: This commitment is subject to the following items as listed below.
       Final acceptance by the Lender must be obtained prior to scheduling the
       loan closing.

FIGURE 13–9
(continued)

It is imperative that we receive this signed commitment letter as soon as possible to ensure a timely closing of your loan. Subject to the conditions hereof, this commitment shall expire on <u>November 25, 1997</u> and thereafter be of no further force and effect.

The undersigned acknowledge and accept the terms of this commitment.

LENDER: BORROWER:

MILLENNIUM BANK

By: <u>Derek Jamison</u>   <u>Patricia Wallis</u>
     Vice President

Date: <u>October 25, 1997</u>   Date: <u>October 25, 1997</u>

FIGURE 13–10
Request for condominium
transfer information

REQUEST FOR CONDOMINIUM TRANSFER INFORMATION

Date: 10/3/97
Our File: 15432
Seller: Parker Properties, Inc.   Buyer: Patricia Wallis
Seller's Unit: Unit 305, Bldg. 2550   Unit Address: 2550 Kingsfield Drive
                                           Any City, Any State

To: Kingsfield Estates Condominium Association

Our firm is representing the Seller of the above-described unit. Please fill out this form and return to our office as soon as possible.

I.   <u>Condominium Maintenance Payments.</u>
   1.   Payment installments: <u>X</u> Monthly   ____ Quarterly
                                   ____ Semi-Annually   ____ Annually
   2.   Amount of each installment: <u>$179.10</u>
   3.   Date upon which last installment payment was made: <u>9/28/97</u>
   4.   Amount of penalty for late payment, if any: <u>$25.00</u>
   5.   Is there a change in the maintenance expected? <u>No</u>
       If so, when? _____ What will be the new payment? _____
II. <u>Special Assessments.</u>
   1.   Are there any special assessments against the above-described unit? If so, please state the amount and when due: <u>None</u>
   2.   Are there any special assessments anticipated within the next twelve months? If so, please describe: <u>None</u>
III. <u>Transfer Fee.</u>
   Is there a transfer fee charged upon transfer of title of the above-described unit? If so, please state the amount: <u>N/A</u>
IV. <u>Interview for Condominium Association Approval.</u>
   Please state the name and telephone number of the individual(s) that must be contacted to set up an interview: <u>Joyce McCarthy</u>
   <u>(000) 032-0078</u>

Dated: <u>October 8, 1997</u>
Kingsfield Condominium Association, Inc.

By: <u>Harold Lipson</u>
    Vice President

Note that the maintenance payments will include the seller's portion of hazard and/or flood insurance. The condominium association insures the structure of the building but not the interior of the unit or its contents. The maintenance payments include the cost of the insurance, the routine maintenance of the building, and any other items specified in the budget as allocated to such payments.

Patricia has already met with the appropriate condominium association committee for an interview and has been approved. The condominium's Certificate of Approval is found in Figure 13–11.

Because one of the parties is a corporate entity, in this instance, the seller, Barbara must verify that the corporation is still in good standing with the secretary of state's office in Any State. She has done so. She must further obtain a certified copy of a corporate resolution in which the board of directors of Parker Properties, Inc., permits the sale of the subject property. She has obtained a copy of the client's articles of incorporation and bylaws and reviewed them to ensure that all procedures have been correctly followed. The corporate resolution was signed in August, and Barbara has obtained the certified copy for the file shown in Figure 13–12.

FIGURE 13–11
Certificate of approval

CERTIFICATE OF APPROVAL

KINGSFIELD CONDOMINIUM ASSOCIATION, INC., an Any State corporation not for profit, the association which administers KINGSFIELD ESTATES Condominium, does hereby certify that the Association has approved the following sale:

Condominium Unit Number:	Unit 305, Building 2550
Seller:	Parker Properties, Inc.
Purchaser:	Patricia Wallis
Date of Approval:	October 28, 1997
	KINGSFIELD CONDOMINIUM ASSOCIATION, INC.

By: _Lillian Keller_
        President

(Corporate Seal)

Attest: _Paul Pearson_
            Secretary

STATE OF ANY STATE
COUNTY OF ANY COUNTY

BEFORE ME, the undersigned authority, personally appeared LILLIAN KELLER and PAUL PEARSON, as President and Secretary respectively of KINGSFIELD CONDOMINIUM ASSOCIATION, INC., an Any State corporation not for profit, who acknowledged before me that they executed the above certificate as such officers of the Corporation and the above certificate is the act and deed of the Corporation.

IN WITNESS WHEREOF, I have hereunto set my hand and official seal this 28th day of October, 1997.

Roberta Hodge
Notary Public
My commission expires: _4/30/99_

RESOLUTION OF THE BOARD OF DIRECTORS OF PARKER PROPERTIES, INC.

I, the undersigned Secretary of Parker Properties, Inc., a corporation duly organized and existing under the laws of the State of Any State, hereby certify that the following is a true copy of a resolution duly adopted by the Board of Directors at a special meeting held on August 14, 1997:

RESOLVED, that the officers of the Corporation and each of them be, and they hereby are, authorized to sell that certain real property as legally described on Exhibit A attached hereto and to execute on behalf of the Corporation all requisite documents and take all other action on behalf of the Corporation as may be necessary or required in connection therewith.

I DO FURTHER CERTIFY that neither the Articles of Incorporation nor the bylaws of the Corporation require any consent of the shareholders for the execution of the documents by the Corporation and that this resolution is not in conflict with any provision of the Articles of Incorporation or the bylaws of the Corporation.

IN WITNESS WHEREOF, I have affixed my name as Secretary and have caused the corporate seal of the Corporation to be hereunto affixed this 14th day of August, 1997.

(Corporate Seal)

Kenneth Ellington
Secretary

FIGURE 13–12
Resolution of the board of directors

The contract does not specify a due date for the preparation of a title commitment. Barbara already has obtained the survey from the seller. From the information gleaned from a title search and examination, as well as the information provided in the survey, Barbara has prepared a title commitment and has submitted it to Patricia. The date indicated on the worksheet is the effective date of the commitment. Schedules A and B of the commitment may be found in Figure 13–13.

Note that the closing worksheet indicates that the client has an existing mortgage on the property in favor of Century Bank. Because Patricia has opted to secure new financing rather than to assume the existing loan, the existing note and mortgage will be paid off at closing. In order to determine what must be paid, Barbara has sent a mortgage estoppel letter to the servicing department of Century Bank, requesting certain payoff information. The due date set forth on the worksheet indicates the target date by which Barbara should either receive a response to the letter or, failing that, call to confirm the items set forth in the letter. A copy of the letter appears in Figure 13–14.

The closing is taking place toward the end of the year. This being the case, the client has already received the annual tax bill for the property, paid it, and forwarded a copy of it to Barbara on the date indicated on the worksheet. The taxes for the year 1997 will be prorated as of the date of closing. If the closing were taking place prior to the client's actual receipt of the current tax bill, Barbara would use the last tax bill for prorating purposes and would make any required adjustments after receipt of the current bill. Note that in some places, real estate taxes are paid quarterly rather than annually. In such a situation, whether the seller has paid the taxes depends on when during the quarter the closing takes place.

FUND COMMITMENT FORM
Schedule A

Commitment No.:   1449898   Effective Date: 10/26/97 at 8:00 a.m.   Agent's File   15432.001
                                                                                      Reference:2440

1. Policy or Policies to be issued:

    OWNER'S: $ 75,200.00

    Proposed Insured:

        Patricia Wallis, a single woman

    MORTGAGEE: $ 67,600.00

    Proposed Insured:

        Millennium Bank, its successors and/or assigns

2. The estate or interest in the land described or referred to in this commitment is a fee simple (if other, specify same) and title thereto is at the effective date hereof vested in:

    Parker Properties, Inc., an Any State corporation

3. The land referred to in this commitment is described as follows:

    Unit 305, Building 2550, of KINGSFIELD ESTATES II, A CONDOMINIUM, according to the DECLARATION OF CONDOMINIUM thereof, recorded in Official Records Book 4676, Page 1342 of the Public Records of Any County, Any State; together with the undivided share of the Common Elements of the Condominium declared in the Declaration of Condominium to be appurtenant thereto.

ISSUED BY

FISHER, ROSS, AND SIMON, P.A.

<u>   3333   </u>
AGENT NO. ———————————— <u>   Ava Ross   </u>
                            AGENT'S SIGNATURE

<u>   1900 N. W. 3rd Avenue   </u> —————————— <u>   Any City   </u> ——— , Any State ————————
    MAILING ADDRESS   CITY   ZIP

Form reproduced through the courtesy of Attorneys' Title Insurance Fund, Inc.

FIGURE 13–13 Title commitment

FUND COMMITMENT FORM

Schedule B

Commitment No.:   1449898

I. The following are the requirements to be complied with:

1. Payment of the full consideration to or for the account of, the grantors or mortgagors.

1. Instruments creating the estate or interest to be insured which must be executed, delivered and filed for record:

    A. Special Condominium Warranty Deed from PARKER PROPERTIES, INC., an Any State corporation to Patricia Wallis, a single woman, conveying premises described under Schedule "A" hereof.

    B. Mortgage from Patricia Wallis to Millennium Bank, encumbering property under Schedule "A" hereof in the original amount of $67,600.00.

II. Schedule B of the policy or policies to be issued will contain exceptions to the following matters unless the same are disposed of to the satisfaction of The Fund:

1. Defects, liens, encumbrances, adverse claims or other matters, if any, created, first appearing in the public records or attaching subsequent to the effective date hereof but prior to the date the proposed Insured acquires for value of record the estate or interest or mortgage thereon covered by this Commitment.

2. Any owner policy issued pursuant hereto will contain under Schedule B the standard exceptions set forth at the inside cover hereof. Any mortgagee policy will contain under Schedule B the standard exceptions unless an affidavit of possession and a satisfactory current survey are submitted, an inspection of the premises is made, it is determined the current year's taxes or special assessments have been paid, and it is determined there is nothing of record which would give rise to mechanics' liens which could take priority over the mortgage (where the liens would otherwise take priority, submission of waivers is necessary).

3. General Taxes for the year 1998 and subsequent years which are not yet due and payable.

4. Restrictions, dedications, conditions, reservations, easements, and other matters set out on the Plat of Kingsfield Estates recorded in Plat Book 37, Page 13, which includes, but is not limited to, easement for utilities, drainage, limited access; drainage right-of-ways; private access easements; restrictions against building or planting on easements; and setbacks, of the Public Records of Any County, Any State.

5. Terms, provisions, covenants, restrictions and easements contained in the Declaration of Condominium of Kingsfield Estates II, a Condominium, recorded in Official Record Book 4676, Page 1342 of the Public Records of Any County, Any State.

Form reproduced through the courtesy of Attorneys' Title Insurance Fund, Inc.

FIGURE 13–13 (continued)

FIGURE 13–14
Mortgage estoppel letter

October 15, 1997

Mortgage Servicing Department

Century Bank
1100 S. Main Street
Any City, Any State

RE: Borrower: Parker Properties, Inc.

        Purchaser: Patricia Wallis
        Property: Unit 305, Building 2550, Kingsfield Estates II
        Street Address: 2550 Kingsfield Drive, #305
                               Any City, Any State

        Loan No: 540031

Dear Sir/Madam:

Please forward to the undersigned a Mortgage Loan Payoff Letter for the above-referenced loan as of November 24, 1997. Our firm has been retained by the Seller of the subject property to conduct the closing on November 24, 1997. In your letter, please indicate the following:

1. Principal balance
2. Annual interest rate and per diem interest
3. Escrow balance and escrow shortage, if any
4. Total payoff amount as of November 24, 1997

Thank you for your assistance in this matter, and should you have any questions, please do not hesitate to contact us.

Sincerely,

Ava Ross, Esquire

The closing worksheet indicates that other items must be prorated as well. Although the closing does not take place until the 24th of November, the worksheet states the due dates for the prorations as the 22nd. This is because Patricia is required to bring a cashier's check to the closing and, therefore, will need to know the exact amount she must pay prior to the date of closing. Thus, Barbara's first task this afternoon is to complete a closing statement to be signed by the parties that itemizes each party's expenses and indicates the cash balance due from the purchaser.

Having input information into her real estate closing software as it has been received, completing the HUD-1 Uniform Settlement Statement should not take much time. The completed HUD-1 statement is found in Figure 13–15.

The software automatically calculates the prorations for the taxes, condominium maintenance, and waste management based on the dates input by Barbara. All three items to be prorated have been paid in advance by the client, so they will appear in the 100s on the HUD-1 statement. Note that the dates for each item differ. Patricia owes Parker Properties for the real estate taxes from the date of closing until the end of the year. Although the condominium has a city address, it is physically located outside the city limits, and therefore, no city taxes accrue. Thus, only county taxes are prorated. The condominium maintenance assessments are paid in advance each month, so

A. SETTLEMENT STATEMENT

United States Department of Housing and Urban Development OMB No. 2502-0265

B. Type of Loan Conventional Uninsured	Loan Number 677377	Mortgage Ins. Case Number	File Number 15432.001

C. Note: This form is furnished to give you a statement of actual settlement costs. Amounts paid to and by the settlement agent are shown. Items marked "p.o.c." were paid outside of closing; they are shown here for informational purposes and are not included in the totals.

D. Name and Address of Borrower: Patricia Wallis, a single woman 235 Crestview Drive, Apt. 205 Any City, Any State	E. Name and Address of Seller: Parker Properties, Inc., an Any State corporation 700 Commercial Boulevard, Suite 360 Any City, Any State TIN: _____
F. Name and Address of Lender: Millennium Bank 1750 Wellington Avenue Any City, Any State	G. Property Location: 2550 Kingsfield Drive Any City, Any State
H. Settlement Agent / Place of Settlement: Fisher, Ross, and Simon, P.A. 1900 N. W. 3rd Avenue Any City, Any State TIN: _____	I. Settlement Date: November 24, 1997

J. Summary of Borrower's Transaction		K. Summary of Seller's Transaction	
100 Gross amount due from borrower		400 Gross amount due to seller	
101 Contract sales price	75,200.00	401 Contract sales price	75,200.00
102 Personal property		402 Personal property	
103 Settlement charges to borrower [1400]	2,716.90	403	
104		404	
105		405	
Adjustments for items paid by seller in advance		Adjustments for items paid by seller in advance	
106 City/town taxes // to //		406 City/town taxes // to //	
107 County taxes 11/24/97 to 12/31/97	125.43	407 County taxes 11/24/97 to 12/31/97	125.43
108 Assessments // to //		408 Assessments // to //	
109 Condo Assn. Maintenance		409 Condo Assn. Maintenance	
110 prorated11/24/97-12/1/97	41.79	410 prorated11/24/97-12/1/97	41.79
111 Solid Waste Authority		411 Solid Waste Authority	
112 prorated11/24/97-9/30/98	143.52	412 prorated11/24/97-9/30/98	143.52
120 Gross Amount Due From borrower	78,227.64	420 Gross Amount Due To Seller	75,510.74
200 Amounts paid by or on behalf of borrower		500 Reductions in amount due to seller	
201 Deposit or earnest money	4,000.00	501 Excess deposit (see instructions)	
202 Principal amount of new loan(s)	67,600.00	502 Settlement charges to seller [1400]	706.00
203 Existing loan(s) taken subject to		503 Existing loan(s) taken subject to	
204		504 Payoff of first mortgage	67,680.00
205		505 Payoff of second mortgage	
206		506 Deposit retained by	
207		507 (Deposit disbursed: 4,000.00)	
208		508	
209 Mortgage in favor of seller		509 Mortgage in favor of seller	
Adjustments for items unpaid by seller		Adjustments for items unpaid by seller	
210 City/town taxes // to //		510 City/town taxes // to //	
211 County taxes // to //		511 County taxes // to //	
212 Assessments // to //		512 Assessments // to //	
213		513	
214		514	
215		515	
216		516	
217		517	
218		518	
219		519	
220 Total Paid By/For Borrower	71,600.00	520 Total Reductions In Amount Due Seller	68,386.00
300 Cash At Settlement From/To Borrower		600 Cash At Settlement To/From Seller	
301 Gross amount due from borrower [120]	78,227.64	601 Gross amount due to seller [420]	75,510.74
302 Less amount paid by/for borrower [220]	71,600.00	602 Less reductions in amount due seller [520]	68,386.00
303 Cash From/(To) Borrower	6,627.64	603 Cash To/(From) Seller	7,124.74

SUBSTITUTE FORM 1099-S SELLER'S STATEMENT: This is important tax information and is being furnished to the Internal Revenue Service. If you are required to file a return, a negligence penalty or other sanction may be imposed on you if this item is required to be reported and the IRS determines that it has not been reported. The information in Boxes E, G, H, and I, the amount on Line 401 and the amount(s) of any real estate tax adjustments appearing on Lines 406 through 412 are reported to the IRS on Form 1099-S.

REQUEST FOR SELLER'S TAXPAYER IDENTIFICATION AND CERTIFICATION: You, the Seller (see Box E) are required by law to provide the Settlement Agent (see Box H) with your correct taxpayer identification number. If you do not provide the Settlement Agent with your correct taxpayer identification number, you may be subject to civil or criminal penalties imposed by law. By signing the following page of this Settlement Statement, you, under penalties of perjury, certify that the number shown on this statement (see Box E - "TIN") is your correct taxpayer identification number.

Pauie Closing System for Windows™

HUD-1 (Rev 3/86)

Form reproduced through the courtesy of Real Estate Expert Systems Associates, Inc.

FIGURE 13–15 HUD-1 Uniform Settlement Statement

L. Settlement Charges						Paid from borrower's funds at settlement	Paid from seller's funds at settlement
700	Total Sales/Broker's Commission Division of commission (line 700) as follows:	Based on $	75,200.00	@	% =		
701	to N/A						
702	to N/A						
703	Commission paid at settlement						
704		Commission retained by					
800	Items Payable In Connection With Loan						
801	Loan origination fee	0.50000 %				338.00	
802	Loan Discount	%					
803	Appraisal fee to:	P.O.C. by Millennium					
804	Credit report to:	P.O.C. by Millennium					
805	Lender's inspection fee						
806	Mortgage insurance application fee to						
807	Assumption fee						
808	Doc. Prep. Fee					150.00	
809							
810							
811							
900	Items Required By Lender To Be Paid In Advance						
901	Interest from 11/24/97 to 12/01/97	14.82000	/ day			103.74	
902	Mortgage insurance premium for	months to					
903	Hazard insurance premium for	years to					
904	Flood insurance premium for	years to					
905							
1000	Reserves Deposited With Lender						
1001	Hazard insurance	months @		per month			
1002	Mortgage insurance	months @		per month			
1003	City property taxes	months @		per month			
1004	County property taxes	2 months @	121.98	per month		243.96	
1005	Annual assessments	months @		per month			
1006	Flood insurance	months @		per month			
1007		months @		per month			
1008							
1100	Title Charges						
1101	Settlement or closing fee to						
1102	Abstract or title search to	Fisher, Ross, and Simon				125.00	
1103	Title examination to						
1104	Title insurance binder to						
1105	Document preparation to						
1106	Notary fees to						
1107	Attorney's fees to Fisher, Ross, Simon	includes above items (	)				700.00
1108	Title insurance fee to	includes above items (	)			712.00	
1109	Lender's coverage	67,600.00	premium	250.00			
1110	Owner's coverage	75,200.00	premium	462.00			
1111	ALTA 4.1 Endorsement					50.00	
1112							
1113							
1200	Government Recording And Transfer Charges						
1201	Recording fees: Deed	12.00	Mortgage	48.00	Release 6.00	60.00	6.00
1202	City/county tax/stamps: Deed		Mortgage	135.20		135.20	
1203	State tax/stamps: Deed	526.40	Mortgage	236.60		763.00	
1204							
1205							
1300	Additional Settlement Charges						
1301	Survey to						
1302	Pest inspection to						
1303	Courier Fees to Fisher, Ross, and Simon					36.00	
1304							
1305							
1306							
1307							
1400	Total Settlement Charges					2,716.90	706.00

I have carefully reviewed the HUD-1 Settlement Statement and to the best of my knowledge and belief, it is a true and accurate statement of all receipts and disbursements made on my account or by me in this transaction. I further certify that I have received a copy of this HUD-1 Settlement Statement.

Borrower:_____ Date:_____ 11/24/97   Seller:_____ Date:_____ 11/24/97
    Patricia Wallis, a single woman   Parker Properties, Inc., an Any State corporation

Borrower:_____ Date:_____   Seller:_____ Date:_____

Borrower:_____ Date:_____   Seller:_____ Date:_____

Borrower:_____ Date:_____   Seller:_____ Date:_____

The HUD-1 Settlement Statement which I have prepared is a true and accurate account of this transaction. I have caused or will cause the funds to be disbursed in accordance with this statement.

Settlement Agent:_____ Date:_____

WARNING: It is a crime to knowingly make a false statement to the United States on this or any similar form. Penalties upon conviction include a fine and imprisonment. For details see Title 18 US Code Section 1001 and Section 1010.

HUD-1 (Rev 3/86)

FIGURE 13-15 (continued)

Patricia owes Parker Properties her share from the date of closing until the first of December. The waste management bill has been paid through the end of September 1998, so Patricia owes Parker Properties her portion of the bill from the date of closing to the last day of September 1998.

The contract and worksheet indicate that Patricia made an earnest money deposit of $4,000 that is being held in escrow by Barbara's firm. This figure appears in line 201 of the HUD-1 statement. Line 202 states the principal amount of the loan as reflected in the loan commitment. From the payoff information received from Century Bank, Barbara inserts the payoff amount of the existing mortgage in line 504.

Barbara moves to the second page of the settlement statement. No real estate broker took part in the transaction, so the 700s pertaining to brokers' commissions are left blank. Patricia is required by her lender, Millennium Bank, to pay a loan origination fee of 0.5%. By simply inserting this number, the software calculates the dollar amount of the loan origination fee automatically. The appraisal fee and credit report fee paid to Millennium Bank are to be paid outside of closing; thus, P.O.C. is typed next to these items. Because they are paid outside of closing, no dollar amount will appear in the borrower's column. Millennium is also charging Patricia a document preparation fee of $150, which Barbara inserts in line 808. Millennium wants Patricia to pay in advance the interest on the loan from the date of closing to the beginning of the following month. Barbara inserts the to-and-from dates and the daily rate, and the software calculates the dollar amount of $103.74.

Because the property in question is a condominium and thus the hazard and flood insurance payments comprise part of each unit owner's monthly maintenance assessments, Millennium Bank is not escrowing sums for the payment of the insurance. However, the bank is requiring that Patricia pay a reserve for the equivalent of two months for the county taxes. The county taxes break down to $121.98 per month.

Barbara's firm is charging $125 for the title search and examination. Costs for the owner's and lender's policies are calculated based on the total coverage of each. The software has made the appropriate calculations. In addition to standard coverage, a condominium endorsement will be issued for the additional fee of $50. Parker Properties is paying for the attorney fees.

The recording fees in the county of Any County are $6.00 per page for each document. Patricia is paying for the recording of the deed and mortgage instrument, while Parker Properties is paying for the recording of the satisfaction of mortgage for the old loan. The amount of $135.20 on line 1202 is the amount of the state intangible tax on the new mortgage loan. It is calculated by multiplying the principal amount of the new loan by the amount of the tax, in this instance, .002. When setting up the software initially, the amount of the tax can be indicated so that the calculation is performed automatically. The same is true of the state documentary stamps. Having input the purchase price and the new loan amount, the software automatically computes the documentary stamp tax based on your tax rate.

Having completed the HUD-1 statement, Barbara can inform Patricia that she will need a check for $6,627.64 on the date of closing. In addition to the HUD-1 statement, Barbara prints out separate buyer's and seller's closing statements that itemize each party's debits and credits in list form. These statements are found in Figures 13–16 and 13–17.

```
                       BUYER'S CLOSING STATEMENT
                                              GF#: 97-15432

   Prepared for:        Prepared by:             Property:
   Patricia Wallis      Fisher, Ross, and Simon  Unit 305, Bldg. 2550

   235 Crestview Dr., #305   1900 N. W. 3rd Ave.
   Any City                  Any City, Any State

   Seller : Parker Properties, Inc.

     Closing date (MO/DY/YR) : 11/24/97      Closer : CLIENT

                                         DEBITS          CREDITS

   Contract Sales Price                    75,200.00
   County taxes          11/24/97 - 12/31/97   125.43
   Condo Assn. Maintenance                      .00
   prorated11/24/97-12/1/97                    41.79
   Solid Waste Authority                        .00
   prorated11/24/97-9/30/98                   143.52
   Deposit or Earnest Money                                4,000.00
   Principal $ of new loan                                67,600.00
   Loan Orig. fee      @ .5000%               338.00
   Doc. Prep. Fee                             150.00
   Interest 11/24/97 - 12/01/97  @   14.82000/day  103.74
   Cnty property taxes  2 mo. @ $   121.98 / mo.   243.96
   Title search to      Fisher,Ross, and Simon    125.00
   Title insurance to   Fisher, Ross, and Simon   712.00
   ALTA 4.1 Endorsement                        50.00
   Recording fees                              60.00
   State tax stamps                           763.00
   Intangible tax on new mortgage             135.20
   Courier Fees to Fisher, Ross, and Simon     36.00
   Funds payable at closing                                6,627.64

                                        _____      _____
                                        $78,227.64      $78,227.64

   Approved:

   _____        _____
   Patricia Wallis               Closing officer or Broker

   Form reproduced through the courtesy of Spencer Systems, Inc.
```

FIGURE 13–16 Buyer's closing statement

Barbara next turns her attention to the preparation of the deed. Her software will automatically insert the names and addresses of the parties, the preparer of the deed, Patricia's social security number, the parcel identification number, and the legal description. If she needs to include customized "subject to" provisions, she can type them into the software file and they will appear under the legal description. Instead, she has chosen to use the standard "subject to" language, indicating Patricia's title is subject to all restrictions, reservations, and limitations that appear on record as well as all future real property taxes. Once signed, witnessed, and acknowledged at closing, the warranty deed will read as shown in Figure 13–18.

```
                         SELLER'S CLOSING STATEMENT
                                                          GF#:  97-15432

    Prepared for:            Prepared by:              Property:
    Parker Properties, Inc.  Fisher, Ross, and Simon   Unit 305, Bldg. 2550

    700 Commercial Blvd.,#360 1900 N. W. 3rd Ave.
    Any City                  Any City, Any State

    Buyer : Patricia Wallis

      Closing date (MO/DY/YR) : 11/24/97       Closer : CLIENT

                                               DEBITS         CREDITS
                                             _____    _____

    Contract Sales Price                                     75,200.00
    County taxes           11/24/97   12/31/97                  125.43
    Condo Assn. Maintenance                                        .00
    prorated11/24/97-12/1/97                                     41.79
    Solid Waste Authority                                          .00
    prorated11/24/97-9/30/98                                    143.52
    Payoff of 1st mtg loan                   67,680.00
    Attorney's fees to     Fisher, Ross, and Simon   700.00
    Recording fees                                6.00
    Funds to seller                           7,124.74
                                             _____    _____
                                             $75,510.74     $75,510.74


    Approved:


    _____        _____
    Hugh Parker, President             Closing officer or Broker
```

FIGURE 13–17 Seller's closing statement

Although the unit is new and sold unfurnished, it does come with standard appliances, lighting fixtures, window screens, and wall-to-wall carpeting. These items are commonly considered fixtures that "go with" the unit. It is common practice in Barbara's firm, however, to complete a bill a sale covering such items to prevent any misunderstandings. The bill of sale, as signed by Hugh Parker on the date of closing, is found in Figure 13–19.

Barbara next turns her attention to completing the seller's affidavit, also referred to as a no-lien affidavit. The state statutes in Any State give a laborer or materialman up to ninety days from the date the last work was completed or the last materials were furnished to the property within which to file a construction lien. This affidavit verifies that no work was done or materials furnished within the last ninety days. The affidavit, as it will appear when signed by Hugh Parker at the closing, is found in Figure 13–20.

Because both the client and Patricia want the existing mortgage lien removed from the property as soon as possible after closing, Barbara prepares a satisfaction of mortgage to be signed by an officer of Century Bank. She will courier the document, together with the check for the loan payoff, the same

Prepared by and return to:

Fisher, Ross, and Simon, P.A.

1900 N. W. 3rd Avenue
Any City,   Any State

Grantees tax identification number: 000505555
Property folio number: 7989594939

Warranty Deed

This Indenture, Made this 24th day of November, 1997 between **Parker Properties, Inc., an Any State corporation**, grantor*, and **Patricia Wallis, a single woman**, grantee*, whose post office address is 235 Crestview Drive, Apt. 205, Any City,   Any State.

*"grantor" and "grantee" are used for singular or plural, as context requires

WITNESSETH: That said grantor, for and in consideration of the sum of TEN AND NO/100 DOLLARS ($10.00) and other valuable considerations to said grantor in hand paid by said grantee, the receipt whereof is hereby acknowledged, has granted, bargained and sold, to the said grantee, and grantee's heirs and assigns forever, the following described land, situate, lying and being in Any County, Any State, to wit:

Unit 305, Building 2550, of KINGSFIELD ESTATES II, A CONDOMINIUM, according to the DECLARATION OF CONDOMINIUM thereof, recorded in Official Records Book 4676, Page 1342 of the Public Records of Any County, Any State; together with the undivided share of the Common Elements of the Condominium declared in the Declaration of Condominium to be appurtenant thereto.

SUBJECT TO RESTRICTIONS, RESERVATIONS AND LIMITATION OF RECORD, IF ANY, AND TAXES FOR THE YEAR 1998 AND SUBSEQUENT YEARS.

and said grantor does hereby fully warrant the title to said land, and will defend the same against the lawful claims of all persons whomsoever.

IN WITNESS WHEREOF, grantor has hereunto set grantor's hand and seal the day and year first above written.

Witnesses:

Rebecca Lawson

William Sanders

PARKER PROPERTIES, INC.,
an Any State corporation

By: Hugh Parker
President

FIGURE 13–18 Warranty deed

STATE OF ANY STATE
COUNTY OF ANY COUNTY

I HEREBY CERTIFY that on this day before me, an officer duly qualified to take acknowledgments, personally appeared HUGH PARKER, President of PARKER PROPERTIES, INC., an Any State corporation to me known to be the person described in and who executed the foregoing instrument and acknowledged before me that he executed the same.

WITNESS my hand and seal in the County and State aforesaid this 24th day of November, 1997.

Ellen Dunning
Notary Public

My Commission Expires: 3/31/99

FIGURE 13–18 (continued)

day so she can have the document returned immediately for recording. A copy of the satisfaction of mortgage, as signed by an officer of the bank, appears in Figure 13–21.

The new mortgage note and mortgage instrument securing the property are not prepared by Barbara, but by Millennium Bank. Patricia is taking out a loan in the amount of $67,600, with a fixed interest rate of eight percent, for a period of thirty years. The mortgage instrument prepared by Millennium Bank has a condominium rider attached to it, by which Patricia promises to abide by the terms of the condominium documents. Additionally, the rider states that Patricia's obligation to maintain hazard insurance is satisfied by the blanket coverage afforded under the condominium association's policy. The rider to the mortgage instrument is found in Figure 13–22.

Both state and federal tax authorities require notification when a sale of real property takes place. As noted in the previous chapter, when the seller is a foreign person or entity and the property being sold is nonresidential property sold for more than $400,000, the Internal Revenue Code requires that at least ten percent of the sales price be withheld for tax purposes. When a nonforeign person or entity is the seller, it is customary for a nonforeign certification (FIRPTA affidavit) to be signed. This certification is not sent to the Internal Revenue Service; rather, it is provided to the purchaser. In such a situation, Barbara prepares the certification to meet the requirements of section 1445 of the Internal Revenue Code, whereby the seller swears under oath that it is not a foreign entity and, therefore, withholding of tax is not required. Barbara does not have to prepare the affidavit for this transaction, however, because the property in question is residential and the purchase price is under $400,000.

Prepared By and Return To:

Fisher, Ross, and Simon, P.A.

1900 N. W. 3rd Avenue
Any City,   Any State

BILL OF SALE, ABSOLUTE

KNOW ALL MEN BY THESE PRESENTS, that **Parker Properties, Inc., an Any State corporation**, transferor, for and in consideration of the sum of TEN AND NO/100 DOLLARS ($10.00) and other good and valuable consideration to transferor paid by **Patricia Wallis, a single woman**, transferee, the receipt whereof is hereby acknowledged, has granted, bargained, sold, transferred and delivered, and by these presents does grant, bargain, sell, transfer and deliver unto transferee, the following goods and chattels:

> All fixed equipment, all window screens, treatments and hardware, all wall-to-wall floor coverings, attached wall coverings and attached lighting fixtures as now installed on the property located at 2550 Kingsfield Drive, Apt. 305, Any City,   Any State.

TO HAVE AND TO HOLD the same unto transferee, transferee's executors, administrators and assigns forever.

AND transferor, for transferor's self and transferor's heirs, executors and administrators, covenant to and with transferee, and transferee's executors, administrators and assigns, that transferor is the lawful owner of the said goods and chattels; that they are free from all encumbrances; that transferor has good right to sell the same aforesaid, and that transferor will warrant and defend the sale of the said property, goods and chattels hereby made, unto transferee said party of the second part his executors, administrators and assigns against the lawful claims and demands of all persons whomsoever.

IN WITNESS WHEREOF, transferor has hereunto set transferor's hand and seal this 24th day of November, 1997.

PARKER PROPERTIES, INC.,
an Any State Corporation

By:___Hugh Parker_____
President

FIGURE 13–19 Bill of sale

PREPARED BY:

FISHER, ROSS, AND SIMON, P.A.

1900 N. W. 3RD AVENUE
ANY CITY, ANY STATE

AFFIDAVIT

STATE OF ANY STATE   )
COUNTY OF ANY COUNTY   )

BEFORE ME, the undersigned authority, personally appeared Hugh Parker, President of Parker Properties, Inc., an Any State corporation ("Affiant") who being by me first duly sworn, on oath, deposes and says:

1. Affiant owns, or is acquiring, an interest in certain property located in Any County , Any State, more particularly described as follows:

> Unit 305, Building 2550, of KINGSFIELD ESTATES II, A CONDOMINIUM, according to the DECLARATION OF CONDOMINIUM thereof, recorded in Official Records Book 4676, Page 1342 of the Public Records of Any County, Any State; together with the undivided share of the Common Elements of the Condominium declared in the Declaration of Condominium to be appurtenant thereto.

2. That the above-described property is free and clear of all liens, taxes, encumbrances and claims of every kind, nature and description whatsoever except for real estate taxes for 1998 and all subsequent years.

3. That within the past 90 days there have been no improvements, alterations or repairs to the above-described property for which the costs remain unpaid, and that within the past 90 days there have been no claims for labor or material furnished for repairing or improving the same, which remain unpaid.

4. That it is in exclusive, full, complete and undisputed possession of said property and that there are no leases, options, claims, unpaid taxes or interest of any kind held thereon, by any other party except:

NONE

5. That there are no construction, mechanic's, or laborer's liens against the above-described property.

6. That the undersigned has not and will not execute any instrument or do any act which would or might in any way affect the title to the described property

7. This Affidavit is made for the purpose of inducing PATRICIA WALLIS, a single woman, to purchase the above-described property from PARKER PROPERTIES, INC. and for the purpose of

FIGURE 13–20 Seller's affidavit

inducing Fisher, Ross, and Simon, P.A., as title agent, to issue a title policy covering such property.

Further Affiant Sayeth Not.   PARKER PROPERTIES, INC., an
                                                               Any State corporation

                                                               _____Hugh Parker_____
                                                                            President

Sworn to and subscribed before me this 24th day of November, 1997.

___Ellen Dunning_____
NOTARY PUBLIC

(Notary Seal)
My Commission Expires: 3/31/99

FIGURE 13–20 (continued)

Barbara next prepares a Department of Revenue of Any State Return for Transfers of Interest in Any State Real Property that will be filed when the deed is recorded. This form is found in Figure 13–23. Note that in the form in Figure 13–23, the address given for Patricia Wallis is the street address for the property purchased because this will be her primary residence once the closing takes place.

Barbara must attend to one more tax matter. As noted in the previous chapter, the Tax Reform Act of 1986 requires that the person, firm, or company handling the real estate closing report the sale to the Internal Revenue Service. This is done on a 1099S form. The form includes the name, address, and tax identification number of the filer; the name, address, and tax identification number of the transferor (seller); the address or legal description of the property; the date of closing; the sales price; and the purchaser's portion of the real estate tax. Figure 13–24 shows the copy supplied to the seller.

After closing, Barbara will send the deed, satisfaction of mortgage from Century Bank, and mortgage instrument in favor of Millennium Bank for recording. She will include a trust account check to cover the recording costs as well as the documentary stamp tax on the deed and mortgage note, and the intangible tax on the new mortgage. The cover letter she sends is found in Figure 13–25.

Once the documents are returned from recording, Barbara prepares the title policies for Patricia and for Millennium Bank. She attaches the ALTA 4.1 endorsement, which is a condominium endorsement insuring the policy holder against loss or damage by reason of such circumstances as the failure of the condominium documents to comply with state statutes and any charges or assessments provided for in the condominium statutes and condominium documents due and unpaid at the date of the policy.

Prepared by:

Fisher, Ross, and Simon, P.A.

1900 N. W. 3rd Avenue
Any City,   Any State

SATISFACTION OF MORTGAGE

KNOW ALL MEN BY THESE PRESENTS: That Century Bank, the owner and holder of that certain mortgage executed by Parker Properties, Inc. , dated March 10, 1995, and recorded in Official Records Book 4678, Page 905, of the Public Records of Any County, Any State, securing payment of the sum of $70,000.00 (original principal amount), and certain promises and obligations set forth in said mortgage deed, upon the property situate in said State and County described as follows, to-wit:

Unit 305, Building 2550, of KINGSFIELD ESTATES II, A CONDOMINIUM, according to the DECLARATION OF CONDOMINIUM thereof, recorded in Official Records Book 4676, Page 1342 of the Public Records of Any County, Any State; together with the undivided share of the Common Elements of the Condominium declared in the Declaration of Condominium to be appurtenant thereto.

hereby acknowledges full payment and satisfaction of said note and mortgage and directs the Clerk of the Circuit Court of said county to cancel the mortgage of record.

IN WITNESS WHEREOF, the owner and holder has executed this Satisfaction of Mortgage the _____ day of _____, 19__.

Witnesses: CENTURY BANK
Eleanor Jacobs

                                                          By: Mark Jansen, Vice President

Robert Spence

STATE OF ANY STATE
COUNTY OF ANY COUNTY

The foregoing instrument was acknowledged before me this 24th day of November 1997 by Mark Jansen, Vice President of Century Bank.

Alice Tompkins
Notary Public

(Seal)

My Commission Expires: April 20, 1998

FIGURE 13–21 Satisfaction of mortgage

FIGURE 13–22
Condominium rider

CONDOMINIUM RIDER

THIS CONDOMINIUM RIDER is made this 24th day of November, 1997, and is incorporated into and shall be deemed to amend and supplement the Security Instrument of same date given by the undersigned ("Borrower") to secure Borrower's Note to MILLENNIUM BANK ("Lender") of the same date and covering the Property described in the Security Instrument and located at: 2550 Kingsfield Drive, Unit 305, Any City, Any State. The Property includes a unit in, together with an undivided interest in the common elements of, a condominium project known as Kingsfield Estates II ("Condominium Project").

Borrower shall perform all of Borrower's obligations under the Condominium Project's Constituent Documents. The "Constituent Documents" are the: (1) Declaration or any other document which creates the Condominium Project; (2) bylaws; (3) code of regulations; and (4) equivalent documents. Borrower shall promptly pay, when due, all dues and assessments imposed pursuant to the Constituent Documents.

So long as the Owners' Association maintains, with a generally accepted insurance carrier, a "master" or "blanket" policy on the Condominium Project which is satisfactory to Lender and which provides insurance coverage in the amounts, for the periods and against the hazards Lender requires, then Lender waives the provision in paragraph 2 of the Security Instrument for the monthly payment to Lender of one-twelfth of the yearly premium installments for hazard insurance on the Property.

If Borrower does not pay condominium dues and assessments when due, then Lender may pay them. Any amounts disbursed by Lender under this paragraph shall become additional debt of Borrower secured by the Security Instrument. Unless Borrower and Lender agree to other terms of payment, these amounts shall bear interest from the date of disbursement at the Note rate and shall be payable, with interest, upon notice from Lender to Borrower requesting payment.

BY SIGNING BELOW, Borrower accepts and agrees to the terms and provisions contained in this Condominium Rider.

Patricia Wallis
Borrower

Barbara then sends the lender, Millennium Bank, the original recorded financing instrument, the original mortgagee's title policy, and a copy of the warranty deed. The cover letter sent with these documents is found in Figure 13–26.

Barbara then turns her attention to the preparation of a residential closing binder index of documents to be provided to Patricia. The index essentially tells the chronology of the closing, starting with the contract through the issuance of the owner's title policy. Each item is numbered, and the corresponding documents are provided in order, separated by dividers that are tabbed and numbered. The completed closing binder index for the documents to be sent to Patricia is found in Figure 13–27.

Barbara next prepares a residential closing binder index for Parker Properties, Inc., as shown in Figure 13–28.

After making copies of all documentation for the office file, Barbara will send these settlement packets to the respective parties and close the file.

DEPARTMENT OF REVENUE OF ANY STATE
RETURN FOR TRANSFERS OF INTEREST IN ANY STATE REAL PROPERTY

PART I:

A.   Grantor (Seller): Parker Properties, Inc., an Any State corporation

B.   Mailing Address: 700 Commercial Boulevard, #360, Any City, Any
State

C.   Grantee (Buyer): Patricia Wallis, a single woman

D.   Mailing Address: 2550 Kingsfield Drive, #305, Any City, Any State

E.   Description of Property: Unit 305, Building 2550, of KINGSFIELD
ESTATES II, A CONDOMINIUM, according to the DECLARATION OF
CONDOMINIUM thereof, recorded in Official Records Book 4676,
Page 1342, of the Public Records of Any County, Any State; together
with the undivided share of the Common Elements of the
Condominium declared in the Declaration of Condominium to be
appurtenant thereto.

F.   Date of Sale: November 24, 1997

G.   Type of Document: General Warranty Deed

H.   Recorded in: Any County, Any State

I.   Total Consideration to Be Paid: $75,200.00

I HEREBY CERTIFY that this return has been examined by me and to the best of
my knowledge and belief is a true and complete return.

_____   _____
Signature of Grantee   Date

_____   _____
Signature of Grantee   Date

PART II: (To be completed by the Clerk of the Circuit Court's Office):

File Number: _____ or O.R. Book _____ Page _____
Clerk's Date Stamp: _____ Date Recorded: _____

FIGURE 13–23
Department of revenue
return for transfers of
interest in real property

Filer's name, street address, city and ZIP code Fisher, Ross, and Simon, P.A. 1900 N. W. 3rd Avenue Any City, Any State	1 Date of closing 11/24/97	OMB No. 1545-0997 **1997**	**Proceeds From Real Estate Transactions**
	2 Gross proceeds 75,200.00		

Filer's Federal identification number 000203123	Transferor's identification number 000998888	3 Address or legal description	**Copy B For Transferor**
Transferor's name Parker Properties, Inc., an Any State corporation Street address (including apt no.) 700 Commercial Boulevard, Suite 360 City, state, and ZIP code Any City, Any State		2550 Kingsfield Drive, Apt. 305 Any City, Any State 4 Transferor received or will receive property or services as part of the consideration (if checked) ☐	This is important tax information and is being furnished to the Internal Revenue Service. If you are required to file a return, a negligence penalty or other sanction may be imposed on you if this item is required to be reported and the IRS determines that it has not been reported.
Account number (optional)		5 Buyer's part of real estate tax $ 125.43	

Instructions for Transferor

Generally persons responsible for closing a real estate transaction must report the real estate proceeds to the Internal Revenue Service and must furnish this statement to you. If the real estate transferred was your main home, file **Form 2119**, Sale of Your Home, with your income tax return even if you sold at a loss or you did not replace your home. If the real estate transferred was not your main home, report the transaction in the applicable parts of **Form 4797**, Sales of Business Property, **Form 6252**, Installment Sale Income, and/or **Schedule D (Form 1040)**, Capital Gains and Losses.

If you sold your home and (1) you did not own it for more than 9 years and (2) it was financed after 1990 under a Federally subsidized program (qualified mortgage bonds or mortgage credit certificates), you may have to recapture part of the subsidy. This will increase your tax. See **Form 8828**, Recapture of Federal Mortgage Subsidy, and **Pub. 523**, Selling Your Home.

Box 1. - Shows the date of closing.

Box 2. - Shows the gross proceeds from a real estate transaction. Gross proceeds include cash and notes payable to you and notes assumed by the transferee (buyer). Box 2 does not include the value of other property or services you received or are to receive. See **Box 4.**

Box 3. - Shows the address of the property transferred or a legal description of the property.

Box 4. - If marked, shows that you received or will receive services or property (other than cash or notes) as part of the consideration for the property transferred. The value of

any services or property (other than cash or notes is not included in box 2.

Box 5. - Shows certain real estate tax on a residence charged to the buyer at settlement. If you have already paid the real estate taxes for the period that includes the sale date, subtract this amount from the amount already paid to determine your deductible real estate tax. But if you have already deducted the real estate tax in a prior year generally report this amount as income on the line for "Other Income" on Form 1040. For more information, see Pub. 523.

FIGURE 13–24 1099-S form

FIGURE 13-25
Sample cover letter

November 25, 1997

Recording Clerk
Circuit Court of Any County
Any County Courthouse
500 Courthouse Road

Any City, Any State

Re: Recording of Documents

Dear Clerk:

Enclosed is our trust account check number 3044, made payable to Clerk, Circuit Court of Any County, Any State, in the amount of $964.20 for the recording of the following documents:

1.	Recording Warranty Deed	$ 12.00
	Documentary Stamps on Deed	$526.40
2.	Recording Mortgage	$ 48.00
	Documentary Stamps on Mortgage	$236.60
	Intangible Tax on Mortgage	$135.00
3.	Recording Satisfaction of Mortgage	$ 6.00

If you have any questions with regard to the above, please do not hesitate to contact me. Please return all recorded documents to my office in the enclosed, self-addressed, stamped envelope. Thank you for your assistance in this matter.

Sincerely,

Barbara Hammond
Legal Assistant to Ava Ross, Esquire

Enc.

FIGURE 13–26
Sample cover letter

December 7, 1997

Mortgage Loan Closing Department
Millennium Bank
1750 Wellington Avenue
Any City, Any State

Re: Patricia Wallis
       2550 Kingsfield Drive, #305
       Any City, Any State

       Loan Number: 677377

Dear Sir/Madam:

In connection with the mortgage loan closing for the above-referenced customer, enclosed are the following items for your files:

1. Copy of conveying title to the subject property to Patricia Wallis, a single woman, from Parker Properties, Inc., dated 11/24/97, and recorded on 11/29/97 in Official Records Book 5120, Page 1003, of the Public Records of Any County, Any State.

2. Original Mortgage encumbering the subject property in favor of Millennium Bank, dated 11/24/97, recorded in Official Records Book 5120, Page 1005, of the Public Records of Any County, Any State.

3. Original Mortgagee Title Insurance Policy Number 698006 issued 12/7/97, providing $67,600.00 of lender's coverage.

The receipt of the enclosed documents should complete your file on this closing. Should you have any further questions, however, please do not hesitate to contact us.

Sincerely,

Barbara Hammond
Legal Assistant to Ava Ross, Esquire

Enc.

RESIDENTIAL CLOSING BINDER INDEX
PARKER PROPERTIES, INC.—WALLIS CLOSING
Property: Unit 305, 2550 Kingsfield Drive
Any City, Any State
Closing Date: November 24, 1997

1. Copy of Contract for Purchase and Sale dated September 28, 1997, between Patricia Wallis, a single woman (Purchaser), and Parker Properties, Inc., an Any State corporation (Seller).
2. Copy of Title Commitment, dated October 26, 1997 (Original previously provided).
3. Copy of Certificate of Approval of Kingsfield Condominium Association, dated October 28, 1997.
4. Copy of Mortgage Instrument by Patricia Wallis, a single woman, in favor of Millennium Bank, dated November 24, 1997.
5. Copy of Note in the amount of $67,600.00 by Patricia Wallis, a single woman, in favor of Millennium Bank, dated November 24, 1997.
6. Original Warranty Deed from Parker Properties, Inc., an Any State corporation, to Patricia Wallis, dated November 24, 1997.
7. Original Bill of Sale from Parker Properties, Inc., an Any State corporation, to Patricia Wallis, dated November 24, 1997.
8. Original Seller's Affidavit from Parker Properties, Inc., an Any State corporation, to Patricia Wallis, dated November 24, 1997.
9. HUD-1 Uniform Settlement Statement, dated November 24, 1997.
10. Buyer's Closing Statement, dated November 24, 1997.
11. Original Owner's Title Insurance Policy No. 739119, issued December 7, 1997.

FIGURE 13–27
Sample residential closing binder index for purchaser

RESIDENTIAL CLOSING BINDER INDEX
PARKER PROPERTIES, INC.—WALLIS CLOSING
Property: Unit 305, 2550 Kingsfield Drive
Any City, Any State
Closing Date: November 24, 1997

1. Copy of Contract for Sale and Purchase, dated September 28, 1997, between Patricia Wallis, a single woman (Purchaser), and Parker Properties, Inc., an Any State corporation (Seller).
2. Original Certificate of Approval by Kingsfield Condominium Association, dated October 28, 1997.
3. Copy of Warranty Deed from Parker Properties, Inc., an Any State corporation, to Patricia Wallis, a single woman, dated November 24, 1997.
4. Copy of Bill of Sale from Parker Properties, Inc., an Any State corporation, to Patricia Wallis, a single woman, dated November 24, 1997.
5. Copy of Seller's Affidavit from Parker Properties, Inc, an Any State corporation, to Patricia Wallis, a single woman, dated November 24, 1997.
6. HUD-1 Uniform Settlement Statement, dated November 24, 1997.
7. Seller's Closing Statement, dated November 24, 1997.
8. Original Satisfaction of Mortgage from Century Bank, dated November 24, 1997.

FIGURE 13–28
Sample residential closing binder index for seller

CHAPTER SUMMARY

1. The key to a successful real estate closing is organization. To aid in organizing a residential closing file, a worksheet is a must. A residential closing worksheet should allow the paralegal to have all pertinent information at his or her fingertips. It should include the names, addresses, telephone numbers, fax numbers, and tax identification numbers of each party. It should contain all relevant information pertaining to lenders, real estate brokers, title companies, and escrow agents. Finally, it should specify the dates and detail all steps that must be taken prior to, during, and following the closing, specifying which party is responsible for each step and which party will be paying for each item.

2. A paralegal will be called upon to prepare not only the closing documents, but also the correspondence to be sent to parties, their attorneys, lenders, brokers, condominium or homeowners' associations, and so forth. The first letter to be sent is the letter confirming the initial appointment with the client. If the client is the seller, he or she should be requested to bring a copy of the contract for sale and purchase (unless your office will be drafting it) and all documentation he or she received at the closing of his or her purchase of the property. If the seller has a survey, he or she should bring that as well. If the client is the buyer, he or she should be asked to bring a copy of the contract for sale and purchase (unless your office is drafting it) and any other documentation provided by the seller at the time of contracting, such as condominium documents.

3. Other correspondence that a paralegal may draft during the course of a real estate closing include letters requesting mortgage payoff or estoppel information, letters requesting the transfer of mortgage papers if the mortgage is to be assumed, letters requesting condominium transfer information, letters pertaining to prorations of taxes if there is the possibility that the prorations will need to be readjusted after closing, and transmittal letters. Letters signed by paralegals should be accurate as to facts and contain no legal advice.

4. Once all parties have signed the required documents at closing, checks have been disbursed, and documents have been recorded, the paralegal must prepare professional packages of the closing documents to be given to the parties. The purchaser is provided with a copy of the contract, a copy of the title commitment (he or she should already have received the original), copies of the financing instrument and note, and the originals of the deed, bill of sale, seller's affidavit, and any other instruments executed by the seller in favor of the purchaser. The purchaser also receives a HUD-1 Uniform Settlement Statement and an owner's title policy.

5. After closing, the seller is provided with a copy of the contract; copies of the deed, bill of sale, seller's affidavit, and any other instruments executed by the seller in favor of the purchaser; and the original satisfaction of mortgage, if applicable. The seller also receives a HUD-1 Uniform Settlement Statement.

REVIEW QUESTIONS

1. Assume that in the hypothetical closing presented in this chapter, city taxes were assessed as well as county taxes. Assume further that the annual calendar-year city taxes were in the amount of $1,560 and that this tax bill was already paid by the seller before the date of closing. Factoring this in, how much cash would be paid by the buyer and how much cash would be due to the seller at closing?

2. Assume that in the hypothetical closing presented in this chapter, the closing date was moved from November 24, 1997, to November 15, 1997. The due dates of which items on the closing worksheet must be changed?

3. After closing, the purchaser receives originals of which documents?

4. After closing, the seller receives originals of which documents?

5. After closing, the lender receives originals of which documents?

ETHICAL QUESTIONS

Some states allow paralegals to conduct real estate closings as long as certain guidelines are met. Assume that your state permits paralegals to conduct real estate closings as long as: (1) the closing is a simple, residential closing; and (2) the paralegal's supervising attorney is available by telephone to handle any question of law that may arise.

Your firm represents the sellers, Aaron and Amy Conaway, who are selling their home to Donald and Sharon Hogan. The closing is scheduled to take place at 2:00 P.M. on Friday at your firm's office. You have prepared the warranty deed, seller's affidavit, bill of sale, and other pertinent documents. Your supervising attorney has reviewed and approved them and has decided to have you conduct the closing, as she has several appointments that day but is planning to be in her office should you need her.

Two hours before the closing, your supervising attorney walks into your office to check in with you before leaving. She has neglected to tell you that she has rescheduled her cross-country flight to attend her brother's weekend wedding. She was originally scheduled to leave at 5:00 P.M., but she rescheduled two of her appointments and is now leaving at 1:00 P.M. You remind her of the Conaway closing, and she tells you to go to the closing and not to worry—everything is in order, and it should go smoothly. What should you do?

PRACTICAL ASSIGNMENTS

Assignment 13:1. Assume that Kingsfield Estates is located within your city, county, and state. Patricia Wallis must move out of state due to a lucrative job offer. She has found a buyer for her condominium unit, and she and the buyer have gone to contract. The contract was signed last Wednesday. Patricia has hired Deborah Sanders, your supervising attorney, to handle the closing. She is scheduled to meet with Deborah five business days from today at 2:00 P.M. Draft a letter confirming the meeting and instruct Patricia regarding the documentation to bring. After review, insert the letter under the "Residential Closings" section of your resource portfolio.

Assignment 13:2. Deborah is putting you in charge of the Wallis closing file. You have reviewed the contract. According to the contract, the sales price of the unit is $86,000. The closing is to take place two months from today's date at 1:00 P.M. The purchaser is David Kern, a single man. His current address is 164 Ferncliff Road, Apt. 106 (your city, county, state). His telephone number is 550-3333. His social security number is 000-70-7070. He does not have a fax number. Patricia was able to keep her old telephone number when she moved to Kingsfield Estates. David has ten days from the date of the contract to make a loan application and thirty days from the date of the contract to procure a loan commitment. He was given the condominium documents by Patricia when he signed the contract. Check your state statutes to determine how many days he has to review them.

David put down a ten percent deposit when he executed the contract. The deposit is with Open Door Realty, 1200 N.W. 4th Street (your city, county, state). Its telephone number is 444-0020, and its fax number is 444-0024. The agent is Wendy Colson. There are no other realtors involved. According to the contract, Patricia is to pay Open Door a five percent commission upon closing.

Your office will not be preparing the title work; an outside title company will be hired. The contract stipulates that the seller must provide the purchaser with a title commitment within fifteen days from the date of the contract. The purchaser is to pay for the title search and examination and for the mortgagee's policy. The seller is to pay for the title commitment and the owner's policy.

David has not hired independent counsel. The contract requires the seller to provide a warranty deed and all other documentation transferring title to the property. With this information in hand, photocopy the blank residential real estate closing worksheet found in your student workbook (the original worksheet is to be used for the workbook assignment) and fill in the relevant information and due dates. (This client number is 1590.) Upon completion and review, insert the worksheet under the "Residential Closings" section of your resource portfolio.

Assignment 13:3. Prepare a request of condominium transfer information to be sent to Kingsfield Condominium Association as well as a certificate of approval to be signed and dated by the condominium officers. In addition, prepare a mortgage estoppel (loan payoff) letter to be sent to Millennium Bank (same address, your city, county, state). After review, insert them under the "Residential Closings" section of your resource portfolio.

Assignment 13:4. David has obtained a loan commitment from Magna Bank, 440 Adams Street (your city, county, state). The bank's telephone number is 322-2200, and its fax number is 322-2020. The loan number is 544006. The loan officer is Anthony Rossi. The principal amount of the loan is $68,800. It is a conventional uninsured loan with a fixed rate of eight percent for a term of thirty years. There is a loan origination fee of one percent, and two points are to be charged. The appraisal and credit report are to be paid to Magna outside of closing. Magna is charging a document preparation fee of $175 and is requiring a three-month reserve for county property taxes.

You have received information back from the condominium association and from Millennium Bank. The monthly maintenance assessments for Patricia's unit are $150. There are no special assessments due or anticipated. The Solid Waste Authority bill has been paid up to the first of next month. The total bill for the year is $165. The payoff amount for Patricia's loan is $65,040.90. The latest tax bill has not been paid yet, and it shows an annual county tax of $1,500.

The title company conducting the examination and preparing the commitment and policies is Premium Title Company, 200 Waterford Road, Suite 103 (your city, county, state). Its telephone number is 440-9977, and its fax number is 440-9978. It is charging $125 for the title examination, $100 for the title commitment, $310 for the mortgagee's policy, and $520 for the owner's policy. There is an additional $50 charge for the ALTA 4.1 endorsement to be attached to the lender's policy. Your firm, Hernandez, Sanders, and Norris, P.A., is acting as closing agent and is charging Patricia a flat rate attorney's fee of $600 for its work on the transaction. Your office address is 263 Republic Avenue (your city and state); the telephone number is 111-0030, and the fax number is 111-0035.

The financing documents to be recorded number seven pages. The contract stipulates that the seller is to pay for the recording of the deed and the satisfaction of mortgage, while the purchaser is to pay for the recording of the financing instruments. Further, the seller is to pay the documentary stamp tax on the deed, while the purchaser is to pay the documentary stamp on the note and the intangible tax, if any, on the financing instrument.

With this information in hand, fill in the additional relevant information on the closing worksheet. Then prepare the HUD-1 Uniform Settlement Statement, photocopying the blank statement provided in your student workbook (the original HUD-1 form is to be used for the workbook assignment). To calculate the recording fees, documentary stamp tax, and intangible tax, use your county's stipulated rates. After review, insert the HUD-1 statement under the "Residential Closings" section of your resource portfolio.

Assignment 13:5. A title update since the date of closing between Parker Properties, Inc., and Patricia shows only the following additions.

a. The satisfaction of mortgage by Century Bank
b. The recording of the deed transferring title from Parker Properties, Inc., to Patricia.
c. The recording of the financing instrument given by Patricia in favor of Millennium Bank

Prepare the following documents to be signed at closing: (a) warranty deed, (b) bill of sale, and (c) seller's affidavit. After review, insert these documents under the "Residential Closings" section of your resource portfolio.

Assignment 13:6. Assume the title policies were issued two weeks from the date of closing. Prepare a residential closing binder index for each of the parties. After review, insert the index behind the worksheet and before the completed closing documents under the "Residential Closings" section of your resource portfolio.

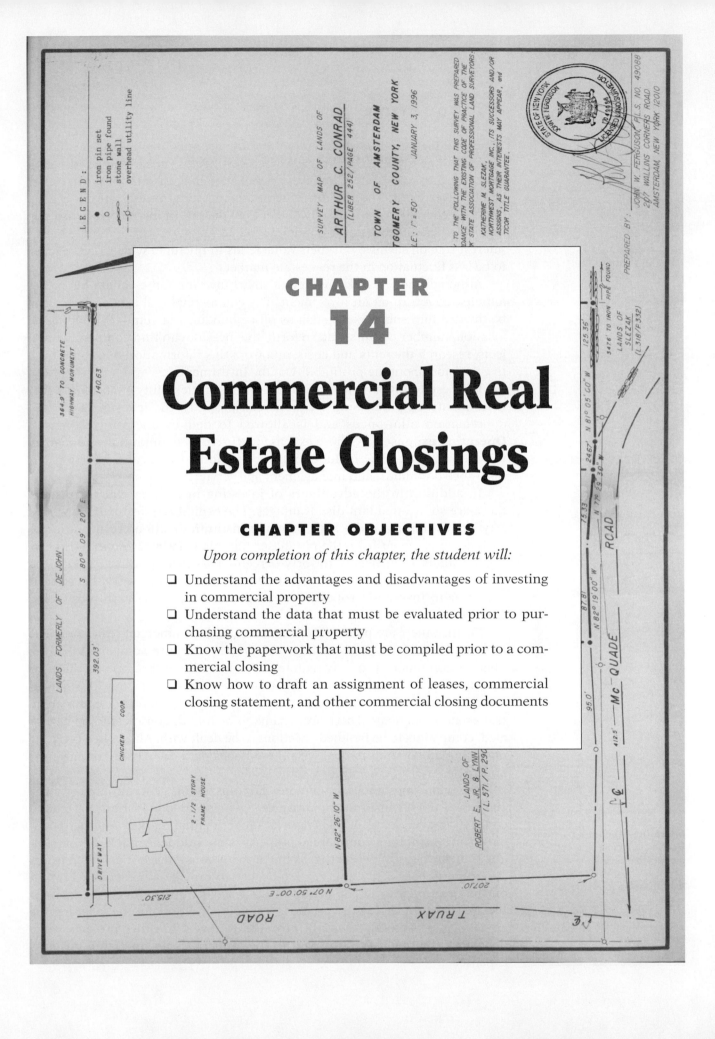

CHAPTER
14

Commercial Real Estate Closings

CHAPTER OBJECTIVES

Upon completion of this chapter, the student will:

❑ Understand the advantages and disadvantages of investing in commercial property
❑ Understand the data that must be evaluated prior to purchasing commercial property
❑ Know the paperwork that must be compiled prior to a commercial closing
❑ Know how to draft an assignment of leases, commercial closing statement, and other commercial closing documents

INTRODUCTION

Individuals and companies looking for avenues of investment have a plethora of possibilities, including savings certificates, stocks and bonds, commodities, and real estate. The investor seeks the highest rate of return on his or her investment. The rate of return on commercial real estate, in a good market, generally is considerably higher than the rate of interest paid on a savings certificate. Stocks and bonds may yield greater returns than a bank's interest rate on savings, but their value tends to fluctuate widely. There tends to be less fluctuation in the real estate market.

Although there is risk involved, a smart investor can estimate his or her anticipated return on an investment. The commercial real estate market can be divided into submarkets, such as office buildings or retail. Depending on location, number of units, and so forth, the investor can find comparable projects, research the rents and costs, and from this information make an objective decision about the profitability of the investment.

Real estate investment also allows more tax flexibility than most other investments. In purchasing a commercial property, the investor is allowed depreciation allowances and is allowed to deduct operating expenses. **Operating expenses** are those expenses incurred in maintaining and managing the property. They include, but are not limited to, real property taxes, insurance premiums, and management and service contracts.

In addition to the advantages of investing in commercial real estate, there are some attendant disadvantages. The capital requirements for property acquisition are quite high. Lending institutions often require a larger cash down payment from the purchaser than they do in residential transactions, usually from twenty to forty percent. This ties up a large portion of the investor's capital in an investment with poor liquidity, because it is harder to turn real property into ready cash than it is with most other investments.

Further, there are management concerns with commercial real estate. The investor must be ready to manage the property or hire someone to do so. There is continuous property maintenance. In addition, because the investor becomes landlord, unless he or she turns the property over quickly, there is more personal involvement and time investment required in a commercial real estate investment. There are tenants to be found, contracts to be negotiated, complaints to be handled, evictions to be dealt with. Although a property manager can be hired to deal with these issues on a daily basis, the investor nonetheless must be involved at some level.

The financing sources for commercial transactions generally are commercial banks and life insurance companies. Savings and loan institutions tend to concentrate their loans in the single-family residential market. Another possible arrangement for a commercial property is the **sale-leaseback.** In this situation, the owner of a property sells the property to an investor and then leases the property back. The rents are established to provide a prearranged return on the investment over the period of the lease. In this manner, the investor receives a guaranteed return on the investment. Additionally, the seller has the advantage of receiving the cash proceeds to invest in other projects while deducting the rental amount paid to the investor as an operating business expense.

operating expenses: Expenses incurred in maintaining and managing property.

sale-leaseback: A situation in which an owner of real property sells the property to an investor and then leases the property back.

A third possibility is seller "take-back" financing, in which the buyer of the property looks not to a lending insitution but to the seller to finance a portion of the transaction, and the buyer executes a promissory note and mortgage in favor of the seller.

As noted in earlier chapters, when one purchases commercial real estate, one must consider numerous factors. A market analysis must be done to determine whether the location and economic climate are conducive to realizing a profit. The investor obtains all data pertaining to the physical site such as surveys and plans, obtains copies of pertinent zoning ordinances, has engineering reports compiled, and so forth. The investor also looks at competitive rental prices currently charged in the locale and comparable occupancy rates.

In addition to looking at the current leases of the prospective seller of a property, the investor must also be able to predict whether future occupancy levels will rise or fall. If the seller's current rent prices appear low in comparison to the competition, the investor will be concerned with the length of the lease terms. If the rents are high, the investor will look to see if the tenants are contractually committed on long leases. In looking at occupancy rates, the investor will take into consideration the under- or oversupply of rental space in the locale.

The investor will want to analyze the property owner's financial records. In addition to the income the property produces, the investor will look at the operating expenses. The investor will need to take reserve requirements into account. **Reserve requirements** are monies set aside for the replacement of items over and above regular maintenance requirements. Reserves may be used to replace a roof or an elevator, for example. The investor is most concerned in determining the **break-even point,** which is the point at which gross income equals the total of fixed costs and variable costs. When a property's gross income exceeds the break-even point, the property begins to realize a profit. **Fixed costs** are costs that remain constant and do not vary according to the income generated. They include such items as real property taxes, insurance, and loan payments. **Variable costs,** on the other hand, are costs that vary according to the income generated. They include such items as advertising costs and managerial fees. The higher the occupancy level needed to break even on the property, the poorer the investment. For example, if a break-even analysis indicates that a ninety-eight percent occupancy rate is necessary to break even, the profitability of the property is virtually nonexistent.

Once an investor contracts to purchase a commercial property, the real estate attorney hired to handle the closing must keep track of numerous documents. The seller must supply the purchaser with the most current list of leases and rent roll. The purchaser will require a list of security deposits held by the seller. Further, the seller will need to obtain tenant estoppel certificates prior to closing. A **tenant estoppel certificate** verifies the terms and conditions of each tenant's lease. Both the purchaser and the purchaser's lender will require these certificates. Additionally, an assignment of leases must be drafted assigning the current leases between the seller and tenants to the purchaser.

The paperwork involved in a commercial closing is considerable, and it will be your responsibility, as paralegal, to keep track of papers submitted by both parties as well as to draft the closing documents. This chapter sets forth

reserve requirements: Monies set aside for the replacement of items over and above regular maintenance requirements.

break-even point: The point at which gross income equals the total of fixed costs and variable costs.

fixed costs: Costs that remain constant and do not vary according to the income generated.

variable costs: Costs that vary according to the income generated.

tenant estoppel certificate: A document that verifies the terms and conditions of a tenant's lease.

a hypothetical commercial closing, providing samples of most documents found in these transactions. As in the case of residential closings, a worksheet should be used as soon as a commercial closing file is opened to help you keep organized.

A commercial closing worksheet will be similar in some respects to a residential closing worksheet, addressing such items as the parties, lenders, brokers, title company, escrow agent, deposits, title work, loan applications, and so forth. Certain items included in a residential closing worksheet, however, will be omitted (for example, condominium association approval, homeowners' association approval), while others will be added. For example, a commercial closing worksheet should include the preparation and execution of tenant estoppel certificates, rent rolls, security deposit lists, schedules of prepaid and delinquent tenants, occupancy/vacancy analysis reports, and the assignment of tenant leases. In addition to tax and other prorations, rents must be prorated between the parties. A commercial closing worksheet is found in the hypothetical closing that follows.

HYPOTHETICAL CLIENT CLOSING

Mansart Corporation owns several commercial properties in town. One of these properties is Tavistock Commercial Plaza, a group of three warehouse buildings. Mansart Corporation wants to get out of the industrial side of commercial properties and focus primarily on office buildings and small shopping centers; therefore, it listed Tavistock Commercial Plaza with Jean Farrell of Farrell Realty. Jean procured a purchaser for the property, WFD Corporation, which recently sold one of its commercial properties and has been looking for another investment to purchase with the sales proceeds.

Gretchen Mansart, president of Mansart Corporation, has hired Ava Ross to represent the company in the transaction. Ava drafted the contract for sale and purchase, and her firm is acting as escrow/closing agent in the transaction. Barbara Hammond, Ava's paralegal, is assisting with the transaction. Upon first opening the client file, Barbara reviewed the contract, which is found in Figure 14–1. The exhibits to the contract are found in Figures 14–2, 14–3, 14–4, and 14–5, respectively.

The property description is a rather lengthy metes and bounds description, so rather than including it in the body of the contract, it is attached as an exhibit (Figure 14–2). The contract lists a purchase price of $2,700,000. Glaringly missing from the contract is a financing provision. This is because WFD Corporation is reinvesting capital from the sale of a recent property and is not obtaining outside financing. According to the contract terms, the seller has ten days from the execution of the contract to provide the purchaser with a title commitment. The seller is to pay for the title examination, the title commitment, and the owner's policy. No mortgagee policy need be prepared, as there is no mortgagee involved. This also means that no financing instrument will be recorded, nor will accompanying fees for recording, documentary stamp tax, and intangible tax be assessed to the purchaser.

The contract stipulates that the purchaser has a forty-five-day inspection period. In this time period, the purchaser may conduct engineering tests and other physical inspections. During this time period, the seller must provide the

AGREEMENT FOR SALE AND PURCHASE

THIS AGREEMENT is entered by MANSART CORPORATION, an Any State Corporation (the "Seller"), and WFD CORPORATION, an Any State Corporation (the "Buyer").

WHEREAS, the Seller is currently the owner of certain warehouse buildings located in the City of Any City, Any State, known as Tavistock Commercial Plaza, and which are legally described in Exhibit A to this Agreement ("Property"), the parties to this Agreement have agreed to the sale and purchase of the Property on the terms hereinafter set forth.

1. **Purchase and Sale.** Subject to all of the terms and conditions of this Agreement, the Seller will sell to the Buyer, and the Buyer will purchase from the Seller, the Property, together with all appurtenances, rights, easements and rights-of-way incident thereto.

2. **Purchase Price.** The purchase price to be paid by the Buyer to the Seller for the Property shall be Two Million Seven Hundred Thousand Dollars ($2,700,000.00) ("Purchase Price").

3. **Deposit.** Upon the execution of this Agreement, the Buyer has deposited with Fisher, Ross, and Simon, P.A. ("Escrow Agent") the sum of Twenty-Five Thousand Dollars ($25,000.00) to be held as an earnest money deposit ("Deposit"), which shall be applied in accordance with the terms of this Agreement. The Deposit shall be placed into an interest-bearing account. Upon closing, any interest earned on the Deposit shall be paid to the Buyer. If this transaction does not close, the interest shall be paid to the party entitled to retain the Deposit under the terms of this Agreement.

4. **Payment of Purchase Price.** At the closing of this transaction, the Buyer will pay to Seller the Purchase Price as follows:
   (a) The Buyer shall deliver a cashier's check to the order of the Seller in the amount of $2,675,000.00.
   (b) The Escrow Agent shall deliver a cashier's check to the order of Seller in the amount of $25,000.00.

5. **Title.** Within ten (10) days of the execution of this Agreement, the Seller shall deliver a Commitment for an Owner's Title Policy in respect of the Property. The Commitment shall obligate the title company to issue to Buyer a title insurance policy in the amount of the Purchase Price, insuring Buyer's title to the Property. If the Commitment reveals any title matters other than the "Permitted Exceptions" enumerated in Exhibit C which render the title other than good and marketable, Buyer shall, within ten (10) days from receipt of the Commitment, notify Seller in writing, specifying the defect(s). Seller shall have thirty (30) days after receipt of such notice in which to cure such defects and furnish to Buyer evidence that all such defects have been cured. If such defects are cured within that time, the sale and purchase shall be closed in accordance with the terms of this Agreement. If Seller cannot cure all such defects within the thirty (30) day period, Buyer shall have the option, to be exercised in its sole discretion, to complete the purchase and to accept title to the Property subject to such defects or to notify Seller in writing that Buyer elects not to complete the purchase, and thereupon, all rights and liabilities of the parties each to the other shall end.

6. **Leases.** None of the leases identified in Exhibit D attached hereto and made a part hereof shall be modified or amended in any material respect after the date hereof without the consent of the Buyer, which consent will not be unreasonably withheld. At closing, Seller shall

FIGURE 14–1
Agreement for sale and purchase

FIGURE 14–1
(continued)

provide Buyer with executed originals of all leases and shall assign all leases to Buyer. Seller shall credit Buyer (together with such certificates of insurance from tenants as may be in Seller's possession) the amount of all deposits and prepaid rent held under the leases. Seller covenants and agrees with Buyer that both Seller and Buyer shall be responsible for the negotiation and execution of each new lease affecting the Property, and no lease shall be executed after the date hereof without the prior written approval of Buyer, which shall not be unreasonably withheld or delayed.

7. <u>Inspection.</u> From and after the effective date of this Agreement, the Buyer shall have forty-five (45) days in which to examine all aspects of the Property to determine whether or not the Property is acceptable and whether the Buyer will conclude the transaction contemplated by this Agreement. Buyer may extend the Inspection Period for fifteen (15) additional days if Buyer has not received its engineering report, environmental report and appraisal within the forty-five (45) day period. During such "Inspection Period," the Seller shall cooperate fully with the Buyer and shall make available to the Buyer copies of all leases and service contracts, together with such building plans, surveys, financial records, operating statements and schedules from tax returns, pertaining to the Property as may be in the Seller's possession and control. The Buyer shall be permitted to conduct a physical inspection of the Property including the performance of testing for environmental or termite problems. By 5:00 p.m. on the final day of the Inspection Period, the Buyer shall notify the Seller in writing whether or not it intends to proceed with the purchase of the Property. If the Buyer fails to notify the Seller of its intention, the Buyer shall be deemed to have elected to proceed with this transaction. If the Buyer elects not to proceed, the Deposit, together with interest thereon, will be returned to the Buyer and this Agreement will be terminated.

8. **Governmental Compliance.** Notwithstanding the Buyer's inspection rights as set forth in Paragraph 7 above, if the Buyer's inspection discloses any condition or situation which is a violation of any governmental law, ordinance, code, zoning or environmental restriction applicable to the Property, the Seller shall be obligated to proceed diligently to cure such condition following receipt of notice from Buyer. The date of closing shall be postponed by the number of days required by Seller to effectuate such cure. However, if the cost to cure such condition exceeds Twenty-Seven Thousand Five Hundred Dollars ($27,500.00), the Seller shall notify the Buyer of such excess cost, and the Buyer shall elect whether or not to pay such cost in excess of Twenty-Seven Thousand Five Hundred Dollars ($27,500.00). If the Buyer does not elect to pay such excess cost, the Seller may elect to terminate this Agreement. In the event of such termination, the Deposit, together with interest thereon, shall be refunded to the Buyer and the parties shall have no further obligations under this Agreement.

9. <u>Closing.</u> The purchase and sale contemplated by this Agreement shall be closed on February 1, 1998. Closing shall occur in the offices of Fisher, Ross, and Simon, P.A., 1900 N.W. 3rd Avenue, Any City, Any State, commencing at 11:00 a.m. Time is of the essence with respect to the parties' obligations to close this transaction.

10. **Seller's Representations and Warranties.** As a material inducement for Buyer to enter into this Agreement and to consummate the closing

FIGURE 14–1
(continued)

hereunder, Seller makes the following representations and warranties to Buyer, which shall survive closing for a period of one year:

(a) Seller has full power and authority to execute and deliver this Agreement and all documents now or hereafter to be delivered by it pursuant to this Agreement ("Seller's Documents") and to perform all obligations arising under this Agreement and under Seller's Documents;

(b) Seller is the owner of fee simple title to the Property, and no other person or entity has or claims any interest therein except as reflected in the Title Commitment;

(c) The Property is free and clear of all obligations for taxes except for ad valorem taxes for the year 1998, not yet due and payable, and for all subsequent years;

(d) The Property is or at the time of Closing will be free and clear of all encumbrances other than those described in the Title Commitment;

(e) Seller has no knowledge of any pending or contemplated condemnation proceedings affecting the Property or any part thereof;

(f) Seller is not aware of any litigation affecting the Property;

(g) There will be no construction liens against the Property at Closing except liens for which adequate security and bonding have been provided by Seller;

(h) All structures upon the Property are being sold "as is." The Seller specifically disclaims any and all warranties or representations (whether express or implied) concerning the physical condition of the Property;

(i) The Rent Roll attached as Exhibit D is true and correct in all material respects;

(j) Except as reflected on the Exhibit D Rent Roll, Seller is aware of no defaults of any tenants under the leases, nor is Seller aware of any claims by a tenant that Seller is in default under any leases;

(k) Seller is unaware of any violations of rules, ordinances and codes of any governmental authority with jurisdiction over the Property;

(l) Seller has received no requests to increase its insurance coverage of the Property;

(m) There has been no rent strike or organized action of the tenants against the Seller during the past twelve (12) months;

(n) The Property is not located within an officially designated historic district.

11. **Buyer's Representations.** As a material inducement for Seller to enter into this Agreement and to consummate the Closing hereunder, Buyer makes the following representations to Seller, which representations shall be true and correct at Closing, as though such representations and warranties were made at and as of the date of Closing:

(a) Buyer has full power and authority to execute and deliver this Agreement and all documents now or hereafter to be delivered by it pursuant to this Agreement ("Buyer's Documents") and to perform all obligations arising under this Agreement and under Buyer's Documents;

(b) This Agreement and Buyer's Documents do not and will not contravene any provision of Buyer's Articles of Incorporation, any present judgment, order, decree, writ or injunction, or any provision of any currently applicable law or regulation.

FIGURE 14–1
(continued)

12. **Seller's Deliveries.** Seller shall deliver to Buyer at Closing the following documents, dated as of the closing date, the delivery and accuracy of which shall be a condition to the consummation of the purchase and sale:

    (a)   Deed. A special warranty deed in recordable form, duly executed by Seller, conveying to the Buyer good and marketable and insurable fee simple title to the Property, subject only to the Permitted Exceptions.

    (b)   Affidavit. A no-lien affidavit in form and content customarily used in Any County, Any State, relating to any activity of Seller at the Property within the period that a lien can be filed based on such activity prior to the closing.

    (c)   Closing Statement. A Closing Statement setting forth the purchase price, deposits, deductions, prorations, fees, recording costs and other items customarily reflected on a Closing Statement in Any County.

    (d)   Assignment of Leases. An assignment of all leases relating to the Property, together with the originals of such leases. Such assignment shall provide for the assumption by Buyer of all obligations under the leases from and after the date of Closing.

    (e)   Estoppel Letters. Estoppel letters in a form substantially similar to Exhibit B from all those tenants who have completed an estoppel letter. Prior to Closing, Seller will mail estoppel letters to all tenants by certified mail, postage prepaid, return receipt requested, and will instruct them to sign and return the estoppel letters.

    (f)   Certified Resolutions. Certified resolutions of the Seller authorizing the entering into and execution of this Agreement and the consummation of each and every transaction contemplated herein.

    (g)   Other Documents. Such other documents as Buyer or its counsel may reasonably require in order to effect the closing of this transaction, together with keys, alarm codes (if any), warranties (if any) and operating manuals (if any).

13. **Buyer's Deliveries.** At Closing, and after the Seller has complied with all of the terms and conditions of this Agreement and has delivered the documents required in Paragraph 13, Buyer shall:

    (a)   Purchase Price. Pay to the Seller by cashier's check or wire transfer the cash portion of the Purchase Price. Seller consents to the use of its closing proceeds to pay off the existing mortgages encumbering the Property.

    (b)   Certified Resolutions. Deliver certified resolutions of the Buyer authorizing the entering into and execution of this Agreement and the consummation of each and every transaction contemplated herein.

14. **Closing and Recording Costs.** Seller shall pay the cost of documentary stamps to be affixed to the deed. Seller shall also pay the cost of the Title Commitment and the cost of an Owner's Title Insurance Policy, together with the cost of recording any documents necessary to render title as required under this Agreement. Buyer shall pay the cost of recording the financing instrument, all intangible tax (if any) pertaining to the Note, and the cost of a Mortgagee's Title Insurance Policy.

15. **Tax Proration and Adjustments.**

    (a)   Adjustments. The following adjustments shall be made between the parties at the Closing: (i) Buyer shall be credited and Seller charged with security deposits or advance rentals in the nature of security

FIGURE 14–1
(continued)

deposits made by tenants under the Leases; (ii) Buyer shall be credited and Seller charged with the aggregate amount of rental abatement, concessions or build-out allowances (if any) under the leases, attributable to the period commencing on the date of the Closing and extending to the date when full rental becomes payable thereunder; and (iii) Seller shall be credited and Buyer charged with transferable deposits under service contracts assumed by Buyer, if any, provided Seller delivers to Buyer at the Closing a letter from the other party to each such service contract, confirming the amount of such deposit and the transferability thereof.

(b)   Prorations. The following shall be prorated between the parties as of the date of the Closing: real estate taxes for the calendar year in which the Closing occurs, water and sewer charges, rent payments under the Leases to the extent actually received by Seller prior to the Closing, charges and fees paid or payable under service contracts which are assigned to Buyer and such other items of income and expense as are customarily prorated in a transaction of this nature.

(c)   Real Estate Taxes and Liens. At Closing, taxes on the Property shall be prorated between the parties on the basis of the taxes paid for the most recent tax year that has been assessed and billed. If the actual taxes for the year of Closing are not determinable at the closing date, the parties agree to reprorate taxes promptly upon issuance of the tax bill for the year of Closing. Special assessment liens certified as of Closing shall be paid by Seller. Pending liens shall be assumed by Buyer.

(d)   Utilities. Seller shall endeavor to have all meters read and final bills rendered for all utilities servicing the Property, including, without limitation, water, gas and electricity, for the period to and including the day preceding the Closing, and Seller shall pay such bills where appropriate, except in the case of utility charges paid or payable by any tenants directly to the utility companies.

(e)   Rent Arrears. At the Closing, Seller shall deliver to Buyer a list of all tenants who are delinquent in the payment of rent, which list shall set forth the amount of each such delinquency, the period to which each such delinquency relates and the nature of the amount due, itemizing separately fixed monthly rent and any additional charges. If the tenant under the lease is in arrears in the payment of rent on the date of Closing, rents received by Buyer from such tenant after the Closing shall be applied in the following order of priority: (i) first to the month in which such rents are received; (ii) then to any rent arrearages for months subsequent to the month in which the Closing occurs; (iii) then to any rent arrearages for the month in which the Closing occurs; and (iv) then to the period for which the tenant in question was in arrears prior to the month in which the Closing occurs. If all or part of any rents, or any escalation charges for real estate taxes, insurance, operating expenses or other charges of a similar nature, received by Seller or Buyer after the Closing are payable to the other party by reason of this allocation, the appropriate sum, less a proportionate share of any reasonable attorneys' fees and other costs and expenses of collection thereof, shall be promptly paid to the other party.

(f)   Proration of Additional Rents. To the extent Seller has received payments from tenants under the Leases for real estate taxes,

FIGURE 14–1
(continued)

operating expenses or other charges of a similar nature, including all amounts noted in Paragraphs 15(b) and 15(d) hereof ("Additional Rents"), and Seller has not expended these monies for the operation of the Property, Seller shall deliver to Buyer (or Buyer's property manager, if so directed by Buyer) the balance of said monies. This delivery shall be in lieu of the prorations provided for in Paragraphs 15(b) and 15(d) except, to the extent any tenant under a Lease is in default in the payments of any Additional Rent, Seller shall deliver an amount to Buyer at the Closing equal to the amount which said tenant is in default in paying. If any Additional Rents are collected by Buyer after the Closing which are attributable in whole or in part to any period prior to the date of the Closing, the Buyer shall pay Seller's proportionate share thereof to Seller within five (5) business days after receipt, less any reasonable attorneys' and accountants' fees and other costs and expenses incurred by Buyer in connection with the collection thereof. Nothing in this Paragraph 15(f) shall be construed as limiting the provisions of Paragraph 15(g) hereof.

(g) <u>Postclosing Adjustment Procedures.</u> Seller and Buyer acknowledge that it may be impossible to make all necessary adjustments at the Closing. Therefore, Seller and Buyer agree that subject to the provisions of Paragraphs 15(c), 15(d), 15(e) and 15(f), all operating revenues, including rental payments, from the Property which relate to the Period prior to the date of the Closing (the "Preclosing Period") shall belong to Seller, including all accrued but unpaid rental payments; and all such revenues applicable to the period on or after the date of the Closing shall belong to Buyer.

(h) <u>Errors.</u> If any errors or omissions are made at the Closing regarding adjustment or prorations, the parties shall make the appropriate corrections promptly after the discovery thereof.

The provisions of this Article 15 shall survive the Closing until all such adjustments and payments have been made.

16. <u>Possession.</u> Buyer shall be granted possession of the Property as of the date of Closing, subject, however, to the possessory interests of the tenants under the Leases.

17. <u>Real Estate Commissions.</u> Seller hereby warrants to Buyer that Seller has not engaged any broker or agent with respect to the purchase and sale of the Property as contemplated by this Agreement other than Farrell Realty and Cromwell Realty. Seller shall indemnify and hold Buyer harmless against any and all liability, cost, damage and expense (including, but not limited to, attorneys' fees and costs of litigation, including appeals) that Buyer shall ever suffer or incur because of any claim by any other broker or agent claiming to have dealt with Seller, whether or not meritorious, for any commission or other compensation with respect to this Agreement or to the purchase and sale of the Property in accordance with this Agreement.

18. <u>Condemnation.</u> In the event of the institution against the record owner of the Property of any proceedings, judicial, administrative or otherwise, relating to the taking, or to a proposed taking, of any portion of the Property by eminent domain, condemnation or otherwise, prior to Closing, then Seller shall notify Buyer promptly and Buyer shall have the option, in its sole and absolute discretion, of either (a) terminating this Agreement, or (b) closing in accordance with the terms of this Agreement, but at such Closing Seller shall assign to Buyer all of its

FIGURE 14–1
(continued)

right, title and interest in and to any net awards that have been or may be made with respect to such eminent domain proceeding or condemnation. Such election must be made by the Buyer within thirty (30) days of the notice furnished by Seller. If Buyer fails to make an election in writing, Buyer shall be deemed to have elected to close in accordance with the terms of this Agreement.

19. **Loss or Damage.** Any loss or damage to the Property between the date of this Agreement and Closing shall not void this Agreement or modify the provisions hereof, provided that Seller at its sole cost and expense shall maintain fire and extended coverage insurance upon the Property to the full insurable value thereof with a loss payable provision endorsement in favor of Seller. Any and all insurance proceeds shall be received by Seller and Seller shall apply such insurance proceeds to the repair or loss of damage to the Property.

20. **Default.** If this transaction does not close solely due to a refusal or default on the part of Buyer, the Deposit placed under this Agreement, together with the interest thereon, shall be delivered by Escrow Agent to Seller as liquidated and agreed upon damages, and thereafter, Buyer shall be relieved from all further obligations under this Agreement; or Seller, at its option, may proceed at law or in equity to enforce its legal rights under this Agreement.

    If this transaction fails to close due to a default on the part of the Seller, then at the option of Buyer, the Deposit, including all interest thereon, shall be returned by Escrow Agent to Buyer, or Buyer may proceed against the Seller only for specific performance of this Agreement. In no event shall the Seller be liable to the Buyer for money damages.

21. **Entire Agreement.** This Agreement constitutes the entire agreement between the parties with respect to the transaction contemplated herein, and it supersedes all prior understandings or agreements between the parties.

22. **Binding Effect.** This Agreement shall be binding upon and inure to the benefit of the parties hereto and their respective successors and assigns.

23. **Survival of Warranties.** No representations, warranties, covenants and agreements specified in this document shall survive the closing, other than those set forth in Paragraphs 16 and 18.

24. **Waiver; Modification.** The failure by Buyer or Seller to insist upon or enforce any of their rights shall not constitute a waiver thereof, and nothing shall constitute a waiver of Buyer's right to insist upon strict compliance with the terms of this Agreement. Either party may waive the benefit of any provision or condition for its benefit which is contained in this Agreement. No oral modification of this Agreement shall be binding upon the parties; any modification must be in writing and signed by the parties.

25. **Government Law; Venue.** This Agreement shall be governed by and construed under the laws of the State of Any State. In the event of any litigation concerning this Agreement, venue shall be in the Eleventh Judicial Circuit of Any State.

26. **Headings.** The paragraph headings as set forth in this Agreement are for convenience of reference only and shall not be deemed to vary the content of this Agreement or limit the provisions or scope of any paragraph herein.

27. **Notices.** Any notice, request, demand, instruction or other communication to be given to either party, except where required by the terms of this Agreement to be delivered at Closing, shall be in writing and shall

FIGURE 14–1
(continued)

be sent by registered or certified mail or by private overnight delivery service, as follows:

If to Buyer:	WFD Corporation c/o Walter F. Davidson 1200 N.W. 30th Street, Suite 200 Any City, Any State
with copy to:	Emily Griffin, Esquire Griffin, Hill, and Colson, P.A. 504 S.E. 6th Avenue, Suite 302 Any City, Any State
If to Seller:	Mansart Corporation c/o Gretchen Mansart 705 N.E. 12th Street, Suite 100 Any City, Any State
with copy to:	Ava Ross, Esquire Fisher, Ross, and Simon, P.A. 1900 N.W. 3rd Avenue Any City, Any State

If forwarded by overnight delivery service, notice shall be effective when received. If forwarded by certified or registered mail, notice shall be effective upon delivery, or, if delivery is refused, upon the first delivery attempt.

28. **Assignment.** This Agreement may be assigned by Buyer. Notwithstanding any assignment, Buyer shall continue to remain responsible for the performance of this Agreement.

29. **Indemnification.** The Seller hereby indemnifies and holds harmless the Buyer from any loss, cost or liability it may incur (including reasonable attorneys' fees) based on any claim arising from the ownership or operation of the Property prior to the date of Closing. Conversely, the Buyer hereunder indemnifies and holds harmless the Seller from any loss, cost or liability it may incur (including reasonable attorneys' fees) based on any claim arising from the ownership or operation of the Property from and after the date of Closing.

30. **Effective Date.** The date of this Agreement shall be the date upon which the last party to sign has executed this Agreement.

The parties have executed this Agreement on the respective dates set forth below.

BUYER:

ATTEST: WFD CORPORATION, an Any State corporation

Mitchell Maynard
Secretary   By: _Walter F. Davidson_
(Corporate Seal)   President

DATE: _November 15, 1997_

SELLER:

ATTEST: MANSART CORPORATION, an Any State corporation

Dean Slater
Secretary   By: _Gretchen Mansart_
(Corporate Seal)   President

DATE: _November 15, 1997_

The undersigned agrees to act as Escrow Agent in accordance with the terms of this Agreement.

Fisher, Ross, and Simon, P.A.
By: *Ava Ross*

The undersigned brokers agree that only upon the closing of the transaction set forth in the forgoing Agreement, they shall each be entitled to receive a commission, payable by the Seller, in the respective amounts described below.

FARRELL REALTY, INC.

By: *Jean Farrell*
   Vice President

Amount: $67,500.00

CROMWELL REALTY, INC.

By: *George Cromwell*
   President

Amount: $67,500.00

SELLER:

MANSART CORPORATION

By: *Gretchen Mansart*
   President

FIGURE 14–1
(continued)

EXHIBIT A
LEGAL DESCRIPTION

A parcel of land being described as Lot 21 and a portion of Lot 4, Block 9, of the PLAT OF SOUTHERN HILLS, SECTION 4, according to the plat thereof recorded in Plat Book 20, Pages 101 through 105, of the Public Records of Any County, Any State, said parcel being more particularly described as follows:

Beginning at the Southeast corner of Lot 10, Block 9, of the aforementioned plat, thence Northerly along the Easterly lines of Lots 10, 11, 12, 13, 14, 15, and 16, Block 9, a distance of 680.68 feet to a point; thence Northerly with a deflection of 4°47'30" to the right along the Easterly lines of Lots 16 and 17, Block 9, a distance of 178.15 feet to a point; thence Easterly along the South line of Lots 19 and 20, Block 9, a distance of 158.43 feet to a point; thence Northerly along the Westerly line of Lot 21, Block 9, a distance of 160.00 feet to a point, said point being the Southeast corner of Lot 21; thence Southerly with a deflection to the left of 13°33'40", a distance of 20.57 feet to a point; thence Easterly with a deflection to the left of 76°26'20", a distance of 53.08 feet to a point; thence Southerly with a deflection to the right of 76°26'20", a distance of 805.66 feet to a point; thence Westerly at right angles to the preceding course, a distance of 72.50 feet to a point; thence Northerly at right angles to the preceding course, a distance of 42.50 feet to a point; thence Westerly at right angles to the preceding course, a distance of 143.56 feet to a point; thence Southerly with a deflection of 89°54'09" to the left, a distance of 118.33 feet to the Northeast corner of Parcel 10 of the City of Any City as recorded in Deed Book 760, Page 301, Public Records of Any County, Any State; thence Westerly along the North line of said Parcel 10, a distance of 70.01 feet to the Northwest corner of Parcel 10; thence Northerly along the East line of Lot 8, Block 9, a distance of 15.83 feet to a point; thence Westerly along the North line of Lot 8, a distance of 36.26 feet to the Southeast corner of Lot 9, Block 9; thence Northerly along the East line of Lot 9, Block 9, a distance of 102.50 feet more or less back to the Point of Beginning.

FIGURE 14–2
Legal description of property

FIGURE 14–3
Tenant's estoppel
certificate

EXHIBIT B
TENANT'S ESTOPPEL CERTIFICATE

Date: _____

TO:

RE: Lease (the "Lease") dated _____ by and between MANSART CORPORATION, an Any State corporation, as Landlord and _____, as Tenant, with respect to Tavistock Commercial Plaza, Suite _____, 1400 S.E. 19th Avenue, Any City, Any State.

To Whom it May Concern:

As Tenant under the above-referenced Lease, the undersigned hereby acknowledges for the benefit of WFD CORPORATION, or its assigns, which has or is about to purchase the above-referenced property, the truth and accuracy of the following statements pertaining to said Lease:

1. The copy of the Lease attached hereto is a true, complete and correct copy, and includes all modifications, amendments or other terms of the Lease.

2. Except as otherwise set forth in Paragraph 7 below, Tenant is paying the full rent stipulated in said Lease, and to the best of its knowledge Tenant is in good standing and not in default or breach of any of its obligations under the Lease.

3. Current monthly base rent under the Lease is $_____, the rent is fully paid through _____, and no monies have been paid to Landlord in advance of the due date except as follows:

Current Operating Expense Reimbursements or other rent due in addition to the current monthly base rent is payable as follows:

Monthly Real Estate Tax and Electricity Charges of $_____
Monthly Other Operating Expense Charges of $_____
and is fully paid through: _____.

The Landlord is presently holding a security deposit in the amount of $_____.

4. The current term of the Lease commenced on _____. Landlord has satisfactorily complied with all of the requirements and conditions precedent to the commencement of the term of the Lease as specified therein. The current term ends on _____ and there are no remaining renewal or extension options except:

5. The Landlord is not, as of the date of this certificate, in default in the performance of the Lease, nor are there any circumstances which, with the passage of time, the giving of notice, or both, would result in a breach or default under the Lease by Landlord, nor are there any existing setoffs, counterclaims, or credits against rentals due or to become due under the Lease, nor are there existing defenses against the enforcement of the Lease by Landlord.

6. Tenant hereby acknowledges that (a) there have been no modifications or amendments to said Lease other than as specifically stated herein; (b) it has no notice of a prior assignment, hypothecation or pledge of rents or of the Lease; and (c) notice of the proposed assignment of Landlord's interest in said Lease may be given it by certified or registered mail, return receipt requested, at the premises.

7. The Tenant has not been granted any options to purchase or unused concession of free rent except:

TENANT:

_____
(Print name)

By: _____

Name: _____

Title: _____

FIGURE 14–3
(continued)

EXHIBIT C
PERMITTED EXCEPTIONS

A. Taxes for 1998 and subsequent years, which are not yet due and payable.
B. Public utilities and building lines as shown on the plat of SOUTHERN HILLS, SECTION 4, recorded in Plat Book 20, Pages 101 to 105, Public Records of Any County, Any State.
C. Covenant creating private road dated March 26, 1982, recorded March 31, 1982, in Official Records Book 2444, Page 58, Public Records of Any County, Any State.
D. Declaration Not to Relocate, Modify, Terminate or Cancel Ingress-Egress Easement dated March 26, 1982, recorded March 31, 1982, in Official Records Book 2444, Page 59, Public Records of Any County, Any State.
E. Declaration of Parking Easement dated March 26, 1982, recorded March 31, 1982, in Official Records Book 2444, Page 60, Public Records of Any County, Any State.
F. Parties in possession under Leases.

FIGURE 14–4
Permitted exceptions

purchaser with building plans, surveys, and financial records pertaining to the property, such as operating statements and tax return schedules. Should, during the course of the inspections, problems arise related to governmental codes, ordinances, zoning, environmental restrictions, and so forth, the purchaser is to immediately inform the seller, and the seller must take steps to cure the defects. Realizing that the costs to remedy these problems may be steep, a dollar limitation is set on the seller's obligation of $27,500. Should the cost to cure the problems exceed this amount, the purchaser may choose to pay the excess or to cancel the contract.

The contract details the steps that may and may not be taken regarding leases between the time of contracting and date of closing. Leases cannot be modified without the consent of the purchaser. Any new leases entered into during this period must be negotiated by both the seller and the purchaser. Upon closing, the seller is to provide the purchaser with all original leases, the security deposits, and prepaid rents, as well as a list of delinquent rents. When and if recovered, the delinquent rents are to be applied in a specified order.

EXHIBIT D
LEASE/RENT ROLL

BUILDING I

UNIT	TENANT	SQ. FT.	DATE OF LEASE	TERM	MONTHLY RENT
101,103	Daltrey Designs	4145	1/1/96	5 yr	2,103.57
105,107,109	Red Carpet Motors	4523	5/1/97	1 yr	2,453.12
111,113	Weller Marble	2010	6/25/96	2 yr	910.34
115,117	Colber Creations	1507.5	5/1/97	1 yr	821.16
119	Brian Buchanan	502	9/1/97	1 yr	288.51
121,123	Naturescape, Inc.	1507.5	6/14/97	2 yr	833.86
125	--------------------	1005	----------	-----	-----------
127	--------------------	1005	----------	-----	-----------
129	Vittorio Furn.	3015	2/22/97	1 yr	1,433.38
131	--------------------	1005	----------	-----	-----------
133,135	Holms Carpet	1005	9/1/96	40 mo	477.00
137,139	Lance Glass	2010	12/1/96	3 yr	1,575.75
141	Gordon's Lawn Maintenance	1005	7/1/97	1 yr	503.50
143	Reynolds Upholstery	1005	4/1/97	1 yr	577.04
145	Stevenson Interiors	1005	8/1/96	2 yr	489.37
147	AVH Builders, Inc.	1005	4/1/97	1 yr	530.00
149,151	Mulligan Linens	2760	10/9/94	5 yr	1,220.77
153	Palladium Cable	1755	4/1/95	3 yr	938.54
155	Matthew Holt	350	2/1/96	3 yr	200.95
157,159	--------------------	3800	----------	-----	-----------

BUILDING II

UNIT	TENANT	SQ. FT.	DATE OF LEASE	TERM	MONTHLY RENT
200	WWP Tire, Inc.	5400	2/3/96	3 yr	2,981.25
202,204,206,208	Car Doctor, Inc.	4420	6/1/96	2 yr	2,217.85
210,212,214	Wincott Enterp.	3315	7/15/95	3 yr	1,485.62
216,218	Murillo Accessories	2210	6/1/97	1 yr	1,001.46
220	J.C. Howell	1005	10/1/97	13 mo	585.65
222,224	Rollins Sprinkler	2210	1/1/97	3 yr	1,098.09
226,228,230,232,234	Flynn Corp.	4972.5	1/15/96	3 yr	2,659.81
236,238	Jeffrey Long	1657.5	1/15/96	3 yr	736.91
240,242	Newton Technology	1455	4/1/97	2 yr	835.41
244	Mansart Corp.	285	----------	-----	----------

BUILDING III

UNIT	TENANT	SQ. FT.	DATE OF LEASE	TERM	MONTHLY RENT
300	----------------------	800	--------	-----	-----------
302,304	Marilyn Callahan	3100	8/1/93	5 yr	1,631.90
306,308	Beverly Enterp.	3100	7/13/96	2 yr	2,141.50
310,312	T.J. McCarthy	3100	2/1/96	3 yr	1,554.00
314,316	Madison Furn.	1892	11/1/96	2 yr	1,218.00
318,320,322	LPR Stucco, Inc.	1080	12/14/97	2 yr	551.20
324	Stockwell, Inc.	3600	9/13/96	2 yr	1,855.00
326	VMV, Inc.	2360	6/24/96	3 yr	1,414.04
328	James Reilly	800	9/22/96	2 yr	551.20
330	Ritter Labs, Inc.	3660	11/3/95	3 yr	1,542.30
332,334,336	Dunmore Systems	1680	3/21/97	2 yr	808.78
338,340,342	Garrett Pool Care	1920	10/1/95	3 yr	968.84
344	----------------------	1005	----------	------	-----------

FIGURE 14–5 Lease/rent roll

Additionally, the seller is to provide the purchaser with tenant estoppel certificates or letters in a format similar to that found in Figure 14–3.

The contract indicates that two real estate brokers were involved in the transaction—Farrell Realty as the listing broker, and Cromwell Realty as the selling broker. They will split a five percent commission.

As both the seller and the purchaser are corporate entities, each must provide the other with certified resolutions from their boards of directors that authorize the sale and purchase of the property in question. Under the terms of the contract, the seller is to prepare the closing statement, as well as the seller's affidavit, an assignment of leases, and the deed. The deed to be delivered is a special warranty deed. Because the property is encumbered with an existing mortgage, the seller must pay off the seller's lender and record a satisfaction of mortgage. Note that the lender in this instance is an insurance company, Scarborough Life Insurance Company.

The scheduled closing date is February 1, 1998. If the closing takes place as scheduled, rents will not have to be prorated. Real estate taxes, however, will be prorated. The seller has not yet received the tax bill for 1998, and therefore, the parties will need to sign a tax proration agreement whereby they agree to readjust the tax proration according to the 1998 tax bill when it is received.

From this initial review of the contract, Barbara filled in the preliminary information on a commercial closing worksheet; other information will be added as it is received. The worksheet appears in Figure 14–6. Note that the file date is November 10, before the contract was signed, as Ava drafted the contract. The due dates listed for the closing statement and various other documents to be prepared by Barbara's firm are two days before the date of closing. As mentioned in the last chapter, the closing statement figures must be provided to the purchaser prior to the date of closing because the purchaser will have to obtain a cashier's check to deliver at closing. Further, both parties need to review the closing documents prior to closing so that if corrections need to be made, they will not delay the closing.

As the closing date is nearing, Barbara reviews the worksheet shown in Figure 14–6 to determine what has already been done and what she must tackle next. She has already prepared a title commitment and delivered it to Emily Griffin, WFD Corporation's attorney, for review. She has sent a letter to her client's lender, Scarborough Life Insurance Company, requesting the payoff figures for a February 1st closing. In return, she has received the payoff statement from Scarborough found in Figure 14–7.

Barbara has prepared a cover letter for Mansart Corporation to deliver with the tenant estoppel certificate forms to each tenant. Barbara has instructed the client to attach a copy of each tenant's lease to that tenant's certificate form. The purchaser will receive the original leases at a later time. The cover letter is found in Figure 14–8. Although the certificates do not have to be presented until closing, the cover letter requests that the tenants return them no later than January 15th, providing some lead time.

Mansart Corporation has already provided WFD Corporation with financial records, including a list of security deposits and a vacancy summary, indicating the percentage of space occupied and vacant. It has submitted a schedule of the tax bills for the last two years, as the current tax bill is as yet

FIGURE 14–6
Commercial closing
worksheet

COMMERCIAL CLOSING WORKSHEET

DATE FILE OPENED: November 10, 1997

ATTORNEY: Ava Ross

PARALEGAL: Barbara Hammond

CLIENT NUMBER: 15480

MATTER NUMBER: 001

CLIENT: _____ BUYER __X__ SELLER _____ LENDER

1. SELLER NAME(S):   Mansart Corporation, an Any State corporation

2. ADDRESS(ES):   705 N.E. 12th Street, Suite 100
                         Any City, Any State

3. PHONE NUMBER(S):   (000) 004-2090
    FAX NUMBER(S):   (000) 004-2095

4. SOCIAL SECURITY NUMBER(S) [IF A BUSINESS ENTITY, FEDERAL TAX
    I.D. NO.]:   000625425

5. BUYER NAME(S):   WFD Corporation, an Any State corporation

6. ADDRESS(ES):   1200 N.W. 30th Street, Suite 200
                         Any City, Any State

7. PHONE NUMBER(S):   (000) 471-7200
    FAX NUMBER(S):   (000) 471-7230

8. SOCIAL SECURITY NUMBER(S) [IF A BUSINESS ENTITY, FEDERAL TAX
    I.D. NO.]:   000644461

9. BUYER'S LENDER: Not applicable

10. ADDRESS:

11. PHONE NUMBER:
    FAX NUMBER:

12. LOAN OFFICER ASSIGNED TO LOAN FILE:

13. LOAN NUMBER:

14. SELLER'S LENDER (IF SELLER HAS EXISTING MORTGAGE ON
    PROPERTY):   Scarborough Life Insurance Company

15. ADDRESS: 500 Chamberlain Street
                         Any City, Any State

16. PHONE NUMBER: (000) 203-6500
    FAX NUMBER: (000) 203-6550

17. LOAN NUMBER: 560816

18. ATTORNEY FOR: __X__ BUYER _____ SELLER _____ LENDER

19. ATTORNEY NAME: Emily Griffin, Esq., Griffin, Hall, and Colson, P.A.

20. ADDRESS: 504 S.E. 6th Avenue, Suite 302
                         Any City, Any State

21. PHONE NUMBER: (000) 154-0500
    FAX NUMBER: (000) 154-0550

22. REAL ESTATE BROKER #1: Farrell Realty (Jean Farrell)

23. ADDRESS: 786 Wisteria Street
                         Any City, Any State

24. PHONE NUMBER: (000) 367-2952
    FAX NUMBER: (000) 367-2953

25. REAL ESTATE BROKER #2: Cromwell Realty (George Cromwell)

26. ADDRESS: 481 Tunbridge Drive
                         Any City, Any State

27. PHONE NUMBER: (000) 259-1778
    FAX NUMBER: (000) 259-1779

28. COMMISSION: 5%   HOW SPLIT: 50/50

29. ESCROW AGENT: Fisher, Ross, and Simon, P.A.

FIGURE 14–6
(continued)

30. ADDRESS: 1900 N.W. 3rd Avenue
                            Any City, Any State
31. PHONE NUMBER: (000) 555-2000
    FAX NUMBER: (000) 555-2020
32. TITLE COMPANY: Fisher, Ross, and Simon, P.A.
33. ADDRESS:

34. PHONE NUMBER:
    FAX NUMBER:
35. STREET ADDRESS OF PROPERTY:
                            Tavistock Commercial Plaza, 3082 Tavistock Drive
                            Any City, Any State
36. LEGAL DESCRIPTION OF PROPERTY:
                            See attached Exhibit
37. PARCEL IDENTIFICATION NUMBER: 7321483300
38. CLOSING:
    (A) DATE: 2/1/98
    (B) TIME: 11:00 a.m.
    (C) PLACE: our offices
39. PURCHASE PRICE: $2,700,000.00
40. LOAN AMOUNT: Not applicable

41. **DEPOSITS:**   **AMOUNT**   **DATE DUE**   **DATE RECEIVED**
    (A) LOT:
    (B) INITIAL: $25,000.00   11/15/97   11/15/97
    (C) ADDITIONAL:

42. ITEMS	DONE BY	DATE DUE	CHARGE TO
Title Search	Seller	11/20/97	Seller
Order Survey	Seller	11/15/97	P.O.C.
Title Examination	Seller	11/20/97	Seller
Title Commitment	Seller	11/25/97	Seller
Remedy Defects			
Issue Policy(ies):			
(a) Owner's	Seller		Seller
(b) Mortgagee's			
(c) Endorsements:			
_____	_____	_____	_____
_____			
Property Appraisal	Seller		P.O.C.
Engineer's Report	Buyer	12/30/97	P.O.C.
Zoning Information	Seller	11/20/97	
Environmental Information	Seller	11/20/97	
Warranty Information	Seller	11/20/97	
Inspections	Buyer	12/30/97	P.O.C.
Loan Application			
Loan Commitment			
Promissory Note			
Mortgage/Deed of Trust			
UCC Financing Forms			
Lease List/Rent Roll	Seller	11/15/97	
Security Deposits List	Seller	12/30/97	
Vacancy Summary	Seller	12/30/97	

FIGURE 14-6
(continued)

ITEMS	DONE BY	DATE DUE	CHARGE TO
Tenant Estoppel Certificates	Seller	1/15/98	
Assignment of Leases	Seller	1/30/98	
Schedule of Prepaid Tenants	Seller	1/30/98	
Schedule of Delinquent Tenants	Seller	1/30/98	
Tenant Notice Letter	Seller	1/30/98	
Assignment/Termination of Management/Service Contracts	Seller	12/31/97	
Mortgage Estoppel Letter	Seller	11/25/97	
Satisfaction of Mortgage/ Deed of Trust	Seller	1/30/98	
Insurance Coverage	Buyer		P.O.C.
Verification of Corporate Status	B and S	S-11/20/97	
Corporate Resolution	B and S	S-10/27/97	
Tax Receipts	Seller	1/30/98	
City Tax Prorated	Seller	1/30/98	
County Tax Prorated	Seller	1/30/98	
Rents Prorated	Seller	1/30/98	
Special Assessments Prorated			
Maintenance Assessments Prorated			
Other Prorations:			
_____	_____	_____	_____
_____	_____	_____	_____
Deed	Seller	1/30/98	
FIRPTA Affidavit	Seller	1/30/98	
Bill of Sale			
Seller's Affidavit	Seller	1/30/98	
Marriage Affidavit			
Closing Statement	Seller	1/30/98	
Recordation of Deed	Seller		Buyer
Recordation of Financing Instrument			
Recordation of UCC Forms			
Recordation of Satisfaction of Mortgage/Deed of Trust	Seller		Seller
Doc. Stamps on Deed	Seller	1/30/98	Seller
Doc. Stamps on Financing Instrument			
Intangible Tax on New Mortgage			
1099S Filed	Seller		
State Revenue Form Filed	Seller		
Disbursement to Seller		2/1/98	
Disbursement to Seller's Lender		2/1/98	
Disbursement to Brokers		2/1/98	
Disbursement to Title Company		2/1/98	
Commercial Closing Binder Index Prepared	Seller		
Documents Mailed to Buyer			
Other:			
Tax Proration Agreement	Seller	1/30/98	
Tax Reproration Letter			
File Closed _____			

PAYOFF STATEMENT

Investor: SCARBOROUGH LIFE INSURANCE COMPANY

Loan #:   560816   Borrower Name/Address:
Date: December 12, 1997 Mansart Corporation
                                  705 N.E. 12th Street, Suite 100
                                  Any City, Any State

Sent to: Property Address:
Fisher, Ross, and Simon, P.A.   3082 Tavistock Drive
Interest Rate: 13.25%   Any City, Any State
Interest Paid Through: 11/30/97

Statement of amount necessary to pay loan in full on February 1, 1998:

Present Balance:	$948,717.49
Interest through January 1, 1998:	$ 10,824.58
Prepayment Penalty (Waived):	$ 0.00
Late Charges Due:	$ 0.00
TOTAL TO PAY LOAN IN FULL:	$959,542.07

Funds received after February 1, 1998, will require the addition of $349.18 interest per day.

Please wire the funds to the following:

Wexford Bank   For Credit to:
100 Kettering Place   Scarborough Life Insurance Company
Any City, Any State   Account #000-7-890778
Attn: Peter Fowler

Please notify our office once the wire has taken place. The Satisfaction of Mortgage will be forward after required funds have been received and processed by the investor.

Sincerely,

Shirley Hayes
Loan Service Administrator

FIGURE 14–7
Payoff statement

December 13, 1997

Dear Tenant:

   We are asking that you complete the enclosed Tenant's Estoppel Certificate, which is attached to a copy of your lease, as soon as possible and return it to us at your earliest convenience. We would appreciate it if you could complete and return the form to us by the January 15, 1998.

   We appreciate your help and thank you for your kind cooperation.

Sincerely,

Mansart Corporation

FIGURE 14–8
Sample cover letter

unavailable. The vacancy summary and schedule of tax bills are found in Figures 14–9 and 14–10, respectively.

Having reviewed all of the items discussed so far, Barbara is ready to draft the closing statement. She will not be using the HUD-1 Uniform Settlement Statement, as this is not a residential closing. Prior to drafting the closing statement and closing documents, Barbara makes several photocopies of certain exhibits attached to the contract, specifically the legal description, the permitted exceptions, and the lease list/rent roll, as one or more of these items will be attached to various documents. The closing statement, as executed by the parties at closing, is found in Figure 14–11.

The purchase price of the property, $2,700,000, is listed on the first line of the settlement statement shown in Figure 14–11. The purchaser put down a $25,000 deposit when it executed the contract, which was put in escrow with

FIGURE 14–9
Vacancy summary

VACANCY SUMMARY

Building I		Building II	
Total units:	29	Total units:	23
Total sq. feet:	35,925	Total sq. feet:	26,930
Units occupied:	25	Units occupied:	22
Sq. feet occupied:	29,110	Sq. feet occupied:	26,645
Units vacant:	4	Units vacant:	1*
Sq. feet vacant:	6,815	Sq. feet vacant:	285*
Vacancy rate (based on # of units):	16%	Vacancy rate (based on # of units):	4%*
Vacancy rate (based on # sq. ft.):	19%	Vacancy rate (based on # sq. ft.):	1%*

Building III	
Total units:	23
Total sq. feet:	27,297
Units occupied:	21
Sq. feet occupied:	25,492
Units vacant:	2
Sq. feet vacant:	1,805
Vacancy rate (based on # of units):	8%
Vacancy rate (based on # sq. ft.):	7%

*Unit/sq. feet is presently occupied by Mansart Corporation as a leasing office.

FIGURE 14–10
Schedule of tax bills

Real Estate Taxes—Warehouse Buildings

Building #	Assessed	Square feet	1996	1997
Building I	$1,240,377.00	35,925	$27,620.52	$28,344.11
Building II	$ 856,481.00	26,645	$19,139.14	$19,644.46
Building III	$1,016,143.00	27,297	$22,702.20	$23,301.34

FIGURE 14–11
Settlement statement

SETTLEMENT STATEMENT

DATE OF CLOSING: February 1, 1998
SELLER: MANSART CORPORATION, an Any State corporation
BUYER: WFD CORPORATION, an Any State corporation
PROPERTY: See Exhibit A attached hereto

	Credit seller	Credit buyer
PURCHASE PRICE (REAL PROPERTY)................	$2,700,000.00	
DEPOSIT: Held by Fisher, Simon, and Ross, P.A...............		$ 25,000.00
TAX PRORATION: Based on $71,289.91 per year; $194.3418 per day x 32 days...........................		$ 6,218.94
SECURITY DEPOSIT LIABILITY: See Schedule Attached		$ 45,341.98
PREPAID RENT: See Schedule Attached...........................		$ 2,797.72
SUBTOTALS..	$2,700,000.00	$ 79,358.64
CREDIT SELLER LESS CREDIT BUYER................	79,358.64	
CASH DUE BEFORE EXPENSES..........................	**$2,620,641.36**	

BUYER'S EXPENSES:
Engineering Report.. 628.00
Record Deed... $ 30.00
TOTAL BUYER'S EXPENSES............................... 658.00

SELLER'S EXPENSES:
Payoff of Outstanding Mortgage .... $ 959,542.07
Record Satisfaction of Mortgage........................ $ 6.00
Documentary Stamps .... $ 18,900.00
Title Insurance .... $ 10,175.00
Title Search.. $ 150.00
Real Estate Commissions .... $ 135,000.00*
TOTAL SELLER'S EXPENSES $1,123,773.07

BUYER'S RECAP:
    CASH DUE BEFORE EXPENSES $2,620,641.36
    PLUS BUYER'S EXPENSES............................. $ 658.00
    NET CASH DUE FROM BUYER **$2,621,299.36**

SELLER'S RECAP:
    CASH DUE BEFORE EXPENSES $2,620,641.36
    PLUS DEPOSIT .... $ 25,000.00
    LESS SELLER'S EXPENSES .... ($1,123,773.07)
    NET CASH DUE TO SELLER **$1,521,868.29**

*Farrell Realty .... $ 67,500.00
 Cromwell Realty... $ 67,500.00

    Buyer and Seller hereby acknowledge that the terms of the Agreement for Sale and Purchase between Buyer and Seller (the "Contract") provide that certain of the obligations of the parties shall survive the Closing (the "Closing") of the sale and purchase contemplated thereby and, to the extent necessary, Buyer and Seller hereby ratify and confirm all such obligations to which the survival language in the Contract is applicable and agree that the provisions of the Contract in which such obligations are stated have survived the Closing and the delivery of the documents at Closing.

FIGURE 14–11
(continued)

> The undersigned Buyer and Seller, having read the forgoing Settlement Statement, do hereby acknowledge and approve the disbursements set forth herein and do hereby authorize and direct Closing Attorney and the Title Agent, as applicable, to disburse the funds in accordance herewith.
>
> APPROVED:
>
> MANSART CORPORATION,   WFD CORPORATION,
> an Any State corporation   an Any State corporation
>
> By: _Gretchen Mansart_   By: _Walter F. Davidson_
>   President   President

Barbara's firm. To prorate the taxes, Barbara took the latest figures for each building, added them together, then divided by 365 to get a daily rate. She then multiplied by the number of days owed by the seller, as the taxes have not yet been paid for 1998. Next, she totaled the security deposit figures to determine the amount to be credited the purchaser, the security deposit list to be attached to the closing statement. Having received a list from the client of those tenants who have prepaid rent, she credited the purchaser accordingly. The schedule of prepaid rents, to be attached as an exhibit to the closing statement, is found in Figure 14–12.

The purchaser has only two expenses that will be paid at closing; one is the recording of the deed, and the other is the cost of the engineering report. The deed is five pages long, as the lengthy legal description and list of permitted exceptions will be attached to it. The list of seller's expenses is longer. As noted earlier, the seller is to pay for all the title work costs, the documentary stamp tax on the deed, the recording of the satisfaction of mortgage, and the real estate commissions. From the payoff statement provided by Scarborough Life Insurance Company, Barbara has inserted the payoff amount to satisfy the seller's outstanding loan obligation.

Barbara next turns her attention to the drafting of the assignment of leases, by which the client assigns all current leases to WFD Corporation. By assigning the leases, the seller is transferring its rights and obligations under the leases to the purchaser. Once completed and reviewed by Ava, Barbara will attach the legal description and lease list/rent roll as exhibits. In some circumstances, the sellers of commercial property assign their current management or service

FIGURE 14–12
Schedule of prepaid rents

Schedule of Prepaid Rents

Building	Unit	Tenant	Amount paid
I	115,117	Colber Creations	$ 821.16 (February)
I	119	Brian Buchanan	$ 288.51 (February)
II	220	J.C. Howell	$ 585.65 (February)
III	328	James Reilly	$1,102.40 (February and March)
		TOTAL	$2,797.72

contracts to the purchaser as well. In this instance, however, the contracts will be terminated, as they expire at the end of 1997, and Mansart Corporation will take responsibility for providing these services for the month of January.

The assignment of leases, as executed by the parties at closing, appears in Figure 14–13.

Barbara has received the list of delinquent tenants to provide to the purchaser at closing. At such time as these rents are paid (if at all), the rent proceeds will first be applied to the month in which the rents are received, then to any rent arrearages for months subsequent to the month in which the closing takes place, then to any rent arrearages for the month of closing, and finally for the period for which the tenant was in arrears prior to the month of closing. This being the case, there may be a situation in which the delinquent rents will have to be apportioned between the seller and the purchaser. The schedule of delinquent tenants appears in Figure 14–14.

Barbara next turns her attention to the drafting of the deed. The contract stipulates that a special warranty deed is to be delivered. The legal description and permitted exceptions will be attached as exhibits to the deed. She also prepares the seller's affidavit and the nonforeign certification, all to be executed by the seller. The deed and nonforeign certification appear in Figures 14–15 and 14–16, respectively. (A sample seller's affidavit was provided in the hypothetical found in the previous chapter. The format of such an affidavit used for a commercial closing would be similar to that used in a residential closing and, therefore, is not included here.)

As mentioned previously, the tax proration set forth on the closing statement is an estimate of the taxes owed, based on the most current tax bill in the seller's possession. It is unlikely that the tax amounts will remain the same in the bill for the 1998 taxes; thus, the parties agree to a reproration when the new tax bill becomes available. The seller and the purchaser, therefore, will sign a tax proration agreement consenting to the adjustment. The agreement prepared by Barbara, as executed by the parties at closing, is found in Figure 14–17.

The tenants must be informed that the sale has been completed and be told where to send their rent checks. Barbara prepares a letter of attornment, sometimes referred to as a tenant notice letter, to be sent to all tenants of Tavistock Commercial Plaza. The letter, as signed by both parties, is found in Figure 14–18.

Barbara then proceeds to prepare the tax filing forms. Upon closing, she will send a trust account check for the amount of the loan payoff to the bank indicated on Scarborough Life Insurance Company's payoff statement for deposit in Scarborough's account. Barbara has prepared the satisfaction of mortgage for Scarborough to execute and send back to her. Along with a cover letter, she encloses a Federal Express envelope with a self-addressed mailing label to be returned immediately to her firm. The cover letter appears in Figure 14–19.

After closing, Barbara will also update the title examination and prepare the owner's policy. When that is done and the deed and satisfaction of mortgage recorded, she will prepare a closing binder index for each party and send them their set of closing documents. When the tax bill arrives, the necessary adjustment will be made. Figure 14–20 provides the letter sent to Mansart Corporation requesting that a check for the tax reproration be sent to WFD Corporation.

ASSIGNMENT OF TENANT LEASES AND ASSUMPTION AGREEMENT

THIS AGREEMENT OF TENANT LEASES AND ASSUMPTION AGREEMENT is executed by and between MANSART CORPORATION, an Any State corporation ("Assignor"), whose post office address is 705 N.E. 12th Street, Suite 100, Any City, Any State, and WFD CORPORATION, an Any State corporation ("Assignee"), whose post office address is 1200 N.W. 30th Street, Suite 200, Any City, Any State.

WITNESSETH:

Assignor has entered into certain tenant leases with tenants covering leased premises located in the buildings located on a certain tract of land situated in Any County, Any State (the "Property"), more particularly described on Exhibit A attached hereto and made a part hereof for all purposes.

Attached hereto as Exhibit B and made a part hereof for all purposes is a true and correct copy of the list of the tenant leases presently in force (the "Leases").

Assignee desires to purchase from Assignor, and Assignor desires to sell and assign to Assignee, the lessor's interest in the Leases and the leasehold estates created thereby.

NOW, THEREFORE, for and in consideration of the sum of Ten and No/100 Dollars ($10.00) and other good and valuable consideration this day paid and delivered by Assignee to Assignor, Assignor does hereby assign, transfer and deliver to Assignee all of Assignor's right, title and interest in and to all Leases pertaining to the warehouse project located on the Property and the leasehold estates created thereby, and all of the rights, benefits and privileges of the lessor thereunder, including without limitation an amount of cash equal to all refundable security, damage or other deposits and unapplied prepaid rentals made under the Leases as shown on the rent roll attached as Exhibit B (the "Rent Roll"), but subject to all terms, conditions, reservations and limitations set forth in the Leases, except Assignor reserves all rights in and to any unpaid rent or other sums due to the Assignor under the Leases attributable to the period of time prior to the date hereof.

TO HAVE AND TO HOLD all and singular the Leases unto Assignee, its successors in interest and assigns, and Assignor does hereby bind itself and its successors to warrant and forever defend all and singular the Leases unto Assignee, its successors in interest and assigns, against every person whomsoever lawfully claiming or attempting to claim the same, or any part thereof, by, through or under Assignor, but not otherwise.

1. It is specifically agreed that Assignor shall not be responsible to the lessees under the Leases for the discharge and performance of any and all duties and obligations to be performed and/or discharged by the lessor thereunder from and after the date hereof. By accepting this Assignment of Tenant Leases and Assumption Agreement and by its execution hereof, Assignee hereby assumes and agrees to perform all of the terms, covenants and conditions of the Leases on the part of the lessor therein required to be performed from and after the date hereof.

2. Assignor hereby certifies that the Rent Roll set forth as Exhibit B attached hereto is a true and correct list of the Leases in effect on the date hereof.

3. All of the covenants, terms and conditions set forth herein shall be binding upon and shall inure to the benefit of the parties hereto and their respective heirs, executors, personal representatives, successors and assigns.

Assignor and Assignee have executed this Assignment of Tenant Leases and Assumption Agreement to be effective as of the 1st day of February, 1998.

WITNESSES:

Alison Simons

Vincent Morris

Kevin Smith

Carol Burton

STATE OF ANY STATE
COUNTY OF ANY COUNTY

ASSIGNOR:
MANSART CORPORATION,
an Any State corporation

By: _Gretchen Mansart_
    President

ASSIGNEE:
WFD CORPORATION,
an Any State corporation

By: _Walter F. Davidson_
    President

The forgoing instrument was acknowledged before me this 1st day of February, 1998, by Gretchen Mansart, President of Mansart Corporation, an Any State corporation, and Walter F. Davidson, President of WFD Corporation, an Any State corporation, who are personally known to me and who acknowledged executing the forgoing document.

WITNESS, my hand and official seal in the State and County last aforesaid this 1st day of February, 1998.

Ellen Dunning
Notary Public
My commission expires: 3/31/99

(Notary Seal)

FIGURE 14–13
(continued)

Schedule of Delinquent Tenants

Building	Unit	Tenant	Amount due
I	145	Stevenson Interiors	$514.37 (January $489.37 & Late Fee)
II	236–238	Jeffrey Long	$756.91 (January $731.91 & Late Fee)
III	332–336	Dunmore Systems	$833.78 (January $808.78 & Late Fee)
		TOTAL	$2,105.06

FIGURE 14–14
Schedule of delinquent tenants

FIGURE 14–15
Special warranty deed

Prepared by and return to:

Ava Ross, Esquire
Fisher, Ross, and Simon, P.A.
1900 N.W. 13th Avenue
Any City, Any State

SPECIAL WARRANTY DEED

   MANSART CORPORATION, an Any State corporation ("Grantor"), whose post office address is 705 N.E. 12th Street, Suite 100, Any City, Any State, for and in consideration of the sum of TEN AND NO/100 DOLLARS ($10.00) paid to Grantor and other good and valuable consideration, the receipt and sufficiency of which are hereby acknowledged, has GRANTED, SOLD and CONVEYED and by these presents does hereby GRANT, SELL and CONVEY unto WFD CORPORA-TION, an Any State corporation ("Grantee"), whose post office address is 1200 N.W. 30th Street, Suite 200, Any City, Any State, that certain land located in Any County, Any State, and being more particularly described in Exhibit A attached hereto and incorporated herein by reference, together with all improvements located on such land (such land and improvements being collectively referred to as the "Property").

   This conveyance is made and accepted subject to all matters (the "Permitted Exceptions") set forth in Exhibit B, attached hereto and incorporated herein by reference.

   TO HAVE AND TO HOLD the Property, together with all and singular the rights and appurtenances pertaining thereto, including all of Grantor's right, title and interest in and to adjacent streets, alleys and rights-of-way, subject to the Permitted Exceptions, unto Grantee and Grantee's successors in interest and assigns forever; and Grantor does hereby bind itself and its successors in interest to warrant and forever defend the Property unto Grantee and Grantee's succes-sors in interest and assigns, against every person whomsoever claiming or to claim the same or any part thereof or interest therein, by, through or under Grantor, but not otherwise, subject, however, to the Permitted Exceptions.

   EXECUTED as of the 1st day of February, 1998.

WITNESSES: MANSART CORPORATION,
                                        an Any State corporation

Alison Simons

                                        By: *Gretchen Mansart*
Vincent Morris   President

STATE OF ANY STATE
COUNTY OF ANY COUNTY

   The forgoing instrument was acknowledged before me this 1st day of February, 1998, by Gretchen Mansart, President of Mansart Corporation, an Any State cor-poration, who is personally known to me and who acknowledged executing the aforesaid document.

   WITNESS, my hand and official seal in the State and County last aforesaid this 1st day of February, 1998.

Ellen Dunning
Notary Public
My commission expires: 3/31/99

(Notary Seal)

FIGURE 14–16
Nonforeign certification

NONFOREIGN CERTIFICATION

Section 1445 of the Internal Revenue Code provides that a transferee of a United States real property interest must withhold tax if the transferor is a foreign person. To inform the transferee that withholding of tax is not required upon the disposition of a United States real property interest by MANSART CORPORATION, an Any State corporation, the undersigned hereby certifies the following:

1. MANSART CORPORATION, an Any State corporation, is the fee owner of the real property located in Any County, Any State, more particularly described in Exhibit A attached hereto.
2. MANSART CORPORATION is conveying the aforedescribed property to WFD CORPORATION, an Any State corporation.
3. MANSART CORPORATION is not a foreign entity (as that term is defined in the Internal Revenue Code and Income Tax Regulations).
4. The Federal Tax Identification Number for MANSART CORPORATION is 000625425.
5. The address of MANSART CORPORATION is 705 N.E. 12th Avenue, Suite 100, Any City, Any State.
6. The officers of MANSART CORPORATION understand that this certification may be disclosed to the Internal Revenue Service by the transferee and that any false statement contained herein could be punished by fine, imprisonment, or both.
7. That this Affidavit is being given for the purpose of providing an exception from the withholding requirements of Internal Revenue Code Section 1445.

Under penalties of perjury, I declare that I have examined this certification and to the best of my knowledge and belief it is true, correct and complete.

ATTEST:

MANSART CORPORATION,
an Any State corporation

Dean Slater
Secretary

By: _Gretchen Mansart_
        President

(Corporate Seal)

STATE OF ANY STATE
COUNTY OF ANY COUNTY

I HEREBY CERTIFY that on this day before me, an officer duly authorized in the State and County aforesaid to take acknowledgments, personally appeared Gretchen Mansart as President of Mansart Corporation, an Any State corporation, and Dean Slater, as Secretary of Mansart Corporation, an Any State corporation, who are personally known to me and who acknowledged executing and attesting to the aforesaid document.

WITNESS, my hand and official seal in the State and County aforesaid this 1st day of February, 1998.

Ellen Dunning
Notary Public
My commission expires: 3/31/99

(Notary Seal)

FIGURE 14-17
Tax proration agreement

TAX PRORATION AGREEMENT

Date: February 1, 1998
Seller: Mansart Corporation
Purchaser: WFD Corporation
Property: Tavistock Commercial Plaza
              3082 Tavistock Drive
              Any City, Any State

Seller and Purchaser agree as follows:

1. The closing on the above-described property took place on the above date.
2. The real estate taxes for the current year were estimated because the tax bill for the current year was not available at the time of closing.
3. The real estate taxes shown on the closing statement of the above date are an estimate only.
4. At the time the tax bill for the current year is available, the real estate taxes shall be reprorated, and any adjustment will be promptly paid by the Seller to the Purchaser.
5. The parties, upon review of the closing statement, shall make readjustments for any typographical or mathematical error(s), and any adjustment made shall promptly be paid as applicable.

SELLER: PURCHASER:

MANSART CORPORATION,   WFD CORPORATION,
an Any State corporation   an Any State corporation

By: _Gretchen Mansart_   By: _Walter F. Davidson_
    President   President

FIGURE 14-18
Letter of attornment

LETTER OF ATTORNMENT

February 1, 1998

RE: NOTICE TO TENANTS OF SALE OF THE TAVISTOCK COMMERCIAL PLAZA, ANY CITY, ANY STATE, TO WFD CORPORATION

Notice is hereby given to the tenants of the Tavistock Commercial Plaza, Any City, Any State (the "Property"), that MANSART CORPORATION, an Any State corporation ("Seller"), has, effective February 1, 1998, sold and conveyed the Property to WFD CORPORATION, an Any State corporation ("Purchaser"), who has assumed all of the obligations of landlord under your lease of a warehouse unit at the Property, accruing after the date hereof, and is responsible for any security deposits delivered by you under the terms of your lease.

Tenants are hereby directed to pay all future rental payments due under the terms of your lease and direct all future inquiries as specified below:

TO: WFD Corporation
        1200 N.W. 30th Street, Suite 200
        Any City, Any State

SELLER: PURCHASER:

MANSART CORPORATION,   WFD CORPORATION,
an Any State corporation   an Any State corporation

By: _Gretchen Mansart_   By: _Walter F. Davidson_
    President   President

FIGURE 14–19
Sample cover letter

February 1, 1998

HAND DELIVERED BY COURIER

Wexford Bank
Attn: Peter Fowler
100 Kettering Place
Any City, Any State

RE: Property: Tavistock Commercial Plaza
                    3082 Tavistock Drive
                    Any City, Any State

       Loan No.:   560816

Dear Mr. Fowler:

    Enclosed you will find our trust account check in the amount of $959,542.07 representing the amount necessary to pay off the above-described loan as set forth in Scarborough Life Insurance Company's payoff statement dated December 12, 1997. A copy of the payoff statement is enclosed. I have also enclosed a Satisfaction of Mortgage for execution by Scarborough Life Insurance Company, to be returned to our offices for recording. A Federal Express envelope with self-addressed mailing label is provided for your convenience.

    If you have any questions, please do not hesitate to contact our offices.

                    Very truly yours,

                    Barbara Hammond
                    Legal Assistant to Ava Ross, Esquire

Enc.

cc: Mansart Corporation

CHAPTER SUMMARY

1. Commercial real estate can be a good investment for those seeking a high rate of return. Although there are risks involved, the investor can minimize those risks by conducting a thorough market analysis in researching comparable projects. The investor must also look at all data pertaining to the subject property, including engineering reports, surveys, plans and specifications, governmental regulations, and the property owner's financial records.

2. When considering the purchase of a commercial property, the investor is most concerned with the break-even point, the point at which gross income equals the total of fixed costs and variable costs. The higher the occupancy rate level needed to break even on the property, the poorer the investment.

3. A purchaser of commercial real estate enjoys certain tax advantages in the form of depreciation allowances and deduction of operating expenses.

4. In purchasing commercial real estate, one must expend large amounts of capital. The cost of commercial projects is high, and lending institutions require larger cash down payments than are required when purchasing residential property. The purchaser's capital is tied up in an investment with poor liquidity, as real estate is harder to convert into ready cash than many other forms of investment.

FIGURE 14–20
Letter requesting a check
for tax reporation

April 30, 1998

Mansart Corporation
705 N.E. 12th Street, Suite 100
Any City, Any State

Attn: Gretchen Mansart, President

Re: Request for Funds After Tax Reproration

Dear Ms. Mansart:

Enclosed is a copy of the current tax bill for Tavistock Commercial Plaza, which has been forwarded to our offices by the Purchaser.

At the time of the closing, the real estate taxes were estimated, since the current tax bill was not available. Now that the actual figures are known, the following is a breakdown of the reprorations:

Amount of Actual Tax Bill:	Building I:	$28,950.20
	Building II:	$20,116.40
	Building III:	$23,976.80
	TOTAL	$73,043.40

Actual Tax Proration ($200.1189 per day x 32 days):	$ 6,403.80
Estimated Tax Proration:	$ 6,218.94
Difference Due (Please pay this amount):	$ 184.86

Please make the check for the difference due payable to and send to the following:

WFD Corporation
1200 N.W. 30th Street, Suite 200
Any City, Any State

Thank you for your prompt attention to this matter. Should you have any questions, please do not hesitate to contact our offices.

Very truly yours,

Ava Ross, Esquire

Enc.

5. The documentation provided by the seller to the purchaser in a commercial transaction includes but is not limited to: (a) a current list of leases and rent roll; (b) a vacancy analysis; (c) surveys, plans, and specifications; (d) a list of security deposits; (e) tenant estoppel certificates; (f) a list of prepaid tenants; (g) a list of delinquent tenants; and (h) an assignment of leases.

6. Tenant estoppel certificates verify the terms and conditions of each tenant's lease. They usually state (a) the term of the lease, (b) the current monthly base rent, (c) any monies paid in advance, (d) current operating expense reimbursements or other rent due in addition to the current monthly base rent, (e) the amount of the security deposit held by the landlord, (f) any free rent concessions, and (g) any options to purchase granted the tenant.

7. On a commercial closing statement, the purchaser must be credited for any earnest money deposits, the security deposits held by the seller, and prepaid rents. Rents for the month of closing must be prorated between the parties.

A list of the security deposits, a schedule of prepaid tenants, and a schedule of delinquent tenants should accompany the closing statement.

8. In addition to the special documentation provided by the seller in a commercial closing, the seller also provides (a) a deed transferring title, (b) a seller's affidavit verifying that there are no outstanding construction or other liens on the property, (c) a bill of sale if there is personal property transferred together with the real property, and (d) a nonforeign certification informing the purchaser that withholding of tax is not required.

REVIEW QUESTIONS

1. What are the advantages and disadvantages of investing in commercial real estate?
2. Provide examples of the following.
   a. Operating expenses
   b. Fixed costs
   c. Variable costs
3. What advantages are there to a seller in a sale-leaseback situation?
4. What documentation must be prepared for a commercial closing that is not prepared for a closing of a single-family residence?
5. What clauses are included in a commercial real estate sales contract that do not appear in a residential contract?

ETHICAL QUESTIONS

Your state's rules of professional conduct include the following rule:

A lawyer shall not give anything of value to a person for recommending the lawyer's services, except that a lawyer may pay the reasonable cost of advertising or written communication permitted by this rule and may pay the usual charges of a not-for-profit lawyer referral service or other legal service organization.

Your supervising attorney is often asked by real estate clients to recommend a good title insurance company. She always suggests Premium Title Company. In return for this favor, the title agents at Premium always suggest your supervising attorney when their customers ask for the name of a good real estate lawyer. Has your supervising attorney violated the above rule by participating in this arrangement?

PRACTICAL ASSIGNMENTS

Assignment 14:1. Assume that Tavistock Commercial Plaza is located in your city, county, and state. WFD Corporation has entered into a contract to sell the warehouses to Cosgrave Properties, Inc. The contract was executed three weeks ago from today's date. Walter F. Davidson, president of WFD Corporation, has hired your supervising attorney, Deborah Sanders, to represent the company in the transaction and act as escrow agent.

Deborah is putting you in charge of the WFD Corporation closing file. According to the contract, the sales price is $3,000,000. The closing is to take place two months from today's date at 9:00 A.M. at your offices, Hernandez, Sanders, and Norris, P.A., 263 Republic Avenue (your city and state), telephone number 111-0030, fax number 111-0035. Cosgrave Properties, Inc.'s address is 600 Chesterfield Drive, Suite 500 (your city and state). Its telephone number is 400-4000, and its fax number is 400-4050. The president of Cosgrave Properties, Inc., is Philip Ruskin.

Upon execution of the contract, Cosgrave put down an earnest money deposit of $150,000, which is being held by your firm in escrow. One broker was involved in the transaction, Jean Farrell of Farrell Realty. According to the terms of the contract, Farrell Realty will be paid a six percent commission by the seller at closing.

Cosgrave Properties, Inc., is represented by legal counsel, Robert Dunne of Henderson, Dunne, and Burnett, P.A. The law firm is located at 840 Camden Street, Suite 206 (your city and state). Its telephone number is 888-8100, and its fax number is 881-8150.

Your office will not be preparing the title work, as an outside title company, Four Quadrants Title Company, has been hired. The company's address is 2700 N.W. 9th Street (your city and state). Its telephone number is 434-7180, and its fax number is 434-7185. The contract stipulates that the seller must provide the purchaser with a title commitment within fifteen days from the date of the execution of the contract. The seller pays for the title search and examination, the title commitment, and the owner's title policy. The purchaser pays for the mortgagee's policy. Four Quadrants is charging $175 for the title search and examination and $125 for the title commitment. The premium for the owner's policy is $11,225 and the premium for the mortgagee's policy is $9,850.

The contract provides that the purchaser has ten days from the date of executing the contract to submit a loan application and thirty days within which to obtain a loan commitment. Cosgrave Properties applied for a loan two business days following the date of execution of the contract and obtained a loan commitment from Wexford Bank last Friday in the amount of $2,000,000. The bank's address is 100 Kettering Place (your city and state). Its telephone number is 160-6000, and its fax number is 160-6060. The loan number is 530736, and the loan officer in charge of the loan file is Ann Graham. Wexford Bank is charging Cosgrave Properties a one percent loan origination fee and a document preparation fee of $200.

Recall that WFD Corporation did not take out a loan to purchase the property; therefore, there is no loan to pay off at closing.

The contract provides a thirty-day inspection period. The survey was delivered to the title company four business days after the signing of the contract. The seller is to prepare a special warranty deed, the seller's affidavit, the closing statement, and all other documents to transfer marketable title. In addition to the title work mentioned earlier, the seller pays the documentary stamps on the deed. Attorneys' fees for each party are to be paid outside of closing. The purchaser is to pay for the recording of the deed (include the legal description and permitted exception exhibits when counting pages), the recording of the financing instrument (eight pages), the documentary stamp tax on the note, and the intangible tax on the financing instrument (if any).

The security deposit liability is $47,504.86. There are no prepaid rents. The total monthly rents for the date of closing are $44,877.81. The current tax bill for the three buildings is as follows:

Building I: $29,640.24
Building II: $21,326.60
Building III: $25,034.20

Photocopy the blank commercial closing worksheet found in your student workbook (the original worksheet is to be used for the workbook assignment). With the information given here, complete the worksheet. (The client number is 1600.) Then prepare a tenant estoppel form and cover letter to be sent to the tenants by WFD Corporation. After review, insert these items under the "Commercial Closings" section of your resource portfolio.

Assignment 14:2. Prepare a closing statement for this transaction. Be sure to prorate the rents for the month of closing. To calculate the recording fees, documentary stamp tax, and intangible tax, use your county's stipulated rates. After review, insert these items under the "Commercial Closings" section of your resource portfolio.

Assignment 14:3. Next prepare the following documents: (a) a special warranty deed (if your state has a different or statutorily prescribed form, use it), (b) a seller's affidavit, (c) a nonforeign certification, (d) an assignment of leases, and (e) a tenant notice letter. After review, insert these items under the "Commercial Closings" section of your resource portfolio.

Assignment 14:4. Define the following key terms.

break-even point   sale-leaseback
fixed costs   tenant estoppel certificate
operating expenses   variable costs
reserve requirements

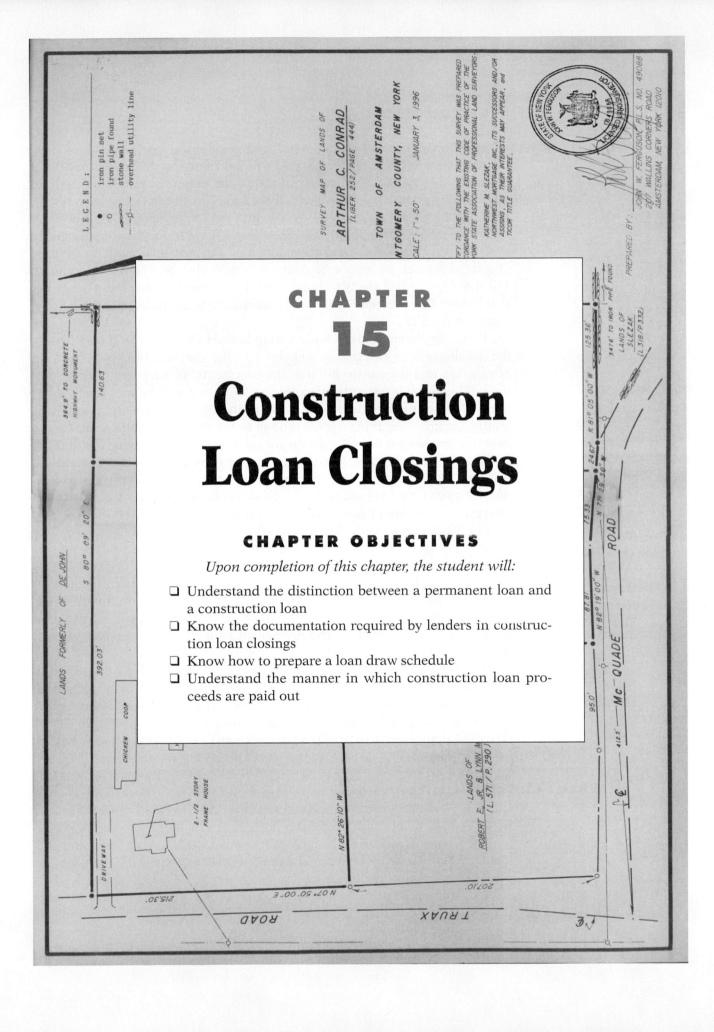

CHAPTER
15

Construction Loan Closings

CHAPTER OBJECTIVES

Upon completion of this chapter, the student will:

❑ Understand the distinction between a permanent loan and a construction loan

❑ Know the documentation required by lenders in construction loan closings

❑ Know how to prepare a loan draw schedule

❑ Understand the manner in which construction loan proceeds are paid out

INTRODUCTION

Developers of both commercial and residential projects rarely have enough capital in their corporate coffers to fund construction projects without the assistance of outside funding. A developer may first purchase the land upon which to build the project and, if the project is not to be started immediately, later seek the financing of the constructed improvements. In this situation, the developer will initially seek out a lender for land acquisition. Typically, this would be a savings and loan or a commercial bank. In the case of a large project, an insurance company might also be a source of funding. The developer, when ready to build, would then need to seek out a construction lender. Commercial banks traditionally have been the best source of construction funding.

If the developer plans to build within a short time after land acquisition, the developer is more likely to seek out a lender that will fund both the land acquisition and the construction of improvements. In such a situation, both the land and the improvements constructed upon it will be collateral for the note. Whether the land and construction funding are obtained separately or jointly, the financing provided will tend to be for a shorter duration than in the case of a permanent loan. A loan for the purchase of land may be for a period of three, five, or ten years. A construction loan is for an even shorter duration. It is only meant to cover the period of construction. Thus, a construction loan often is given for a one-year period, with available extensions. Additionally, the interest charged on a construction loan typically is higher than that charged on a permanent residential loan.

If the improved property is not sold in a timely manner, the developer must then seek out a permanent lender to cover the outstanding debt obligation until the property is sold. The permanent loan will be similar to a typical long-term mortgage. In essence, the permanent lender pays off the construction loan, plus the lot funding if it has not been paid off, and the construction lender is out of the picture. The permanent loan then operates like an ordinary, long-term mortgage loan.

A construction lender is concerned with every aspect of the construction process, both prior to and during the actual construction of the improvements. It will require submission of all plans and specifications for approval. If the borrower is building in a subdivision that must be approved by HUD/FHA, the construction lender will want copies of any subdivision reports issued by HUD/FHA to assure that the improvements will satisfy these requirements.

A construction lender will also want verification that the architect, engineer, and general contractor used on the project are properly licensed. Further, it will request copies of all contracts entered into by the borrower and these parties as well as copies of the building permit and the notice of commencement filed prior to the start of construction. The lender will then require copies of all inspection reports made at each stage of construction.

As is the case with other commercial loans, the lender will want to verify that the zoning classification permits the intended use of the property and that no rezoning applications or variances have been submitted or are under consideration.

Rather than paying out the entirety of the loan amount in one lump sum, a construction lender pays out funds to the borrower according to a draw schedule. The paying of loan funds in installments permits the lender to retain some control over the project, thereby reducing the lender's risk. The draw schedule will break down the construction project into various phases (for example, floor slab completed, drywall completed) and/or into percentages of completion (for example, intervals of ten percent completion). As each stage is completed, the borrower will make a request for the next draw. Once a request is submitted, the lender will check the progress schedule to determine whether the borrower is approved for the next draw. The lender will want to make sure that all requisite inspections have been passed up to that point, and that all items covered on previous draws have been paid for by submission of lien waivers from the various subcontractors and materialmen. In addition to inspections by city and county inspectors, the lender may have its own inspectors report on the project. It is common practice for the lender to set the draw schedule so that the amount of each draw is for less than the value of the actual work performed. In this way, the lender is protecting its collateral.

Because the principal is paid out in stages, the total amount of principal outstanding at any given time will vary. This means that the amount of interest accruing on the loan will also vary from month to month. If the interest rate is not fixed but variable, as is often the case with construction loans, the interest computations can be quite complex.

The general contractor of the project plays an integral role as well. The construction lender wants assurances that the general contractor will be able to complete the improvements within the projected time schedule. The general contractor, unless it is also the borrower, will not be in privity of contract with the lender. Therefore, if the general contractor defaults on its contract, the lender has no recourse. Thus, some construction lenders will require that the general contractor post a performance bond guaranteeing completion on schedule. The construction lender also will want verification that the general contractor is carrying adequate workers' compensation and liability coverage.

Both the hazard insurance and title insurance policies will be structured differently in a construction loan scenario than in the average residential or commercial closing. Because the principal amount of the loan and the value of the construction project increases over time, the insurance policies will be written in such a manner as to correspondingly increase coverage.

As one can see, a construction loan closing is an intricate process. There is no such thing as a "typical" construction loan closing. The amount of financing in question is often large, and the circumstances differ from project to project. As a result, all terms of a loan commitment, note, and mortgage are subject to negotiation and must be tailored to meet the needs of the parties.

This chapter takes you through a hypothetical construction loan closing. Although construction loan closings may take place separately from the closing for the sale and purchase of land, the hypothetical presented shows the lot purchase and construction closing as part of the same transaction. In this manner, you, as a paralegal, acquire a better understanding of how these two transactions work together. Your law firm may use separate closing worksheets for land funding, construction loan closings, and other real estate closings. The worksheet utilized in the hypothetical closing that follows can be used for a construction loan closing that does not involve the sale and purchase of property, or it can be used for a combined transaction.

HYPOTHETICAL CLIENT CLOSING

Upon consulting her tickler file, Barbara sees that she has planned to spend this morning reviewing a client's file for an upcoming closing and preparing the last of the requisite documents for her supervising attorney, Ava Ross. The closing combines a construction loan closing and the closing for the sale and purchase of the property upon which the construction is to take place. The client is Maxwell Development Corporation, a company that specializes in high-end homes. It typically develops exclusive country club developments.

Maxwell Development Corporation's president, Thomas Maxwell, has noticed a recent resurgence in popularity of an older development in his county, Crosswinds Country Club. It is a yachting community, and as waterfront property is scarce, those who can afford it have been buying the remaining waterfront vacant lots and constructing expensive homes on them.

Through a local realtor, Thomas was made aware of two lots that were becoming available within Crosswinds. The owners are foreign nationals, Malcolm and Katherine Bryant, who live in London, England, and bought the properties as investments a number of years ago. Now retired, they wish to sell the lots to free up some capital. They have listed the properties with Arcadia Realty. The realtor who was Thomas's contact, Vantage Point Realty, saw the listing on the Multiple Listing Service and informed Thomas of the availability of these lots.

Maxwell Development Corporation contracted with the Bryants for the purchase of the property on January 23, 1998, the closing to take place on March 18, 1998. Because the Bryants live abroad and do not have a local attorney, the contract specifies that the buyer's attorney will conduct the title examination, prepare the closing documents, and arrange for the title policies. Thomas has hired Ava Ross to represent his company in this transaction. The Bryants are planning to fly in for the closing.

The client file was opened by Barbara on January 29th. When first opening the file, Barbara reviewed the signed contract to assist her in completing the construction closing worksheet her firm utilizes for its construction loan closings. As more documents have been submitted for Ava's review by the lender, Millennium Bank, Barbara has been able to ascertain the lender's requirements to close the transaction.

Barbara reviews the closing worksheet to refresh her memory as to what steps have already been taken and what remains to be done. The closing worksheet is found in Figure 15–1.

The closing worksheet indicates several dates. According to the sales contract, Maxwell Development Corporation has thirty days from signing the contract to obtain a loan commitment. The purchase of the lots is conditioned upon securing not only the lot funding but also the construction funding. Maxwell Development has obtained construction funding from Millennium Bank before for other projects and has a good relationship with the bank. Thus, Millennium Bank was the first bank Thomas contacted, and upon

FIGURE 15–1
Construction loan
closing worksheet

CONSTRUCTION LOAN CLOSING WORKSHEET

DATE FILE OPENED: 1/29/98
ATTORNEY: Ava Ross
PARALEGAL: Barbara Hammond
CLIENT NUMBER: 15500
MATTER NUMBER: 001
CLIENT: __X__ BUYER   _____ SELLER   _____ LENDER

1. SELLER NAME(S):   Malcolm Bryant and Katherine Bryant, Husband and
                     Wife

2. ADDRESS(ES):   109 St. Martin's Lane
                     London, England

3. PHONE NUMBER(S): (0494)022-474 FAX NUMBER(S): (0494)022-536

4. SOCIAL SECURITY NUMBER(S) [IF A BUSINESS ENTITY, FEDERAL TAX.
   I.D NO.]:   Foreign nationals—withhold ten percent of sales price as
                     per IRS requirements

5. BUYER NAME(S):   Maxwell Development Corporation

6. ADDRESS(ES):   580 Franklin Avenue, Suite 400
                     Any City, Any State

7. PHONE NUMBER(S): (000) 011-9898 FAX NUMBER(S): (000) 011-9860

8. SOCIAL SECURITY NUMBER(S) [IF A BUSINESS ENTITY, FEDERAL TAX
   I.D. NO.]:   000330054

9. CONSTRUCTION LENDER: Millennium Bank

10. ADDRESS: 1750 Wellington Avenue
                     Any City, Any State

11. PHONE NUMBER: (000) 041-4000   FAX NUMBER: (000) 041-4100

12. LOAN OFFICER ASSIGNED TO LOAN FILE: Erica Hiller

13. LOAN NUMBER: 800100

14. SELLER'S LENDER (IF SELLER HAS EXISTING MORTGAGE ON PROPERTY):
                     Not applicable

15. ADDRESS:

16. PHONE NUMBER: FAX NUMBER:

17. LOAN NUMBER:

18. ATTORNEY FOR: _____ BUYER   _____ SELLER   __X__ LENDER

19. ATTORNEY NAME: Craig Fox (In-House Counsel for Millennium)

20. ADDRESS: 1750 Wellington Avenue
                     Any City, Any State

21. PHONE NUMBER: (000) 041-4200   FAX NUMBER: (000) 041-4202

22. ATTORNEY FOR: _____ BUYER   __X__ SELLER   _____ LENDER

23. ATTORNEY NAME: Not applicable

FIGURE 15–1
(continued)

24. ADDRESS: _____

25. PHONE NUMBER: _____ FAX NUMBER: _____

26. REAL ESTATE BROKER #1: Arcadia Realty (Andrew Sage, realtor)

27. ADDRESS: 360 Poplar Drive
Any City, Any State

28. PHONE NUMBER: (000) 031-3535   FAX NUMBER: (000) 031-3536

29. REAL ESTATE BROKER #2: Vantage Point Realty (Marsha Meyers, realtor)

30. ADDRESS: 618 Coolidge Street
Any City, Any State

31. PHONE NUMBER: (000) 050-4424   FAX NUMBER: (000) 050-4425

32. COMMISSION: 5%   HOW SPLIT: 50/50

33. ESCROW AGENT: Fisher, Ross, and Simon, P.A.

34. ADDRESS: 1900 N.W. 3rd Avenue
Any City, Any State

35. PHONE NUMBER: (000) 555-2000   FAX NUMBER: (000) 555-2020

36. TITLE COMPANY: In-house

37. ADDRESS: _____

38. PHONE NUMBER: _____ FAX NUMBER: _____

39. STREET ADDRESS OF PROPERTY:
230 Crosswinds Avenue, Any City, Any State (Lot 60)
232 Crosswinds Avenue, Any City, Any State (Lot 61)

40. LEGAL DESCRIPTION OF PROPERTY:
Lot 60 in Block 10 of CROSSWINDS COUNTRY CLUB
SUBDIVISION, according to the plat thereof recorded in
Plat Book 36 at Pages 60 through 66 inclusive of the
Public Records of Any County, Any State.
Lot 61 in Block 10 of CROSSWINDS COUNTRY CLUB
SUBDIVISION, according to the plat thereof recorded in
Plat Book 36 at Pages 60 through 66 inclusive of the
Public Records of Any County, Any State.

41. PARCEL IDENTIFICATION NUMBER: 8488007439 (Lot 60); 8488100221(Lot 61)

42. CLOSING:
(A) DATE: March 18, 1998
(B) TIME: 11:00 a.m.
(C) PLACE: our offices

43. PURCHASE PRICE: $750,000.00

44. LOAN AMOUNT: $1,425,000.00

45. **DEPOSITS:**

	AMOUNT	DATE DUE	DATE RECEIVED
(A) LOT:			
(B) INITIAL:	$50,000.00	1/23/98	1/23/98
(C) ADDITIONAL:			

46.

ITEM	**DONE BY**	**DATE DUE**	**CHARGE TO**
Title Search	Buyer		Buyer/Seller split
Order Survey	Buyer	2/2/98	Buyer

FIGURE 15–1
(continued)

ITEM	DONE BY	DATE DUE	CHARGE TO
Title Examination	Buyer	2/14/98	Buyer/Seller split
Title Commitment	Buyer	2/14/98	Included above
Remedy Defects			
Issue Policy(ies):			
(a) Owner's	Buyer		Seller
(b) Mortgagee's	Buyer		Buyer
(c) Endorsements:			
Variable rate	Buyer		Buyer
Six Construction			
Updates	Buyer		Buyer
Property Appraisal	Lender	2/25/98	Buyer
Engineer's Report	Buyer	2/25/98	Buyer
Preparation of Plans			
and Specifications	Buyer	2/20/98	Buyer
Submission of Plans			
and Specifications	Buyer	2/25/98	
Loan Application	Buyer	2/3/98	Buyer
Submission of			
Financial Statements	Buyer	2/6/98	
Loan Commitment	Lender	2/23/98	
Promissory Note	Lender	3/18/98	
Mortgage/Deed of Trust	Lender	3/18/98	
Draw Schedule	Lender	3/18/98	
UCC Financing Forms			
Performance Bond			
General Construction			
Contract			
Contractor's Certification	Buyer	2/25/98	
Architect's Contract	Buyer	1/27/98	
Architect's Certification	Buyer	2/25/98	
Engineer's Contract	Buyer	1/28/98	
Engineer's Certification	Buyer	2/25/98	
Building Permit	Buyer		
Notice of Commencement	Buyer		
List of Required Inspections	Buyer	2/25/98	
Request for Payment Forms	Lender		
HOA Approval	Buyer	3/3/98	
Mortgage Estoppel Letter			
Satisfaction of Mortgage/			
Deed of Trust			
Insurance Coverage	Buyer	3/9/98	Buyer
Verification of			
Corporate Status	Buyer	1/29/98	
Corporate Resolution	Buyer	1/14/98	
Tax Receipts	Seller	2/21/98	
City Tax Prorated			
County Tax Prorated	Buyer	3/16/98	Seller
Special Assessments			
Prorated			
Maintenance Assessments			
Prorated	Buyer	3/16/98	Buyer
Other Prorations:			
_____			
_____			

FIGURE 15–1
(continued)

ITEM	DONE BY	DATE DUE	CHARGE TO
Deed	Buyer	3/18/98	
FIRPTA Affidavit			
Marriage Affidavit	Buyer	3/18/98	
Closing Statement	Buyer	3/16/98	
Recordation of Deed	Buyer		Buyer
Recordation of Financing Instrument	Buyer		Buyer
Recordation of UCC Forms			
Recordation of Satisfaction of Mortgage/Deed of Trust			
Doc. Stamps on Deed	Buyer		Seller
Doc. Stamps on Financing Instrument	Buyer		Buyer
Intangible Tax on New Mortgage	Buyer		Buyer
1099S Filed	Buyer		
State Revenue Form Filed	Buyer		
Disbursement to Seller		3/18/98	
Disbursement to Seller's Lender			
Disbursement to Brokers		3/18/98	
Disbursement to Title Company		3/18/98	
Construction Loan Binder Index Prepared	Buyer		
Documents Mailed to Buyer			
Other:			
_____			
_____			
File Closed	_____		

submission of the required documents, Maxwell Development was approved within the contractually stipulated time period. A copy of the loan commitment is found in Figure 15–2. Figures 15–3 and 15–4 are exhibits to the commitment.

Millennium Bank requires copies of licensure certification of the general contractor (in this instance, Thomas Maxwell), the architect, and the engineer. It also requires copies of contracts entered into by Maxwell Development Corporation and the architect and engineer. As Maxwell Development Corporation will be both the owner of the properties and the contractor, no copy of the contract between the owner and contractor is necessary. The dates indicated for these items on the worksheet are the dates Thomas delivered the items to Millennium.

Because the two lots are located within a community that has a homeowners' association, Maxwell Development Corporation has gone through the formality of obtaining approval of its purchase by the Crosswinds Country Club Homeowners' Association. The information provided by the association indicates that the maintenance assessments have been paid through June, so

FIGURE 15–2
Loan agreement

LOAN AGREEMENT

THIS AGREEMENT entered into as of the 10th day of February, 1998, by and between MAXWELL DEVELOPMENT CORPORATION, an Any State corporation (the "Borrower"), and MILLENNIUM BANK, having an office at 1750 Wellington Avenue, Any City, Any State (the "Lender").

WITNESSETH:

WHEREAS, the Borrower desires to acquire the Premises hereinafter described and to construct certain Improvements hereinafter described thereon; and

WHEREAS, the Borrower has made application to the Lender for a loan in connection with the acquisition of the Premises and the construction of the Improvements which loan has been approved by the Lender.

NOW THEREFORE, in consideration of the promises set forth herein and other good and valuable consideration, receipt of which is hereby acknowledged, the parties agree as follows:

1. The loan shall be in the principal amount of ONE MILLION, FOUR HUNDRED TWENTY-FIVE THOUSAND AND NO/100 DOLLARS ($1,425,000.00) and shall be secured by a first mortgage upon the Premises described in Exhibit A attached hereto and made a part hereof, and the Improvements. The terms and conditions of this loan, including without limitation the terms of payment of the interest on and principal amount of this loan, are further set out in the note and mortgage executed in connection with this loan.

2. The Improvements shall be constructed in accordance with the plans and specifications approved by the Lender. No changes, additions or deletions shall be made in the plans and specifications without the prior written approval of the Lender. The Improvements shall be constructed in accordance with the applicable building code and all other applicable laws, ordinances and regulations, federal, state or local. The Borrower shall obtain all required permits and approvals in connection with the construction of the Improvements. The Borrower agrees to construct the Improvements in a continuous and diligent manner. The Borrower shall record and post a Notice of Commencement pursuant to Any State Statutes, after the recording of the mortgage executed in connection with this loan and before the commencement of construction, and shall designate therein the Lender as someone to receive a copy of all notices given pursuant to Any State Statutes.

3. The Borrower understands and agrees that the Lender is in no way liable or responsible for the quality of construction, labor performed, or materials used in the construction of the Improvements. As between the Borrower and the Lender, the Borrower shall have the sole responsibility as to the quality of said items. During the progress of construction, the Borrower shall make personal inspections or arrange for a third party to do so in its behalf.

4. Authorized agents of the Lender shall at all times have the right to enter upon the Premises during the course of construction in order to ascertain the progress of construction of the Improvements.

5 The net proceeds of this loan plus any other funds required in connection with this Agreement shall be disbursed from time to time by the Lender during the progress of construction of the Improvements for labor performed and materials furnished in connection therewith. Such disbursements shall be made only upon the written request of the Borrower, or its duly authorized agent, except as hereinafter set forth. Disbursements shall be made at the times and under the terms and

FIGURE 15–2
(continued)

conditions as shall from time to time be designated by the Lender. Prior to any such disbursement, the Lender may require that a satisfactory inspection of the progress of the construction be made by its inspectors or inspectors selected by the Lender, that a satisfactory title update be obtained and/or that partial or full releases of construction liens be provided from the subcontractors or others. The Lender shall have the right to make payments in connection with disbursements directly to a subcontractor or other person entitled thereto rather than to the Borrower.

6. The Lender shall have the right to disburse, without the written request of the Borrower or its duly authorized agent, funds required to release the Premises from the lien of any recorded construction lien, provided, however, that the Lender shall give Borrower not less than fifteen (15) days prior written notice of its intention to procure such release. The Borrower hereby releases the Lender from all liability in connection with any disbursement made pursuant to this section.

7. The Borrower specifically agrees that the Lender shall be under no duty or obligation whatsoever to disburse any portion of the loan proceeds whenever it is the opinion of the Lender that the undisbursed portion of the loan is not sufficient to pay all remaining costs of the Improvements. In such event, the Lender shall have the right to require from the Borrower and the Borrower agrees to pay to the Lender such additional amount as the Lender then deems necessary, in addition to the undisbursed portion of the loan, to pay in full all remaining costs of the Improvements. Such additional amount shall be paid to the Lender within ten (10) days after its demand.

8. Anything to the contrary set forth herein or in the note executed in connection with this loan notwithstanding, interest shall only be payable from time to time on the portion of this loan which has been disbursed.

9. The Borrower agrees not to transfer or convey, directly or indirectly, its interest in the Premises prior to the completion of the Improvements and the issuance of a certificate of occupancy without the prior written approval thereof and of the transferee or grantee by the Lender.

10. A default under this Agreement shall constitute a default under the note and the mortgage executed in connection with this loan.

11. During the construction of the Improvements, the Borrower agrees to provide and keep in force at all times at Borrower's cost such builder's risk and flood insurance as Lender may reasonably require, such insurance to be with insurance companies and in form, substance and amount satisfactory to Lender.

12. The Borrower understands and agrees that the Lender must be in receipt of a satisfactory foundation survey, evidence of Hazard Insurance and evidence of Flood Insurance (if applicable) prior to release of first disbursement and a satisfactory Title Insurance Policy prior to release of the second disbursement.

13. The Borrower agrees to execute from time to time such other documents and instruments as the Lender may reasonably require in connection with this loan and to comply with such other terms and conditions of this loan as Lender may from time to time reasonably impose; provided such terms and conditions are not unusual or uncustomary in connection with loans such as this loan.

The Borrower agrees to reimburse the Lender from time to time for all its reasonable fees, expenses and costs in connection with this loan, including without limitation, inspection fees and title update charges.

FIGURE 15–2
(continued)

14. The relationship between the Borrower and the Lender in connection herewith and with the Premises and the Improvements is a lending relationship and in no way whatsoever constitutes a joint venture.

15. The Borrower and the Lender each hereby expressly waive all rights to a trial by jury in any action arising out of this loan.

16. All notices hereunder or in connection with this loan shall be given by first-class certified mail, return receipt requested, to the parties at their respective addresses given above or at such other addresses as each may from time to time so notify the other.

17. This Agreement together with the other documents and instruments in connection herewith constitute the entire agreement between the parties, and no oral statements heretofore or hereafter made by either party or their agents shall be a part hereof.

18. This Agreement may not be modified, altered or amended except by an instrument in writing executed by the parties hereto.

19. This Agreement shall be interpreted, construed and enforced in accordance with the laws of the State of Any State and shall be legally binding upon the parties and their respective successors and assigns.

IN WITNESS WHEREOF, the parties have caused this Agreement to be executed, intending to be legally bound, as of the day and year first above mentioned.

ATTEST: MAXWELL DEVELOPMENT CORPORATION,
                                           an Any State corporation
_Natalie Lang_____   By: _Thomas Maxwell_____
Secretary   President
(SEAL)

ATTEST: MILLENNIUM BANK, an Any State corporation
_Brad Carter_____   By: _Gillian Powers_____
Secretary   Vice President

Maxwell Development will owe the Bryants its share of the paid assessments at closing.

The hazard insurance coverage required by Millennium Bank to cover the constructed improvements will be purchased by Maxwell Development Corporation outside of closing. Therefore, Millennium Bank will not require the setting aside of reserves for the hazard insurance that would appear on the closing statement. However, Millennium does require an interest reserve, the setting aside of reserves to cover the payment of interest on the loan for a specified number of months or as a specified sum. Further, it had an appraisal of the property conducted, the cost of which is charged to Maxwell Development.

Inasmuch as Maxwell Development is a corporate entity, it has provided Barbara with a certificate of good standing from the secretary of state's office that will, in turn, be given to the Bryants at closing. Thomas has also supplied Barbara with a certified copy of a corporate resolution in which the board of directors approved the purchase of the lots and the application of appropriate funding.

A survey was ordered from ABC Survey Company, and from this and the information gleaned from the title search and examination, Barbara has

FIGURE 15-3
Description of property

EXHIBIT A

Lot 60 in Block 10 of CROSSWINDS COUNTRY CLUB SUBDIVISION, according to the plat thereof recorded in Plat Book 36 at Pages 60 through 66, inclusive, of the Public Records of Any County, Any State.

Lot 61 in Block 10 of CROSSWINDS COUNTRY CLUB SUBDIVISION, according to the plat thereof recorded in Plat Book 36 at Pages 60 through 66, inclusive, of the Public Records of Any County, Any State.

FIGURE 15-4
Loan disbursements authorization

LOAN DISBURSEMENTS AUTHORIZATION

Date: February 10, 1998
Property: 230 Crosswinds Avenue   232 Crosswinds Avenue
                 Any City, Any State   Any City, Any State

From the proceeds of my/our mortgage loan, you are authorized to disburse to the Bank the amounts charged or incurred by it for appraisal, credit reports, document preparation, service fees, title and survey in connection with said loan.

You are further authorized to make the following additional disbursements:

INTEREST FROM FILING DATE TO THE FIRST OF THE NEXT FILING MONTH	$ (TO BE BILLED WITH THE FIRST REGULARLY SCHEDULED INTEREST BILLING)
TO MILLENNIUM BANK 1.5 POINTS	$ 21,375.00
TO MILLENNIUM BANK APPRAISAL FEE	$ 675.00
TO MILLENNIUM BANK INTEREST RESERVE	$ 92,250.00
TO MILLENNIUM BANK DOC. PREP. FEE	$ 100.00
TO MILLENNIUM BANK INSPECTION FEES	$ AS BILLED
TO FISHER, SIMON, AND ROSS TITLE CHARGES	$ AS BILLED
TO FISHER, SIMON, AND ROSS LOT ADVANCE	$ 500,000.00

If the loan is a construction loan, the balance of the net proceeds shall be credited to the applicable construction loan account for disbursement as construction progresses.

If the loan is for Home Improvement, you may disburse the net proceeds as construction progresses or upon full completion thereof, as you may determine to be appropriate.

PAYOFFS WILL INCLUDE INTEREST TO DATE OF RECEIPT IF REQUIRED BY DEBT HOLDER

MAXWELL DEVELOPMENT CORPORATION,
an Any State corporation

By: *Thomas Maxwell*
      President

---

prepared a title commitment. The date indicated on the worksheet is the effective date of the commitment. Schedules A and B of the commitment may be found in Figure 15–5. Notice the note found at the end of Schedule B. Because a construction loan is involved, the amount of money furnished at closing by Millennium Bank is not the total amount of the loan. The remainder will be

FUND COMMITMENT FORM
Schedule A

Commitment No.: 1501125   Effective Date: 02/14/98 at 10:30 a.m.   Agent's File Reference: 2580

1. Policy or Policies to be issued:

    OWNER'S: $ 750,000.00

    Proposed Insured:

        Maxwell Development Corporation, an Any State corporation

    MORTGAGEE: $ 1,425,000.00

    Proposed Insured:

        Millennium Bank, its successors and/or assigns

2. The estate or interest in the land described or referred to in this commitment is a fee simple (if other, specify same)
    and title thereto is at the effective date hereof vested in:

    Malcolm Bryant and Katherine Bryant, Husband and Wife as tenants by the entirety

3. The land referred to in this commitment is described as follows:

    Lot 60 in Block 10 of CROSSWINDS COUNTRY CLUB SUBDIVISION, according to the plat thereof recorded in Plat
    Book 36 at Pages 60 through 66, inclusive, of the Public Records of Any County, Any State.

    Lot 61 in Block 10 of CROSSWINDS COUNTRY CLUB SUBDIVISION, according to the plat thereof recorded in Plat
    Book 36 at Pages 60 through 66, inclusive, of the Public Records of Any County, Any State.

ISSUED BY

FISHER, ROSS, AND SIMON, P.A.

	3333	Ava Ross
	AGENT NO.	AGENT'S SIGNATURE

1900 N. W. 3rd Avenue	Any City	, Any State
MAILING ADDRESS	CITY	ZIP

FIGURE 15–5 Maxwell Development Corporation title commitment

FUND COMMITMENT FORM

Schedule B

Commitment No.:   1501125

I.   The following are the requirements to be complied with:

1.   Payment of the full consideration to or for the account of, the grantors or mortgagors.

2.   Instruments creating the estate or interest to be insured which must be executed, delivered and filed for record:

   A.   Warranty Deed from Malcolm Bryant and Katherine Bryant, Husband and Wife, to Maxwell Development Corporation.

   B.   Mortgage executed by Maxwell Development Corporation in favor of Millennium Bank in the original principal sum of $1,425,000.00.

   C.   Proof of payment of all association fees and assessments.

   D.   Current survey of the property, properly certified, showing no encroachments or other adverse matters.

II. Schedule B of the policy or policies to be issued will contain exceptions to the following matters unless the same are disposed of to the satisfaction of The Association:

1.   Defects, liens, encumbrances, adverse claims or other matters, if any, created, first appearing in the public records or attaching subsequent to the effective date hereof but prior to the date the proposed Insured acquires for value of record the estate or interest or mortgage thereon covered by this Commitment.

2.   Any owner policy issued pursuant hereto will contain under Schedule B the standard exceptions set forth at the inside cover hereof. Any mortgagee policy will contain under Schedule B the standard exceptions unless an affidavit of possession and a satisfactory current survey are submitted, an inspection of the premises is made, it is determined the current year's taxes or special assessments have been paid, and it is determined there is nothing of record which would give rise to mechanics' liens which could take priority over the mortgage (where the liens would otherwise take priority, submission of waivers is necessary).

3.   Taxes for the year 1998 and all subsequent years.

4.   Matters as shown on the Plat of Crosswinds Country Club Subdivision, recorded in Plat Book 27, Page 75, of the Public Records of Any County, Any State.

Form reproduced through the courtesy of Attorneys' Title Insurance Fund, Inc.

FIGURE 15–5 (continued)

5. Restrictions, covenants, conditions and stipulations as contained in instrument dated June 20, 1979, recorded June 23, 1979 in Official Records Book 386, Page 602, and further amended in Official Records Book 1003, Page 127, and further amended in Official Records Book 2907, Page 515, all of the Public Records of Any County, Any State. The foregoing instruments create or contain provisions which establish the right to create an easement on the land and provide for private charges or assessments.

6. Terms and provisions of all agreements and franchises pertaining to the cost, installation, operation and maintenance of gas, water and/or sewer facilities. Any lien as provided by Chapter 230, Any State Statutes, in favor of any city, town, or county authority for unpaid service charges for service by any water sewer or gas system supplying the lands described herein.

NOTE: PENDING DISBURSEMENT OF THE FULL PROCEEDS OF THE LOAN SECURED BY THE MORTGAGE COVERED BY THIS POLICY, THIS POLICY INSURES ONLY TO THE EXTENT OF THE AMOUNT ACTUALLY DISBURSED BUT INCREASES AS EACH DISBURSEMENT IS MADE IN GOOD FAITH AND WITHOUT ANY ACTUAL KNOWLEDGE OF ANY DEFECTS IN, OR OBJECTIONS TO THE TITLE, UP TO THE FACE AMOUNT OF THIS POLICY.

Form reproduced through the courtesy of Attorneys' Title Insurance Fund, Inc.

FIGURE 15–5 (continued)

paid in disbursements according to the draw schedules. The title policy covers the amount disbursed, with the coverage increasing as each disbursement is made.

No existing mortgage is outstanding against the properties, so no mortgage estoppel letter is necessary. The closing is taking place in the first quarter of the year. This being the case, the sellers have not yet received the current tax bill for the properties, so prorations for real property taxes will be based on the most recent bill and adjusted later if and as necessary. Maxwell Development Corporation will be paying the taxes when due, so the Bryants' share of the taxes for 1998 will be deducted from what is owed by Maxwell.

Three and one-half percent of Maxwell Development's closing costs will be funded by loan proceeds, so this will be indicated on the closing statement.

Having input information into her real estate closing software as it has been received, Barbara is able to complete the HUD-1 Uniform Settlement Statement with ease. The completed HUD-1 statement is found in Figure 15–6.

The construction draw account is indicated on line 104 of the statement. The amount of the homeowners' association maintenance, previously paid by the Bryants, which is owed by Maxwell, appears on line 105.

The contract and worksheet indicate that Maxwell Development made an earnest money deposit of $50,000, which is being held in escrow by Barbara's firm. The figure appears on line 201 of the HUD-1 statement. Line 202 states the principal amount of the total loan, and line 204 indicates that portion of

A. SETTLEMENT STATEMENT

United States Department of Housing and Urban Development   OMB No. 2502-0265

B. Type of Loan	Loan Number	Mortgage Ins. Case Number	File Number
Conventional Uninsured	800100		15500.001

C. Note: This form is furnished to give you a statement of actual settlement costs. Amounts paid to and by the settlement agent are shown. Items marked "p.o.c." were paid outside of closing, they are shown here for informational purposes and are not included in the totals.

D. Name and Address of Borrower:	E. Name and Address of Seller:
Maxwell Development Corporation, an Any State corporation 580 Franklin Avenue, Suite 400 Any City, Any State	Malcolm Bryant and Katherine Bryant 109 St. Martin's Lane London, England TIN: _____

F. Name and Address of Lender:	G. Property Location:
Millennium Bank 1750 Wellington Avenue Any City, Any State	230 Crosswinds Avenue Any City, Any State

H. Settlement Agent / Place of Settlement:	I. Settlement Date:
Fisher, Ross, and Simon, P.A. 1900 N.W. 3rd Avenue Any City, Any State TIN: _____	March 18, 1998

J. Summary of Borrower's Transaction		K. Summary of Seller's Transaction	
100 Gross amount due from borrower		**400 Gross amount due to seller**	
101 Contract sales price	750,000.00	401 Contract sales price	750,000.00
102 Personal property		402 Personal property	
103 Settlement charges to borrower [1400]	129,455.50	403	
104 Construction Draw Acct	796,017.20	404	
105 HOA Maint. thru 6/30/98	380.61	405	
Adjustments for items paid by seller in advance		Adjustments for items paid by seller in advance	
106 City/town taxes / / to / /		406 City/town taxes / / to / /	
107 County taxes / / to / /		407 County taxes / / to / /	
108 Assessments / / to / /		408 Assessments / / to / /	
109		409	
110		410	
111		411	
112		412	
120 Gross Amount Due From borrower	**1,675,853.31**	**420 Gross Amount Due To Seller**	**750,000.00**
200 Amounts paid by or on behalf of borrower		**500 Reductions in amount due to seller**	
201 Deposit or earnest money	50,000.00	501 Excess deposit (see instructions)	
202 Principal amount of new loan(s)	1,425,000.00	502 Settlement charges to seller [1400]	121,865.00
203 Existing loan(s) taken subject to		503 Existing loan(s) taken subject to	
204 Lot Funding $500,000.00		504 Payoff of first mortgage	
205 Closing Costs		505 Payoff of second mortgage	
206 funded $36,732.80		506 Deposit retained by	
207		507 (Deposit disbursed: 50,000.00)	
208		508	
209 Mortgage in favor of seller		509 Mortgage in favor of seller	
Adjustments for items unpaid by seller		Adjustments for items unpaid by seller	
210 City/town taxes / / to / / 13,839.53 / 365 days		510 City/town taxes / / to / / 13,839.53 / 365 days	
211 County taxes 01/01/98 to 03/18/98	2,881.66	511 County taxes 01/01/98 to 03/18/98	2,881.66
212 Assessments / / to / /		512 Assessments / / to / /	
213		513	
214		514	
215		515	
216		516	
217		517	
218		518	
219		519	
220 Total Paid By/For Borrower	**1,477,881.66**	**520 Total Reductions In Amount Due Seller**	**124,746.66**
300 Cash At Settlement From/To Borrower		600 Cash At Settlement To/From Seller	
301 Gross amount due from borrower [120]	1,675,853.31	601 Gross amount due to seller [420]	750,000.00
302 Less amount paid by/for borrower [220]	1,477,881.66	602 Less reductions in amount due seller [520]	124,746.66
303 Cash From/(To) Borrower	**197,971.65**	**603 Cash To/(From) Seller**	**625,253.34**

SUBSTITUTE FORM 1099-S SELLER'S STATEMENT: This is important tax information and is being furnished to the Internal Revenue Service. If you are required to file a return, a negligence penalty or other sanction may be imposed on you if this item is required to be reported and the IRS determines that it has not been reported. The information in Boxes E, G, H, and I, the amount on Line 401 and the amount(s) of any real estate tax adjustments appearing on Lines 406 through 412 are reported to the IRS on Form 1099-S.

REQUEST FOR SELLER'S TAXPAYER IDENTIFICATION AND CERTIFICATION: You, the Seller (see Box E) are required by law to provide the Settlement Agent (see Box H) with your correct taxpayer identification number. If you do not provide the Settlement Agent with your correct taxpayer identification number, you may be subject to civil or criminal penalties imposed by law. By signing the following page of this Settlement Statement, you, under penalties of perjury, certify that the number shown on this statement (see Box E - "TIN") is your correct taxpayer identification number.

Rawi   Closing System for Windows™

HUD-1 (Rev 3/86)

Form reproduced through the courtesy of Real Estate Expert Systems Associates, Inc.

FIGURE 15–6 HUD-1 Uniform Settlement Statement

L. Settlement Charges							Paid from borrower's funds at settlement	Paid from seller's funds at settlement
700	Total Sales/Broker's Commission		Based on $ 750,000.00	@	5.00000	% = 37,500.00		
	Division of commission (line 700) as follows:							
701	18,750.00	to	Arcadia Realty					
702	18,750.00	to	Vantage Point Realty					37,500.00
703	Commission paid at settlement							
704			Commission retained by					
800	Items Payable In Connection With Loan							
801	Loan origination fee		%					
802	Loan Discount		1.50000 %				21,375.00	
803	Appraisal fee to:	Millennium Bank					675.00	
804	Credit report to:							
805	Lender's inspection fee							
806	Mortgage insurance application fee to							
807	Assumption fee							
808	Interest Reserve						92,250.00	
809	Doc. Prep. Fee						100.00	
810								
811								
900	Items Required By Lender To Be Paid In Advance							
901	Interest from	/ /	to	/ /		/ day		
902	Mortgage insurance premium for		months to					
903	Hazard insurance premium for		years to					
904	Flood insurance premium for		years to					
905								
1000	Reserves Deposited With Lender							
1001	Hazard Insurance		months @		per month			
1002	Mortgage insurance		months @		per month			
1003	City property taxes		months @		per month			
1004	County property taxes		months @		per month			
1005	Annual assessments		months @		per month			
1006	Flood insurance		months @		per month			
1007			months @		per month			
1008								
1100	Title Charges							
1101	Settlement or closing fee to	Fisher, Ross, and Simon					100.00	
1102	Abstract or title search to	Fisher, Ross, and Simon					90.00	90.00
1103	Title examination to	Fisher, Ross, and Simon					100.00	100.00
1104	Title insurance binder to							
1105	Document preparation to							
1106	Notary fees to							
1107	Attorney's fees to	Fisher, Ross, Simon		includes above items (		)	900.00	
1108	Title insurance fee to			includes above items (		)	4,805.00	3,925.00
1109	Lender's coverage	1,425,000.00	premium	4,805.00				
1110	Owner's coverage	750,000.00	premium	3,925.00				
1111	Variable Rate Mortgage Endorsement						25.00	
1112	6 Construction Updates						1,050.00	
1113								
1200	Government Recording And Transfer Charges							
1201	Recording fees:	Deed	12.00	Mortgage	36.00	Release	48.00	
1202	City/county tax/stamps:	Deed		Mortgage	2,850.00		2,850.00	
1203	State tax/stamps:	Deed	5,250.00	Mortgage	4,987.50		4,987.50	5,250.00
1204								
1205								
1300	Additional Settlement Charges							
1301	Survey to	ABC Survey Company					100.00	
1302	Pest inspection to							
1303	FIRPTA Withholding IRS							75,000.00
1304								
1305								
1306								
1307								
1400	Total Settlement Charges						129,455.50	121,865.00

I have carefully reviewed the HUD-1 Settlement Statement and to the best of my knowledge and belief, it is a true and accurate statement of all receipts and disbursements made on my account or by me in this transaction. I further certify that I have received a copy of this HUD-1 Settlement Statement.

Borrower: _____ Date: _____ 03/18/98   Seller: _____ Date: _____ 03/18/98
Maxwell Development Corporation, an Any State corporation   Malcolm Bryant

Borrower: _____ Date: _____   Seller: _____ Date: _____ 03/18/98
                                                 Katherine Bryant

Borrower: _____ Date: _____   Seller: _____ Date: _____

Borrower: _____ Date: _____   Seller: _____ Date: _____

The HUD-1 Settlement Statement which I have prepared is a true and accurate account of this transaction. I have caused or will cause the funds to be disbursed in accordance with this statement.

Settlement Agent: _____ Date: _____
   WARNING: It is a crime to knowingly make a false statement to the United States on this or any similar form. Penalties upon conviction include a fine and imprisonment.
   For details see Title 18 US Code Section 1001 and Section 1010.

HUD-1 (Rev 3/86)

FIGURE 15–6 (continued)

the loan which covers the funding of the purchase of the lots. Line 205 indicates the dollar amount of Maxwell Development's closing costs that are funded by loan proceeds. Only county taxes are assessed against the properties, as Crosswinds Country Club lies just outside the city limits. The prorated county taxes appear on line 210. As no outstanding mortgage loan must be paid off, line 504 remains blank.

Barbara noted on the worksheet that two brokers were involved in this transaction. Their respective commissions appear on lines 701 and 702. Millennium Bank is charging Maxwell Development one and one-half percent of the loan amount as discount points. This appears on line 802. Additionally, Millennium is charging Maxwell Development the cost of the appraisal and a document preparation fee, and the bank is requiring an interest reserve. These items complete the 800s.

The title charges and attorney's fee appear in the 1100s. Maxwell Development is paying the nominal closing fee. The fees for the title search and examination are split between the parties on lines 1102 and 1103. Maxwell's attorneys' fees appear on line 1107. Maxwell is paying for the lender's title policy, and the Bryants are paying for the owner's title policy, as indicated on line 1108. Maxwell Development is paying for the required endorsements.

The document recording fees are incurred by Maxwell Development. It further pays the intangible tax on the new mortgage and the documentary stamp tax on the financing instrument. The Bryants are paying the documentary stamp tax on the deed.

The survey charge appears on line 1301 of the HUD-1 statement. Note line 1303: because the Bryants are foreign nationals, ten percent of the sales price must be withheld by law for federal taxes. Having completed the HUD-1 statement, Barbara can inform Thomas that Maxwell Development must submit a cashier's check in the amount of $197,971.65 at closing.

Barbara next turns her attention to the preparation of the deed. The software automatically inserted the pertinent information. Because Barbara had inputted each lot as a separate legal description, that is the way they will appear on the deed. Once signed, witnessed, and acknowledged at closing, the warranty deed will read as shown in Figure 15–7.

A bill of sale is not prepared because the properties in question are vacant lots. Similarly, a no-lien affidavit is not prepared. The new mortgage note and mortgage instrument securing the properties and subsequent improvements to be built on them have been prepared by Millennium's in-house attorney, Craig Fox. He has sent copies to Ava for review. The mortgage instrument is not included here (sample mortgage instruments and deeds of trust are found in Chapter 10). The note, found in Figure 15–8, is an open-ended mortgage note. The note is for an initial period of one year, but may be extended. The note is also a variable rate note, for the 9.75% interest indicated is only for the remainder of the month of closing. Thereafter, each quarter, the interest accrues at 1.5% above the prime rate of the bank.

Included with the financing instruments are the draw schedule (Figure 15–9) and a sample form for requesting disbursements (Figure 15–10).

Maxwell Development Corporation has received a list of required inspections from the county building department, and Barbara has forwarded a copy

Prepared by and return to:

Fisher, Ross, and Simon, P.A.

1900 N. W. 3rd Avenue
Any City,   Any State

Grantee's tax identification number: 000330054
Property folio number: 8488007439; 8488100221

Warranty Deed

This Indenture, Made this 18th day of March, 1998 between **Malcolm Bryant and Katherine Bryant,** Husband and Wife, grantor*, whose post office address is 109 St. Martin's Lane, London, England, and **Maxwell Development Corporation, an Any State corporation,** grantee*, whose post office address is 480 Franklin Avenue, Suite 400, Any City,   Any State.

*"grantor" and "grantee" are used for singular or plural, as context requires

WITNESSETH: That said grantor, for and in consideration of the sum of TEN AND NO/100 DOLLARS ($10.00) and other valuable considerations to said grantor in hand paid by said grantee, the receipt whereof is hereby acknowledged, has granted, bargained and sold, to the said grantee, and grantee's heirs and assigns forever, the following described land, situate, lying and being in Any County, Any State, to wit:

Lot 60 in Block 10 of CROSSWINDS COUNTRY CLUB SUBDIVISION, according to the plat thereof recorded in Plat Book 36 at Pages 60 through 66, inclusive, of the Public Records of Any County, Any State.

Lot 61 in Block 10 of CROSSWINDS COUNTRY CLUB SUBDIVISION, according to the plat thereof recorded in Plat Book 36 at Pages 60 through 66, inclusive, of the Public Records of Any County, Any State.

SUBJECT TO RESTRICTIONS, RESERVATIONS AND LIMITATION OF RECORD, IF ANY, AND TAXES FOR THE YEAR 1998 AND SUBSEQUENT YEARS.

and said grantor does hereby fully warrant the title to said land, and will defend the same against the lawful claims of all person whomsoever.

FIGURE 15–7 Warranty deed

IN WITNESS WHEREOF, grantor has hereunto set grantor's hand and seal the day and year first above written.

Witnesses:

Kelly Hunter   *Malcolm Bryant*

Jeffrey Stanford   *Katherine Bryant*

STATE OF ANY STATE
COUNTY OF ANY COUNTY

I HEREBY CERTIFY that on this day before me, an officer duly qualified to take acknowledgments, personally appeared MALCOLM BRYANT and KATHERINE BRYANT, to me known to be the persons described in and who executed the foregoing instrument and acknowledged before me that they executed the same.

WITNESS my hand and seal in the County and State aforesaid this 18th day of March, 1998.

Ellen Dunning
Notary Public

My commission expires: 3/31/99

FIGURE 15–7 (continued)

of the list to Millennium Bank. A copy of the inspection list appears in Figure 15–11.

Barbara next prepares a continuous marriage affidavit to be signed by each of the Bryants at closing. Once signed, it will read as shown in Figure 15–12. Then she prepares the federal and state tax reporting documents. Millennium Bank requires a building permit and a Notice of Commencement to be obtained as soon as possible. Barbara prepares the Notice of Commencement that will be filed as soon as the building permit is obtained. The Notice of Commencement for Lot 60 appears in Figure 15–13.

Once the closing has been held and the documents recorded, Barbara will prepare the title policies and submit closing binders to each party.

FIGURE 15–8
Mortgage note

MORTGAGE NOTE

Executed at Any City, Any State

$1,425,000.00 (U.S.)   March 18, 1998

FOR VALUE RECEIVED, the undersigned (sometimes referred to as "Borrower") promises to pay to the order of MILLENNIUM BANK, an Any State corporation (hereinafter called the "Bank" or, with its successors and assigns, the "holder"), at its principal office at 1750 Wellington Avenue, Any City, Any State, or at such other place as the holder hereof from time to time may designate in writing, the principal sum of ONE MILLION FOUR HUNDRED TWENTY-FIVE THOUSAND and no/100 Dollars ($1,425,000.00 U.S.), with interest as hereinafter provided. Interest on the unpaid principal balance of this Note from time to time outstanding shall accrue at the rate of NINE AND THREE-QUARTERS percent (9.75%) per annum from the date of this Note until the end of the current calendar month and, during each loan quarter thereafter, at a rate equal to ONE AND ONE-HALF percent (1.50%) per annum above the Prime Rate of the Bank, as in effect on the twentieth (20th) day of the calendar month immediately preceding such loan quarter. The term "loan quarter" shall mean each period of three (3) consecutive calendar months commencing on the first day of the first calendar month after the day hereof. The Prime Rate is not necessarily the lowest interest rate offered or charged by the Bank at any given time.

All accrued interest shall be due and payable on the first day of each calendar month hereafter commencing on May 1, 1998, and continuing until the entire indebtedness evidenced by this Note is fully paid, provided that the entire unpaid principal and all accrued interest thereon, if any, shall be due and payable in full on March 18, 1999 (the "maturity date"); provided, however, that if Borrower is not then in default under any of the terms, provisions or conditions of this Note, the Mortgage (hereinafter defined), the Agreement (hereinafter defined), or any document related thereto, the maturity date of this Note shall be automatically extended for a period of six (6) months, on and subject to the same terms, provisions and conditions as provided herein, and an extension fee in an amount equal to one-half of one percent (1/2%) of the original principal amount of this Note shall be added to and deemed to be a portion of the unpaid principal balance of this Note as of the original maturity date.

Interest shall be determined for each day by multiplying a daily interest factor (based on the annual interest rate then in effect divided by 360) by the unpaid principal balance outstanding for such day. Interest shall be calculated and accrue on each advance of the principal of this Note from and including the day on which such advance is made.

The holder may apply any and all amounts received by it in such manner as the holder in its discretion may determine. Any payment may be applied at the option of the holder to the repayment of any sums advanced by the holder for payment of taxes, assessments, casualty insurance premiums, or for keeping, maintaining and/or protecting the property subject to the Mortgage (hereinafter defined); or the holder may require said sums so advanced to be repaid together with interest thereon at a rate which is five percent (5%) per annum higher than the rate of interest accruing from time to time in accordance with the provisions of the first paragraph of this Note, in addition to the required monthly installments. If

FIGURE 15–8
(continued)

any of the aforesaid monthly installments or any sum required to be paid pursuant to the Mortgage or the Agreement (hereinafter defined) is not paid within ten (10) days after the same is due and payable, the holder hereof, at its option, and in addition to any other remedies available to it, may charge the Borrower a "late charge" of eight percent (8%) of each unpaid monthly installment and/or sum, to reimburse the holder hereof for the extra expense involved in handling delinquent payments.

The Borrower may prepay this Note in full or in part at any time without pre-payment charge. The aforesaid monthly installments are to be paid each and every calendar month irrespective of any prepayment until this Note is paid in full, and the holder hereof may, without notice, at its option, apply all or part of any such prepayment to the payment of any monthly installments not made when due.

If more than one person or entity signs this instrument, each undertaking herein is a joint and several obligation of each of the undersigned, and the fore-going warrant of attorney to confess judgment is a joint and several warrant of attorney.

This Note is secured by an Open-End Mortgage of even date from MAXWELL DEVELOPMENT CORPORATION to Bank on real estate located at 230 Crosswinds Avenue, Any City, Any State, and 232 Crosswinds Avenue, Any City, Any State (the "Mortgage"). The terms, covenants, conditions, stipulations and agreements contained in the Mortgage entered into by and between the undersigned and the Bank is hereby made a part of this Note to the same extent as if fully set forth herein.

BORROWER

ATTEST: MAXWELL DEVELOPMENT CORPORATION,
                                 an Any State corporation

Natalie Lang   By: _Thomas Maxwell_
Secretary   President

(SEAL)

FIGURE 15–9
Draw schedule

MILLENNIUM BANK
CONSTRUCTION LOAN DRAW SCHEDULE

Name of Borrower: Maxwell Development Corporation

Name of Contractor: Maxwell Development Corporation

Legal Description: Lot 60 Block 10 CROSSWINDS COUNTRY CLUB SUBDIVISION
Lot 61 Block 10 CROSSWINDS COUNTRY CLUB SUBDIVISION

Buyer: Spec

A. Loan Amount $1,425,000.00
B. Lot Takedown $ 500,000.00
C. Closing Costs Funded $ 36,732.80
D. Construction Fund $ 796,017.20

Appraised Value: $ 760,000.00
Sales Price: $ 750,000.00

LOT 60 DRAW SCHEDULE:

Draw Requested	% Completed	Description	Amount Requested
1	10%	Floor Slab–Bldg Survey	$39,800.86
2	10%	Tie Beam	$39,800.86
3	10%	Roof in Dry	$39,800.86
4	10%	Partitions Up	$39,800.86
5	10%	Drywall or Lath & Plaster	$39,800.86
6	10%	Stucco	$39,800.86
7	10%	Roof Complete	$39,800.86
8	10%	Cabinets & Tile Installed	$39,800.86
9	10%	Complete Except Floors, Landscaping, Misc.	$39,800.86
10	10%	Complete	$39,800.86

LOT 61 DRAW SCHEDULE:

Draw Requested	% Completed	Description	Amount Requested
1	10%	Floor Slab–Bldg Survey	$39,800.86
2	10%	Tie Beam	$39,800.86
3	10%	Roof in Dry	$39,800.86
4	10%	Partitions Up	$39,800.86
5	10%	Drywall or Lath & Plaster	$39,800.86
6	10%	Stucco	$39,800.86
7	10%	Roof Complete	$39,800.86
8	10%	Cabinets & Tile Installed	$39,800.86
9	10%	Complete Except Floors, Landscaping, Misc.	$39,800.86
10	10%	Complete	$39,800.86
		TOTAL:	$796,017.20

FIGURE 15–10
Sample form for
requesting disbursements

MILLENNIUM BANK
REQUEST FOR PAYMENT

OWNER: <u>Maxwell Development Corporation</u>   LOAN NUMBER: <u>800100</u>
JOB ADDRESS: _____
LEGAL DESCRIPTION: _____

_____

CONTRACTOR: <u>Maxwell Development Corporation</u>
MAKE PAYMENT TO: <u>Maxwell Development Corporation</u>
AMOUNT: _____

THIS PAYMENT COVERS THE FOLLOWING ITEMS ON PROGRESS SCHEDULE SHOWN:

ITEM	%	CONSTRUCTION STAGE
_____	10	Floor Slab–Building Survey
_____	10	Tie Beam
_____	10	Roof in Dry
_____	10	Partitions Up
_____	10	Drywall or Lath & Plaster
_____	10	Stucco
_____	10	Roof Complete
_____	10	Cabinets & Tile Installed
_____	10	Complete Except Floors, Landscaping, Misc.
_____	10	Complete

OTHER: _____

_____

The undersigned hereby certifies that all materials and/or labor covered by this Request for Payment have been used in construction of Improvements on subject property and that all Items covered on previous Requests have been paid for.

The Owner hereby approves this requisition, requests payment of same by MILLENNIUM BANK, and charges thereof against the above Loan Number.

_____   _____
Contractor   Owner

_____   _____
Date   Date

Approved for payment from MILLENNIUM BANK by: _____
Date: _____

FIGURE 15–11
Inspection list

REQUIRED INSPECTIONS

PERMIT TYPE: SINGLE FAMILY RESIDENCE   PERMIT NUMBER:

	CODE	DESCRIPTION	DATE
1.	500	TEMPORARY SERVICE	_____
2.	200	FOUNDATION	_____
3.	400	UNDERGROUND ROUGH PLUMBING	_____
4.	510	SLAB ELECTRIC	_____
5.	600	SLAB MECHANICAL	_____
6.	3000	BUILDING LOCATION SURVEY	_____
7.	210	SLAB	_____
8.	3001	BUILDING ELEVATION SURVEY	_____
9.	220	COLUMNS	_____
10.	230	TIE BEAM	_____
11.	240	ROOF SHEATHING	_____
12.	241	WALL SHEATHING	_____
13.	420	TOPOUT PLUMBING	_____
14.	410	ROUGH PLUMBING	_____
15.	415	ROUGH TANK & LINE	_____
16.	412	ROUGH GAS	_____
17.	528	ELECT. CEILING ROUGH	_____
18.	520	ROUGH ELECTRIC	_____
19.	4002	LOW VOLTAGE ROUGH	_____
20.	610	ROUGH MECHANICAL	_____
21.	260	FRAMING	_____
22.	300	INSULATION	_____
23.	270	EXTERIOR LATHING	_____
24.	280	INTERIOR LATHING	_____
25.	450	FINAL PLUMBING	_____
26.	529	ELECT. CEILING FINAL	_____
27.	530	FINAL ELECTRIC	_____
28.	4001	LOW VOLTAGE FINAL	_____
29.	620	FINAL MECHANICAL	_____
30.	440	SPRINKLER SYSTEM	_____
31.	430	SEWER	_____
32.	413	FINAL GAS	_____
33.	445	SOLAR ENERGY SYSTEMS	_____
34.	900	ENVIRONMENTAL FINAL	_____
35.	710	DRIVE/SIDEWALK ROUGH	_____
36.	730	LOT GRADING	_____
37.	740	DRIVEWAY ROCK BASE	_____
38.	700	PAVING/DRAINAGE FINAL	_____
39.	310	FINAL BUILDING	_____
40.	3049	TERMITE CERTIFICATE	_____
41.	4050	INSULATION CERTIFICATE	_____
42.	215	PATIO SLAB	_____
43.	255	FINAL ROOF	_____

PREPARED BY:

FISHER, ROSS, AND SIMON, P.A.

1900 N. W. 3RD AVENUE
ANY CITY, ANY STATE

CONTINUOUS MARRIAGE AFFIDAVIT

STATE OF ANY STATE
COUNTY OF ANY COUNTY

BEFORE ME, the undersigned authority, duly authorized to administer oaths and take acknowledgments, personally appeared Malcolm Bryant and Katherine Bryant ("Affiants"), who being first duly cautioned and sworn, depose and say:

1.   That Affiants are the owners of the following described property:

> Lot 60 in Block 10 of CROSSWINDS COUNTRY CLUB SUBDIVISION, according to the plat thereof recorded in Plat Book 36 at Pages 60 through 66, inclusive, of the Public Records of Any County, Any State.

> Lot 61 in Block 10 of CROSSWINDS COUNTRY CLUB SUBDIVISION, according to the plat thereof recorded in Plat Book 36 at Pages 60 through 66, inclusive, of the Public Records of Any County, Any State.

2.   That Affiants were married on June 7, 1965; that they have lived together as husband and wife continuously from that date; that the said marriage was never dissolved by a divorce proceeding; and at the present time they are husband and wife.

FURTHER AFFIANTS SAYETH NAUGHT.

Malcolm Bryant

Katherine Bryant

Sworn to and subscribed before me this 18th day of March, 1998.
Ellen Dunning
NOTARY PUBLIC

(Notary Seal)

My Commission Expires:3/31/99

FIGURE 15–12 Continuous marriage affidavit

FIGURE 15–13
Notice of commencement

This instrument prepared by:
Ava Ross, Esquire
Fisher, Ross, and Simon, P.A.
1900 N.W. 3rd Avenue
Any City, Any State

NOTICE OF COMMENCEMENT

TO WHOM IT MAY CONCERN:

Notice is hereby given, in accordance with the statutes of Any State, of the commencement of Improvements to the following described property, to-wit:

1. Description of Property:
   a. Street Address:
      230 Crosswinds Avenue, Any City, Any State
   b. Legal Description:
      Lot 60 in Block 10 of CROSSWINDS COUNTRY CLUB SUBDIVISION, according to the plat thereof recorded in Plat Book 36 at Pages 60 through 66, inclusive, of the Public Records of Any County, Any State.
2. General Description of Improvements: Single-family residence
3. Owner Information: Maxwell Development Corporation, an Any State corporation
   580 Franklin Avenue, Suite 400
   Any City, Any State
4. Contractor: Maxwell Development Corporation, an Any State corporation
   580 Franklin Avenue, Suite 400
   Any City, Any State
5. Surety (if any):   Not applicable
6. Lender: Millennium Bank
   1750 Wellington Avenue
   Any City, Any State
7. In addition to itself, Owner designates the following upon whom notices or other documents may be serviced under the Any State Construction Lien Law:

   Millennium Bank
   1750 Wellington Avenue
   Any City, Any State
8. Expiration date of Notice of Commencement [the expiration date is one (1) year from the date of recording unless a different date is specified]:_____

Executed this _____ day of _____, 1998.

MAXWELL DEVELOPMENT CORPORATION,
an Any State corporation

By: _____
         President

STATE OF ANY STATE
COUNTY OF ANY COUNTY

   Sworn to and subscribed before me this _____ day of _____, 1998, by Thomas Maxwell as President of Maxwell Development Corporation, an Any State corporation.

_____
Notary Public
My commission expires:

CHAPTER SUMMARY

1. A construction loan is a short-term loan covering the construction costs of a project. Its term typically is for one to two years, with stipulated extensions. It may be obtained separately or in conjunction with a land acquisition loan. The interest rate charged on a construction loan often is higher than that charged on permanent residential loans.

2. A permanent loan is a long-term loan obtained once construction is completed. It is obtained either by the borrower/developer or the subsequent purchaser of the property. The permanent lender pays off the construction loan.

3. Prior to closing, the construction lender will require submission of the following: (a) all plans and specifications; (b) engineering reports; (c) verification of zoning; (d) verification of licensure of architects, engineers, and general contractors; (e) copies of contracts between the borrower and architects, engineers, and general contractors; (f) title examination; and often (g) a performance bond from the general contractor.

4. After closing and recording of the financing instrument, the lender will require copies of the building permit and notice of commencement prior to construction. Prior to release of each draw, the lender will require verification that all requisite inspections have been passed and that all items covered by previous draws have been paid.

5. Although the lender prepares the loan commitment, note, financing instrument, and draw schedule, all terms are subject to negotiation. Because each transaction will vary significantly from the next, documents should be tailored to meet the needs of the parties.

REVIEW QUESTIONS

1. What documents are required by construction lenders that are not required to be submitted in an average residential closing?
2. What is a draw schedule and how does it work?
3. What is the typical duration of the following?
   a. A loan for lot funding
   b. A loan for construction funding
   c. A permanent loan
4. How is the structuring of hazard and title insurance policies different in a construction loan situation than in the average residential or commercial closing?
5. What documents must be obtained and/or filed after recording of the financing instrument and prior to construction?

ETHICAL QUESTIONS

Prior to your career as a paralegal, you worked for several years as a loan officer in a bank. This afternoon a client, David Dreyden, the president of Dreyden Development Corporation, telephones your office to speak to your supervising attorney. He has just received a loan agreement for a construction project and has some legal questions pertaining to two of the items in the agreement. When you inform him that your supervising attorney is out of the office, he responds that he knows your banking background and that you could probably answer the questions just as well if not even better than your supervising attorney. In fact, you are familiar with the items in question, as you used to process many construction loan agreements. What should you do?

PRACTICAL ASSIGNMENTS

Assignment 15:1. Prepare a buyer's closing statement and a seller's closing statement for the Maxwell Development Corporation–Bryant transaction.

Assignment 15:2. Contact your city building department and obtain a copy of the list of required inspections for the construction of:

a. a single-family residence.
b. a multistory office building.
c. a strip shopping center.

Insert these inspection lists under the "Construction Loan Closings" section of your resource portfolio.

Assignment 15:3. Assume that Crosswinds Country Club is located within your city, county, and state and that Maxwell Development Corporation has hired your supervising attorney, Deborah Sanders, to represent it. Andrew Sage, the realtor from Arcadia Realty, has just listed another vacant lot for sale in Crosswinds. It is owned by QRP Properties, Inc. Having sold the homes built on spec on the other two properties in Crosswinds for a nice profit, Thomas Maxwell is anxious to find similar opportunities. Having been informed of the availability of the lot by Andrew, Thomas contracts with the president of QRP Properties, Quentin Prescott, for its purchase. The contract was signed on the first of last month, and the closing is scheduled to take place one month from today's date. The closing is contingent upon Maxwell Development Corporation's ability to procure funding for both the acquisition of the lot and for the construction costs.

The purchase price of the lot is $400,000. Its parcel identification number is 3390044652. Its street address is 305 North Star Road (your city, county, and state). Its legal description is as follows:

> Lot 38 in Block 12 of CROSSWINDS COUNTRY CLUB SUBDIVISION, according to the plat thereof recorded in Plat Book 36 at Pages

60 through 66, inclusive, of the Public Records of (your county and state).

There is only one realtor involved, Arcadia Realty. According to the contract, the real estate commission is six percent. The seller is represented by legal counsel, Lawrence Ottley of Ottley, Grant, and Williams, P.A., 450 Burr Road (your city and state). His telephone number is 077-7000, and his fax number is 077-7070. According to the terms of the contract, it is the seller's responsibility to prepare the general warranty deed and any other necessary documents for the transfer of the property to buyer. The seller is also the party responsible for obtaining approval from the homeowners' association, ordering the survey, conducting the title search and examination, and providing the title commitment and title policies. The contract stipulates that the seller is to pay for the title search and examination as well as the owner's policy, while the buyer is to pay for the mortgagee's policy and any endorsements. The seller's law firm is charging its client a flat fee of $800 for attorneys' fees. It is also acting as escrow/closing agent. No separate fee will be charged for this service.

Your firm, Hernandez, Sanders, and Norris, P.A., located at 263 Republic Avenue (your city and state), is charging Maxwell Development Corporation a flat fee of $500 to review all documents and coordinate matters with the construction lender. Your telephone number is 111-0030, and your fax number is 111-0035.

According to the contract, Maxwell Development Corporation has one month from the date of contract to obtain financing. Thomas applied for a loan the business day following the date of execution of the contract and obtained a loan commitment two weeks ago (from today's date) from Millennium Bank. The loan number is 777645. The total amount of the loan is $800,000, $300,000 of which is allocated to lot funding. None of the closing costs are funded. The remainder of the loan amount is allocated for the construction draw account.

Millennium is requiring an interest reserve of $43,000, and is charging a document preparation fee of $125 and an appraisal fee of $650. It is also charging two discount points and a loan origination fee of 0.5%. Millennium requires the submission of copies of the contracts with the architect and engineer, as well as copies of all certifications. Thomas submitted them one week from the date of the loan commitment. He submitted his company's financial statements at the time of making the loan application. The loan commitment requires Maxwell Development Corporation to purchase hazard insurance to cover the constructed improvements. The insurance will be purchased outside of closing. Millennium's in-house counsel, Craig Fox, is preparing the financing instrument, note, and draw schedule.

The seller has hired Premium Title Company to do the title search and examination and to prepare the commitment and policies. Its address is 200 Waterford Road, Suite 103 (your city and state). Its telephone number is 440-9977, and its fax number is 440-9978. It received the survey ordered by the seller from ABC Survey Company. The charge to the seller for the survey is $110. Premium Title Company is charging $175 for the title search and examination, $1,870 for the owner's coverage, $4,075 for the mortgagee's coverage, and $25 each for the endorsements. There is a variable rate mortgage endorsement and six construction updates.

Maxwell Development Corporation paid an earnest money deposit of $40,000 at time of contracting, which has been deposited with the seller's attorney. The homeowners' association maintenance assessment has been paid for by the seller through the end of this quarter. The amount paid for the quarter is $800. The county property taxes for the year are $7,758.75. The property is located just outside the city limits, so there are no city taxes assessed. The seller has an outstanding loan on the property in the amount of $286,230 with Century Bank, which is located at 1100 South Main Street (your city and state). Its telephone number is 023-2300, and its fax number is 023-3333.

The contract stipulates that the buyer is responsible for paying the recording fees for the financing instrument and the deed. The deed is two pages long, and the financing instrument is six pages long. The seller is responsible for paying the recording fee for the satisfaction of mortgage. The seller is also responsible for the documentary stamp tax on the deed, while the buyer is responsible for the documentary stamp tax on the mortgage and the intangible tax (if any) on the new mortgage. To calculate the recording fees, documentary stamp tax, and intangible tax, use your county's stipulated rate.

With this information in hand, photocopy the blank construction loan closing worksheet and HUD-1 statement in your student workbook (the originals are to be used for the workbook assignment). Complete the worksheet. (The client number is 1620.) Then prepare the closing statement for this transaction. After review, insert these items under the "Construction Loan Closings" section of your resource portfolio.

Assignment 15:4. Now assume that instead of working for Deborah Sanders, you are a paralegal working with Craig Fox at Millennium Bank. You have been asked to draft an open-end mortgage note for the transaction described in Assignment 15:3. The interest on the principal balance will accrue at the rate of nine percent per annum until the end of the calendar month of the date of closing and, during each loan quarter thereafter, at a rate equal to one percent per annum above the prime rate of the bank as in effect on the twentieth day of the calendar month immediately preceding the loan quarter. The note shall be for an initial period of one month but, if the borrower is not in default at the end of this period, may be extended for an additional six months. The extension fee is equal to three-fourths of one percent of the original principal amount of the note. A late charge of ten percent of each unpaid monthly installment will be charged if the monthly payments are not paid within ten days after they are due. After review, insert this document under the "Construction Loan Closings" section of your resource portfolio.

Assignment 15:5. Assume you are still working with Craig Fox at Millennium Bank. He has asked you to draft a draw schedule for this transaction. There are to be ten draw requests, as per the draw schedule provided in the hypothetical closing, each occurring when ten percent of the improvements are completed. Using the description list provided in the draw schedule in the hypothetical closing, prepare a draw schedule for this construction loan. After review, insert this document under the "Construction Loan Closings" section of your resource portfolio.

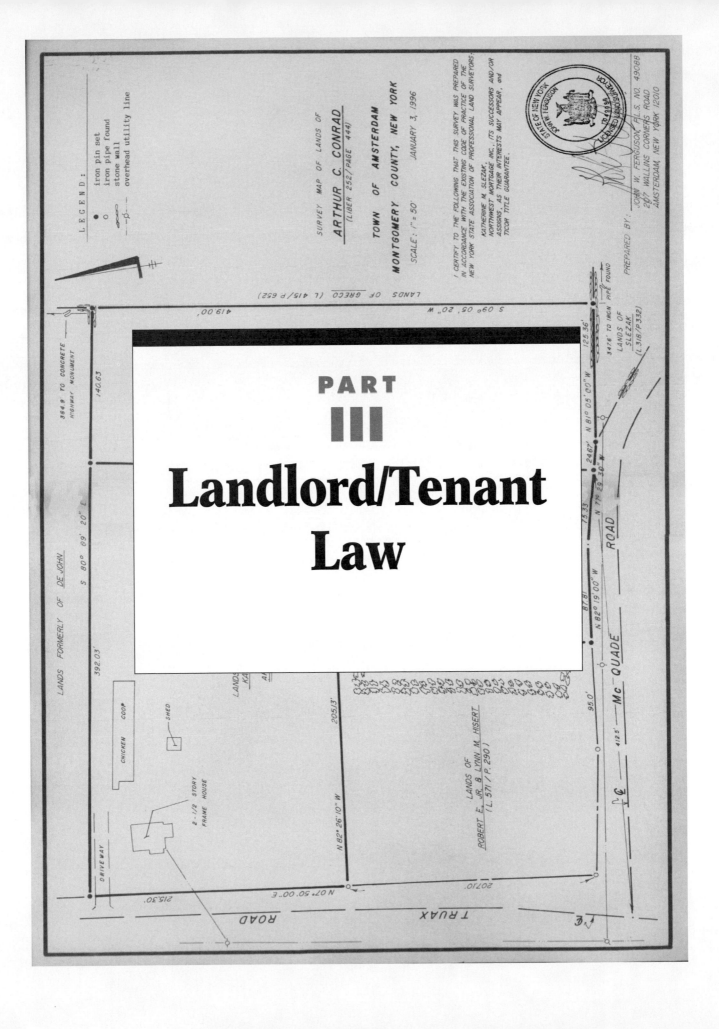

PART

III

Landlord/Tenant Law

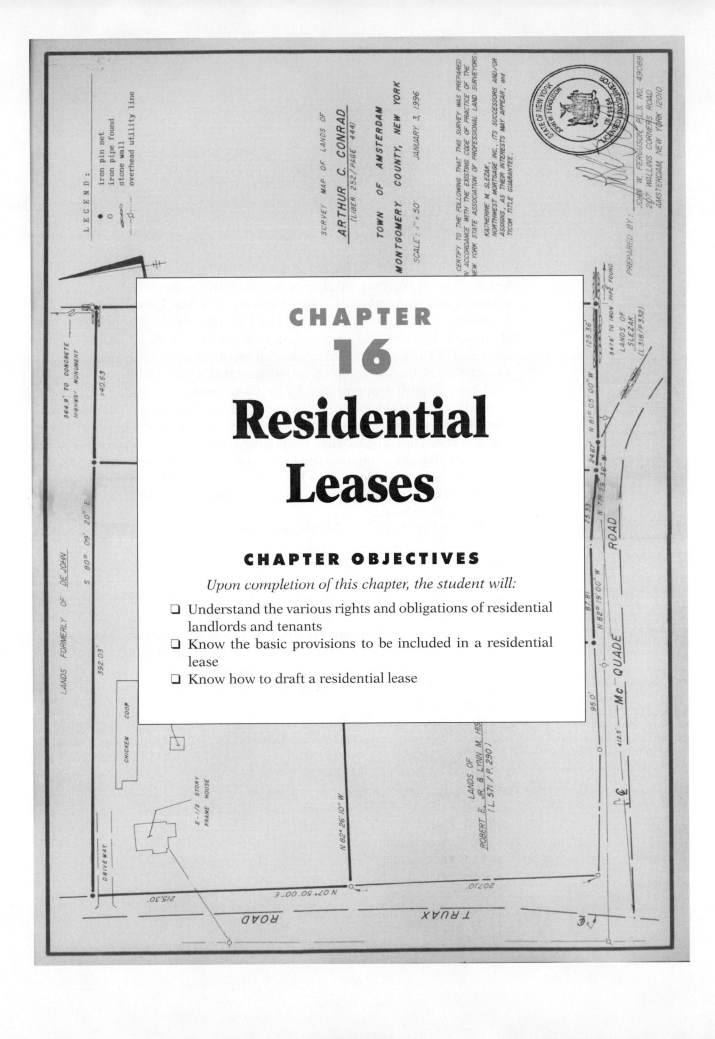

CHAPTER
16

Residential Leases

CHAPTER OBJECTIVES

Upon completion of this chapter, the student will:

❑ Understand the various rights and obligations of residential landlords and tenants

❑ Know the basic provisions to be included in a residential lease

❑ Know how to draft a residential lease

INTRODUCTION

A **lease** serves two functions. First, a lease operates as a contract, expressing the terms and conditions mutually agreed upon by the lessor and lessee. Second, a lease operates as an instrument of conveyance, similar to a deed, conveying from the lessor to the lessee a leasehold estate that includes the right of exclusive possession, but not ownership, in real property for a period of time in return for the payment of rent. The lessee retains a reversionary right in the real property.

Residential leases are governed not only by the common law of contracts, but also by state statutes. In addition to state statutes that apply to general real property law, a number of states have adopted the Uniform Residential Landlord and Tenant Act (URLTA). The URLTA, originally approved by the National Conference of Commissioners on Uniform State Laws in 1972 and amended in 1974, was created in recognition of the trend in state law to move away from the English common law treatment of residential leaseholds.

Under English common law, the landlord-tenant relationship was treated primarily as a conveyance of a leasehold, rather than as a contractual relationship. Therefore, the covenants made by each party were considered independent covenants, and as such, the failure of the lessor to abide by his or her covenants did not relinquish the lessee from his or her covenants (or vice versa). Over the years, state laws have recognized that the obligations arising under a residential landlord-tenant relationship should be treated as interdependent obligations.

The URLTA embodies this principle and attempts to treat both parties evenhandedly, covering such issues as the landlord's obligation to maintain the premises, the tenant's obligation to maintain the premises, landlord remedies, tenant remedies, and a tenant's protection against retaliation by the landlord for complaints. At the time of this writing, the URLTA has been adopted by the following states: Alaska, Arizona, Connecticut, Florida, Hawaii, Iowa, Kansas, Kentucky, Michigan, Mississippi, Montana, Nebraska, New Mexico, Oklahoma, Oregon, Rhode Island, South Carolina, Tennessee, Virginia, and Washington. In addition to common law and state statutes, federal laws, such as the **Tenants' Eviction Procedures Act of 1976,** and local ordinances regulate some residential leases.

Many states allow for the recording of long-term leases in the county in which the leased premises is located. In some states, a **memorandum of lease** may be recorded rather than the actual lease, the memorandum providing only such skeletal information as the names of the lessor and lessee and a description of the leased premises to put others on notice of a transfer of physical possession of the property. However, neither the actual lease nor a memorandum are recorded in most instances. The lessee's physical presence on the property puts third parties on notice of the lessee's leasehold interest in the property.

Paralegals working in the area of real estate law are often asked by their supervising attorneys to review or prepare residential leases. It is important, therefore, that you understand the rights and duties of both lessor and lessee in a residential tenancy. This chapter focuses on these rights and duties, both from the standpoint of general real property law and of the URLTA. The

lease: A document that conveys a leasehold interest in real property which includes the right of possession, but not ownership, for a period of time in return for the payment of rent.

Tenants' Eviction Procedures Act of 1976: A federal act that mandates eviction procedures to be followed for residential tenants in government-subsidized, multiunit buildings.

memorandum of lease: A document providing skeletal information of a lease, such as the names of the lessor and lessee and a description of the leased premises. This document is recorded in the county in which the leased premises is located to put others on notice of a transfer of physical possession of the property.

chapter continues with a discussion of common lease provisions and ends with a look at how a lease might be drafted to meet a hypothetical client's needs.

RIGHTS AND DUTIES OF THE LANDLORD

Historically, a landlord (the *lessor)* had no duties to provide a tenant (the *lessee)* with a habitable premises, unless a lease so provided. It was the lessee's responsibility to inspect the premises, and the lessee was assumed to take the premises as he or she found it under the doctrine of *caveat emptor* (let the buyer beware). A lessor had no common law duty to make needed repairs to a leased premises. Indeed, it could be stated that it was in the lessor's best interests not to repair, for if the lessor was negligent in the manner in which repairs were made, the lessor could be held liable for resulting injuries. On the other hand, if the lessor neither agreed to make nor actually made repairs, the lessor could not be held liable for injuries suffered by the lessee or third parties as a result of dangerous conditions on the leased premises unless those conditions could not have been discovered by reasonable inspection of the premises.

However, because a lessor retained exclusive control over *common areas,* such as hallways, sidewalks, and stairwells, the lessor did have the duty to keep those areas safe, and neglect of a dangerous condition in a common area would lead to potential liability. The lessor's responsibility for common areas has carried over to current law and has been extended to include all fixtures and equipment located in common areas, such as laundry appliances in a common laundry room and exercise equipment in a common exercise room.

The law has expanded over time to increase the nature of a residential lessor's duties. Most states now require that the landlord be held responsible for maintaining the premises in a habitable condition. Section 2.104(a) of the URLTA, for instance, requires that a landlord

1. comply with the requirements of applicable building and housing codes materially affecting health and safety;
2. make all repairs and do whatever is necessary to put and keep the premises in a fit and habitable condition;
3. keep all common areas of the premises in a clean and safe condition;
4. maintain in good and safe working order and condition all electrical, plumbing, sanitary, heating, ventilating, air-conditioning, and other facilities and appliances, including elevators, supplied or required to be supplied by the landlord;
5. provide and maintain appropriate receptacles and conveniences for the removal of ashes, garbage, rubbish, and other waste incidental to the occupancy of the dwelling unit and arrange for their removal; and
6. supply running water and reasonable amounts of hot water at all times and reasonable heat except where the building that includes the dwelling unit is not required by law to be equipped for that purpose, or the dwelling unit is so constructed that heat or hot water is generated by an installation within the exclusive control of the tenant and supplied by a direct public utility connection.

What constitutes compliance with applicable building, health, and safety codes can vary considerably from state to state. Statutory law or local ordinances may require that the lessor provide pest control services and/or smoke detection devices. Subsection (c) of section 2.104 of the URLTA provides that if the leased premises is a single-family residence, the lessor and lessee may agree in writing that the lessee will be responsible for trash removal; for the supply of running water, hot water, and heat; and for specified repairs. Further, subsection (d) provides that a lessee and a lessor of a leased premises other than a single-family residence may enter into a written lease in which the lessee is responsible for specific repairs, but only if the repair work is not necessary to cure the lessor's noncompliance with applicable building, health, and safety codes.

A lease may expand upon the maintenance duties listed above. A lessor, however, cannot negate his or her statutory responsibilities by inclusion of a lease provision in which the lessee waives the right to a warranty of habitability. Such a provision is unconscionable. In some states, a lessor, while responsible for maintaining and repairing the premises, is allowed to charge the lessee for such services.

Should a lessor fail to maintain the leased premises in a habitable condition, most states allow the lessee legal recourse. Some states require that the lessee provide the lessor with written notice of the lessor's material noncompliance and provide an opportunity to cure before terminating the lease. The lessee may be allowed to make the necessary repairs, or hire someone qualified to do so, and then deduct the cost of the repairs against rent owed. Alternatively, the lessee may be allowed to remain in the premises but *abate* the rent. **Abatement of rent** is a deduction from the rent owed for the diminishment in value of the premises caused by the lack of maintenance.

If the lessor's noncompliance is so egregious as to render the premises uninhabitable by local building, health, or safety code standards, the lessee may not be able to remain on the premises due to the defective conditions. Under these circumstances, the lessor is said to have *constructively evicted* the lessee. Should constructive eviction occur, a lessee is entitled to move out of the premises and will not be held responsible for the rent due for the remainder of the lease term. Constructive eviction is discussed in Chapter 18.

Section 4.101(a) of the URLTA provides that a lessee may deliver written notice to the lessor specifying the acts or omissions constituting noncompliance and indicating that the lease will terminate if the acts or omissions are not cured within a statutorily prescribed time period. The section further provides that the lease will be terminated as provided in the notice, subject to the following:

1. If the breach is remediable by repairs, the payment of damages, or otherwise, and the landlord adequately remedies the breach before the date specified in the notice, the rental agreement shall not terminate by reason of the breach.
2. If substantially the same act or omission that constituted a prior noncompliance of which notice was given recurs within [state statute specifies the time period] months, the tenant may terminate the rental agreement upon at least [state statute specifies the time

abatement of rent: A deduction from the rent owed for the diminishment in value of the premises caused by the lack of maintenance.

period] written notice specifying the breach and the date of termination of the rental agreement.

3. The tenant may not terminate for a condition caused by the deliberate or negligent act or omission of the tenant, a member of the tenant's family, or other person on the premises with the tenant's consent.

In addition to any remedies available to a lessee for the lessor's failure to maintain and repair the premises, city and county ordinances may impose fines on the lessor for noncompliance.

Most states prohibit the lessor from interrupting essential services, such as electricity, gas, heat, and water. If these services are willfully or negligently interrupted and the interruption is not corrected after proper notice is given, a lessee may be allowed an abatement of rent, may take measures to reinstall the services and deduct the cost from rent owed, or may move out temporarily until such time as the services are reinstalled. In the latter instance, the lessee will not be liable for rent during the period in which the services are interrupted and may recover the cost of reasonably suitable housing.

For the protection and preservation of the leased and surrounding property as well as the welfare of the lessee and third parties, a lessor may impose reasonable rules and regulations regarding the use of the leased premises. It is not uncommon, for example, for a lessor to disallow pets, particularly in furnished premises, or require additional security deposits to cover any potential damage. A lessor may prohibit the playing of loud music before or after certain hours for the welfare of other tenants or may prohibit barbecuing on a balcony. Section 3.102(a) of the URLTA allows a lessor to impose rules and regulations upon the use of a leased premises upon the following conditions:

1. The purpose of the rule or regulation is to promote the convenience, safety, or welfare of the tenants in the premises; preserve the landlord's property from abusive use; or make a fair distribution of services and facilities held out for the tenants generally
2. The rule or regulation is reasonably related to the purpose for which it is adopted
3. It applies to all tenants in the premises in a fair manner
4. The rule or regulation is sufficiently explicit in its prohibition, direction, or limitation of the tenant's conduct to fairly inform the tenant of what the tenant must or must not do to comply
5. It is not for the purpose of evading the obligations of the landlord
6. The tenant has notice of it at the time the tenant enters into the rental agreement, or when it is adopted

To ensure the protection of the premises and the lessee's compliance with reasonably imposed rules and regulations, state law allows a lessor to inspect the premises periodically. As noted in the lease provisions section in the following text, these inspections must be made at reasonable times and with the consent of the lessee, whose consent cannot be unreasonably withheld.

If a lessee defaults or breaches a lease agreement, a lessor's remedies may include money damages or injunctive relief. Often a lease will include a remedies provision. Section 4.201 of the URLTA specifies the remedies available to the lessor for a lessee's noncompliance with a rental agreement. Under this section, should the lessee breach the lease or fail to maintain the leased premises, the lessor may send written notice to the lessee specifying the acts or omissions constituting the breach and notifying the lessee that the lease will terminate if violations are not corrected within a statutorily prescribed time period. It further states that if the lessee has previously committed the same violation, the lessor need not give the lessee a second opportunity to cure and instead may simply provide written notice that the lessor is terminating the lease within a specified time period.

Neither those states adopting the URLTA nor any other state allows a lessor to evict a lessee without following some degree of due process of law. At common law, a lessor had the right to forcibly remove a lessee for failure to pay rent as well as a right to *distress*, also referred to as *distraint for rent*. **Distress** is the right to seize a lessee's goods to satisfy a rent arrearage. The present statutory trend is away from self-help measures and toward court-supervised proceedings. Section 4.205(b) of the URLTA abolishes distraint for rent. Although some states do consider personal property left behind in a leased premises to be abandoned when the lessee abandons the property, and therefore allow the lessor to dispose of the personal property as he or she sees fit, most states consider it unconstitutional to seize personal property by forcible entry to satisfy an outstanding rent obligation without going through formal notice and hearing procedures.

To remove a lessee lawfully, due process typically requires that a lessor bring a *suit for possession*. This procedure is known as *actual eviction*, covered at length in Chapter 18 of the text. Prior to evicting a lessee, a lessor must serve notice upon the lessee. State statutes dictate the prescribed notice period and the manner in which such notice is to be served. Once proper notice has been served, the lessee files a complaint with the court requesting permission to evict the lessee and retake possession of the leased premises. The lessee is allowed to respond to the complaint. Should the lessee fail to do so, a court may award judgment in favor of the lessor, which judgment will be executed by the sheriff or other court-appointed official. Whether contested or not, until the court renders judgment, the lessor is not entitled to harass the lessee or to interrupt the lessee's essential services. Once the judgment is rendered, the sheriff will oversee the removal of the lessee and the lessee's property from the premises. If the lessee is leasing a unit in a multiunit building owned or subsidized by the government, the lessor must comply with the federal Tenants' Eviction Procedures Act of 1976, which contains its own notice and procedural requirements.

In addition to evicting the lessee, the lessor may claim back rents owed. Once the lessee is evicted, however, the lease is terminated, and many states will not allow the lessor to recover future rents unless the lease contains a provision for their collection. Even so, state statute may require that the lessor attempt to mitigate damages by finding another lessee for the premises.

distress: The right to seize a lessee's goods to satisfy a rent arrearage.

RIGHTS AND DUTIES OF THE TENANT

A lessee is responsible for more than the prompt payment of rent. State law imposes minimum duties on the conduct of lessees, consistent with local health and safety codes. A lessee must maintain the interior of the leased premises in a clean and safe condition and must use all appliances in a reasonable manner. Although normal wear and tear is expected when one leases property, a lessee must not negligently or willfully destroy property or allow others invited onto the premises to do so. Section 3.101 of the URLTA requires a lessee to

1. comply with all obligations primarily imposed upon tenants by applicable provisions of building and housing codes materially affecting health and safety;
2. keep that part of the premises that the tenant occupies and uses as clean and safe as the condition of the premises permits;
3. dispose from the dwelling unit all ashes, garbage, rubbish, and other waste in a clean and safe manner;
4. keep all plumbing fixtures in the dwelling unit or used by the tenant as clean as their condition permits;
5. use in a reasonable manner all electrical, plumbing, sanitary, heating, ventilating, air-conditioning, and other facilities and appliances including elevators in the premises;
6. not deliberately or negligently destroy, deface, damage, impair, or remove any part of the premises or knowingly permit any person to do so; and
7. conduct oneself and require other persons on the premises with the tenant's consent to conduct themselves in a manner that will not disturb the neighbor's peaceful enjoyment of the premises.

Under the URLTA, there is no affirmative duty placed upon a lessee to repair the premises; instead, there is an affirmative duty to use the premises in such a manner as to preserve its condition. Nonetheless, a lease may include a provision obligating the lessee to make specific repairs. A lessee may not make alterations or improvements to a leased premises unless the lease so provides. Further, most states hold the lessee liable for unsafe conditions caused by the lessee that injure the lessee or a third party.

If a lessee fails to maintain the premises in a proper manner, many states allow the lessor, after providing written notification of the violation and having given the lessee the statutorily prescribed time period within which to cure, to enter the premises and make any necessary repairs, which may then be charged to the lessee. In some states, or if the lease so provides, failure to maintain the premises may be considered a material breach of the lease and grounds for termination.

Upon taking lawful possession of a leased premises, a lessee is entitled to a covenant of quiet enjoyment of the premises. This covenant not only pertains to intrusions by third parties, but also pertains to unreasonable intrusions or harassment by a lessor. Most states allow a lessee to seek injunctive relief against a lessor's unlawful entry and may additionally allow recovery of attorneys' fees. Further, many states, including those adopting the URLTA, protect a lessee from retaliatory conduct by the lessor. Section 5.101 of the URLTA prohibits a lessor from increasing rent, decreasing services, or threatening eviction in retaliation for complaints lodged against the lessor by the lessee. Further, this section allows a legal presumption of retaliatory conduct if the lessee's complaint was made within a statutorily specified time period prior to the resulting conduct.

Many states have recognized **tenant unions** as a proper means for lessees to find strength in numbers. Lessees forming tenant unions believe that retaliatory conduct is minimized in the face of structured grievance procedures and the requirement of negotiating through elected representatives. Tenant unions may, through their representatives, consolidate tenant complaints, negotiate favorable rent agreements, and ensure compliance with maintenance requirements.

LEASE PROVISIONS

A lease is a contract and, as such, must meet the four basic criteria for a contract in order to be legally binding: (1) offer and acceptance, (2) consideration, (3) capacity to contract, and (4) a legal subject matter. The first criterion, offer and acceptance, implies that the parties, the lessor and lessee, have mutually agreed to the terms of the contract. The second criterion, consideration, implies that each party has provided something of legal value—typically, the payment of rent in exchange for occupation of the leased premises and the accompanying *covenant of quiet enjoyment*, which is the right to possession free from interference. The third criterion, capacity to contract, implies that all parties are of legal age and sound mind when entering into the contract. The fourth criterion, a legal subject matter, implies that the objectives of the contract are legal. To ensure that this last criterion is met, most written contracts include a *severability* provision, discussed later, stating that should any provision in the contract be invalid, it is severed from the remaining provisions which will continue in force.

Not all leases have to be in writing in order to be legally binding on the parties in the majority of states. In most states, however, the statute of frauds requires that contracts for a term of more than one year be in writing.

As is the case with other contracts, a residential lease may be customized to suit the objectives of the parties to the agreement. While some lessors choose to use standardized lease forms for their expediency and low cost, this is not always suitable. Even if standard leases are used, the parties must understand each provision in terms of their rights and obligations and should be informed that standard lease forms may, and should, be modified to achieve the objectives of both parties.

Standard leases are not always drafted with evenhandedness; many of their provisions are drafted in favor of the lessor. A prospective lessee often feels he or she has unequal bargaining power. Nonetheless, the use of a standardized lease form is not unconscionable in and of itself, so both prospective lessees and prospective lessors should review the lease with an attorney before signing. Ideally, the parties to a lease should have an attorney draft the agreement. Although the specifics will vary, most residential leases contain similar components.

Parties

The *parties* to the lease should be indicated. The lessee may be dealing directly with the lessor or may be dealing with an agent. The lessor's legal

tenant unions: Organizations that elect representatives to consolidate tenant complaints, negotiate favorable rent agreements, and assure compliance with maintenance requirements.

name should appear on the lease. If the lessor is a corporation, the lease may need to be approved by the directors or stockholders of the corporation by adoption of a corporate resolution (a formal expression of the decision of a group, adopted by vote). If the lessor is an individual and that individual is married, it is advisable that the names of both the individual and his or her spouse appear on the lease as lessors.

The rental of a condominium or a cooperative may require the approval of a committee of condominium or cooperative owners. Some condominium documents limit the number of times a unit may be rented in a year (for example, only once per year), and some specify the minimum rental periods (for example, three months or longer). If the lessor is the owner of a condominium or cooperative unit, approval procedures and applicable rules should be checked.

The lease should list as lessees all adults who will be living in the leased premises. For example, if Amy Anderson wants to rent a two-bedroom apartment with her good friend Carla Carrington, both names should appear as lessees on the lease. This way, the lessor may hold both Amy and Carla, or either of them, legally responsible for the entire rental payment. The lease should also specify the *number* of parties occupying the premises, indicating separately the number of adults and the number of children. Many zoning ordinances limit the number of persons per square footage.

Use of the Premises

Zoning ordinances may limit the *use* of the premises to single-family residential purposes, and the lease should acknowledge that the premises will be used only for such purposes. For example:

The premises shall be used and occupied by Lessee exclusively as a private, single-family residence, and no part thereof shall be used at any time during the term of this lease by Lessee for the purpose of carrying on any business, profession, or trade of any kind. Lessee shall comply with all laws, ordinances, rules, and orders of appropriate governmental authorities affecting the occupancy, preservation, and cleanliness of the leased premises.

Description of the Premises

An adequate *description* of the premises should be included. If a single-family house is being leased, the street address often will be adequate. If an apartment is being leased, the street address of the building together with the apartment number should be sufficient. Some states may require the inclusion of a legal description of the premises, so state statutes should be checked. Apartment units are often provided with designated parking spaces. If applicable, designated parking spaces should be noted on the lease.

Lease Term and Renewal

The *lease term* provision should indicate the date the lease commences and the date the lease terminates. If the lessor intends to give the lessee the right to *renew* the lease at the expiration of the lease term, a provision should be included specifying the notice required for election to renew and the terms of renewal. The renewal terms may be included in the original lease or in an addendum to be attached to the original lease. A renewal provision may read as follows.

> *Lessor grants to Lessee the option to renew this lease at the expiration thereof, provided said option is exercised by written notification given by Lessee to Lessor at least ninety (90) days prior to the expiration of this lease. Said renewal shall be accomplished by the execution of an addendum to this lease.*

In addition to or in place of a renewal provision, a lease may give a lessee the option to purchase the premises, usually at a predetermined price, the option to be kept open for a specified time period. This *option to purchase* provision may provide added incentive by crediting rent paid toward the purchase price.

Rent

It is advisable to include in the *rent* provision the total amount of rent due for the entire term of the lease, as well as the number of periodic installments, the amount of each, the date they are to commence, and the date each subsequent installment is due (for example, the first of each month). If some or all utilities are included as part of the rent payment, this should be specified. Where the rental payment is to be made may be included in the rent provision or in the *notice* provision of the lease. The following is a sample rent provision.

> *Lessee agrees to pay Lessor, without demand, as rent for the premises the total amount of Nine Thousand Six Hundred Dollars ($9,600.00), payable in twelve installments of Eight Hundred Dollars ($800.00) per month in advance on the first day of each calendar month beginning May 1, 1998, at the following address: 4500 Commercial Drive, Any City, Any State.*

Some longer leases contain a built-in mechanism for incremental rent increases during the lease period. One type of lease that does this is an **index lease,** which ties the rent to the government cost-of-living index or some similar index, requiring periodic changes in the rent amount as determined by the index. It should be noted that if a lease is calculated this way, there is a chance of a cost-of-living decrease, which will then be translated into a rent decrease. Another type of lease that accomplishes similar results is a *graduated lease,* which provides for rent increases on specified dates in predetermined amounts.

The lessor may wish to include certain penalties for late rent or returned rent checks. These penalties may be part of the rent provision or may be put into a separate provision. For example:

> *Lessee agrees to pay a late charge fee of five percent (5%). If the rental payment is made by check and said check is refused by the designated bank for any reason, Lessee shall be required to redeem said check from Lessor with money order or cashier's check for rent covered by said check*

index lease: A lease that contains a built-in mechanism for incremental rent increases during the lease period, tying the rent to the governmental cost-of-living index or some similar index.

plus a Twenty-Five Dollar ($25.00) service charge and to make all future payments by money order, or certified or cashier's check.

Deposits

Most lessors will require a *security deposit* from the lessee, either when signing the lease or when the lessee first moves into the leased premises. This deposit cannot be treated as rent. The amount of the security deposit may equal one month's rent or may be some other amount. Statutory law prohibits placement of the security deposit in the lessor's personal bank account; rather, it should be kept in a separate account similar to an escrow or trust account. State statutes may include detailed rules regarding security deposits.

Many states set maximum limits on the amount that may be collected (for example, one month's rent), as does section 2.101 of the URLTA. Some statutes give the lessor the choice of placing security deposits in either interest-bearing or noninterest-bearing accounts. If placed in an interest-bearing account, who receives the interest? Statutory law may dictate that the lessee receives the interest, or it may be silent on the matter, making the payment of interest a point of negotiation between the parties. In either case, a security deposit provision in a lease should specify not only the amount of the deposit but also the type of account in which it will be placed, who receives the interest, if any, when the interest will be paid, the conditions under which the security deposit will be returned, and when it will be returned. For example:

> *Upon execution of this lease, Lessee shall pay a security deposit in the amount of Seven Hundred and Fifty Dollars ($750.00). Said security deposit shall be placed in an interest-bearing account bearing an interest rate of five percent (5%). Accrued interest shall be paid to Lessee at the end of each year in which the lease remains in force. Said security deposit shall be returned in full within ten (10) days after termination of this lease if Lessee returns the premises in good condition, normal wear excepted.*

Statutory law may provide that security deposits must be returned within a prescribed time period as well as provide procedures that must be followed if they are retained. For example, some statutes provide that the lessor has a specified number of days to return the security deposit with interest, if any, or in which to give the tenant written notice of the lessor's intention to impose a claim on the deposit and the reason for imposing the claim. Upon receipt of this notice, the lessee is then given a specified number of days within which to object to the claim. Failure of the landlord to abide by the governing law may mean the imposition of punitive or double damages in some states.

In addition to requiring ordinary security deposits, many lessors will require a *pet deposit* if the lease allows the lessee to bring a pet onto the premises. Here again, the lease should indicate the amount of the pet deposit, the conditions under which it will be returned, if refundable, and when it will be returned. If there are any size limitations or other restrictions imposed on the keeping of a pet, these should also be indicated. For example:

One pet under twenty-five pounds will be allowed. A Five Hundred Dollar ($500.00) pet fee (nonrefundable) must be paid upon the signing of the lease. Pets must be leashed when outside.

Although state statutes cover security deposits, many do not cover pet deposits, so the deposit is left as a point of negotiation between the parties. Further, if pets are not allowed, a statement to that effect should be included, such as the following.

By the execution of this lease, the Lessee warrants to the Lessor that the Lessee does not have a pet, and further, the Lessee understands that it cannot harbor a pet in this unit during the term and/or extension of this lease.

The Fair Housing Amendments of 1988 prohibit discrimination against handicapped individuals, and therefore, blind or deaf persons may not be charged additional deposits or be evicted because they have guide dogs.

Advance Rent

It is common to request *advance rent* upon execution of a lease. A lessor may require payment of first month's rent, last month's rent, or both. It is important that the lease clearly distinguish between monies collected as deposits and monies collected as advance rent. If the monies collected from the lessee are deemed a security deposit, the lessor may not apply those monies to the last month's rent. Additionally, security and other deposits are not considered taxable income to the lessor, unlike advance rents, which are considered as such.

Personalty

It is not uncommon to lease furnished premises. The lease should indicate whether the leased premises are furnished or unfurnished. If furnished, an exhibit should be attached to the lease listing all items contained in the leased premises, preferably room by room, and indicating the condition of each item. This exhibit should be signed by both the lessor and lessee acknowledging the accuracy of the list.

As a further precaution, the lessor may choose to photograph or videotape the items prior to turning the premises over to the lessee. The photographs or videotape can then serve as a record of the contents and their condition should a dispute later arise. Even when a premises is leased unfurnished, it is good practice for the lessor to do a "walk-through" with the lessee, taking note of the condition of all appliances, cabinetry, plumbing fixtures, floor coverings, and window treatments, and signing a statement acknowledging their condition.

Insurance

Insurance coverage is another provision to be included in the lease. It is common for state statutes to require lessors of apartment complexes to carry fire, windstorm, and public liability insurance. However, the personal contents of a rented unfurnished apartment or home are not covered by this insurance, and the lessee must obtain renter's insurance to protect his or her personal property, as in the following provision.

> *It is the Lessee's responsibility to insure all personal property. The Lessee acknowledges and accepts that the Lessor will not be responsible for any loss, theft, or damage to the Lessee's property resulting from any act, occurrence, or event.*

Indemnity

A lease may include an *indemnity* provision, sometimes called an *injury or loss* provision, which safeguards the lessor from any potential liability as a result of personal injury or losses suffered by the lessee or any other person on the leased premises. For example:

> *Unless caused by the willful conduct of Lessor or Lessor's agents, Lessee hereby indemnifies and holds Lessor harmless from any and all suits, actions, damages, liability and expenses in connection with the loss of life, bodily injury or property damage arising from or out of any occurrence in, upon, at or from the premises or the occupancy or use by Lessee of said premises or any part thereof, or occasioned wholly or in part by any act or omission of Lessee, Lessee's agents, contractors, servants, invitees or licensees.*

A word of caution is warranted here. In a number of states, including those that have adopted the URLTA, provisions exculpating the lessor entirely from all wrongdoing or limiting any liability of the lessor arising under law are illegal (see section 1.403(a)(4) of the URLTA). Therefore, state statutes should be checked prior to drafting an indemnification provision, and great care should be taken in its drafting.

Maintenance and Repairs

A *maintenance* or *repairs* provision should outline the responsibilities of each party for maintaining and/or repairing the premises. If the lease is silent, many state statutes indicate the duties of the parties. In most states, the lessor is responsible for structural and exterior repairs, and the lessee is responsible for the maintenance of the interior of the premises, unless the lease provides otherwise. Nonetheless, including a maintenance/repairs provision in the lease allows the parties to elaborate on and clarify these obligations. For example:

> *Lessor will maintain the exterior of the apartment, including but not limited to the exterior walls, doors, windows, and other exterior features, in good condition. Lessee will maintain the interior of the apartment in good and clean condition and in a state of good repair at all times, and shall use and maintain all mechanical equipment, to-wit: kitchen appliances, plumbing fixtures and air-conditioning equipment, strictly in accordance with the suggestions and requirements of the manufacturer thereof, and regulations that may from time to time be promulgated by Lessor.*

As noted earlier, the lessor upon notice is allowed by state law to enter the leased premises for *inspection* and repair purposes. In a number of states, a lessor may enter at any time for protection of the premises and may enter at a reasonable time and upon reasonable notice to the lessee for the purpose of repairing the premises. Further, some state statutes provide that a lessor may enter when necessary (1) with the consent of the lessee, (2) in case of emergency, (3) when the lessee unreasonably withholds consent, and (4) if the lessee is absent from the premises for a statutorily prescribed time period. The lessor also will desire entry toward the expiration of the lease term in order to show the premises to prospective new lessees, potential purchasers, or mortgagees. A sample entry and inspection provision follows.

At reasonable times during the term of this lease and any renewal thereof the Lessor and Lessor's agents shall have the right to enter the premises to inspect and to protect the condition of the premises and to repair or to alter the premises and all of Lessor's property contained therein. Lessor reserves the right, at reasonable times during the last sixty (60) days of the term of this lease, to show the premises to prospective lessees

Alterations

A lessee may desire to make certain *alterations* or *improvements* to the interior of the leased premises. It is advisable that the lease contain a provision requiring that any and all alterations and/or improvements be made only with the written consent of the lessor. This is of particular importance because of the issue of construction liens. If the lessee fails to pay a wallpaper hanger, for example, the wallpaper hanger may, depending on state law, have a statutory right to file a construction lien against the lessor's property. While it is difficult for a lessor to protect himself or herself from such a happening, the lessor should be aware of this possibility.

The lessor could include a provision stating that the tenant has no power or authority to create liens on the property. However, while this provision will be binding on the tenant, it will not be binding on subcontractors or laborers who are third parties. Thus, the lessor could sue the tenant for breach of contract if a construction lien is filed against the property, but would still have to deal with the lienor. Additionally, the lessor runs the risk of injury to a subcontractor or one of the subcontractor's employees. To guard against this liability, any written consent should include, as a prerequisite to work commencing, that the lessee supply the lessor with written evidence that all persons performing work on the premises carry workers' compensation and any other necessary insurance.

The characterization of these improvements is important. Depending on the nature of the improvements, they may be considered fixtures. The question then becomes whether they are affixed in such a manner that they remain with the premises upon the expiration of the lease. The alterations provision may indicate that all alterations and improvements remain on the premises. The following is a typical example of an alterations and improvements provision.

Without the prior written consent of Lessor, Lessee shall make no alterations or improvements to the premises including, but not necessarily limited to, interior painting and wallpapering. The Lessee shall have no power or authority to create any lien or allow any lien to attach to the premises. If any such lien attaches, the Lessor shall have the option of paying or discharging the lien, and the Lessee agrees to reimburse the Lessor for all expenses incurred. All alterations, changes and improvements in and about the premises made by Lessee with the exception of Lessee's movable personal property and Lessee's fixtures, removable without damage to the premises, shall become the property of Lessor and remain on the premises at the expiration of the lease.

Casualty

Unforeseen events happen and often leave damage in their wake. Therefore, a lease should include a provision stipulating how the parties will treat *casualty* or *destruction* to the premises caused through no fault of either party. In the event of a fire, flood, or other casualty that renders the total premises uninhabitable, it is customary that the lease is terminated.

Sometimes even severe damage, although less than total destruction, may be cause for terminating a lease. What are the options if the leased premises is partially destroyed? Some provisions allow abatement of all or a portion of the rent until repairs are completed. Other provisions allow a choice between abatement of rent and termination of the lease, the choice given to one or both parties. If repairs are possible but the premises is rendered uninhabitable while the repairs are in progress, who pays for the lessee's temporary accommodation? Again, this is something that must be negotiated by the parties. The following sample provision provides one option.

If the premises, or any part thereof, shall be partially damaged by fire or other casualty not due to Lessee's negligence, willful act or that of Lessee's agents, family, or visitors, Lessor shall have the option of promptly repairing the premises or of terminating this lease. In the event that Lessor elects to repair the premises, Lessor and Lessee acknowledge and agree that Lessee's sole remedy, if any, against Lessor, shall be a reasonable abatement of rent, the computation of said abatement to be based upon the extent to which the premises are rendered uninhabitable.

Subordination

Often the leased premises will be mortgaged. As a condition for obtaining financing, a lessor may have had to agree to obtain *subordination agreements* from all present and future lessees. A subordination agreement states that the lessee's interests in the premises legally are inferior to those of the financial institution, the mortgagee. Instead of executing a separate subordination agreement, the lessor may choose to include a subordination provision in the lease, such as the following ones.

This lease and Lessee's interest hereinunder are and shall be subordinate to any liens or encumbrances now or hereinafter placed upon the premises by Lessor, all advances made under any such liens or encumbrances, the interest payable upon any of such liens or encumbrances, and any and all renewals or extensions of such liens or encumbrances.

Even absent wording to the effect, if a mortgagee or some other person or entity with title superior to that of the lessee should evict the lessee from the premises, the lessee will not be held responsible for the remaining rent owed on the lease.

Assignment and Subletting

Most leases include a provision pertaining to *assignment* and *subletting* of the premises by the lessee. The terms *assignment* and *subletting* are not synonymous. A lessee who transfers all of his or her interest in a lease has *assigned* the lease. A lessee who transfers less than all of his or her interest in a lease has *subletted* the leased premises.

In either circumstance, the original lessee remains legally liable to the lessor for all rents owed under the lease unless the lessor agrees to work a *novation*, which is a substitution of an original party to a contract for a new party, the substitution relieving the substituted party of all legal obligations under the contract. With an assignment, the assignee typically makes rental payments to the lessor, but with a sublet, the sublessee makes rental payments to the original lessee who, in turn, makes rental payments to the lessor. A lessor generally allows either the assignment of the lease or the subletting of the premises only with his or her prior written consent. A provision that prohibits assignment but is silent with regard to subletting (or vice versa) will be narrowly construed by the courts and will not be read to prohibit both. A typical assignment and subletting provision reads as follows.

Without the prior written consent of Lessor, Lessee shall not assign this lease, or sublet the premises or any part thereof. An assignment or sublet without the prior written consent of Lessor shall be void and shall, at Lessor's option, constitute a default under this lease.

Default

A crucial provision in a lease is the *default* provision. This provision specifies the circumstances or actions constituting default by one or both parties. It is not uncommon in residential leases to find that although this clause emphasizes conduct of the lessee constituting grounds for default, it may tend to omit breaches in performance by the lessor. A lessee's remedies in the event of default or breach by the lessor, however, are governed by state statutory law, and the omission of such remedies in the lease does not negate them.

If the lessee defaults, the lessor usually is required to provide written notice to the lessee of the default and to specify a time period within which the lessee may attempt to cure. If the lessee has defaulted on the lease by failure to pay rent, provision may be made for interest on the rent after default. This provision may include a listing of remedies available to the nonbreaching party, or the available remedies may be set forth in a separate provision. For example:

If Lessee defaults in the payment of rent, or any part, or if Lessee breaches or defaults in performance of or in compliance with, or violates any term or condition of this lease, at the option of the Lessor, the lease shall terminate, and Lessor may take action for eviction as provided by state statute, re-enter the premises and retake possession, recover damages, including court costs incurred and attorneys' fees, and take any further action provided under law. Lessee shall be given five (5) days written notice of any default in rental payment and seven (7) days written notice of any violation of this lease.

In the event the lessor breaches or defaults, the usual remedy available to the lessee is money damages. Should the lessor default by failing to provide services required under either the lease or state statute, the provision may allow the lessee to hire contractors to supply the necessary services and then charge back the cost of the services against the amount of rent due under the lease. In most states, the prevailing party in a breach of contract action is not entitled to attorneys' fees and costs unless the contract so specifies. Therefore, it is necessary to include a statement to that effect in any remedies provision if that intention is desired by the parties.

Abandonment

It is common for a lease to include an *abandonment* provision separate from a default provision, indicating the actions that may be taken by a lessor should a lessee abandon the leased premises. Statutory law typically dictates the actions a lessor may and may not take under these circumstances, and an abandonment provision should be in accordance with state statutory law. As stated earlier in this chapter, some states allow the lessor to lay claim to any personal property the lessee leaves behind in the leased premises, such as in the following sample provision, and may make a distinction between forcible entry for seizure of property and the claiming of abandoned property.

If Lessee abandons the premises, Lessor may, at Lessor's option, take possession of the premises without becoming liable to Lessee for damages. If Lessor's right of re-entry is exercised following abandonment of the premises by Lessee, Lessee agrees that Lessor may consider any personal property belonging to Lessee that is left in the premises to also have been abandoned, in which case Lessee agrees that Lessor may dispose of all such personal property in any manner Lessor deems proper, and Lessee hereby relieves Lessor of all liability for doing so.

Miscellaneous Provisions

All leases contain a *notice* provision, indicating the manner in which as well as the address to which written notification should be sent to the parties. Additionally, leases usually include several *boilerplate* provisions, which are standard provisions found in most contracts. These may include a clause specifying that this lease is meant to represent the *entirety of the agreement* between the parties and that no prior written or oral understandings apply. Additionally, the lease may contain a *severability* provision which states that an invalid portion of the lease shall be severed from the remainder, which shall otherwise remain in full force and effect. Further, the lease may indicate that the law of a certain state controls if any matter concerning the lease is litigated by the parties.

Finally, care should be taken in the execution of a lease. If the lease is to be signed by an agent of either party, that agent's authority must be verified, and the agent's representative capacity should be indicated beneath the appropriate signature line. Similarly, if the lessor is a corporation, only an officer with the requisite authority to bind the corporation may sign the lease. Usually the corporate resolution approving the lease will indicate which corporate officials have the authority to sign. If not, then the corporation's bylaws or state statutes may specify who may sign contracts on behalf of the corporation.

If the lessor is a partnership, many state statutes provide that the actions of any partner may bind the partnership unless a partnership agreement provides otherwise. A lessee may request either that all partners in the partnership sign the lease or that the lessee be given written verification that the signing partner has the authority to bind the partnership to the lease.

If the parties will record the lease, state statutory law should be followed for the recording of instruments. Many states require that recorded instruments be both witnessed and notarized.

Paralegals may be actively involved in drafting or reviewing residential leases. They may be involved in information gathering by interviewing clients, or they may be asked to draft a lease from the attorney's notes. Even if the law firm has a standard residential lease agreement in its computer files, a paralegal must, as with any other contract, customize the lease to obtain the desired results for the client. If the law firm has a residential lease worksheet, this will prove invaluable in ensuring that all necessary information is obtained prior to drafting the lease. It is advisable, as stated earlier, to include, as an attachment to the lease, a listing of the items found in each room of the premises, providing a description of each item and an assessment of its condition. A sample worksheet and lease attachment are found in the hypothetical client matter that follows.

HYPOTHETICAL CLIENT MATTER

Checking her tickler file as soon as she arrives at the office this morning, Barbara notices that she has scheduled the drafting of the Munson lease. Michael and Mary Munson are new clients, referred to Ava Ross by another client. Mary is a physics professor at a local university and has been offered a position as visiting professor over the summer and through the following academic year at a university in the Washington, D.C. area. The Washington university will provide housing for the Munsons in Arlington, Virginia. The Munsons own a home in Any State that they desire to rent for the period they will be away, and they have found prospective tenants, the Russells.

Raymond Russell is being transferred by his company from his present location in Raleigh, North Carolina, to a position with a subsidiary company located in Any State. The Russells want to rent a house for a year before making the commitment to purchase a home in Any State. The Russells have two school-age children and a golden retriever. They are particularly enthusiastic about renting from the Munsons because the Munsons' house is located in a very good school district. Further, many potential lessors will not allow pets, but the Munsons are agreeable to leasing to pet owners. The Russells have provided references to the Munsons, and having checked the references, the Munsons are ready to have a lease drafted.

They met yesterday afternoon with attorney Ava Ross, who asked Barbara to sit in on the meeting. After a preliminary discussion, Ava asked Barbara to take the Munsons into the conference room to obtain the necessary information to draft the lease. Barbara used her residential lease worksheet to guide her as she worked with the Munsons. The Munsons are taking their furniture with them to Arlington, Virginia, as the house provided by the university is unfurnished. The Munsons are requiring a $1,000 security deposit and a $500 pet deposit to be paid upon the signing of the lease, but they have decided not to ask for first or last month's rent based on the strength of the Russells' references.

At this point, the Munsons believe they will only be in the Washington, D.C. area for a year, so they do not want to give the Russells an automatic renewal option or an option to buy. However, they do want to leave themselves open to negotiating an extension of the lease should they stay in D.C. longer than expected.

Ava has discussed with them the applicable law in Any State regarding such topics as repairs, indemnification for injury or loss, and eviction. The statutory law of Any State prohibits provisions attempting to exculpate and indemnify lessors from all wrongdoing, and therefore, Ava has advised the clients against including such an indemnification provision in their lease. However, the statutory law of Any State does allow for distraint of a tenant's property in the case of abandonment, and Ava has suggested that the lease contain a provision that parallels state law on this issue. Ava has also advised the Munsons to make a videotape of the premises prior to turning the premises over to the Russells. This videotape will provide evidence of the condition of the premises prior to leasing should a dispute later arise.

Barbara now pulls out the Munsons' folder and reviews the completed worksheet, which reads as shown in Figure 16–1.

Having reviewed the worksheet, Barbara is ready to proceed with the drafting of the lease. She has a skeletal form for a residential lease in her computer files; it contains some of the provision headings she will incorporate into the clients' lease, as well as many of the boilerplate provisions found in standard contracts. (Even boilerplate provisions must be scrutinized to make sure they are applicable in each client's situation.) Using this form and her worksheet as guides, she drafts the agreement shown in Figure 16–2.

When meeting with the Munsons yesterday afternoon, Barbara worked with them on a list of fixtures that will remain in the house during the lease term. These fixtures included floor, lighting, and window treatments as well as kitchen, bathroom, and laundry appliances. Using this list, Barbara drafts an exhibit to be attached to the lease and signed by all parties (see Figure 16–3). This exhibit assures that all parties understand what will remain in the premises and that all parties agree that the items are delivered at the commencement of the lease in the condition indicated on the exhibit.

FIGURE 16–1
Residential lease
worksheet

RESIDENTIAL LEASE WORKSHEET

DATE OF INTAKE: March 19, 1998
ATTORNEY: Ava Ross
PARALEGAL: Barbara Hammond
CLIENT NUMBER: 2231
MATTER NUMBER: 0001
PERSON RESPONSIBLE
FOR INTAKE: Barbara Hammond

1. LESSOR: Michael and Mary Munson

2. ADDRESS: 813 Ridge Lake Boulevard
                         Any City, Any State

3. TELEPHONE: (000) 445-7896   FAX: not applicable

4. LESSEE: Raymond and Robin Russell

5   ADDRESS: 250 Wilcox Street
                         Raleigh, North Carolina

6. TELEPHONE: (919) 888-3333   FAX: (919) 888-3330

7. ADDRESS OF LEASED PREMISES (Include legal description if
    applicable):   813 Ridge Lake Boulevard
                         Any City, Any State

8. PREMISES IS   ____ FURNISHED   X UNFURNISHED
                       (complete contents sheet and
                       attach to lease as exhibit)

9. NUMBER OF OCCUPANTS: 2 ADULTS   2 CHILDREN

10. PETS: X ALLOWED   ___ NOT ALLOWED
    IF ALLOWED, SPECIFY NUMBER, TYPE, SIZE, AND ANY CONDITIONS:
    One dog. Lessee shall pay additional deposit for pet upon execution of
    lease, deposit to be returned with security deposit if premises returned
    in good condition.

11. ASSIGNED PARKING SPACE (If applicable): not applicable

12. LEASE TERM:
    (A)   BEGINNING DATE: June 1, 1998
    (B)   ENDING DATE: May 31, 1999

13. USE OF PREMISES: Premises is to be used for single-family residential
                     purposes only.

14. RENT:
    (A)   TOTAL AMOUNT: $15,600.00
    (B)   PAID IN 12 INSTALLMENTS OF $1,300.00
    (C)   COMMENCEMENT DATE: June 1, 1998
    (D)   DUE DATE EACH INSTALLMENT: First of each month

15. SECURITY DEPOSIT FOR PREMISES:
    (A)   AMOUNT: $1,000.00
    (B)   PLACED IN: ___ INTEREST-BEARING ACCOUNT
                      X NONINTEREST-BEARING ACCOUNT

FIGURE 16–1
(continued)

(C)   IF PLACED IN INTEREST-BEARING ACCOUNT, SPECIFY PROCE-
DURE FOR PAYMENT OF INTEREST: not applicable

(D)   RETURN OF SECURITY DEPOSIT (Specify conditions, time period
after termination of lease, etc.): Security deposit to be returned in
full within 15 days after termination of lease if premises returned
in good condition, normal wear excepted.

16.   OTHER REQUIRED DEPOSITS (Pets, etc.): $500.00 pet deposit to be
returned in full within 15 days after termination of lease if no evidence
of damage to premises by pet.

17.   ADVANCE RENTS: ___ FIRST MONTH   ___ LAST MONTH
                             ___ BOTH   TOTAL: $ N/A

18.   UTILITIES PAID BY LESSOR: All utilities to be paid by Lessees.

19.   UTILITIES PAID BY LESSEE: Lessees are responsible for paying all utilities.

20.   INSURANCE: Lessors shall obtain and continue in force for the
duration of the lease term an insurance policy covering loss or damages to the premises by fire or other perils up to full replacement
value. Lessors shall not be responsible for loss or damages to any furniture or other contents belonging to the Lessees. It is the responsibility
of the Lessees to obtain renters' insurance covering such losses.

21.   REPAIRS TO BE DONE BY LESSOR: Lessors shall be responsible for all
repairs to exterior walls, windows, doors, roof, and any other exterior
features of the premises. Lessors shall also be responsible for all
repairs to air-conditioning and heating units.

22.   REPAIRS TO BE DONE BY LESSEE: Lessees shall be responsible for all
repairs to the interior of the premises, including plumbing and electrical repairs. Lessees shall be responsible in addition for the upkeep of
the front, side, and back yards of the premises.

23.   ALTERATIONS/IMPROVEMENTS BY LESSEE: Upon obtaining the written
consent of the Lessors, the Lessees may make alterations or improvements to the interior of the premises at Lessees' expense. Any alterations and/or improvements so made shall remain the property of the
Lessors at the termination of the lease. Prior to any alterations or
improvements made to the interior of the premises, Lessees shall provide Lessors with written evidence that all laborers are covered by
workers' compensation and any other necessary insurance. Lessees
additionally warrant that the premises of Lessors shall not be subject to
any liens for improvements contracted for by Lessees.

24.   FIXTURES: The fixtures supplied by Lessors on Exhibit A to the lease
shall remain the property of the Lessors at the termination of the lease.
Any furniture, appliances, and other personal property supplied by the
Lessees that may be removed without damage to the premises shall
remain the property of the Lessees at the termination of the lease.

25.   OPTION TO RENEW: Should the Lessees desire to extend the lease,
they shall provide the Lessors with at least 60 days' written notice prior
to the termination of the lease. If the Lessors are agreeable to extending the lease, an addendum to the lease shall be executed by the parties.

FIGURE 16–1
(continued)

26. ASSIGNMENT: Lessees shall not assign this lease without first obtaining the written consent of the Lessors. Lessors may sell, transfer or assign all or any part of their interest in the premises without the consent of the Lessees.

27. SUBLETTING: Lessees shall not sublet all or any portion of the premises without first obtaining the written consent of the Lessors.

28. PENALTIES:

(A) LATE RENT: Rent received after the 8th of each month shall be considered late rent and a $25.00 late fee shall apply. If rent is not received by the 20th of the month, the Lessees shall be considered in default of this lease and the default provision shall apply.

(B) RETURNED CHECKS: A $25.00 fee shall be charged for the first returned check. Should any subsequent check be returned for any reason, the Lessees shall be considered in default of this lease and the default provision shall apply.

(C) OTHER: not applicable

29. SUBORDINATION: This lease and the Lessees' interest hereunder are and shall be subordinate to any liens or encumbrances now or hereinafter placed upon the premises by the Lessors, all advances made under any such liens or encumbrances, the interest payable upon any such liens or encumbrances, and any and all renewals or extensions of such liens or encumbrances.

30. DESTRUCTION OF PREMISES: In the event the premises is destroyed by fire, flood, earthquake, or other act of God, or any other casualty not caused by the Lessees, the lease shall be considered terminated as of the date of the happening of such event. The Lessees shall be responsible for any rents due up to that date, and the Lessors shall refund any rents paid for occupancy beyond that date. Should only part of the premises be destroyed, the rent shall be adjusted accordingly in proportion to the percentage of the premises so destroyed. If more than 25% of the premises is destroyed, the Lessees shall have the option of paying the adjusted rent or terminating the lease.

31. INDEMNIFICATION: not to be included

32. DEFAULT:

(A) SPECIFY CONDITIONS CONSTITUTING DEFAULT: Failure by Lessees to pay rent or the payment of rent after the 20th of the month shall be considered default. Failure to maintain the plumbing and electrical systems in good condition or failure to make necessary repairs to said systems or other necessary repairs to the interior of the premises shall be considered default. Failure to maintain the front, side, and back yards of the premises, or using the premises for any purpose other than as a single-family residence, shall be considered default. Having any persons or animals living at the premises other than those specified in the lease shall be considered default. Failure to comply with applicable health codes shall be considered default.

(B) TIME PERIOD IN WHICH TO CURE: Lessees shall be given written notice of any default and shall be given five days from receipt of

FIGURE 16–1
(continued)

such notice to correct. If Lessees have, since the commencement of the lease, received prior written notice from the Lessors of the same or a similar violation, the Lessors, at their option, may choose to give the Lessees five days from receipt of written notice to correct or may choose to pursue those remedies for default available to the Lessors under the terms of this lease.

33. REMEDIES: Should the Lessees be in default of the lease and fail to cure the default, having been properly notified of such default as provided above, the Lessors may declare the lease terminated; enter and retake possession of the premises; remove all persons, animals, and property from the premises; and may sue for any outstanding balance and any damages sustained, including attorneys' fees and costs. Should the Lessors unlawfully terminate the lease, the Lessees may sue for any money damages sustained, including attorneys' fees and costs.

34. ABANDONMENT: If Lessees abandon the premises, Lessors may, at their option, take possession of the premises without becoming liable to the Lessees for damages. If the Lessors' right of re-entry is exercised following abandonment of the premises by the Lessees, the Lessees agree that the Lessors may consider any personal property belonging to the Lessees that is left in the premises to also have been abandoned, in which case the Lessees agree that the Lessors may dispose of all such personal property in any manner the Lessors deem proper, and the Lessees hereby relieve the Lessors of all liability for doing so.

35. NOTICES:
    (A) TO LESSOR: Michael and Mary Munson
                     1203 S.E. 14th Court
                     Arlington, Virginia
    (B) TO LESSEE: Raymond and Robin Russell
                     813 Ridge Lake Boulevard
                     Any City, Any State

36. ADDITIONAL PROVISIONS: Entry of Lessors: Lessors or their authorized agents may enter premises at reasonable times to inspect. Also, unless an addendum has been executed extending the term of the lease, the Lessors or their authorized agents may show the premises to prospective tenants at reasonable times during the last sixty days of the lease term.

FIGURE 16–2
Residential lease
agreement

RESIDENTIAL LEASE AGREEMENT

BY THIS LEASE, made and entered into this _____ day of _____ , 19___ , by and between MICHAEL AND MARY MUNSON (LESSORS) and RAYMOND AND ROBIN RUSSELL (LESSEES), the LESSORS agree to lease an unfurnished, single-family residence located at 813 Ridge Lake Boulevard, Any City, Any State, to the LESSEES under the following terms and conditions.

I.   **LEASE TERM.** The lease term shall commence on June 1, 1998 and end on May 31, 1999.

II. **NUMBER OF OCCUPANTS.** During the term of this lease, the premises shall be occupied by no more than two adults and two children.

III. **USE OF PREMISES.** The premises is to be used for single-family residential purposes only.

IV. **RENT.** The total amount of rent due under the terms of this lease is Fifteen Thousand Six Hundred Dollars ($15,600.00), to be paid in monthly installments of One Thousand Three Hundred Dollars ($1,300.00); payment to commence on June 1, 1998 and to continue to be due on the first day of each month until the expiration of this lease.

V.   **SECURITY DEPOSITS.** The LESSEES agree, upon the signing of this lease, to pay a security deposit in the amount of One Thousand Dollars ($1,000.00). Said deposit shall be placed by the LESSORS in a non-interest-bearing account and shall be returned in full within fifteen (15) days after the termination of this lease if LESSEES return the premises in good condition, normal wear excepted.

VI. **PETS.** LESSEES shall be allowed one dog in or about the premises and, upon the signing of this lease, shall pay a Five Hundred Dollar ($500.00) pet deposit, said deposit to be returned in full within fifteen (15) days after the termination of this lease if there is no evidence of damage to the premises caused by the dog.

VII. **UTILITIES.** LESSEES are responsible for paying all utilities, including but not limited to telephone, gas, and electricity.

VIII. **INSURANCE.** LESSORS shall obtain and continue in force for the duration of the lease term an insurance policy covering loss or damages to the premises by fire or other perils up to full replacement value. LESSORS shall not be responsible for loss or damages to any furniture or other personal property belonging to the LESSEES. It is the responsibility of the LESSEES to obtain renters' insurance covering such losses.

IX. **REPAIRS BY LESSORS.** LESSORS shall be responsible for all repairs to exterior walls, windows, doors, roof, and any other exterior features of the premises. LESSORS shall also be responsible for all repairs to air-conditioning and heating units.

X.   **REPAIRS BY LESSEES.** LESSEES shall be responsible for all repairs to the interior of the premises, including plumbing and electrical repairs. In addition, LESSEES shall be responsible for the upkeep of the front, side, and back yards of the premises.

FIGURE 16–2
(continued)

XI. **ALTERATIONS AND IMPROVEMENTS.** Upon obtaining the written consent of the LESSORS, the LESSEES may make alterations or improvements to the interior of the premises at LESSEES' expense. Any alterations and/or improvements so made shall remain the property of the LESSORS at the termination of the lease. Prior to the commencement of any alterations or improvements, Lessees shall provide the Lessors with written evidence that all laborers are covered by workers' compensation insurance and any other necessary insurance. The Lessees warrant that the premises of the Lessors shall not be subject to any liens for improvements contracted for by the Lessees.

XII. **FIXTURES.** The fixtures supplied by LESSORS on Exhibit A to the lease shall remain the property of the LESSORS at the termination of the lease. Any furniture, appliances, and other personal property supplied by the LESSEES that may be removed without damage to the premises shall remain the property of the LESSEES at the termination of the lease.

XIII. **RENEWAL OPTION.** Should the LESSEES desire to extend the lease, they shall provide the LESSORS with at least sixty (60) days' written notice prior to the termination of the lease. If the LESSORS are agreeable to extending the lease, an addendum to the lease shall be signed by the parties.

XIV. **ASSIGNMENT.** The LESSEES shall not assign this lease without first obtaining the written consent of the LESSORS. LESSORS may sell, transfer, or assign all or any part of their interest in the premises without the consent of the LESSEES.

XV **SUBLETTING.** The LESSEES shall not sublet all or any part of the premises without first obtaining the written consent of the LESSORS.

XVI. **ENTRY BY LESSORS.** The LESSORS or their authorized agents may enter at reasonable times to inspect the premises. Unless an addendum has been signed by the parties extending the term of the lease, the LESSORS or their authorized agents may show the premises to prospective tenants at reasonable times during the last sixty (60) days of the lease term.

XVII. **PENALTIES.**

(A) Rent received after the 8th of each month shall be considered late rent and a Twenty-Five Dollar ($25.00) late fee shall apply. If rent is not received by the 20th of the month, the LESSEES shall be considered in default of this lease and the default provision shall apply.

(B) A Twenty-Five Dollar ($25.00) fee shall be charged for the first returned rent check. Should any subsequent rent check be returned for any reason, the LESSEES shall be considered in default of this lease and the default provision shall apply.

XVIII. **SUBORDINATION.** This lease and the LESSEES' interest hereunder are and shall be subordinate to any liens or encumbrances now or hereinafter placed upon the premises by the LESSORS, all advances made under any such liens or encumbrances, the interest payable upon any of such liens or encumbrances, and any and all renewals or extensions of such liens or encumbrances.

FIGURE 16–2
(continued)

XIX. **DESTRUCTION OF PREMISES.** In the event the premises is destroyed by fire, flood, earthquake, or other act of God or any other casualty not caused by the LESSEES, the lease shall be considered terminated as of the date of the happening of such event. The LESSEES shall be responsible for any rents due up to that date, and the LESSORS shall refund any rents paid for occupancy beyond that date. Should only part of the premises be destroyed, the rent shall be adjusted accordingly in proportion to the percentage of the premises so destroyed. If more than twenty-five percent (25%) of the premises is destroyed, the LESSEES shall have the option of paying the adjusted rent or terminating the lease.

XX. **DEFAULT.** The LESSEES shall be considered in default of this lease if they:

(A)   fail to pay rent or pay rent after the 20th of the month;

(B)   fail to maintain the plumbing and electrical systems in good condition or fail to make necessary repairs to these systems or other necessary repairs to the interior of the premises;

(C)   fail to maintain the front, side, and back yards of the premises;

(D)   use the premises for any purpose other than as a single-family residence;

(E)   have any persons or animals living in or about the premises other than those specified in the lease; or

(F)   fail to comply with applicable health codes.

The LESSEES shall be given written notice of any default and shall be given five (5) days from receipt of such notice to correct. If LESSEES have, since the commencement of the lease, received prior written notice from the LESSORS of the same or similar violation, the LESSORS, at their option, may choose to give the LESSEES five (5) days from receipt of written notice to correct or may choose to pursue those remedies for default available to the LESSORS under the terms of the lease.

XXI. **REMEDIES.** Should the LESSEES be in default of the lease and fail to cure such default, having been properly notified of such default as provided above, the LESSORS may declare the lease terminated; enter and retake possession of the premises; remove all persons, animals, and property from the premises; and may sue for any outstanding balance and any damages sustained, including attorneys' fees and costs. Should the LESSORS unlawfully terminate the lease, the LESSEES may sue for any money damages sustained, including attorneys' fees and costs.

XXII. **ABANDONMENT.** If the LESSEES abandon the premises, the LESSORS may, at their option, take possession of the premises without becoming liable to the LESSEES for damages. If the LESSORS' right of re-entry is exercised following abandonment of the premises by the LESSEES, the LESSEES agree that the LESSORS may consider any personal property belonging to the LESSEES that is left in the premises to also have been abandoned, in which case the LESSEES agree that the LESSORS may dispose of all such personal property in any manner the LESSORS deem proper, and the LESSEES hereby relieve the LESSORS of all liability for doing so.

FIGURE 16–2
(continued)

XXIII. NOTICES. All rental payments and written notices to the LESSORS shall
be sent to the following address: Michael and Mary Munson
1203 S.E.14th Court
Arlington, Virginia
All written notices to the LESSEES shall be sent to the following address:
Raymond and Robin Russell
813 Ridge Lake Boulevard
Any City, Any State

XXIV. WAIVER. No waiver of any breach by any party of the terms of this lease
shall be deemed a waiver of any subsequent breach.

XXV. GOVERNING LAW. This lease shall be construed and governed in
accordance with the laws of the State of Any State.

XXVI. ENTIRE AGREEMENT. This lease shall constitute the entire agreement
between the parties, and any understanding or representation of any
kind prior to the date of this lease shall not be binding upon the parties.

XXVII. MODIFICATION. Any modification to this lease shall be enforceable
only by a written document signed by each party.

XXVIII. SEVERABILITY. If, for any reason, any provision of this lease is held
invalid, the other provisions of this lease shall remain in effect, insofar
as is consistent with law.

IN WITNESS WHEREOF, the parties have executed this lease on the day and
year first above written.

LESSORS:

_____
Michael Munson

_____
Mary Munson

LESSEES:

_____
Raymond Russell

_____
Robin Russell

FIGURE 16–3
List of fixtures

EXHIBIT A

The following items are considered fixtures that shall remain with the LESSORS at the termination of the lease:

ROOM	CONDITION
I. KITCHEN	
kitchen cabinets	good
terracotta tile floor	good
recessed lighting	good
almond miniblinds	good
almond Amana side-by-side refrigerator	good
almond Amana stove and self-cleaning oven	good
almond Amana microwave oven	good
almond Amana dishwasher	good
II. DEN	
terracotta tile floor	good
track lighting	good
almond vertical blinds	good
built-in wall unit	good
III. LIVING ROOM	
off-white wall-to-wall carpeting	good
track lighting	good
off-white damask draperies	good
IV. DINING ROOM	
off-white wall-to-wall carpeting	good
brass chandelier	good
off-white damask draperies	good
V. MASTER BEDROOM	
off-white wall-to-wall carpeting	good
rose damask draperies	good
VI. MASTER BATH	
off-white tile floor	good
off-white cabinets	good
recessed lighting	good
off-white American Standard pedestal sink	good
off-white American Standard toilet	good
stall shower	good
off-white American Standard jacuzzi tub	good
VII. BEDROOM #2	
off-white wall-to-wall carpeting	good
off-white miniblinds	good
VIII. BEDROOM #3	
rose wall-to-wall carpeting	good
rose miniblinds	good
IX. BEDROOM #4	
light blue wall-to-wall carpeting	good
light blue miniblinds	good
X. BATHROOM #2	
off-white tile floor	good
recessed lighting	good
off-white sink/cabinet combination	good
off-white American Standard toilet	good
off-white American Standard tub/shower combination	good
XI. BATHROOM #3	
off-white tile floor	good

FIGURE 16–3
(continued)

ROOM	CONDITION
recessed lighting	good
off-white sink/cabinet combination	good
off-white American Standard toilet	good
XII. LAUNDRY ROOM	
terracotta tile floor	good
fluorescent lighting	good
white Kenmore clothes washer	good
white Kenmore clothes dryer	good

The parties hereby acknowledge that the above fixtures are in the condition above stated as of _____ , 19__ .

LESSORS: LESSEES:

_____   _____
Michael Munson   Raymond Russell

_____   _____
Mary Munson   Robin Russell

CHAPTER SUMMARY

1. Residential leasing is governed by the common law of contracts and real property, as well as by federal, state, and local statutory law. The modern trend, reflected in the Uniform Residential Landlord and Tenant Act and in many state statutes, is to provide an equitable distribution of rights and obligations between lessors and lessees.

2. Although historically a lessee took possession of the leased premises under the theory of caveat emptor, present state law requires that a lessor maintain the premises in a habitable condition. Failure to do so could give rise to suit under the possible theories of breach of contract, negligence, and/or strict liability.

3. Lessors may impose reasonable restrictions on the use of the leased premises for the protection of the premises and the welfare of others. A lessor may also enter the leased premises after notice and at reasonable times for the purpose of inspection or repair.

4. Upon breach of a lease by the lessee, a lessor may avail himself or herself of contractual or statutory remedies which may include injunctive relief, money damages, and/or termination of the lease. However, a lessor may not evict a lessee without following statutorily prescribed procedures.

5. State statutes require that a lessee maintain the leased premises in a clean and safe condition. A lessee is responsible not only for his or her actions in the leased premises, but also for the actions of third parties invited onto the premises.

6. Upon taking possession of the leased premises, a lessee is entitled to a covenant of quiet enjoyment which provides protection from intrusions by third parties as well as unreasonable intrusions by the lessee. The Uniform Residential Landlord and Tenant Act and many state

statutes protect the lessee from retaliatory conduct on the part of the lessor.

7. Should the lessor breach a lease agreement, a variety of remedies may be available to the lessee, depending on the terms of the agreement and state law. A lessee may be entitled to rent abatement, rent withholding, lease termination, money damages, or injunctive relief, based on the nature of the lessor's breach.

8. At a bare minimum, a residential lease should include the names of the parties, a description of the leased premises, the lease term, and the rent amount. A well-drafted lease will include other provisions as well, such as provisions governing security deposits, advance rents, utilities, insurance, repairs, alterations or improvements, assignment and subletting, and default.

REVIEW QUESTIONS

1. Explain the duties of a landlord regarding the maintenance of a residential leased premises.
2. Explain the duties of a tenant regarding the maintence of a residential leased premises.
3. What legal recourse does a residential tenant have if the landlord fails to maintain the leased premises?
4. What remedies are available to a landlord if a residential tenant breaches the lease?
5. What basic provisions should be included in a residential lease?

ETHICAL QUESTIONS

Your supervising attorney has met with client Christa Connolly, who needs a residential lease drafted. After taking down the pertinent information, your supervising attorney turns the task over to you. Christa needs the lease no later than the end of the week. You have drafted the lease and put it on your supervising attorney's desk for review three days ago. It is now Friday, and you notice the lease has not yet been reviewed. The client has already phoned twice to check on its progress. When you mention this, your supervising attorney says she has been too busy to get around to it, that she trusts your work and she does not need to look at it. She tells you to call the client and tell her the lease is prepared and ready to be picked up. What should you do?

PRACTICAL ASSIGNMENTS

Assignment 16:1. Research your state statutes regarding the respective maintenance and repair obligations of residential lessors and lessees as well as those statutes regarding a residential lessor's rights of access to the leased premises. Photocopy the relevant statutes and insert them under the "Leases" section of your resource portfolio.

Assignment 16:2. Research your state statutes pertaining to the handling of security deposits by residential lessors. Photocopy the relevant statutes and insert them under the "Leases" section of your resource portfolio.

Assignment 16:3. Research your state statutes to determine whether indemnity provisions may be included in residential leases in your state. Photocopy the relevant statutes and insert them under the "Leases" section of your resource portfolio.

Assignment 16:4. Research your state statutes to determine the remedies available to a residential lessor for a lessee's noncompliance with a rental agreement. Photocopy the relevant statutes and insert them under the "Leases" section of your resource portfolio.

Assignment 16:5. This morning Deborah Sanders, your supervising attorney, met with client Todd Weller. Todd has recently purchased a duplex and plans on living in one half of the duplex and renting out the other half. Jason and Jennifer Marshall are the potential lessees. Todd needs a lease drafted and has spent some time with Deborah going over the particulars. Deborah, in turn, hands her notes to you and asks you to draft a lease. The property to be leased is located at 200 Royce Road (your city, county, and state) and is to be rented unfurnished. The lease term is one year, commencing on the first of next month. The total rent is $10,800, to be paid in monthly installments of $900 on or by the first of each month. The rent does not include utilities. Any rent check received later than the fifth of the month is subject to a $30 late fee. Rent past due by the tenth of the month constitutes a breach of the lease. Todd requires the payment of the first month's rent and a security deposit of $800 upon the signing of the lease. The security deposit will be put in a noninterest-bearing account and will be refundable within ten business days after the termination of the lease if the premises is left in good condition.

The area is zoned residential exclusively, so the premises may only be used for residential purposes. No pets are allowed on the leased premises. Todd agrees to make all necessary repairs to the exterior walls, doors, windows, roof, and air-conditioning, heating, and plumbing facilities. The Marshalls are responsible for keeping the interior in sanitary and good condition. Todd will allow the Marshalls to repaint the interior of the premises, but they may not make any alterations or improvements, or assign or sublet the lease, without first receiving Todd's written consent. Todd has the right to enter the leased premises at reasonable times and upon notice for the purposes of inspection and repair, and he reserves the right, during the last two months of the lease term, to show the premises to potential lessees at reasonable times and upon notice.

Todd is not liable for any loss, theft, or damage to property, or injury to or death of any person on or about the leased premises, and the Marshalls agree to indemnify and hold Todd harmless for such damage, injury, or death. Should the Marshalls want to renew the lease, they must inform Todd in writing of their intention within sixty days prior to the expiration of the lease. The terms for renewal will be set forth either on an addendum to this lease or by the execution of a new lease. Should the Marshalls choose not to renew, they will surrender the leased premises at the expiration of the lease term in good condition, reasonable wear and tear excepted. Failure of either Todd or the Marshalls to perform any or all of the terms of the lease constitutes a breach. The nonbreaching party shall provide a ten-day written notice setting forth the nature of the breach to the defaulting party. If at the end of the ten-day period, the breach is not cured, the nonbreaching party may take any action provided under state law, including the recovery of reasonable attorneys' fees and costs. In addition to these provisions, the standard boilerplate clauses regarding notice, severability, governing law, and so forth should be included.

With this information, draft the lease. Upon review, insert the lease under the "Leases" section of your resource portfolio.

Assignment 16:6. Define the following key terms.

abatement of rent	memorandum of lease
distress	tenant unions
index lease	Tenants' Eviction Procedures Act of 1976
lease	

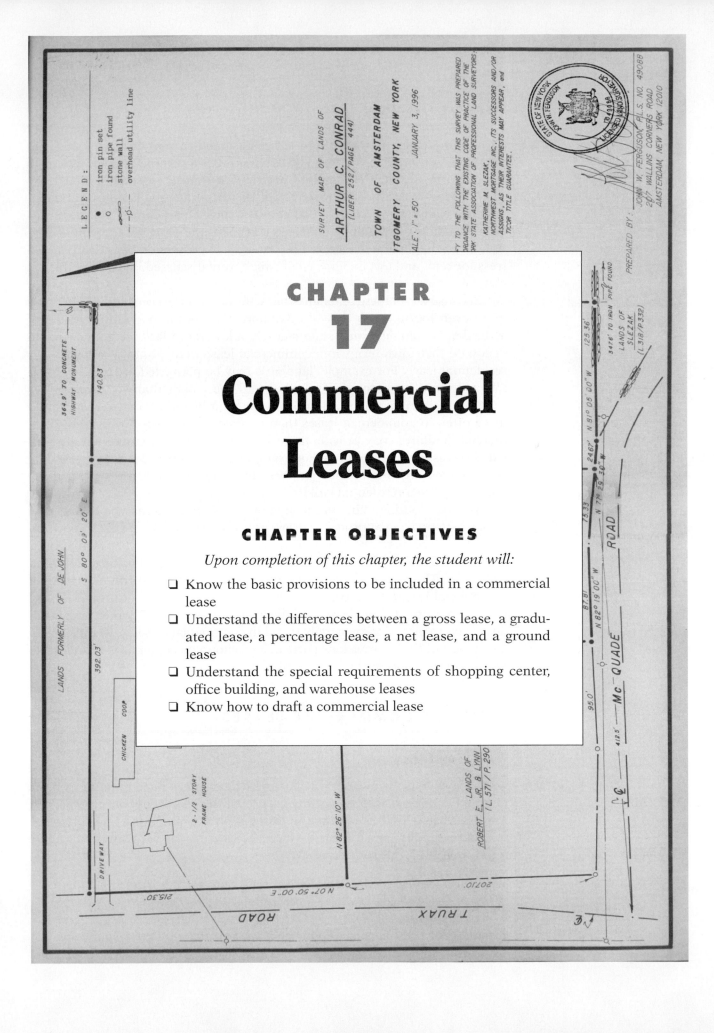

CHAPTER
17

Commercial Leases

CHAPTER OBJECTIVES

Upon completion of this chapter, the student will:

❑ Know the basic provisions to be included in a commercial lease

❑ Understand the differences between a gross lease, a graduated lease, a percentage lease, a net lease, and a ground lease

❑ Understand the special requirements of shopping center, office building, and warehouse leases

❑ Know how to draft a commercial lease

INTRODUCTION

Commercial leases are those leases designed to rent space for business purposes. Although, at the time of this writing, no commercial equivalent to the Uniform Residential Landlord and Tenant Act exists, state statutes typically address the respective responsibilities of commercial landlords and tenants. In many states, commercial statutes parallel residential statutes, with their focus on the handling of security deposits, landlord and tenant obligations regarding maintenance and repair, right of possession upon default, distress for rent, and tort liability, all of which were discussed in detail in the last chapter.

Because a commercial tenant's bargaining power is considered to be on a more even footing with that of a landlord than is the bargaining power of a residential tenant, some state statutes allow more latitude for parties to negotiate their own terms in a commercial lease than would be allowed in a residential lease. For example, landlords may be permitted, by agreement, to allocate more maintenance and repairs to the tenant than would normally occur in residential leases. Additionally, indemnification provisions are found more often in commercial leases than in residential leases. Conversely, commercial landlords may provide more services for their tenants than are provided by residential landlords. For example, a commercial lease may stipulate that the landlord is to provide janitorial and security services over and above those found in a residential building.

As a paralegal working in the area of real estate, you may be called upon by your supervising attorney to review or draft commercial leases. To perform these tasks competently, you need to know the distinctions between various types of commercial leases, as well as the provisions found in most commercial leases. This chapter begins with a discussion of the most common types of commercial leases: the gross lease, the graduated lease, the ground lease, the percentage lease, the net lease, and the triple net lease. The chapter then introduces you to provisions generally found in commercial leases, and ends with a discussion of those provisions particular to shopping center, office, and warehouse leases, respectively.

TYPES OF COMMERCIAL LEASES

The Gross Lease

A **gross lease** is a lease in which the lessee pays a fixed amount as basic rent and is not required to pay any portion of the lessor's operating expenses. A gross lease is used most often in less complex transactions, such as in the case of warehouse and executive office suite leases. The following is a sample rent provision for a gross lease.

> *Tenant shall pay unto Landlord a total rent of Four Thousand Eight Hundred Dollars ($4,800.00) per annum, together with any applicable use tax, commencing on April 1, 1998 until the end of the Lease Term. Said rent shall be paid without demand, in equal monthly installments, in advance, on the first day of each calendar month of the Lease Term.*

gross lease: A lease in which the lessee pays a fixed amount as basic rent and is not required to pay any portion of the lessor's operating expenses.

The Graduated Lease

Commercial leases usually are long-term, requiring the lessor to take into consideration the role of inflation, adjustable mortgage rates, and other factors that may raise the lessor's costs over the lease term. A **graduated lease** is a lease that contains a rent adjustment clause, allowing for the increase and, less often, the decrease of the rent to be paid over the term of the lease. This clause may be tied to the consumer price index or some other commonly used index. The consumer price index typically is used because it is adjusted annually and is tied to the concept of purchase power. In some cases, a lessor may simply provide that the rent will be increased by a specified percentage each year of the lease term, regardless of whether the lessor's actual costs increase, decrease, or remain the same. A typical rent adjustment provision follows.

> *The base rent shall be Twenty-Five Thousand Dollars ($25,000.00), plus any applicable sales or use tax, for the first year of the Lease Term, said base rent to be adjusted on the first day of each subsequent year of the Lease Term in the same percentage as any increase in the Consumer Price Index.*

The Percentage Lease

A **percentage lease,** commonly used by retail centers, is a lease in which, in addition to the base rent, the lessee is obligated to pay a specified percentage of the lessee's sales receipts to the lessor. Although the percentage may be negotiated by the parties to the lease, the National Association of Realtors® publishes a listing of the percentages used most often with various types of retail and service businesses. Many variations of this form of lease are possible.

Some percentage leases base computations on gross sales figures, while others base computations on net sales figures. Definitions of "gross" or "net" sales should be included in the lease to avoid ambiguity. Some leases include sales made by mail order, while others do not. The stated percentage of sales receipts may be required to be paid regardless of the total amount of gross (or net) sales accrued, or may "kick in" only after sales reach a stated level.

The lessor will require access to the financial records of each lessee to verify that the correct amounts are paid. These records usually are provided to the lessor for inspection quarterly, semiannually, at the end of the lessee's fiscal year, the end of a calendar year, or the end of each year of the lease term. Similarly, the lessee may be required to pay the stated percentage at the end of the year (fiscal, calendar, or otherwise) or may be required to make monthly, quarterly, or semiannual estimated payments, adjusting the payment amounts accordingly at the end of the lessee's fiscal year. The following provides an example of a percentage provision.

> *Tenant shall pay unto Landlord the base rent of Twenty Thousand Dollars ($20,000.00) per annum, plus any applicable sales and use tax, said base rent to be paid without demand in equal monthly installments. In addition to the base rent, Tenant shall pay unto Landlord Three Percent (3%) of Tenant's annual gross sales for all annual gross sales over the aggregate sum of Five Hundred Thousand Dollars*

graduated lease: A lease that contains a rent adjustment clause, allowing for the increase and, less often, the decrease of the rent to be paid over the term of the lease.

percentage lease: A lease in which, in addition to the base rent, the lessee is obligated to pay a specific percentage of the lessee's sales receipts to the lessor.

($500,000.00). "Gross sales" is herein defined to include all sales made on the leased premises, or by mail, telephone, or fax from the leased premises, including those sales made to employees.

The Net Lease

A **net lease** is a lease in which the lessee pays a base rent, plus a pro rata share of some of the lessor's operating expenses. The targeted operating expenses may include, but need not be limited to, real property taxes, utilities, insurance, and maintenance charges. Under a **triple net lease,** a lessee pays a pro rata share of all of the lessor's expenses. A net lease or triple net lease provision should define the term *operating expenses* very clearly. Because the lessee is paying a portion of the operating expenses, the lessee may request inspection of the lessor's records with respect to such expenses, including tax assessments from the property appraiser's office, utility bills, and contracts with insurance and maintenance companies. A triple net provision is set forth below.

This lease is a triple net lease. Landlord is not responsible for any Operating Expenses arising from or relating to the Premises. Tenant shall pay Ten Percent (10%) of all Operating Expenses as said Expenses are defined in this lease. Tenant shall pay estimated Operating Expenses in equal quarterly installments as such amounts shall be estimated from time to time by Landlord, adjustments to be made accordingly at the end of each year of the Lease Term. For the purposes of this Lease "Operating Expenses" shall mean any amounts paid or payable, whether by Landlord or by others on behalf of Landlord, arising out of Landlord's ownership, maintenance, operation, repair, replacement and administration of the Office Building.

The Ground Lease

A **ground lease** is a lease for a parcel of vacant real property. The lease period may be for up to ninety-nine years or some similar exceedingly lengthy period. The leased property is then used for the construction of a commercial premises, be it a shopping center, office building, or industrial complex. The purpose of the ground lease is to defray the costs of purchasing the real property upon which the structure is built. A lessee may deduct the entirety of the rent payments on the land as a business expense. If the lessee purchased the land, only a portion of the mortgage payments would be deductible—specifically, that portion allocated to interest. This tax advantage might very well make a vacant parcel more attractive to a business looking to build on a large scale. Additionally, since a lessee is not buying the land, only leasing it, a ground lease will decrease the amount of financing required because the lessee will require a loan only for the construction of improvements (for example, the office building, the shopping center), not for the purchase of the land upon which the improvements will be located.

The lending institution, on the other hand, may disfavor a ground lease because upon default of the construction loan by the lessee and subsequent foreclosure, the lending institution will step into the shoes of the lessee, acquiring only a leasehold, rather than a freehold, interest in the land itself.

net lease: A lease in which the lessee pays a base rent, plus a pro rata share of some of the lessor's operating expenses.

triple net lease: A lease in which the lessee pays a pro rata share of all of the lessor's expenses.

ground lease: A lease for a parcel of vacant real property.

The lending institution, as mortgagee, therefore will want to include, in any construction loan agreement, provisions protecting its position. For example, the mortgagee might require that the lessor subordinate its title to the land in favor of the mortgagee. Barring such a provision, the mortgagee may require a provision that allows the mortgagee to cure any default by the lessee under the lease and seek repayment from the lessee.

BASIC ELEMENTS OF A COMMERCIAL LEASE

Parties

Many of the basic provisions of a commercial lease are quite similar to those provisions found in a residential lease. The opening paragraph of the lease names the *parties* to the lease and often includes the date upon which the lease is signed by the parties. Unlike a residential lease in which one party, the lessor, is often a business entity entering into the lease with an individual tenant, a commercial lease typically is an agreement entered into by two business entities.

The lessor is often a corporation, partnership, limited partnership or limited liability company and must be identified as such on the lease (for example, Prestige Commercial Enterprises, Inc., an Any State corporation or Prestige Commercial Group, an Any State partnership). Likewise, the lessee is often a business entity renting office or retail space, and the lessee's proper legal name should appear on the lease.

It is common for an individual to enter into a commercial lease on behalf of a yet-to-be-created corporation. For example, Arlene Tyson may scout out potential retail space for a new business selling household accessories. She may want to secure a lease in a prime location before the space is taken by someone else, even if the articles of incorporation for the new business, Panache Accessories, Inc., have yet to be drafted and filed with the secretary of state's office. If Arlene enters into a commercial lease agreement before the corporation is legally created, she is signing the lease as a promoter, not as an officer, of the corporation. This means that she is individually liable for payment of the rent and the observance of all conditions of the lease. Therefore, the lease requires a clause allowing Arlene to assign her interest in the leased premises to the new corporation once the corporation is legally created by the filing of the articles of incorporation and the issuing of a certificate of incorporation by the secretary of state.

If the lessee is a corporation or a limited liability company, the lessor may want certain personal guarantees with regard to the rent. In these businesses, the owners (shareholders in a corporation or members in a limited liability company) are not personally liable for business debts. Conceivably, a corporation or limited liability company may not have enough money in the corporate account to cover all business obligations. If this business entity is a lessee and fails to pay rent, the lessor's only recourse is to seek a judgment against the business assets, which may be insufficient; the lessor cannot recover from the owners personally.

To guard against this contingency, the lessor will want to investigate the potential lessee's financial status. Further, the lessor may require that the individual owners enter as parties to the lease as well as entering into the lease as officers of the corporation. Or, instead of having the owners enter as parties, the lessor may require that the corporation be the named party and the individual owners sign as personal guarantors. Another option is to require sufficient deposits and advance rents (including last month's rent) to make it costly for the lessee to abandon the premises.

Description of the Premises

The introductory paragraph setting forth the parties to the lease is followed by a provision *describing the leased premises*. This provision will include the street address, the square footage of the leased space and, if office space, the suite number or, if warehouse space, the bay number, and fixtures provided. This provision may also include a description of designated parking, or the designated parking may be contained in a separate provision. The following provisions are examples of premises and parking provisions.

> **Premises.** *Landlord does lease unto Tenant the retail premises located in the retail center known as Magnolia Plaza, 2300 Independence Avenue, Any City, Any State, consisting of approximately 2,000 square feet, including all plumbing, electrical, sewerage, heating, air-conditioning, and other utilities fixtures thereof, together with the use of all common areas.*

> **Parking.** *The Tenant shall use the parking spaces that extend immediately in front of and/or immediately to the rear of the demised premises.*

Lease Term and Renewal

The *lease term* provision in a commercial lease usually provides for a longer rental period than is found in residential leases. One reason for this is that a commercial tenant often invests a great deal of money in improvements, alterations, and trade fixtures to conform the rental space to the needs of the business. For example, a restaurant renting space in a mall or strip center may spend considerable time and money outfitting the space with the kitchen equipment and decor necessary to create just the right ambience. Another reason for the lengthier lease terms found in commercial leases is the fact that, unless the business is a well-recognized chain name, it will need to remain in one location for an extended period before it becomes well known. An example of a lease term provision follows.

> *The term of this Lease shall be 36 months commencing upon January 1, 1998 ("Commencement Date") and ending December 31, 2001 ("Expiration Date"). At the expiration of this Lease, Tenant will vacate and surrender the Premises to Landlord in accordance with the terms hereof and said Premises shall be in a broomclean condition.*

If the lessor intends to give the lessee the right or option to *renew* the lease, the terms and conditions for the renewal should be set forth either as a provision within the lease or as an addendum to the lease. The lease renewal period may be for the same length or for a different length than the original lease term and typically will be at a higher base rent price. A renewal provision may read as follows.

> Provided that Tenant is in good standing and has performed all of the terms and conditions under this Lease, the Tenant shall have the option to extend the Lease for an additional thirty-six (36) months on the same terms and conditions of this Lease by giving Landlord three (3) months advance written notice of its intent to exercise this option. Said notice shall be delivered by certified mail, return receipt requested. The base rent for the renewal period will be:

> | | |
> |---|---|
> | Year 1: | $20,000.00 |
> | Year 2: | $20,500.00 |
> | Year 3: | $21,000.00 |

> Except as otherwise provided herein, the terms and conditions of the Lease remain in full force and effect.

Early Termination

Conversely, the lease may include a provision permitting the lessee to *terminate the lease* prior to the lease's expiration date. For new businesses, this is a particularly attractive provision because of the risk involved with new business ventures. Most businesses do not realize profits until their second or third year, and many new entrepreneurs find they do not have the capital resources to hold out for the duration. A provision permitting early termination may provide for the payment of a penalty in exchange for release from the lease obligations; nonetheless, the penalty required usually is much less than what the lessee would contractually be obligated to pay under the full lease term.

If the commercial building or center is mortgaged, the lending institution's approval may be required for early termination. The lending institution's loan to the lessee is secured by the real property and the improvements thereon (for example, the building or center). The value of the improvements increases proportionately with the percentage of space rented. In order to safeguard the value of its collateral, the lending institution may, as part of the loan agreement, prohibit early termination of leases. The following is an example of an early termination provision.

> Provided that the Tenant shall have been in good standing and has performed all of the terms and conditions under this Lease, the Tenant shall have the option to shorten the term of the Lease to eighteen (18) months by giving the Landlord three (3) months advance written notice of its intent to exercise this option. Said notice shall be delivered by certified mail, return receipt requested. The Tenant agrees to pay the Landlord one (1) month's rent as a penalty for the early termination of this Lease Agreement. Payment of the penalty must be tendered at the same time as the notice to exercise this option.

Use of the Premises

The *use of the premises* should be clearly stated. This provision should specify that the tenant's use of the premises must comply with all state, county, and city regulations, including occupational licensing and zoning regulations. This provision may also state that the lessee cannot use the premises in such a manner as to cause an increase in the payments of, or invalidate, the lessor's insurance policies. The following is a sample use provision.

> *Tenant shall use the Premises solely for the purpose of selling retail cloth-ing and accessories and for no other use or purpose whatsoever. Tenant shall comply with all laws, ordinances, rules and regulations of applica-ble governmental authorities respecting the use, operation and activities of the Premises. Tenant shall not make any use of the Premises which would make void or voidable any policy of fire or extended coverage insurance covering the Premises.*

Rent

The drafting of the *rent* provision is dependent on the type of commercial lease agreement. As noted earlier, the lease may be a gross lease, a percent-age lease, a net lease, a triple net lease, a graduated lease, or a lease combining several different characteristics, such as a triple net lease with a graduated rent schedule for the minimum base rent. Because commercial leases custom-arily are long-term leases, the lessor will want to include a rent adjustment mechanism in the lease to hedge against inflation and increased costs, includ-ing the costs of any adjustable rate mortgage on the property.

The rent provision should specify the total base rent, the amount to be paid in each installment, the date upon which each installment is due, and any costs to be paid in addition to the base rent. In many states, the lessor is required to collect applicable sales and use tax. The lessor may impose in the rent provision or in a separate provision a penalty for the *late payment of rent.*

> *Tenant agrees to pay to Landlord rent at the annual rate of Twenty-Four Thousand Dollars ($24,000.00) plus any sales and use tax which Tenant covenants to pay to Landlord in equal monthly installments of Two Thousand Dollars ($2,000.00) plus applicable sales and use tax in advance of the first day of each calendar month of each year of the term, without prior demand. Upon Tenant's failure to pay rent when the same is due, Tenant shall pay to Landlord, as liquidated damages for such fail-ure, six percent (6%) of the delinquent sum per day for each day such payment of rent is delinquent.*

Taxes

Apart from sales and use taxes, a commercial lease should cover the pay-ment of any and all other applicable *taxes,* setting forth each party's responsi-bility for payment. In a triple net lease, for example, the lessee is responsible for its pro rata share of the lessor's real estate taxes on the property. Even in gross leases, a lessor may tie payment of additional rent to the lessor's increased real estate taxes and assessments. Additionally, the personal prop-erty and trade fixtures of the lessee have a bearing on the assessed value of the lessor's shopping center or office building, and the lessor may desire to include a provision in which the lessee is required to pay for any increase in taxes resulting from such a situation, as in the following sample provision.

Landlord shall pay all real estate taxes and insurance relating to Trident Towers. Tenant shall be liable for all insurance premiums and taxes levied against personal property and trade fixtures placed by Tenant in and about the demised premises. If any such taxes are levied against Landlord or Landlord's property and Landlord pays same or if the assessed value of Landlord's property is increased by the inclusion thereof, Tenant, upon demand, shall pay to Landlord the taxes resulting from such increase in assessment.

Security Deposit

Just as in the case of residential leases, commercial leases contain a provision setting forth the amount of the *security deposit* to be paid by the lessee, the type of account in which the deposit will be held, the conditions under which the deposit will be returned, and the time at which the deposit will be returned. Some state statutes specify the time period within which a lessor must return a security deposit.

Upon execution of this Lease, Tenant shall pay Landlord a security deposit in the amount of one (1) month's rent. The security deposit shall not constitute the payment of Minimum Rent, or any portion thereof, but shall be returned to Tenant within ten (10) business days following the expiration of the Lease Term and the observance and performance by Tenant of all conditions and obligations stated in this Lease. The security deposit shall not bear interest.

Advance Rents

The lessor will want to collect any *advance rents* upon the signing of the commercial lease, usually the first and last month's rent. Note that inasmuch as most commercial leases have a duration of several years and include a rent adjustment provision, the last month's rent often is greater than the first month's rent.

Upon execution of this Lease, Tenant shall pay to Landlord the first and last month's rent (plus the security deposit provided elsewhere in this Lease), which amounts are as follows:

First month's rent: $1,457.77 plus sales tax
Last month's rent: $1,516.84 plus sales tax

Utilities

A commercial lease may provide that the lessee is responsible for all *utilities*, that the lessor is responsible for all utilities, that each party is responsible for a specified percentage of the utility costs, or that each party is responsible for specified utility charges. If the lessee is a tenant in an executive office suite, for example, the lessor often pays for all utilities during normal business hours. In a retail shopping center, on the other hand, it is common for the lessee to be responsible for all utilities. A lessor may agree to pay utility charges as long as such charges do not exceed a certain amount and may charge the lessee for any increased amount, such as in the following provision.

Landlord at its expense will furnish electrical (that consumed by normal office equipment), water, and sewer for Tenant. Air conditioning and heating will be provided Monday through Friday from 8:00 a.m. to 5:30 p.m., excluding legal holidays. If, in any calendar year during the Lease Term or any renewal or extension thereof, the annual electrical or water/sewer rates are greater than the same charges for the prior calendar year, tenant shall pay, in addition to the rent herein fixed, a pro rata amount, equal to that ratio of the amount of gross square feet in the Trident Towers to the gross square feet of Tenant, of said increase for said utility services.

Signs and Advertising

The lessee will want to advertise its business in a manner that will attract the most customers. The lessor will want to ensure uniformity in signage and will want to make sure that all signage complies with local ordinances. A commercial lease should contain a provision pertaining to *signs and advertising* that clearly specifies the type of signage and advertising permitted, those not permitted, and the allocation of costs for signage, such as the following provision.

Tenant will not exhibit, inscribe, paint or affix any sign, advertisement, notice or other lettering on any part of the outside of the Premises, or inside the Premises if visible from the outside, without first obtaining Landlord's prior approval thereof, which approval shall not be unreasonably withheld or delayed. Tenant shall present to the Landlord plans and specifications for such signage at the time the approval is sought. Tenant shall only install signs which conform with applicable codes of the city of Any City, and said signs shall be in conformance with Landlord's criteria for signage. Tenant shall pay all costs of installation and maintenance of the sign, and the cost of obtaining all necessary government permits and approvals.

Insurance

The lessor normally carries fire insurance and public liability insurance. However, the lessor may require that the lessee carry certain types of *insurance* as well. The lessee may be required to carry public liability insurance for the leased premises as well as workers' compensation and employer's liability insurance to cover employees.

Tenant shall, at its sole expense, provide and maintain in force during the entire term of this Lease, and any extension or renewal hereof, public liability insurance with limits of coverage not less than One Million Dollars ($1,000,000.00) for death or bodily injury for any one occurrence and One Million Dollars ($1,000,000.00) for any property damage or loss from any one accident. Each such policy of insurance shall name as the insured thereunder both the Landlord and the Tenant. Further, Tenant shall maintain, at all times during the term of the Lease, workers' compensation at legally required levels.

Further, should the lessee remodel the leased premises, the lessor will require that the lessee or the lessee's contractor carry builder's risk insurance.

Additionally, the lessee may choose to carry insurance covering lessee's personal property. This is quite common in the lease of warehouse space, particularly in instances where the lease expressly states that the lessor relinquishes all responsibility for any loss to personal property caused by theft or damage to the leased premises.

> *The Personal Property of Tenant shall be kept, stored or maintained in and on the Premises at Tenant's sole risk, and Landlord shall have no liability for any loss or damage caused to the Personal Property from any source whatsoever. If Tenant desires insurance coverage for said Personal Property, it must be obtained by Tenant at Tenant's sole cost and expense.*

Indemnity

Although *indemnity* provisions may be found in both residential and commercial leases, these provisions are more common in commercial leases. Recall from the last chapter that an indemnity provision safeguards the lessor from any potential liability as a result of personal injury or losses suffered by the lessee or any other person on the leased premises. Some states frown upon indemnity provisions that exculpate the lessor from all liability (for example, the lessor's own negligence as well as the lessee's negligent acts), so state statutes must be checked carefully before drafting an indemnity provision. A typical indemnity provision reads as follows.

> *Tenant shall protect, indemnify and hold harmless Landlord, Landlord's agents, employees, licensees and invitees from and against any and all claims of loss or damage to property and of injury to or death of persons arising out of or in connection with the acts or negligence of Tenant, its agents, employees, licensees or invitees in or about the Premises.*

Maintenance and Repairs

The *maintenance and repairs* provision should address the responsibilities of each party for maintaining and/or repairing the premises. As is the case with residential leases, state statutes require the lessor to comply with the requirements of all applicable building and health codes and to maintain the structural components of the leased premises in good repair. Some state statutes make it the obligation of the lessor to keep the plumbing in reasonable condition, while others only designate this responsibility to the lessor with regard to residential leases.

In some situations, the lessor provides all maintenance, but the costs are passed on to the lessee. In other situations, the lessor provides maintenance of all structural components and common areas (at the cost of either the lessor or the lessee, as designated in the lease), and the lessee is responsible for the maintenance (and all costs thereof) of the interior of the premises unless the lease provides otherwise. If the potential lessee is to be charged a pro rata share of the common maintenance costs, it is advisable that the lessee ask to see the maintenance fees charged to lessees over the past few years before signing the lease. The following provisions exemplify a common delegation of maintenance duties.

> ***Maintenance and Repairs by Landlord.*** *Landlord covenants to keep the following in good order, repair and condition: (i) the structure of the Office Building; (ii) the mechanical, electrical and other base building systems (except as may be installed by or be the property of Tenant); (iii) the entrances, sidewalks, corridors, parking areas and other facilities from time to time comprising the Common Areas. So long as Landlord is acting in good faith, Landlord shall not be responsible for any damages caused to Tenant by reason of failure of equipment or facilities serving the Office Building or delays in the performance of any work for which Landlord is responsible pursuant to this Lease.*

> ***Maintenance and Repairs by Tenant.*** *Tenant shall, at its sole cost, maintain the Premises, in good order, condition and repair, exclusive of base building, mechanical, plumbing and electrical systems, all to a standard consistent with a first-class Office Building, with the exception only as to those which are the obligation of Landlord as set forth above. All repairs and maintenance performed by Tenant in the Premises shall be performed by contractors designated or approved by Landlord.*

Lessor's Access to Premises

Even if the lessor is not responsible for repairs to the interior of the leased premises, the lessor may need access in order to carry out structural or mechanical repairs. Further, the lessor will require access to the leased premises to show the premises to potential mortgagees, purchasers, or, toward the end of the lease term, to prospective lessees. In most states, the lessor can enter the leased premises at any time for the protection of the premises. In nonemergency situations, the lessor may enter at reasonable times to repair, make alterations, or show the premises. A standard *inspection* provision follows.

> *Tenant agrees that Landlord, its agents and representatives may enter upon the Premises from time to time to inspect the same and to make such repairs, alterations and improvements to the Premises as may be necessary in Landlord's judgment. Tenant agrees further that Landlord, its agents and representatives may show the Premises to prospective purchasers or mortgagees of the Premises from time to time during the Term.*

Alterations

Commercial lessees typically want to make *alterations* or improvements to the leased space over and above the installation of trade fixtures. This can be arranged in several ways. The lessor can make such alterations for the tenant as a *build-out* (discussed later under special provisions), and the cost of the alterations can be factored into the annual rent or be charged separately. This type of arrangement may be preferable to the lessor. The lessor may own several commercial properties and have experienced, licensed contractors working for the lessor who can move the project along quickly.

Additionally, the lessor may prefer to handle the alterations to prevent potential problems with construction liens. Contractors and subcontractors can attach construction liens on real property for the costs of improvements and, if payment is not forthcoming, foreclose on the property to collect monies owed. If a lessee hires contractors to make alterations to the leased premises and fails to pay them, the lessor's property can be thus encumbered.

The lessor's mortgagee may have reservations about the alterations provision. In many states, the priority of construction liens works retroactively, the priority of the lien determined not by the date of recording but by the day the first work was done or materials supplied by the contractor to the site. If the lending institution's mortgage was recorded after this date, the contractor's lien would be superior to that of the lending institution.

Even if the lending institution has no such concerns because its mortgage was recorded before the construction of the building or center commenced, the lending institution may be wary of alterations clauses that delegate the responsibility of the alterations work to the lessor. If the lessor fails to perform the alterations work, does the work improperly, or causes undue delay in the performance of the work, the lessee may be entitled, under the terms of the lease, to cancel the lease.

If the lessor does not want to undertake the alterations, a provision can be drafted to require the lessor's approval of all plans including the requirement that the lessor be provided with all drawings and specifications, the lessor's approval of all contractors performing the alterations, and the lessor's indemnification against all liens.

> **Tenant's Alterations.** *Tenant shall have the right to make nonstructural interior alterations to the Premises which are not visible from outside the Premises (excluding electrical, mechanical and HVAC alterations). Tenant shall submit to Landlord details of the proposed work including drawings and specifications prepared by qualified architects or engineers conforming to good engineering practice. All such alterations shall be performed at the sole cost of Tenant, and in accordance with drawings and specifications approved in writing by Landlord.*

> **Liens.** *Tenant shall promptly pay for all materials supplied and work done in respect of the Premises so as to ensure that no lien is recorded against any portion of the real property upon which the Office Building is erected or against Landlord's or Tenant's interest therein.*

Trade Fixtures

In addition to or as part of remodeling and alterations, commercial tenants install *trade fixtures* in the leased premises. Although the law in most states allows the tenant to remove and take trade fixtures as long as the premises are restored to their original condition, the trade fixtures provision should clearly spell out what may be removed and what must remain on the premises. The lease should delineate leasehold improvements and trade fixtures. Leasehold improvements, such as partitions, usually become the property of the lessor, whereas trade fixtures, such as display cases in a retail store, remain the property of the lessee.

All Leasehold Improvements, other than trade fixtures listed on Exhibit A, shall immediately upon their placement in the Premises become Landlord's property without compensation to Tenant. Tenant may, during the Term, in the usual course of its business, remove its trade fixtures, provided that Tenant is not in default under this Lease.

Casualty

Most commercial leases contain a *casualty* provision setting forth the rights of the parties in the event of a fire or other damage to the premises. If the damage makes the premises untenantable, the lessor typically has the option of terminating the lease or rebuilding. The lessor will be concerned about the adequacy of the insurance proceeds to cover all costs of rebuilding and, therefore, will desire a casualty provision that does not obligate the lessor to rebuild. Should the lessor choose to rebuild, the question of whether the rent is abated while rebuilding is in progress is material to both parties. If the lessee has business interruption insurance, rent abatement may not apply.

If the option of rebuilding is chosen by the lessor, the time period within which the lessor must rebuild should be specified. Additionally, the question of whether the lessor is responsible for rebuilding the lessee's leasehold improvements should be addressed in the casualty provision, such as in the following provision.

In the event any improvements on the Office Building site are rendered untenantable by fire or other casualty, Landlord shall have the option of terminating this Lease or rebuilding, and in such event, written notice of the election by Landlord shall be given to Tenant within thirty (30) days after the occurrence of such casualty. In the event Landlord elects to rebuild, Landlord shall not be obligated to rebuild the Tenant's Improvements.

Rules and Regulations

The lessor of a commercial premises often promulgates *rules and regulations* that must be followed by all lessees (and often the lessees' employees, licensees, invitees, and customers). These regulations usually include, but need not be limited to, rules pertaining to the common areas of the premises, including the passages, stairways, and elevators; rules pertaining to safety concerns; rules pertaining to signage; rules pertaining to defacement of the premises; rules pertaining to storage and to disposal of discarded materials; and rules pertaining to delivery and moving of freight.

The lessor will want to include a statement that the lessor may alter the rules enumerated if in the best interests of the building or center, or add reasonable and appropriate rules to those specifically enumerated. If the regulations are lengthy, they may be attached to the lease as an addendum.

Tenant covenants that the rules and regulations attached as an addendum to this Lease, and such other and further rules and regulations as Landlord may make, being in the Landlord's judgment needful for the safety, care and cleanliness of the Office Building and Premises or for the comfort of tenants, shall be observed by Tenant and by the agents, clerks, servants and visitors of Tenant.

In addition to ordinary rules and regulations, the lessor wants to make certain that the lessees comply not only with licensing and zoning laws but also with state and federal environmental laws. The owners of real property can face both civil and criminal penalties for disposal of hazardous substances and other prohibited practices. The lessor, therefore, may want to attract the lessee's attention to the necessity for compliance by setting forth the lessee's covenant of compliance in a separate provision, such as the following.

Tenant hereby covenants that it will strictly comply with any and all local, state and federal environmental rules, regulations, ordinances and statutes. In the event Tenant violates any such rules, regulations, ordinances, or statutes, Landlord may terminate this Lease. Tenant shall be liable for all clean-up costs and any other costs connected with any such violation, including any and all imposed fines and penalties.

Subordination

As noted earlier, the commercial premises are often mortgaged. As a condition for obtaining financing, the lessor may be required to have all present and future lessees sign subordination agreements, subordinating their rights in the leased premises to the rights of the lending institution. A *subordination* provision states that the lessee agrees to sign a subordination agreement should it be required.

It is specifically understood and agreed by and between the Landlord and the Tenant that the Landlord may, from time to time, secure a construction and/or first mortgage on the demised premises from a recognized lending institution, and that this Lease is and shall be subordinate to the lien of said construction and/or first mortgage; and the Tenant agrees that it will execute such subordination or other documents or agreements as may be requested or required by such lending institution.

Estoppel Certificates

The lending institution typically requires the lessor/mortgagor to provide estoppel certificates signed by all lessees verifying the terms and conditions of their leases. Thus, a commercial lease may contain an *estoppel certificate* provision, similar to the following one.

At any time and from time to time, upon not less than ten (10) days prior notice by Landlord or Landlord's Mortgagee (the "Requesting Party"), Tenant shall comply with, execute, acknowledge and deliver in writing to the Requesting Party an estoppel certificate certifying the terms of this Lease, including a statement that this Lease is unmodified and in full force and effect, or if there have been modifications, that the Lease is in full force and effect as modified, and stating the modifications and such further information with respect to the Lease or the Premises as the Requesting Party may reasonably request.

Assignment and Subletting

The *assignment or subletting* of the leased premises is of concern to both parties, as well as to any mortgagee of the leased premises. The lessee wants a way out of paying rent without defaulting on the lease if business is slow. In such a situation, the lessee would ultimately like the ability to terminate the lease early or, failing that, the ability to assign the lease to another party, making that other party, the assignee, primarily liable under the lease and the original lessee only secondarily liable.

The lessor, on the other hand, entered the lease with the lessee based on the financial status of the lessee and that of any guarantors executing the lease. The lessor may not want to negate the lessee's primary liability and that of any guarantors by approving an assignment unless the lessor believes, after thorough investigation, that the prospective assignee is a better business risk than the lessee. The lessor certainly will not agree to a provision allowing assignment of the lease without the lessor's prior written approval.

The lessor might be more willing to allow the lessee to sublet the leased premises. In this way, the lessee remains obligated to the lessor, while the sublessee is obligated to the lessee. Even if the lessor consents to subletting, the lessor will want to be assured that the sublessee agrees to abide by all terms and conditions of the original lease.

> *Tenant shall not enter into, consent to, or permit any transfer of this Lease without the prior written consent of Landlord in each instance, which consent shall not be unreasonably withheld, but shall be subject to Landlord's rights hereunder. Landlord shall, within thirty (30) days after having received such notice and all requested information, notify Tenant either that it consents or does not consent to the transfer. If Landlord fails to give any timely notice, Landlord shall be deemed to have refused consent to the transfer.*

Default and Remedies

Most *default and remedies* provisions in commercial leases focus on the lessee's default and the lessor's available remedies. If the lessee defaults, the lessor wants a swift resolution, either a timely cure by the lessee or the lessee's vacating of the premises, together with acceleration of all rent for the entire lease term. State law may severely restrict the remedies available to the lessor, so state statutes should be checked carefully prior to drafting this provision.

This provision should specify the actions constituting a default by tenant, the time period in which to cure, and the default remedies. Should the lessor default, the typical remedies available to the lessee are the termination of the lease and money damages, where applicable. The lessor will be concerned with the prospect of having property encumbered by a judgment lien and may seek to include a provision limiting the lessee's remedies. Again, state statutes should be checked to determine whether the desired limitations are permitted. Sample default and remedies provisions follow.

> **Default.** *A default by Tenant shall be deemed to have occurred hereunder if and whenever: (A) any Minimum Rent is in arrears by the fifth of the*

month, whether or not any notice or demand for payment has been made by Landlord; (B) any Additional Rent is in arrears and is not paid within five (5) days after written demand by Landlord; or (C) Tenant has breached any of its obligations under this Lease (other than payment of Rent) and Tenant fails to remedy such breach within fifteen (15) days (or such shorter period as may be provided in this Lease).

Default Remedies. *In the event of any default hereunder by Tenant, then without prejudice to any other rights which may be exercised by Landlord: (A) Landlord may terminate this Lease by notice to Tenant and retake possession of the Premises for Landlord's account; (B) Landlord may enter the Premises as Agent of Tenant to take possession of any property of Tenant on the Premises, to store such property at the expense and risk of Tenant or sell or otherwise dispose of such property in such manner as Landlord may see fit without notice to Tenant, which shall be credited toward any Rent owed Landlord pursuant hereunder; (C) Landlord may accelerate all Rent for the entire Term.*

Should the lessee remain in the leased premises after the expiration of the lease term, some state statutes provide that a month-to-month tenancy is created and that the parties are entitled to such rights and notice as is applicable under such a tenancy. However, if permitted under state law, the holding over of a commercial lessee may be considered by the parties to create only a tenancy at sufferance. State law should be consulted before drafting a *holding over* provision.

If Tenant remains in possession of the Premises after the end of the Term hereof, there shall be no tacit renewal of this Lease, and Tenant shall be deemed to be under a month-to-month tenancy. Tenant shall pay to Landlord an amount equal to the last monthly installment paid under the Lease for each month or portion thereof Tenant remains on the Premises. All other obligations of Tenant under this Lease shall be applicable to Tenant during the period in which Tenant is a month-to-month tenant.

Miscellaneous Provisions

Finally, a commercial lease will contain many of the boilerplate provisions found in most contracts, albeit altered where necessary to suit the needs of the parties. These provisions include a *notice* provision, specifying the manner in which parties are required to give notice to each other. A *waiver* provision typically is included, specifying that the excusal by one party of any default by the other shall not be a waiver with respect to any continuing or subsequent defaults. A *governing law* provision specifies the state law under which the lease shall be construed, while a *severability* provision provides that should any provision in the lease be found to be invalid, that provision shall be severed from the lease and the rest of the lease shall remain in full force and effect. Additionally, a provision will be included which indicates that the lease, plus any addendums or exhibits attached to it, constitutes the *entire agreement* between the parties and that no modification of this lease can be made except by a writing executed by the lessor and the lessee. The next section of this chapter discusses the special concerns or provisions specifically found in shopping center leases, executive office suite leases, and warehouse leases.

SPECIAL PROVISIONS

Shopping Centers

When retail space is rented out to a shopping center lessee, the lessee rarely moves into the space without alterations. If the lessee is a restaurant, it typically will require more extensive alterations to the interior space than a boutique; nonetheless, interior build-out should be addressed by the parties.

The commencement date of the lease term may be the date of signing the lease, the date the work on alterations commences, or the date on which the alterations are completed. Sometimes these alterations are undertaken by the lessee, but often they are undertaken by the lessor. The cost of alterations may be factored into the rent or may be charged separately. If the lessor undertakes the alterations, the architectural plans and drawings should be attached to the lease as an exhibit. Likewise, any alterations for which the lessee is responsible should be approved by the lessor and attached as a lease exhibit. All agreed-upon alterations should then be referred to in a provision within the text of the lease, such as the following.

> *Landlord will, at its sole expense, perform all work specified to be performed by Landlord, more specifically set forth in Exhibit A attached hereto and entitled "Landlord Improvements." Tenant will, at its sole expense, perform all other work necessary to complete the Premises for its business purposes, more specifically set forth in Exhibit B attached hereto and entitled "Tenant Improvements."*

Parking is another major concern of shopping center lessees. Lessees want to be assured that their customers will have adequate parking space with easy access to their stores and may require a minimum number of guaranteed parking spaces per store or per square footage of rental space. They will also be concerned with the safety of their customers and will desire proper lighting in the parking lot if the center will be open at night, as well as possible security patrols. The costs for security, lighting, and parking lot maintenance often are factored into the operating costs to be paid by the lessees. An example of a shopping center parking provision follows.

> *Tenant shall be allotted four (4) reserved parking spaces for its customers in the front parking area. In addition, Tenant's customers shall have the nonexclusive use of all nonreserved parking areas. Landlord shall provide one (1) roaming security patrol guard in the front and rear parking areas during the hours of 5:00 p.m. to 9:00 p.m. on those evenings the shopping center is open for business. The parking areas in front of the shopping center are intended primarily for customers of the center. Tenant and Tenant's employees are to park in the rear parking area.*

A more controversial area of concern is that of competing businesses within the shopping center. The lessee usually desires an exclusivity provision in the lease, acknowledging that the lessor shall not rent out space to stores in competition with the lessee. The lessee will argue that to succeed in a particular location, and thus to be a lucrative tenant, the lessee requires such a provision. Under certain circumstances, this may make sense, such as in the instance of a florist located in a small strip center. Two or more competing florists in the strip center would most likely have a difficult time sustaining business, and one of the florists might find it could not survive and move out, leaving the lessor with vacant space.

On the other hand, a larger shopping center may be able to incorporate two or more similar businesses, such as a large shopping mall which often contains several men's, children's, and women's boutiques as well as several department stores and restaurants. Even in a smaller shopping center, the lessor's conception for the center may include similar businesses—for example, a center for high fashion designer clothing boutiques necessarily will include more than one such boutique; likewise, a center for home furnishings and home accessories necessarily will include more than one furniture store. Additionally, the lessor's mortgagee may prohibit the inclusion of an exclusivity provision in the lease, since the mortgagee will want to provide as much flexibility in rentals as possible.

If an exclusivity provision is included in the lease, it should be drafted carefully. The lessor should not prohibit other stores from selling the same goods (for example, jewelry); rather, the lessor should agree not to rent space to another business that is in direct competition with the lessee or is in the same primary business as the lessee. The lessor would not want to be prohibited, for example, from renting space to a clothing boutique that also sold costume jewelry as accessories when the lessor signed a contract containing an exclusivity provision with a store selling gold and other fine jewelry. A sample exclusivity provision follows.

> *Landlord agrees not to rent other space in the shopping plaza, during the term of this Lease and any extensions thereof, to others whose primary business is the sale of exercise equipment. The term "exercise equipment" is defined for the purposes of this Lease as treadmills, stair machines, rowing machines, bench presses, free weights, and similar equipment. It does not include the sale of exercise clothing or footwear. The term "primary business" is defined for the purposes of this Lease as a business in which fifty percent (50%) or more of the inventory of the business is comprised of exercise equipment.*

Stores in shopping centers often are required to keep uniform store hours. If a lessee fails to abide by the required hours, this breach of contract not only affects the lessee but also may have an impact on other tenants. For example, if the center is closed on Sundays but a lessee keeps its store open on Sunday, this causes confusion among shopping center customers and could breed resentment among the tenants. Conversely, a lessee may not want to keep open on evenings designated as evening shopping center hours. The shopping center's advertising and marketing may depend on uniformity. Further, city and county ordinances may regulate business hours. The center's policy on store hours should be set forth clearly in the lease.

Tenant's business shall remain open during designated store hours, namely: Monday, Tuesday, and Thursday, 10:00 a.m. to 9:00 p.m.; Wednesday, Friday and Saturday, 10:00 a.m. to 6:00 p.m.; Sunday, 12:00 p.m. to 5:00 p.m. The shopping plaza shall be closed for business on the following holidays: Christmas Day and Easter Sunday. Should Tenant desire to close the Premises for the taking of inventory, Tenant must first obtain the permission of Landlord. Failure of Tenant to abide by the terms of this provision shall be considered a default of this Lease.

Finally, a lessor may require lessees to contribute to the promotion of the shopping center. This is commonly done by the formation of merchants' associations, which develop advertising budgets and allocate expenses for the advertising costs on a pro rata basis. The lessor typically contributes a specified percentage of the designated budget and reserves approval rights for all advertising copy and promotions.

Executive Office Suites

An executive office suite lessee usually is a short-term tenant as compared with a lessee in a shopping center. The lessees of an executive office suite are looking for ways in which to minimize their overhead costs. They do not want to hire secretarial support staff or spend the money on conference rooms or reference libraries. In keeping overhead to a minimum, they are not interested in extensive alterations to the rented space. They are looking for space in an office building that provides secretarial support services, access to common business facilities, and, occasionally, furnished premises.

The costs of certain services, such as switchboard services, are included in the monthly rent. Other services, such as photocopying and keyboarding, may be included in the monthly rent or, more often, may be available to the lessee who will be charged per transaction. The services to be provided should be outlined in the text of the lease or should appear as an exhibit attached to the lease.

Landlord shall provide a switchboard operator to answer incoming calls of Tenant during the workday hours of 8:30 a.m. to 5:30 p.m., Mondays through Fridays. Tenant shall have access to the Secretarial Support Center. The charges for Secretarial Support services are listed on Exhibit A attached to this Lease.

Executive suite buildings may provide conference rooms that may be reserved by lessees. Some buildings may also include professional libraries, such as law libraries, that may be shared by attorneys who are sole practitioners and who would find the cost of a creating and maintaining a law library prohibitive. Rules for the use of common facilities should be included in the lease or as an exhibit to the lease, such as the following provisions.

Use of the switchboard system for advertising, promotion or toll-free numbers which solicit a high volume of calls is strictly prohibited. The additional volume of these calls and messages places extraordinary pressures on the system and detrimentally impacts the timely response to all Tenants. If it is discovered that the switchboard number is being employed for these purposes, Management will forward all calls to the Tenant's voicemail.

Use of the conference room is on a reservation basis, usually at least twenty-four (24) hours in advance. If the telephone in the conference room is to be used in connection with a meeting to be conducted therein, it is necessary that arrangements for use of the phone be made at the same time the room is reserved.

Additionally, any furniture, furnishings, and equipment to be supplied in the leased space by the lessor should be inventoried and each item should be set forth, including but not limited to such items as telephone equipment, desks, desk chairs, side chairs, credenzas, file cabinets, and pictures.

Warehouses

Warehouse or storage space leases often are less complex than shopping center or office leases. The amount of rent paid is small and the rental term short in comparison. No alterations are made to the premises, and maintenance is minimal. Unlike a retail or office situation, the lessee of warehouse space may be located out of state, giving rise to a concern on the part of both parties.

The lessor wants assurances that out-of-state checks will pass muster. The lessee wants assurances that a delayed rent check will not result in the sale of the stored property as damages. To minimize these concerns, the lessor may require the lessee to open an account in a local bank, may charge a fee for returned checks, or may simply charge a high security deposit. Further, the lessee may be given a specified grace period for late rent (with penalties, if desired by lessor) before a default occurs. The lease may also require that the lessor provide notice before taking advantage of any rights of distraint afforded by state statute.

A major concern of the lessor is the storage of dangerous or illegal items on the premises. Most warehouse leases include provisions forbidding the storage of hazardous or toxic substances, illegal substances, and animals on the premises, such as the following.

Tenant shall not keep anything within the Premises that would increase the insurance premium costs or invalidate any insurance policy carried by Landlord on the Premises, including, but not limited to, petroleum products, explosives, firearms, volatile or flammable chemical products, any toxic products, and any domesticated animals or pets.

Sometimes a lessee will rent warehouse space and attempt to operate a business out of the rented space, such as automobile repairs or customizing. If the zoning allows for such use, the lessor may be amenable to renting the space for this or similar purposes. In this instance, employees and customers of the lessee will be entering the premises, and the lessor should require employers' liability, public liability, and workers' compensation insurance as well as require an indemnity provision. Under no circumstances should a lessee conduct a business on the premises without the prior knowledge and approval of the lessor. A lessor may include a provision forbidding the conduct of any business, such as the following.

The Premises may be used and occupied by Tenant only for the purpose of storing and removing the personal property of Tenant. Tenant shall perform no other labor or service, or conduct any business of any kind whatsoever thereon. Tenant shall comply with the requirements of all constituted public authorities and with the terms of all laws, statutes, ordinances, rules, regulations and orders of all federal, state, county and city authorities, commissions, departments and agencies exercising jurisdiction over the Premises.

Paralegals may actively be involved with the drafting or reviewing of any of the leases discussed here. Commercial leases usually are negotiated more vigorously than residential leases, and lease forms found in office supply stores often will not suffice. A paralegal should use a commercial lease worksheet in both the drafting and reviewing of a lease. In drafting a lease, the worksheet will assure the paralegal that all important provisions are discussed with the client. In reviewing a lease, the worksheet will serve as a checklist of provisions that should be included, or at least considered, before signing a lease. A sample completed worksheet is provided in the hypothetical client matter that follows.

HYPOTHETICAL CLIENT MATTER

Sandor Commercial Group, Inc., is a client of attorney Ava Ross specializing in buying and revitalizing commercial properties. In the past Ava has drafted retail and warehouse leases as well as handled several commercial closings for this client. Yesterday Ava met with Robert Sandor, President of Sandor Commercial Group, Inc., to discuss a leasing matter. Barbara Hammond, her paralegal, was asked to sit in on the meeting. Having recently acquired a downtown office building, Robert plans to turn the building into executive suites and needs an executive suite lease drafted that can be used as a standard lease form for prospective tenants.

Robert has prepared a list of rules and regulations to be attached to the lease as an exhibit, and he has asked Ava to review the list to ensure that the rules are not in contravention with state law. He has also provided Ava with a tenant cost breakdown sheet to be attached to the lease as an exhibit, itemizing the breakdown of amenity costs, such as switchboard services, as well as move-in costs, such as switchboard programming and required deposits.

After Ava discussed the particulars of the executive suite lease with Robert, she asked Barbara to take Robert into the conference room to complete a commercial lease worksheet to be used in the drafting of the lease. This morning Barbara pulls the client file to begin drafting the executive suite lease. She reviews the worksheet, which reads as shown in Figure 17–1.

From a review of the worksheet, Barbara knows that the lease is to be a gross lease. This particular building has an underground garage secured by electronic gates. This garage will be used by the tenants, the parking lot spaces allotted to clients and customers of the tenants. The tenants will access the garage by using a garage door opener. Therefore, in addition to the security deposit, the landlord is requiring a garage door opener deposit.

The landlord will provide varied switchboard services, having the tenant select the option that best suits the tenant's needs. The offices will come equipped with basic office furnishings. These furnishings will be inventoried on an attached exhibit. Tenants will have access to a conference room and will be allowed to use it for eight hours each month at no additional cost. Tenants will not be allowed to offer secretarial, administrative, or support services that directly compete with those provided by the landlord.

Although Any State's residential landlord and tenant statutes prohibit provisions attempting to exculpate and indemnify lessors from all wrongdoing, Any State's commercial landlord and tenant statutes permit indemnification provisions as long as such provisions are not unconscionable. Therefore, a standard commercial indemnification provision will be included in this lease. Additionally, according to state statutes, a month-to-month tenancy is created automatically should a commercial tenant hold over after a lease term expires unless the term is renewed by an agreement of the parties. Thus, the holding over provision in this lease will parallel state law. From this worksheet, Barbara drafts the lease shown in Figure 17–2.

Once the lease is reviewed by Ava and approved by the client, the three exhibits shown in Figures 17–3, 17–4, and 17–5 will be attached to it: (1) an inventory of each suite's furnishings, (2) the rules and regulations of the office building, and (3) the new tenant move-in cost breakdown.

FIGURE 17–1
Commercial lease worksheet

COMMERCIAL LEASE WORKSHEET

DATE OF INTAKE:	March 23, 1998
ATTORNEY:	Ava Ross
PARALEGAL:	Barbara Hammond
CLIENT NUMBER:	2150
MATTER NUMBER:	0009
PERSON RESPONSIBLE	
FOR INTAKE:	Barbara Hammond
1. LESSOR:	Sandor Commercial Group, Inc.
2. ADDRESS:	1600 Adams Avenue, Suite 300
	Any City, Any State
3. TELEPHONE:	(000) 223-4455 FAX: (000) 223-4776
4. LESSEE:	Not applicable; preparation of standard lease form.
5. ADDRESS:	Not applicable
6. TELEPHONE:	N/A FAX: N/A
7. TYPE OF LEASE:	(A) X GROSS __NET __TRIPLE NET
	__PERCENTAGE __OTHER

FIGURE 17–1
(continued)

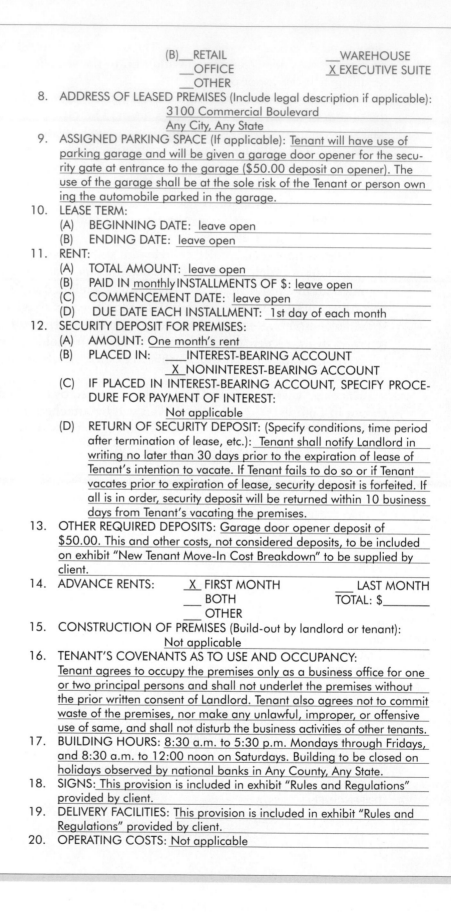

(B) __ RETAIL   __ WAREHOUSE
    __ OFFICE   X EXECUTIVE SUITE
    __ OTHER

8. ADDRESS OF LEASED PREMISES (Include legal description if applicable):
   3100 Commercial Boulevard
   Any City, Any State

9. ASSIGNED PARKING SPACE (If applicable): Tenant will have use of parking garage and will be given a garage door opener for the security gate at entrance to the garage ($50.00 deposit on opener). The use of the garage shall be at the sole risk of the Tenant or person owning the automobile parked in the garage.

10. LEASE TERM:
    (A) BEGINNING DATE: leave open
    (B) ENDING DATE: leave open

11. RENT:
    (A) TOTAL AMOUNT: leave open
    (B) PAID IN monthly INSTALLMENTS OF $: leave open
    (C) COMMENCEMENT DATE: leave open
    (D) DUE DATE EACH INSTALLMENT: 1st day of each month

12. SECURITY DEPOSIT FOR PREMISES:
    (A) AMOUNT: One month's rent
    (B) PLACED IN: __ INTEREST-BEARING ACCOUNT
                      X NONINTEREST-BEARING ACCOUNT
    (C) IF PLACED IN INTEREST-BEARING ACCOUNT, SPECIFY PROCEDURE FOR PAYMENT OF INTEREST:
        Not applicable
    (D) RETURN OF SECURITY DEPOSIT: (Specify conditions, time period after termination of lease, etc.): Tenant shall notify Landlord in writing no later than 30 days prior to the expiration of lease of Tenant's intention to vacate. If Tenant fails to do so or if Tenant vacates prior to expiration of lease, security deposit is forfeited. If all is in order, security deposit will be returned within 10 business days from Tenant's vacating the premises.

13. OTHER REQUIRED DEPOSITS: Garage door opener deposit of $50.00. This and other costs, not considered deposits, to be included on exhibit "New Tenant Move-In Cost Breakdown" to be supplied by client.

14. ADVANCE RENTS: X FIRST MONTH   __ LAST MONTH
                        __ BOTH   TOTAL: $_____
                        __ OTHER

15. CONSTRUCTION OF PREMISES (Build-out by landlord or tenant):
    Not applicable

16. TENANT'S COVENANTS AS TO USE AND OCCUPANCY:
    Tenant agrees to occupy the premises only as a business office for one or two principal persons and shall not underlet the premises without the prior written consent of Landlord. Tenant also agrees not to commit waste of the premises, nor make any unlawful, improper, or offensive use of same, and shall not disturb the business activities of other tenants.

17. BUILDING HOURS: 8:30 a.m. to 5:30 p.m. Mondays through Fridays, and 8:30 a.m. to 12:00 noon on Saturdays. Building to be closed on holidays observed by national banks in Any County, Any State.

18. SIGNS: This provision is included in exhibit "Rules and Regulations" provided by client.

19. DELIVERY FACILITIES: This provision is included in exhibit "Rules and Regulations" provided by client.

20. OPERATING COSTS: Not applicable

FIGURE 17–1
(continued)

21. UTILITIES PAID BY LESSOR: Lessor to provide air conditioning and heating for the leased premises and common areas in landlord's judgment sufficient to reasonably cool or heat the building and electric current for common areas and the leased premises (for details, see provision 27).

22. UTILITIES PAID BY LESSEE: All other utilities not included under provision 27 below.

23. INSURANCE: Tenant shall maintain, at all times during the term of the lease, workers' compensation and employer's liability insurance at legally required levels for the benefit of all employees entering the building. Tenant shall maintain at its sole cost and expense any and all insurance covering contents owned by tenant.

24. REPAIRS TO BE DONE BY LESSOR: All repairs to be done by landlord, as landlord deems necessary for safety, preservation or convenience of tenant or other occupants.

25. REPAIRS TO BE DONE BY LESSEE: None

26. ALTERATIONS TO PREMISES: Tenant shall have no right to alter, modify or improve the premises in any fashion.

27. LANDLORD SERVICES: (a) Landlord shall furnish the following services during workday hours of 8:30 a.m. to 5:30 p.m. on Mondays through Fridays, and 8:30 a.m. to 12:00 noon on Saturdays, inclusive on normal business days, except holidays observed by national banks in Any County, Any State: (i) elevator service in common with other tenants; (ii) air conditioning and heating for the leased premises and the common areas in landlord's judgment sufficient to reasonably cool or heat the leased premises; (iii) water for ordinary lavatory purposes; (iv) common use restrooms; (v) janitorial services during nonbusiness hours, except Saturdays and Sundays; and (vi) electric current for common areas and leased premises.
(b) Landlord shall furnish the following services during workday hours of 8:30 a.m. to 5:15 p.m. on Mondays through Fridays on normal business days, except holidays observed by national banks in Any County, Any State: (i) receive, sort and distribute mail; (ii) switchboard (tenant will select one of the following): switchboard operator to answer all incoming calls, tenant to answer incoming calls when tenant is on premises, tenant to answer all incoming calls. There shall be no abatement, set-off or apportionment of rent payable by tenant relative to the failure of landlord to furnish any of the services in paragraph (a) or the making of any repairs or maintenance.

28. RULES AND REGULATIONS: Tenant agrees that it, and its agents, representatives, officers, guests, clients and customers will comport themselves in a businesslike manner so as not to disrupt other tenants and will abide by the landlord's rules and regulations as set forth in an exhibit attached to the lease (exhibit to be supplied by client).

29. LANDLORD'S RIGHT OF ACCESS: Landlord shall have the right to enter the premises at reasonable hours to examine the premises and for the purpose of making such repairs, additions and alterations as landlord shall deem necessary for the safety, preservation or convenience of tenant or other occupants. No entry by the landlord shall constitute a breach of the covenant of quiet enjoyment, nor a retaking of possession by the landlord.

30. HOLDING OVER: If tenant remains in possession of the premises after the lease term, there shall be no tacit renewal of the lease, and tenant shall be deemed a month-to-month tenant.

FIGURE 17–1
(continued)

31. OPTION TO RENEW: This provision is not to be included in the standard lease form; client will negotiate this on an individual basis.

32. ASSIGNMENT: Not permitted without prior written consent of landlord.

33. SUBLETTING: Not permitted without prior written consent of landlord.

34. PENALTIES:
  (A) LATE RENT: If tenant has not paid rent by the 5th day after it is due and payable, then tenant agrees to pay an administrative late charge of $10.00 per day to landlord.
  (B) RETURNED CHECKS: This provision not to be included.
  (C) OTHER: Not applicable

35. SUBORDINATION: This provision not to be included.

36. DESTRUCTION OF PREMISES: This provision not to be included.

37. INDEMNIFICATION: Tenant shall indemnify, defend and hold harmless landlord against any expense, loss or liability paid, suffered or incurred, including attorneys' fees (at both the trial and appellate levels) as a result of any breach by tenant, its agents, customers or visitors of any agreement in this lease or as a result of tenant's use or occupancy of the premises, or the carelessness, negligence or improper conduct of tenant, its agents, customers or visitors.

38. DEFAULT:
  (A) SPECIFY CONDITIONS CONSTITUTING DEFAULT: Default in payment of rent or if tenant violates any covenant in the lease or rules and regulations set forth in the attached exhibit.
  (B) TIME PERIOD IN WHICH TO CURE: Tenant immediately becomes a tenant at sufferance and landlord shall be entitled to re-enter and retake possession immediately.
  (C) REMEDIES: In the event that legal action is necessary to recover possession of premises, rental payments, damages, or to enforce the provisions of this lease, tenant agrees to pay to landlord reasonable attorneys' fees (including the cost of any appeal), and all court costs and other incidental costs. If landlord fails to perform any covenant, term or condition of this lease, tenant shall recover a money judgment against landlord, such judgment to be satisfied only out of the proceeds of sale received upon execution of judgment and levy thereon against the right, title and interest of landlord in the office complex located at 3100 Commercial Boulevard, Any City, Any State, as the same may then be encumbered and the landlord shall not be otherwise liable for any deficiency. In no event shall tenant have the right to levy execution against any property of landlord other than the office complex described above.

39. ABANDONMENT: It shall be a default if tenant abandons the premises. Such abandonment shall not release tenant from the future obligation to pay rent for the duration of the lease, even if landlord shall retake the premises.

40. NOTICES:
  (A) TO LESSOR: Sandor Commercial Group, Inc.
        1600 Adams Avenue, Suite 300
        Any City, Any State
  (B) TO LESSEE: At the premises

41. ADDITIONAL PROVISIONS: (A) Condition of Premises: Tenant acknowledges that it has inspected the premises and all furniture, fixtures and equipment contained therein and further acknowledges that they are in satisfactory condition and accepts the premises, furniture,

FIGURE 17–1
(continued)

fixtures and equipment in their current condition "as is" without requiring landlord to make any repairs or replacement thereof. (B) Personal Property: Tenant agrees that any personal property brought onto the premises is done so at tenant's own risk and if any loss or damage occurs, landlord is not liable. (C) Noncompetitive Office Equipment Use: Tenant shall be allowed to place a typewriter, computer system, facsimile machine and file cabinet in the premises for the sole use of its business, and said equipment shall not be used to offer services to other tenants in such manner as to be deemed competitive with the Executive Office Support Services Center. (D) Conference Room: Use of the conference room is on a reservation basis, usually at least 24 hours in advance. For the first 8 hours of use each month there is no charge to the tenant; for each hour beyond that, per month, the charge is $10.00 per hour. (E) Furniture/Equipment: Landlord has supplied tenant with furniture and equipment for tenant's exclusive use during the lease term, as set forth on an attached exhibit. At the expiration of the lease term, tenant shall surrender all furniture and equipment in the same condition as when the lease commenced and be responsible for any damage, normal wear and tear excepted.

FIGURE 17–2
Lease

EXECUTIVE SUITE LEASE

THIS LEASE is made this _____ day of _____, 199__ , between _____, hereinafter referred to as "Landlord," and _____, hereinafter referred to as "Tenant."

WITNESSETH:

That Landlord hereby lets unto Tenant for a term commencing on _____ , and ending _____, the following described premises: Executive Suite(s) _____ located at 3100 Commercial Boulevard, Any City, Any State, hereinafter referred to as the " Leased Premises"; the terms and conditions of this Lease being set forth below:

I. RENT. The monthly rent for the term of the Lease is $_____ per month, being due and payable without demand on the first (1st) day of each month. In addition, Tenant shall pay any state sales tax or use tax, together with each payment of rent. If Tenant has not paid the rent by the fifth (5th) day after it is due and payable, then Tenant agrees to pay an administrative late charge of $10.00 per day to Landlord. Tenant shall also pay the following to Landlord:

$_____ paid the execution hereon as rent for the month(s) of _____, including sales tax;

$_____ security deposit;

$_____ one (1) garage door opener deposit;

$_____ total deposit.

II. SERVICES.

(A) Landlord shall furnish the following services during workday hours of 8:30 a.m. to 5:30 p.m. on Mondays through Fridays, and 8:30 a.m. to 12:00 noon on Saturdays, inclusive (except where otherwise specified) on normal business days, except holidays observed by national banks in Any County, Any State:

FIGURE 17–2
(continued)

(i)   elevator service in common with other tenants;

(ii)   air conditioning and heating for the Leased Premises and the common areas in Landlord's judgment sufficient to reasonably cool or heat the Leased Premises;

(iii)   water for ordinary lavatory purposes;

(iv)   common use restrooms;

(v)   janitorial services during nonbusiness hours, except Saturdays and Sundays; and

(vi)   electric current for common areas and the Leased Premises.

(B)   Landlord shall furnish the following services during workday hours of 8:30 a.m. to 5:15 p.m. on Mondays through Fridays on normal business days, except holidays observed by national banks in Any County, Any State:

(i)   receive, sort and distribute mail;

(ii)   switchboard (select one):

    ____ switchboard operator to answer incoming calls

    ____ Tenant to answer incoming calls when Tenant is on the Leased Premises

    ____ Tenant to answer all incoming calls

Tenant agrees to follow and abide by the Rules for the Communication System as attached hereto in Exhibit B and made a part hereto.

(C)   There shall be no abatement, set-off or apportionment of rent payable by Tenant relative to the failure of Landlord to furnish any of the services listed in Paragraph (A) above or the making of any repairs or maintenance.

III.   <u>USE</u>. The Tenant agrees to occupy the Leased Premises only as a business office for one or two principal persons and shall not underlet the same or any part thereof, or assign this Lease, without the prior written consent of the Landlord. Tenant also agrees not to suffer or commit any waste of the Leased Premises, nor make any unlawful, improper or offensive use of same, and shall not disturb the business activities of Landlord or other tenants.

IV.   <u>CONDITION OF PREMISES</u>. Tenant acknowledges that it has inspected the Leased Premises and all furniture, fixtures and equipment contained therein, and further acknowledges that they are in satisfactory condition and accepts the Leased Premises, furniture, fixtures and equipment in their current condition, "as is," without requiring Landlord to make any repairs or replacement thereof.

V.   <u>ABANDONMENT</u>. It shall be a default if Tenant abandons the Leased Premises. Such abandonment shall not release Tenant from the future obligation to pay rent for the duration of the Lease, even if Landlord shall retake the Leased Premises. Tenant shall, at the termination of said tenancy, quietly yield up the Leased Premises, together with Landlord's furnishings, if any, in as good and tenantable condition in all respects as the same were at the beginning of the Lease Term.

VI.   <u>DEFAULT</u>. It is agreed that if any default is made in the payment of rent as above set forth, or if Tenant violates any covenant of the Lease, Tenant shall forthwith become a tenant at sufferance, and the Landlord shall be entitled to re-enter and retake possession immediately. In the event that legal action is necessary to recover possession of the Leased Premises, rental payments, damages, or to enforce the provisions of this Lease, the Tenant agrees to pay to Landlord reasonable attorney's fees (including the cost of any appeal), and all court costs and other incidental costs.

FIGURE 17–2
(continued)

VII. **RULES AND REGULATIONS.** This Lease is subject to rules, regulations and control of Landlord, and Tenant agrees to comply with same as adopted from time to time. Tenant agrees that it and its agents, representatives, officers, guests, clients and customers shall at all times comport themselves in a businesslike manner so as not to disrupt, interfere or impair the ability of the Landlord and other tenants to conduct their business affairs. Continued violation of this provision after written notice from the Landlord shall constitute a default of this Lease. Tenant agrees to follow and abide by the Rules and Regulations as attached hereto in Exhibit B and made a part hereof.

VIII. **REPAIRS AND ALTERATIONS.** Tenant shall have no right to alter, modify or improve the Leased Premises in any fashion. Landlord shall have the right to enter the Leased Premises at reasonable hours to examine the same and for the purpose of making such repairs, additions and alterations as Landlord shall deem necessary for safety, preservation or convenience of Tenant or other occupants of the building. No entry by the Landlord or its agents pursuant to a right granted in this Lease shall constitute a breach of the covenant of quiet enjoyment, nor a retaking of possession by the Landlord.

IX. **SUBLETTING AND ASSIGNMENT.** Tenant shall not sublet, assign or transfer its rights under this Lease without the prior written consent of the Landlord. In the event of a permitted transfer, all covenants and agreements herein contained shall extend to and bind the heirs, personal representatives, successors and assigns of each party hereto.

X. **INDEMNIFICATION.** Tenant shall indemnify, defend and hold harmless Landlord against any expense, loss or liability paid, suffered or incurred, including attorneys' fees (at both trial and appellate levels) as a result of any breach by Tenant, its agents, customers or visitors of any agreement in this Lease, or as a result of the carelessness, negligence or improper conduct of Tenant, its agents, customers or visitors.

XI. **PERSONAL PROPERTY.** Tenant agrees that any personal property brought onto the Leased Premises is done so at Tenant's own risk and if any loss or damage occurs, Landlord is not liable.

XII. **INSURANCE.** Tenant shall maintain, at all times during the term of this Lease, workers' compensation and employer's liability insurance at legally required levels for the benefit of all employees entering the building as a result of or in connection with their employment by Tenant. Tenant shall maintain at its sole cost and expense any and all insurance covering contents owned by Tenant, if any.

XIII. **TENANT'S REMEDIES FOR LANDLORD'S BREACH.** If Landlord shall fail to perform any covenant, term or condition of the Lease upon Landlord's part to be performed and, as a consequence of such default, Tenant shall recover a money judgment against Landlord, such judgment shall be satisfied only out of the proceeds of sale received upon execution of such judgment and levy thereon against the right, title and interest of Landlord in the office complex located at 3100 Commercial Boulevard, Any City, Any State, as the same may then be encumbered, and the Landlord shall not be otherwise liable for any deficiency. It is understood that in no event shall Tenant have any right to levy execution against any property of Landlord other than its interest in the office complex as described above. In the event of the sale or other transfer of Landlord's rights, title and interest in the Premises of the office complex, Landlord shall be released from all liability and obligations hereunder.

FIGURE 17–2
(continued)

XIV. <u>**SUPPORT SERVICES/RULES AND REGULATIONS**</u>. The Executive Suite Support Services and Rules and Regulations are attached hereto by separate schedule and are incorporated into this Lease by reference.

XV. <u>**NONCOMPETITIVE OFFICE EQUIPMENT USE**</u>. Tenant shall be allowed to place a typewriter, computer system, facsimile machine and file cabinet in the Leased Premises for the sole use of its business and said equipment shall not be used to offer services to other Tenants in such manner as to be deemed competitive with the Executive Office Support Services Center.

XVI. <u>**CONFERENCE ROOM**</u>. Use of the conference room is on a reservation basis, usually at least twenty-four (24) hours in advance. For the first eight (8) hours of use each month, there is no charge to the Tenant; for each hour beyond that, per month, the charge is $10.00 per hour.

XVII. <u>**HOLDING OVER**</u>. If Tenant remains in possession of the Premises after the Lease Term, there shall be no tacit renewal of this Lease, and Tenant shall be deemed to be under a month-to-month tenancy. Tenant shall pay to Landlord an amount equal to the Monthly Rent stated in the Lease for each month or portion thereof Tenant remains on the Premises. All other obligations of Tenant under this Lease shall be applicable to Tenant during the period in which Tenant is a month-to-month tenant.

XVIII. <u>**PARKING**</u>. Use of the parking garage shall be at the sole risk of the Tenant or the person owning any automobile parked in the underground garage. The Landlord shall in no event be liable for any loss, destruction, theft or damage to said automobiles or property contained therein.

XIX. <u>**VACATION OF PREMISES**</u>. Tenant shall notify Landlord, in writing no later than thirty (30) days prior to the Lease expiration, of its intentions to vacate the Leased Premises. If Tenant fails to notify Landlord in writing as specified or vacates the Leased Premises prior to the Lease expiration, Tenant's security deposit will be forfeit. If, upon inspection by management, the Leased Premises is in good condition and all other provisions of this Lease have been met by Tenant, Tenant's security deposit shall be returned to Tenant within ten (10) business days after the vacation of the Leased Premises by Tenant.

XX. <u>**FURNISHINGS AND EQUIPMENT**</u>. Landlord has supplied Tenant with furnishings and equipment for Tenant's exclusive use during the term of this Lease as attached hereto in Exhibit A and made a part hereof. At the expiration of the term of this Lease, Tenant shall surrender all furnishings and equipment listed in Exhibit A in the same condition as when the Lease commenced and be responsible for any damage, normal wear and tear excepted.

XXI. <u>**NOTICES**</u>. Any notice, consent or other instrument required or permitted to be given under this Lease shall be in writing and shall be delivered in person, or sent by certified mail, return receipt requested, postage prepaid, or by Federal Express or similar overnight courier service, address (a) if to Landlord, Sandor Commercial Group, Inc., 1600 Adams Avenue, Suite 300, Any City, Any State; (b) if to Tenant, at the Leased Premises.

IN WITNESS WHEREOF, the parties have hereunto set their hands of the date first above written.

WITNESSES:

LANDLORD:
Sandor Commercial Group, Inc.

BY: _____
Agent/Owner

_____

Title: _____

_____

TENANT:

BY: _____

_____

Title: _____

FIGURE 17–2
(continued)

EXHIBIT A
SUITE _____ INVENTORY

The following is a list of the items contained in the above-referenced suite.

Description	Quantity
Executive desk(s)	_____
Executive chair(s)	_____
Credenza(s)	_____
Telephone(s)	_____
Waste basket(s)	_____
Side chair(s)	_____
Picture(s): list name,	_____
artist's name, and picture	
number for each picture below:	

_____
_____
_____
_____
_____
_____
_____

Tenant agrees not to nail, pin, or tape any items to the office walls which have been wallpapered.

_____   _____
Tenant   Owner/Agent

FIGURE 17–3
Suite inventory

FIGURE 17–4
Rules and regulations

EXHIBIT B
RULES AND REGULATIONS

1. Tenant, its officers, agents, servants and employees shall not block or obstruct any of the entries, passages, doors, elevators, elevator doors, hallways or stairways of building or garage, or place, empty or throw any rubbish, litter, trash or material of any nature into such areas, or permit such areas to be used at any time except for ingress and egress of Tenant, its officers, agents, employees, patrons, licensees, customers, visitors or guests.

2. The movement of furniture, equipment, machines, merchandise or materials within, into or out of the leased premises or building shall be restricted to time, method and routing of movement as determined by Landlord upon request from Tenant, and Tenant shall assume all liability and risk to property, leased premises and building in such movement. Tenant shall not move furniture, machines, equipment, merchandise or materials within, into or out of the building or leased premises without having first obtained a written permit from Landlord twenty-four (24) hours in advance.

3. No signs, door plaques, advertisements or notices shall be displayed, painted or affixed by Tenant, its officers, servants, employees, patrons, licensees, customers, visitors or guests in or on any part of the outside or inside of the building or leased premises without prior written consent of Landlord, and then only of such color, size, character, style and material and in such places as shall be approved and designated by Landlord. Signs on doors and entrances to leased premises shall be placed thereon by a contractor designated by Landlord and paid for by Tenant.

4. Landlord will maintain an alphabetical Directory Board on the ground floor lobby of the building containing one name of each Tenant. Additional listings will be limited to only those required by law.

5. Landlord will not be responsible for lost or stolen personal property, equipment, money or any articles taken from the leased premises or the building regardless of how or when loss occurs.

6. Tenant, its officers, agents, servants and employees shall not install or operate any refrigerating, heating or air-conditioning apparatus or carry on any mechanical operation or bring onto the leased premises or the building any inflammable fluids or explosives without written permission of Landlord.

7. Tenant, its officers, agents, servants or employees shall not use the leased premises or the building for housing, lodging or sleeping purposes or for the cooking or preparation of food without the prior written consent of the Landlord.

8. No additional locks shall be placed on any door in the building without the prior consent of Landlord. Landlord will furnish two keys to each lock on doors in the leased premises, and Landlord, upon the request of Tenant, shall provide additional duplicate keys at Tenant's expense. Landlord may at all times keep a pass key to the leased premises. All keys shall be returned to the Landlord upon termination of the Lease.

9. No space in the building shall, without the prior written consent of the Landlord, be used for manufacturing, public sales, the storage of merchandise or the sale or auction of merchandise, goods or property of any kind.

FIGURE 17–4
(continued)

10. Canvassing, soliciting and peddling in the building are prohibited, and each Tenant shall cooperate to prevent the same. In this respect, Tenant shall promptly report such activities to the Property Manager's office.

11. The work of Landlord's janitors or cleaning personnel shall not be hindered by Tenant after 6:00 p.m., and such work may be done at any time when the offices are vacant. The windows, doors and fixtures may be cleaned at any time. Tenant shall provide adequate waste and rubbish receptacles, cabinets, bookcases, map cases, etc., necessary to prevent unreasonable hardship to Landlord in discharging its obligation regarding cleaning services. In this regard, Tenant shall also empty all glasses, cups and other containers holding any type of liquid whatsoever.

12. Tenant will be responsible for any damage to the leased premises, including carpeting and flooring, as a result of rust or corrosion of file cabinets, roller chairs, metal objects or spills of any type of liquid.

13. Tenants employing laborers or others outside of the building shall not have their employees paid in the building but shall arrange to pay their payrolls elsewhere.

14. Tenant shall not make or permit any use of the leased premises or building facilities which, directly or indirectly, is forbidden by law, ordinance or governmental or municipal regulations, code or order or which may be disreputable or dangerous to life, limb or property.

15. Tenant shall permit Landlord or its agents to enter the leased premises to make inspection, repairs, alterations or additions in or to the leased premises or the building and at any time in the event of any emergency shall permit Landlord to perform any acts related to the safety, protection, preservation, reletting or improvement of the leased premises or building.

16. Landlord shall have the right to exclude any person from the building other than during customary business hours, and any person in the building will be subject to identification by the employees and agents of Landlord. All persons in or entering the building shall be required to comply with the security policies of the building. If Tenant desires any additional security for the premises, Tenant shall have the right (with the advance written consent of the Landlord) to obtain such additional service at Tenant's sole cost and expense.

17. In keeping up with the passing of the Clean Air Act of Any State, Management requests that there be no smoking in the leased premises, the lobby, the elevators, the restrooms or any of the other Common Areas.

Initials:

_____
Tenant

_____
Landlord

FIGURE 17–5
New tenant move-in cost
breakdown

EXHIBIT C
NEW TENANT MOVE-IN COST BREAKDOWN

I. AMENITY COST BREAKDOWN

Furniture	$ 0
Switchboard	$ 50.00 per month
One phone line	$ 0
Second phone line	$ 25.00 per month
Voicemail	$ 0
Parking	$ 20.00 per month, secured covered garage
A/C after hours and weekends	Available
Secretarial services	$ 0
Conference room	8 hours per month free; $10.00 each extra hour per month

Amenities	$ 95.00
Rent for Suite _____	$_____
Total Package	$_____

II. MOVE-IN COST BREAKDOWN

Switchboard programming	$140.00
Keys	$ 0
Directory listing	$ 0
Door signage	$ 0 (suite number and company name)
Security deposit	One month's rent
Garage door opener deposit	$50.00

One time move-in costs	$140.00
Garage opener deposit	$ 50.00
Security deposit	$_____
First month's rent	$_____
Total move-in costs	$_____

Initials:

_____
Tenant

_____
Landlord

CHAPTER SUMMARY

1. A gross lease is a lease in which the tenant pays a fixed basic rent and the landlord remains responsible for all operating expenses, whereas under a net lease, the tenant, in addition to paying a fixed basic rent, incurs a proportionate share of some or all of the landlord's operating costs.

2. A graduated lease is a lease that allows for rent adjustment (typically upward) over the term of the lease by tying the rent provision to the consumer price index or by providing an increase of a specified percentage of the annual rental payment.

3. A percentage lease, quite popular in retail rentals, requires that the tenant, in addition to paying a fixed basic rent, pay the landlord a stated percentage of the tenant's sales receipts (gross or net). A percentage lease

provision should include the requisite percentage figure, a definition of the term *sales*, the conditions under which the provision goes into effect (for example, after annual gross sales exceed a stated figure), and the manner of payment (for example, quarterly, annually).

4. A ground lease is a lease of vacant land for an exceptionally lengthy period of time, allowing the tenant to construct a commercial building on the leased land. The result of a ground lease is the separation of ownership of the land and the improvements to the land.

5. The basic provisions of a commercial lease are similar to those found in a residential lease. The parties, leased premises, rental term, security deposit, and advanced rent should all be specified clearly. The responsibility for utilities, repairs, maintenance, and insurance should be allocated. The conditions constituting default and the applicable remedies should be noted. In addition to these common provisions, commercial leases often include more complex rent payment and alterations provisions as well as provisions pertaining to business hours, signage, delivery facilities, parking, and rules and regulations of the building or center.

6. Of particular concern in shopping center leases are the build-out, parking, exclusivity (competing business), and business hours provisions. The parties should designate clearly the nature of the build-out work to be done, the party responsible for performing the work, and the allocation of expenses for the work. The parking provision should specify the number of allocated parking spaces per tenant and any parking restrictions. The exclusivity provision, if included, should be carefully worded to protect the tenant from direct competition while allowing complementary businesses. The business hours provision should emphasize uniformity of hours within the center and conformity with city and county ordinances.

7. An executive office suite provides a tenant with a professional atmosphere and minimal overhead costs. Rather than hiring full- or part-time support staff, the tenant has access to support services provided by the lessor. The lease should designate the preferred services and indicate whether the cost of such services is included in the monthly rent or is charged separately. Rules and regulations for the use of common business facilities should be included, and any furniture, furnishings, and equipment provided by the lessor should be inventoried.

8. Although warehouse leases typically are less complex than other commercial leases, certain provisions should be of concern to the parties. If the lessee is located out of state, a provision should be included in the lease to safeguard the lessor against bad checks while, at the same time, protecting the lessee (in the event of a late or lost check) from the lessor's self-help remedies. Further, the lease should include provisions prohibiting the storage of hazardous materials and, unless otherwise agreed, prohibiting the conduct of any business on the leased premises.

REVIEW QUESTIONS

1. Distinguish between the following:
   a. A net lease and a triple net lease
   b. A graduated lease and a percentage lease
2. What operating expenses incurred by a lessor might a lessee be obliged to pay under a triple net lease?
3. What advantages, if any, are there to signing a ground lease rather than purchasing a parcel of real property for the construction of a commercial premises?
4. What basic provisions should be included in a commercial lease?
5. What special provisions should be included in the following?
   a. A shopping center lease
   b. An executive office suite lease
   c. A warehouse lease

ETHICAL QUESTIONS

Sandra Gordon, an associate with your law firm, graduated from law school one year ago. Tim Benton, a senior partner of the firm, had originally placed Sandra in the family law department of the firm because of Sandra's experience with the family law clinic for legal aid clients that was run by her law school. Tim now believes Sandra should gain experience in other departments and has asked Sandra to work in the real estate department. Sandra loves family law and has neither experience nor interest in real estate; however, she wants to continue to work for this law firm, so she grudgingly accepts the reassignment.

You have been asked to work with Sandra as well as with your present supervising attorney. This morning Sandra met with a client who just purchased a small warehouse and wants a lease drafted for use with future lessees. Sandra hands you a copy of a retail center percentage lease and a legal pad on which Sandra has scratched a few notes, including the name of the client, the address of the warehouse, the size of the warehouse units, the required deposits, and the average monthly rent. She asks you to copy the retail lease verbatim and just insert the information on the legal pad. You inform Sandra that you have several warehouse leases on file that would be more appropriate than the retail center percentage lease. Sandra very sharply insists that you follow her instructions. You know that Sandra's inexperience will become apparent to the client if you follow her instructions and that the document will not best serve the client's needs. What should you do?

PRACTICAL ASSIGNMENTS

Assignment 17:1. Research your state statutes pertaining to the handling of security deposits by commercial lessors. Photocopy the relevant statutes and insert them under the "Leases" section of your resource portfolio.

Assignment 17:2. Research your state statutes to determine whether indemnity provisions may be included in commercial leases in your state. Photocopy the relevant statutes and insert them under the "Leases" section of your resource portfolio.

Assignment 17:3. Research your state statutes regarding the respective maintenance and repair obligations of commercial lessors and lessees as well as those statutes regarding a commercial lessor's rights of access to the leased premises. Photocopy the relevant statutes and insert them under the "Leases" section of your resource portfolio.

Assignment 17:4. Research your state statutes regarding the remedies available to a commercial lessor in the event of a lessee's default on a lease. Additionally, research your state statutes to determine the type of tenancy cre ated when a commercial lessee holds over at the expiration of the lease term. Photocopy the relevant statutes and insert them under the "Leases" provision of your resource portfolio.

Assignment 17:5. Your supervising attorney, Deborah Sanders, has met with a new client, Daniel Daventry, President of Daventry Properties, Inc. Daventry Properties is close to completion of an industrial park and ware house project named Daventry Industrial Park, and Daniel wants a lease drafted that he can use for all future industrial park and warehouse tenants. Deborah hands you a notepad with the particulars and asks that you draft the lease.

Daventry Properties, Inc., is to be the lessor of the project, which is located at 735 Baynham Drive (your city, county, and state). The leased premises of each future lessee will be described by bay number and square footage of space rented. Although a duration of term provision must be included, the actual term will vary from tenant to tenant, so blank spaces must be left for the commencement and expiration dates. Similarly, a general rent provision must be included, with the actual amount of the rent to be filled in at a later date. Rent payments are to be sent to the manager's office on the project premises, bay number 101.

The lessor will be collecting security deposits from each lessee, said deposits to be returned upon expiration of the lease. In addition to the minimum rent, each tenant shall pay (1) all utility services that may be provided to the premises, including but not limited to water, sewer, gas, electric, telephone, and garbage; and (2) all sales and use taxes due as a result of business conducted on the premises and personal property taxes assessed against the personalty situated on the leased premises.

The client wants a subordination clause included in the lease whereby the lease shall be subordinate to any mortgage upon the premises and in which each tenant agrees to execute any subordination documents required by the lending institution. Further, each tenant must, during the full term of the lease, carry workers' compensation, employers' liability, and public liability insurance in the following amounts: $100,000 each person, $300,000 each accident, and $50,000 property damage.

The tenants must keep the interior portion of the leased premises and improvements thereon in a good state of repair. No tenant may assign his or her lease or sublet the premises without the written consent of the lessor. No tenant will occupy or use the leased premises for any unlawful purpose or in any manner that may increase the standard rate of fire, windstorm, extended coverage, and liability insurance.

The lessor requires uniformity in signage and has the sole discretion to determine its material and size. The lessor, at its option, may order and install signs from one source at the cost and expense of the tenants. If the premises is partially damaged by fire or other casualty but is not untenantable, leaving not less than 60% of the leased floor space usable for the tenant's purposes, the lessor has the option to begin rebuilding of the premises with due diligence or to elect not to rebuild. Lessor must notify the tenant of its option within thirty days of the date the damage occurred.

Within ninety days from the expiration of the lease term, the tenant must notify the lessor in writing, sent certified mail, of its intention to vacate at the end of the lease term or renegotiate a new lease. If the tenant fails to do so within this time period, the lessor has the right to rent the premises at the expiration of the lease.

Failure to pay rents according to the terms of the lease shall constitute a breach, and the lessor may, at its option, elect to declare the entire rent for the balance of the term due and payable, may take possession of the premises and rent it for the account of the tenant, or may avail itself of any other remedies permitted by state law. All furniture, goods, and fixtures brought onto the leased premises by a tenant are considered security for the payment of rent. If the lessor must proceed to suit to collect rent, the tenant will pay a reasonable attorney fee and any costs incurred by the lessor.

Any trade fixtures installed by a tenant remain the property of the tenant and may be removed by the tenant at the expiration of the lease, provided the removal is done without damage to the premises. If damage is incurred by the removal, the tenant shall be responsible for the costs of repair. In addition to these provisions, the lease should include the standard boilerplate provisions. Upon completion and review of the lease, insert it under the "Leases" section of your resource portfolio.

Assignment 17:6. Define the following key terms.

graduated lease	net lease
gross lease	percentage lease
ground lease	triple net lease

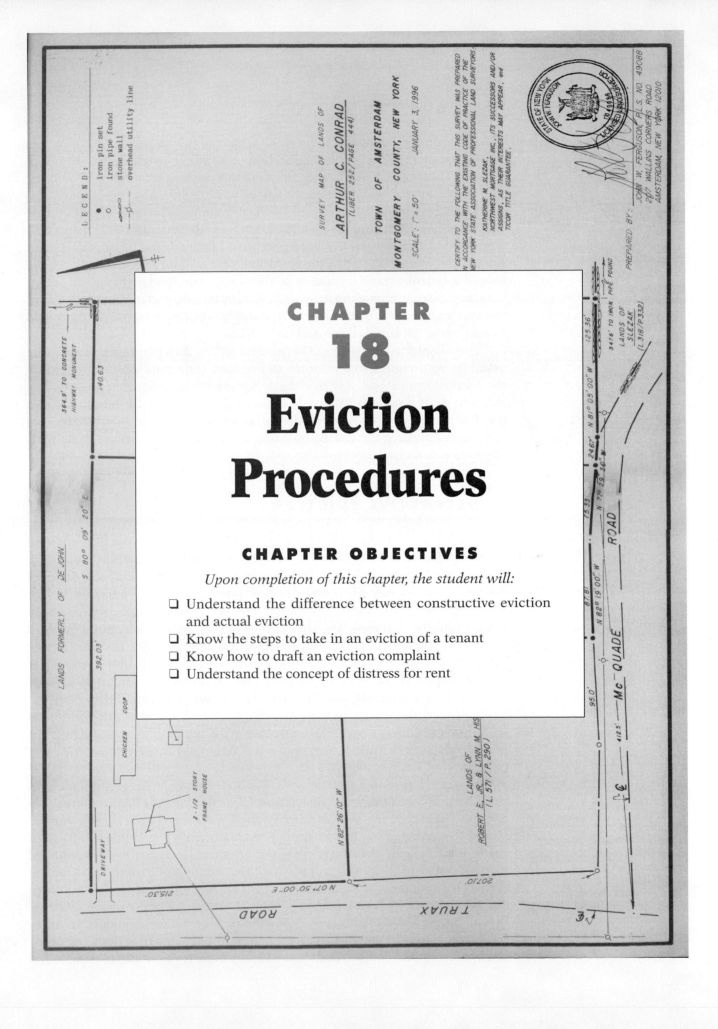

CHAPTER
18
Eviction Procedures

CHAPTER OBJECTIVES

Upon completion of this chapter, the student will:

- ❑ Understand the difference between constructive eviction and actual eviction
- ❑ Know the steps to take in an eviction of a tenant
- ❑ Know how to draft an eviction complaint
- ❑ Understand the concept of distress for rent

SURVEY MAP OF LANDS OF
ARTHUR C. CONRAD
(LIBER 252/PAGE 444)
TOWN OF AMSTERDAM
MONTGOMERY COUNTY, NEW YORK
SCALE: 1" = 50'   JANUARY 3, 1996

LEGEND:
● iron pin set
○ iron pipe found
⊸⊸ stone wall
--o-- overhead utility line

I CERTIFY TO THE FOLLOWING THAT THIS SURVEY WAS PREPARED IN ACCORDANCE WITH THE EXISTING CODE OF PRACTICE OF THE NEW YORK STATE ASSOCIATION OF PROFESSIONAL LAND SURVEYORS.

KATHERINE M. SLEZAK, NORTHWEST MORTGAGE INC., ITS SUCCESSORS AND/OR ASSIGNS, AS THEIR INTERESTS MAY APPEAR, and TICOR TITLE GUARANTEE.

PREPARED BY:
JOHN W. FERGUSON, P.L.S. NO. 49088
207 WALLINS CORNERS ROAD
AMSTERDAM, NEW YORK 12010

INTRODUCTION

The last two chapters have focused on the rights and obligations of parties to residential and commercial leases, both as set forth in statutory law and as set forth in the agreements made between the parties themselves. Should the landlord or tenant fail to perform as agreed or as required by state statute, certain remedies are available. Leases very rarely address the issue of a landlord's breach, yet a tenant may have a legal remedy available to him or her, should a landlord fail to maintain the leased premises, through the filing of a lawsuit for constructive eviction. A landlord has several more remedies available should a tenant breach a lease. A landlord may sue the tenant for breach of contract, may terminate the lease and evict the tenant, and in some states may, through an action for distress for rent, have the tenant's personal property sold to reimburse the landlord for back rent owed.

This chapter addresses each of these remedies. As a paralegal, you may be asked by your supervising attorney to research your state statutes regarding the legal remedies available to either a tenant or a landlord, or you may be asked to draft a notice of termination, an eviction complaint or a complaint for distress for rent, or a stipulation of settlement between the parties. This chapter emphasizes the procedural steps to be taken in securing a legal remedy for a default under a lease.

CONSTRUCTIVE EVICTION

To evict a tenant is to deprive the tenant of the possession of the leased premises. Eviction can occur through the bringing of a suit for possession of the leased premises by the landlord because of a breach of the lease by the tenant or because of the retention of possession of the premises by the tenant after the expiration of the lease. The bringing of a suit for possession is called **actual eviction,** and the procedures through which actual eviction are accomplished are discussed in detail in the following text. An actual eviction is distinguishable from abandonment or a voluntary surrender by the tenant. If the tenant abandons the premises, the tenant is considered to have voluntarily surrendered the leased premises. Further, if the landlord asks the tenant to leave the premises and the tenant agrees to do so, removing himself or herself together with his or her belongings from the premises, a voluntary surrender has occurred rather than an actual eviction.

In contrast to actual eviction, eviction of a tenant can occur through constructive eviction. **Constructive eviction** happens when the landlord breaches the lease in such a manner as to make the leased premises unusable for the purpose(s) stated in the lease. Through such a breach, the landlord, although not forcibly ejecting the tenant from the premises, is depriving the tenant of the enjoyment of the premises for which the tenant contracted. Constructive eviction can occur through either an act or an omission by the landlord directly or by one of the landlord's agents. In a case of constructive eviction, the tenant may bring suit against the landlord for money damages. In order for a tenant to claim a constructive eviction, the landlord's actions (or omissions) must appear to have been intentionally done (or omitted) to deprive the

actual eviction: The bringing of a suit for possession of leased premises.

constructive eviction: The breach by a landlord of a lease in such a manner as to make the leased premises unusable.

tenant of possession or permanently to interfere with the tenant's beneficial use or enjoyment of the whole or a part of the leased premises. A mere act or default on the part of the landlord without the requisite accompanying intent is not sufficient to constitute a constructive eviction. The intention to evict may be indicated by the nature and character of the landlord's actions.

In order for a tenant to claim a constructive eviction, the tenant must leave the leased premises within a reasonable time after the occurrence of the wrongful act. The timing of the vacating of the premises can be tricky. For example, if the landlord's breach is a failure to repair and the tenant vacates the leased premises before giving the landlord a reasonable opportunity to make the required repair, it is difficult to prove constructive eviction. The landlord may have had every good intention to repair the premises. On the other hand, if the tenant waits too long in vacating the premises, there is the problem of proving that the landlord's breach made the premises uninhabitable. After all, the tenant continued to reside in the premises after the breach! The burden of showing that the leaving of the premises took place within a reasonable period of time is on the tenant. What constitutes a reasonable period of time, therefore, depends upon the circumstances of each case. The question is a question of fact to be decided by the finder of fact (a judge in a bench trial, a jury in a jury trial). Delay in vacating the leased premises may be excused by showing that the tenant relied upon the promises of the landlord to correct the defects complained of. A tenant loses the right to vacate the premises if, before carrying out the intention to vacate, the cause for the constructive eviction has ceased to exist.

What actions or omissions may warrant the bringing of an action for constructive eviction? The interference by a landlord with the tenant's right of ingress and egress to the leased premises, such as by changing the locks or using a bootlock or similar device, may constitute a constructive eviction. The termination or continued interruption of water, gas, heat, or other utility service by the landlord, even if the utility service is under the control of the landlord, may constitute eviction. Failure of the tenant to pay for these services does not permit the landlord to terminate the services.

In those states that follow the Uniform Residential Landlord and Tenant Act, a tenant may, in an action for constructive eviction against a landlord for these violations, recover treble (triple) damages, plus attorneys' fees and costs. Section 4.107 of the Uniform Residential Landlord and Tenant Act states:

If a landlord unlawfully removes or excludes the tenant from the premises or willfully diminishes services to the tenant by interrupting or causing the interruption of heat, running water, hot water, electric, gas, or other essential service, the tenant may recover possession or terminate the rental agreement. The tenant may recover an amount not more than [3] months' periodic rent or [threefold] the actual damages sustained by him, whichever is greater and reasonable attorney's fees.

The Uniform Residential Landlord and Tenant Act also has safeguards in place to prevent a landlord from taking retaliatory action against a tenant who complains about a landlord's violation of a contractual or statutory obligation. Section 5.101 provides:

A landlord may not retaliate by increasing rent or decreasing services, or by bringing or threatening to bring an action for possession after (1) the tenant has complained to a governmental agency charged with responsibility for enforcement of a building or housing code of a violation applicable to the premises materially affecting the health and safety; or (2) the tenant has complained to the landlord of a violation of the landlord's duty under the Uniform Act to maintain the premises; or (3) the tenant has organized or become a member of a tenants' union or similar organization. If the landlord acts in violation of these provisions, the tenant is entitled to the remedies provided in Uniform Act Section 4.107 (recovery of possession or termination of rental agreement and recovery of damages) and has a defense in any retaliatory action against him for possession. In an action by or against the tenant, evidence of a complaint within [1] year before the alleged act or retaliation creates a presumption that the landlord's conduct was in retaliation, but the presumption does not arise if the tenant made the complaint after notice of a proposed rent increase or diminution of services.

The landlord may, however, bring an action for possession if (1) the violation of the applicable building or housing code was caused primarily by lack of reasonable care by the tenant, a member of his family, or other person on the premises with his consent, or (2) the tenant is in default in rent, or (3) compliance with the applicable building or housing code requires alteration, remodeling, or demolition which would effectively deprive tenant of use of the dwelling unit.

If the landlord makes every attempt to comply with his or her contractual obligations regarding the maintenance of the leased premises and finds that compliance within a reasonable period of time is beyond his or her control (such as in the case of fire or natural disaster), the landlord and tenant may agree to terminate the lease, or, in the case of a commercial tenant with a long-term lease, the landlord and tenant may agree that the tenant vacate and cease paying rent until such time as the premises are returned to a usable condition.

EVICTION PROCEDURES

A landlord may not retake possession of a leased premises unless the tenant abandons or voluntarily surrenders the premises, or suit for eviction is brought and a writ of possession is issued by a court. The procedure for evicting a tenant varies significantly from state to state. The time it takes to complete an eviction procedure varies as well, depending on several factors, such as the presence or absence of state statutes providing for **summary proceedings** (short and simple proceedings) and the actions taken by the tenant to defend his or her right to possession.

In addition, the Tenants' Eviction Procedures Act of 1976 mandates eviction procedures to be followed for residential tenants in government-subsidized, multiunit buildings. The purpose of this act is to ensure that residential tenants in government-subsidized housing are provided with reasons for termination in a proper notice and are informed of their right to defend themselves at a court hearing. As noted, self-help remedies such as changing

summary proceedings: Short and simple proceedings used to dispose of certain controversies.

locks or shutting off utilities will result in the landlord's liability for punitive damages. A suit for eviction may be brought against a tenant who has violated one or more terms of a lease or against a tenant who holds over after the expiration of a lease. The most common grounds for bringing an eviction suit are the holding over of a tenant or the tenant's failure to pay rent.

Holdover Tenants

Before a landlord can evict a tenant and retake the premises, the lease must be legally terminated. If neither party breaches the lease, then the lease ordinarily terminates at the expiration of the lease term unless the lease is renewed by the parties. If the lease is indefinite as to the term of duration, or if the parties have agreed that the tenant may continue on at the expiration of the written lease but have not entered into another lease agreement, then the tenancy created is a tenancy at will (recall the earlier discussion of this concept in Chapter 2). Either the landlord or the tenant may terminate a tenancy at will if proper notice of termination is given as required by statute (usually thirty days for a month-to-month tenant). The time required for the notice varies in length, depending upon the rental period involved. As a practical matter, the notice should be written and service of the notice should be made by personal delivery, by registered or certified mail with return receipt requested, or by posting on the premises. State statutes may dictate the form or contents of this type of notice. An example of a notice of termination of a tenancy at will is found in Figure 18–1.

More commonly, an original or renewed lease will have a definite expiration term. If the tenant remains in the premises after the expiration of the lease term without the consent of the landlord, the tenant is considered to have "held over." If an eviction proceeding is brought against a tenant who has

FIGURE 18–1
Notice of termination of tenancy at will

March 26, 1998

CERTIFIED MAIL #P223274556
RETURN RECEIPT REQUESTED

TO: Andrew Atkins
       Apt. 203, Camelot Apartments
       525 Lancelot Drive
       Any City, Any State

Notice is hereby given that your tenancy at will in the premises located at Apt. 203, Camelot Apartments, 525 Lancelot Drive, Any City, Any State, shall be terminated as of May 1, 1998, or thirty days after service of this notice on you, whichever is later in time.

Demand is made that you surrender the premises by 12:01 a.m. on that date.

Excaliber Luxury Rentals, Inc.
450 N.W. 9th Street, Suite 500
Any City, Any State

By: *Gerald Hargreaves*
       President, Excaliber Luxury
       Rentals, Inc.

held over, a landlord may not be required to provide notice of termination prior to filing a complaint for eviction. Nonetheless, it is good practice for a landlord to send a certified letter to the tenant prior to the expiration of the lease indicating the landlord's intent not to renew (see Figure 18–2). In this way, should the tenant hold over after the expiration of the lease term, the landlord has written evidence that the tenant is not continuing on with the consent of the landlord.

In some states, a landlord may collect double rent from a tenant who holds over after the expiration of the lease. In states allowing collection of double rent, the landlord must give the tenant notice of his or her intention to collect the double rent. The double rent may be requested as money damages as part of the eviction proceeding. If, however, the landlord accepts payment from the tenant in the amount agreed upon in the lease after the lease expires, double rent may not be collected.

Once the lease is terminated, a holdover tenant may be removed from the premises by initiating an eviction proceeding in compliance with state statutes. The process for bringing an eviction suit against a holdover is similar to that of bringing an eviction suit against a tenant who has breached the lease agreement. This process is discussed in the next subsection.

Eviction for Breach of Lease

In most states, a landlord must give a tenant the opportunity to cure a breach of the lease before the landlord can terminate the lease and begin

FIGURE 18–2
Notice of landlord's intention not to renew lease

March 26, 1998

CERTIFIED MAIL #P312100448
RETURN RECEIPT REQUESTED

TO: Dean and Pamela Hendricks
        Apt. 400, Ocean Breeze Apartments
        702 Wavecrest Drive
        Any City, Any State

Dear tenants:

This letter serves as a reminder that your lease of Apt. 400, Ocean Breeze Apartments located at 702 Wavecrest Drive, Any City, Any State, expires on May 31, 1998. Please be advised that Seaside Properties, Inc., does not intend to renew or extend your lease. The keys to your apartment should be delivered to the property manager on or before May 31, 1998, together with your forwarding address for return of your security deposit if the premises are returned in satisfactory condition. Should an inspection reveal any damages to the premises, the cost of repairs will be deducted from your security deposit and the balance of the deposit, if any, shall be returned accordingly.

Sincerely,

Michelle St. John, President
Seaside Properties, Inc.
800 Blue Water Drive, Suite 100
Any City, Any State

eviction proceedings. The landlord's first step is to provide the tenant with a notice of the breach and a demand that the breach be cured within a specified time period. The time given within which to cure will vary from state to state and may vary depending upon the type of action constituting the breach (for example, nonpayment of rent; failure to abide by the rules of the apartment building regarding pets, loud music, parking, subleasing, and so forth).

If the breach is something other than nonpayment of rent, a typical notice will inform the tenant of the violation of the lease; will demand that the breach be cured within the statutorily specified time period; will inform the tenant that if the breach is not cured within that time period, the lease will be terminated; and will warn the tenant that if the same or a similar wrongful action occurs within a year, the lease will automatically terminate without a further opportunity provided for cure. State statutes commonly provide that the notice be mailed, hand delivered, or posted on the leased premises. If the notice is mailed, the tenant may be entitled to extra days to offset the time it takes for notice to reach the tenant. An example of this type of notice is provided in Figure 18–3.

If the breach is not cured within the time period set forth in the notice, a second notice normally follows, informing the tenant that the lease is terminated and demanding that the tenant vacate the premises. State statutes may require that the tenant be given a specified period of time within which to

FIGURE 18–3
Notice of breach

TO: Lydia Richards
        Apt. 303, Jefferson Park Apartments
        1000 Jefferson Street
        Any City, Any State

You are hereby notified that you have breached your duties to maintain the leased premises located at 1000 Jefferson Street, Apt. 303, being occupied by you, as is required by Section 70.70 of the state statutes as follows:

1. Failure to remove all garbage from the dwelling unit in a clean and sanitary manner
2. Failure to use and operate plumbing and electrical facilities in a reasonable manner

In addition, you have materially breached paragraphs seven and twelve of the rental agreement. If these defaults are not remedied within seven days after the date of delivery of this notice, the rental agreement shall terminate on that date. If you remain in possession of the premises after termination, you will be charged double rent for any holdover period, as permitted by Section 70.102 of the state statutes.

                    Franklin Residential Leasing, Inc.
                    400 Franklin Avenue, Suite 105
                    Any City, Any State

CERTIFICATE OF SERVICE

I HEREBY CERTIFY that a copy of the above notice was delivered to the above-named tenant by posting on the premises on the 26th day of March, 1998.

Alice Franklin
President, Franklin Residential Leasing, Inc.

vacate once the tenant is formally notified of the termination of the lease, such as in the sample notice provided in Figure 18–4.

If the tenant's breach of the lease agreement is the nonpayment of rent, the notice procedure is similar, but state statutes should be checked because the amount of time allotted for cure may be different. Please note that federal statutes apply to public housing. For example, tenants in public housing must be given a fourteen-day notice for nonpayment of rent and a thirty-day notice for other breaches of the lease agreement. When counting out the days of the notice period, most states do not include the date of delivery of the notice in the calculation, nor do they include weekends and holidays. If the tenant receives a notice and cures the breach within the time period specified in the notice, the landlord may not evict the tenant.

Preparation of the Eviction Complaint

Should a tenant fail to cure and the lease is terminated, the next step is to begin an eviction suit. A suit is initiated by filing a complaint with the clerk of court. A landlord may hire an attorney to bring suit or may represent himself or herself in the matter. Many landlords believe that the expense of attorneys' fees will negate or exceed a judgment for back rent owed by the tenant. In turn, many attorneys choose not to handle evictions because the fees they can reasonably charge for such cases do not warrant the time spent.

Some attorneys charge a nominal fee to advise a client on the proper procedures to follow in an eviction, and the client then proceeds with self-representation. If the landlord believes that the tenant will fight the eviction, the case may become more complex and may be best handled by an attorney.

FIGURE 18–4
Notice of termination of lease

TO: Lydia Richards
        Apt. 303, Jefferson Park Apartments
        1000 Jefferson Street
        Any City, Any State

You are hereby notified that your lease is terminated effective immediately. You have seven days from delivery of this notice of termination to vacate the premises. This action is taken because of your failure to cure your breach of Section 70.70 of the state statutes and your failure to cure your breach of paragraphs seven and twelve of the rental agreement within the seven-day period allotted.

If you remain in possession of the premises after seven days from delivery of this notice of termination, you will be charged double rent for any holdover period, as permitted by Section 70.102 of the state statutes.

Franklin Residential Leasing, Inc.
400 Franklin Avenue, Suite 105
Any City, Any State

CERTIFICATE OF SERVICE

I HEREBY CERTIFY that a copy of the above notice was delivered to the above-named tenant by posting on the premises on the 4th day of April, 1998.

Alice Franklin
President, Franklin Residential Leasing, Inc.

Note also that if the landlord is a corporation, the landlord must be represented by legal counsel because a corporation is a legal entity separate and apart from its shareholders, directors, and officers and, therefore, cannot be represented by them in court.

State statutes may provide a statutory form for complaint and summons to be used in eviction proceedings and will indicate the court in which the complaint must be filed (for example, county court, circuit court). Therefore, when you are preparing an eviction complaint for a client, check state statutes first. The complaint should be filed in the county in which the leased premises is located. The complaint begins with the caption, naming the court in which the case will be heard, the case number, and the parties involved. The case number will be assigned by the clerk of court when the complaint is filed at the courthouse. Following the caption is the pleading designation, indicating that the pleading is a complaint for tenant eviction.

The body of the complaint should be double-spaced and may include one or more counts. The removal of the tenant from the leased premises and the retaking of the premises by the landlord is one count. If the landlord is also asking for back rent, this would be an additional count in the complaint. If the landlord is evicting a holdover tenant, the first count of the complaint would be a count for the eviction of the tenant, and the second count would be for money damages for the holdover period (for example, rent for each day the tenant remains on the premises after the termination of the lease, or double rent in states that so allow). A copy of any notice(s) delivered to the tenant and a copy of the lease agreement (if written) should be attached as exhibits to the complaint.

In closing, the complaint must include a prayer for relief that tells the court what relief is requested by the landlord/plaintiff. The prayer for relief typically includes a request for possession of the property, rent owed (if any), and court costs. If the lease agreement stipulates that a prevailing party in litigation is entitled to attorneys' fees, then attorneys' fees may be included in the prayer for relief as well. If a jury trial is desired, it must be requested. The complaint will be signed by either the landlord/plaintiff or the attorney representing the landlord. Some states require eviction complaints to be verified complaints. A **verified complaint** is a complaint that is signed and sworn to by the plaintiff, attesting that all allegations within the complaint are true to the plaintiff's best knowledge and belief. Have your attorney review the complaint prior to asking the client for his or her signature. Figure 18–5 provides an example of a verified complaint to evict a tenant for breach of a lease other than nonpayment of rent.

Before filing the complaint, make a copy for the client file, a copy for the client, and a copy to bring with the original to the clerk's office. The next step is to prepare the summons. As noted, state statute may dictate the form of the summons. The summons will inform the tenant/defendant of the suit filed against him or her and specify the time period within which he or she must file an answer. An original summons must be prepared for each defendant. The summons will be signed by the clerk of the court. All states require filing fees to be paid before a complaint is processed. Have a check for the appropriate amount cut, together with any sheriff's fees that may be required for the service of the complaint.

verified complaint: A complaint that is signed and sworn to by the plaintiff, attesting that all allegations within the complaint are true to the plaintiff's best knowledge and belief.

FIGURE 18–5
Complaint for
tenant eviction

IN THE COUNTY COURT FOR ANY COUNTY, ANY STATE

CASE NO.

WENDY S. MANNING,
    Plaintiff,

vs.

GLENN MURRAY,
    Defendant. /   **COMPLAINT FOR TENANT EVICTION**

Plaintiff, WENDY S. MANNING, sues Defendant, GLENN MURRAY, and alleges:

1. This is an action to evict Defendant from real property located in Any County, Any State.
2. Plaintiff owns the real property described as Apt. 301, Madison Apartments, 211 Greentree Lane, Any City, Any County, Any State.
3. Defendant has possession under a written lease agreement, a copy of which is attached hereto and made a part hereof as Exhibit A.
4. Defendant failed to comply with the terms of the rental agreement as follows:

    Defendant is operating a business on the real property in contravention of county zoning regulations and in contravention of the lease agreement.

5. Plaintiff served Defendant with a notice on March 13, 1998, demanding that Defendant cure the breach, but Defendant failed to do so. A copy of the notice is attached hereto and made a part hereof as Exhibit B.
6. Plaintiff served Defendant with a notice of termination on March 24, 1998, but Defendant has failed to vacate the premises. A copy of the notice of termination is attached hereto and made a part hereof as Exhibit C.

WHEREFORE, Plaintiff demands judgment against Defendant for possession of the real property and costs.

DATED: April 6, 1998.

        Wendy S. Manning
        Plaintiff
        607 Centennial Drive
        Any City, Any State
        (000) 444-9988

STATE OF ANY STATE
COUNTY OF ANY COUNTY

BEFORE ME, the undersigned authority, personally appeared WENDY S. MANNING, who after being duly sworn deposes and says she has read the foregoing complaint and it is true and correct to her best knowledge and belief.

SWORN TO AND SUBSCRIBED before me this _____ day of April, 1998.

        _____
        Notary Public, State of Any State
        My commission expires:

Most states allow a complaint to be served by either a sheriff or a private, court-approved process server. Ordinarily, the complaint must be served on the tenant personally, but posting of the complaint and summons on the premises may be permitted if several attempts at personal service have failed. Again, state statutes should be checked in this regard.

The time period within which the tenant has to respond to the eviction complaint varies from state to state. In states that permit summary proceedings, the time period in which to respond to an eviction complaint may be considerably shorter than the time period allotted for responses to other types of complaints. Once the tenant is properly served, one of several things may occur. The first possibility is that the tenant will contact the landlord or the landlord's attorney and try to negotiate. If the tenant's breach is for nonpayment of rent and the landlord believes the tenant is both willing and able to correct the breach, the parties may be able to reach an agreement and avoid eviction.

If an agreement is reached, it should be formalized in a stipulation. A **stipulation** is an agreement made by opposing sides in a lawsuit regulating a matter pertaining to the suit. From the landlord's perspective, the stipulation should include an acknowledgment by the tenant of the amount owed, set out an agreed-upon payment schedule for the back rent, and set forth the payments required to be made in the future until the expiration of the lease. The stipulation should further provide that if all payments are made according to this schedule, the landlord will dismiss the suit; however, if the payments are not made, the tenant agrees that the landlord may proceed with the suit. If state law allows, the stipulation should provide that if the tenant fails to make payment, the tenant waives the right to a court hearing and allows the landlord to proceed to summarily evict and retake possession. An example of a stipulation is found in Figure 18–6.

A second possibility is that after receiving the summons and complaint, the tenant fails to respond within the allotted time, or fails to appear at the hearing. Should this occur, the next step is to prepare a motion for default, requesting that the clerk of court enter a default judgment or order of judgment against the tenant. Once a default judgment or order is entered, state statutes typically allow the landlord to obtain a final judgment against the tenant as well as a writ of possession. A **writ of possession** is a court order issued to the sheriff ordering the sheriff to remove the tenant from the property. A sheriff's fee commonly is charged to have the sheriff execute the writ. State law may require that the writ be posted for a specified number of days before the sheriff can carry out the instructions in the writ.

A third possibility, especially if the tenant has other debts owing in addition to the back rent owed the landlord, is for the tenant to file a bankruptcy petition. As soon as a bankruptcy petition is filed, the tenant, as a bankruptcy petitioner, receives an automatic stay. The *automatic stay* is a court order that automatically suspends all proceedings against the petitioner until the bankruptcy petition is dismissed or the petitioner's debts are discharged by the court. The automatic stay commences at the time the petition is filed. Once the landlord is notified by the tenant or the bankruptcy court that the tenant has filed for bankruptcy, all actions by the landlord against the tenant must cease. The only action the landlord may take at this point is to request a *relief from stay* by filing a motion with the bankruptcy court. If granted, the bankruptcy court may permit the landlord to proceed against the tenant for back rent. Note that the automatic stay granted to the tenant by the filing of the bankruptcy petition only pertains to monies owed by the tenant up to the date of filing and does not include future rental payments under the lease.

stipulation: An agreement made by opposing sides in a lawsuit regulating a matter pertaining to the suit.

writ of possession: A court order issued to the sheriff ordering the sheriff to remove a tenant from leased property.

FIGURE 18-6
Stipulation

IN THE COUNTY COURT FOR ANY COUNTY, ANY STATE

CASE NO. 98-1303

MADELINE GRAYSON,
    Plaintiff,

vs.

PAULINE MILLER,
    Defendant.   **STIPULATION**

_____/

The parties to this action hereby stipulate as follows:

1. The Defendant acknowledges the sum of One Thousand Two Hundred Dollars ($1,200.00) to be due and owing to the Plaintiff.

2. In partial payment of the above sum, the Defendant agrees to immediately pay the Plaintiff the amount of Six Hundred Dollars ($600.00), and the balance of the above sum will be paid as follows: $200.00 due on April 13, 1998; $200.00 due on April 20, 1998; and $200.00 due on April 30, 1998.

3. Further, the Defendant agrees to pay the Plaintiff the sum of Six Hundred Dollars ($600.00) on the first day of each month as provided in the lease agreement. Defendant agrees to make these monthly installments in cash.

4. If all of the above-stated sums are paid as per this stipulation, this action shall be dismissed by the Plaintiff. If any of the above-stated sums are not paid as per this stipulation, the Plaintiff shall, upon the filing with the court of an Affidavit of Nonpayment, be entitled to a Writ of Possession and shall be entitled to a money judgment for any such payments as are in default. Defendant agrees to waive her right to a hearing on Plaintiff's application for said writ and application for money judgment.

Dated this 6th day of April, 1998.

_Madeline Grayson_____   _Pauline Miller_____
Plaintiff   Defendant

A fourth possibility is that the tenant files an answer in response to the complaint. In the answer, the tenant may include any applicable defenses. For example, the tenant may say that the landlord accepted the rent after serving the notice or filing the complaint, or may say that the landlord failed to maintain the premises and the tenant was withholding rent until the landlord made the required repairs. If the tenant raises the latter defense, the tenant must be able to show that notice of noncompliance with maintenance requirements was provided by the tenant to the landlord and that the landlord was given an opportunity to make the necessary repairs.

In some states, the tenant is required to pay into the court registry the rent owed before the tenant will be allowed to defend himself or herself in court. If the tenant disputes the amount owed, the tenant may pay the amount the tenant believes is owed into the registry. Once the complaint is answered, the suit will proceed to hearing and possibly to trial. If the tenant has paid money into the registry, the landlord may request those funds by motioning for a release of funds.

As in the case of a default judgment, should the landlord win the suit, a final judgment will be ordered in favor of the landlord and a writ of possession issued. A tenant is given the right to appeal, state statutes specifying the time period within which a tenant must file a notice of appeal. If a tenant files such a notice, a landlord may file a motion for a supersedeas bond. A **supersedeas bond** is a bond required when one is appealing a judgment. The amount of the bond may be set by the court to cover the amount owed to the landlord.

If back rent is owed, state law may permit a landlord to collect interest on the owed rent, the interest running from the date the rent became due until the date of judgment. To collect back rent, the landlord has several options; however, none of them may prove adequate. State law, while permitting the garnishment of wages to satisfy a money judgment, may also place restrictions on the wages that may be garnished. For example, in many states, the wages of the "head of household" are exempt from garnishment. *Head of household* may be broadly defined to include anyone who provides a specified amount of support to one or more dependents. If the tenant owns real property, a lien may be placed against the property. To do so, the landlord must obtain a certified copy of the judgment from the clerk of court and then record that judgment in every county in which the tenant owns real property.

Another method of attempting to collect back rent is to assert the **landlord's lien** on the personal property that the tenant has brought onto the leased premises and have the tenant's property sold to satisfy the judgment. Landlords, by statute, are given a lien on certain personal property of the tenant as soon as the tenant moves property onto the premises. The property covered by the lien may vary, depending upon whether the tenant was a residential or a nonresidential tenant. In residential tenancies, it is common for the lien to cover only property actually on the premises, and even then, some states may mandate that there are certain items that are exempt from collection (for example, personal property owned by the tenant up to the value of $1,000, beds and bedclothes). It often is difficult to ascertain what property falls within the category of property "usually kept on the premises."

The property must belong to the tenant before it is subject to a lien at all, and the landlord's lien does not attach until its title is in the tenant's name. For example, if the tenant has possession of property under a conditional sales contract, the lien does not exist. In nonresidential tenancies, state statute may permit the lien to cover all nonexempt personal property, whether located on or off the leased premises. Further, the general rule is that if the personal property is subject to a perfected security interest or lien before it is brought onto the leased property, the landlord's lien will be inferior to that lien, but it will be superior to those perfected or accruing after the property is brought onto the premises.

DISTRESS FOR RENT

In some states, a landlord's lien is enforced by a summary proceeding known as *distress for rent* (also referred to as *distraint*). This is a proceeding that is not part of an eviction proceeding but, rather, is a separate action to which some landlords resort rather than resorting to eviction. In

supersedeas bond: A bond required when one is appealing a court judgment.

landlord's lien: A lien given by statute to a landlord on certain personal property of a tenant.

common law, this term applied to the right of a landlord to seize a tenant's goods in a nonjudicial proceeding to satisfy the nonpayment of rent. Today, distress for rent procedures are regulated by state statute and require the posting of a bond before a sheriff will levy upon a tenant's property and prohibit the tenant from moving his or her property. In some of the states that do permit distraint, this remedy only pertains to nonresidential leases and has been specifically abolished with regard to residential leases.

As in an eviction proceeding, the initial pleading in distress proceedings is a complaint filed by the landlord or the landlord's attorney. The complaint is similar to an eviction complaint. It sets forth allegations of ownership of the property by the plaintiff, existence of a lease agreement, the amount of rent owed by the tenant/defendant, and a prayer for relief for damages. Once the complaint has been filed, the clerk of court will require the landlord to post a **distress bond** before issuing a distress writ. The bond must be made payable to the defendant, often in a sum at least double the sum demanded and conditioned to pay all costs and damages the defendant may sustain should the landlord's suit be found to be improper. The bond must be in a form approved by the clerk and, unless a cash bond is posted, must be with surety. An example of a distress bond is found in Figure 18–7.

distress bond: A bond posted by a landlord in a distraint proceeding.

FIGURE 18–7
Distress bond

IN THE COUNTY COURT OF ANY COUNTY, ANY STATE
CASE NO. 98-1310

HOWARD ROWLAND,
Plaintiff,

vs.

JOAN KING,
Defendant.
_____/

DISTRESS BOND

We, HOWARD ROWLAND as principal, and AAA SURETY COMPANY, as surety, are bound to Defendant, JOAN KING, in the sum of Two Thousand Dollars ($2,000.00) for the payment of which we bind ourselves, our heirs, personal representatives, successors and assigns, jointly and severally.

THE CONDITION OF THIS BOND is that if the Plaintiff shall pay all costs and damages that the Defendant sustains in consequence of the Plaintiff's improperly suing out the distress writ in this action, then this bond is void; otherwise it remains in force.

SIGNED AND SEALED ON this 7th day of April, 1998.

Howard Rowland
As Principal

Kenneth Alpert
President of AAA Surety Company
as Surety

Approved on April 7, 1998.

_____
Deputy Clerk of Court

Once the distress complaint and bond have been filed by the landlord, the court issues a **distress writ** commanding the sheriff to summon the defendant to answer the complaint. The court also instructs the sheriff either to collect from the tenant the amount claimed by the landlord as unpaid rent or to take custody of a sufficient amount of the tenant's nonexempt property to satisfy the claim if the tenant does not move for dissolution of the writ. The distress writ requires the tenant to serve written defenses to the complaint within the statutorily prescribed time period after service. The writ also enjoins the tenant from damaging, disposing of, secreting, or removing any property liable to distress from the leased premises after the time of service of the writ until the sheriff levies on the property, the writ is vacated, or the court otherwise orders. Figure 18–8 provides an example of a distress writ.

It is common for state statutes to allow a tenant to recover distrained property by posting a bond with the sheriff. Should a tenant fail to respond to the complaint, resulting in a default judgment, or should the matter be brought to trial, resulting in a verdict in favor of the landlord, the sheriff will be instructed to levy on the tenant's nonexempt property and sell it at a public sheriff's sale. The proceeds will be applied toward the payment of the judgment against the tenant.

distress writ: A court order commanding the sheriff to summon the defendant to answer the complaint in a distraint proceeding.

FIGURE 18–8
Distress writ

IN THE COUNTY COURT OF ANY COUNTY, ANY STATE

CASE NO. 98-1310

HOWARD ROWLAND,
      Plaintiff,

vs.

JOAN KING,
      Defendant.   **DISTRESS WRIT**
_____/

THE STATE OF ANY STATE:

To the Sheriff of Any County, Any State:

    YOU ARE COMMANDED to serve this writ and a copy of the complaint on Defendant, Joan King.

    This distress writ subjects all property liable to distress for rent on the following property in Any County, Any State: Apt. 205, Huntley Manor Apartments, 880 Guildford Street, Any City, Any County, Any State.

    The Defendant is enjoined from damaging, disposing of, secreting, or removing any property liable to be distrained from the rented property after the service of this writ until the sheriff levies on the property or this writ is vacated or the court otherwise orders. If the Defendant does not move for dissolution of the writ, the court may order the sheriff to levy on the property liable to distress forthwith after twenty (20) days from the time the complaint in this action is served. The amount claimed in the complaint is the sum of $1,000.00, with interest and costs.

DATED: April 7, 1998.

                                       _____
                                       County Judge

HYPOTHETICAL CLIENT MATTER

When Barbara enters her office this morning, she checks her tickler file to determine the priority of her tasks. She finds a reminder to call Jack Cameron, president of Cameron Properties, Inc., the firm's client, to find out whether a tenant delinquent in rent payments has paid in full or whether eviction procedures should be initiated. Cameron Properties, Inc., is one of the largest developers of residential rental properties in the state and a long-time client of Fisher, Ross, and Simon, P.A., owning eighteen residential rental properties throughout the state. Barbara's supervising attorney, Ava Ross, does not ordinarily handle evictions herself; rather, she advises clients wishing to initiate eviction procedures on how to handle an eviction themselves. However, the client in this instance is a corporation, Cameron Properties, Inc., which is considered a legal entity separate and apart from its owners and managers. Because only individuals may represent themselves in court, a corporate officer, such as Jack Cameron as president, is not allowed to represent the corporation in court. Further, Cameron Properties is an important, long-standing client; therefore, Ava has agreed to handle evictions for Cameron Properties whenever the need arises.

Jack Cameron had contacted the law office several days ago after receiving information from one of his property managers that a tenant, Lee Jeffries, was now two months delinquent in rent payments. When Mr. Jeffries was delinquent on one month's rent, the property manager attempted to contact him, only to find out that Mr. Jeffries was in the hospital for minor surgery. The property manager was informed that Mr. Jeffries would be bringing a check for the delinquent rent to the property manager's office as soon as he was out of the hospital. Mr. Jeffries failed to do so, and when the next month's rent became due, the property manager went over to Mr. Jeffries's apartment. Mr. Jeffries was not at home, but neighboring tenants confirmed that he was out of the hospital and that they had seen him recently. The apartment did not appear to be abandoned.

The statutory laws of Any State allow for summary eviction proceedings against residential tenants. The first step is the delivery of a three-day notice of termination, demanding payment in full of all rent owed or surrender of the premises. In Any State, delivery of this notice may be made in person or by posting the notice on the premises. Barbara had prepared such a notice, which was signed by Jack Cameron and posted on the door of Mr. Jeffries's apartment. A copy of the notice in the client file reads as shown in Figure 18–9.

Neither Barbara nor Ava have heard from the client since the notice was posted, so Barbara calls the client's office and is informed that Mr. Jeffries has not paid the delinquent rent nor surrendered the premises, and that the client wishes to proceed with the eviction. Barbara, in turn, informs Ava of the situation, who asks Barbara to prepare the necessary eviction documents. According to the file notes, the amount of back rent owed by Mr. Jeffries is $1,500. In Any State, eviction matters typically are heard in the county courts unless the amount in dispute is over $15,000. Because the property in question is located in Any County, the eviction complaint must be filed in Any County (the concepts of jurisdiction and venue are discussed in detail in the next chapter on real estate litigation). The

FIGURE 18–9
Three-day notice
of termination

THREE-DAY NOTICE

TO: Lee Jeffries
       350 Jacaranda Street, Apt. 201
       Any City, Any State

YOU ARE HEREBY NOTIFIED that you are indebted to the undersigned in the sum of $1,500, for the rent and use of the premises known as Apartment 201, Cameron Apartments, 350 Jacaranda Street, Any City, Any County, Any State, now occupied by you and that the undersigned demands payment of said rent or that you surrender possession of said premises within three (3) days (excluding Saturdays, Sundays, and legal holidays) from the date of delivery of this notice, to-wit: on or before the 10th day of April, 1998.

                          Cameron Properties, Inc.
                          1200 Commercial Avenue, Suite 300
                          Any City, Any State
                          (000) 222-8888

CERTIFICATE OF SERVICE

I HEREBY CERTIFY that a copy of the above notice was delivered to the above-named tenant by posting on the premises on the 7th day of April, 1998.

                          Jack Cameron
                          President, Cameron Properties, Inc.

---

forms accompanying the Rules of Civil Procedure in Any State provide forms for an eviction summons and an eviction complaint. These statutory forms are on file on Barbara's computer. She proceeds to access the form for a residential eviction summons and completes it as shown in Figure 18–10.

A case number will be assigned to the matter when the complaint and summons are filed with the clerk of court. The clerk will sign the summons and have it, together with the complaint, served upon Mr. Jeffries by a sheriff. Note that because the laws of Any State allow for summary proceedings for evictions, the amount of time the defendant/tenant has to respond to the summons and complaint is shorter than it would be in other types of litigation. In Any State, the defendant/tenant must respond within five days (excluding weekends and holidays).

Barbara next pulls up the statutory form of eviction complaint on her computer screen and proceeds to customize it accordingly. This complaint has two separate counts, or causes of action. The first count is for eviction of Mr. Jeffries from the premises and the return of the premises to Cameron Properties, Inc. The second count is for money damages in the amount of rent owed to date, plus the costs of bringing the proceeding.

In Any State, before an eviction is allowed, the court must be satisfied that the defendant/tenant is not a member of any branch of the military services of the United States. The court requires assurance that the defendant/tenant is not being deprived of an opportunity to come into court and defend himself or herself because he or she is away on a military assignment. Therefore, the complaint must include a statement that the landlord has knowledge that the defendant/tenant is

FIGURE 18–10
Residential eviction
summons

IN THE COUNTY COURT OF ANY COUNTY, ANY STATE

CASE NO.

CAMERON PROPERTIES, INC.,
an Any State corporation,
      Plaintiff,

vs.

LEE JEFFRIES,
      Defendant.

_____/

EVICTION SUMMONS/RESIDENTIAL

TO: LEE JEFFRIES, Defendant
       350 Jacaranda Street, Apt. 201
       Any City, Any State

PLEASE READ CAREFULLY

You are being sued by CAMERON PROPERTIES, INC. to require you to move out of the place where you are living for the reasons given in the attached complaint.

You are entitled to a trial to decide whether you can be required to move, but you MUST do ALL of the things listed below. You must do them within FIVE (5) days (not including Saturday, Sunday, or any legal holiday) after the date these papers were given to you or to a person who lives with you or were posted at your home.

THE THINGS YOU MUST DO ARE AS FOLLOWS:

(1)   Write down the reason(s) why you think you should not be forced to move. The written reason(s) must be given to the court clerk at Any County Courthouse, 2000 Justice Avenue, Any City, Any County, Any State.

(2)   Mail or take a copy of your written reason(s) to:
       Ava Ross, Esquire
       Plaintiff's Attorney
       Fisher, Ross, and Simon, P.A.
       1900 N.W. 3rd Avenue
       Any City, Any State

(3)   Give the court clerk the rent that is due. You MUST pay the clerk the rent each time it becomes due until the lawsuit is over. Whether you win or lose the lawsuit, the judge may pay this rent to the landlord.

(4)   If you and the landlord do not agree on the amount of rent owed, give the court clerk the money you say you owe. Then before the trial you must ask the judge to set up a hearing to decide what amount should be given to the court clerk.

IF YOU DO NOT DO ALL OF THESE THINGS WITHIN 5 WORKING DAYS, YOU MAY BE EVICTED WITHOUT A HEARING OR FURTHER NOTICE.

THE STATE OF ANY STATE

To Each Sheriff of the State: You are commanded to serve this summons and a copy of the complaint in this lawsuit on the above-named defendant.

DATED on _____, 19__.

                                   Clerk of the County Court

                                   By:_____

                                   Deputy Clerk

not a member of the armed services. After the complaint is reviewed and signed by Ava, Barbara will make photocopies of the notice of termination and the lease to be attached to the complaint as exhibits. The complaint and summons will be filed with the clerk of court, together with the appropriate filing fees and sheriff's fees. The completed complaint reads as shown in Figure 18–11.

FIGURE 18–11
Complaint for tenant eviction

IN THE COUNTY COURT FOR ANY COUNTY, ANY STATE

CASE NO.

CAMERON PROPERTIES, INC.,
an Any State corporation,
    Plaintiff,

vs.

LEE JEFFRIES,
    Defendant.   **COMPLAINT FOR TENANT EVICTION**
_____/

    Plaintiff, CAMERON PROPERTIES, INC., sues Defendant, LEE JEFFRIES, and alleges:

<u>COUNT I</u>

1. This is an action to evict Defendant from real property in Any County, Any State.
2. Plaintiff owns the following described real property in said county: Apartment 201, Cameron Apartments, 350 Jacaranda Street, Any City, Any County, Any State.
3. Defendant has possession of the property under a written agreement to pay rent of Seven Hundred and Fifty Dollars ($750.00) per month, a copy of which is attached as Exhibit A.
4. Defendant failed to pay rent due March 1, 1998 and April 1, 1998.
5. Plaintiff served Defendant with a notice on April 7, 1998 to pay the rent or deliver possession, but Defendant refuses to do either. A copy of said notice is attached as Exhibit B.
6. Defendant is not in the military service of the United States.

<u>COUNT II</u>

7. This is an action for rent which is past due.
8. Defendant owes Plaintiff the sum of One Thousand Five Hundred Dollars ($1,500.00) for past due rent plus rent accruing during the pendency of this action.

    WHEREFORE, Plaintiff demands judgment for possession of the property, damages for back rent against Defendant, and costs.

DATED: _____

                    FISHER, ROSS, AND SIMON, P.A.
                    1900 N.W. 3rd Avenue
                    Any City, Any State
                    (000) 232-7000
                    Attorneys for Plaintiff

                    By: _____
                          Ava Ross, Esquire
                          Any State Bar No.123456

If Mr. Jeffries fails to respond to the complaint within five days of service, the client can proceed with a motion for default against him, having a default entered by the clerk of court. Barbara prepares the motion for default and default shown in Figure 18–12, which will be kept in the file until the statutory time for a response from Mr. Jeffries has expired.

If Mr. Jeffries fails to respond and a default is entered against him, the court will sign a final judgment order, ordering the payment of the back rent and the surrender of the apartment. The court will also issue a writ of possession giving the sheriff's department the authority to remove Mr. Jeffries from the premises. Barbara prepares the final judgment order and the writ of possession the client wishes the court to sign after entry of default, both of which are shown in Figures 18–13 and 18–14.

FIGURE 18–12
Motion for default
and default

IN THE COUNTY COURT OF ANY COUNTY, ANY STATE

CASE NO.

CAMERON PROPERTIES, INC.,
an Any State corporation,
     Plaintiff,

vs.

LEE JEFFRIES,   **MOTION FOR DEFAULT**
     Defendant.   **AND DEFAULT**
_____/

    Plaintiff, CAMERON PROPERTIES, INC., moves for entry of a Default by the Clerk of Court against the Defendant, LEE JEFFRIES, for failure to serve any paper on Plaintiff or file any paper as required by law.

    I HEREBY CERTIFY that no copy of answer or other pleading of the Defendant in the above-styled cause has been served upon the Plaintiff.

                              FISHER, ROSS, AND SIMON, P.A.
                              1900 N.W. 3rd Avenue
                              Any City, Any State
                              (000) 232-7000
                              Attorneys for Plaintiff

                              By: _____
                                  Ava Ross, Esquire
                                Any State Bar No. 123456

DEFAULT

    A Default is entered in this action against the Defendant named in the foregoing motion for failure to serve or file any paper as required by law.

    DONE AND ORDERED at Any City, Any County, Any State, this _____ day of _____, 1998.

                              Clerk of the County Court

                              By: _____
                                Deputy Clerk

FIGURE 18–13
Final judgment

IN THE COUNTY COURT FOR ANY COUNTY, ANY STATE

CASE NO.

CAMERON PROPERTIES, INC.,
an Any State corporation,
      Plaintiff,

vs.

LEE JEFFRIES,
      Defendant.   **FINAL JUDGMENT**
_____/

    This cause came on to be heard before me upon the Plaintiff's verified complaint, and default having been duly entered herein, it is

ORDERED AND ADJUDGED

1. That Final Judgment be entered in favor of the Plaintiff against the Defendant for possession of the premises located at Apt. 201, Cameron Apartments, 350 Jacaranda Street, Any City, Any County, Any State, for which let Writ of Possession issue forthwith.
2. That the Plaintiff recover from the Defendant back rent in the amount of $1,500.00, together with costs in the amount of $75.00, for which sums let execution issue forthwith.

    DONE AND ORDERED at Any City, Any County, Any State on this _____ day of _____, 1998.

                                                     _____
                                                     County Judge

FIGURE 18–14
Writ of possession

IN THE COUNTY COURT FOR ANY COUNTY, ANY STATE

CASE NO.

CAMERON PROPERTIES, INC.,
an Any State corporation,
      Plaintiff,

vs.

LEE JEFFRIES,
      Defendant.   **WRIT OF POSSESSION**
_____/

THE STATE OF ANY STATE:

    To All Sheriffs of said State:

    YOU ARE HEREBY COMMANDED, in accordance with the Final Judgment entered herein, forthwith to remove all persons from the following described premises located in Any County, Any State: Apt. 201, Cameron Apartments, 350 Jacaranda Street, Any City, Any State; and to put the Plaintiff or its agent in full and immediate possession thereof, and to take with you the force of the County if same is required, after twenty-four hours notice conspicuously posted on the premises.

    WITNESS my hand and seal of said Court this _____ day of _____, 1998.

                                                       Clerk of the County Court

                                                      By: _____
                                                      Deputy Clerk

CHAPTER SUMMARY

1. Actual eviction refers to a lawsuit brought by a landlord for repossession of the leased premises after the termination of a lease. Constructive eviction refers to a lawsuit brought by a tenant for wrongful dispossession of the leased premises caused by the landlord's failure to maintain the premises in a habitable condition.

2. In order to be successful in a suit for constructive eviction, a tenant must first vacate the premises and then show that the landlord's actions were intentionally done to deprive the tenant of possession or enjoyment of the premises.

3. Landlords may not avail themselves of self-help remedies to remove a tenant from the leased premises. A landlord must follow statutory procedures for eviction. A tenant may be evicted only after the lease is legally terminated. A tenant may be evicted for holding over after the expiration of the lease, for failure to pay rent, or for breach of any provision of the lease agreement.

4. In situations other than one involving a holdover tenant, the landlord must give the tenant an opportunity to cure the breach prior to terminating the lease and bringing suit for eviction. The time period within which to cure is set by state statute.

5. Landlords and tenants, if individuals (not corporations), may represent themselves in court or may choose to hire an attorney. If the lease agreement so stipulates, a landlord or tenant represented by an attorney may be awarded attorneys' fees as part of the damages award should he or she prevail in the suit. Court costs also are awarded to the prevailing party.

6. Eviction complaints are similar to other types of complaints and include the court caption, separate counts for each cause of action, and a prayer for relief. Copies of notices sent to a tenant and a copy of the lease agreement should be attached to the complaint as exhibits. Some states require that eviction complaints be verified complaints.

7. To collect back rent, a landlord who is successful in an eviction suit may (1) attempt to garnish the tenant's wages, (2) attempt to execute judgment against any real property owned by the tenant by recording a certified copy of the judgment in each county in which the tenant owns real property, or (3) attempt to execute judgment by selling that portion of the tenant's personal property that is subject to a landlord's lien.

8. A distress for rent proceeding is a summary proceeding permitted in some states as a remedy for collecting rent owed. The landlord files suit, posts a bond, and obtains a distress writ ordering the sheriff to levy upon the personal property of the tenant, sell it, and distribute the proceeds to the landlord.

REVIEW QUESTIONS

1. What actions by a landlord constitute a constructive eviction?
2. What remedies are available to a tenant in a suit for constructive eviction?
3. Under what circumstances may a landlord retake possession of a leased premises?
4. List the steps to be taken to evict a tenant for breach of a lease agreement.
5. How does a distress for rent proceeding differ from an eviction proceeding?

ETHICAL QUESTIONS

While your supervising attorney is out of the office, Tom Hanson, another attorney with your law firm, knowing that you are a notary public, enters your office and asks you to notarize a document that he says needs to be filed immediately at the courthouse. You look at the document and see that it is a verified complaint to be signed by Donald Wilkinson. Donald Wilkinson's signature already appears on the signature line, and the client is nowhere in sight. You ask Tom where Mr. Wilkinson is, because you need to verify the signature before notarizing the document. Tom informs you that Mr. Wilkinson is out of town on vacation and that the complaint needs to be filed today to prevent the statute of limitations from running out on his cause of action, so Tom signed the document in his place and now needs it notarized. He tells you the client will not mind. What should you do?

PRACTICAL ASSIGNMENTS

Assignment 18:1. Research your state statutes to find your state's
a. eviction statutes.
b. statutory forms for eviction complaint and summons (if available).
c. statutes and forms for distress for rent (if available).
Photocopy the statutes and forms and insert them accordingly under the "Leases" section of your resource portfolio.

Assignment 18:2. Assume that you drafted the eviction complaint for Cameron Properties, Inc., set forth in Figure 18–11. Further assume that Cameron Properties, Inc., Cameron Apartments, and Lee Jeffries are located in your city, county, and state and that Cameron Properties, Inc., was incorporated in your state. The complaint has been filed and served upon Mr. Jeffries. Your supervising attorney tells you that Mr. Jeffries called the office to work out a settlement with your client. Your supervising attorney has spoken with the client, and the client has agreed to allow Mr. Jeffries to remain in the apartment under the following conditions: Mr. Jeffries is to pay $750 to the client immediately upon signing a stipulation and is to pay another $750 within ten days from signing the agreement. In addition, Mr. Jeffries must make all future rent payments on the first of each month in cash. If Mr. Jeffries abides by these terms, the action will be dismissed; should he fail to abide by any of these terms, he agrees to waive his right to further hearing, and the client may file an affidavit of nonpayment and obtain a writ of possession. Your supervising attorney asks you to draft a stipulation in accordance with these terms and conditions.

Assignment 18:3. Define the following key terms.

actual eviction	stipulation
constructive eviction	summary proceedings
distress bond	supersedeas bond
distress writ	verified complaint
landlord's lien	writ of possession

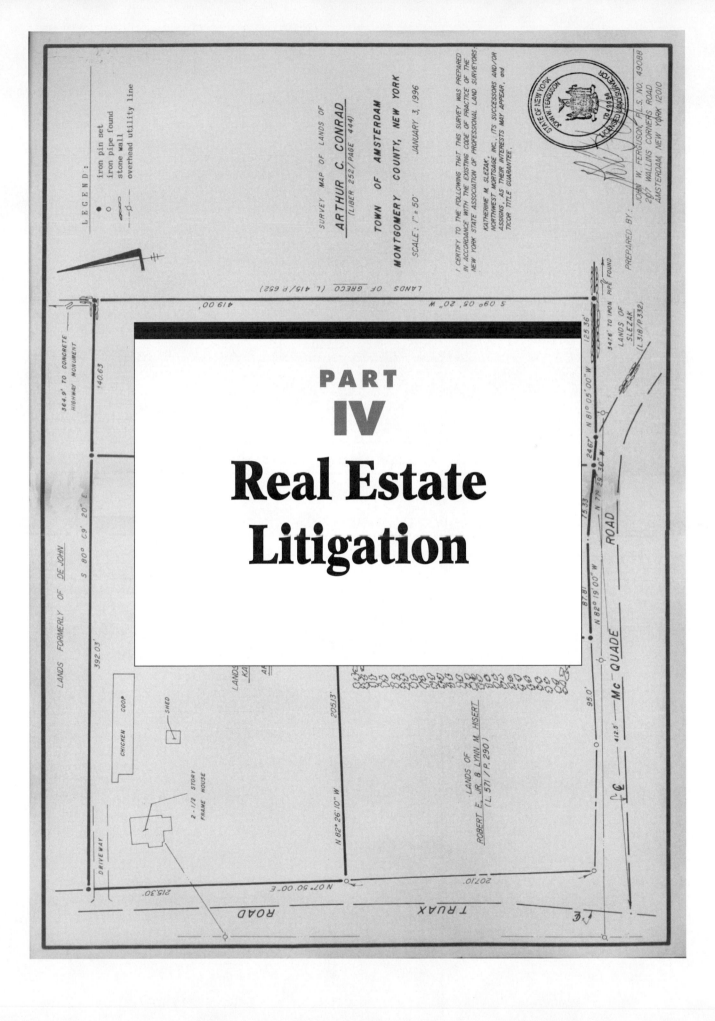

PART IV

Real Estate Litigation

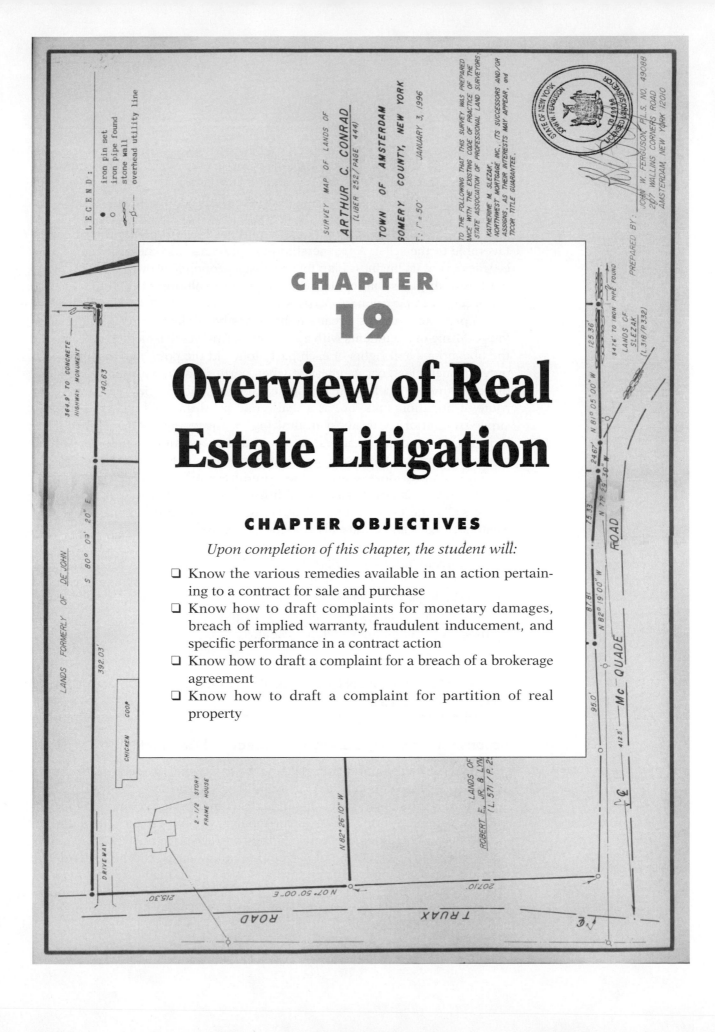

CHAPTER
19

Overview of Real Estate Litigation

CHAPTER OBJECTIVES

Upon completion of this chapter, the student will:

❑ Know the various remedies available in an action pertaining to a contract for sale and purchase

❑ Know how to draft complaints for monetary damages, breach of implied warranty, fraudulent inducement, and specific performance in a contract action

❑ Know how to draft a complaint for a breach of a brokerage agreement

❑ Know how to draft a complaint for partition of real property

INTRODUCTION

People enter real estate transactions with the best intentions. A couple may be buying their first home and, in so doing, engaging in the largest financial commitment they have made to date; yet they sign the contract for sale and purchase with positive expectations. A seller and broker enter into a brokerage agreement, both having the expectation that the broker will quickly find a buyer ready, willing, and able to purchase the property on terms most favorable to the seller. A partnership may purchase income-producing property as part of its business plan for increased economic growth, never imagining future disputes that could bring about a dissolution of the business and the necessity to partition property.

In previous chapters, great emphasis has been placed on careful, scrupulous drafting of documents with an eye toward preventive medicine, clarifying the obligations and rights of each party to avoid the possibility of future disputes. Nonetheless, occasions arise when parties clash and attempts to settle disputes amicably fail. In such instances, one or both parties may choose the route of litigation, and you, as a real estate paralegal, will be asked by your supervising attorney to assist in drafting or answering complaints, drafting motions, conducting legal research and discovery, and participating in all aspects of bringing the case to a successful resolution for the client.

This chapter does not attempt to address all stages of the litigation process, which is best left to a civil litigation course; nor does it attempt to address all areas of real estate litigation. Instead, it focuses on three areas real estate attorneys and paralegals come across most often: (1) litigation of contracts for sale and purchase and construction contracts, (2) litigation of brokerage agreements, and (3) partition of real property. A fourth area, mortgage foreclosure, is covered separately in the next chapter. This chapter discusses each of the litigation matters stated above by looking at the remedies available to the respective parties involved in the dispute and the steps to be taken in drafting a complaint on behalf of a client.

ACTIONS PERTAINING TO CONTRACTS FOR SALE AND PURCHASE

Actions for Monetary Damages for Breach of Contract

The terms of a contract for sale and purchase typically specify the amount recoverable by the nonbreaching party. Damages for breach by a buyer may be either the retention of the deposit; liquidated damages agreed upon in the contract for sale and purchase; a suit for monetary damages, the calculation of which will be the difference between the contract price and the fair market value of the property (this latter remedy is known as the **benefit of the bargain);** or a suit for specific performance (this last remedy is discussed later in this section). Should the buyer's actions indicate bad faith or actions constituting a tort (for example, fraud), separate causes of action may be brought in addition to the cause of action for breach of contract, and additional damages may be awarded.

benefit of the bargain: A monetary remedy in a breach of contract action calculated as the difference between the contract price and the fair market value of the property.

Damages for breach by the seller may be the return of the deposit; liquidated damages agreed upon in the contract for sale and purchase; a suit for monetary damages, the calculation of which includes the deposit(s) paid by the buyer together with interest, expenses of investigating title (if any), and the cost of improvements made by the buyer with the approval of the seller in contemplation of the conveyance; or a suit for specific performance.

As noted in Chapter 7, care and attention must be paid to the drafting of a contract for sale and purchase because the contract dictates the procedures for the rest of the real estate transaction. Poorly drafted provisions may come back to haunt a client and his or her counsel should the client find the other party has breached the contract. For example, the parties to the contract may have agreed that retention (or, conversely, return) of the deposit will be the sole remedy of the parties in the event of breach. Suppose, in this instance, that the contract requires an initial deposit upon signing of the contract and an additional deposit fifteen days later. Suppose further that the buyer breaches the contract and refuses to make the additional deposit. Is the seller entitled to the additional deposit as damages for breach, or is the seller only entitled to that portion of the deposit that has already been paid?

The answer to this question can sometimes be determined by the wording of the remedies provision of the contract for sale and purchase. However, where the remedies provision simply mentions "deposit" and does not provide greater detail, it is quite possible for the court to find that the seller is entitled only to that portion of the deposit that has been paid by the buyer.

Similarly, great care must be given to the drafting of a liquidated damages provision to prevent a court from interpreting it as a penalty provision that is unenforceable against the breaching party. **Liquidated damages** are damages the amount of which represents a reasonable sum to be paid to the nonbreaching party for damages suffered as a result of the breach of contract for sale and purchase. For a liquidated damages provision to be upheld, the first requirement is that the damages suffered must be difficult to compute with any degree of certainty, thus causing the parties to agree upon the stipulated sum. For example, suppose the seller is a developer and the contract calls for a particular model of home to be built on the real property within a specified period of time. It may be difficult to calculate with any degree of certainty the amount of damages suffered by a buyer if the construction is delayed, so the parties may agree to a stipulated sum as liquidated damages for each day of delay.

The second requirement for upholding a liquidated damages provision is that the stipulated sum must not be grossly disproportionate to the amount of damages that one would reasonably expect to be suffered as a result of the breach. Take note that if the remedies provision of a contract for sale and purchase includes both a liquidated damages clause and a clause that allows the nonbreaching party to bring suit for monetary damages, there is great likelihood that the liquidated damages clause will be construed as a penalty because the inclusion of the option of bringing suit for monetary damages implies that the parties believe actual monetary damages can be ascertained. It follows, then, that if actual monetary damages can be ascertained, there is no need for a liquidated damages provision, which implies that actual damages are difficult to ascertain.

liquidated damages:
Damages the amount of which represents a reasonable sum to be paid to the nonbreaching party for damages suffered as a result of a breach of contract.

In circumstances in which a suit to recover monetary damages is a viable option, a court generally awards a successful seller-plaintiff the difference between the contract price for the real property and the current fair market value of the property. Current fair market value ordinarily is determined by the testimony of a property appraiser who will evaluate the property in question against the recent selling price of other comparable properties. For example, suppose an appraiser testifies that properties comparable to the property in question have currently sold for $265,000. Suppose further that the buyer, under contract, agreed to a purchase price of $310,000. A court finding for the seller would award the seller a sum of $45,000, even though the property may be worth only $265,000 on today's market, because the court will give the seller the benefit of the bargain agreed upon by the parties. If the buyer made a bad bargain and agreed to pay a sum now found to be higher than the current fair market value, that is the buyer's loss. The seller is entitled to that for which he or she bargained.

A successful plaintiff-buyer in a suit for monetary damages will be awarded the return of any deposits paid, together with interest, and the costs for expenses incurred. For example, suppose a buyer contracted with a seller and paid the seller a $20,000 deposit at the time of executing the contract. Suppose further that the buyer hired an attorney to conduct a title examination (the attorney charges $200 for this service), hired a landscape architect (with the express approval of the seller) to prepare a landscape plan (the landscape architect charges $150 for this service, this charge to be applied toward the actual landscaping should the buyer hire the landscape architect for the job), and so forth. The buyer would be able to recover the $20,000 deposit, plus accrued interest at the current rate of interest, the title examination fee, the landscape architect fee, and any other costs and expenses reasonably incurred in reliance on the seller's contractual promise to close the transaction. **Punitive damages** (damages designed to punish or to serve as an example) generally are not recoverable in a breach of contract action except in special circumstances (for example, fraud).

In addition to monetary damages, the plaintiff may be entitled to attorneys' fees as the prevailing party. An attorneys' fees provision is often included in a contract for sale and purchase. Under contract law, attorneys' fees may not be recovered by the prevailing party from the losing party unless the contract so provides. If attorneys' fees are recoverable according to the contract, the complaint for breach of contract should include a statement that the plaintiff had to hire counsel as a result of the defendant's breach and, therefore, the plaintiff is entitled to attorneys' fees. For recovery of these fees, the court may require testimony from expert witnesses as to the reasonableness of the fees. Once a judgment is obtained in favor of the plaintiff, an affidavit of proof of fees will be submitted by the plaintiff's counsel.

Prior to drafting a complaint for breach of contract for sale and purchase, proper jurisdiction must be determined. **Jurisdiction** refers to the authority of a court to hear a matter. Courts must have proper **subject matter jurisdiction** (jurisdiction over the subject matter of the litigation, in this instance, money) as well as *personal jurisdiction*, also referred to as **in personam jurisdiction** (jurisdiction over the persons involved in the litigation). In some states, jurisdiction for contract rights affecting title to real property may be in the county in which the real property is located.

punitive damages: Damages designed to punish or serve as an example.

jurisdiction: The authority of a court to hear a matter.

subject matter jurisdiction: Jurisdiction over the subject matter of the litigation.

in personam jurisdiction: Jurisdiction over the persons involved in litigation.

Lawsuits for monetary damages are lawsuits for **legal remedies,** brought in courts of law, whereas lawsuits for **equitable remedies** (remedies administered according to fairness, such as injunctions and actions for specific performance) are brought in courts of equity. In determining which court of law has proper subject matter jurisdiction over the suit, the amount of the damages in question typically is central. Courts of law are divided into a hierarchy of levels, determined by jurisdictional amount. For example, a small claims court in a particular state may hear cases that do not exceed $3,000, the county court may hear cases that exceed $3,000 but do not exceed $15,000, and the circuit court may hear cases that exceed $15,000. To determine proper subject matter jurisdiction, the contract must be reviewed to determine the purchase price and to determine any amounts already paid by the defendant as deposits.

A court has personal jurisdiction over the plaintiff because the plaintiff, by initiating the lawsuit, gives the court power over him or her. A court acquires personal jurisdiction over a defendant by **service of process** (the serving of a summons and the complaint upon the defendant by a sheriff or court-approved process server).

The next step is to determine appropriate venue. **Venue** refers to the proper location to bring the suit. State statutes dictate appropriate venue for various types of lawsuits. In breach of contract actions, proper venue ordinarily is either the county in which the defendant resides, the county in which the contract was executed, or the county in which the contract was breached. Since venue statutes vary from state to state, however, your state's statutes should be checked.

The terms of the contract for sale and purchase should be scrutinized to determine the obligations of the parties, the timing of those obligations, and any conditions placed on those obligations. For example, a contract may stipulate that the buyer's obligations are subject to the buyer obtaining a fixed mortgage in a specified amount at a specified fixed rate within a specified period of time. The contract may further state that if the buyer fails to acquire a mortgage loan meeting these specifications, the buyer may be released from the contract and all deposits are to be returned. If the provision says nothing about the buyer having to use his or her "best efforts" to acquire financing, nor specifies that the buyer has to make application for a mortgage loan within a specified number of days after the signing of the contract, the buyer's exact obligations are uncertain. How much effort must the buyer make to secure financing? If the buyer goes through the motions but makes little effort, the buyer, under the terms of this provision, may not be in breach if the buyer fails to obtain financing within the specified time period.

In another example, suppose a title examination shows red flags such as judgment liens and construction liens against the property. If the contract states that the seller has a specified period of time after being informed of such defects to correct the same, the buyer must allow the seller the opportunity to cure, even if it delays closing, as long as such delay is within the time period specified for cure of title defects. If the buyer does not do so and refuses to close, the buyer will be in breach of contract. Thus, every provision must be scrutinized in this manner. A copy of the contract for sale and purchase should be attached to the complaint as an exhibit. If a jury trial is desired, this must be specifically requested.

legal remedies: Remedies awarded in courts of law, such as monetary damages.

equitable remedies: Remedies administered according to fairness, such as injunctions or actions for specific performance.

service of process: The serving of a summons and complaint upon the defendant by a sheriff or court-approved process server.

venue: The proper location to bring a lawsuit.

A complaint for breach of contract of sale and purchase must contain the following:

1. Jurisdictional facts
2. The existence of a contract for sale and purchase (attach a copy as an exhibit to the complaint)
3. Breach of the contract by the defendant
4. Allegations establishing the plaintiff's full performance under the contract, or a statement that the plaintiff is ready, willing, and able to perform under the contract
5. Damages sustained by plaintiff as a result of defendant's breach
6. If attorneys' fees are recoverable, the necessity of plaintiff's having to employ legal counsel to bring this action
7. Prayer for relief
8. Signature of the attorney

Just as in any other type of litigation, when drafting a complaint, a summons form should also be prepared for the clerk of court's signature when the complaint is filed. A check for the appropriate filing fees must be included when filing the complaint. A case number will be assigned to the case by the clerk of the court. When a lawsuit is brought for monetary damages, a notice of lis pendens should not be filed. Recall from Chapter 9 that a notice of lis pendens is a notice that is recorded when a lawsuit affects title to a particular parcel of property, putting third parties on notice that the property is the subject matter of litigation. The notice is recorded in the county in which the real property is located. In a suit for monetary damages, the title to the real property contracted for is not affected. The only dispute is whether money is owed to one party and, if so, how much. Figure 19–1 provides an example of a complaint for breach of a contract for sale and purchase.

In his or her answer to the complaint, the defendant may attempt to raise one or more defenses to the action. If the plaintiff has waited too long to file suit, the defendant may raise the *statute of limitations* as a defense. The statute of limitations places limits on the time period in which suit may be brought on various matters. Each state has its own statute, and thus state law should be checked. The statute of limitations is an absolute defense, regardless of the worthiness of the plaintiff's cause.

Another possible defense is that the contract is unenforceable. If, for example, the plaintiff and the defendant had an oral contract for the sale and purchase of the real property, an oral contract would be unenforceable because, as noted in Chapter 7, the statute of frauds dictates that a contract pertaining to an interest in real property must be supported by a writing in order to be enforceable. Another defense that might be raised is that certain conditions precedent have not been met by the opposing party, and therefore, the defendant is not yet obligated to perform under the contract.

A defendant may also include in his or her answer to the complaint a counterclaim for breach of contract against the plaintiff, alleging that the plaintiff breached the contract, not the defendant. The counterclaim must include all of the allegations found in a breach of contract suit.

FIGURE 19–1
Complaint for breach of
contract for sale and
purchase

IN THE CIRCUIT COURT OF THE FOURTH JUDICIAL CIRCUIT
IN AND FOR ANY COUNTY, ANY STATE

CASE NO. 98-1350

PAUL GRANT and
CAROLINE GRANT,
     Plaintiffs,

vs.

SIMON PAYSON and
FELICIA PAYSON,
     Defendants.   **COMPLAINT**
_____/

    COME NOW the Plaintiffs, PAUL GRANT and CAROLINE GRANT, by and through their undersigned counsel, and sue the Defendants, SIMON PAYSON and FELICIA PAYSON, and allege as follows:

1. This is an action for damages in excess of Fifteen Thousand Dollars ($15,000.00).
2. On or about the 12th day of January, 1998, in Any County, Any State, Plaintiffs and Defendants entered into and executed a written contract for sale and purchase of real property located in Any City, Any State, a copy of which is attached hereto and made a part hereof as Exhibit A.
3. All conditions precedent to bringing this cause of action have occurred.
4. On or about March 29,1998, the Plaintiffs tendered a deed to the subject real property to the Defendants and requested them to make the payments required of them according to the terms of said contract, which Defendants refused to do.
5. As a result of their failure to close and accept the deed, the Plaintiffs have been damaged in an amount in excess of Fifteen Thousand Dollars ($15,000.00).
6. As a result of their failure to close and accept the deed, the Plaintiffs have been forced to hire an attorney to bring this action and to pay their attorney a reasonable fee for her services herein.

    WHEREFORE, Plaintiffs demand judgment against the Defendants for a sum in excess of $15,000.00 together with court costs and a reasonable attorney's fee.

DATED: April 14, 1998.

                     FISHER, ROSS, AND SIMON, P.A.
                     1900 N.W. 3rd Avenue
                     Any City, Any State
                     (000) 232-7000
                     Attorneys for Plaintiffs

                     By: _____
                          Ava Ross, Esquire
                          Any State Bar No. 123456

Actions for Fraudulent Inducement

When a prospective buyer approaches a seller or a seller's agent (for example, a real estate broker) for information concerning the real property for sale, a buyer is entitled to full disclosure of any defects or other pertinent information regarding the property. Intentional misrepresentation or even omission of relevant facts concerning the real property constitutes fraud. If the buyer is induced to purchase the property because of the intentional misrepresentations or omissions, the buyer has grounds to bring suit for fraudulent inducement. The buyer may choose to rescind a fraudulently induced sale of real property and sue for recovery of the purchase price paid.

Alternatively, the buyer may continue to hold title to the real property and bring an action against the seller or the seller's agent who has induced the fraudulent sale and recover the damages the buyer has suffered as a consequence of the fraud. Those damages are the difference between the actual value of the property at the time of the contract and the value the property would have had if the facts and representations of the seller had been true.

Prior to bringing an action for fraudulent inducement, the proper jurisdiction should be determined. Because this action is one for monetary damages, the proper jurisdiction will be determined by the amount of the damages incurred. Proper venue typically is the county in which the defendant resides, the county where the real property is located, or the county in which the agreement was made.

Next, a determination should be made regarding who made the misrepresentations. Did the broker representing the seller make the misrepresentations, or were they made directly by the seller? If they were made directly by the seller and the broker was unaware of these fraudulent statements, the appropriate party to bring suit against is the seller. If the misrepresentations were made by the broker, both the broker and the seller should be brought into the suit as defendants. The seller is the broker's principal and, thus, is responsible for representations made by the broker.

The misrepresentations (or omissions) should be described with specificity in the complaint. If the misrepresentations were made in written form, the document containing the misrepresentations should be attached to the complaint as an exhibit. The complaint must include allegations that the misrepresentations were material to the transaction, that they were intentional, that they were made to induce the buyer to purchase the property, and that the buyer relied on the misrepresentations to his or her detriment. As noted, if a jury trial is desired, this must be specifically stated in the prayer for relief.

In summary, a complaint for fraudulent inducement should set forth the following:

1. Jurisdictional facts
2. Ownership of the real property by the defendant at the time of contracting
3. Description of the real property
4. Agreement made between plaintiff and defendant
5. Allegations of fraudulent misrepresentations (or omissions) made by defendant
6. Allegations that the misrepresentations were made to induce the plaintiff to purchase the property
7. Allegations that the misrepresentations relate to material facts
8. Allegations that the misrepresentations were false and the defendant knew them to be false at the time of making the misrepresentations

9. Plaintiff's reliance on the misrepresentations
10. Damages suffered by plaintiff as a result of the fraudulent misrepresentations
11. Prayer for relief
12. Signature of the attorney

Figure 19–2 sets forth a sample complaint for fraudulent inducement.

The defendant in a fraudulent misrepresentation action may raise one or more defenses in his or her answer to the complaint. First, just as in the case of a breach of contract action, if the plaintiff waited too long to bring suit, the defendant may raise the statute of limitations as an absolute defense. Alternative defenses are that the misrepresentation was not intentional or the misrepresentation did not go to a material fact that would have induced the plaintiff to enter into, or not enter into, the contract.

Actions for Breach of Implied Warranty

When a buyer purchases a product, such as a television, a lawnmower, or an automobile, there is an implied warranty that the product is fit for the particular purpose for which it was bought. This is called an **implied warranty of fitness and merchantability.** This implied warranty also pertains to the purchase of a house or building and the contents therein. This implied warranty survives after the closing on the property. If an item in the purchased premises is defective, the buyer may have an action for breach of implied warranty. This action is only available to an original purchaser, not to subsequent purchasers, and may not be available in all states, so state statutes must be checked.

To be successful in an action for breach of implied warranty, the buyer must be able to show damage on account of the breach. Further, this damage must result in the decrease of value of the property as a whole, not simply of the item complained of. For example, if the water heater is found to be defective, that in and of itself may not be enough for a successful action under breach of implied warranty, for it is doubtful that the defective water heater would result in a diminution of the value of the property. This is especially the case if the current appraised value of the property is greater than the purchase price contracted for. If, however, there is a serious structural defect in the property, such as cracks in the foundation walls, the floors not being level, and so forth, it is quite likely that these defects would result in the diminution of the value of the property.

An action for breach of implied warranty is one that requests monetary damages for the devaluation of the property. The calculation of damages is the difference between the purchase price of the property and the value of the property in its present, defective condition. Alternatively, if the plaintiff has hired contractors to repair the damages, the monetary damages are the costs incurred for the repairs done and that need to be done in the future.

Jurisdiction for a breach of implied warranty action is based on the amount of monetary damages sought. Proper venue typically is the county in which the defendant resides, the county in which the contract for sale and purchase was executed, or the county in which the property is located (where the breach occurred). The complaint should set forth allegations concerning the execution of the contract for sale and purchase, the delivery of the property, specific details regarding the defects amounting to breach of implied

implied warranty of fitness: An implied warranty that a product is fit for the particular purpose for which it was bought.

IN THE CIRCUIT COURT OF THE SECOND JUDICIAL CIRCUIT
IN AND FOR ANY COUNTY, ANY STATE

CASE NO. 98-1362

EDWARD FULLER and
WENDY FULLER,
     Plaintiffs,

vs.

KURT HARRINGTON,
     Defendant.   **COMPLAINT**

_____/

    COME NOW the Plaintiffs, EDWARD FULLER and WENDY FULLER, by and through their undersigned counsel, and sue the Defendant, KURT HARRINGTON, and allege as follows:

1. This is an action for damages in excess of Fifteen Thousand Dollars ($15,000.00).
2. On January 18, 1998, Defendant was the owner of the following described real property:

   ALL THAT TRACT of land lying and being situated in the Northeast quarter of the Northwest quarter of the Southwest quarter of Section 3, Township 15 North, Range 5 East, Any County, Any State.

3. Plaintiffs and Defendant entered into negotiations for the sale of the above-described real property and a structure on it under which the Plaintiffs agreed to pay to the Defendant the sum of Three Hundred Thousand Dollars ($300,000.00). During the negotiations that resulted in the sale to the Plaintiffs, Defendant represented to the Plaintiffs that the property was properly zoned for both residential and commercial uses.
4. The representation was made by the Defendant with the intention that the Plaintiffs rely on such representation.
5. The representation relates to an existing, material fact.
6. Defendant knew the representation was false.
7. Plaintiffs, believing the Defendant's representation to be true, relied on it and as a result entered into a contract for sale and purchase with the Defendant on January 18, 1998, and thereafter concluded the sale by payment to the Defendant of the purchase price of Three Hundred Thousand Dollars ($300,000.00). The Defendant then conveyed the property to the Plaintiffs.
8. Defendant's fraudulent representation became known to the Plaintiffs on April 4, 1998 when the Plaintiffs went to apply for an occupational license for their business which they planned on conducting from the above-described property and were told by the clerk at City Hall that the above-described property was zoned for residential use only.
9. As a result of being fraudulently induced to purchase the real property from the Defendant, the Plaintiffs have suffered damages in excess of Fifteen Thousand Dollars ($15,000.00).

    WHEREFORE, the Plaintiffs demand judgment against the Defendant for damages in excess of Fifteen Thousand Dollars ($15,000.00).

FIGURE 19-2
(continued)

DATED: April 17, 1998.

FISHER, ROSS, AND SIMON, P.A.
1900 N.W. 3rd Avenue
Any City, Any State
(000) 232-7000
Attorneys for Plaintiffs

By: _____

        Ava Ross, Esquire
        Any State Bar No. 123456

warranty, a request for repairs to be made, a refusal to make necessary repairs, and damages to the plaintiff as a result of the breach, as noted in the following checklist:

1. Jurisdictional facts
2. Plaintiff's ownership of the property
3. Existence of a contract for sale and purchase (attach a copy as an exhibit)
4. Allegation of implied warranty that defendant was to deliver property in condition of fitness
5. Allegations of breach of implied warranty
6. Allegations of demands for repair made by plaintiff and defendant's refusal to make repairs
7. Damages sustained by plaintiff as a result of defendant's breach
8. Prayer for relief
9. Signature of the attorney

Breach of implied warranty actions happen most commonly (but not exclusively) in construction contract situations. Often a construction contract will contain a warranty clause that the contractor/developer warrants that the house/building being constructed meets specified standards. Further, the warranty clause may provide that the contractor/developer gives the buyer a warranty on the structure, heating, air conditioning, and appliances for a specified time period (often, one year). A written warranty is an express warranty rather than an implied warranty, and if an express warranty is included in the contract for sale and purchase and is not honored, the plaintiff has grounds to bring an additional cause of action for breach of express warranty. A sample complaint for breach of implied warranty is found in the hypothetical lawsuit section at the end of this chapter.

In answer to a complaint for breach of implied warranty, a defendant may resort to the statute of limitations, if applicable. If the defect is structural, the defendant may state that the structure was built in exact accordance with approved plans and specifications. Lenders often require inspection of the property prior to closing. For example, if an FHA loan was obtained to finance the purchase, the FHA requires submittal of plans and specifications for inspection and, before closing, makes a final inspection report to ensure that construction is in compliance with these plans and specifications. If the plaintiff financed the purchase of the property through an FHA loan, the defendant may raise the FHA inspections as a defense.

Actions for Specific Performance

An action for *specific performance* is a lawsuit whereby the plaintiff asks the court to order the defendant to specifically perform under the terms of the contract. If the breaching party is the buyer, the seller asks the court to order the buyer to pay the purchase price stated in the contract. If the breaching party is the seller, the buyer asks the court to order the seller to deliver title to the real property in return for the buyer's payment of the purchase price.

In order to bring an action for specific performance of a real estate contract, two requirements must be met. The first requirement is that the real estate contract must be supported by a writing in compliance with the statute of frauds. An exception to this requirement is carved out by the courts in permitting an oral contract to be specifically enforced if partially performed. Partial performance occurs when (1) payment (full or partial) of consideration is made by the buyer, (2) possession of the property is taken by the buyer, and (3) valuable improvements to the property are made by the buyer with the consent of the seller. The buyer has the burden of proving the existence and partial performance of an oral contract for the sale and purchase of real property by evidence that is "definite and certain," clearly a higher burden of proof than the "preponderance of the evidence" standard used in most civil cases.

The second requirement that must be met in order to bring an action for specific performance is a showing that the plaintiff has no adequate remedy at law. If the contract contains a liquidated damages provision, the inclusion of this provision indicates that the parties to the contract agreed to a stipulated monetary sum to be awarded in the event of breach. A proper liquidated damages provision (one that is not a disguised penalty) provides for monetary damages, agreed upon by the parties at the time of contracting. In this situation, the courts will deem that an adequate remedy at law is indeed available to the complaining party. Further, should the contract provide for alternate remedies, for example, a stipulated sum as liquidated damages or, in the alternative, suit for specific performance, the courts will again find that inasmuch as the parties themselves came up with an alternative to specific performance, the parties concede that monetary damages (for example, the liquidated damages sum) can be considered an adequate remedy for breach.

Note that should the courts allow an action for specific performance, this decision does not preclude the courts from awarding monetary damages in addition to specific performance if the monetary damages are necessary in order to restore the parties to their respective positions prior to the breach. For example, the seller may have problems in clearing title defects. If the buyer is willing to accept the property with the title defects, the seller cannot use the title defects as an excuse to back out of the transaction. If the seller does so, the buyer may sue for specific performance, and if specific performance is awarded, the courts may additionally reduce the price of the property accordingly to reflect the diminished value of the title to the property.

The first step in initiating a suit for specific performance, as is the case in a suit for monetary damages, is determining proper jurisdiction. Because an action for specific performance is an equitable action, only courts of equity may hear the case. In most states, the equity courts are the circuit courts. Therefore, a statement that the action is one for specific performance in and of itself is a statement of jursidiction. Equitable actions are tried by judge without a jury; therefore, a jury trial is not requested. Applicable venue statutes must be checked. Proper venue most commonly will be in any one of three places: (1) where the defendant resides, (2) where the property in question is located, or (3) where the breach of contract occurred.

Once proper jurisdiction and venue are determined, attention must be turned to the contract itself. Just as in a breach of contract action for monetary damages, all of the terms of the contract must be scrutinized, together with any addendums and modifications, to ascertain the exact obligations of each party and to determine whether the plaintiff has fulfilled all of his or her obligations. The obligations of the seller or buyer under the contract and the actions taken by them must be specifically pled in a complaint for specific performance. Therefore, if a buyer seeks specific performance of a contract for sale and purchase, the buyer must allege in the complaint that payment under the contract has been made or tendered by him or her, or that he or she has been ready, willing, and able to pay, or that he or she has been excused from performance. Once the contract has been reviewed, a notice of lis pendens should be prepared to be filed in the public records of the county in which the property is located, together with any bond that may be required to maintain the lis pendens on the property. A notice of lis pendens is appropriate in an action for specific performance because the relief sought affects title to the property.

A complaint for specific performance must include the following:

1. Jurisdictional facts
2. Allegations setting forth the ownership of the real property (by plaintiff or defendant) and the description of the property
3. The existence of a contract for sale and purchase (attach copy as an exhibit to the complaint)
4. Breach of the contract for sale and purchase by the defendant
5. Allegations establishing plaintiff's full performance under the contract, or a statement that the plaintiff is ready, willing, and able to perform under the contract
6. Lack of any adequate remedy at law
7. Damages sustained by plaintiff as a result of defendant's breach
8. Prayer for relief
9. Signature of the attorney

Figure 19–3 provides an example of a notice of lis pendens. Figure 19–4 provides an example of a complaint for specific performance.

As a defensive matter, the defendant in an action for specific performance may choose to attack the validity of the contract being sued upon. If the plaintiff delays in bringing suit, the defendant may raise the **doctrine of laches.** This doctrine, similar to the statute of limitations, is premised on the principle of vigilance and propounds that equity aids those who are vigilant, not those who "sleep" on their rights. Therefore, if a plaintiff neglects to assert a claim for an unreasonable length of time, this neglect, together with other circumstances causing prejudice to the defendant, will bar relief by a court of equity. Whether or not a defense of laches will be sustained in any case will depend

doctrine of laches: A doctrine similar to the statute of limitations, premised on the principle of vigilance, which states that if a plaintiff neglects to assert a claim for an unreasonable length of time, the neglect, together with other circumstances causing prejudice to the defendant, will bar relief by a court of equity.

FIGURE 19–3
Notice of lis pendens

IN THE CIRCUIT COURT OF THE FIFTH JUDICIAL CIRCUIT
IN AND FOR ANY COUNTY, ANY STATE

CASE NO. 98-1534

LYLE SEATON and
ELAINE SEATON,
     Plaintiffs,

vs.

EVERGREEN PROPERTIES, INC.,
an Any State corporation,
     Defendant.   **NOTICE OF LIS PENDENS**
_____/

TO DEFENDANT EVERGREEN PROPERTIES, INC., AND ALL OTHERS WHOM IT MAY CONCERN:

YOU ARE NOTIFIED of the institution of this action by Plaintiffs against you seeking specific performance of that certain written real estate contract for sale and purchase of the following described property located in Any County, Any State:

> Lot 18, Block 9, EVERGREEN ESTATES subdivision, a subdivision of a portion of Section 17, Township 4 South, Range 20 East, Any County, Any State, according to the plat of said subdivision recorded in Plat Book 30, Page 11 of the public records of Any County, Any State.

DATED: May 8, 1998.

FISHER, ROSS, AND SIMON, P.A.
1900 N.W. 3rd Avenue
Any City, Any State
Attorneys for Plaintiffs

By: _____
     Ava Ross, Esquire
     Any State Bar No. 123456

upon all of the relevant circumstances surrounding the contract for sale and purchase and the period between the making of the contract and the filing of the action for specific performance.

Breach of a Construction Contract

A construction contract is similar to an ordinary contract for sale and purchase. The contractor hired to build a house or building may also be the developer from which the buyer purchased the lot, or the buyer may have purchased the lot from one party (entering into a contract for sale and purchase with that party for the real property) and then entered into a separate contract with another party (the contractor) to build a structure on the property. For this reason, the term *owner* will be used in this discussion rather than *buyer* when referring to the party acquiring the contractor's services. Every state has its own statutes regarding the qualifications and licensing of contractors. Research on qualifications and licensing becomes important in a situation in which suit is brought based on the contractor's negligence. If the

IN THE CIRCUIT COURT OF THE FIFTH JUDICIAL CIRCUIT
IN AND FOR ANY COUNTY, ANY STATE

CASE NO. 98-1534

LYLE SEATON and
ELAINE SEATON,
    Plaintiffs,

vs.

EVERGREEN PROPERTIES, INC.,
an Any State corporation,   **COMPLAINT FOR SPECIFIC**
    Defendant.   **PERFORMANCE**
_____/

COME NOW the Plaintiffs, LYLE SEATON and ELAINE SEATON, by and through their undersigned counsel, and sue the Defendant, EVERGREEN PROPERTIES, INC., and allege as follows:

1. This is an action for specific performance of a contract for the sale of real estate in Any County, Any State.

2. At all material times, Defendant was and is now the owner of the following-described real property:

    Lot 18, Block 9, EVERGREEN ESTATES subdivision, a subdivision of a portion of Section 17, Township 4 South, Range 20 East, Any County, Any State, according to the plat of said subdivision recorded in Plat Book 30, Page 11 of the public records of Any County, Any State.

3. On or about January 14, 1998, Plaintiffs as buyers and Defendant as seller entered into and executed a written contract for sale and purchase pertaining to the above-described real property, a copy of which is attached hereto and is made a part hereof as Exhibit A.

4. Plaintiffs have been and are now ready, willing and able to comply with the terms of said contract by paying the purchase price set forth in said contract to the Defendant and have indicated same to the Defendant.

5. Notwithstanding this, the Defendant has failed to perform and continues to refuse to perform the Defendant's obligations under the terms of said contract.

WHEREFORE, Plaintiffs demand judgment requiring the Defendant to specifically perform the Defendant's obligations under the terms and conditions of said contract and for such other relief as the Court deems just.

DATED: May 8, 1998.

          FISHER, ROSS, AND SIMON, P.A.
          1900 N.W. 3rd Avenue
          Any City, Any State
          (000) 232-7000
          Attorneys for Plaintiffs

          By: _____
             Ava Ross, Esquire
             Any State Bar No. 123456

FIGURE 19–4
Complaint for specific performance

contractor fails to meet state qualifications and licensing requirements, most states allow recovery of punitive damages (for example, three times the actual damages) plus attorneys' fees and costs.

An action pertaining to a construction contract normally involves disputes regarding (1) performance by the contractor according to the requirements of the plans and specifications (or noncompliance therewith), (2) changes in the plans and specifications, (3) failure of the owner or the owner's agent (for example, an architect, engineer) to provide something upon which the contractor's performance depends, (4) failure of the contractor to complete performance for the maximum guaranteed costs, (5) incomplete performance, (6) time of completion, or (7) time or amount of payment.

A contractor will sometimes do more work than the construction contract calls for. Under certain circumstances, compensation may be allowed for this extra work. The terms specified in the construction contract should address the issue of whether a contractor is entitled to payment for certain work in addition to the contract price. The general rule is that when parties enter into a construction contract, and during the course of construction alterations or changes are requested by the buyer in the form of extras and otherwise, the owner has an obligation to pay the reasonable cost of such extras in addition to the stipulated sum named by the parties in the original contract.

As an added protection to both parties, it is common for a construction contract to include a provision stating that the contractor will not execute any extra work or make any modifications or alterations in the work described in the specifications and plans unless ordered in writing by the owner or the owner's named agent, or claim pay for extra work, modifications, or alterations unless the written order is produced. There are situations, however, where alteration of plans and specifications is made necessary by the requirements of a city or county ordinance. In these situations, compensation is adjusted to include the additional costs incurred by compliance with the ordinance.

An owner is not required to pay the agreed-upon contract price for defective work. If full payment has not yet been made to the contractor, the owner may deduct the difference between the contract price and the value of the inferior work, plus the amount of any direct damages caused by existing defects. If the defects are not discovered until after the work is completed and full payment is made, the owner, as noted earlier in the discussion of breach of implied warranty, is entitled to bring suit for the difference between the contract price paid and the value of the structure in its defective condition. If, however, a contractor builds the structure in strict conformance with the plans and specifications given to him or her, the contractor is not liable for defects in the work due to the plans and specifications, and the contractor is entitled to receive the agreed-upon contract price for his or her services. In this instance, suit must be brought against the drafter of the plans and specifications.

If a contractor breaches the contract in such a manner as to make it necessary for the buyer to hire another contractor to complete the work, the breaching contractor may not recover the value of his or her services if the owner spent more than the original contract price to complete the job properly. In a situation in which the breaching contractor fails to complete the work, he or she may recover the value of his or her services only for the work completed, and not in excess of the contract price. Note that if the contractor has failed to complete the construction, the owner has a duty to mitigate his or her damages.

It is common for construction contracts to contain a provision mandating that disputes between the parties be referred to professionals, such as architects or engineers, for arbitration. If the parties have agreed to arbitration, the arbitrators, rather than the courts, determine the rights of the parties.

A complaint for breach of a construction contract includes the following:

1. Jurisdictional facts
2. The existence of a construction contract (attach a copy as an exhibit to the complaint)
3. Breach of the construction contract by the defendant
4. Allegations establishing the plaintiff's full performance under the contract, or a statement that the plaintiff is ready, willing, and able to perform under the contract
5. Damages sustained by plaintiff as a result of defendant's breach
6. If attorneys' fees are recoverable, the necessity of plaintiff's having to employ legal counsel to bring this action
7. Prayer for relief
8. Signature of the attorney

Figure 19–5 provides an example of a complaint for breach of a construction contract in which the contractor failed to complete performance of his or her contractual obligations for the maximum guaranteed costs, requiring the owner to hire another contractor to complete the job.

ACTIONS BY REAL ESTATE BROKERS

Although an action by a real estate broker to recover earned commissions is not an action for breach of the contract for sale and purchase per se, the action does relate to the sale and purchase of real property and may stem from a breach of that agreement by the buyer or seller. The real estate broker, for example, might have found a buyer ready, willing, and able to purchase the seller's property, and at some point after the contract for sale and purchase had been executed by both the buyer and seller, the buyer may have attempted to back out of the transaction. The broker, having met his or her obligations to his or her principal (in most cases, the seller) believes he or she is entitled to the agreed-upon commission. The seller, on the other hand, disgruntled to find himself or herself with an unclosed transaction, may be unwilling to pay the commission.

A cause of action available to a broker seeking to recover commissions due will be brought against the broker's employer/principal. The most common situations giving rise to a cause of action against the employer/principal are failure to pay a commission because the sale was never consummated due to the fault of either buyer or seller, or else the employer's simple refusal to pay a commission on a consummated transaction. Occasionally, an action may be brought against another party, such as a buyer who, by making fraudulent representations, induced the seller who employed the broker to breach the broker agreement.

In a real estate brokerage action, jurisdiction will be determined by the amount of monetary damages claimed, as is the case in a breach of contract

IN THE CIRCUIT COURT OF THE SEVENTH JUDICIAL CIRCUIT
IN AND FOR ANY COUNTY, ANY STATE

CASE NO. 98-1566

LISA S. OWENS,
      Plaintiff,

vs.

PETERSON CONSTRUCTION COMPANY,
      an Any State corporation,
      Defendant.   **COMPLAINT**
_____/

    COMES NOW the Plaintiff, LISA S. OWENS, by and through her undersigned counsel, and sues the Defendant, PETERSON CONSTRUCTION COMPANY, and alleges as follows:

1.   This is an action for damages that exceed Fifteen Thousand Dollars ($15,000.00).

2.   Plaintiff is an individual residing at 711 Cardinal Drive, Any City, Any County, Any State.

3.   At all times mentioned in this complaint, Defendant was a corporation organized and existing under the laws of Any State, with its principal place of business located at 305 S.W. 5th Avenue, Any City, Any County, Any State.

4.   On February 9, 1998, Plaintiff and Defendant entered into a contract for the construction of a house for Plaintiff to be located at 711 Cardinal Drive, Any City, Any County, Any State. Construction was to be completed for a maximum sum of Two Hundred and Seventy-Five Thousand Dollars ($275,000.00). A copy of this contract is attached hereto and made a part hereof as Exhibit A.

5.   Plaintiff has at all times been ready, willing, and able to perform her part of the contractual obligations. Plaintiff has paid or tendered payment to Defendant in the amount of Two Hundred Thousand Dollars ($200,000.00). The balance due on the contract, the sum of Seventy-Five Thousand Dollars ($75,000.00), has been retained by the Plaintiff until such time as the Defendant fully performs the contractual agreement between the parties by completing the following items: (i) completion of the driveway, (ii) installation of the landscaping in the front and back of the house, and (iii) installation of the swimming pool.

6.   Defendant has breached the contract between the parties as a result of Defendant's failure to complete the contractual agreement as set forth above.

7.   In addition, Defendant represented to the Plaintiff that construction of the house, including landscaping and swimming pool, could be completed for a maximum of Two Hundred and Seventy-Five Thousand Dollars ($275,000.00). Defendant now refuses to accept the Plaintiff's tender of the sum of Seventy-Five Thousand Dollars ($75,000.00) as payment in full and is instead attempting to charge amounts in excess of the agreed maximum contractual price.

8.   As a result of the Defendant's breach, the Plaintiff has been forced to hire another contractor to complete the work in an amount in excess of the balance due on the above-described contract, causing the Plaintiff to pay in excess of the agreed maximum contract price for the work for which the parties originally contracted.

WHEREFORE, Plaintiff requests judgment against the Defendant for damages in excess of Fifteen Thousand Dollars ($15,000.00), together with costs of suit, and such other and further relief as the court may deem proper.

DATED: May 13, 1998.

FISHER, ROSS, AND SIMON, P.A.
1900 N.W. 3rd Avenue
Any City, Any State
(000) 232-7000

By: _____
Ava Ross, Esquire
Any State Bar No. 123456

FIGURE 19–5
(continued)

for sale and purchase in which the plaintiff is seeking monetary damages rather than specific performance. An action for specific performance is not available in a real estate brokerage action because the broker agreement is a contract for services for which a remedy at law, monetary damages, is available. Proper venue is the same in an action for commission as it is in any other contract action. A broker does not have the right to file a notice of lis pendens against the real property because the lawsuit does not concern title to the real property but, rather, concerns the payment of commission. Neither can the broker file a lien against the real property for payment of commission prior to filing suit. The broker did not perform labor or furnish material in the improvement of real property. Should the broker be successful in the lawsuit and obtain a judgment against the employer/principal, the broker is then able to file a judgment lien, as is the case in any successful lawsuit brought by a plaintiff against a defendant.

State statutes require that a broker must allege and prove his or her licensing under the laws of the state. Only properly licensed brokers (or properly licensed real estate salespersons) may be paid commission. For example, if the broker's license was up for renewal prior to entering into the broker agreement with the employer/principal and the broker's license had expired at the time of contracting and was renewed at a later date, the broker was not properly licensed at the time he or she entered the agreement, and thus the agreement would be invalid.

The complaint must also allege the precise nature of the employment in question. When drafting this section of the complaint, the drafter should take into consideration whether the employment was procured by the seller or buyer; whether the contract was oral or written; whether it was an open listing, an exclusive listing, or an exclusive-right-to-sell; whether under the contract, the broker was to procure a prospect on terms subject to negotiation or on terms specifically prescribed by the employer; and whether the payment of the commission was conditioned on the consummation of the real estate transaction (that is, conditioned on the real estate closing rather than on simple procurement of a ready, willing, and able buyer). If the contract is a written contract, a copy should be attached to the complaint as an exhibit.

If the employer acted through an agent, as in the case of a corporate employer acting through one of its officers, directors, or shareholders, the complaint should indicate the relationship between the agent and the employer. Further, the complaint should allege that the agent was authorized to act on behalf of the corporation. Real estate brokers do not typically ask to see corporate resolutions authorizing this agency relationship prior to entering into a broker agreement (the existence or nonexistence of such a resolution will be determined through the discovery period prior to trial). Nonetheless, the complaint should allege that the agent at all times mentioned was duly authorized to act on behalf of the principal and employ real estate brokers to procure a buyer for the real property, to agree to the compensation to be paid the broker, and to agree on the terms for sale.

The next step in drafting the complaint is to allege full performance by the broker. Performance is the broker's consideration in return for commission. When a broker is employed to find a buyer ready, willing, and able to purchase the property, the broker simply alleges that he or she did so and does not have to allege that the real estate transaction was completed. If, however, the broker is employed to procure a buyer on specific terms dictated by the seller, the complaint must allege that the broker procured a buyer in specific accordance with those terms.

In outline form, the complaint must contain the following elements:

1. Jurisdictional facts
2. Licensing of broker under state statute
3. Allegations setting forth ownership of the real property
4. If the defendant is a corporation, allegations of agency relationship between defendant and defendant's agent
5. Existence of contract for brokerage services (attach copy as an exhibit)
6. Allegations establishing the amount of the agreed-upon commission
7. Allegations setting forth the conditions of performance by plaintiff
8. Allegations of breach of contract by defendant
9. Allegations establishing plaintiff's full performance
10. Allegations of damages sustained by plaintiff as a result of defendant's breach
11. Prayer for relief
12. Signature of the attorney

Figure 19–6 provides an example of a complaint for breach of a brokerage agreement.

ACTIONS FOR PARTITION OF REAL PROPERTY

partition: An action by the court dividing real property held by joint tenants, tenants in common, or tenants in partnership.

The term **partition** refers to the dividing of real property held by joint tenants or by tenants in common, or held jointly by business partners in a tenancy in partnership, into separate and distinct parcels so that each joint owner may hold his or her portion in severalty. Recall from Chapter 2 that ownership in severalty refers to property ownership by an individual owner taking title in fee simple, with the according rights to use and ultimately

IN THE CIRCUIT COURT OF THE FOURTH JUDICIAL CIRCUIT
IN AND FOR ANY COUNTY, ANY STATE

CASE NO. 98-1581

JAY MONROE,
     Plaintiff,

vs.

BDA INVESTMENT PROPERTIES, INC.,
an Any State Corporation,   **COMPLAINT**
     Defendant.

_____/

COMES NOW the Plaintiff, Jay Monroe, by and through his undersigned counsel, and sues Defendant, BDA INVESTMENT PROPERTIES, INC., and alleges as follows:

1. This is an action for damages that exceed $15,000.00.
2. At all times hereinafter mentioned, Plaintiff was and still is a duly licensed real estate broker under the laws of the State of Any State.
3. At all times hereinafter mentioned, Defendant was and still is a domestic corporation duly organized and existing under the laws of the State of Any State.
4. At all times hereinafter mentioned, Defendant was and still is the owner of a parcel of real property described as:

    > ALL THAT TRACT of land lying and being in the Southwest quarter of the Southwest quarter of Section 2, Township 33 South, Range 10 East, Any County, Any State

5. At all times hereinafter mentioned, Christopher Ryan was an officer, shareholder, and director of Defendant and was authorized to act for and on behalf of Defendant to employ real estate brokers to procure a buyer for the above-described property and to agree to the terms and conditions upon which the above-described property was to be sold.
6. On or about March 19, 1998, Defendant, acting by or through the duly authorized agent named above, employed Plaintiff to procure a ready, willing and able buyer for the above-described property upon the terms and conditions set forth in the exclusive-right-to-sell listing agreement, a copy of which is attached hereto and made a part hereof as Exhibit A.
7. Defendant agreed to pay the Plaintiff the sum of six per cent (6%) of the purchase price of the above-described property as commission.
8. Thereafter Plaintiff procured a buyer, Reilly Development Corp., ready, willing and able to purchase the property at a price and on terms and conditions satisfactory to Defendant, said purchase price being One Million Dollars ($1,000,000.00), and Defendant agreed to enter into a formal written contract for sale and purchase of the above-described property.
9. Defendant thereafter wrongfully and without justification failed and refused to enter into the formal written contract and failed and refused to sell the property to the buyer procured by Plaintiff.
10. Plaintiff has duly performed all of the terms and conditions to be performed by Plaintiff under Plaintiff's contract with Defendant.
11. There is now due and owing from Defendant to Plaintiff the sum of Sixty Thousand Dollars ($60,000.00), with interest from March 20, 1998, no part of which has been paid, although payment has been demanded.

FIGURE 19–6
Complaint for breach of a brokerage agreement

FIGURE 19–6
(continued)

WHEREFORE, Plaintiff demands judgment for damages against Defendant.
DATED: May 15, 1998.

> FISHER, ROSS, AND SIMON, P.A.
> 1900 N.W. 3rd Avenue
> Any City, Any State
> (000) 232-7000
> Attorneys for Plaintiff
>
> By: _____
>
>   Ava Ross, Esquire
>   Any State Bar No. 123456

dispose of the property in any manner the individual owner chooses. Property held as tenancy by the entirety (with each spouse owning one hundred percent of the property) cannot be partitioned. Upon dissolution of marriage, however, the spouses become tenants in common, at which point the property may be partitioned if one of the parties so requests. If properly pled, the property may be partitioned as a part of the dissolution proceedings. When an action for partition is properly brought, all controversies about the title to the real property or other matters relating to the property should be settled in that action.

For example, suppose an income-producing property is held as a tenancy in partnership by the partners of a general partnership. A dispute arises about the managing partner's handling of the accounts regarding the income from the property. This, as well as other problems within the partnership, leads to an action to partition the property. As part of the action to partition, the court may order that an accounting be carried out regarding the partnership's accounts. Similarly, a mortgage held by one owner against part of the real property may be foreclosed in a partition action. If one co-owner has made improvements to the jointly held real property, that co-owner cannot charge the other co-owner(s) for the improvements. However, the co-owner who made the improvements may, in a partition action, have set off to him or her that portion of the real property on which the improvements were made, leaving the other co-owners portions of the remaining property equal in value to the portion given to him or her, without taking into account the value of the improvements.

Partition is available only when the plaintiff has possession or a right to immediate beneficial possession of the real property. It cannot be enforced if there is a life estate outstanding. For example, in a situation where a testator, survived by a wife (his second marriage) and adult children from his first marriage, devises a life estate to a parcel of land to his wife, naming his children as remaindermen, his children cannot bring an action for partition of the property during the wife's lifetime because they have no standing to do so inasmuch as they have no right to immediate beneficial possession of the real property. Once the wife dies, the children, as joint owners in fee simple, may, if they so choose, bring an action to partition.

It is necessary when drafting a complaint for partition to have complete title information on the property in question. There may be outstanding mortgages against a fractional interest, conveyances of fractional interests among the co-owners or to third parties, or judgment liens against a co-owner. If all parties having interests in or liens upon the land in question are not brought into the partition action as necessary parties, a second action may be necessary. If the only parties with an interest in the real property are the co-owners, only the co-owners are necessary parties to the action.

A complaint for partition should allege the following:

1. Statement that this is an action for partition
2. Jurisdictional facts (proper jurisdiction is the county in which the real property is located)
3. A description of the real property
4. The names and places of residence of other persons interested in the lands
5. The manner in which title is held by the owners and the quantity held by each
6. Any other matters necessary to enable the court to adjudicate the rights and interests of the parties
7. Statement regarding the divisibility or indivisibility of the real property
8. Prayer for relief
9. Signature of the attorney

If the complaint seeks other incidental relief, it should be alleged. In addition, if the plaintiff seeks some particular equity, such as consideration for improvements placed by him or her on the common property, the circumstances entitling the special treatment should be included.

If the real property is divisible, a court typically appoints commissioners, a special master, or the clerk of the court to partition the property. The court-appointed official will determine the proper share to be allotted to each owner and will employ a surveyor to draw up a survey showing the property as it is to be partitioned. The official will then file a report with the clerk of court that describes the real property divided and the share allotted to each party. If the real property is indivisible, the court will appoint a special master of the clerk of the court to sell the real property at a private or public sale.

Once a purchaser is procured, the sale must be approved by the court before the conveyance of title to the purchaser is made. It is generally the clerk of the court who issues a certificate of sale. The proceeds of the sale of the real property are deposited with the court for disbursement to the parties. If the plaintiff wants the property sold at a private sale, a statement to this effect must be included in the complaint. Each party to the action is bound by the judgment of the court to pay his or her proportionate share of the costs, including attorneys' fees. In a case involving indivisible property in which the property is sold, the court may order costs and fees retained out of the proceeds from the sale. All taxes due at the time of sale also are paid out of the purchase price. If state statute so provides, the reasonable fees and expenses of the commissioners, special masters, surveyors, and such usually are taxed as an item of costs.

A sample complaint for partition is provided in Figure 19–7. A sample judgment is provided in Figure 19–8.

618   REAL ESTATE LITIGATION

FIGURE 19–7
Complaint for partition

IN THE CIRCUIT COURT OF THE THIRD JUDICIAL CIRCUIT
IN AND FOR ANY COUNTY, ANY STATE

CASE NO. 98-1590

ROBERTA M. PRESCOTT,
      Plaintiff,

vs.

LAWRENCE T. PRESCOTT,
      Defendant.   **COMPLAINT FOR PARTITION**
_____/

COMES NOW the Plaintiff, ROBERTA M. PRESCOTT, by and through her undersigned counsel, and sues the Defendant, LAWRENCE T. PRESCOTT, and alleges as follows:

1. This is an action for partition of real property.
2. The property sought to be partitioned is in Any County, Any State and is described as follows:

    Lot 6 in Block 8 of WEDGWOOD ESTATES, 2ND SECTION, according to the plat thereof, recorded in Plat Book 1099, Page 5, of the Public Records of Any County, Any State.

3. The property was acquired by Bertram C. Prescott by deed dated November 4, 1979, who died testate on June 15, 1985, leaving surviving him a widow, Marjory E. Prescott, since deceased, and two children: Plaintiff, ROBERTA M. PRESCOTT, and Defendant, LAWRENCE T. PRESCOTT. In and by his last will and testament, Bertram C. Prescott devised the above-described real property to his wife, Marjory E. Prescott, as a life estate, naming his two children, the Plaintiff and the Defendant, as remaindermen.
4. The probate of the estate of Bertram C. Prescott decreed the parties to this action are equal owners of the real property. Their places of residence are set beneath their respective names.

    ROBERTA M. PRESCOTT
    29 Willow Lane
    Any City, Any State

    LAWRENCE T. PRESCOTT
    621 N.E. 17th Avenue
    Any City, Any State

5. The property is indivisible and is not subject to partition in kind without prejudice to its owners.

WHEREFORE, the plaintiff respectfully demands that a partition of the property be ordered.

DATED: May 16, 1998.

                          FISHER, ROSS, AND SIMON, P.A.
                          1900 N.W. 3rd Avenue
                          Any City, Any State
                          (000) 232-7000
                          Attorneys for Plaintiff

                          By: _____
                            Ava Ross, Esquire
                            Any State Bar No. 123456

FIGURE 19–8
Judgment for partition

IN THE CIRCUIT COURT OF THE THIRD JUDICIAL CIRCUIT
IN AND FOR ANY COUNTY, ANY STATE

CASE NO. 98-1590

ROBERTA M. PRESCOTT,
　Plaintiff,

vs.

LAWRENCE T. PRESCOTT,
　Defendant.　　　　　　　**JUDGMENT FOR PARTITION**
_____/

　　This action was heard before the court. On the evidence presented, the court finds that the property sought to be partitioned is indivisible and is not subject to partition in kind without prejudice to its owners, and it is
　　ADJUDGED that:

1. ROBERTA M. PRESCOTT and LAWRENCE T. PRESCOTT are equal owners of real property located in Any County, Any State, described as follows:

   Lot 6 in Block 8 of WEDGWOOD ESTATES, 2ND SECTION, according to the plat thereof, recorded in Plat Book 1099, Page 5, of the Public Records of Any County, Any State.

2. The property is indivisible and none of it is subject to partition without prejudice to its owners.

3. Patricia Andrews, a practicing attorney of this court, is appointed special master to sell the premises in the manner provided for sales in such cases by state statute. The sale, if public, shall be made within the legal hours of sale, at public auction, to the highest bidder, on the steps of the Any County Courthouse, at Any City, Any State, after publishing notice once each week for four consecutive weeks prior to the sale, in a newspaper regularly published and in general circulation in Any County, Any State. If the special master can secure an offer of a fair price for the premises at a private sale, prior to the date of public sale, she shall report such offer, with her recommendations, to this court.

4. This court retains jurisdiction of this action to enforce this judgment.

ORDERED on this 19th day of May, 1998, at Any County, Any State.

　　　　　　　　　　　　　　　　_____
　　　　　　　　　　　　　　　　Circuit Judge

HYPOTHETICAL CLIENT MATTER

　　This afternoon Ava Ross met with clients Amanda and Brad Hartley who are distressed and frustrated over problems with the house constructed for them fifteen months ago in Royalton Estates, a community developed by RBR Construction Company. Full payment of the contract price was made at time of completion of the work. In the past couple of months, the Hartleys have found cracks in the foundation walls with resulting leakage causing further structural damage, cracks in the tiles and walls of the bathrooms, window sills separating from the walls, baseboards splitting, and the sliding glass doors separating from the facings, leaving space between the doors.

The Hartleys made several attempts within the past month and a half to contact Roger Robinson, the president of RBR Construction Company, over the phone to no avail. They then sent him a demand letter by certified mail, return receipt requested, specifying the repairs to be made. Roger Robinson replied by phone, telling the Hartleys that more than a year has passed since the work was completed and that it is RBR Construction Company's policy to make necessary repairs only within the first year after completion. Roger Robinson further stated that a certain degree of "settling" of a house is to be expected. The Hartleys consulted with another contractor who gave them an estimation of the costs for repairing the defects and has begun work in making the repairs. The Hartleys wanted to know if there was any recourse they could take against RBR Construction Company. They brought a photocopy of the original contract, the demand letter with the return receipt, and copies of the repair bills to date with them, together with the estimated costs of completion of the repair work. Ava discussed the possibility of a lawsuit and explained what would be entailed if suit were brought. The Hartleys decided to go ahead with the litigation.

After meeting with the Hartleys, Ava turns over their file, containing notes of the meeting and photocopies of the documents received from the Hartleys, to Barbara and asks her to draft a complaint for breach of implied warranty of a construction contract. The statute of limitations for bringing a breach of implied warranty action in Any State is three years, so there is no bar to the Hartley's action. Barbara first reads through the construction contract carefully to determine whether it contains any express warranties from the contractor because such warranties could be the basis for an additional cause of action. Seeing no express warranty language, she then notes that the business address of the defendant is located in Any County. Further, the property in question (the location of the breach) is located in Any County. Therefore, the complaint should be filed in Any County.

Barbara next looks at the repairs bills accrued and the estimated costs of future repair work. The total costs exceed fifteen thousand dollars, which is the threshold requirement for bringing suit in circuit court in Any State. In addition to asking for the costs of these repairs, the Hartleys will be asking for damages for the diminution of the value of the property. With the information gathered together in the client file, Barbara proceeds to draft the complaint shown in Figure 19–9 for Ava's review and signature.

Barbara next prepares a summons to be served on RBR Construction Company. Once Ava reviews and signs the complaint, Barbara will make a copy of the summons for the office file, three copies of the complaint (one for the client, one for the office file, and one to be stamped by the clerk when the original is filed), have checks cut for filing fees and sheriff's fees, and mail the original and one copy of the complaint, together with the summons, checks, cover letter, and addressed, stamped envelope (for return of the stamped complaint), to the clerk of the court for filing.

FIGURE 19–9
Complaint for breach of
implied warranty

IN THE CIRCUIT COURT OF THE FOURTH JUDICIAL CIRCUIT
IN AND FOR ANY COUNTY, ANY STATE
CASE NO.

BRAD HARTLEY and
AMANDA HARTLEY,
     Plaintiffs,

vs.

RBR CONSTRUCTION COMPANY,
an Any State corporation,
     Defendant.   /   **COMPLAINT**

    COME NOW the Plaintiffs, BRAD HARTLEY and AMANDA HARTLEY, by and
through their undersigned counsel, and sue the Defendant, RBR CONSTRUCTION
COMPANY, and allege as follows:

1. This is an action for damages that exceed Fifteen Thousand Dollars
($15,000.00).
2. Plaintiffs are now, and at all times mentioned in this complaint were, the
owners of real property located at 65 Baron Court, Any City, Any
County, Any State.
3. At all times relevant to the events described in this complaint, Defendant
was a professional building contractor, having its principal office
located at 901 State Street, Suite 205, Any City, Any County, Any State.
4. On October 1, 1996, the Plaintiffs entered into a written contract with
the Defendant for the construction by the Defendant of a residential
house, for use by the Plaintiffs and their family. A copy of the contract,
containing the plans and specifications for the house, is attached hereto
and made a part hereof as Exhibit A.
5. An implied term of the contract was that the Defendant would construct
the house in a manner that meets ordinary standards reasonably to be
expected of living quarters of comparable kind and quality. Plaintiffs
relied on the Defendant to construct a house meeting these standards of
fitness.
6. On or about February 4, 1997, the Defendant informed the Plaintiffs
that construction of the house was completed and executed and delivered to the Plaintiffs a warranty deed.
7. On or about March 10, 1998, the Plaintiffs discovered that the
Defendant had failed to construct the house in a reasonable manner in
that the foundation walls have cracked resulting in leakage and other
structural damage, the tiles and walls of the bathrooms have cracked,
the window sills have separated from the walls, the baseboards have
split, and the sliding glass doors have separated from the facings, leaving space between the doors.
8. On March 27, 1998, the Plaintiffs sent the Defendant a written demand
letter, certified mail, return receipt requested, demanding that the
Defendant repair the deficiencies in construction of the house. A copy of
the demand letter and the return receipt are attached hereto and made
a part hereof as Exhibit B. The Defendant, however, has refused to
make such repairs.
9. As a result of the Defendant's failure to honor the Plaintiffs' request, the
Plaintiffs have employed contractors to repair the damage at a cost to
date of Eighteen Thousand Dollars ($18,000.00).
10. Plaintiff is reasonably certain to suffer additional damages in the future
in the sum of Twenty Thousand Dollars ($20,000.00) for the repair of

FIGURE 19–9
(continued)

defects caused because of the Defendant's breach of the implied warranty of fitness in failing to properly construct the Plaintiffs' house. Such repairs are necessary to make the house a safe and suitable place for housing the Plaintiffs and their family.

11. The Plaintiffs have suffered additional damage for diminution of the value of the house because it is constructed in an improper manner.

12. The Defendant should have foreseen that all of the items of damage would occur due to the Defendant's failure to construct the house in a manner that meets ordinary standards reasonably to be expected of living quarters of comparable kind and quantity.

WHEREFORE, the Plaintiffs respectfully demand judgment against the Defendant for damages in excess of Fifteen Thousand Dollars ($15,000.00), together with costs of suit, and such other and further relief as the court may deem proper.

DATED: _____

FISHER, ROSS, AND SIMON, P.A.
1900 N.W. 3rd Avenue
Any City, Any State
Attorneys for Plaintiffs

By: _____
    Ava Ross, Esquire
    Any State Bar No. 123456

CHAPTER SUMMARY

1. The remedies available to a buyer or seller in an action for breach of contract for sale and purchase will be either the return (or retention) of the deposit(s), liquidated damages, a suit for monetary damages, or a suit for specific performance.

2. A liquidated damages provision will only be upheld by a court if the actual damages incurred by a party are difficult to calculate and, thus, a reasonably agreed-upon sum has been arrived at in the contract. If a contract for sale and purchase gives the nonbreaching party the option of recovering liquidated damages or bringing suit for monetary damages, the liquidated damages provision will not be upheld. Similarly, if the contract gives the nonbreaching party the option of recovering of monetary damages or bringing suit for specific performance, the court will not allow specific performance because the contract provides an adequate remedy at law.

3. In a suit brought by the seller for monetary damages, a court typically allows the seller the "benefit of the bargain" for which the seller contracted by awarding the seller the difference between the contract price for the real property and the current fair market value of the property. In a suit brought by a buyer for monetary damages, a court typically awards the return of any deposits, together with interest, and the costs for expenses incurred by the buyer in reliance on the contract. Attorneys' fees are recoverable by the prevailing party only if the contract for sale and purchase so stipulates. Punitive damages ordinarily are not recoverable.

4. Separate causes of action may be brought for fraudulent inducement and breach of implied warranty, if applicable. Fraudulent inducement occurs if the first party, through intentional misrepresentations or omissions of material facts by the second party or the second party's agent, is induced to enter into a contract for sale and purchase. A breach of implied warranty occurs if some aspect of the property is defective, resulting in a decrease of value of the property.

5. Actions pertaining to construction contracts typically involve disputes over the quality of the work performed by the contractor, changes requested or required by law, failure to complete the contracted work, the timing of completion, or the timing or amount of payment. If the work performed by a contractor is defective, the owner may deduct the difference between the contract price and the value of the inferior work. If another contractor has to be employed to complete the work, the breaching contractor may not recover the value of his or her services if the owner spent more than the original contract price to complete the job properly.

6. In an action for breach of a brokerage agreement by the broker's employer-principal, a broker must allege compliance with state licensing requirements, the precise nature of the employment in question including the conditions of performance by the broker, and the broker's full performance of his or her obligations under the contract.

7. A partition is the dividing of real property held by joint tenants, tenants in common, or tenants in partnership. Through a partition action, divisible property is divided so that each joint owner can hold his or her respective share in severalty. Indivisible property is sold by court order and the proceeds from the sale distributed proportionately.

REVIEW QUESTIONS

1. Distinguish between the concept of legal remedies and the concept of equitable remedies.
2. List the items that must be included in an action for breach of contract for sale and purchase.
3. What defense might a defendant raise in an action for breach of contract for sale and purchase?
4. What remedies are available to a party fraudulently induced into entering a contract for sale and purchase?
5. Explain the procedure by which a court partitions real property.

ETHICAL QUESTIONS

In the past several months, you have noticed a number of articles in paralegal journals discussing the practice of double billing. Double billing is billing more than one client for the same billable time. These articles indicate that this practice happens quite often. For example, a paralegal may be asked to interview a witness in the next county and, on the drive to and from the office, make follow-up calls to several other clients on a cell phone provided by the law office. Is it appropriate to bill the client whose witness you interviewed for the time spent in traveling to see the witness, and also to bill the clients telephoned during that time? The American Bar Association published an opinion on this matter, stating that it is unethical to charge more than one client for the same hours of work.

You have drafted a complaint for breach of a construction contract and have been asked by your supervising attorney to take the complaint, summons, and filing fee down to the courthouse for filing. You have also been asked, while there, to do some research on a title matter for another client. Is it inappropriate to do both? What if only one client is billed for the time spent?

PRACTICAL ASSIGNMENTS

Assignment 19:1. Research your state statutes regarding proper venue and statute of limitations for the following causes of action.
  a. Breach of contract
  b. Breach of implied warranty
  c. Fraudulent misrepresentation

Photocopy the relevant statutes and insert them under the "Litigation" section of your resource portfolio.

Assignment 19:2. Obtain a copy of your county's summons form and insert it under the "Litigation" section of your resource portfolio.

Assignment 19:3. Telephone the clerk of court's office and find out the filing fees and sheriff's fees applicable in your county. Insert this information under the "Litigation" section of your resource portfolio.

Assignment 19:4. Your supervising attorney, Deborah Sanders, has asked you to draft a complaint for breach of contract for sale and purchase. The client is the buyer, Terrence Mason. He contracted eight months ago from today's date to purchase a house from Victor and Laura Stowe for the purchase price of $200,000.00. Upon execution of the contract, Terrence gave the Stowes a down payment of $20,000.00. The closing was supposed to take place one month ago from today's date. Terrence was prepared to go through with the closing and was willing and able to pay the remainder of the purchase price and his share of the closing costs. However, the Stowes backed out of the closing at the last minute and refuse to close. The contractual remedies include suit for monetary damages. Therefore, a suit for specific performance would not be appropriate.

In addition to the down payment, Terrence has incurred costs for title examination, surveying, and roof and termite inspection that total $700. Further, Terrence sold his house in reliance on the closing and has been paying rent for the past two months of $800 a month. Because the rented apartment was too small to fit all of his furniture, Terrence had to rent storage space for most of his furniture until he moved into the new house and, therefore, has been paying storage rent of $200 a month for the past two months. In addition, he has hired your law firm to bring suit, and the contract stipulates that the prevailing party is entitled to attorneys' fees. Assume the contract was executed in your county, that all the parties reside in your county, and that the house in question is located in your county.

Draft a complaint for monetary damages for breach. The name and address of your firm (Hernandez, Sanders, and Norris, P.A., 263 Republic Avenue, your city, your state) should appear above Deborah's signature line. Deborah's bar number is 654321. After completion and review, insert the complaint under the "Litigation" section of your resource portfolio.

Assignment 19:5. Define the following key terms.

benefit of the bargain	liquidated damages
doctrine of laches	partition
equitable remedies	punitive damages
implied warranty of fitness	service of process
in personam jurisdiction	subject matter jurisdiction
jurisdiction	venue
legal remedies	

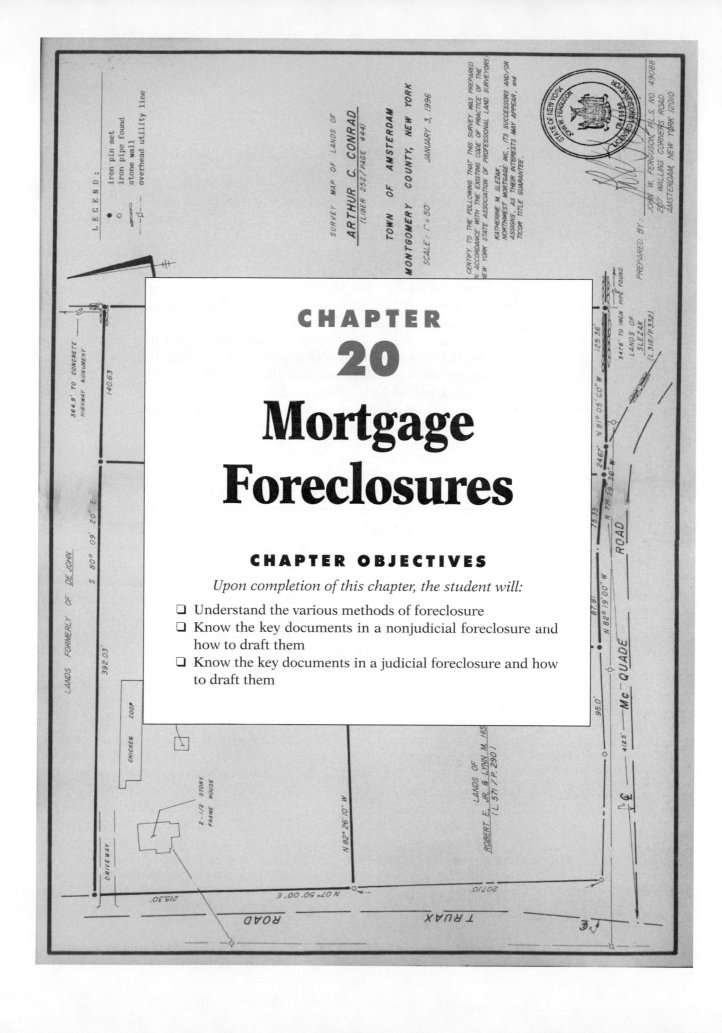

CHAPTER
20

Mortgage Foreclosures

CHAPTER OBJECTIVES

Upon completion of this chapter, the student will:

❑ Understand the various methods of foreclosure
❑ Know the key documents in a nonjudicial foreclosure and how to draft them
❑ Know the key documents in a judicial foreclosure and how to draft them

INTRODUCTION

In the best of all possible worlds, a loan transaction is advantageous to both lender and borrower. The borrower obtains the funds necessary to purchase property he or she could not otherwise afford, while the lender makes a profit by "selling" money to the borrower at a specified interest rate. If the borrower makes each payment on time, the parties can continue a satisfactory relationship. Unfortunately, borrowers can find themselves in situations where they default on one or more payments, which causes problems for both parties. The lender becomes anxious about its investment and may seek to accelerate the loan and/or foreclose on the collateral property to prevent a loss. The borrower becomes anxious both about keeping his or her real property and keeping a good credit rating.

This chapter begins by looking at arrangements that may be worked out between the borrower and lender to prevent foreclosure. It then explores the various foreclosure methods available, focusing on the documents a paralegal working in a real estate law firm, or in the legal department of a lending institution, may be asked to prepare by his or her supervising attorney, including but not limited to demand letters, notices of default, notices of lis pendens, complaints, various motions, and affidavits.

ARRANGEMENTS TO PREVENT FORECLOSURE

A borrower in default and a lender may work out an arrangement short of foreclosure. One possibility is a **reinstatement of loan.** This is particularly applicable if the loan is secured by a standard FNMA/FHLMC mortgage instrument. This instrument provides for the borrower's right to reinstate a loan if certain conditions are met. The borrower is required to pay all delinquent sums and late charges, as well as take any reasonable actions the lender may require to ensure that the lender's interest in the real property is protected and the borrower's obligation to pay under the terms of the note and mortgage remain unimpaired.

When the borrower has low equity and is unable to cure default on the loan, yet wants to prevent the expense of defending a foreclosure action while preserving his or her credit rating, the borrower may sign over to the lender a **deed in lieu of foreclosure.** A lender may save itself the expense of bringing a foreclosure suit by accepting this arrangement. Prior to such acceptance, the lender's considerations include such factors as the value of the property and the existence of junior lienholders. If the appraised value of the property is less than the outstanding debt owed to the lender, the lender may not accept a deed in lieu of foreclosure because by accepting the deed, the lender may be relinquishing rights to pursue a deficiency judgment against the borrower for the difference between the value of the real property and the amount of the remaining outstanding debt. If there are junior liens against the real property, the lender, by accepting the deed in lieu of foreclosure, will have to satisfy those junior lienholders before the lender can deliver clear title to a prospective purchaser of the property.

A third possibility is to work out an agreement between the borrower and the lender that does the following: (1) acknowledges the default, (2) modifies

reinstatement of loan: An arrangement in lieu of foreclosure, whereby a borrower pays all delinquent sums and late charges and takes any reasonable actions the lender may require to ensure both that the lender's interest in the real property is protected and that the borrower's obligation to pay under the terms of the note and mortgage remain unimpaired.

deed in lieu of foreclosure: A deed to mortgaged property given by a borrower to the lender in order to prevent foreclosure.

the loan repayment terms, and (3) outlines measures to protect the lender's interests. In the latter instance, the lender may, for example, require that a quitclaim deed be delivered to a trustee with the understanding that the deed will not be recorded except in the event of another default by the borrower. The lender may also require that another appraisal of the property be done, with the borrower paying the costs of the appraisal.

THE CONCEPT OF FORECLOSURE AND LIEN PRIORITY

If none of these remedies are applicable or acceptable, the lender will move to foreclose on the real property. **Foreclosure** is the legal procedure whereby real property is sold to repay a debt to a creditor who has a lien on the real property. The sale may be made to the creditor bringing the foreclosure action, another creditor, or a third party. In this chapter, the creditor in question is the lending institution that has a senior lien on the real property. The lienholder bringing a foreclosure action, however, may be a judgment creditor, the holder of a construction lien, the holder of a second mortgage, the United States government as holder of a tax lien, and so forth.

In many circumstances, a junior lienholder may bring a foreclosure action before action is taken by a senior lienholder. The reason for this lies in the manner in which payment is made in the event of foreclosure. When property is sold in a foreclosure sale, there is a priority in which lienholders are paid from the foreclosure proceeds. The lienholder with the highest priority, often the holder of a first mortgage, is paid first. Junior lienholders only receive proceeds after the senior lienholder's debt is paid in full. If there are no funds left over to pay the lienholder with the second highest priority, neither that lienholder nor lienholders of lesser priority receive anything from the foreclosure sale. This commonly is the case because the foreclosed property is sold to the highest bidder. The senior lienholder will bid the full amount of its outstanding debt obligation. If there are no other bidders, the senior lienholder acquires the property for that amount, which leaves nothing remaining for the other lienholders.

If a junior lienholder wants to protect its interests, it will foreclose and buy the property, usually for the amount of the outstanding debt obligation under the second mortgage, and take title to the property subject to the existing first mortgage. Because the value of the real property will be greater than the outstanding debt obligation under the second mortgage, the junior lienholder will sell the property and pay off all senior lienholders.

TYPES OF FORECLOSURE

The type of foreclosure method applicable in a given situation generally will depend on whether the state in which the real property is located is a state that uses deeds of trust or one that uses mortgages as the primary security instrument. In lien theory states, mortgages are the primary security instruments. The lender-mortgagee is given a lien against, rather than title to, the real property and, therefore, must bring a judicial action of foreclosure to

foreclosure: The legal procedure whereby real property is sold to repay a debt to a creditor who has a lien on the real property.

perfect its lien. In title theory states, deeds of trust are the primary security instruments. The trustee has title rights to the real property and, therefore, under the power-of-sale clause contained in the deed of trust, is allowed to sell the real property in a nonjudicial foreclosure. Additionally, a few states have special foreclosure methods, which are discussed in the following text.

Nonjudicial Foreclosure

Recall from the discussion of deeds of trust in Chapter 10, that there are three parties to a deed of trust: (1) the trustor (borrower), (2) the trustee, and (3) the beneficiary (lender). The trustee is an independent party, normally a title, trust, or escrow company. When a borrower obtains a loan, the borrower signs a deed of trust as trustor to the trustee for the benefit of the lender-beneficiary. This deed allows the trustee to sell the property in question if the borrower fails to meet his or her loan obligations. Additionally, the borrower signs a promissory note which is given to the lender setting forth the terms for paying back the loan. If the borrower fails to meet his or her obligations under the note, the lender-beneficiary notifies the trustee. The trustee then proceeds to sell the property under the powers granted to the trustee in the deed of trust.

Before initiating the foreclosure process, the lender may be required, under state law, to send a letter to the borrower informing the borrower of the default and making demand for payment. As this is not a prerequisite in all states to bringing a nonjudicial foreclosure action, state statutes must be checked. The demand may be for the delinquent payment, penalty charges, and attorneys' fees (if an attorney has been hired to handle the matter); or the demand may be for the total sum outstanding on the note, together with interest according to rights granted in an acceleration clause in the deed of trust. A sample demand letter appears in Figure 20–1.

If a demand letter is sent and the borrower fails to respond, the trustee will begin the foreclosure process. The first step in the nonjudicial foreclosure process is the preparation of a notice of default. The **notice of default** typically is recorded in the recorder's office in the county in which the property is located. A notice of default ordinarily includes the following information: (1) the name of the trustee, (2) the name of the trustor, (3) the name of the beneficiary, (4) the legal description of the property, (5) the amount and date of the default, (6) the statutorily prescribed time period within which to respond, (7) the recording information pertaining to the deed of trust, (8) the recording information pertaining to the notice of default, (9) the party to contact for payment to stop foreclosure, and (10) a statement that the property may be sold without court action and that the borrower may lose legal rights if he or she does not act within the time period stated. A sample notice of default is provided in Figure 20–2.

Once a notice of default has been recorded and a copy sent to the borrower, a statutorily prescribed waiting period (for example, three months), commences, usually referred to as a **redemption period.** Most states in which deeds of trust are used provide for a redemption period. During this period, the borrower may prevent foreclosure by paying the amounts owed plus interest and penalties, or by negotiating an agreement with the lender. If one of these avenues is taken by the borrower, or if the borrower has made all

notice of default: A notice informing a borrower that he or she is in default, setting forth the amount and date of the default, the period within which to respond, and the consequences if he or she does not act within the prescribed period.

redemption period: A statutorily prescribed period of time within which a borrower may prevent foreclosure by paying the amount(s) owed, plus interest, and penalties, or by negotiating an agreement with the lender.

FIGURE 20–1
Demand letter

February 19, 1998

CERTIFIED MAIL #P432163445
RETURN RECEIPT REQUESTED

Mr. Thomas Trent
423 Grasemere Terrace
Any City, Any State

RE: Loan No. 511884

Dear Mr. Trent:

Please be informed that you are in default under the above-referenced loan as you have failed to make your monthly payment of $950.00, which was due on the first day of February. As a result of this default, the lender, Any County First National Bank, declares the entire indebtedness due and payable and demands that you make immediate payment by cashier's check of the outstanding principal balance of $98,398.00, together with interest of $3,887.00. Failure to pay the above-cited sum by March 3, 1998 may result in foreclosure and sale of the following property:

Lot 9 in Block 33, MANSFIELD PARK ESTATES, a subdivision according to the plat thereof as recorded in Plat Book 58, Page 18, of the Public Records of Any County, Any State.

Unless you dispute the validity of this debt within thirty (30) days of your receipt of this notice, the debt shall be assumed valid. Should you notify us in writing within the thirty (30) day period that the debt is in dispute, steps will be taken to verify the debt, and verification shall be forwarded to you.

Sincerely,

Ava Ross, Esquire
Fisher, Ross, and Simon, P.A.

cc: Any County First National Bank, N.A.

---

required payments prior to the filing and recording of a notice of default, the borrower will request that a **notice of rescission** (sometimes referred to as a *satisfaction of default notice)* be recorded.

A notice of rescission normally includes the following information: (1) the name of the trustee, (2) the name of the trustor, (3) the name of the beneficiary, (4) the legal description of the property, (5) the recording information pertaining to the deed of trust, (6) the recording information pertaining to the notice of default, (7) a statement that the notice of default is rescinded, (8) a statement that such rescission does not amount to a waiver of any breach or default nor impair any rights to remedies available to the trustee, and (9) a statement that all obligations under the deed of trust are reinstated.

If the borrower's default payment amount is not in dispute, and the borrower fails to satisfy the default obligation or fails to reach an agreement with the lender to extend the payment date or otherwise work out negotiated terms for paying off the debt within the statutorily prescribed period after the notice of default is recorded, the next step is the publication of a **notice of trustee's sale.** The publication requirements vary from state to state. Publication

notice of rescission: A notice that rescinds a notice of default in a nonjudicial foreclosure.

notice of trustee's sale: A notice published in a newspaper of general circulation in the county in which the real property is located announcing the details of the sale of the real property in a nonjudicial foreclosure action.

632 REAL ESTATE LITIGATION

FIGURE 20–2
Notice of default

RECORDING REQUESTED BY:
Any City Trust Company

AND WHEN RECORDED MAIL TO:

Any City Trust Company
669 N.W. 10th Street
Any City, Any State

Attn: Valerie Winslow   Reference No.: 123456

IMPORTANT NOTICE

IF YOUR PROPERTY IS IN FORECLOSURE BECAUSE YOU ARE BEHIND IN YOUR PAYMENTS, IT MAY BE SOLD WITHOUT ANY COURT ACTION, and you may have the legal right to bring your account in good standing by paying all of your past due payments plus permitted costs and expenses within three months from the date this Notice of Default was recorded. This amount is $1,900.00 as of March 1, 1998, and will increase until your account becomes current. You may not have to pay the entire unpaid portion of your account, even though full payment was demanded, but you must pay the amount stated above. After three months from the date of recordation of this document (which date of recordation appears hereon), unless the obligation being foreclosed upon permits a longer period, you have only the legal right to stop the foreclosure by paying the entire amount demanded by your creditor. To find out the amount you must pay, or to arrange for payment to stop the foreclosure, or if your property is in foreclosure for any other reason, contact:

ANY COUNTY FIRST NATIONAL BANK
1000 COMMERCIAL AVENUE
ANY CITY, ANY STATE

If you have any questions, you should contact a lawyer or the government agency which may have insured your loan.

Remember, YOU MAY LOSE LEGAL RIGHTS IF YOU DO NOT TAKE PROMPT ACTION.

THE FOLLOWING COPY OF "NOTICE," THE ORIGINAL OF WHICH WAS FILED FOR RECORD ON MARCH 6, 1998 IN THE OFFICE OF THE RECORDER OF ANY COUNTY, ANY STATE, IS SENT TO YOU INASMUCH AS AN EXAMINATION OF THE TITLE TO SAID TRUST PROPERTY SHOWS YOU MAY HAVE AN INTEREST IN THE TRUSTEE'S SALE PROCEEDINGS.

NOTICE OF DEFAULT

NOTICE IS HEREBY GIVEN: THAT ANY CITY TRUST COMPANY is duly appointed Trustee under a Deed of Trust dated October 8, 1994 executed by THOMAS TRENT as Trustor, to secure certain obligations in favor of ANY COUNTY FIRST NATIONAL BANK, N.A. as beneficiary recorded October 9, 1994 as Instrument No. 947 in Book 455, Page 107, of Official Records in the Office of Recorder of Any County, Any State, describing land therein as:

Lot 9 in Block 33, MANSFIELD PARK ESTATES, a subdivision according to the plat thereof as recorded in Plat Book 58, Page 18, of the Public Records of Any County, Any State

said obligations including a note for the total sum of $100,000.00 that a breach of, and default in, the obligations for which such Deed of Trust is security has occurred in that payment has not been made of:

$1,900.00

that by reason thereof, the present beneficiary under such Deed of Trust has deposited with said duly appointed Trustee, such Deed of Trust and all documents evidencing obligations secured thereby, and the undersigned does hereby declare all sums secured thereby immediately due and payable and does hereby elect to cause the trust property to be sold to satisfy the obligations secured thereby.

Any City Trust Company

By: _____

Valerie Winslow, President

Dated: March 6, 1998.

FIGURE 20–2
(continued)

typically is made in a newspaper of general circulation in the county in which the property is located, or it may be made in a newspaper that primarily carries legal notices. State law also may require the recording of the notice of trustee's sale.

A notice of trustee's sale ordinarily includes the following information: (1) the name of the trustee; (2) the name of the trustor; (3) the name of the beneficiary; (4) a legal description of the property and the street address; (5) the date of the sale; (6) the time of the sale; (7) the location of the sale; (8) the recording information pertaining to the deed of trust; (9) the recording information pertaining to the notice of default; (10) the party conducting the sale; (11) the unpaid balance, together with advances, costs, and expenses; (12) the manner in which payment for the property is to be made (for example, cashier's check, cash); and (13) a disclaimer regarding warranty of title of the property. An example of a notice of trustee's sale is provided in Figure 20–3.

During the publication period of the notice of trustee's sale, the borrower may attempt to prevent foreclosure by paying the entire outstanding balance, plus interest, penalties, costs, and expenses, or by reaching a negotiated agreement with the lender. Alternatively, the borrower may forestall foreclosure by filing for bankruptcy. Should the borrower fail to avail himself or herself of these alternatives, the public auction and sale of the property will proceed. In most deed of trust states, the redemption period ends prior to or on the date of the sale. However, some state statutes may allow a redemption period to continue even after the sale, so state statutes should be checked carefully. The lender, the borrower, or a third party may purchase the property at the foreclosure sale. After the sale, the purchaser of the property receives a trustee's deed, similar to the example provided in Figure 20–4.

As a paralegal working in the legal department of a trust, title, or escrow company, in the legal department of a lending institution, or in a law firm, you

RECORDING REQUESTED BY:
Any City Trust Company

AND WHEN RECORDED MAIL TO:
Any City Trust Company
669 N.W. 10th Street
Any City, Any State

Attn: Valerie Winslow
      TS#654321   SPACE ABOVE THIS LINE FOR RECORDER'S USE
_____

NOTICE OF TRUSTEE'S SALE
NOTICE

YOU ARE IN DEFAULT UNDER A DEED OF TRUST DATED OCTOBER 8, 1994. UNLESS YOU TAKE ACTION TO PROTECT YOUR PROPERTY, IT MAY BE SOLD AT A PUBLIC SALE. IF YOU NEED AN EXPLANATION OF THE NATURE OF THE PRO-CEEDING AGAINST YOU, YOU SHOULD CONTACT A LAWYER.

ON June 29, 1998, at 10:00 A.M., ANY CITY TRUST COMPANY, as duly appointed Trustee under and pursuant to Deed of Trust executed by THOMAS TRENT as Trustor for the benefit and security of ANY COUNTY FIRST NATIONAL BANK, N.A. as Beneficiary, dated October 8, 1994, and recorded as Instrument No. 947, Book 455, Page 107, on October 9, 1994, Any County, Any State

WILL SELL AT PUBLIC AUCTION TO HIGHEST BIDDER FOR CASH, A CASHIER'S CHECK DRAWN ON A STATE OR NATIONAL BANK, A STATE OR FEDERAL CREDIT UNION, OR A STATE OR FEDERAL SAVINGS AND LOAN ASSOCIATION DOMICILED IN THE STATE OF ANY STATE (payable at time of sale in lawful money of the United States) at

ANY COUNTY COURTHOUSE
400 MARSHALL AVENUE
ANY COUNTY, ANY STATE

all right title and interest conveyed to and now held by it under said Deed of Trust in the property situated in said County and State described as:

Lot 9 in Block 33, MANSFIELD PARK ESTATES, a subdivision according to the plat thereof as recorded in Plat Book 58, Page 18, of the Public Records of Any County, Any State

The street address and other common designation, if any, of the real property above is purported to be:

423 Grasemere Terrace, Any City, Any State

THE UNDERSIGNED TRUSTEE DISCLAIMS ANY LIABILITY FOR INCORRECT INFORMATION FURNISHED.

THAT said sale is made without covenant or warranty regarding title, possession, or encumbrances, or as to insurability of title.

THE total amount of the unpaid balance of said obligations, together with advances and estimated costs and expenses, is $103,506.00.

FIGURE 20–3
(continued)

THAT notice of breach of said obligation and election to sell real property was recorded as Instrument No. 115 in Book 612, Page 4, on June 6, 1998, of the Official Records of the County Recorder of Any County, State of Any State.

Trustee or party conducting Sale   ANY CITY TRUST COMPANY
                                       669 N.W. 10TH STREET
                                       ANY CITY, ANY STATE

Dated: June 8, 1998.   ANY CITY TRUST COMPANY

By:_____
Valerie Winslow, President

may be called upon to prepare any or all of the documents discussed in the preceding text if you work in a deed of trust state. In assisting an attorney in a deed of trust foreclosure, the following checklist should prove helpful.

DEED OF TRUST FORECLOSURE CHECKLIST

1. Review deed of trust and note carefully, noting:
   a. The proper names of all parties
   b. The legal description of the property
   c. The total amount of the debt obligation
   d. The payment terms
   e. The rights conferred upon each party in the event of default
   f. The recording information pertaining to the deed of trust
2. Determine whether a demand letter is required (or desired) to be sent prior to filing and recording a notice of default. If required or desired, include:
   a. The name of the lender
   b. The amount of the default and date it was due
   c. The demand terms (for example, default amount plus penalties, acceleration of the total outstanding obligation)
   d. Date by which default must be corrected
   e. Legal description of the property
   f. Date by which to notify lender or trustee in the event the borrower disputes the default amount
3. Prepare notice of default
4. Ascertain recording fee for recording notice of default and send original notice, together with applicable recording fee, to county recorder's office
5. Mail copy of notice of default to borrower and to lender
6. If borrower corrects default prior to or after recording of notice of default:
   a. Prepare a notice of rescission
   b. Ascertain recording fee for recording notice of rescission and send original notice, together with applicable recording fee, to county recorder's office
7. If borrower fails to correct default within redemption period:
   a. Prepare notice of trustee's sale

FIGURE 20–4
Trustee's deed

RECORDING REQUESTED BY:
Any City Trust Company

AND WHEN RECORDED MAIL TO:
Any City Trust Company
669 N.W. 10th Street
Any City, Any State

Attn: Valerie Winslow

_____ SPACE ABOVE THIS LINE FOR RECORDER'S USE

MAIL TAX STATEMENTS TO:
Robert Pearson
519 S.W. 6th Avenue   **Trustee's Deed Upon Sale**
Any City, Any State   **Trustee Sale No. 654321**

The undersigned Grantor declares:
  (1) The Grantee herein was not the foreclosing beneficiary.
  (2) The amount of the unpaid debt together with costs was $103,506.00.
  (3) The amount paid by the Grantee at the trustee sale was $104,500.00.
  (4) The documentary transfer tax is $679.25.
  (5) The survey fee is $75.00.
  (6) Said property is in the City of Any City, and ANY CITY TRUST COMPANY
       (herein called Trustee), as the duly appointed Trustee under the Deed of
       Trust hereinafter described, does hereby grant and convey, but without
       warranty, express or implied, to

                    ROBERT PEARSON, a single man

(herein called Grantee), all of its right, title and interest in and to that certain
property situated in the City of Any City, County of Any County, State of Any State,
described as follows:

       Lot 9 in Block 33, MANSFIELD PARK ESTATES, a subdivision according to
       the plat thereof as recorded in Plat Book 58, Page 18, of the Public
       Records of Any County, Any State

TRUSTEE STATES THAT:

This conveyance is made pursuant to the powers conferred upon Trustee by that
certain Deed of Trust dated October 8, 1994 and executed by THOMAS TRENT as
trustor, and recorded on October 9, 1994 in Book 455, Instrument No. 947, Page
107, of Official Records of Any County, Any State, and after fulfillment of the conditions specified in said Deed of Trust authorizing this conveyance.

Default occurred as set forth in a Notice of Default and Election to Sell which was
recorded in the office of the Recorder of said County.

All requirements of law regarding the mailing and recording of copies of notices
and the posting and publication and recording of copies of the Notice of Sale
have been complied with.

Said property as sold by said Trustee at public auction on June 29, 1998 at the
place named in the Notice of Sale, in the County of Any County, Any State, in
which the property is situated, Grantee being the highest bidder at such sale,
became the purchaser of said property and paid therefor to said Trustee the
amount bid, being $104,500.00, in lawful money of the United States, or by the
satisfaction, pro tanto, of the obligations then secured by said Deed of Trust.

FIGURE 20–4
(continued)

IN WITNESS WHEREOF, said ANY CITY TRUST COMPANY, as Trustee, has this day, caused its corporate name and seal to be hereunto affixed by its President and Secretary, thereunto duly authorized by resolution of its Board of Directors.

Dated: July 10, 1998.   ANY CITY TRUST COMPANY

By: _____
Valerie Winslow, President

By: _____
Curtis Emerson, Secretary

(corporate seal)

STATE OF ANY STATE
COUNTY OF ANY COUNTY

On this 10th day of July, 1998, before me, the undersigned, a Notary Public in and for the County and State aforesaid, personally appeared VALERIE WINSLOW known to me to be the President and CURTIS EMERSON known to me to be the Secretary of the corporation that executed the within instrument, and known to me to be the persons who executed the within instrument on behalf of the corporation therein named, and acknowledged to me that such corporation executed the same, pursuant to its laws, or a resolution of its Board of Directors.

_____
Notary Public, State of Any State
My commission expires:

    b. *Publish notice of trustee's sale according to state statutory requirements*
    c. *If required by state statute, record notice of trustee's sale*
    d. *Arrange for public auction and sale of the property*
    e. *Prepare trustee's deed*
    f. *After receiving proceeds from purchaser, record the trustee's deed and provide to purchaser*

Judicial Foreclosure

A judicial foreclosure is a court proceeding in which (1) the court awards judgment against the borrower on the promissory note and (2) all title rights in the secured real property held by the borrower are foreclosed and the property sold to pay the debt. Mortgages typically are foreclosed through judicial foreclosure.

Prior to initiating a judicial action, the lender's attorney usually sends a demand letter to the delinquent borrower specifying the nature and amount of the default, the action required to cure the default, the date by which the default must be cured, and the actions that may be taken by the lender should the borrower fail to cure the default by the specified date. A sample demand letter, together with samples of documents pertaining to judicial foreclosures, may be found in the hypothetical foreclosure suit provided at the end of this chapter.

Should the borrower fail to meet the terms of the demand letter, a judicial foreclosure will be initiated by the filing of a complaint in the trial court in the county in which the real property is located. A judicial foreclosure generally is a lengthier procedure than a nonjudicial foreclosure. The borrower is a defendant in the suit and has the right to raise defenses against the foreclosure action.

Prior to the filing of a complaint, one must determine all necessary parties to the suit. All necessary parties are those individuals or entities having an interest in the real property inferior (lesser in priority) to the interest of the lender. This includes the borrower and all junior lienholders. To determine the identity of any and all junior lienholders, the title work on the real property should be updated by obtaining a partial abstract from the date the lender's mortgage was recorded to the present date (see Chapter 11 for a detailed discussion of abstracts). The holders of any junior liens must be named as defendants in the suit. If the property in question is rental property, tenants are considered parties having a leasehold interest in the property and, therefore, must be joined in the action.

Next, state statutes must be checked to determine if court rules require that a particular form of complaint be used in the action. A foreclosure complaint should include a count for foreclosure and a separate count for money damages. If there is a risk that the property's value may diminish because the property has been abandoned or poorly maintained, or if the property is rental property, an additional count should be included in the complaint requesting the appointment by the court of a *receiver*. A receiver will protect the lender's interests by maintaining the property and, if applicable, by generating appropriate rents from income-producing property. A copy of the note and a copy of the mortgage should be attached to the complaint as exhibits. Some states require that the filed complaint be a verified complaint.

A notice of lis pendens (discussed in Chapter 9) should be filed at the same time the complaint is filed, putting third parties on notice that the real property is the subject matter of pending litigation. Service of process upon all parties is set out in state civil procedure statutes. Service of process is carried out by serving a summons and a copy of the foreclosure complaint on each defendant. In the event a borrower cannot be personally served, state statute may permit *constructive service* (service by publication or other methods). In these instances, an affidavit of diligent search and inquiry may be required to be filed setting forth the steps taken by the plaintiff-lender to attempt to find and personally serve the defendant-borrower.

The summons, served personally or constructively, states the statutorily prescribed time period within which the defendant-borrower must respond to the complaint. Should the defendant fail to respond within this time period, the plaintiff's attorney will move for a default judgment against the defendant.

The **Soldiers' and Sailors' Relief Act,** a federal statute, mandates that in any court action in which a defendant fails to appear through submission of a responsive pleading, the plaintiff is required to file an affidavit swearing to the best of his or her knowledge and belief that the defendant is not in one of the branches of military service, before a default judgment may be rendered against the defendant. In order to prepare such an affidavit, the lender's attorney must obtain certificates of status from each branch of service. This procedure is time-consuming and should be commenced as soon as the complaint is filed. Letters should be sent to

Soldiers' and Sailors' Relief Act: A federal statute which mandates that in any action in which a defendant fails to appear through the submission of a responsive pleading, the plaintiff is required to file an affidavit swearing that to the best of his or her knowledge and belief, the defendant is not in one of the branches of the military service, before a default judgment may be rendered against the defendant.

each branch of the military, providing the defendant's name, date of birth, social security number, and any other relevant identifying information. Each letter should also state the reason for requesting the certificate and be accompanied by a check made payable to the appropriate official in the required amount.

If the defendant was served by publication, state law may require the appointment of an **attorney ad litem** to represent the defendant's interests. If this is the case, a motion for appointment of attorney ad litem should be prepared, together with a court order appointing an attorney ad litem before the case proceeds further. If an attorney ad litem is appointed, it is his or her task to attempt to ascertain the whereabouts of the defendant and to determine the defendant's military status.

Once the certificates of military status have been received and it is determined that the defendant's failure to respond is not due to his or her military posting, a motion for default and an affidavit as to nonmilitary service are prepared. Additionally, if permitted by state statute and court rules, a motion for summary final judgment may be prepared, together with supporting affidavits establishing the sums owed to the plaintiff-lender on the loan, the sums owed for court costs, and the sums owed for attorneys' fees.

A final hearing is then scheduled, and notice of the hearing is sent to the parties. The court requires the original note and mortgage. At the hearing, the plaintiff's attorney will present the court with a final judgment order for the judge to sign authorizing a judicial sale. State statute dictates the prescribed form for a notice of sale and the requisite publication period of the notice.

After the sale is completed, the clerk of the court typically issues a certificate of sale. Title to the property will be transferred to the buyer by a sheriff's deed or a referee's deed. Transfer of title to the real property may be delayed, however, pending the closure of the permitted redemption period during which the borrower may redeem the property by repaying the amount of the loan plus court costs, interest, and penalties. If the Internal Revenue Service has placed a federal tax lien on the property, it must be given written notice of the foreclosure sale twenty-five days prior to the date of the sale. The Internal Revenue Service is entitled to redeem the property up to one hundred and twenty days after the date of the sale. Other lienholders also have certain rights of redemption, so state statutes should be researched before an attempt is made to resell the property.

A paralegal working in a real estate law firm or in the legal department of a lending institution may be asked to prepare any or all of the documents just mentioned. In assisting an attorney with a judicial foreclosure, the following checklist may prove helpful.

MORTGAGE FORECLOSURE CHECKLIST
1. *Review mortgage and note carefully, noting:*
   a. *The proper names of all parties*
   b. *The legal description of the property*
   c. *The total amount of the debt obligation*
   d. *The payment terms*
   e. *The rights conferred upon each party in the event of default*
   f. *The recording information pertaining to the mortgage*

attorney ad litem: An attorney appointed by the court to protect a defendant's interests.

2. *Prepare the demand letter that includes:*
    a. *The name of the lender*
    b. *The amount of the default and date it was due*
    c. *Demand terms (for example, default amount plus penalties, acceleration of the total outstanding obligation)*
    d. *Date by which default must be corrected*
    e. *Legal description of the property*
    f. *Date by which to notify lender in the event the borrower disputes the default amount*
    g. *The consequences should borrower fail to act within the specified time period*
3. *Obtain updated partial abstract to determine junior lienholders*
4. *If income-producing property, ascertain names of all tenants*
5. *Prepare complaint including counts for foreclosure, money damages, and, if applicable, appointment of a receiver. Attach copies of note and mortgage as exhibits.*
6. *Prepare a summons for each defendant*
7. *Make appropriate number of copies of complaint for the clerk and a copy of each summons for office file*
8. *Prepare a notice of lis pendens*
9. *File the complaint and notice of lis pendens with applicable filing fee and sheriff's fee. Have clerk sign summonses.*
10. *Obtain certificates of military status of defendant from each branch of service by sending letter with requisite information and fee*
11. *If personal service fails, prepare affidavit of diligent search and inquiry and serve by publication*
12. *If required by state statute, prepare motion for appointment of attorney ad litem to represent defendant served by publication, together with order appointing attorney ad litem*
13. *Should borrower fail to respond to complaint, prepare and file:*
    a. *motion for default*
    b. *motion for summary final judgment*
    c. *affidavit as to nonmilitary service*
    d. *affidavit of indebtedness*
    e. *affidavit of costs*
    f. *affidavit as to attorneys' fees*
14. *Schedule final hearing*
15. *Obtain original note and mortgage*
16. *Prepare final judgment order*
17. *Prepare notice of sale and publish as per state statutory requirements*

Strict Foreclosure

strict foreclosure: A foreclosure method used primarily in Connecticut and Vermont in which a court hearing is held to determine the mortgagee's right to foreclose. If the mortgagee's right is authorized, the court awards the real property to the mortgagee without requiring the mortgagee to bid for the property at a public sale.

Strict foreclosure is a foreclosure method used primarily in Connecticut and Vermont. It differs from judicial foreclosure in that the real property serving as collateral for the loan is not sold. A court hearing is held to determine the mortgagee's right to foreclose. If the mortgagee's right is authorized, the court simply awards the real property to the mortgagee without requiring the mortgagee to bid for the property at a public sale. In a judicial foreclosure, should proceeds be left over after the plaintiff and junior lienholders are paid, the remaining proceeds are handed over to the defendant. In a strict fore-closure, the defendant receives nothing because no sale has taken place.

Entry Foreclosure

Entry foreclosure is another foreclosure method that is used only in a few New England states. It is similar to strict foreclosure in that no sale of the real property takes place. Instead, upon default by the borrower, the lender forecloses by taking possession of the real property and holding possession for a specified time period, after which legal title to the property passes to the lender.

entry foreclosure: A foreclosure method used only in a few New England states in which the lender forecloses by taking possession of the real property for a specified time period, after which legal title to the property passes to the lender.

HYPOTHETICAL CLIENT MATTER

Barbara has set aside some time this afternoon to work on a foreclosure file. The client is Any County First National Bank. Any County First National Bank made a residential mortgage loan to Leonard and Joyce Dryden. The Drydens became delinquent on their monthly payments, and Any County First National Bank contacted attorney Ava Ross to initiate proceedings against the Drydens. The demand letter shown in Figure 20–5 was sent to the Drydens demanding cure of their default.

The demand letter was received but the Drydens did not respond to the letter, and upon Ava's instruction, Barbara prepared and filed the complaint shown in Figure 20–6.

The Notice of Lis Pendens shown in Figure 20–7 was filed with the complaint shown in Figure 20–6.

Personal service upon the Drydens was perfected, but they have failed to file a responsive pleading. The statutory time period for filing a response has expired, and Ava has asked Barbara to prepare the appropriate motions and supporting affidavits to proceed with the foreclosure. The first document Barbara prepares is a motion for default (see Figure 20–8). The top half of the document embodies the motion, while the bottom half contains the default to be signed by the clerk of the court.

Barbara next prepares a motion for final summary judgment (see Figure 20–9). This motion will be accompanied by numerous supporting affidavits to establish the sums owed to Any County First National Bank for the outstanding debt obligation plus interest and penalties, the amount expended on costs, and the amount expended on attorneys' fees in pursuing this action.

Barbara next checks the file to make sure all certificates of military status have been received. Because personal service was perfected on the Drydens, there was no necessity for having an attorney ad litem appointed. Therefore, the responsibility for obtaining the requisite certificates fell upon Barbara. The certificates verify that neither Leonard nor Joyce Dryden are active members of the military. Barbara proceeds to prepare an affidavit as to nonmilitary service

FIGURE 20–5
Demand letter

April 7, 1998

CERTIFIED MAIL #P332261355
RETURN RECEIPT REQUESTED

Mr. and Mrs. Leonard Dryden
894 Colonial Avenue
Any City, Any State

RE: Loan No. 655344

Dear Mr. and Mrs. Dryden:

The undersigned law firm has been retained to represent Any County First National Bank, N.A. We have been informed that you presently are in default under the above-referenced loan by failing to make payment due March 1, 1998 and all subsequent payments. You are required, in order to cure this default, to forward to Any County First National Bank certified funds in the total amount of $1,937.24. This amount consists of the following: payments due March 1, 1998 and April 1, 1998, totaling $1,762.24; late charges in the amount of $50.00; and attorneys' fees in the amount of $125.00. If the funds are forwarded after May 1, 1998, then you must add an additional $881.12 to the above total sum. The above total sum must be paid no later than May 10, 1998 in order to cure the default. Failure to do so may result in acceleration of the total outstanding balance of your loan secured by your mortgage and judicial foreclosure and sale of the following described real property:

Lot 18 in Block 6, LONGFORD ESTATES, a subdivision according to the plat thereof as recorded in Plat Book 103, Page 59, of the Public Records of Any County, Any State.

According to the terms of the mortgage securing the above-referenced loan, you have the right to reinstate after acceleration, as well as the right to raise any applicable defense in any foreclosure proceeding. Should you fail to cure the default as specified above, the terms of your promissory note hold you responsible for the costs and fees incurred by Any County First National Bank for any further legal proceedings in this matter.

Unless you dispute the validity of this debt within thirty (30) days of your receipt of this letter, we will assume that the debt is valid. Should you notify us in writing within the thirty (30) day period that you are disputing this debt, we will proceed to obtain verification of the debt from Any County First National Bank and forward the verification to you.

Sincerely,

Ava Ross, Esquire

cc: Any County First National Bank, N.A.

affidavit of indebtedness: A sworn statement attesting to the amounts owed to the affiant by a party.

(see Figure 20–10), which will be signed by Vincent Gray, the loan officer assigned to the Dryden loan file.

Barbara then prepares an **affidavit of indebtedness** (see Figure 20–11), also to be signed by Vincent. This affidavit sets forth the date of execution of the note and mortgage, the date of recording of the mortgage, the Official Records book

FIGURE 20–6
Complaint for mortgage foreclosure

IN THE CIRCUIT COURT OF THE THIRD JUDICIAL CIRCUIT
IN AND FOR ANY COUNTY, ANY STATE

CASE NO. 98-4011

ANY COUNTY FIRST NATIONAL BANK, N.A.,
a national banking association,
                    Plaintiff,

vs.

LEONARD DRYDEN and JOYCE DRYDEN,
                    Defendants.
_____/

COMPLAINT FOR MORTGAGE FORECLOSURE

Plaintiff, ANY COUNTY FIRST NATIONAL BANK, N.A., by and through its undersigned counsel, sues Defendants, LEONARD DRYDEN and JOYCE DRYDEN, and alleges:

COUNT I—ACTION FOR MORTGAGE FORECLOSURE

1. This is an action to foreclose a mortgage on real property in Any County, Any State.
2. On May 10, 1995, Defendants executed and delivered a Promissory Note and a Mortgage securing payment of the Note to Plaintiff. The Mortgage was recorded on May 11, 1995, in Official Records Book 1190 at page 15, of the public records of Any County, Any State, and mortgaged the property described in the Mortgage then owned by and in possession of the mortgagor, a copy of the Mortgage and a copy of the Note being attached hereto and made a part hereof as Exhibits A and B.
3. Plaintiff owns and holds the Note and Mortgage.
4. The property is now owned by Defendants who hold possession.
5. Defendants have defaulted under the Note and Mortgage by failing to pay the payment due March 1, 1998, and all subsequent payments.
6. Plaintiff declares the full amount payable under the Note and Mortgage to be due.
7. Defendants owe Plaintiff $102,186.65 that is due on principal on the Note and Mortgage, interest from February 1, 1998, and title search expense for ascertaining necessary parties to this action.
8. Plaintiff is obligated to pay Plaintiff's counsel a reasonable fee for services rendered.

WHEREFORE, Plaintiff demands judgment foreclosing the Mortgage and, if the proceeds of the sale are insufficient to pay Plaintiff's claim, a deficiency judgment.

COUNT II—DAMAGES

9. This is an action for damages that exceed Fifteen Thousand Dollars ($15,000.00).
10. Plaintiff realleges and incorporates herein the allegations contained in paragraphs 2 through 8 above.
11. Defendants owe Plaintiff those sums of money set forth in paragraph 7 above.

WHEREFORE, Plaintiff demands judgment for damages against Defendants.

DATED: May 12, 1998.

> FISHER, SIMON, AND ROSS, P.A.
> 1900 N.W. 3rd Avenue
> Any City, Any State
> (000) 232-7000
> Attorneys for Plaintiff
>
> By: _____
> Ava Ross, Esquire
> Any State Bar No. 123456

IN THE CIRCUIT COURT OF THE THIRD JUDICIAL CIRCUIT
IN AND FOR ANY COUNTY, ANY STATE

CASE NO. 98-4011

ANY COUNTY FIRST NATIONAL BANK, N.A.,
a national banking association,
            Plaintiff,

vs.

LEONARD DRYDEN and JOYCE DRYDEN,
            Defendants.
_____/

NOTICE OF LIS PENDENS

TO DEFENDANTS LEONARD DRYDEN AND JOYCE DRYDEN, AND ALL OTHERS
WHOM IT MAY CONCERN:

YOU ARE NOTIFIED of the institution of this action by Plaintiff against you seeking to foreclose a mortgage on the following property in Any County, Any State:

> Lot 18 in Block 6, LONGFORD ESTATES, a subdivision according to the
> plat thereof as recorded in Plat Book 103, Page 59, of the Public Records
> of Any County, Any State.

DATED on May 12, 1998.

> FISHER, ROSS, AND SIMON, P.A.
> 1900 N.W. 3rd Avenue
> Any City, Any State
> (000) 232-7000
> Attorneys for Plaintiff
>
> By: _____
> Ava Ross, Esquire
> Any State Bar No. 123456

IN THE CIRCUIT COURT OF THE THIRD JUDICIAL CIRCUIT
IN AND FOR ANY COUNTY, ANY STATE
CASE NO. 98-4011

ANY COUNTY FIRST NATIONAL BANK, N.A.,
a national banking association,
                    Plaintiff,

vs.

LEONARD DRYDEN and JOYCE DRYDEN,
                    Defendants.
_____/

MOTION FOR DEFAULT

Plaintiff, ANY COUNTY FIRST NATIONAL BANK, N.A., by and through its undersigned counsel, moves for entry of Default by the Clerk against Defendants LEONARD DRYDEN and JOYCE DRYDEN for their failure to serve any paper on the undersigned since the filing of the complaint.

DATED: _____ 1998.

                              FISHER, ROSS, AND SIMON, P.A.
                              1900 N.W. 3rd Avenue
                              Any City, Any State
                              (000) 232-7000
                              Attorneys for Plaintiff

                              By: _____
                                   Ava Ross, Esquire
                                   Any State Bar No. 123456

DEFAULT

A Default is entered in this action against the Defendants named in the above Motion, for their failure to serve or file any paper as required by law.

DATED: _____ 1998.

                              ROSEMARY HIGGINS
                              Clerk of the Court

                              By: _____
                                   Deputy Clerk

Copies furnished to:
Ava Ross, Esquire
Leonard Dryden
Joyce Dryden

FIGURE 20–8
Motion for default

and page numbers at which the mortgage was recorded, and a breakdown on the amounts owed to the client.

In addition to the sums listed in the affidavit of indebtedness, certain sums were expended as costs incurred in bringing the foreclosure proceeding. In this instance, the costs incurred were the filing fee for filing the complaint, the sheriff's

FIGURE 20–9
Motion for summary
judgment of foreclosure

IN THE CIRCUIT COURT OF THE THIRD JUDICIAL CIRCUIT
IN AND FOR ANY COUNTY, ANY STATE

CASE NO. 98-4011

ANY COUNTY FIRST NATIONAL BANK, N.A.,
a national banking association,
           Plaintiff,

vs.

LEONARD DRYDEN and JOYCE DRYDEN,
           Defendants.

_____/

MOTION FOR SUMMARY JUDGMENT OF FORECLOSURE

COMES NOW the Plaintiff, ANY COUNTY FIRST NATIONAL BANK, N.A., by and through its undersigned counsel, and hereby moves this Court for entry of a Summary Final Judgment of Foreclosure and for attorneys' fees and costs in this cause, and as grounds therefore would show as follows:

1. This is an action to foreclose a Mortgage on real property located in Any County, Any State.
2. There is no material issue of law or fact in this cause, and Plaintiff is entitled to entry of a Summary Final Judgment of Foreclosure in its favor as a matter of law.
3. Service of process has been properly perfected upon the Defendants.
4. Plaintiff has an interest superior to any interest of the Defendants in and to the real property more particularly described as follows:

   Lot 18 in Block 6, LONGFORD ESTATES, a subdivision according to the plat thereof as recorded in Plat Book 103, Page 59, of the Public Records of Any County, Any State

5. Plaintiff attaches to this Motion the following supporting affidavits:
   (a)   Affidavit as to Nonmilitary Service
   (b)   Affidavit of Indebtedness
   (c)   Affidavit as to Costs
   (d)   Affidavit as to Attorneys' Fees

WHEREFORE, Plaintiff requests entry of a Summary Final Judgment of Foreclosure and for attorneys' fees and costs in this cause.

FISHER, SIMON, AND ROSS, P.A.
1900 N.W. 3rd Avenue
Any City, Any State
(000) 232-7000
Attorneys for Plaintiff

By: _____
Ava Ross, Esquire
Any State Bar No. 123456

fee, and the cost of obtaining the partial abstract from a title company to ascertain whether any liens were filed against the property since the recording of the client's mortgage. With these costs noted, Barbara prepares an affidavit as to costs (see Figure 20–12).

IN THE CIRCUIT COURT OF THE THIRD JUDICIAL CIRCUIT
IN AND FOR ANY COUNTY, ANY STATE

CASE NO. 98-4011

ANY COUNTY FIRST NATIONAL BANK, N.A.,
a national banking association,
        Plaintiff,

vs.

LEONARD DRYDEN and JOYCE DRYDEN,
        Defendants

_____/

AFFIDAVIT AS TO NONMILITARY SERVICE

STATE OF ANY STATE
COUNTY OF ANY COUNTY

BEFORE ME, the undersigned authority, personally appeared VINCENT GRAY who, being first duly sworn, says as follows:

1. Affiant is an employee of Plaintiff in this matter and is authorized to make this affidavit on its behalf.
2. The statements made herein are made upon Affiant's own personal knowledge.
3. To the best of Affiant's knowledge and belief, Defendants, LEONARD DRYDEN and JOYCE DRYDEN, are over eighteen years of age.
4. To the best of Affiant's knowledge and belief, Defendants have not been on active duty in the military service of the United States since the filing of this action.

FURTHER AFFIANT SAYETH NOT.

_____
Vincent Gray, Affiant

Sworn to and subscribed before me this _____ day of _____, 1998, by VINCENT GRAY, personally known to me.

_____
Notary Public, State of Any State
My commission expires:

FIGURE 20–10
Affidavit as to nonmilitary service

Finally, Barbara refers to the applicable rule in the Any State Bar Code of Professional Responsibility pertaining to the factors to consider when awarding attorneys' fees. The factors set forth in the rule help the court determine whether the attorneys' fees presented are reasonable. Factors commonly considered are the difficulty of the matter, the rates customarily charged for similar matters, and the rates the attorney charges similar clients for such services. Some states require an additional affidavit from an attorney outside the firm corroborating that the fees charged in the case before the court are reasonable, but no such additional affidavit is required by the courts in Any State. The affidavit as to attorneys' fees prepared by Barbara is shown in Figure 20–13.

IN THE CIRCUIT COURT OF THE THIRD JUDICIAL CIRCUIT
IN AND FOR ANY COUNTY, ANY STATE

CASE NO. 98-4011

ANY COUNTY FIRST NATIONAL BANK, N.A.,
a national banking association,
             Plaintiff,

vs.

LEONARD DRYDEN and JOYCE DRYDEN,
             Defendants.

_____/

AFFIDAVIT OF INDEBTEDNESS

STATE OF ANY STATE
COUNTY OF ANY COUNTY

BEFORE ME, the undersigned authority, this day personally appeared VINCENT GRAY who, being first duly sworn, says as follows:

1. Affiant is an employee of the Plaintiff in this matter and is authorized to make this affidavit on its behalf.
2. The statements made herein are made upon Affiant's own personal knowledge.
3. On May 10, 1995, Defendants executed and delivered to Plaintiff a Promissory Note. The Mortgage was recorded on May 11, 1995 in Official Records Book 1190, Page 15, of the public records of Any County, Any State. A copy of the Note and Mortgage are attached as Exhibits A and B.
4. The Plaintiff is the holder and owner of said Note and Mortgage.
5. The real property is owned by Defendants, who have possession of the property.
6. Defendants have defaulted under said Note and Mortgage by failing to make the payment due March 1, 1998 and all subsequent payments.
7. Defendants owe Plaintiff the following amounts:

(a)	Principal due on Note and Mortgage	$102,186.65
(b)	Interest from February 1, 1998 to June 12, 1998	1,629.25
	(Interest after the above date at the rate of $12.25 per day)	
(c)	Late charges	100.00
(d)	Taxes and insurance	0
	TOTAL	$103,915.90

8. Plaintiff has retained the services of Fisher, Simon, and Ross, P.A. to represent it in this action and is obligated to pay said law firm a reasonable fee for services rendered.

FURTHER AFFIANT SAYETH NOT.

_____
Vincent Gray, Affiant

Sworn to and subscribed before me this _____ day of _____, 1998, by VINCENT GRAY, who is personally known to me.

_____
Notary Public, State of Any State
My commission expires:

IN THE CIRCUIT COURT OF THE THIRD JUDICIAL CIRCUIT
IN AND FOR ANY COUNTY, ANY STATE

CASE NO. 98-4011

ANY COUNTY FIRST NATIONAL BANK, N.A.,
a national banking association,
Plaintiff,

vs.

LEONARD DRYDEN and JOYCE DRYDEN,
Defendants.

_____/

AFFIDAVIT AS TO COSTS

STATE OF ANY STATE
COUNTY OF ANY COUNTY

BEFORE ME, the undersigned authority, this day personally appeared Ava Ross, Esquire who, being first duly sworn, deposes and says as follows:

1. She is the attorney for the Plaintiff in this action and is familiar with the costs expended by, or on behalf of, the Plaintiff.
2. The costs expended by the Plaintiff in this action are as follows:

(a)	Clerk of the Court, Any County	$ 80.00
(b)	Sheriff, Any County	20.00
(c)	Any City Title Company	200.00
	TOTAL	$300.00

FURTHER AFFIANT SAYETH NOT.

_____
Ava Ross, Affiant

Sworn to and subscribed before me this _____ day of _____, 1998, by AVA ROSS, ESQUIRE, who is personally known to me.

_____
Notary Public, State of Any State
My commission expires:

FIGURE 20–12
Affidavit as to costs

FIGURE 20–13
Affidavit as to
attorneys' fees

IN THE CIRCUIT COURT OF THE THIRD JUDICIAL CIRCUIT
IN AND FOR ANY COUNTY, ANY STATE

CASE NO. 98-4011

ANY COUNTY FIRST NATIONAL BANK, N.A.,
a national banking association,
                    Plaintiff,

vs.

LEONARD DRYDEN and JOYCE DRYDEN,
                    Defendants.

_____/

AFFIDAVIT AS TO ATTORNEYS' FEES

STATE OF ANY STATE
COUNTY OF ANY COUNTY

BEFORE ME, the undersigned authority, this day personally appeared AVA ROSS, ESQUIRE of Fisher, Simon, and Ross, P.A., who after being first duly sworn, deposes and says to the best of her knowledge and belief as follows:

1. She is the attorney for the Plaintiff in this action and has been practicing law in the State of Any State since 1980.
2. The following time at the following rates has been expended on this action:
   (a) 3.00 hours by attorney at the rate of $150.00 per hour
   (b) 4.00 hours by paralegal at the rate of $75.00 per hour
   The above hourly rates represent Affiant's fee arrangement with her client.
3. The above-mentioned hourly rate is a rate which is customarily charged for similar matters and one which the Affiant customarily charges similar clients for such services.
4. The hours expended as set forth on the attached Statement for Services are a reasonable amount of time to have spent on this action.

FURTHER AFFIANT SAYETH NOT.

_____
Ava Ross, Affiant

Sworn to and subscribed before me this _____ day of _____, 1998, by AVA ROSS, ESQUIRE, who is personally known to me.

_____
Notary Public, State of Any State
My commission expires:

CHAPTER SUMMARY

1. When a borrower is in default on a loan, the borrower may seek various remedies to prevent foreclosure on the real property securing the loan. The borrower may attempt to reinstate the loan under the currently existing loan terms, may attempt to enter into a loan modification agreement, may give the lender a deed in lieu of foreclosure, or, as a final measure, may file for bankruptcy.

2. Foreclosure is the process whereby the real property securing a loan is sold and the proceeds used to pay the outstanding debt. However, two types of foreclosure methods exist in which no sale takes place. The first is strict foreclosure in which a court hearing determines a lender's right to foreclose, after which the property is transferred to the lender. The second is entry foreclosure in which the lender simply takes possession of the property and, after a stipulated time period, receives title to the property. Strict foreclosure and entry foreclosure are only used in certain New England states.

3. Nonjudicial foreclosure primarily occurs in deed of trust states. Rather than filing a lawsuit, the trustee records a notice of default setting forth the particulars of the default and notifying the borrower that the property may be sold without court action if the borrower does not act within the stated time period. After the prescribed waiting period expires, a notice of trustee's sale is published and a public auction is held.

4. In assisting an attorney with a nonjudicial foreclosure, a paralegal may be called upon to prepare the following: (1) a demand letter, (2) a notice of default, (3) a notice of trustee's sale, and (4) a trustee's deed.

5. Mortgages typically are foreclosed through judicial foreclosure. Although the actual procedure varies from state to state, a judicial foreclosure begins with the filing of a complaint, naming the borrower, and all other parties with interests inferior to those of the plaintiff, as defendants in the suit. Should the borrower fail to respond to the complaint, a default judgment may be entered against him or her. Upon final hearing, the court will authorize the public sale of the real property. Most states allow a redemption period after the sale, during which time the borrower can redeem the property by paying off the loan plus all penalties, costs, and attorneys' fees.

6. In assisting an attorney with a judicial foreclosure, a paralegal may be called upon to prepare the following: (1) a demand letter, (2) a complaint, (3) a notice of lis pendens, (4) a motion for default, (5) a motion for summary final judgment, and (6) various supporting affidavits.

REVIEW QUESTIONS

1. What remedies might a borrower seek to prevent foreclosure?
2. Outline the steps to be taken in a nonjudicial foreclosure.
3. Outline the steps to be taken in a judicial foreclosure.
4. Explain the manner in which lienholders are paid in the event of a foreclosure.
5. Distinguish between (a) strict foreclosure and (b) entry foreclosure.

ETHICAL QUESTIONS

You spent two hours on your computer preparing foreclosure documents for a lending institution client. This is the first time your supervising attorney has been asked to file a foreclosure, so you were preparing the documents from scratch. As you were completing the documents, a sudden power outage occurred, and when the power came back on, you found that you lost all of the prepared documents and that you had to start all over again, a task that took an additional two hours. You are now preparing a time slip for the hours spent on this task. How many hours should you bill the client for?

PRACTICAL ASSIGNMENTS

Assignment 20:1. Research your state statutes regarding foreclosure procedures. Photocopy the relevant statutes and insert them under the "Litigation" section of your resource portfolio.

Assignment 20:2. Your supervising attorney, Deborah Sanders, represents client Midas National Bank, a national banking association. Midas National Bank has contacted Deborah regarding customers who were delinquent on their loan payments. The customers in question are Dennis and Linda Davidson, residing at 230 Bantry Lane (your city, your state). The Davidsons have failed to make the monthly payment of $1,000 that was due the first of last month. Deborah asks that you draft a demand letter for her signature. The loan number is 111222. In the letter, demand immediate payment by cashier's check of the outstanding principal of $120,000, together with interest of $4,000, within thirty days from today's date. State that failure to pay within this time period may result in foreclosure on the property. The legal description of the property in question is:

> Lot 1 in Block 4, ENFIELD CHASE, a subdivision, according to the plat thereof, as recorded in Plat Book 58, Page 18, of the Public Records of (your county and state).

After review, insert the demand letter under the "Litigation" section of your resource portfolio.

Assignment 20:3. Now assume that thirty days have passed without a response from the Davidsons, who are now an additional month behind on their loan payments. Further assume that you live in a title theory state that utilizes deeds of trust as the primary financing instrument. Prepare a notice of default. The trustor is Marcus Catesby of Premium Trust Company, located at 700 Coolidge Street (your city and state). The reference number is 111222. The deed of trust was executed in favor of Midas National Bank on July 1, 1995, and recorded on July 2, 1995, at book 600, page 100, of the official records of your county and state. Midas National Bank's address is 920 Eisenhower Avenue (your city and state). After review, insert the notice under the "Litigation" section of your resource portfolio.

Assignment 20:4. Now assume that instead of living in a title theory state, you live in a lien theory state in which mortgages are the primary financing instruments, and instead of a deed of trust, the Davidsons executed a mortgage that was recorded at the book and page number given. Prepare a foreclosure complaint and a notice of lis pendens based on the information provided in Assignment 20:3, with the changes indicated in this assignment. Remember to include the following information: name and address of your firm, which is Hernandez, Sanders, and Norris, P.A., 263 Republic Avenue (your city and state); the telephone number, which is (your area code) 222-3333; and Deborah's bar number is 654321 under her signature. After review, insert the complaint and notice of lis pendens under the "Litigation" section of your resource portfolio.

Assignment 20:5. Define the following key terms.

affidavit of indebtedness
attorney ad litem
deed in lieu of foreclosure
entry foreclosure
foreclosure
notice of default

notice of rescission
notice of trustee's sale
redemption period
reinstatement of loan
Soldiers' and Sailors' Relief Act
strict foreclosure

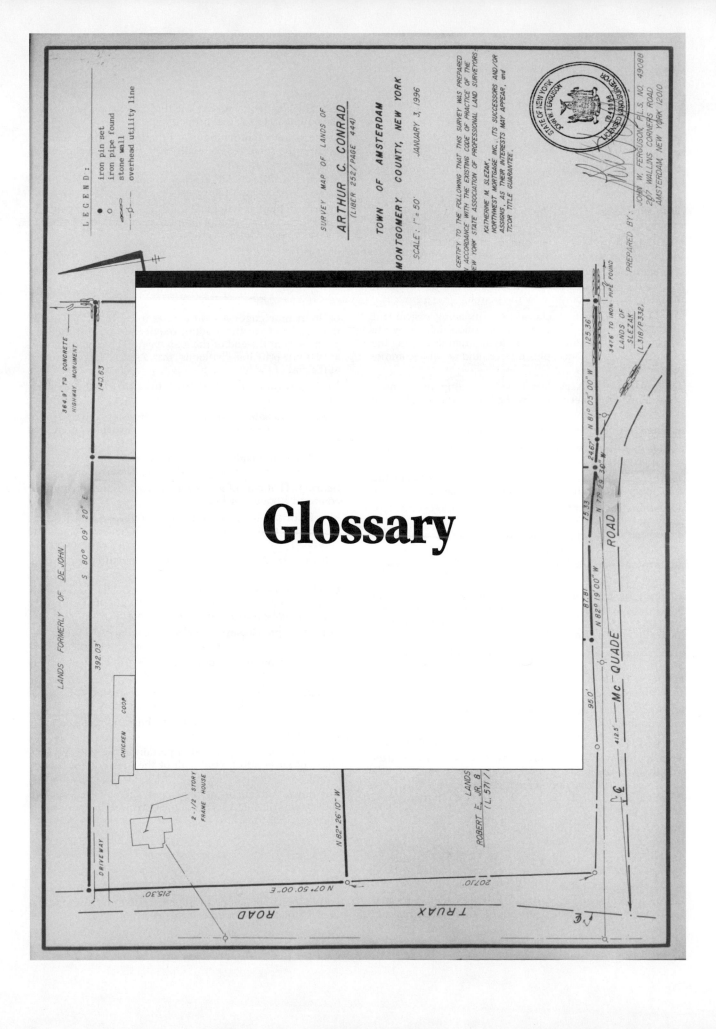

Glossary

A

ABA standards: Standards of ethical conduct for persons in the legal profession set forth in the American Bar Association's Model Code of Professional Responsibility and Model Code of Professional Conduct.

abatement of rent: A deduction from the rent owed for the diminishment in value of the premises caused by the lack of maintenance.

abstract of title: A copy or condensed version of each document pertaining to a particular parcel of real property.

abstractor's certificate: A certificate that states the records the abstractor has examined, any records not examined, and the dates covered by the search.

acceleration clause: A clause in a financing instrument that permits the lender, at its option, upon default by the borrower, to accelerate the entire loan amount, making the full outstanding balance, plus interest and penalties, immediately due.

accounting: A broker's duty in safeguarding any monies, documents, or property held by the broker on behalf of the principal.

acreage: A tract of undeveloped real property.

actual eviction: The bringing of a suit for possession of leased premises.

actual notice: Direct knowledge a person has about the ownership and condition of title of real property.

adjustable rate loan: A loan in which the interest rate typically starts lower than that of a fixed rate loan, and then periodically changes in relation to an index rate, such as the rate on Treasury securities.

adjustment period: The period between one rate change and the next for an adjustable rate loan.

advance fee trust account: A special escrow account in which advance fees paid to a broker are deposited. These fees may be used for advertising and other expenses incurred in marketing real property.

adverse possession: The acquisition of title to real property through taking possession of land that belongs to another without the owner's consent and retaining possession for a statutorily prescribed period of time.

affidavit of indebtedness: A sworn statement attesting to the amounts owed to the affiant by a party.

agent: A person authorized to act on behalf of another.

American Land Title Association (ALTA): An organization that was created to meet the demands for uniform title insurance protection nationwide. It has devised title commitment and title policy forms that are used in many parts of the country.

amortized loan: A loan in which level payments are made throughout the life of the loan.

anchor store: A major lessee in a shopping center, typically a major department store or, in the case of a neighborhood center, a supermarket.

annual percentage rate (APR): The true interest rate on a loan, which includes charges added such as points and mortgage insurance.

appurtenant easement: An easement given to confer a benefit to adjacent real property.

arc: The length of a curved line that makes up a segment of the boundary of the real property.

assumption of mortgage: A situation in which a buyer assumes personal responsibility for payment of the seller's existing mortgage loan.

attorney ad litem: An attorney appointed by the court to protect a defendant's interests.

attorney-client privilege: A rule of evidence law that prevents a court from compelling the revelation of communications between lawyer and client.

B

balloon mortgage: A loan calling for periodic payments that are less than the amount required to pay off the loan completely at the end of the loan term. The remaining balance of the principal "balloons" into a single, large payment at the end of the loan term.

Bank Insurance Fund (BIF): A fund that insures depositors' accounts.

bargain and sale deed: A deed that transfers the real property itself rather than transferring any particular interest in the property.

base line: An imaginary line running east and west used in the government survey method of legal descriptions.

bearing: That part of a call which provides the direction or course of a boundary line.

benefit of the bargain: A monetary remedy in a breach of contract action calculated as the difference between the contract price and the fair market value of the property.

bill of sale: A document that transfers title to personal property.

blockbusting: The attempt to get homeowners to list their property for sale by stating or implying that minority groups may be moving into the neighborhood.

bona fide purchaser for value: Someone who purchases property in good faith and for valid consideration.

break-even point: The point at which gross income equals the total of fixed costs and variable costs.

broker: A person licensed under state law to facilitate a real estate transaction in return for compensation.

brokerage: The name given to the business engaged in by real estate brokers.

bulk transfer laws: Laws that pertain to the sale and purchase of all or substantially all of the inventory of a business.

buy-down: A financing arrangement whereby the seller will "buy down" the interest rate of the borrower's loan for a certain period of time.

C

call: A short segment providing the course and distance of a line of a metes and bounds legal description.

cash sale: A sale in which a buyer pays cash for the property and does not acquire financing from a lending institution.

certificate of eligibility: A certificate that states the maximum available loan guaranty entitlement for a veteran.

chain of title: The geneology of a particular parcel of real property.

check: A measurement of land that is twenty-four miles square.

Chinese Wall: A situation in which an attorney or paralegal is isolated from a client case for conflict of interest reasons.

chord: A straight line drawn from the starting point of an arc to the end point of an arc.

client trust fund account: An account separate from the law firm's regular business account in which fee advances, deposit money, closing proceeds, and/or escrowed funds are placed.

commercial bank: A lender that is a major source of construction loans, short-term loans, and home improvement loans.

common elements: Those areas of a condominium development that all of the owners use in common, such as the grounds on which the condominium building is located, the roof, the exterior walls and structural components, the parking lot, and any recreational facilities.

community property: All property, both real and personal, acquired during marriage by either spouse, in states that recognize this concept.

competence: Having the necessary legal skill to perform a given task and devoting the requisite time to that task to do a thorough job for the client.

competitive market analysis: A comparison of prices of properties similar to the seller's property that have recently been sold.

condemnation: The process by which private property is taken by federal, state, and local governments for public use.

condominium: A form of ownership in which the property owner owns the interior of a unit, plus an undivided interest, expressed as a percentage interest, in the common elements of the condominium complex.

condominium association: An association comprised of unit owners that sets rules and manages the operation of the condominium.

confidentiality: An ethical concept prohibiting a lawyer and others in a law firm from voluntarily disclosing information about a client matter.

conflict of interest: A situation in which a lawyer's professional judgment might be affected because of business or personal interests.

construction lien: A statutory lien placed on real property by persons or entities providing labor or materials for the improvement of real property.

constructive eviction: The breach by a landlord of a lease in such a manner as to make the leased premises unusable.

constructive notice: Notice legally presumed because of the recording of documents in the public records.

contingency fee: An attorney's fee that is contingent upon the client reaching settlement or winning in court. The payment the attorney receives is set forth as a percentage of the settlement or court award.

continuous marriage affidavit: A sworn statement verifying the marital status of the sellers.

conventional loan: A loan made by a private lender in which the lender usually does not have any insurance or guarantee from a third party, such as a government agency, backing the loan should the borrower fail to meet his or her loan obligations.

cooperative: A multiunit building owned by a corporation. One purchases stock in the corporation, which entitles the purchaser of the stock to enter into a long-term lease with the corporation.

correction lines: Every fourth township line above and below a baseline. At each correction line, the range lines are remeasured to a distance of six miles.

covenant: A promise or guarantee.

credit union: A cooperative association in which members make savings deposits. Credit unions pay interest on the savings accounts and permit members to borrow money for both short-term and long-term residential loans.

curtesy: The provision the law makes for a widower to make a legal claim to an interest in his deceased wife's real property.

D

declaration of condominium: The document that legally creates a condominium.

declaration of covenants and restrictions: A document setting forth the rights and restrictions of property owners within a planned unit development.

declaratory judgment: A judgment sought when the parties to a lawsuit want a judicial decree on their status and rights with regard to a particular matter.

deed: A formal written instrument that conveys title to real property from one party to another.

deed in lieu of foreclosure: A deed to mortgaged property given by a borrower to the lender in order to prevent foreclosure.

deed of trust: A three-party financing instrument between the trustor/ borrower, beneficiary/lender, and trustee. The borrower, as trustor, signs legal title to the real property in question to the trustee as collateral for the loan, while the borrower remains in physical possession of the property.

deed restrictions: Restrictive covenants contained in a deed transferring property from seller to buyer.

deficiency judgment: A court judgment for the difference between the sale of real property in a foreclosure action and the outstanding loan debt.

demand deposit: An account in which the depositor may take out his or her money on demand; a checking account.

diligence: Attentiveness and care.

distress: The right to seize a lessee's goods to satisfy a rent arrearage.

distress bond: A bond posted by a landlord in a distraint proceeding.

distress writ: A court order commanding the sheriff to summon the defendant to answer the complaint in a distraint proceeding.

doctrine of imputed disqualification: A doctrine which provides that the entire body of lawyers in a firm are treated as one for conflict of interest purposes.

doctrine of laches: A doctrine similar to the statute of limitations, premised on the principle of vigilance, which states that if a plaintiff neglects to assert a claim for an unreasonable length of time, the neglect, together with other circumstances causing prejudice to the defendant, will bar relief by a court of equity.

documentary stamps: A tax imposed on the transfer of real property.

dower: The provision the law makes for a widow to lay legal claim to an interest in her deceased husband's real property.

dual agency: An agency situation in which a broker represents both the seller and the buyer in the same transaction.

due-on-sale clause: A clause in a loan document which states that should the real property securing the loan obligation be sold, the total amount outstanding on the loan becomes immediately due.

E

earnest money: A sum of money paid by a buyer at the time of entering a contract to indicate the buyer's intention of carrying out the terms of the contract.

easement: The enforceable right to use the real property of another for a particular purpose.

easement in gross: An easement given to benefit a particular individual or entity rather than one given to confer a benefit to real property.

effective date: The date upon which a contract becomes legally binding on all parties.

elective share: A spouse's statutory right to a fractional share of real and personal property owned by the deceased spouse at the date of death.

eminent domain: The right of federal, state, and local governments and certain public and quasi-public corporations and utilities to take private property for public use.

encroachment: An illegal intrusion of a building or appurtenance onto the property of another.

encumbrance clause: A deed clause setting forth any encumbrances on the real property conveyed, such as mortgages, leases, liens, easements, or restrictions.

endorsement: A form provided by the title insurer that is used for the amendment of any information that has appeared as part of a title commitment or title policy.

entry foreclosure: A foreclosure method used only in a few New England states in which the lender forecloses by taking possession of the real property for a specified time period, after which legal title to the property passes to the lender.

Equal Credit Opportunity Act (ECOA): A federal law enacted to prevent discrimination in making credit available to consumers.

equitable remedies: Remedies administered according to fairness, such as injunctions or actions for specific performance.

equitable right of redemption: The right to buy back real property at any time prior to a forced sale by paying the full amount of the debt owed and all additional charges.

escheat: The right of reversion of title to private property in their jurisdictions, given to state and local governments.

escrow account: An account in a bank, savings and loan, credit union, or similar financial institution that is held by a third party and into which funds are deposited to be held until the happening of a stated event.

escrow closing: A closing in which a third party acts as escrowee and receives closing documents deposited by each party, whereupon the escrowee proceeds to close the transaction.

estate for years: An estate that continues for a designated period.

exclusive listing: A listing agreement in which the seller agrees to list the property with no broker other than the listing broker for the term of the agreement. As an exclusive agent, the listing broker is entitled to receive compensation if the listing broker or any person other than the seller procures a buyer within the listing term.

exclusive-right-to-sell listing: A listing agreement in which the listing broker is entitled to a commission if anyone procures a buyer within the listing term.

F

Federal Deposit Insurance Corporation (FDIC): An institution that insures depositors' accounts.

Federal Home Loan Mortgage Corporation (FHLMC): A corporation established to provide a secondary market, primarily for conventional loans.

Federal National Mortgage Association (FNMA): A governmentally regulated corporation that buys and services conventional, FHA, and VA residential loans that meet its specific guidelines.

Federal Truth in Lending Act: A federal law requiring lenders to make full disclosure of all costs incurred in obtaining credit.

fee simple absolute: An estate that grants the property owner each of the four basic property rights.

FHA loan: A loan insured by the Federal Housing Administration. The FHA insures loans for owner-occupied one-to-four family dwellings.

fictitious name: A name other than one's legal name under which one operates a business.

fiduciary duty: A duty held by a person in a special position of trust (for example, the duty of care, obedience, diligence, loyalty).

fiduciary lender: A lender that has a fiduciary duty to its principals.

Financial Institutions Reform, Recovery and Enforcement Act (FIRREA): A federal law that restructured the savings and loan regulatory and insurance systems, giving management of insurance funds for savings and loans to the FDIC.

fixed costs: Costs that remain constant and do not vary according to the income generated.

fixture: An object that at one time was personal property but has, through the process of attachment to real property, become part of the real property.

flat fee: An attorney's fee set forth as a sum certain for the performance of a specified task.

flat fee sale: An arrangement in which, for a flat fee, a broker evaluates and photographs a property, inserts a property description in a special directory, and provides For Sale signs to the seller.

foreclosure: The legal procedure whereby real property is sold to repay a debt to a creditor who has a lien on the real property.

fraudulent misrepresentation: Misrepresentation made with an intent to mislead or deceive.

freehold estate: An estate of indeterminable duration.

G

gap period: The period between the effective date of the commitment and the recording date of the instruments giving rise to the interest being insured.

general lien: A lien that is not secured by any particular parcel of real property and, therefore, may affect all nonexempt property of a debtor.

general warranty deed: A deed by which the grantor states that he or she has valid title and will defend that title against any defect arising from the actions of the grantor or those of the grantor's predecessors. This type of deed provides the greatest degree of protection for the grantee.

government lot: An irregular-sized tract of land labeled by government surveyors.

Government National Mortgage Association (GNMA): A division of HUD that works in tandem with the FNMA in the secondary market assisting lending institutions with low-income housing projects.

government survey method: A method of legal description, established by the United States Congress, that works on a grid system.

graduated lease: A lease that contains a rent adjustment clause, allowing for the increase and, less often, the decrease of the rent to be paid over the term of the lease.

graduated payment mortgage: A loan in which the borrower's monthly payments during the first years of the loan term are reduced and the deferred portions of the payments are added onto the monthly payments made in later years.

grantee: The person or entity to whom title to real property is conveyed.

granting clause: A deed clause that contains the words of conveyance expressing the grantor's intention of transferring the real property. It also includes the recital of consideration and description of the property to be conveyed.

grantor: The person or entity conveying title of real property to another.

gross lease: A lease in which the lessee pays a fixed amount as basic rent and is not required to pay any portion of the lessor's operating expenses.

ground lease: A lease for a parcel of vacant real property.

growing equity mortgage: A loan in which the borrower quickly increases his or her equity in the real property by increasing the amount of the monthly payments by a certain percentage each year according to a schedule. This increase is applied to the principal in order to pay the loan off by an earlier maturity date than would be applicable in a standard loan.

guide meridians: Every fourth range line east and west of the principal meridian.

H

habendum clause: A deed clause describing the type of estate being conveyed to the grantee(s).

homestead property: The primary dwelling house or residence of the head of household plus adjoining land.

hourly fee: An attorney's fee based upon the amount of time the attorney spends on a client matter.

I

implied warranty of fitness: An implied warranty that a product is fit for the particular purpose for which it was bought.

index lease: A lease that contains a built-in mechanism for incremental rent increases during the lease period, tying the rent to the governmental cost-of-living index or some similar index.

in personam jurisdiction: Jurisdiction over the persons involved in litigation.

installment contract: A contract in which at least one payment under the contract is made after the close of the taxable year of sale.

intangible tax: A tax imposed for the right to issue, execute, sell, assign, trade in, or receive income from intangible property.

interest rate cap: A limitation on the amount an interest rate can increase on an adjustable rate loan.

J

joint tenancy: A form of concurrent ownership in which two or more persons have undivided interests in property, with right of survivorship.

jurisdiction: The authority of a court to hear a matter.

L

landlord's lien: A lien given by statute to a landlord on certain personal property of a tenant.

lease: A document that conveys a leasehold interest in real property which includes the right of possession, but not ownership, for a period of time in return for the payment of rent.

leasehold estate: An estate of determinable duration.

legal description: A precise delineation of a specific parcel of real property that sets the property apart from other parcels of real estate.

legal remedies: Remedies awarded in courts of law, such as monetary damages.

license: A personal right to perform specified activities on the real property of another.

lien: A claim or charge against property for payment of a debt.

lien theory: A legal theory pertaining to financing instruments maintaining that a financing instrument serves as a lien on the secured real property.

lien waiver: A document indicating that a subcontractor has been paid and will not be subjecting real property to liens.

life estate: An estate in which the grantor conveys title to real property to another for a period of time measured by somebody's life.

life estate pur autre vie: A life estate granted for the lifetime of someone other than the grantee.

liquidated damages: Damages the amount of which represents a reasonable sum to be paid to the nonbreaching party for damages suffered as a result of a breach of contract.

lis pendens: A notice recorded when a lawsuit affects title to a particular parcel of real property.

listing agreement: A contract between a seller and a broker.

littoral rights: Water rights pertaining to a landowner whose property abuts a lake, ocean, or sea.

loan commitment: A document outlining the terms under which the lender will loan a specified amount to the borrower. Once accepted by the borrower, it becomes a contract.

loan origination fee: A fee charged by lenders to process a loan application.

loan-to-value ratio: The correspondence between the value of the real property to serve as collateral for a loan and the amount of the loan.

M

maker: The borrower signing a promissory note.

margin: The amount of percentage points a lender adds to the index rate to come up with an ARM interest rate.

marketable title: Title to real property that is free from encumbrances which would bring down the value of the real property or create reasonable doubt or controversy.

master association: An umbrella association that provides management services and decision-making functions to smaller condominiums.

master plan: A plan created by a local planning commission that provides for land use, conservation, circulation, noise regulation, and public facilities in a given area.

memorandum of lease: A document providing skeletal information of a lease, such as the names of the lessor and lessee and a description of the leased premises. This document is recorded in the county in which the leased premises is located to put others on notice of a transfer of physical possession of the property.

merchants' association: An organization consisting of the merchants of a shopping center whose primary purpose is the promotion of the common good of the center.

metes and bounds method: A method of legal description that outlines the boundary lines of a parcel of real property by establishing a starting point called the point of beginning, describing the course and distance each boundary line travels from that point around the perimeters of the property and back again, returning to the point of beginning.

millage rate: A rate used in computing ad valorem real property taxes.

monetary judgment: An award of monies to a plaintiff if he or she wins a lawsuit.

monument: A natural or manmade object that is permanent and fixed.

mortgage: A two-party security instrument between the mortgagor/borrower and the mortgagee/lender that describes the property serving as collateral for the loan and sets forth the rights of the lender should the borrower default.

mortgage banking company: A private corporation that originates loans for other lenders and investors for which it receives a servicing fee.

mortgage broker: A licensed individual who acts as a middleman in a financing transaction, bringing lenders and borrowers together in return for a placement fee.

mortgagee: The lender.

mortgagee estoppel letter: A letter specifying the amount to be paid to satisfy an outstanding loan debt.

mortgagee's policy (MP): A title policy issued to insure the mortgage lien that a lender is acquiring.

mortgagee's policy leasehold (MPL): A title policy issued to insure the mortgage lien that a lender is acquiring in a leasehold estate.

mortgage insurance premium: An insurance premium charged on FHA loans. These premiums are collected into the FHA's Mutual Mortgage Insurance Fund to insure lenders against bad loans.

mortgagor: The borrower.

multiple listing service: An organization of brokers who agree to publicize their listings to all other broker members through the use of the service.

mutual savings bank: A lending institution found primarily in the Northeast that is owned by the depositors, who are the investors. The depositor-investors receive a return on their investment through the payment of interest on their savings accounts. Mutual savings banks make loans for both residential and income-producing properties.

N

National Association of Legal Assistants (NALA): A voluntary national paralegal association.

negative amortization: A situation in which the interest cost that is not covered by the monthly payments is added to the unpaid principal balance, leaving the borrower owing the lender more than the borrower did at the beginning of the loan.

net lease: A lease in which the lessee pays a base rent, plus a pro rata share of some of the lessor's operating expenses.

net listing: A listing agreement in which the seller specifies the net amount of money he or she must receive in order to sell the property. Under the terms of the agreement, the broker receives any monies in excess of this specified amount as commission.

nonconforming use: Also referred to as *preexisting use*. Permission given to a property owner who has built an improvement on land prior to the enactment of a zoning ordinance to continue to use the land in the same manner as before.

nonforeign certification: A statement certifying that the seller is not a foreign person as that term is defined in section 1445 of the Internal Revenue Code, and that monies need not be withheld from the sale for tax purposes.

notice of commencement: A document recorded by a property owner indicating the date upon which construction began on the property.

notice of default: A notice informing a borrower that he or she is in default, setting forth the amount and date of the default, the period within which to respond, and the consequences if he or she does not act within the prescribed period.

notice of nonresponsibility: A notice posted on a construction site by the owner of the property to avoid legal responsibility for unauthorized work done or unauthorized materials furnished.

notice of rescission: A notice that rescinds a notice of default in a nonjudicial foreclosure.

notice of trustee's sale: A notice published in a newspaper of general circulation in the county in which the real property is located announcing the details of the sale of the real property in a nonjudicial foreclosure action.

notice statute: A recording statute whereby the notice a subsequent purchaser has of a previous purchaser's deed is imperative in determining the priority of title to the real property.

notice to owner: A document that puts a property owner on notice of those parties expecting payment for work or materials incorporated into the owner's real property.

O

open listing: The granting of a nonexclusive right to solicit and receive offers on the seller's real property.

operating expenses: Expenses incurred in maintaining and managing property.

option contract: A contract in which the seller gives a potential buyer the exclusive right, within a specified limited time period, to purchase real property. The potential buyer pays the seller for this exclusive right.

owner's policy (OPM): A marketability policy, extending insurance coverage against loss or damage because of the inability to sell the property in the future because of title defects.

owner's policy leasehold (OPL): A title policy used to insure the title that the purchaser of a leasehold is acquiring.

P

partition: An action by the court dividing real property held by joint tenants, tenants in common, or tenants in partnership.

party wall easement: An easement on the part of a shared partition wall between two properties.

payee: The lender as receiver of a promissory note.

percentage lease: A lease in which, in addition to the base rent, the lessee is obligated to pay a specific percentage of the lessee's sales receipts to the lessor.

personal property: All property that is not considered real property.

PITI: A loan payment that is comprised of principal, interest, taxes, and insurance.

planned unit development (PUD): A subdivision containing individual lots with common areas controlled by a homeowners' association.

plat map: A survey that breaks down a tract of land into blocks referenced by letter or number.

plat method: A method of legal description that describes real property by making reference to its location on a plat map recorded in the land records in the county in which the property is located.

point of beginning: A readily identifiable point that is the starting point of a metes and bounds legal description of the subject real property.

points: A lending charge, sometimes referred to as *discount points*. Each point is equal to one percent of the loan amount.

police powers: Those powers given to the federal government and to the states by their constitutions to create laws necessary for the protection of public health, safety, and welfare.

power-of-sale clause: A clause in a deed of trust that gives the trustee the power to sell the real property serving as collateral for a loan at public auction if the borrower defaults on his or her loan obligation.

premises clause: The opening paragraph of a deed, setting forth the date of execution of the deed, the parties to the deed, and, in states that so require, the addresses of the parties.

prescriptive easement: An easement created when a person adversely uses the property of another for a statutorily specified time period.

principal: The person upon whose behalf an agent is authorized to work.

principal meridian: An imaginary line running north and south used in a government survey method of legal description.

private mortgage insurance (PMI): Insurance from private insurance providers that insures the portion of a loan which exceeds the typical conventional loan-to-value ratio.

profit à prendre: The right to remove certain items from another's land or to remove a portion of the land.

promissory note: A written promise to repay a debt on agreed-upon terms and conditions. The note is the legal evidence of the borrower's intentions to repay the debt.

prorations: Charges that are apportioned between the parties.

punitive damages: Damages designed to punish or serve as an example.

purchase money mortgage sale: A sale in which the seller finances all or a portion of the purchase price of the property, the buyer executing a mortgage instrument and mortgage note in favor of the seller.

Q

quitclaim deed: A deed in which the grantor transfers whatever interest he or she may have without making any warranties regarding the quality of the title.

R

race-notice statute: A recording statute premised on protecting a bona fide purchaser for value without notice if he or she is the first to record the deed to real property.

race statute: A recording statute whereby priority of claim to title of real property is determined literally by a race to the recording office.

radius: The distance between any point on a curved line and the center of an imaginary circle that could be drawn if that curved line was extended to form a full circle.

range lines: Imaginary lines located at each six-mile interval, running in a north and south direction parallel to a principal meridian.

real estate agent: A real estate salesperson or real estate broker.

Real Estate Investment Trust (REIT): A trust that accumulates funds by selling beneficial interests in the trust to members of the public. The trust then invests in various types of loans, typically construction loans and loans for larger real estate projects.

Real Estate Settlement Procedures Act (RESPA): A federal law requiring the lender to provide the borrower with a good faith estimate of closing costs within three days from the date the loan application is submitted. It also requires the use of a uniform settlement statement for all nonexempt transactions.

real property: Property comprised of land and all things affixed to it, as well as natural objects on or growing on the land.

realtor: A licensed real estate broker who voluntarily becomes a member of a local board of realtors that is affiliated with the National Association of Realtors®.

recording: Delivering a document to the appropriate government official for transcription into a plat book, deed book, mortgage book, or official records book.

recording statute: A statute that prescribes the requirements for recording a document and that determines the priority of rights to real property if there are conflicting claims.

reddendum clause: A deed clause reserving some right in the real property for the grantor or imposing a restriction on the use of the property by the grantee.

redemption period: A statutorily prescribed period of time within which a borrower may prevent foreclosure by paying the amount(s) owed, plus interest, and penalties, or by negotiating an agreement with the lender.

redlining: Denying a loan or presenting different terms or conditions for a loan based upon the composition of the neighborhood or other discriminatory reasons.

reinstatement of loan: An arrangement in lieu of foreclosure, whereby a borrower pays all delinquent sums and late charges and takes any reasonable actions the lender may require to ensure both that the lender's interest in the real property is protected and that the borrower's obligation to pay under the terms of the note and mortgage remain unimpaired.

reserve requirements: Monies set aside for the replacement of items over and above regular maintenance requirements.

respondeat superior: "Let the master answer." A legal doctrine that holds the principal legally responsible for the actions of the agent.

restrictive covenants: Private restrictions imposed on the use of private property.

retainer agreement: A contract between an attorney and client that sets forth the manner in which the client will be billed for the attorney's work.

reverse annuity mortgage: A situation in which a real property owner who has one hundred percent equity in his or her home borrows against that equity and receives monthly payments from the lender over a period of years. Upon the owner's death, the property is sold, and the loan is repaid from the proceeds.

riparian rights: Water rights pertaining to a landowner whose property abuts a river, stream, or similar watercourse.

S

sale-leaseback: A situation in which an owner of real property sells the property to an investor and then leases the property back.

sale subject to existing mortgage: A situation in which a buyer becomes responsible for the seller's payments under an existing mortgage, but the seller remains primarily liable under the mortgage note.

satisfaction of judgment: A document recorded to evidence the satisfaction of a debt and the removal of an encumbrance from real property.

satisfaction of mortgage: A document recorded to evidence the payment in full of a mortgage loan.

savings and loan association: A lending institution that primarily makes residential, conventional loans but, on occasion, makes FHA and VA loans.

Savings Association Insurance Fund (SAIF): A fund that insures savings and loan deposits.

secondary market: A market for the purchase and sale of existing mortgages.

section: A measurement of land that is one mile square and contains 640 acres.

seisin clause: A deed clause whereby the grantor warrants that he or she is the rightful owner of the property in question and thereby has the right and power to convey the property to the grantee.

seller's affidavit: A sworn statement signed by the seller stating that there are no existing liens on the property that would encumber the purchaser's title.

separate property: Property that is (1) acquired by a spouse prior to marriage, (2) income from property acquired by a spouse prior to marriage unless commingled in a manner that makes it community property, (3) acquired solely through separate funds, or (4) acquired by gift, will, or descent, unless the gift or will clearly indicates that the property is given to both husband and wife.

service of process: The serving of a summons and complaint upon the defendant by a sheriff or court-approved process server.

shared appreciation mortgage: A loan in which the lender lends money at a lower interest rate in return for a share in the appreciated value of the real property when the property is sold.

Sherman Act: A federal antitrust law protecting against unlawful restraints in trade and commerce, such as monopolies and price-fixing.

single agency: A broker who represents only one principal in a transaction.

Soldiers' and Sailors' Relief Act: A federal statute which mandates that in any action in which a defendant fails to appear through the submission of a responsive pleading, the plaintiff is required to file an affidavit swearing that to the best of his or her knowledge and belief, the defendant is not in one of the branches of the military service, before a default judgment may be rendered against the defendant.

special assessment: An assessment for shared improvements that enhance the value of real property.

special exception: Permission given to a property owner to use property for a use undesignated in that area.

special warranty deed: Also known as a limited warranty deed. A deed by which the grantor, in conveying title to real property, only warrants that he or she has done nothing to encumber the property, but does not provide further assurances with regard to the grantor's predecessors.

specific lien: A lien that is secured by a particular parcel of real property.

statute of frauds: A state statute indicating which contracts must be in writing and signed by the party to be charged in order to be legally enforceable.

statute of limitations: A statute indicating the time periods within which a suit must be brought or be forever barred.

steering: The attempt to guide prospective homeowners into one neighborhood as opposed to another based on the racial, religious, or ethnic composition of a particular neighborhood.

stipulation: An agreement made by opposing sides in a lawsuit regulating a matter pertaining to the suit.

straight loan: A loan in which the borrower makes periodic interest payments, with the entire principal paid at the end of the loan term.

strict foreclosure: A foreclosure method used primarily in Connecticut and Vermont in which a court hearing is held to determine the mortgagee's right to foreclose. If the mortgagee's right is authorized, the court awards the real property to the mortgagee without requiring the mortgagee to bid for the property at a public sale.

subagent: Someone who is authorized by an agent to aid in a transaction for a principal, if authorized under the original agency agreement.

subject matter jurisdiction: Jurisdiction over the subject matter of the litigation.

subordination agreement: An agreement by which one party agrees that his or her interest in real property should have lower priority than the interest to which it is being subordinated.

summary proceedings: Short and simple proceedings used to dispose of certain controversies.

supersedeas bond: A bond required when one is appealing a court judgment.

T

tax base: The total assessed value of all taxable real property in a taxing authority's jurisdiction.

tenancy at sufferance: A tenancy occurring after the expiration of a lease, in which a tenant remains in possession of the property without the landlord's consent.

tenancy at will: A tenancy that begins as an estate for years, with the tenant remaining on the property by agreement with the landlord after the estate for years expires.

tenancy by the entirety: A form of concurrent ownership by husband and wife, in which each spouse has an undivided interest and right of survivorship.

tenancy from period to period: A leasehold that continues for successive intervals until one party to the agreement provides the other party with notice of termination of the tenancy.

tenancy in common: A form of concurrent ownership in which two or more persons have undivided interests in property but which does not confer the right of survivorship.

tenant estoppel certificate: A document that verifies the terms and conditions of a tenant's lease.

Tenants' Eviction Procedures Act of 1976: A federal act that mandates eviction procedures to be followed for residential tenants in government-subsidized, multiunit buildings.

tenant unions: Organizations that elect representatives to consolidate tenant complaints, negotiate favorable rent agreements, and assure compliance with maintenance requirements.

tenendum clause: A deed clause indicating the improvements that are being conveyed together with the land, such as the buildings built on the land.

1099 form: A federal tax reporting form for the reporting of real property sales transactions.

testimonium clause: A deed clause in which the deed is executed, witnessed, and acknowledged.

tickler system: A method of keeping track of priorities and deadlines.

time share: The purchase of the right to use real property for a limited, specified period of time each year.

title commitment: A document that sets forth the status of the title of a particular parcel of real property and the terms under which a title policy for the property will be issued.

title insurance: Insurance of an owner of real property or another having an interest in the real property against loss brought about by encumbrances, defective titles, invalidity, or adverse claim to the title.

title search: The search of the public records to determine if title to real property is marketable.

title theory: A legal theory pertaining to financing instruments which maintains that a financing instrument transfers conditional title in the secured real property to the lender.

Torrens certificate: In states that utilize the Torrens system, a certificate, issued by the registrar of title, that is the actual legal title to the real property.

Torrens system: A method for determining title to real property through the institution of a lawsuit.

township: A measurement of land that is six miles square, or thirty-six miles.

township lines: Imaginary lines that are located at each six-mile interval running in an east-west direction parallel to a baseline.

tract index: An index compiled by a description of parcels of real property.

transaction broker: A broker who acts as a "middleman" between the parties by simply bringing the parties together, but does not actively represent either party.

triple net lease: A lease in which the lessee pays a pro rata share of all of the lessor's expenses.

V

VA loan: A loan made to veterans by approved lenders for residential, owner-occupied property and guaranteed by the Veterans Administration.

variable costs: Costs that vary according to the income generated.

variance: Permission given to a property owner to deviate from strict compliance with all or part of a zoning ordinance.

venue: The proper location to bring a lawsuit.

verified complaint: A complaint that is signed and sworn to by the plaintiff, attesting that all allegations within the complaint are true to the plaintiff's best knowledge and belief.

W

wraparound loan: A loan that allows a borrower to pay off an existing loan to obtain additional financing from a second lender. The second lender provides the borrower with a new loan, charging a higher interest rate than the first lender. The second lender then assumes payment of the existing first mortgage loan.

writ of attachment: A court order that prevents a party to a lawsuit from conveying title to property, real or personal, while the suit is pending.

writ of execution: A court order that directs the sheriff to levy upon real property and sell it at a sheriff's sale.

writ of possession: A court order issued to the sheriff ordering the sheriff to remove a tenant from leased property.

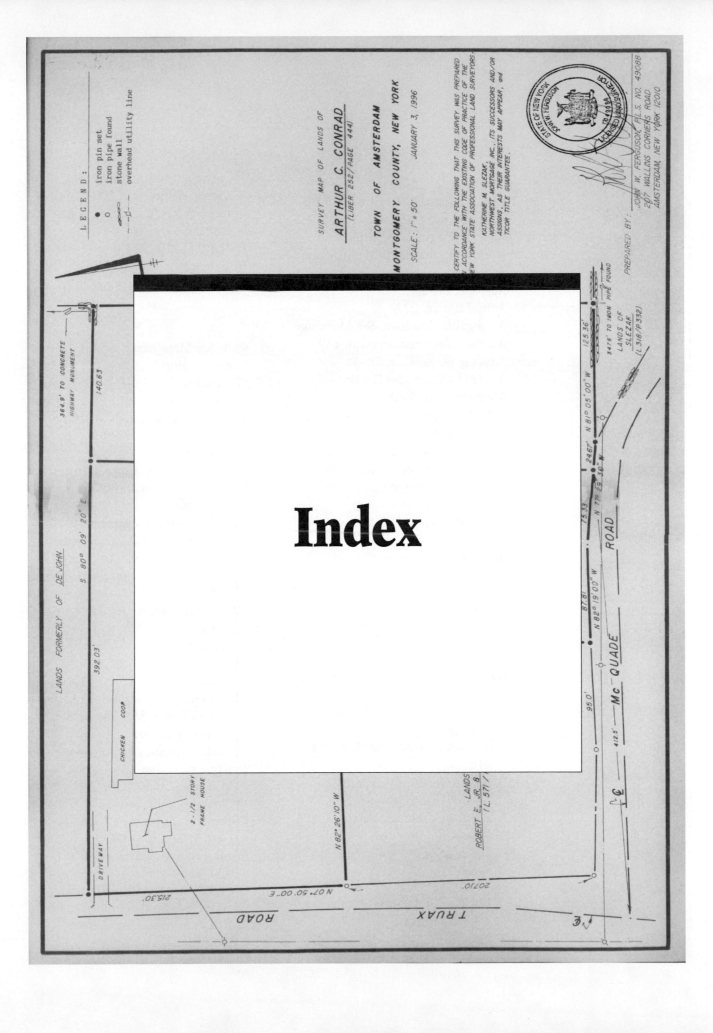

Index

INDEX